AN INFOGRAPHIC JOURNEY

An Infographic Journey Through the Neurobiology of Emotion

Visualizing Emotions: The Art of Fear

Editors

FAISAL R. JAHANGIRI

HANIYA QAVI - KHADEEJA MOOSA

Copyright © 2024 Global Innervation LLC.

All rights reserved.

ISBN: 9798332353901

AN INFOGRAPHIC JOURNEY

DEDICATION

This book is dedicated to all the students who bravely explored the depths of fear and emotions and those who seek to understand them. May this book inspire empathy, curiosity, and resilience. Thank you for turning complex feelings into art, making the invisible visible to everyone.

AN INFOGRAPHIC JOURNEY

Table of Contents

Acknowledgment — i
Preface — iii

Chapter 1 Fear — 1

- What is fear?
- Causes of fear
- Modern fear
- Imagination, perception, and belief's effect on fear
- Can animals experience fear?

Chapter 2 Categorizing Fear — 21

- Rational and irrational fears
- Types of fear
- Fear and manipulation

Chapter 3 Life with Fear — 35

- Effects of fear
- Is fear beneficial or harmful?
- Beneficial Fear
- Unfavorable fear

Chapter 4 The Body on Fear — 59

- Bodily effects of fear

Chapter 5 Anxiety — 71

- What is anxiety?
- Fear vs. Anxiety
- Effects of anxiety
- How is anxiety beneficial?

Chapter 6 Anxiety Disorders — 95

- Generalized anxiety disorder
- Social anxiety
- Hypochondriasis
- Phobias

Chapter 7 Emotions   119

- Defining emotions
- Theories of emotion
- LeDoux vs Papez theory

Chapter 8 Emotion, Memory, and Predictions   141

- Memory and emotion
- Predictive coding
- The emotional motor system

Chapter 9 The Nervous System   153

- Development of neuroscience
- What makes up the nervous system?
- Autonomic nervous system
- Sympathetic vs Parasympathetic nervous system
- Right vs left cortex
- Insula
- Other important structures in the nervous system
- Sensory pathways

Chapter 10 The Amygdala   168

- What is the amygdala?
- Activation of the amygdala
- Emotion and the amygdala
- Exteroception and interception
- Functional aspects of the amygdala
- Connections of the amygdala
- Sensory routes to the amygdala
- Damage to the amygdala
- Kluver-Bucy syndrome

Chapter 11 Neurobiology of Emotion   195

- The Limbic System
- Neurobiology of fear and anxiety
- Functional aspects of emotion
- Neurobiology of anxiety

Chapter 12 Detection of Threat   217

- HPA Axis
- Stress and disease
- HPA and HPG Axis

Chapter 13 Oxytocin and Other Molecules   231

- Molecules that affect emotion
- Oxytocin
- Acetaminophen
- Estradiol
- Other molecules
- Risk of medication

Chapter 14 Neuroplasticity   251

- What is neuroplasticity?
- Adaptive vs maladaptive neuroplasticity
- Maternal neuroplasticity

Chapter 15 Diseases of the Nervous System   275

- Neuroplasticity Disorders
- Tinnitus

Chapter 16 Pain   293

- Phantom pain
- Deafferentation pain
- Neuropathic pain

Chapter 17 Treatment and Technology   309

- Importance of knowledge
- Therapy
- Vagus nerve Stimulation
- Deep brain stimulation

Contributors   325

About the Authors and Illustrator   329

AN INFOGRAPHIC JOURNEY

ACKNOWLEDGMENT

We extend our deepest gratitude to Haniya, Khadeeja, and Zainab for their invaluable contributions to this book. Haniya's meticulous attention to detail, Khadeeja's perceptive suggestions, and Zainab's artistic talents made this project possible. Your dedication and editorial proficiency have significantly elevated the quality of our work. We sincerely appreciate your hard work and commitment to bringing our vision to life.

AN INFOGRAPHIC JOURNEY

PREFACE

Welcome to "An Infographic Journey Through the Neurobiology of Emotions: Visualizing Emotions: The Art of Fear," an exceptional and enlightening book crafted by students for students. This compilation of infographics goes beyond the ordinary, serving as a gateway to unravel the intricate and often misconstrued realm of fear and other emotions. Emotions significantly influence our daily encounters, shaping our thoughts, actions, and connections. By translating these intricate emotional concepts into clear and captivating visuals, we aim to make comprehending emotions more accessible and impactful.

Fear is a complex and deeply ingrained human emotion. It can manifest as a response to an immediate threat, such as encountering a wild animal, or in anticipation of a perceived danger, like public speaking. While fear can serve to protect us by encouraging caution, it can also hinder us when it becomes overwhelming or irrational. A thorough understanding of fear, from its biological underpinnings to its psychological and social ramifications, can help us navigate our lives more effectively. This book utilizes infographics to offer a comprehensive, multi-dimensional perspective on fear, making it more accessible and relatable. By gaining insight into fear, we can learn to manage it and harness its power to our advantage.

Infographics are an ideal medium for this exploration. They combine the precision of data with the appeal of visual storytelling, making complex information more digestible and engaging. Each infographic in this book has been thoughtfully designed by students to highlight key aspects of fear and emotions. Through vivid visuals and succinct explanations, we aim to make the science of emotions accessible to everyone, regardless of their background or prior knowledge, because we believe everyone has the right to understand and manage their emotions.

One of the core themes we explore is the biological basis of fear. Fear is deeply rooted in our physiology, involving intricate processes within our brain and body. We delve into how the brain detects threats, focusing on the amygdala's role, and examine the hormonal responses that prepare us for fight or flight. By visualizing these processes, we clearly show how fear operates biologically, giving you a comprehensive understanding of the connection between our physical and emotional responses.

Psychology plays a crucial role in shaping our experience of fear. Fear is not just a biological reflex; our thoughts, experiences, and environment also influence it. This book examines how fear can be conditioned and learned, how it impacts our decision-making, and how it can manifest in both rational and irrational ways. We explore concepts such as phobias, anxiety disorders, and the cognitive mechanisms that drive fear-based behaviors. We aim to make these psychological concepts more relatable and easier to understand through infographics, fostering empathy and awareness.

AN INFOGRAPHIC JOURNEY

Fear possesses significant social and cultural dimensions. It can serve as a mechanism for social control, a trigger for collective behavior, and a reflection of cultural values and anxieties. We delve into the representation of fear in media, politics, and art and its role in shaping societal norms and attitudes. Our infographics analyze the role of fear in historical events, its portrayal in literature and film, and its impact on public opinion and policy. By connecting individual experiences of fear to broader social phenomena, we provide a comprehensive perspective on how this emotion influences our world.

The book serves as an invitation to delve into the intricate world of fear and emotions through the medium of infographics. By melding scientific data, psychological insights, and artistic design, we offer a distinctive viewpoint on these influential facets of human experience. We aim to render the intangible tangible, converting abstract emotions into lucid visual representations that foster comprehension and empathy. Whether you are a student, a professional, or intrigued by the science of emotions, "An Infographic Journey Through the Neurobiology of Emotions: Visualizing Emotions: The Art of Fear" presents a comprehensive and captivating roadmap to one of life's most fundamental elements, tailored for all curious minds.

Faisal R. Jahangiri

AN INFOGRAPHIC JOURNEY

CHAPTER 1

Fear

Everything to Know About Fear

By Bhargava Murari and Abdullah Farhat, Spring 2024

The Neurobiology of Fear and Its Impact on Mental Health

Fear is one of the fundamental emotions in humans for thousands of years. Evolution has allowed this emotion to be deeply ingrained and integrated within us as a survival mechanism. This survival mechanism has been a focal point of study for countless researchers around the globe for decades. All humans are programmed to experience fear both internally and externally. When we experience something, we take in endless amounts of visual and emotional stimuli, which get integrated by the various circuits and mechanisms in our brain. Recent neuroscience studies have revealed that intricate neural pathways are responsible for our fear responses within the human brain.

While delving into the pathways of fear is important, it is crucial to acknowledge that numerous mental illnesses are deeply associated with this emotion. Conditions like certain anxiety disorders, phobias, and stress disorders like PTSD often is associated with fear as a central component. Researchers gain valuable insights into these disorders by comprehending the neural mechanisms behind fear responses. This enhanced understanding not only enriches our comprehension of human behavior but also provides invaluable insights into the development and treatment of various mental health disorders characterized by excessive fear and anxiety.

The Brain's Fear Circuitry

The brain's fear circuitry lies in the amygdala, an almond-shaped structure within the temporal lobes. Serving as an emotional center, the amygdala processes and integrates fear-related information. When confronted with a potential threat, sensory inputs from the environment are rapidly conveyed to the amygdala for evaluation. This assessment entails discerning the threat's relevance and potential danger based on past experiences and learned associations. The amygdala's response to fear-inducing stimuli is modulated by complex interactions with other brain regions, including the prefrontal cortex, hippocampus, and brainstem. Notably, the ventromedial prefrontal cortex within the prefrontal cortex plays a critical role in regulating emotional responses and decision-making processes associated with fear. It aids in contextualizing fear-inducing stimuli and modulating the intensity of fear responses based on cognitive information. Furthermore, the hippocampus, crucial for memory formation and retrieval, provides contextual information about past experiences, facilitating the encoding and consolidation of fear-related memories. Disruptions in the hippocampal-amygdala circuitry have been implicated in the development of mental health issues like post-traumatic stress disorder (PTSD), which is characterized by the activation of fear responses triggered by traumatic memories.

Neurotransmitters and Fear Regulation

The transmission of signals within the brain's fear circuitry relies on various neurotransmitters and chemical messengers facilitating communication between neurons. Among these neurotransmitters, gamma-aminobutyric acid (GABA) and glutamate are important in regulating fear responses. GABA, the primary inhibitory neurotransmitter, attenuates neural activity and diminishes anxiety by inhibiting neurons firing in the amygdala. Dysfunction in GABAergic neurotransmission is implicated in anxiety disorders such as generalized anxiety disorder (GAD) and panic disorder. Conversely, glutamate, the brain's primary excitatory neurotransmitter, facilitates the transmission of fear-related signals within the amygdala and interconnected regions. Abnormalities in glutamatergic neurotransmission are observed in individuals with PTSD and other trauma-related disorders.

Impact of Chronic Stress on Fear Circuitry

Chronic stress, stemming from prolonged exposure to adverse life events or environmental stressors, exerts a profound impact on the brain's fear circuitry, rendering individuals more susceptible to anxiety and mood disorders. At the crux of this process lies the hypothalamic-pituitary-adrenal (HPA) axis, a fundamental neuroendocrine system governing the body's stress response. Under stress, the hypothalamus releases corticotropin-releasing hormone (CRH), triggering the pituitary gland to secrete adrenocorticotropic hormone (ACTH), which then ACTH stimulates the adrenal glands to release cortisol, which is a coping mechanism for stress. Persistent activation of the HPA axis and sustained elevation of cortisol levels exert harmful effects on the brain, particularly impacting the hippocampus and prefrontal cortex. Chronic stress-induced alterations in these brain regions may compromise their ability to regulate fear responses effectively, predisposing individuals to anxiety disorders and depression.

Implications for Mental Health Treatment

Understanding the impact of fear on mental health treatment is imperative for developing diverse therapeutic options. Cognitive-behavioral therapy (CBT) and pharmacotherapy emerge as primary approaches. CBT, a non-invasive method, focuses on restructuring thought patterns and behaviors to reduce amygdala activation while bolstering prefrontal regulation. Pharmacotherapy targets neurotransmitter levels in the brain's fear circuitry, providing rapid relief, particularly for severe or treatment-resistant conditions. Despite their differences, both approaches aim to alleviate distress and enhance functioning. CBT equips individuals with coping mechanisms and resilience, whereas pharmacotherapy offers immediate symptom relief and stabilization. Integrating these approaches optimizes outcomes, fostering holistic mental health care. Additionally, emerging research underscores the potential of neuromodulation techniques such as transcranial magnetic stimulation (TMS) and deep brain stimulation (DBS) for targeting specific brain regions involved in fear processing and regulation. While TMS provides a non-invasive alternative with fewer procedural risks, DBS offers greater precision and long-term efficacy, albeit with a more invasive approach. These innovative therapies hold significant promise for reshaping the landscape of mental health treatment, providing new avenues for individuals seeking relief from debilitating symptoms. These approaches offer promising avenues for personalized treatment interventions, directly modulating neural activity and restoring balance within the fear circuitry without invasiveness.

Conclusion

In summary, the neurobiology of fear has a complex neural circuit involving the neurotransmitter systems and neuroendocrine pathways, which collectively influence an individual's emotional responses to threatening stimuli. As neuroscience advances, certain mechanisms of fear are continuously being researched and discovered. Specifically, the underlying mechanisms of fear regulation and dysregulation undoubtedly allow us to gain valuable insights into the pathophysiology of anxiety as well as trauma-related disorders. By comprehending how fear manifests in the brain and how we can find ways to modulate it, researchers and clinicians can develop more targeted and efficacious interventions for individuals struggling with excessive fear and anxiety. Furthermore, diverse therapeutic approaches and innovative techniques provide us with a comprehensive toolkit for addressing the multifaceted nature of fear-related mental health disorders, ultimately helping individuals reclaim control over their well-being.

References

1. Møller, A. R. (2019). Neurobiology of Fear and Other Emotions. Springer.
2. LeDoux, J. E. (2012). Rethinking the Emotional Brain. Neuron, 73(4), 653–676. doi: 10.1016/j.neuron.2012.02.004
3. McEwen, B. S., & Gianaros, P. J. (2011). Stress- and Allostasis-Induced Brain Plasticity. Annual Review of Medicine, 62(1), 431–445. doi: 10.1146/annurev-med-052209-100430
4. Nunez, Kirsten. "TMS Therapy: What It Treats, Benefits, Side Effects, and Costs." *Healthline*, Healthline Media, 20 Jan. 2021, www.healthline.com/health/tms-therapy.
5. Tovote, Philip, et al. "Neuronal Circuits for Fear and Anxiety." *Nature News*, Nature Publishing Group, 20 May 2015, www.nature.com/articles/nrn3945.

AN INFOGRAPHIC JOURNEY

DEFINITIONS OF FEAR

- Fear is an unpleasant feeling that is caused by the belief that something may occur.
- Fear can sometimes be associated with pleasure. An example of this is watching horror films.
- Concerns, angst, and apprehension are all words used to describe fear.
- Pain warns about what occurs in the present while fear warns about what may occur in the future.

PSYCHOLOGIST
According to psychology, fear is an innate emotion that creates a biochemical response among all organisms and presents in a highly emotional manner.

NEUROSCIENTIST
Fear is classified as something that engages certain parts of the brain, specifically the emotional brain. Neuroscientists associate fear with the nuclei of the amygdala.

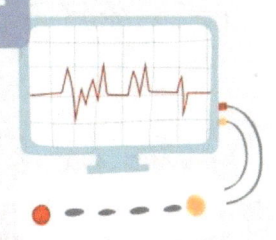

PHYSICIAN
In medicine, fear can be associated with disorders, such as anxiety and depression, and is seen as something that can be treated

NEUROPHYSIOLOGIST
Fear is grouped with behavioral issues. Neurophysiologists aim to eliminate the cause of these symptoms.

Vyshnavi Poruri, Fall 2023

Infographic #1:
Taha Ahmed

THE CONCEPT OF FEAR

01. WHAT IS FEAR?
Fear can be described as an unpleasant experience that can be measured objectively and only is assessed by the person who experiences the fear. It could also be recognized as a complex feeling of being afraid.

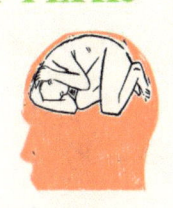

02. WHAT ARE THE TYPES OF FEAR?
Various forms of fear include:
- Rational fear
- Irrational fear
- Chronic fear
- Misdirected fear
- Acute fear
- Enjoyable fear
- Fear from phantom risks
- Fear that may be either purposeful or unintentional.

03. THE CAUSES OF FEAR:
Fear can be impacted by a range of factors, encompassing both external and internal influences, distinct mental visualizations, and enduring anxieties that may stem from prior experiences. The intensity of fear is contingent upon the perceived level of threat.

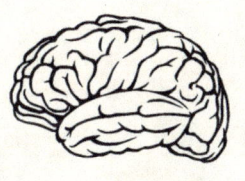

04. WHAT ARE WORDS THAT DESCRIBE FEAR:
Several terms that convey the emotion of fear are: concerns, angst, and apprehension.

05. HOW DOES FEAR AFFECT OUR BODY?
Fear has profound impacts on physiological functions. The body's autonomic system experiences notable changes, characterized by a reduction in parasympathetic activity and an elevation in sympathetic activity.

Taha Ahmed, Spring 2024

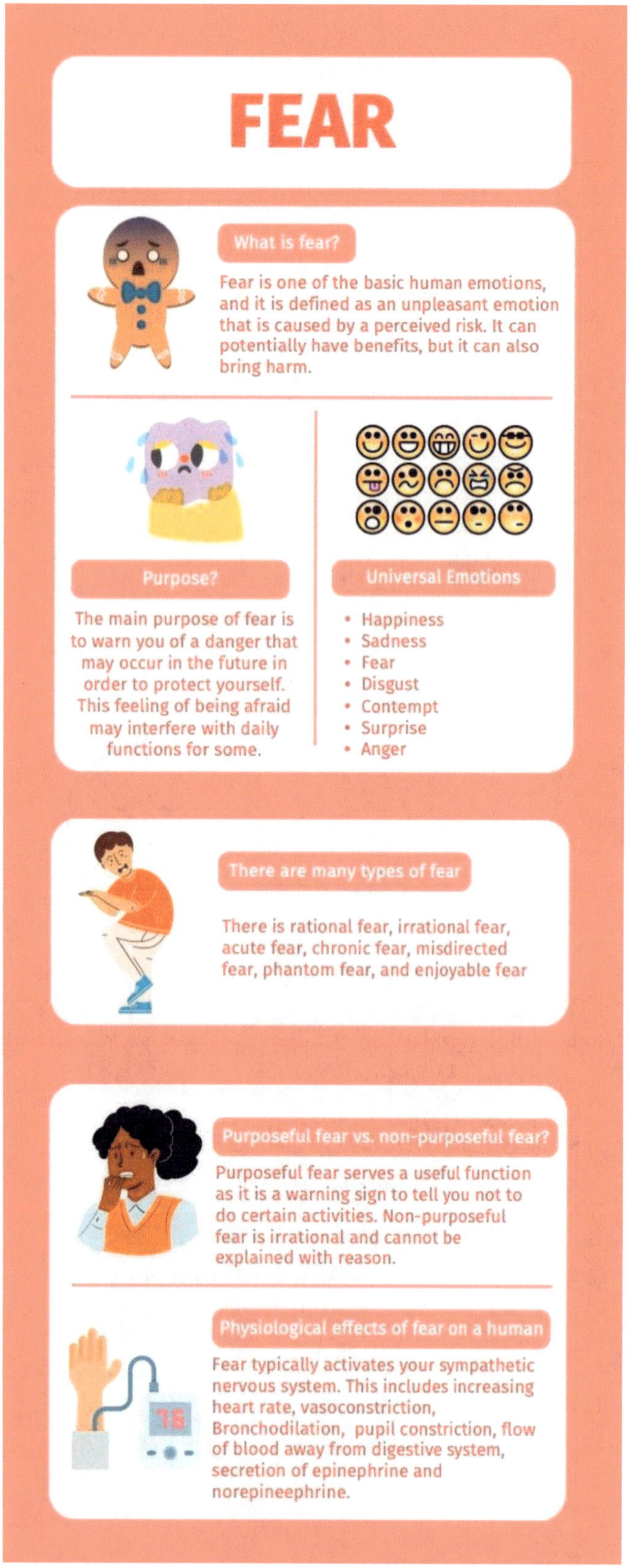

AN INFOGRAPHIC JOURNEY

FEAR

What is fear?
Fear is one of the basic human emotions, and it is defined as an unpleasant emotion that is caused by a perceived risk. It can potentially have benefits, but it can also bring harm.

Purpose?
The main purpose of fear is to warn you of a danger that may occur in the future in order to protect yourself. This feeling of being afraid may interfere with daily functions for some.

Universal Emotions
- Happiness
- Sadness
- Fear
- Disgust
- Contempt
- Surprise
- Anger

There are many types of fear
There is rational fear, irrational fear, acute fear, chronic fear, misdirected fear, phantom fear, and enjoyable fear

Purposeful fear vs. non-purposeful fear?
Purposeful fear serves a useful function as it is a warning sign to tell you not to do certain activities. Non-purposeful fear is irrational and cannot be explained with reason.

Physiological effects of fear on a human
Fear typically activates your sympathetic nervous system. This includes increasing heart rate, vasoconstriction, Bronchodilation, pupil constriction, flow of blood away from digestive system, secretion of epinephrine and norepineephrine.

Ajay Tunikipati, Fall 2023

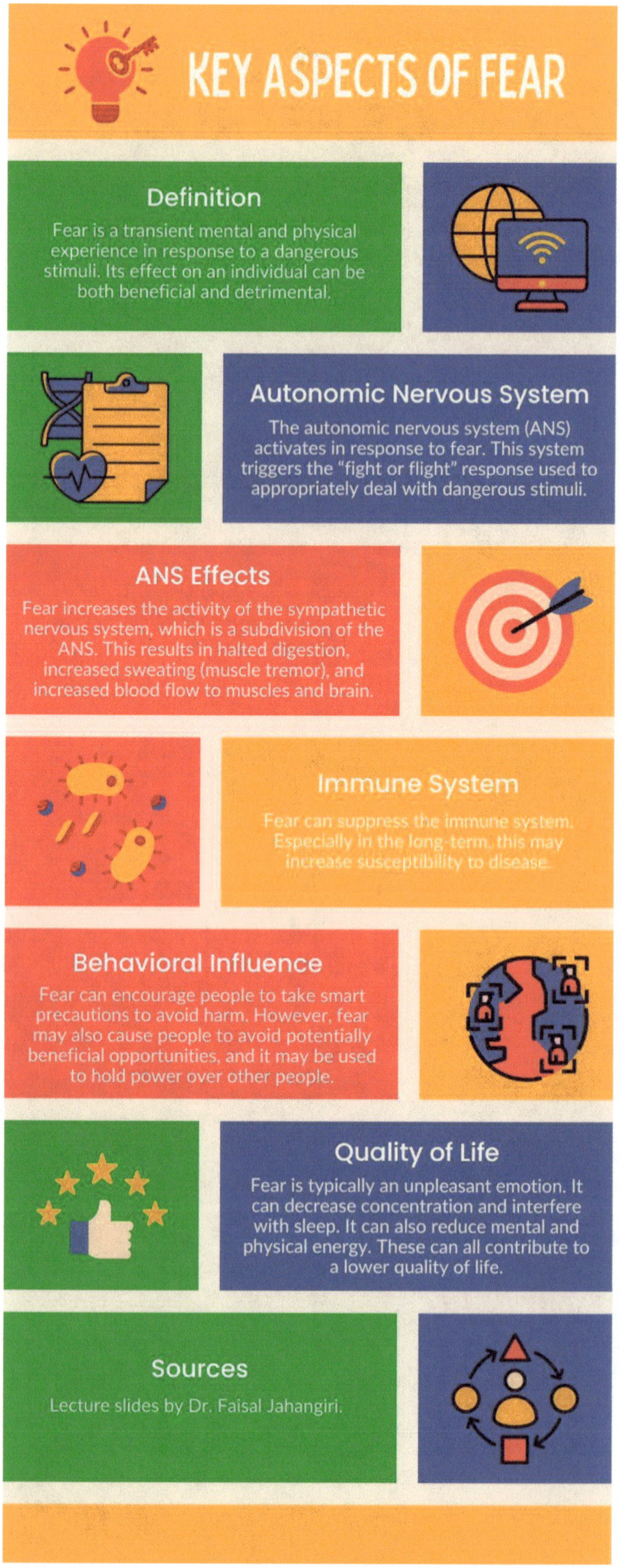

KEY ASPECTS OF FEAR

Definition
Fear is a transient mental and physical experience in response to a dangerous stimuli. Its effect on an individual can be both beneficial and detrimental.

Autonomic Nervous System
The autonomic nervous system (ANS) activates in response to fear. This system triggers the "fight or flight" response used to appropriately deal with dangerous stimuli.

ANS Effects
Fear increases the activity of the sympathetic nervous system, which is a subdivision of the ANS. This results in halted digestion, increased sweating (muscle tremor), and increased blood flow to muscles and brain.

Immune System
Fear can suppress the immune system. Especially in the long-term, this may increase susceptibility to disease.

Behavioral Influence
Fear can encourage people to take smart precautions to avoid harm. However, fear may also cause people to avoid potentially beneficial opportunities, and it may be used to hold power over other people.

Quality of Life
Fear is typically an unpleasant emotion. It can decrease concentration and interfere with sleep. It can also reduce mental and physical energy. These can all contribute to a lower quality of life.

Sources
Lecture slides by Dr. Faisal Jahangiri.

Vijaya Dutt, Fall 2023

AN INFOGRAPHIC JOURNEY

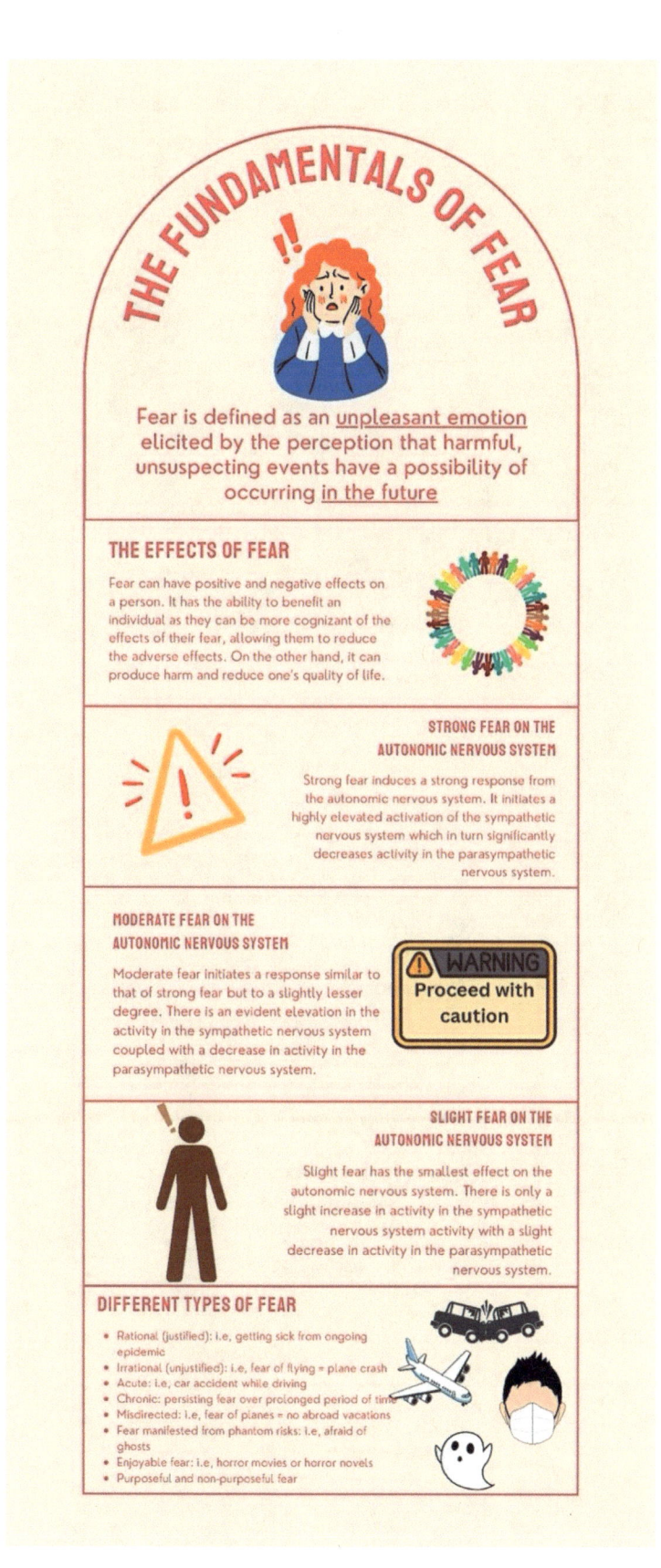

Dannah Bagcal, Spring 2024

Pradyun Sangineni, Fall 2023

AN INFOGRAPHIC JOURNEY

CAUSES OF FEAR

By Vyshnavi Poruri

Signals from the environment, internal sources (ie. pain), and thoughts, memories, and imagination are all known to cause fear.

Prediction of the Future
- Fear is a worry about what can happen in the future.
- Therefore, someone's fear is based on the person's ability to predict the future.
- Fearing the wrong future may cause unnecessary worrying

Focusing on Risks that are Very Small
- Many people worry about events that they cannot control over ones they have control over.
- ex: many people are more afraid of terrorism than catching influenza.

Matters that a Person has No Control Over
- Politics
- Weather
- Natural catastrophes

Harmless Matters that cause Fear
- Arachnophobia: fear of spiders
- Acrophobia: fear of heights
- cynophobia: fear of dogs
- Trypanophobia: fear of injection
- Mysophobia: fear of germs
- Ornithophobia: fear of birds

Vyshnavi Poruri, Fall 2023

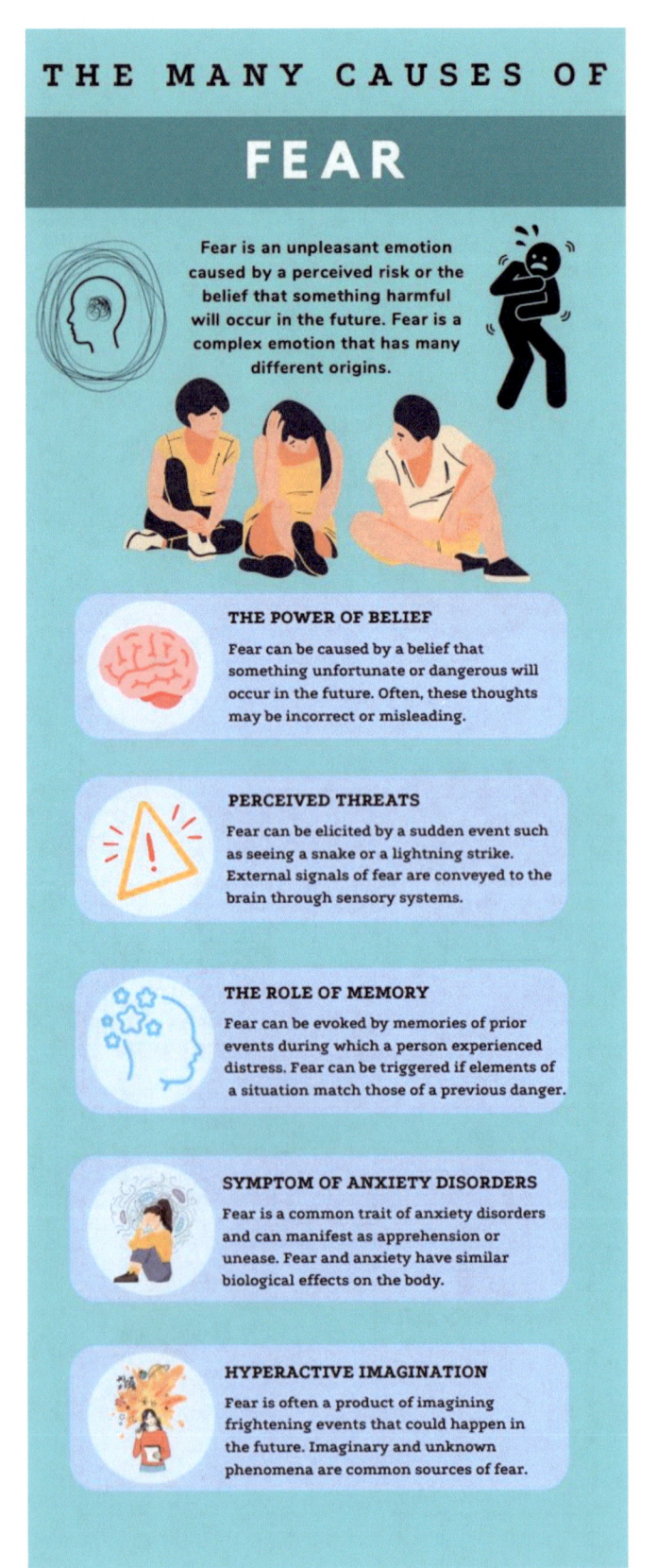

THE MANY CAUSES OF FEAR

Fear is an unpleasant emotion caused by a perceived risk or the belief that something harmful will occur in the future. Fear is a complex emotion that has many different origins.

THE POWER OF BELIEF
Fear can be caused by a belief that something unfortunate or dangerous will occur in the future. Often, these thoughts may be incorrect or misleading.

PERCEIVED THREATS
Fear can be elicited by a sudden event such as seeing a snake or a lightning strike. External signals of fear are conveyed to the brain through sensory systems.

THE ROLE OF MEMORY
Fear can be evoked by memories of prior events during which a person experienced distress. Fear can be triggered if elements of a situation match those of a previous danger.

SYMPTOM OF ANXIETY DISORDERS
Fear is a common trait of anxiety disorders and can manifest as apprehension or unease. Fear and anxiety have similar biological effects on the body.

HYPERACTIVE IMAGINATION
Fear is often a product of imagining frightening events that could happen in the future. Imaginary and unknown phenomena are common sources of fear.

Megha Akkineni, Fall 2023

AN INFOGRAPHIC JOURNEY

the Causes of Fear
Anisah Bakshi

the Handling of Uncertainties
We can only accurately determine the likelihood of very few fixed events. This uncertainty of most events is therefore, the cause of many people's fears.

Internal vs External Sources
Fear can result from external/environmental sources. The brain acts as a mediator to makes sense of the sensory input than can elicit fear. Fear can also be the result of internal sources such as thoughts, hellucinations, and memories.

Fear can be Real of Imagined
The loss of a loved one or getting in a car accident are examples of real fears. Moreover, fear is caused by a person perceiving a threat which can vary from realistic to harmless. Phantom fears include the fear of conversation or fear of success/failure.

Fear of Harmless or Unlikely Events
Examples of **harmless** fears:
- Fear of certain animals (arachnophobia, cynophobia, ornithophobia)
- Fear of flying or heights (pteromerhanophobia, acrophobia)

Examples of **unlikely** fears:
- Fears of death from a catastrophic event or environmental disaster.
- Fears of catching a highly unlikely virus or sickness such as the plague in 2023.

Fear is Generally Misplaced
Most people fear the wrong things causing them to worry inappropriately. This can lead to choices and lifestyles that are not beneficial. People seek control over their fate even when statistically, it may be safer to make a different choice but with less control.

Anisah Bakshi, Fall 2023

---

5 CAUSES OF FEAR
BY: HIMA PRAVEEN

1. GENETICS
Some people are prone to having more fear than others solely due to the alterations in their brain chemistry. This means they are more vulnerable to developing phobias due to their genetics.

2. EVOLUTIONARY INSTINCTS
Some fears are innate, which is seen as a type of survival mechanism that helps us in situations where threats are perceived. The physical response from this biochemical reaction is the 'fight or flight' response, which helps the body respond to the danger in the environment.

3. LEARNED HISTORY
This may include childhood experiences that have led to learned fears. This means that if a child has a parent who is prone to anxiety about the unknown, the child can also develop this fear by learning from the parent. This highlights that fear can stem from what is learned.

4. NEGATIVE EXPERIENCES
Some experiences, such as abuse and accidents, could have triggered the development of a phobia. Many fears can be traced back to childhood experiences, some of which might have been traumatic. This means that simply witnessing or hearing about a negative experience could have been enough to trigger a phobia or fear.

5. PHYSICAL SYMPTOMS
Many fears occur because they lead to physical symptoms in response to certain actions. For example, a common fear is the fear of heights because being at a high elevation can induce dizziness and discomfort in the stomach. To avoid these physical sensations, a fear of heights may develop.

Sources:
Fritscher, L. (2023, April 11). The Psychology of Fear. Verywell Mind. https://www.verywellmind.com/the-psychology-of-fear-2671696
Mayo Foundation for Medical Education and Research. (2023, June 9). Specific phobias. Mayo Clinic. https://www.mayoclinic.org/diseases-conditions/specific-phobias/symptoms-causes/syc-20355156
Pratt, E. (2022, January 4). Fear of the unknown: Definition, symptoms, causes, treatment. Verywell Health. https://www.verywellhealth.com/fear-of-the-unknown-5208919

Hima Praveen, Fall 2023

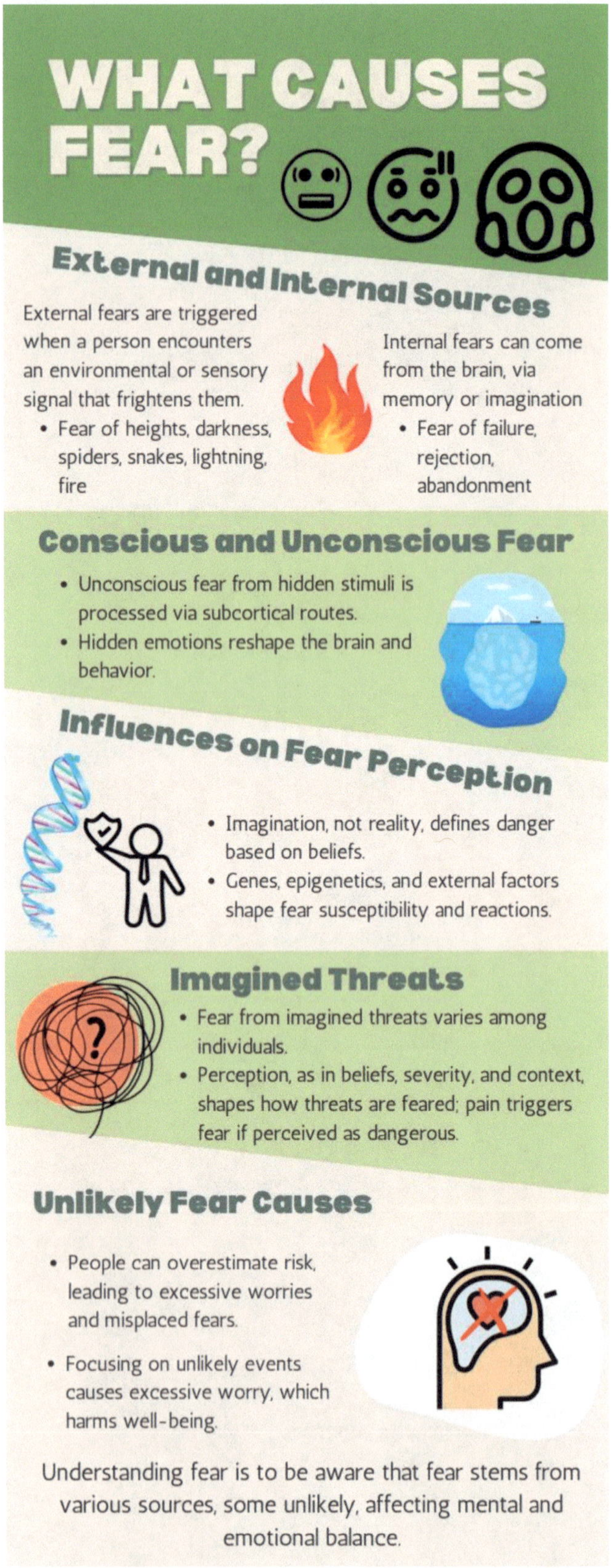

AN INFOGRAPHIC JOURNEY

WHAT CAUSES FEAR?

External and Internal Sources

External fears are triggered when a person encounters an environmental or sensory signal that frightens them.
- Fear of heights, darkness, spiders, snakes, lightning, fire

Internal fears can come from the brain, via memory or imagination
- Fear of failure, rejection, abandonment

Conscious and Unconscious Fear
- Unconscious fear from hidden stimuli is processed via subcortical routes.
- Hidden emotions reshape the brain and behavior.

Influences on Fear Perception
- Imagination, not reality, defines danger based on beliefs.
- Genes, epigenetics, and external factors shape fear susceptibility and reactions.

Imagined Threats
- Fear from imagined threats varies among individuals.
- Perception, as in beliefs, severity, and context, shapes how threats are feared; pain triggers fear if perceived as dangerous.

Unlikely Fear Causes
- People can overestimate risk, leading to excessive worries and misplaced fears.
- Focusing on unlikely events causes excessive worry, which harms well-being.

Understanding fear is to be aware that fear stems from various sources, some unlikely, affecting mental and emotional balance.

Natalie Laguer Torres, Fall 2023

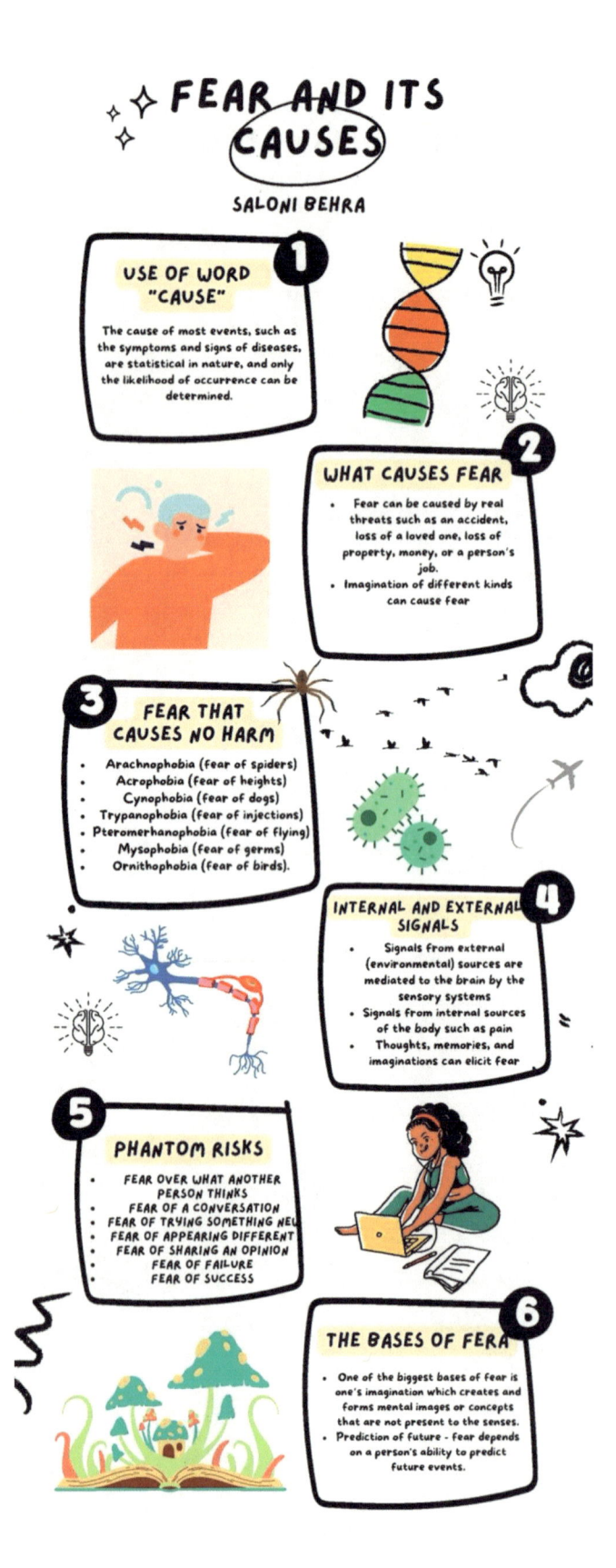

FEAR AND ITS CAUSES
SALONI BEHRA

1. USE OF WORD "CAUSE"
The cause of most events, such as the symptoms and signs of diseases, are statistical in nature, and only the likelihood of occurrence can be determined.

2. WHAT CAUSES FEAR
- Fear can be caused by real threats such as an accident, loss of a loved one, loss of property, money, or a person's job.
- Imagination of different kinds can cause fear

3. FEAR THAT CAUSES NO HARM
- Arachnophobia (fear of spiders)
- Acrophobia (fear of heights)
- Cynophobia (fear of dogs)
- Trypanophobia (fear of injections)
- Pteromerhanophobia (fear of flying)
- Mysophobia (fear of germs)
- Ornithophobia (fear of birds)

4. INTERNAL AND EXTERNAL SIGNALS
- Signals from external (environmental) sources are mediated to the brain by the sensory systems
- Signals from internal sources of the body such as pain
- Thoughts, memories, and imaginations can elicit fear

5. PHANTOM RISKS
- FEAR OVER WHAT ANOTHER PERSON THINKS
- FEAR OF A CONVERSATION
- FEAR OF TRYING SOMETHING NEW
- FEAR OF APPEARING DIFFERENT
- FEAR OF SHARING AN OPINION
- FEAR OF FAILURE
- FEAR OF SUCCESS

6. THE BASES OF FEAR
- One of the biggest bases of fear is one's imagination which creates and forms mental images or concepts that are not present to the senses.
- Prediction of future - fear depends on a person's ability to predict future events.

Saloni Nehra, Spring 2024

AN INFOGRAPHIC JOURNEY

Factors that Increase Fear and Anxiety
By: Talha Maqsood

False Information
Incorrect information is spread widely, causing fear of matters that are not as threatening.

Economic Situation
Because of economic situations of the home or of the country of origin, fear might be implanted of a downfall of society.

Increased Crime
Crimes becoming rampant in a certain area induces fear and anxiety in the community

Increased Suicide
Increased depression, anxiety, and suicide leads to more fear and anxiety.

Healthcare
When healthcare insurance and expenses rise up, fear and anxiety of injury start to arise as well.

Talha Maqsood, Spring 2023

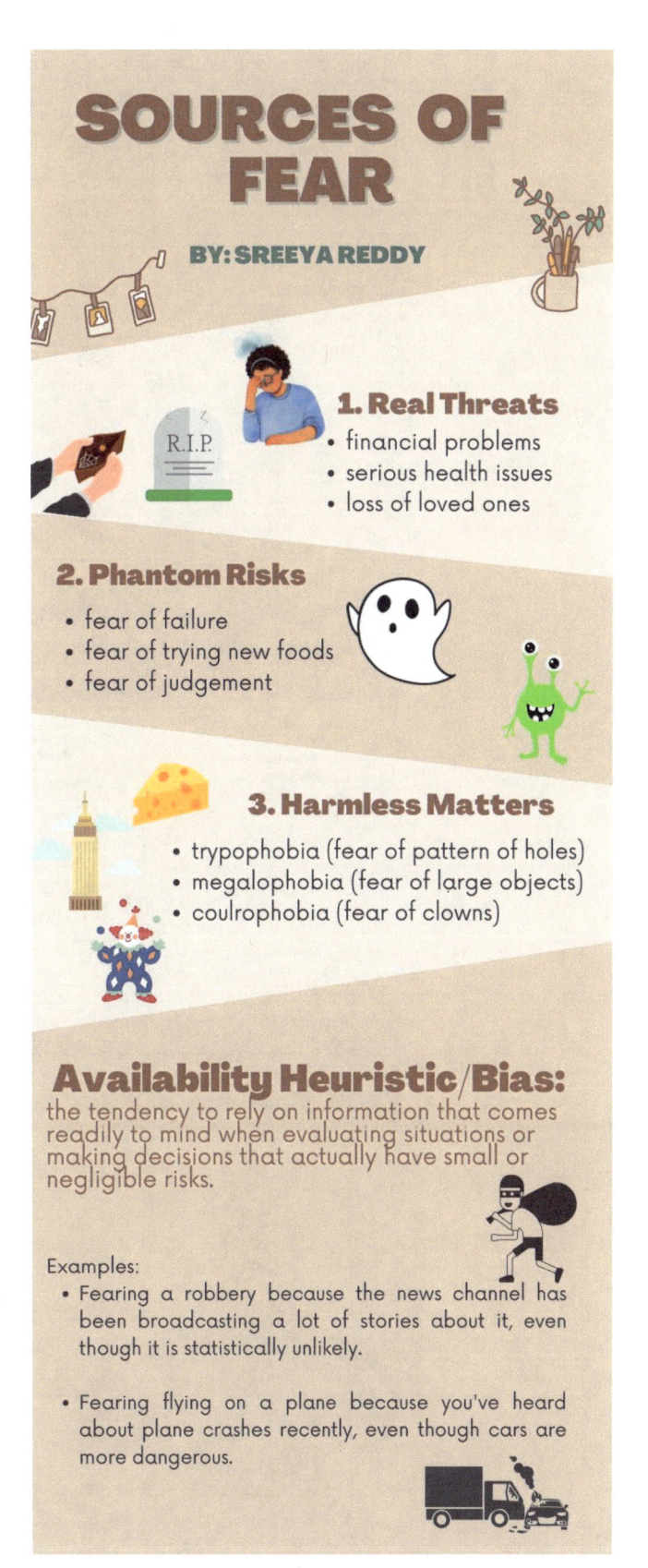

SOURCES OF FEAR
BY: SREEYA REDDY

1. Real Threats
- financial problems
- serious health issues
- loss of loved ones

2. Phantom Risks
- fear of failure
- fear of trying new foods
- fear of judgement

3. Harmless Matters
- trypophobia (fear of pattern of holes)
- megalophobia (fear of large objects)
- coulrophobia (fear of clowns)

Availability Heuristic/Bias:
the tendency to rely on information that comes readily to mind when evaluating situations or making decisions that actually have small or negligible risks.

Examples:
- Fearing a robbery because the news channel has been broadcasting a lot of stories about it, even though it is statistically unlikely.
- Fearing flying on a plane because you've heard about plane crashes recently, even though cars are more dangerous.

Sreeya Reedy, Spring 2023

Causes of Fear

MOST events, such natural disasters and disease, are statistical in the sense that there occurrence can be measured.

Yet many people still fear theses events and others.

Factors That Elicit Fear

- External sources
- Internal sources
- Imagination

→ Fear

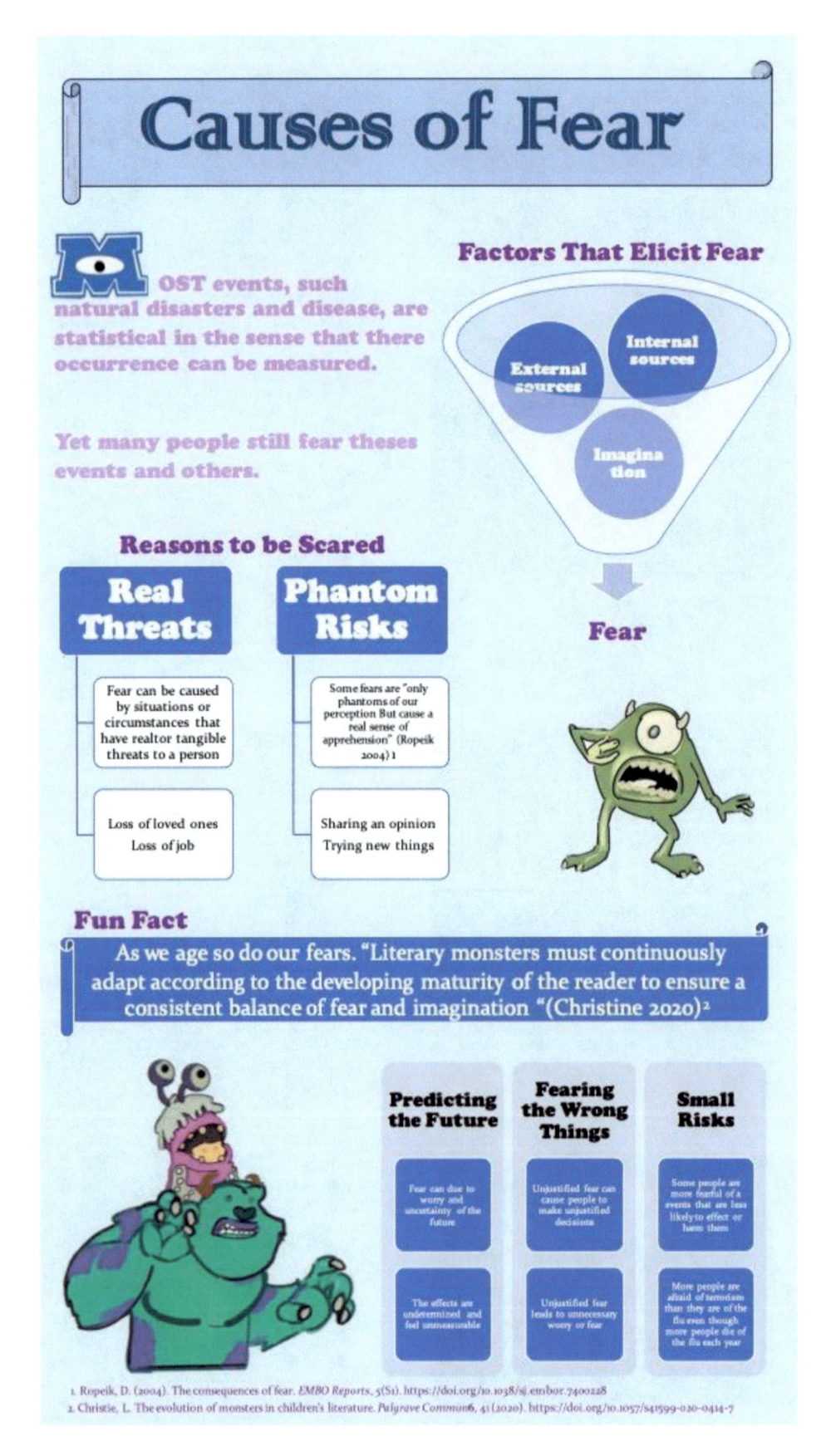

Reasons to be Scared

Real Threats
- Fear can be caused by situations or circumstances that have realtor tangible threats to a person
- Loss of loved ones
- Loss of job

Phantom Risks
- Some fears are "only phantoms of our perception But cause a real sense of apprehension" (Ropeik 2004) [1]
- Sharing an opinion
- Trying new things

Fun Fact

As we age so do our fears. "Literary monsters must continuously adapt according to the developing maturity of the reader to ensure a consistent balance of fear and imagination" (Christine 2020) [2]

Predicting the Future
- Fear can due to worry and uncertainty of the future
- The effects are undetermined and feel unmeasurable

Fearing the Wrong Things
- Unjustified fear can cause people to make unjustified decisions
- Unjustified fear leads to unnecessary worry or fear

Small Risks
- Some people are more fearful of a events that are less likely to effect or harm them
- More people are afraid of terrorism than they are of the flu even though more people die of the flu each year

1. Ropeik, D. (2004). The consequences of fear. *EMBO Reports*, 5(S1). https://doi.org/10.1038/sj.embor.7400228
2. Christie, L. The evolution of monsters in children's literature. *Palgrave Commun* 6, 41 (2020). https://doi.org/10.1057/s41599-020-0414-7

Anna Awa, Fall 2023

AN INFOGRAPHIC JOURNEY

Sources of FEAR

01 External Sources

Environmental stressors can elicit fear
Mediated by the brain and sensory systems

Internal Sources 02

Signals from the body can elicit fear
Examples include pain and self worth

03 Imaginations

Thoughts, imaginations and memories about future or previous events can elicit fear.

Example: Thinking about the MCAT or remembering the exam can cause fear

Nehal Dave, Spring 2024

AN INFOGRAPHIC JOURNEY

WHAT'S WORTH WORRYING ABOUT

Crista Thyvelikakath

Fear of events unlikely to occur and/or that are out of your control may not be worth the anxiety.

PURPOSEFUL	PROBLEMATIC
Influenza — There is use in fearing catching the flu, especially when it is flu season because the flu is very common. There are also many ways to lower your chance of catching the flu.	**Failure** — Such a subjective concept should not be so feared. There are few failures that are impossible to come back from, and success looks different to everyone.
Car Accidents — Car accidents are much more frequent and likely to cause harm. Practicing defensive driving, wearing a seatbelt, and avoiding distractions can save lives.	**Flying** — Airplane crashes are extremely unlikely. Many do not fear driving as much as flying, despite the statistics being much more concerning. You also have little control over risks when flying.
Losing Money — It is important to be smart with your money by budgeting, saving money, and not wasting money. You get to decide what happens to your money.	**Terrorism** — The average person can do little to combat terrorism. Facing a terrorist attack is also highly unlikely, and there is little anyone can do to decrease the low risk.
Drugs — Know the risks involved with what you put into your body. Consult a doctor when using any drug, including prescription or over-the-counter.	**Sharks** — Despite how the media portrays sharks, most are not out to kill humans. It is extremely unlikely to get attacked by a shark, so the fear is not worth avoiding a trip to the beach.

Crista Thyvelikakath, Spring 2023

CAUSES OF FEAR

The Past — reminders of trauma from a previous activities

Phobias — can be a persistent feeling toward an activity, object or situation

The Unknown — the belief of not knowing what is coming in the future

Human-made Fear — can come from work, society, government, and even families.

Social Anxiety Disorder — an intense feeling of not being embraced by others

Tamjeed Islam, Spring 2023

Fear Induced by Modern Society
BY: AKASH SIVAKUMAR

1 Economic Fears
In a modern society, the fear of economic survival grows each day. With debts and cost of living increasing each day, there is a fear of economic collapse on both a personal and societal level.

2 Technology Induced Fears
With the growing reach of technology, there is a rise in accessibility to information and other people. Unfortunately, there is also more false information spread through technology and causing fear.

3 Crime Rate
There is an increase in crimes in modern society causing an increase in fear for personal safety. For example, the number of murders increased from 205 to 254 from 2019 to 2020 in the DFW area.

4 Educational Burdens
Increasing competition brings out the fear of succeeding in the academic setting and the cost of education rises each year adding another economic fear.

5 Drug Usage
In modern society, access to drugs is easier, which is causing a rise in drug usage and physical harm. These trends are a consequence of increasing fears.

Akash Sivakumar, Fall 2023

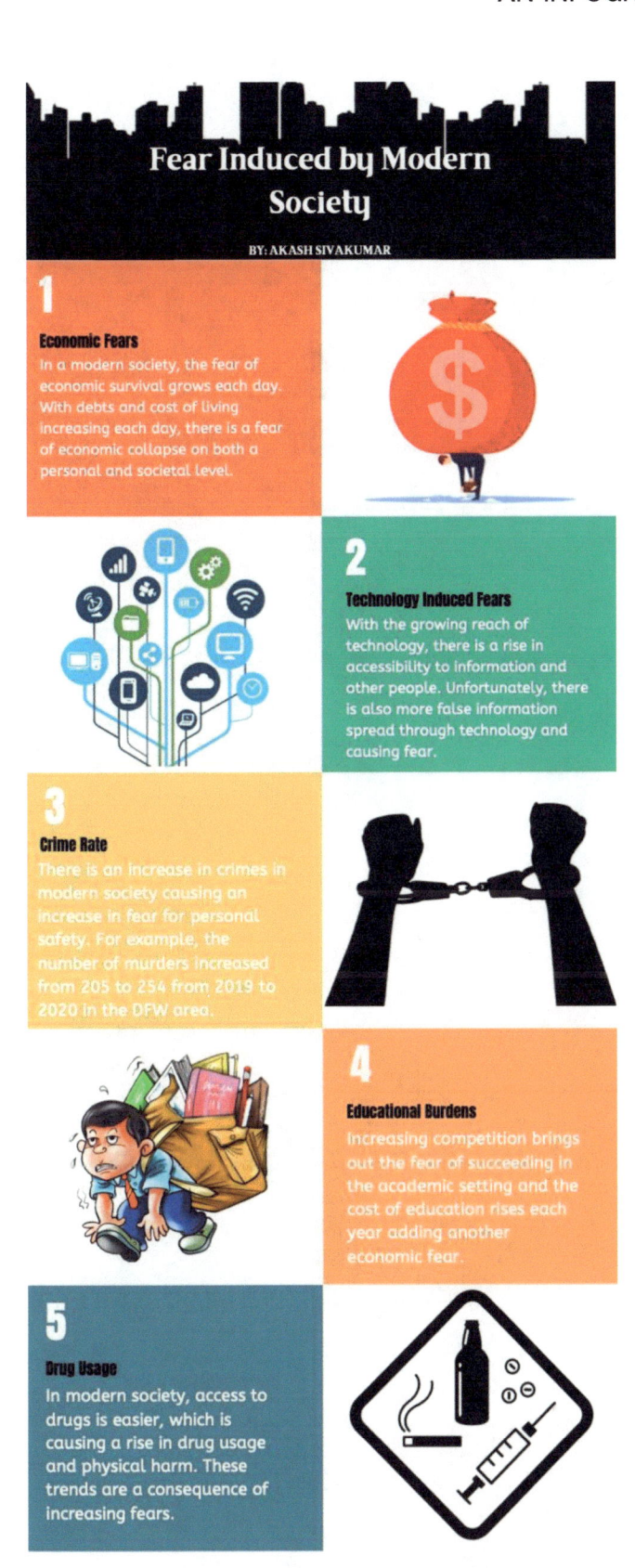

Recent Causes of Increased Fear
Pranavi Maddipatla

01 HEALTHCARE
The COVID-19 pandemic has heightened fear related to the rising costs of healthcare and caused anxiety over whether individuals would be able to continue to be able to access healthcare.

02 INDIVIDUAL RELIANCE
Recent build-up of frustration and lack of faith in the federal government has led many people to believe that they can no longer trust those in power to keep them safe, thus increasing fear and anxiety.

03 SOCIAL MEDIA
Increased connectivity between different communities across social media platforms has increased the spread of intimidating news articles as well as misinformation, leading individuals to fear for their safety.

04 POLITICS
Oftentimes politics have centered on influencing people by using fearmongering as a strategy to exaggerate potential causes for concern, resulting in increased anxiety for the general public.

References
Rothman, L. (2016, January 6). Why Americans are more afraid than they used to be. Time. https://time.com/4158007/american-fear-history/

Pranavi Maddipatla, Fall 2023

AN INFOGRAPHIC JOURNEY

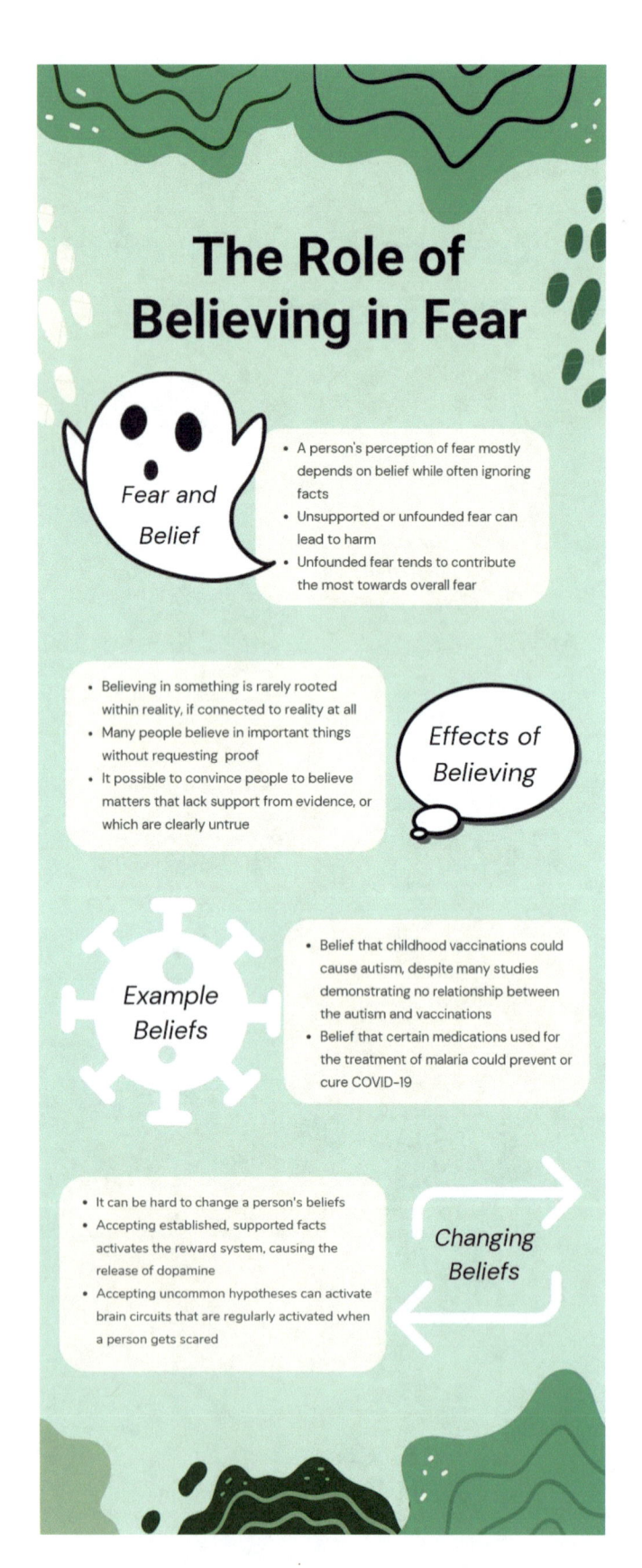

The Role of Believing in Fear

Fear and Belief
- A person's perception of fear mostly depends on belief while often ignoring facts
- Unsupported or unfounded fear can lead to harm
- Unfounded fear tends to contribute the most towards overall fear

Effects of Believing
- Believing in something is rarely rooted within reality, if connected to reality at all
- Many people believe in important things without requesting proof
- It possible to convince people to believe matters that lack support from evidence, or which are clearly untrue

Example Beliefs
- Belief that childhood vaccinations could cause autism, despite many studies demonstrating no relationship between the autism and vaccinations
- Belief that certain medications used for the treatment of malaria could prevent or cure COVID-19

Changing Beliefs
- It can be hard to change a person's beliefs
- Accepting established, supported facts activates the reward system, causing the release of dopamine
- Accepting uncommon hypotheses can activate brain circuits that are regularly activated when a person gets scared

Anonymous, Spring 2023

THE POWER OF BELIEVING & CONFIRMATION BIAS

It is often difficult to change what a person believes due to the facts activating the reward system releasing dopamine in the brain.

Believing is something loosely related to reality that many people believe matters of importance without requesting evidence.

Using confirmation bias (favoring information confirming your previous existing beliefs) activates the reward pathway in the brain.

The "reward" pathway runs from the ventral tegmental area (VTA) that released dopamine when experiencing pleasurable stimulus.

SO JUST KEEP BELIEVING!

Kayla Pham, Spring 2023

AN INFOGRAPHIC JOURNEY

FEAR & IMAGINATION

basis of fear
often imagination is the basis of fear due to the mind's ability to create images or concepts that are not present to the senses, so the fear of danger may not be rooted in reality

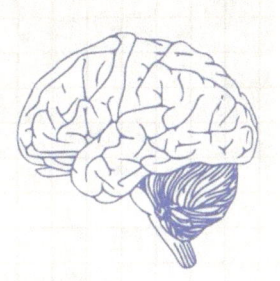

future prediction
fear depends on a person's ability to predict future events since fear is a worry about what can happen in the future although these occurences are uncertain

people fear the wrong things
fearing the wrong things causes unnecessary worry and leads to what is known as unjustified fear which may cause people to make unfavorable decisions.

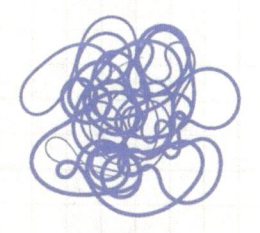

focusing on small risks
the fear for more unlikely occurrences tend to be focused on much more than what's statistically more likely.
examples:
- much more fear of natural disaster than getting influenza
- wanting a gun at home in case of intruders, when having a gun at home is much more dangerous statistically than an intruder

Zahra Zafar, Spring 2024

Infographic #3
Our Perception of Fear

We tend to worry about the wrong things
Our fears, more often than we may think, are misdirected and can in turn result in missed opportunities, failures, and poor decision making. We worry about things that we have no control over and ignore things that are obvious to cause harm.

How can we decide what we should and shouldn't worry about?
It's important to think logically and understand that our fears may be associated with risks. These risks are usually based in perception rather than actuality when it comes to worries and fears. It's important to come to terms with the facts. What is true and what isn't. What absolutely can hurt us and what more than likely cannot, despite what we feel.

How we react differently
Not everyone reacts to fear in the same way. Some of us may face it head on. Some may avoid it, some may even freeze up completely and may be unable to react. We sometimes tend to come up with our own coping mechanisms for our fear, such as using humor to lighten the mood, or simply seeking social support from friends and/or family.

Our perception of fear
Fear is different to each and every single one of us. No two people fear the same exact things the same exact way. This is because the fears we experience are not static, rather they are dependent on miscellaneous things that encapsulate our identity, such as social status, wealth, security, and most notably, our past experiences.

How our beliefs control our fears and reactions
Our beliefs can strongly influence how we react when we are afraid. We fear what we definitively believe to be true and this can be difficult. It is difficult to change one's beliefs. Once someone believes something and fears it, it is highly unlikely that they will no longer fear it.

Sources Used: Møller, A.R. Sensory Systems: Anatomy and Physiology, Aage R. Møller Publishing, 2014.

Zaki Khan, Fall 2023

AN INFOGRAPHIC JOURNEY

Fear and our Imagination
By: Shrujin Shah

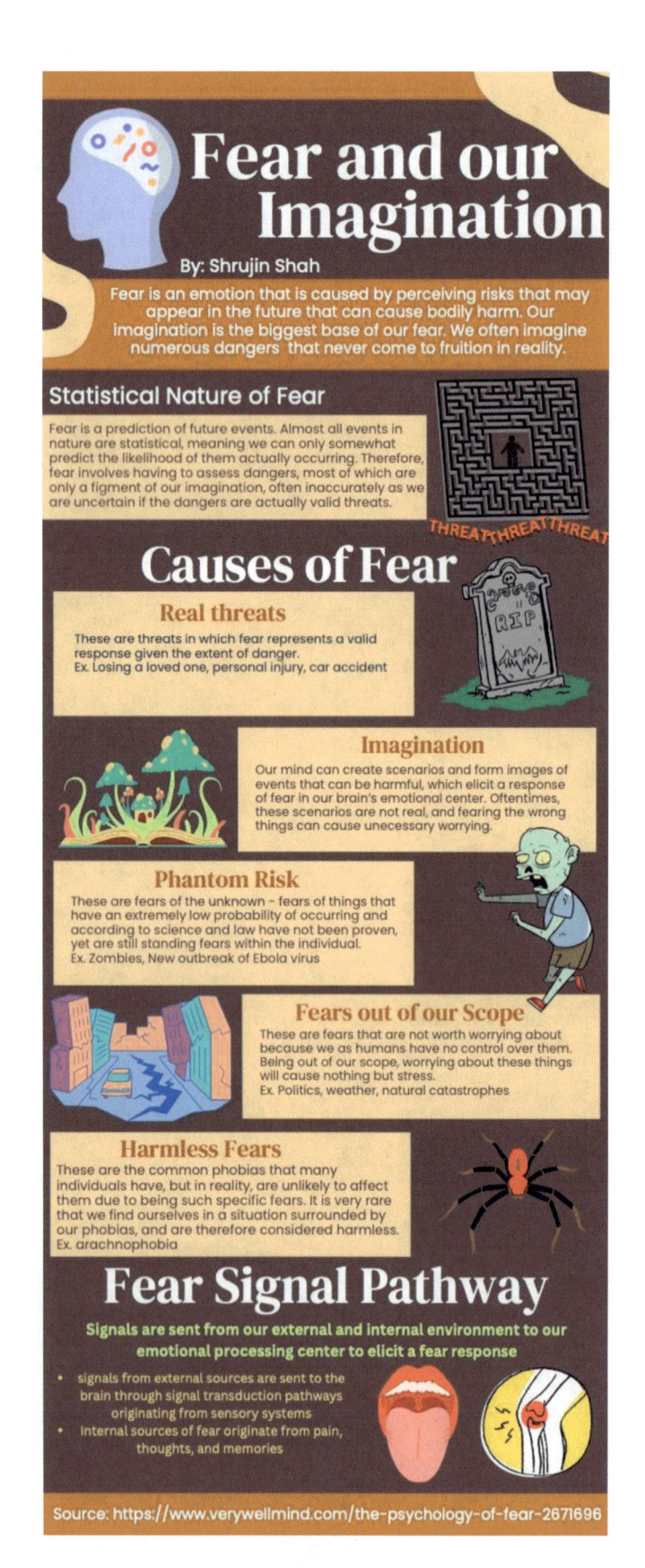

Fear is an emotion that is caused by perceiving risks that may appear in the future that can cause bodily harm. Our imagination is the biggest base of our fear. We often imagine numerous dangers that never come to fruition in reality.

Statistical Nature of Fear
Fear is a prediction of future events. Almost all events in nature are statistical, meaning we can only somewhat predict the likelihood of them actually occurring. Therefore, fear involves having to assess dangers, most of which are only a figment of our imagination, often inaccurately as we are uncertain if the dangers are actually valid threats.

Causes of Fear

Real threats
These are threats in which fear represents a valid response given the extent of danger.
Ex. Losing a loved one, personal injury, car accident

Imagination
Our mind can create scenarios and form images of events that can be harmful, which elicit a response of fear in our brain's emotional center. Oftentimes, these scenarios are not real, and fearing the wrong things can cause unecessary worrying.

Phantom Risk
These are fears of the unknown - fears of things that have an extremely low probability of occurring and according to science and law have not been proven, yet are still standing fears within the individual.
Ex. Zombies, New outbreak of Ebola virus

Fears out of our Scope
These are fears that are not worth worrying about because we as humans have no control over them. Being out of our scope, worrying about these things will cause nothing but stress.
Ex. Politics, weather, natural catastrophes

Harmless Fears
These are the common phobias that many individuals have, but in reality, are unlikely to affect them due to being such specific fears. It is very rare that we find ourselves in a situation surrounded by our phobias, and are therefore considered harmless.
Ex. arachnophobia

Fear Signal Pathway
Signals are sent from our external and internal environment to our emotional processing center to elicit a fear response

- signals from external sources are sent to the brain through signal transduction pathways originating from sensory systems
- Internal sources of fear originate from pain, thoughts, and memories

Source: https://www.verywellmind.com/the-psychology-of-fear-2671696

Shrujin Shah, Fall 2023

BELIEFS AND FEAR

THE ROLE OF BELIEF
An individual's beliefs that something unfortunate or dangerous may happen in the future, as well as interpretation of signals, may elicit fear. Beliefs often determine what to fear and to what extent

IMAGINATION
Beliefs concerning fear are often based on imagination as opposed to reality. As fear-based imagination can lead us to believe something is true with minimal evidence, people's perceptions of the source and extent of dangers tend to be rooted in incorrect information.

SIGNALS OF BELIEF-BASED FEAR
Pain, injury, or other signals from within the body can elicit fear if a person believes it is a source of danger, such as a disease

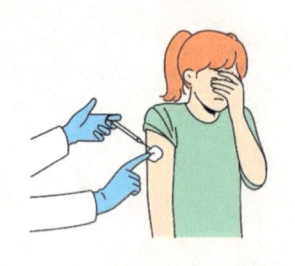

Fear may also be elicited if a person perceives a signal or stimulus as a threat. As beliefs are often based on incorrect information, an individual's fear is often based on phantom risks or of harmless matters, such as an injection (trypanophobia)

Minaal Atif, Spring 2024

18

AN INFOGRAPHIC JOURNEY

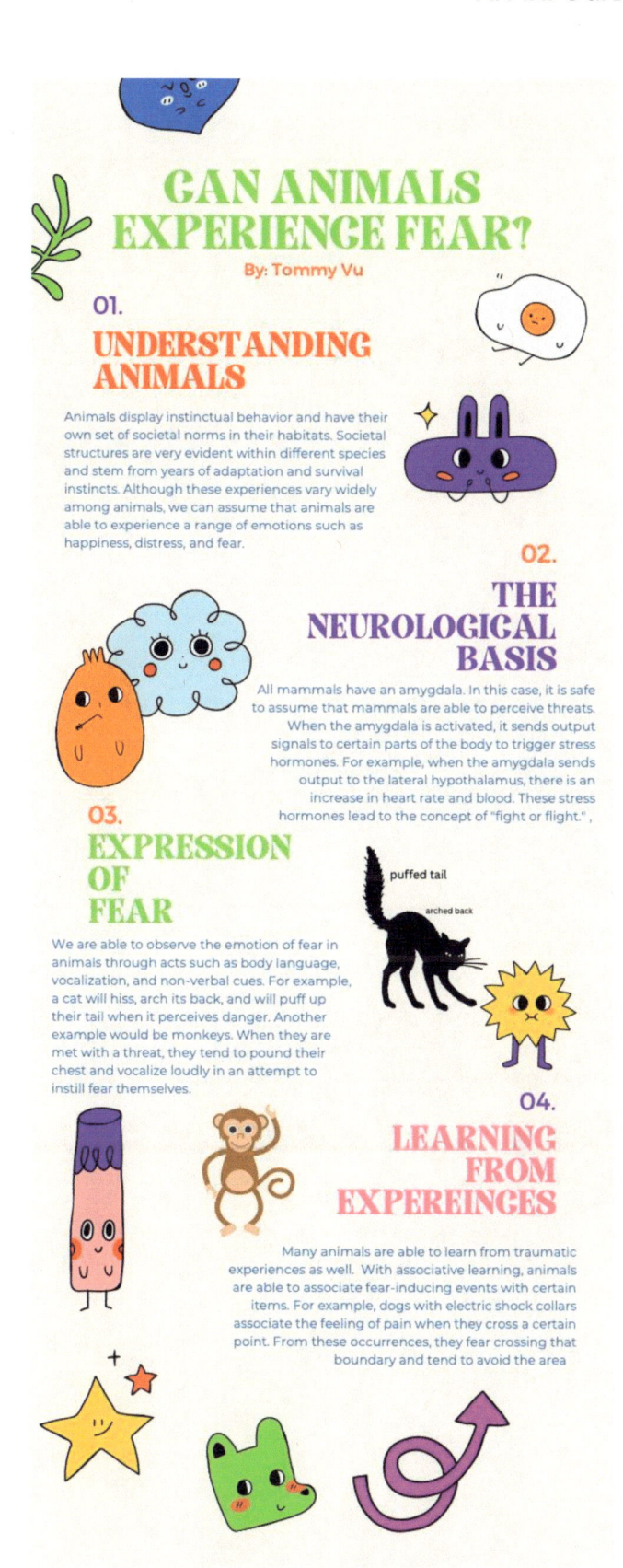

Tommy Vu, Fall 2023

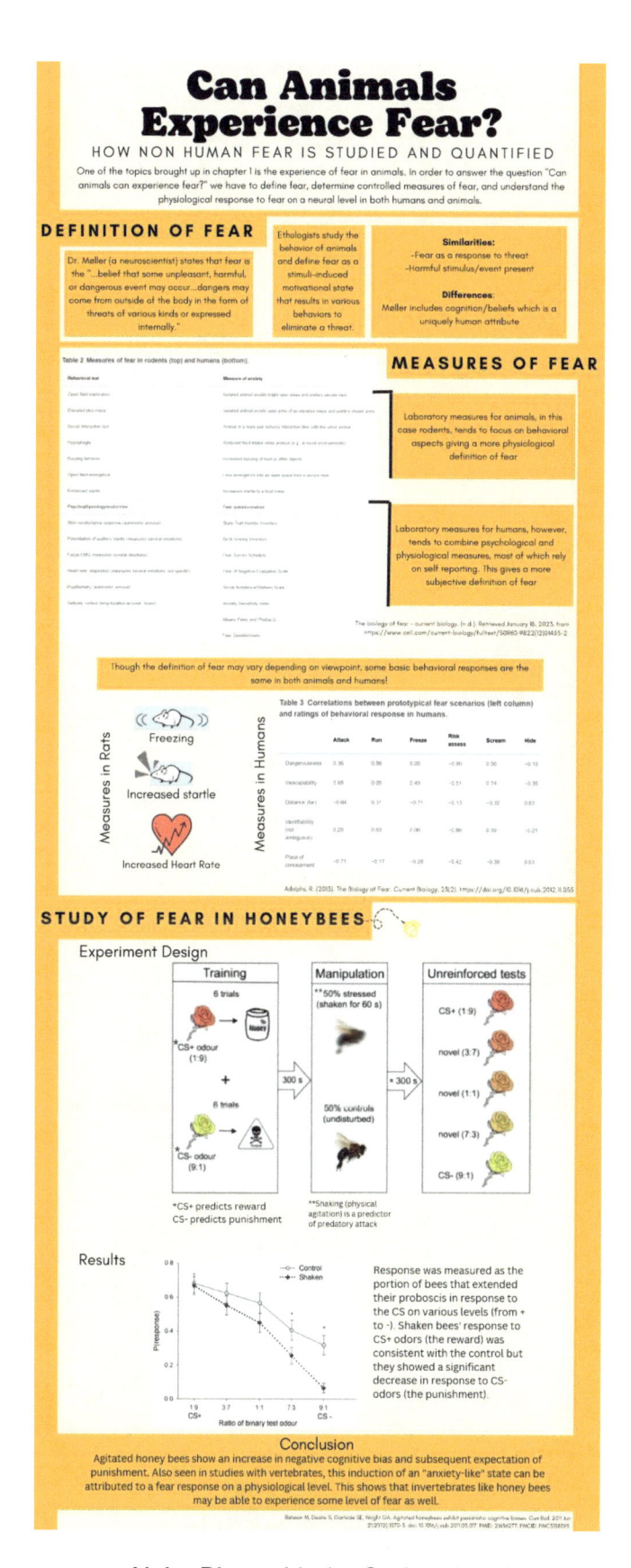

Neha Bhupathiraju, Spring 2023

AN INFOGRAPHIC JOURNEY

CHAPTER 2

Categorizing Fear

The Multifaceted Nature of Fear: Understanding Its Manifestations, Effects, and Interventions

By Nabeeha F. Hassan, Spring 2024

Fear is a universal human emotion, with its expressions, triggers, and impacts varying widely across the globe. Studies examining the prevalence of specific phobias reveal a range of 3% to 15% globally (Eaton 2018), underscoring the pervasive and multifaceted nature of fear in our lives. To delve deeper into this complex psychological and physiological experience, it is crucial to define fear and explore its nuances, from rational to irrational manifestations, its far-reaching effects on the human body, and the strategies that can be employed to mitigate its negative consequences.

At the outset, fear can be defined as an unpleasant, highly subjective emotional state that cannot be objectively measured or quantified. It is an emotion primarily concerning potential future events and the belief that something hazardous or threatening may occur, leading to harm, injury, or other undesirable outcomes. While pain serves as a warning about present occurrences, fear alerts us to potential future dangers, triggering a cascade of physiological responses aimed at protecting the body. Interestingly, fear can be a source of enjoyment for some individuals, as evidenced by the widespread popularity of horror movies and thrill-seeking activities.
However, excessive, uncontrolled fear can significantly diminish an individual's quality of life and interfere with daily functioning, underscoring the need for a deeper understanding of this complex emotion.

Professionals from diverse academic and clinical backgrounds, such as psychologists, neuroscientists, physicians, and clinical neurophysiologists, approach the study of fear from varying perspectives, each offering unique insights. For instance, a psychologist may define fear as a complex emotional state that results in physical and psychological changes, influencing an individual's thoughts, behaviors, and overall well-being. In contrast, a neuroscientist may define fear as a specific pattern of brain activity, particularly in the brain's emotional centers, such as the amygdala nuclei.

Within the broad category of fear, there are several distinct subtypes, each with its characteristics and implications. These include rational (justified) fear, irrational fear, acute fear, chronic fear, misdirected fear, fear from phantom risks, enjoyable fear, purposeful fear, and non-purposeful fear. Rational (justified) fear may stem from events such as the loss of a loved one, contracting a severe illness, financial hardship, becoming a victim of crime, or experiencing a harmful accident. On the other hand, irrational fear is often directed towards dangers that never materialize, as predictions about what is genuinely hazardous are frequently inaccurate and based on distorted perceptions or cognitive biases. Fear can also be categorized by its intensity, with strong fear triggering a robust fight-or-flight response, moderate fear causing elevated sympathetic activity and decreased parasympathetic activity, and slight fear resulting in a more subtle elevation in sympathetic activity and lower-than-normal parasympathetic activity.

The far-reaching effects of fear on the human body are well-documented, with the autonomic nervous system responding accordingly. Typically, the activity of the parasympathetic nervous system decreases. In contrast, the sympathetic nervous system's activity increases, leading to physiological changes, such as increased heart rate, elevated blood pressure, and heightened muscle tension. Fear can also profoundly influence our actions, encouraging us to take precautionary measures to reduce the risks of trauma or illness, such as using seat belts, getting vaccinated, and maintaining a healthy lifestyle. However, people often exhibit a distorted perception of risk, underestimating the importance of certain events and overestimating the importance of others, as exemplified by the disproportionate fear of Ebola compared to the more prevalent and deadly influenza virus in the United States.

Both external and internal sources can trigger fear. Internal sources include pain, thoughts, memories, and imaginations, while external sources encompass real threats, such as accidents, loss of loved ones, or loss of property, money, or employment. Many fears also originate from matters that pose no actual harm, such as phobias of spiders, heights, dogs, injections, flying, or frogs. People are also often afraid of events beyond their control, including politics, weather, natural disasters, and unlikely occurrences, such as death from a catastrophic event or a rare disease.

Interestingly, knowledge and understanding have helped reduce some forms of fear. Advancements in areas like vaccination, healthy lifestyle promotion, and prenatal care have alleviated certain fears by providing individuals with the tools and information to mitigate specific risks. Similarly, scientific and clinical studies have demonstrated the potential for various preventive measures, such as vitamin D3 supplementation, blood pressure management, and physical exercise, to reduce the risk of diseases like cancer and stroke significantly. However, the medical profession has been slow to promote the widespread adoption of these preventive strategies, highlighting the need for a more proactive approach to addressing the root causes of fear.

In addition to these preventive measures, developing effective therapeutic interventions has also played a crucial role in helping individuals manage their fears. Cognitive-behavioral therapy (CBT), for example, is highly effective in treating a wide range of fear-related disorders, such as phobias, panic attacks, and generalized anxiety. By challenging distorted thought patterns, improving coping strategies, and gradually exposing individuals to their feared stimuli in a controlled environment, CBT can help individuals develop a more rational and adaptive response to fear-inducing situations. Similarly, the use of medications, such as selective serotonin reuptake inhibitors (SSRIs) and benzodiazepines, can be a valuable complement to psychological interventions, providing short-term relief and reducing the physiological symptoms of fear.

Beyond individual-level interventions, public health initiatives and policy changes can also be crucial in addressing the social and environmental factors contributing to fear. For instance, improving community safety, enhancing emergency preparedness, and promoting mental health literacy can help reduce the prevalence and impact of fear-related disorders. Additionally, advocating for increased funding and research in the field of fear and anxiety can lead to a better understanding of the underlying mechanisms and the development of more effective prevention and treatment strategies.

In conclusion, fear, though a natural and adaptive emotion, can profoundly impact individuals' lives, ranging from rational caution to debilitating anxieties. Understanding the intricacies of fear, from its neurobiological foundations to its diverse manifestations, is essential for developing targeted interventions to mitigate its negative consequences. By promoting knowledge, fostering rational risk assessments, and advocating for preventive and therapeutic measures, we can navigate the complexities of fear and cultivate resilience in the face of uncertainty, ultimately enhancing individual and societal well-being.

References

- Dr. Faisal Jahangiri and his class

- Eaton, W. W., Bienvenu, O. J., & Miloyan, B. (2018). Specific phobias. The lancet. Psychiatry, 5(8), 678–686. https://doi.org/10.1016/S2215-0366(18)30169-X

Being Afraid for the Wrong Reasons

Rational fears are fears of real matters such as contracting a serious illness or being involved in a car accident. They are justified because they can cause harm to a person's everyday life.

Illnesses and car crashes are serious dangers to our well being!

Irrational fears are fears that cannot cause harm to a person. Many people discriminate against those who are different from themselves. Xenophobia for example, is an irrational fear and hatred of international citizens. This is an irrational fear because people are not a threat to us because of their differences.

People are made from the same origin, and thus there is no reason to fear people's differences on the basis of race, sexuality, or socioeconomic status.

Juveria Ali, Spring 2023

AN INFOGRAPHIC JOURNEY

IRRATIONAL FEARS

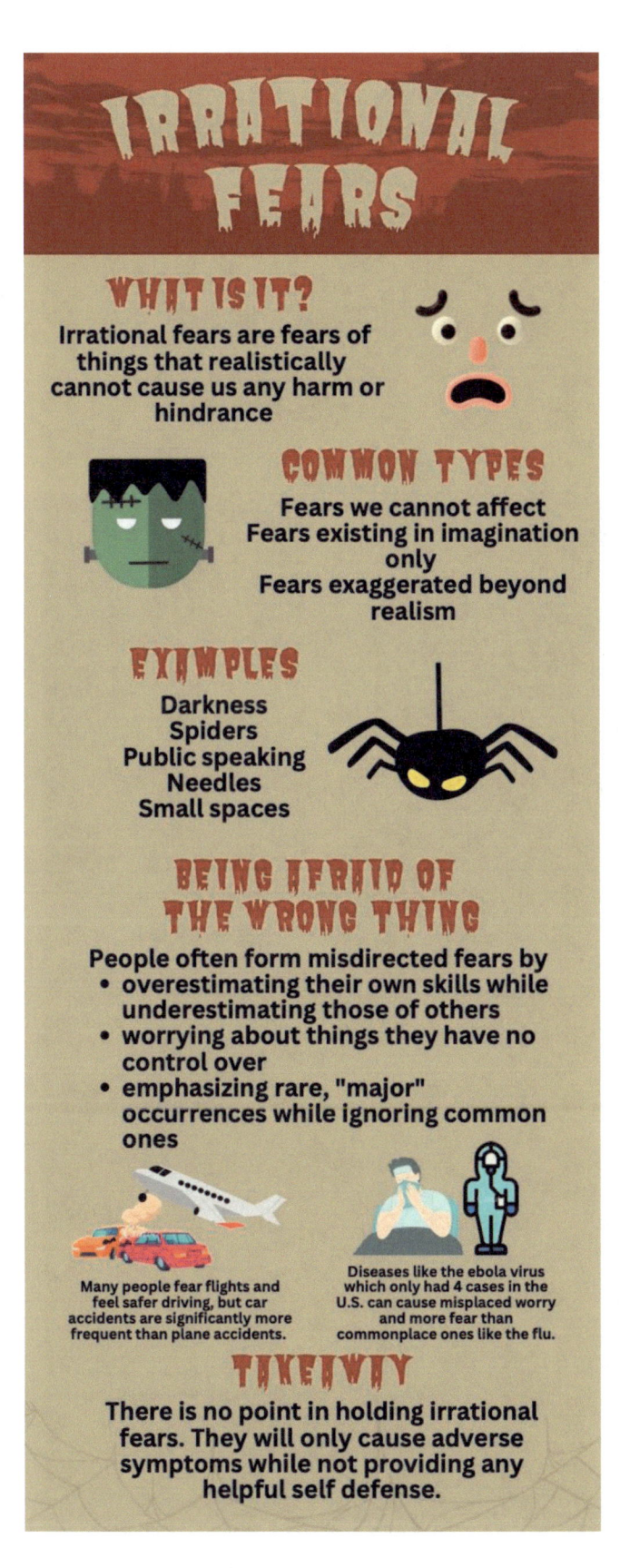

WHAT IS IT?
Irrational fears are fears of things that realistically cannot cause us any harm or hindrance

COMMON TYPES
Fears we cannot affect
Fears existing in imagination only
Fears exaggerated beyond realism

EXAMPLES
Darkness
Spiders
Public speaking
Needles
Small spaces

BEING AFRAID OF THE WRONG THING
People often form misdirected fears by
- overestimating their own skills while underestimating those of others
- worrying about things they have no control over
- emphasizing rare, "major" occurrences while ignoring common ones

Many people fear flights and feel safer driving, but car accidents are significantly more frequent than plane accidents.

Diseases like the ebola virus which only had 4 cases in the U.S. can cause misplaced worry and more fear than commonplace ones like the flu.

TAKEAWAY
There is no point in holding irrational fears. They will only cause adverse symptoms while not providing any helpful self defense.

Aman Mohammad, Fall 2023

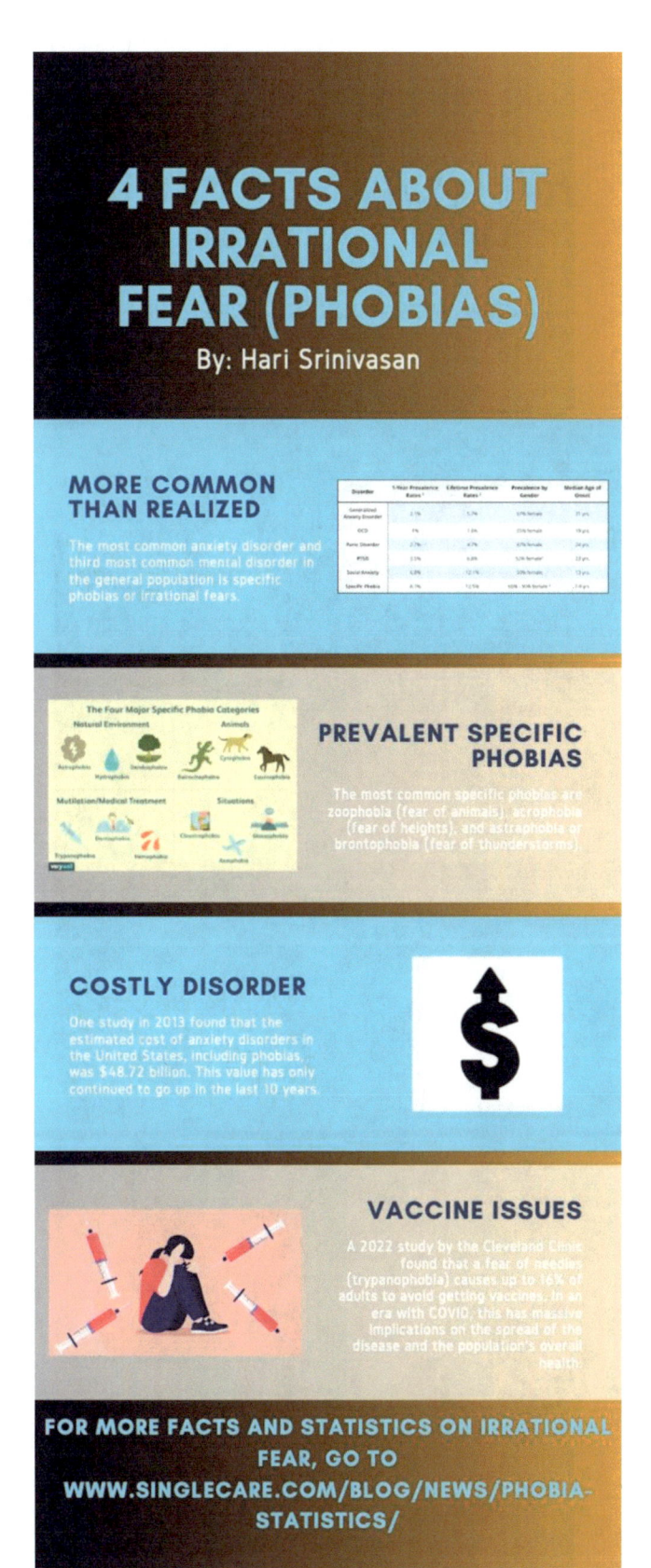

---

4 FACTS ABOUT IRRATIONAL FEAR (PHOBIAS)
By: Hari Srinivasan

MORE COMMON THAN REALIZED
The most common anxiety disorder and third most common mental disorder in the general population is specific phobias or irrational fears.

PREVALENT SPECIFIC PHOBIAS
The most common specific phobias are zoophobia (fear of animals), acrophobia (fear of heights), and astraphobia or brontophobia (fear of thunderstorms).

COSTLY DISORDER
One study in 2013 found that the estimated cost of anxiety disorders in the United States, including phobias, was $48.72 billion. This value has only continued to go up in the last 10 years.

VACCINE ISSUES
A 2022 study by the Cleveland Clinic found that a fear of needles (trypanophobia) causes up to 16% of adults to avoid getting vaccines. In an era with COVID, this has massive implications on the spread of the disease and the population's overall health.

FOR MORE FACTS AND STATISTICS ON IRRATIONAL FEAR, GO TO
WWW.SINGLECARE.COM/BLOG/NEWS/PHOBIA-STATISTICS/

Hari Srinivasan, Fall 2023

AN INFOGRAPHIC JOURNEY

SOURCES OF RATIONAL FEAR OF HARM

A few examples of what humans realistically think about that leads them to become fearful.

LOSS OF SPOUSE OR CHILD
No individual would want their loved one to pass especially at the most unpredictable moments.

GETTING SEVERE DISEASE
Unknown cures for high-complex viruses can lead a person to create a scenario in their head if they unexpectedly contract it one day.

BEING A VICTIM OF A CRIME
Influence of National News and the crimes that are presented to the public can allow a person to think whether they are the next victim.

HAVING A TRAFFIC ACCIDENT
Constant drunk driving and reckless driving present on the news.

Skyla Lopez, Spring 2023

RATIONAL VS IRRATIONAL FEAR

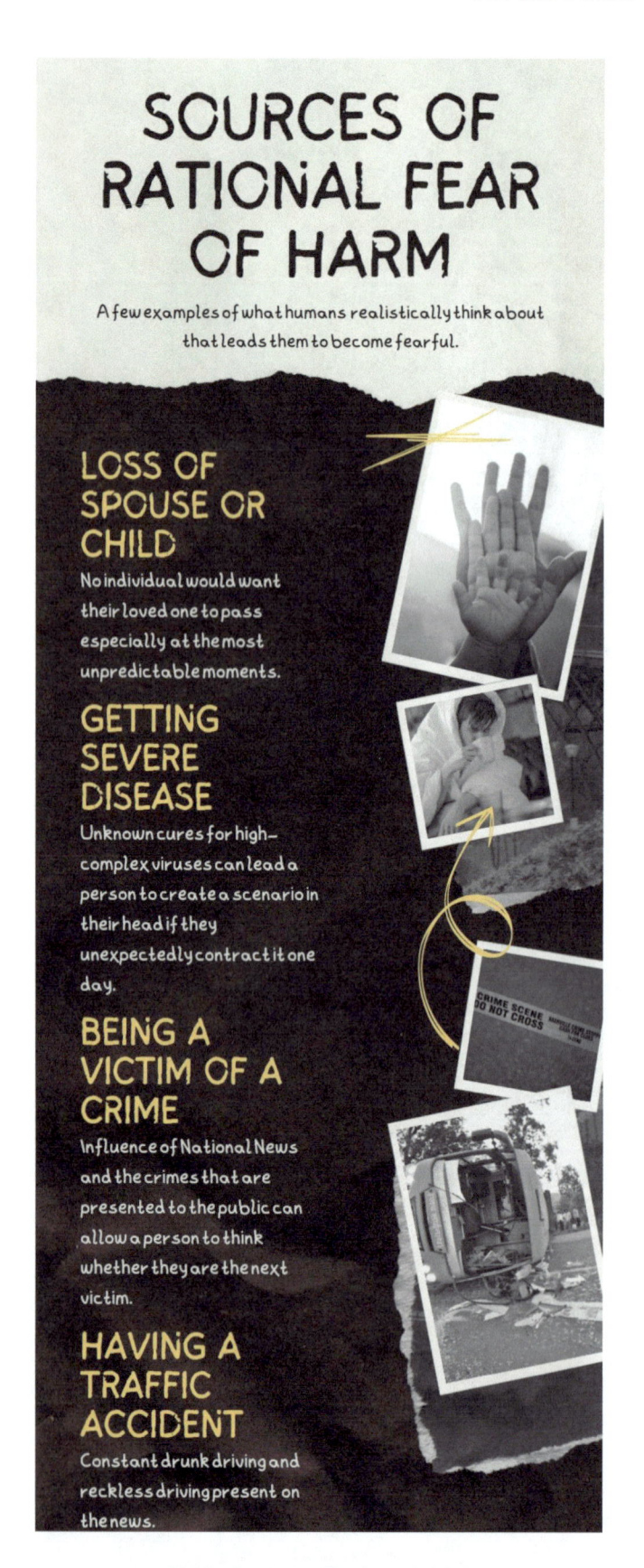

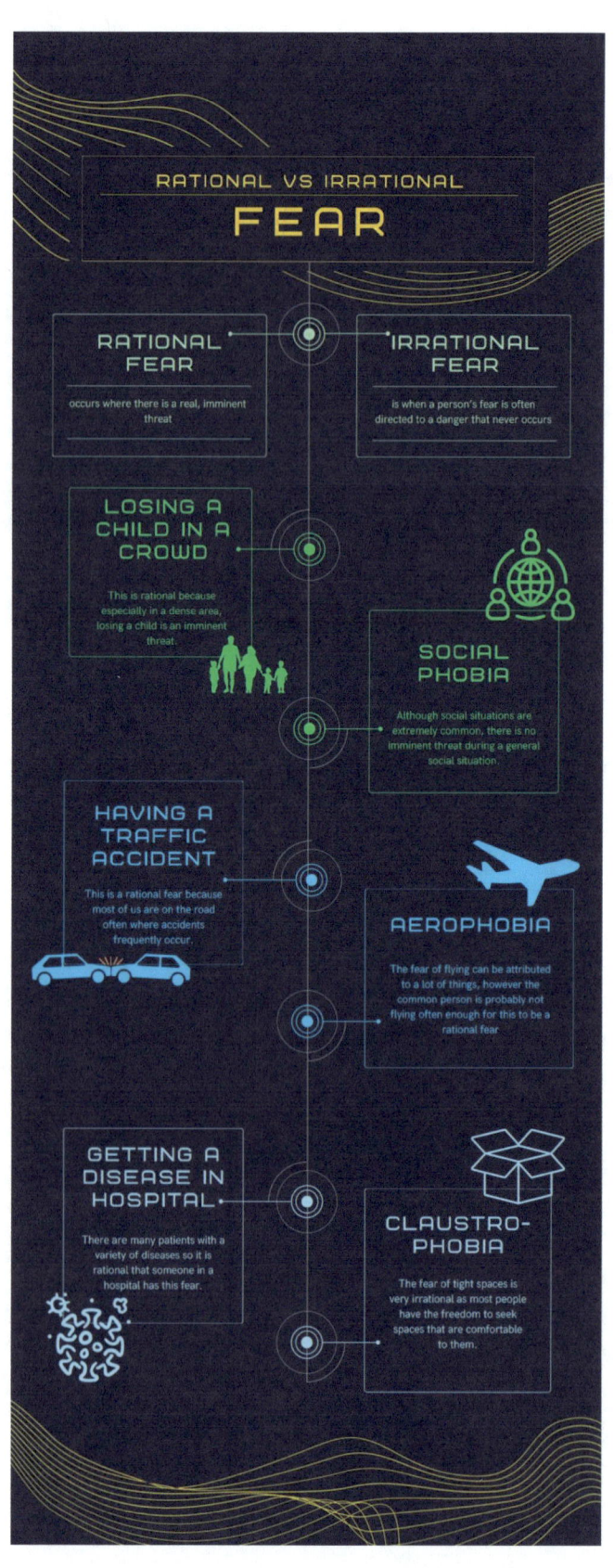

RATIONAL FEAR
occurs where there is a real, imminent threat

IRRATIONAL FEAR
is when a person's fear is often directed to a danger that never occurs

LOSING A CHILD IN A CROWD
This is rational because especially in a dense area, losing a child is an imminent threat.

SOCIAL PHOBIA
Although social situations are extremely common, there is no imminent threat during a general social situation.

HAVING A TRAFFIC ACCIDENT
This is a rational fear because most of us are on the road often where accidents frequently occur.

AEROPHOBIA
The fear of flying can be attributed to a lot of things, however the common person is probably not flying often enough for this to be a rational fear

GETTING A DISEASE IN HOSPITAL
There are many patients with a variety of diseases so it is rational that someone in a hospital has this fear.

CLAUSTRO-PHOBIA
The fear of tight spaces is very irrational as most people have the freedom to seek spaces that are comfortable to them.

Shreya Saride, Spring 2023

AN INFOGRAPHIC JOURNEY

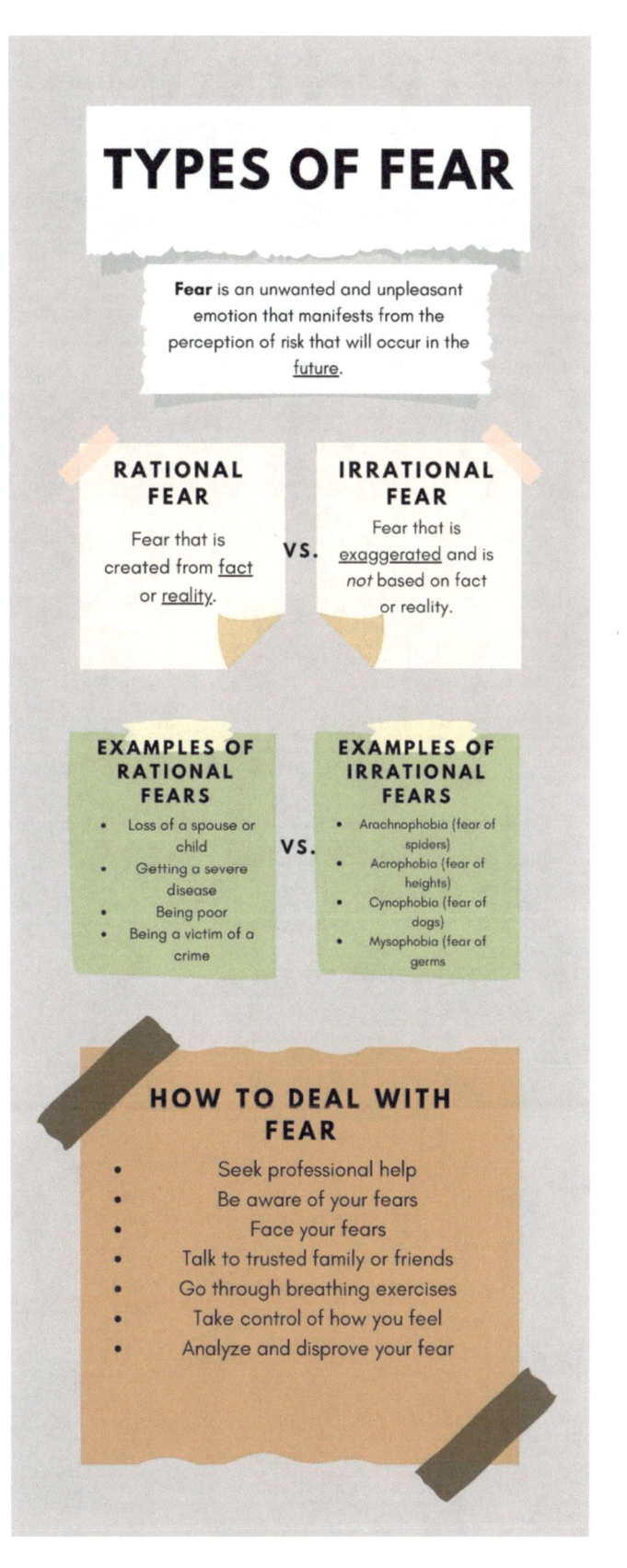

Irrational Fear: Causes and Effects
By: Naomi Kurian

What is Irrational Fear?
Irrational fear, also commonly known as phobia, is uncontrollable fear due to certain things, environments, or activities that restricts one from daily activities.

Causes of Irrational Fear
- past traumatic events
- learned reaction from childhood
- reaction to previous panic attack
- long term stress
- genetic factors

Effects of Irrational Fear
There are physical and psychological symptoms of irrational fear. Some physical effects include fainting, hot flashes, nausea, etc. Some psychological effects are fear of dying, fear of fainting, extreme anxiety, panic attacks, etc.

Examples of Irrational Fears
Irrational fears can be due to any regular object, place, activity, etc. Some examples include:
- insects
- school
- enclosed places
- driving
- germs

Treatment for Irrational Fears
The most commonly prescribed treatment for irrational fears is Cognitive Behavioral Therapy (CBT) where a practical approach is decided to decrease the fear. This may occur through gradual exposure to the fear to desensitize the patient from the fear.

Naomi Kurian, Spring 2024

TYPES OF FEAR

Fear is an unwanted and unpleasant emotion that manifests from the perception of risk that will occur in the <u>future</u>.

RATIONAL FEAR
Fear that is created from <u>fact</u> or <u>reality</u>.

vs.

IRRATIONAL FEAR
Fear that is <u>exaggerated</u> and is *not* based on fact or reality.

EXAMPLES OF RATIONAL FEARS
- Loss of a spouse or child
- Getting a severe disease
- Being poor
- Being a victim of a crime

vs.

EXAMPLES OF IRRATIONAL FEARS
- Arachnophobia (fear of spiders)
- Acrophobia (fear of heights)
- Cynophobia (fear of dogs)
- Mysophobia (fear of germs

HOW TO DEAL WITH FEAR
- Seek professional help
- Be aware of your fears
- Face your fears
- Talk to trusted family or friends
- Go through breathing exercises
- Take control of how you feel
- Analyze and disprove your fear

Dannah Bagcal, Spring 2024

AN INFOGRAPHIC JOURNEY

7 DIFFERENT KINDS OF FEAR
By: Shrujin Shah

Fear is an emotion that is caused by perceiving risks that may appear in the future that can cause bodily harm. There are various kinds of fear that all act as a warning signal for dangers in our environment and make us afraid.

Rational (justified) Fear
Rational fear comes from a completely justified source that is perceived by many to be dangerous and has the possibility to cause immense pain (physically or mentally) or bodily injury.
Ex. Coronavirus, Loss of a child, Car accident

Irrational (unjustified) Fear
An irrational fear represents fear of a threat that never occurs or a fictional future danger that has no chance of actually harming the individual. People with an irrational fear will go to extreme lengths to avoid situations involving a fear that is not actually present.
Ex. Deserted on island

Chronic Fear / Acute Fear
Chronic fear represents fears that have affected our brain and well-being for a long period of time and have the possibility to cause many physical and mental health complications such as ADHD and clinical depression. This is the opposite of acute fear, which is fear that is only temporary and based on current circumstances.
Ex. Constant fear of failure

Fear from Phantom Risks
This is a fear of things that do not exist.
Ex. Zombies, Ghosts

Enjoyable Fears
This is a fear that stimulates our brain to crave more of a particular activity since we find it enjoyable. Individuals genuinely enjoy the feelings of adrenaline (raised heart rate, palpitations, pounding heart) that is obtained from these sources of fear.
Ex. Rollercoasters, Horror movies

Purposeful Fear
Purposeful fear describes a situation when fear is used as a warning sign for our body. Purposeful fear is usually felt as a general defense system to protect our body from immediate dangers in our surroundings. Through evolution, fear was used as a defense mechanism with the purpose of keeping an animal/individual's guard up.
Ex. Earthquake, Predator vs. Prey

Shrujin Shah, Fall 2023

DIFFERENT TYPES OF FEAR

GENERAL DEFINITION
Fear is a natural emotional response to future events that imply or are perceived to imply a danger. Fear is crucial for survival, however excessive fear can impact daily functions and emotional well-being.

RATIONAL & IRRATIONAL
Also known as justified and unjustified fears. Rational fears are based in logic and reason to measure the danger levels of a particular stimulus or situation. Irrational fears have many layers and are not based in reason. An example of a rational fear is fear of going out due to a pandemic.

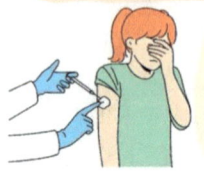

ACUTE
Triggered by a stimulus or specific situation, acute fears are typically intense phobias that do not seem to match the actual level of danger posed. For example, the fear of needles can be triggered by vaccines and the individual may experience heightened anxiety during doctor appointments

CHRONIC
A long-lasting state of fear or generalized sense of worry. Can couple with external stressors, traumatic experiences, or it is not always tied to a single event. This sense of excessive worry can impact one's daily lives. In some cases, it can lead to physical illnesses as well.

MISDIRECTED
Misdirected fear often overlaps with irrational fear in the sense that it is not based on a realistic threat. For example, arachibutyrophobia is the fear of peanut butter sticking to the roof of the mouth. Peanut butter isn't usually seen as an actual danger which is what makes this misdirected.

PHANTOM RISK
Fear of situations, objects, or people that do not exist or lack evidence proving its reality. It is commonly influenced by media portrayal and misinformation. An example of this is one having a fear of ghosts, spirits, and hauntings.

ENJOYABLE
Fear that is experienced in a safe environment and provides pleasure and excitement over distress is seen as enjoyable. This is one of the ways that fear can be beneficial as it is a way for individuals to better understand themselves and their emotions. Examples of enjoyable fears are watching horror movies, playing thriller games, rollercoasters, etc.

PURPOSEFUL & NOT
Purposeful fears are seen as a useful survival mechanism that is thought to have evolved within humans. For example, the fear of heights may have evolved to prevent fall injuries. Not purposeful fears are not linked to a survival mechanism and somewhat overlap with irrational fears.

Sneha Sharma, Spring 2024

AN INFOGRAPHIC JOURNEY

TYPES OF FEAR

1. RATIONAL FEAR
Justified fears
- Protects individuals from dangerous environments
- Pandemics, gun violence, poisons

2. IRRATIONAL FEAR
Unjustified fears
- Caused by non-dangerous factors
- Choosing to drive long distances to avoid flying due to a fear of flights

3. ACUTE FEAR
Sudden emergencies
- Can be caused by past experiences
- Fear of car accidents or sudden illness (heart attacks, strokes)

4. CHRONIC FEAR
Long-term fears
- Physical health (minor symptoms evolving to cancer)
- Fear of death by old age

5. MISDIRECTED FEAR
Illogical fears
- Superstitions (opening an umbrella indoors, breaking a mirror)
- Fear of harmless creatures

6. FEAR OF PHANTOM RISKS
Fear of what does not exist
- Risks not backed by science
- Threats: Ghosts, zombies, apocalypses

7. ENJOYABLE FEAR
Voluntary fears
- Satisfaction from fear-causing actions
- Riding rollercoasters, watching horror movies

8. PURPOSEFUL/NOT PURPOSEFUL FEAR
Difference between fears directed to a risk or the wrong matter
- Beneficial when identifying valid harms

Devaditya Ray, Fall 2023

Types of Fear

THE DEFINITION OF FEAR
- Unpleasant emotion
- Occurs when a person believes a negative event will happen in the future
- Part of the body's defense systems
- Encourages behaviors that reduce the risk of harm

TYPES OF FEAR

JUSTIFIED
- Proportional to the likelihood an event will happen and the consequences if it did
  Two Types:
- Purposeful: leads to actions that reduce the risk of harm
- Not purposeful: does not lead to productive action
  Example:
- Fear of COVID, leading to getting the vaccine

IRRATIONAL
- Disproportionate fear of harmless, imaginary, or unlikely events and objects
- Many common fears are irrational
  Examples:
- Fear of flying
- Fear of spiders

ACUTE
- Lasts only a short time
  Example:
- Fear of failing a test that dissipates after taking the test

CHRONIC
- Lasts for an extended period of time
- Detrimental to physical health
- Can be a sign of an anxiety disorder

Allyson Macfee, Spring 2024

AN INFOGRAPHIC JOURNEY

2 TYPES OF FEAR
IRRATIONAL & RATIONAL

01 WHAT IS IRRATIONAL FEAR?
Unjustified fears of matters that cannot cause any harm or inconvenience or signal damage of any kind to a person. Tend to be exaggerated beyond what is realistic and imaginative.

02 WHAT IS RATIONAL FEAR?
Justified fears of real matters such as harm to a person's body or damaging effects on a person's everyday life.

03 EXAMPLE FOR IRRATIONAL FEAR:
Being afraid of totally harmless things, such as salamanders and/or spiders are a form of irrational fear.

04 EXAMPLE FOR RATIONAL FEAR:
Walking on the street when it's dark because of the risk of robbery (being a victim of crime), fear of illness, fear of falling.

05 BENEFITS FOR BOTH
Taking matters of appropriate precautions can be beneficial such as getting vaccinated to prevent getting sick.

06 CONSEQUENCES FOR BOTH
Often people's worries are in vain. Consequently, this can lead to sickness, excessive worry, anxiety, and fatigue.

Tabatha Vaca Nieves, Spring 2023

THREE TYPES OF FEAR

Strong Fear
A flight or fight reaction, which is marked by decreased parasympathetic activity and increased sympathetic activity, can be triggered by a significant fear. Both increased awareness and tremors in the muscles may result from this physiological response. Extreme terror can make it difficult to engage in cognitive activity because the fight-or-flight response takes precedence. It's crucial to remember that this increased awareness is a normal, adaptive process that gets the body ready to respond to perceived threats.

Moderate Fear
Elevated sympathetic activity and decreased parasympathetic activity can be brought on by moderate fear. An increase in attentiveness and a reduction in relaxation are the characteristics of this physiological reaction. The sympathetic nervous system's activation can trigger a mild fight-or-flight response, preparing the body to react to imagined dangers. The body's adaptive reaction to mild to moderate levels of fear is reflected in this balance between sympathetic and parasympathetic activity.

Slight Fear
While retaining lower than normal parasympathetic activity, slight fear causes a small rise in sympathetic activity. This physiological reaction is indicative of a little activation of the stress response in the body, which causes a minor elevation in alertness. This degree of fear is characterized by a balance between sympathetic and parasympathetic activity, which points to a controlled and adaptive physiological response to perceived dangers and supports a raised but controllable state of arousal.

Emma Siddiqui, Spring 2024

The 5 Different Types of FEAR

BEWARE: MAY CAUSE FEAR

1. RATIONAL FEAR
Rational fear occurs when there is a potentially dangerous event or object. There is real, imminent danger. Examples include a harmful accident or being a victim of a crime.

2. IRRATIONAL FEAR
Irrational fear is often directed towards danger that never occurs. Unlike rational fears, there is no actual threat. Examples include phobias such as a fear of flying or a fear of heights.

3. ACUTE FEAR
Have you ever feared of getting into an accident while driving? This is acute fear! Something suddenly causing fear.

4. CHRONIC FEAR
Chronic fear can be characterized by constant worrying, nervousness, and tension. This type of fear can lead to headaches/migraines, and muscle aches leading into fibromyalgia.

5. ENJOYABLE FEAR
Do you enjoy watching horror movies? You're most likely experiencing enjoyable fear! This is a result of the highly enjoyable adrenaline rush caused by fear.

Kayla Pham, Spring 2023

PHANTOM FEARS
BY ELSA CHITTET

DEFINITION: Fear may be caused by a person's belief that something unfortunate or dangerous may happen in the future

EXAMPLES

FEAR OVER WHAT ANOTHER PERSON THINKS
One may judge of being watched and judged by others, effecting work, school, and other daily activities.

FEAR OF A CONVERSATION
These fears make us self-conscious and anxious about conversation with strangers and acquaintances, leading us to avoidance and isolation.

FEAR OF TRYING SOMETHING NEW
Being fearful of the unknown, it causes individuals to stick to familiar experiences and restrict themselves from unlocking their full potential.

FEAR OF APPEARING DIFFERENT
This involves a fear of being belittled or criticized for your choices in front of others. This causes one to blend into the crowd rather than expressing how one would truly desire.

FEAR OF SHARING AN OPINION
Similarly, the fear of expressing one's opinion is derived from the fear of being judged. It prevents one's true thoughts being spoke and being vulnerable to the public.

FEAR OF FAILURE
Fear of failing can cause individuals to do nothing and prevent us from moving forward in progress missing opportunities in the way.

FEAR OF SUCCESS
Individuals are fearful of success due to the possibility of fearing failure through these added responsibility. It involves being afraid of achievement, often to the point that people will sabotage themselves.

Elsa Chittet, Spring 2024

AN INFOGRAPHIC JOURNEY

4 FLAVORS OF FEAR
Shohini Ghosh

Rational
Rational fear is reasonable fear, usually felt in times of danger. Examples includes being followed at night and contracting a deadly disease.

Irrational
Irrational fear is directed at something that is not dangerous or the prediction of danger is wrong. These types of fears are in vain.

Chronic
Chronic fear can have physical effects on the body such as migraines, chronic body pain, and weak immune system.

Enjoyable
Some people like to enjoy fear because there is a feeling of danger which causes fear, but no risk of harm. This can be done by going on a rollercoaster or watching a horror movie.

DIFFERENT TYPES OF FEAR

RATIONAL & IRRATIONAL
Rational fears include things that may cause harm to a person's body or damaging effects on a person's everyday life or loss of property. Common examples of rational fear are fear of illness or of falling. Irrational fears include things that can't cause harm or signal damage of any kind. These fears may also just exist in a person's imagination. Some examples of irrational fear are the fear of salamanders or spiders.

ACUTE & CHRONIC
Thoughts and memories can elicit both acute and chronic fears. An example of an acute fear is the feeling of an immediate danger to the body, such as a hostile person or animal, or a car accident. Examples of chronic fears would be fears that occur over a long period of time and create physical effects such as headaches or muscle aches.

MISDIRECTED
Misdirected fears can also be referred to as worries. Worries describe a kind of misdirected fear that can be harmful to both the body and the mind as it can cause stress and decrease the quality of life. Some examples of misdirected worries are worrying about something that cannot be proven or disproven, or worrying about terrorism in the USA when the risk of being harmed by an intoxicated driver is much higher.

PHANTOM RISKS
Phantom risks are the fear of the unknown or the fear of things that don't actually exist. An example of phantom risks would be the fear of ghosts.

ENJOYABLE
Fear is often regarded as an unpleasant feeling. However, some individuals experience pleasure or joy from watching horror movies or riding rollercoasters. While these things may produce a feeling of danger, there is no risk associated with that fear. That being said, real-life experiences from a threatening person with a weapon are very different than watching a horror movie.

PURPOSEFUL & NOT PURPOSEFUL
Fear can be purposeful as it can be used to identify a specific risk. Fears can also be purposeful but not beneficial if fear is directed to matters that pose no risk. For example, being afraid of harmless objects or events. Fears that are not purposeful are fears that are directed to the wrong matter or if there is no specific target that can be identified.

SOURCES
Free design tool: Presentations, video, social media | CANVA. Canva. (n.d.). https://www.canva.com/
Møller, A. R. (2019). Neurobiology of Fear and other Emotions. Aage R Møller Publishing.

Shohini Ghosh, Spring 2023

Tiffany Nouanesengsy, Fall 2023

AN INFOGRAPHIC JOURNEY

3 WAYS FEAR CAN BE A MANIPULATOR

Fear can be used as a weapon to manipulate a single person or even an entire population. Let's learn about the different ways this can occur.

WHAT CAN FEAR DO?

Fear is a commonly used weapon to terrorize people. A common example of this is when modern politicians fabricate misleading information about opposing candidates to dissuade citizens from electing the opposing candidacy.

FEAR MONGERING

This form of fear can be induced by deliberately causing alarm to the public regarding certain issues. Most times fear mongering can be irreversible because people are uncomfortable changing their minds. An example of this would be when car commercials mention having fewer passenger airbags which can evoke fear in a family because it can cause them harm.

FEAR FOR THE GAIN OF MONEY

People can manipulate information for personal gain such as for money. This type of fear is commonly seen in movies when a person is kidnapped or threatened for answers.

WEAPON IN WARS

For several years, fear has been used as a weapon for wars or as a means to solve conflicts. Religious wars are an example of this which have lasted for centuries. Fear can also be exacerbated through the use of real weaponary to manipulate the public into following a groups' rules and laws.

EXAMPLES

Fear can consume our daily life and may cause irrational fears regarding events otherwise deemed non-threatening. Other common examples fear is used as a manipulator include purchasing unecessary types of insurances or signing up for services that are not needed.

Source: Neurobiology of Fear and Other Emotions, Aage R. Moller

Devapriya Baiju, Fall 2023

MANIPULATION BY FEAR

HOW IS IT USED?

Fear can be used by a person to manipulate another to the point of committing crimes or achieve their own personal goal. All the person has to do is learn what the other is really scared of and hold it over their head.

An example of this can be seen in governments...
- Fear is used to keep citizens under control. The most common example of this being laws and their consequences if broken.

Fear is one of the most efficient methods for manipulation.

WHAT CAN IT DO?

This is usually done to get a person subdued and under the control of the manipulator. It's one of the most effective ways to dominate a person. It makes one pliable and submissive. Making them go along with whatever is asked of them.

"THE ONLY THING WE HAVE TO FEAR IS FEAR ITSELF." - FRANKLIN D. ROOSEVELT

The manipulation of fear can be used by...
- Bosses to intimidate employees
- A person to terrorize their spouse
- Police officers to enforce law

Alicia Gonzalez, Spring 2023

33

AN INFOGRAPHIC JOURNEY

CHAPTER 3

Life with Fear

Fear and the Impact on the COVID-19 Vaccination

By Mark Nguyen, Spring 2024

On March 11, 2020, the World Health Organization (WHO) declared COVID-19 a pandemic. This led to the halting of life as we know it, including closing schools, restaurants, and malls. Loss of taste, shortness of breath, and a dry cough quickly became well-known and rightfully feared tell-tale signs of the virus. Scientists and research labs began to work rapidly to develop a vaccine to combat the virus's spread. After months of rigorous testing and safety protocols, the Pfizer-BioNTech COVID-19 mRNA vaccine was authorized for emergency use in individuals 16 years and older on December 11, 2020. At this point, it was believed that the tides would turn in the fight against the novel coronavirus.

Despite the expansion of the availability of the mRNA vaccine, the safety and efficacy of it was heavily scrutinized in the United States. The public remained hesitant to receive the vaccine due to concerns over the rapid development and potential side effects, rallying against the CDC's recommendations. Many quoted a small number of anecdotal stories of severe side effects, such as some cases of people having blood clots from one of the vaccines, further exacerbating fears over the safety of the vaccine. Other factors that affected the public perception of the vaccine were based on political ideologies and the concerns over mandatory vaccinations leading to the infringement of one's autonomy. These decided to make the vaccinations highly controversial due to the fear and skepticism of their safety, further delaying the end of the pandemic.

The widespread vaccine resistance posed a significant challenge to achieving herd immunity in the US. Herd immunity, a term often mentioned in the context of the pandemic, is achieved when a threshold percentage of the population becomes immune, either through vaccination or previous infection. This reduces the likelihood of transmission to individuals who lack immunity. A formula can determine the threshold for herd immunity, $I_c = 1 - (1/R_o)$, where

Ro is the basic reproductive number indicating how many secondary cases are generated by a singular primary case. Initially, herd immunity seemed within reach as transmission rates were low. However, the disease evolved, becoming more transmissible. This was mainly due to the fear of safety concerns and the lack of action regarding vaccination, pushing the threshold for herd immunity out of reach.

The significant role of fear during the pandemic demonstrates how it can harm our health. Fear is one of the seven universal emotions, including anger, happiness, disgust, sadness, and surprise. Fear is caused by signals from external (environmental) or internal (body) sources that can elicit the emotion. The body's internal alarm is a complex and unpleasant emotion caused by the perceived risk of harmful events that may occur in the future. Once triggered, it causes an elevation in sympathetic activity and a decrease in parasympathetic activity, which prepares the body for fight-or-flight. Although fear is generally viewed as a negative emotion, it can have many benefits, such as receiving the COVID-19 vaccine due to the fear of contracting a fatal disease. As mentioned earlier, fear can also have many adverse effects, such as producing extreme reactions unrelated to the perceived risk of consequences.

Fear can manifest in various ways, from rational (justified) fears about bona fide dangers to irrational (unjustified) fears triggered by unlikely threats. Additional types of fear include acute fear, chronic fear, misdirected fear, fear from phantom risks, enjoyable fear, and fear that is purposeful. Unjustified fear can lead to overestimating risks while underestimating more common dangers. This was seen with the COVID-19 vaccine, as isolated anecdotal stories of severe side effects deterred many individuals from receiving the life-saving vaccination. Knowing these various types of fear is paramount to understanding how fear can interrupt or extend daily life.

Statistics and fear go hand in hand, influencing how individuals perceive and react to risks. Almost every event a person can encounter involves probabilities. For instance, the probability of contracting a deadly disease or the likelihood of fatality from an earthquake can both be determined by statistics. Fear is, instead, often based upon one's imagination and depends on their ability to predict future events. Generally, people focus on risks that are small and unlikely to occur when they should fear other, more likely risks. In the case of the COVID-19 pandemic, data has shown that individuals in Texas who were not vaccinated were 26x more likely to die when compared to those with a vaccination in 2022. In 2024, unvaccinated Texans, compared to Texans vaccinated with the updated bivalent booster, were 11x more likely to die of a COVID-19-associated illness. This shows that public mistrust of the COVID-19 vaccines and fear, in general, still have residual effects today that could have been easily prevented. The spread of knowledge and awareness of statistics such as this will help individuals put their minds at ease about their rational and irrational fears.

Understanding how fear works and its mechanism will allow us to regulate our emotions healthily and appropriately. Based on what we know, the main area in the brain that controls the fear response in humans is the amygdala, a part of the limbic system. The limbic system is a collection of structures involved in emotion, behavior, long-term memory, motivation, and olfaction. The amygdala communicates with many different structures in the brain, such as the hypothalamus, reticular formation, PAG, and the nucleus of the Vagus nerve. The amygdala's connections to other brain parts will elicit fear or pain symptoms, depending on which structure it releases signals to. There are many theories on how the basis of emotions is formed in the brain. LeDoux and his students theorize that the basis of human emotions includes the amygdala, stating that this structure is the center of the neural circuit of the emotional brain. As we advance technology and neuroscience in the 21st century, we hope to one day understand entirely the complex emotion of fear.

People should not wait until it is too late to treat their conditions. Few individuals use readily available resources for the prevention of many severe diseases. Instead, people should be proactive in preventing their health from faltering by following guidelines from educated community organizations and members. We need to urge policymakers to implement ways to educate the masses on not allowing hearsay to lead them to detrimental health practices and to promote awareness of effective preventative strategies instead. In addition, advancing technology and knowledge in neuroscience will allow us to regulate our fear so that we do not succumb to detrimental fear.

References

1. "CDC Museum COVID-19 Timeline." Centers for Disease Control and Prevention, 15 Mar. 2023, www.cdc.gov/museum/timeline/covid19.html.
2. "Coronavirus Disease 2019 (COVID-19) - Symptoms and Causes." Mayo Clinic, 14 July 2023, www.mayoclinic.org/diseases-conditions/coronavirus/symptoms-causes/syc-20479963.
3. "COVID-19 Deaths by Vaccination Status Dashboard | Texas DSHS." Texas Department of State Health Services (DSHS),nwww.dshs.texas.gov/covid-19-coronavirus-disease-2019/covid-19-vaccine-information/c ovid-19-cases-deaths.
4. "FDA Approves First COVID-19 Vaccine." U.S. Food and Drug Administration, 23 Aug. 2021, www.fda.gov/news-events/press-announcements/fda-approves-first-covid-19-vaccine.
5. "Herd Immunity and COVID-19: What You Need to Know." Mayo Clinic, 4 Nov. 2023, www.mayoclinic.org/diseases-conditions/coronavirus/in-depth/herd-immunity-and-coronavirus/art-20486808.
6. Moller, Aage R. Neurobiology of Fear, Anxiety and Other Emotions. 2019.
7. Plans-Rubió, Pedro. "Percentages of Vaccination Coverage Required to Establish Herd Immunity against SARS-CoV-2." Vaccines, vol. 10, no. 5, 2022, p. 736.

AN INFOGRAPHIC JOURNEY

Helen Nguyen
FEAR AND LIFE OF A PERSON

WHAT CAN FEAR DO TO A PERSON?

- The mental experience of fear is often accompanied by bodily reactions that aim at placing the body in alarm mode.
  - Activation of the autonomic nervous system
  - Suppressing the immune system
  - Affecting a person's mood
  - Reducing a person's quality of life
  - Consuming a person's time

THE BENEFITS AND DISADVANTAGES OF FEAR

BENEFITS
- Warn about dangers
  - From outside the body
  - From inside the body (diseases)
- Prepare the body for "Flight or fight"
- Preventive actions such as:
  - Vaccinations
  - Healthy lifestyle
  - Using safety belts
  - Buying insurances

DISADVANTAGES
- Reduces the quality of life
- Danger to the body by activating stress reactions
- May prevent a person from opportunities that may have been beneficial
- Fear can change the function of many organs in a person's body
- Use of fear as a weapon to control people

OTHER UNFAVORABLE EFFECTS OF FEAR

- To be fearful is unpleasant and it reduces a person's quality of life
- Fear absorbs mental and physical energy
- Fear makes it difficult to concentrate on mental tasks and it can interfere with sleep
- Fear may make people make unfavorable decisions
- Misdirected fear may prevent a person from opportunities that could have been beneficial

FEAR CAN HAVE TREMENDOUS NEGATIVE EFFECTS

- The negative effect from the current pandemic from the infections by the corona virus is mainly from the fear it creates on many people world wide and not from the number of people who have died
- Similar number of people have died from other, often preventable causes, with little or no attention from the news organizations
- Example: 80,000 died one year in the USA from the influenza with little or no attention from the news organizations

SOURCES: BLACKBOARD. (2020). WEEK 10. CHAPTER 5. PART 1. FEAR & LIFE OF A PERSON - ... RETRIEVED OCTOBER 27, 2023, FROM UTDALLAS.EDU WEBSITE: HTTPS://ELEARNING.UTDALLAS.EDU/WEBAPPS/BLACKBOARD/EXECUTE/CONTENT/FILE?CMD=VIEW&CONTENT_ID=_7107587_1&COURSE_ID=_335276_1

Helen Nguyen, Fall 2023

FEAR AND LIFE OF A PERSON

AFFECT IN THE LIFE
Like other emotions, fear can affect a person's quality of life. Fear often affects basic body functions through its effects on the autonomic nervous system increasing a person's blood pressure and heart rate, and causing sweating causing muscle tremors. Fear may increase the risk of some diseases

AFFECTS ON THE PERSON
- Activation of the autonomic nervous system.
- Suppressing the immune system.
- Affecting a person's mood.
- Reducing a person's quality of life.
- Consuming a person's time.

ACTIVATION OF THE ANS
Activation of the sympathetic part of the autonomic nervous system causes increased blood pressure, increased heart rate, and sweating. Reducing the activity of the parasympathetic part of the autonomic nervous system causes, suppression of functions related to digestion, decreasing the blood supply to digestive organs, and increasing the blood supply to muscles and the brain

BENEFITS OF FEAR
Prepare for future dangers and prevent a person from engaging in risky activity. Part of the body's protection systems (like pain). Warns (correctly) about risks to the integrity and proper function of systems of a person's body

MECHANISM
- There are several systems in the brain that serve the purpose of survival and actions to take when a threat of one kind or another occurs
- A fast direct action is initiated through the nonclassical sensory system "fast and dirty"; a more refined response to various forms of fear may occur through the classical sensory system, "slow and accurate"

Melanie Cruz, Spring 2023

38

AN INFOGRAPHIC JOURNEY

How Fear Impacts People

How Fear affects Life:
- Affects basic body functions through the **autonomic nervous system (ANS)**:
    - increased blood pressure, heart, rate, sweating, and muscle tremors

What can fear do to a person?:
- fear places the body in **alarm mode**:
    - suppresses **immune response**
    - affects **mood** and reduces **quality of life**
    - consumes a person's **time**

Activation of the ANS:
- reducing the activity of the parasympathetic part of the ANS causes:
    a. suppression of functions related to digestion
    b. decreasing blood supply to digestion organs
    c. increasing the blood supply to brain and muscles

Beneficial effects of fear
- prepares for **future danger** and prevents engagement in risky activity
- part of the **body's protection system**
- **warns** about risks to proper function of body

Alyssa Tran, Fall 2023

AN INFOGRAPHIC JOURNEY

THE EFFECTS OF FEAR
BY: TOMMY VU

1. WHAT IS FEAR?
As defined in our lecture slides, "Fear is an unpleasant experience that cannot be measured objectively and only is assessed by the person who experiences the fear." This emotion can be associated with the six common emotions such as anger, disgust, fear, happiness, sadness, and surprise.

2. THE DIFFERENT KINDS OF FEAR
The different kinds of fear include:
- Rational/Irrational fear
- Acute fear
- Chronic Fear
- Fear from phantom risks
- Misdirected Fear
etc.

3. CAUSES OF FEAR
Fear usually stems from "real threats" such as physical accidents, the death of a loved one, financial stability, etc. However, there are other versions of fear such as "Phantom risks." Examples of Phantom risks include fear of conversation, fear of failure, fear of success, etc.

4. EFFECTS OF FEAR
Fear is related to mood disorders such as anxiety and depression. An intense amount of fear may result to said disorders. According to Everyday Health, the activation of the hypothalamus-pituitary-adrenal axis leads to the release of the stress hormone, cortisol, into the bloodstream.

5. SOURCES OF INFORMATION
Week 2. Chapter 1. Part 1. Fear Lecture Video
Week 2. Chapter 1. Part 2. Causes of Fear
https://www.everydayhealth.com/emotional-health/all-about-fear/#:~:text=Some%20research%20has%20linked%20chronic,may%20also%20be%20psychological%20consequences.

Tommu Vu, Fall 2023

Effects of Fear on a Person

What Fear Can Do to People
Fear is a mental state that triggers physical responses in the body to prepare for alarm. These responses involve activating the autonomic nervous system, suppressing the immune system, affecting mood, reducing the individual's quality of life, and consuming their time.

Beneficial Effects of Fear
Fear can also have several beneficial effects, including preparing individuals for potential future dangers, dissuading them from engaging in risky activities, and serving as a protective mechanism, akin to pain. Additionally, fear can accurately warn individuals about risks to the integrity and proper functioning of their body's systems.

Unfavorable Effects of Fear on a Person
Fear can have a range of harmful effects on individuals. It reduces the quality of life by activating stress reactions in the body, making it unpleasant and energy-draining. This fear-induced stress can hinder concentration, disrupt sleep, and lead to unfavorable decision-making. Additionally, misdirected fear may prevent individuals from pursuing potentially beneficial opportunities.

Activation of the autonomic nervous system
When the sympathetic part is activated, it results in increased blood pressure, a higher heart rate, and increased sweating. Conversely, reducing the activity of the parasympathetic part leads to the suppression of digestive functions, reduced blood supply to digestive organs, and an increase in blood supply to muscles and the brain.

Citations
- https://elearning.utdallas.edu/webapps/blackboard/execute/content/file?cmd=view&content_id=_7107587_1&course_id=_335276_1

Sahana Dhananjayan, Fall 2023

AN INFOGRAPHIC JOURNEY

PRANAVI MADDIPATLA

4 MOST COMMON FEAR RESPONSES

ONE — Fight: Fight is an aggressive response to fear which causes an individual to become combative as a defense mechanism to protect themselves from a perceived threat.

TWO — Flight: Flight involves an individual removing themselves from the situation that they feel fear towards to attempt to save themselves.

THREE — Freeze: Freezing occurs when an individual becomes immobile in face of a threat, sometimes known as "playing dead" to wait until the situation causing them fear has passed.

FOUR — Fawn: Fawning is a pacifying response to the threat in order to appease whatever or whoever is causing them to feel fear in the situation, in an attempt to mask distress.

REFERENCES

- Zingela, Z., Stroud, L., Cronje, J., Fink, M., & van Wyk, S. (2022, July 15). The psychological and subjective experience of catatonia: a qualitative study. BMC Psychology, 10(1). https://doi.org/10.1186/s40359-022-00885-7
- It's so much more than just 'fight or flight' – PTSD UK. (n.d.). https://www.ptsduk.org/its-so-much-more-than-just-fight-or-flight/
- Bracha, H. S. (2004, September). Freeze, Flight, Fight, Fright, Faint: Adaptationist Perspectives on the Acute Stress Response Spectrum. CNS Spectrums, 9(9), 679–685. https://doi.org/10.1017/s1092852900001954

EFFECTS OF FEAR & THREATS

HOW DOES FEAR IMPACT QUALITY OF LIFE?
The mental experience of fear is accompanied by bodily reactions that aim at placing the body in alarm mode. Some things that occur are activation of the autonomic nervous system, impression of the immune system, impact on a person's mood, decreased quality of life, and consumption of a person's time.

AUTONOMIC NERVOUS SYSTEM VS PARASYMPATHETIC NERVOUS SYTEM
Activation of the ANS causes increased blood pressure, heart rate, and sweating. Reduction of the PNS causes suppression of functions related to digestion, decreased blood supply to digestive organs, and increased blood supply to muscles and the brain.

BENEFITS OF FEAR
Some benefits of fear are preparing for future dangers to prevent a person from engaging in risky activity, warning about dangers from outside and inside the body, putting the body in an alarmed condition, and preparing the body for "flight or fight". Some examples of preventive actions that may be related to fear regarding diseases are vaccinations, a healthy lifestyle, the use of safety belts, and insurance.

UNFAVORABLE EFFECTS OF FEAR
Fear can cause damage to the body by activating stress reactions and changing the functions of many organs. It can also promote diseases, be used as a weapon to control people, and overall reduce a person's quality of life as it absorbs mental and physical energy and makes it difficult to concentrate and sleep.

FEAR ON A BIGGER SCALE
Fear is often the main cause of harm that is associated with catastrophic events. More specifically, during the COVID-19 pandemic, it caused fear that it has induced, but not over the number of deaths it had caused. The fear of contracting the virus has changed human behavior and has made some individuals more vigilant.

SOURCES:
FREE DESIGN TOOL: PRESENTATIONS, VIDEO, SOCIAL MEDIA | CANVA. CANVA. (N.D.). HTTPS://WWW.CANVA.COM/
MØLLER, A. R. (2019). NEUROBIOLOGY OF FEAR AND OTHER EMOTIONS. AAGE R MØLLER PUBLISHING.

Pranavi Maddipatla, Fall 2023 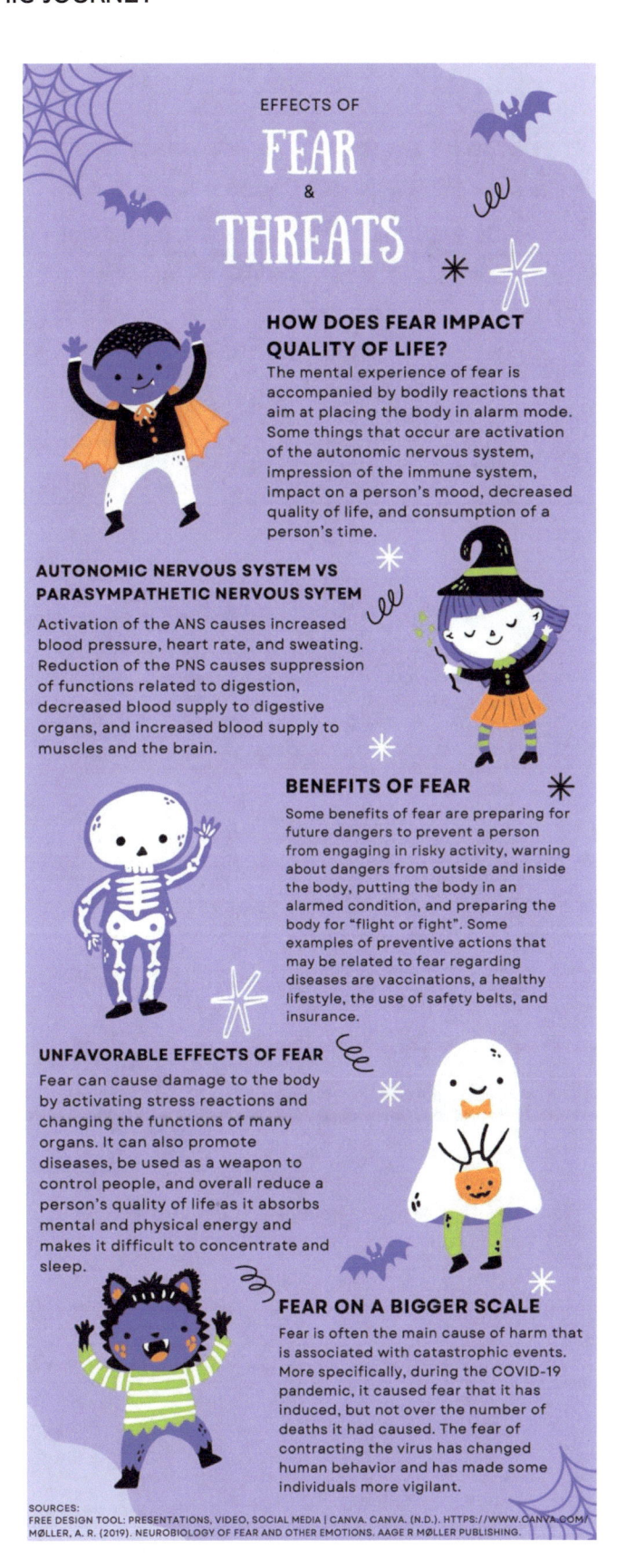   Tiffany Nouanesengsy, Fall 2023

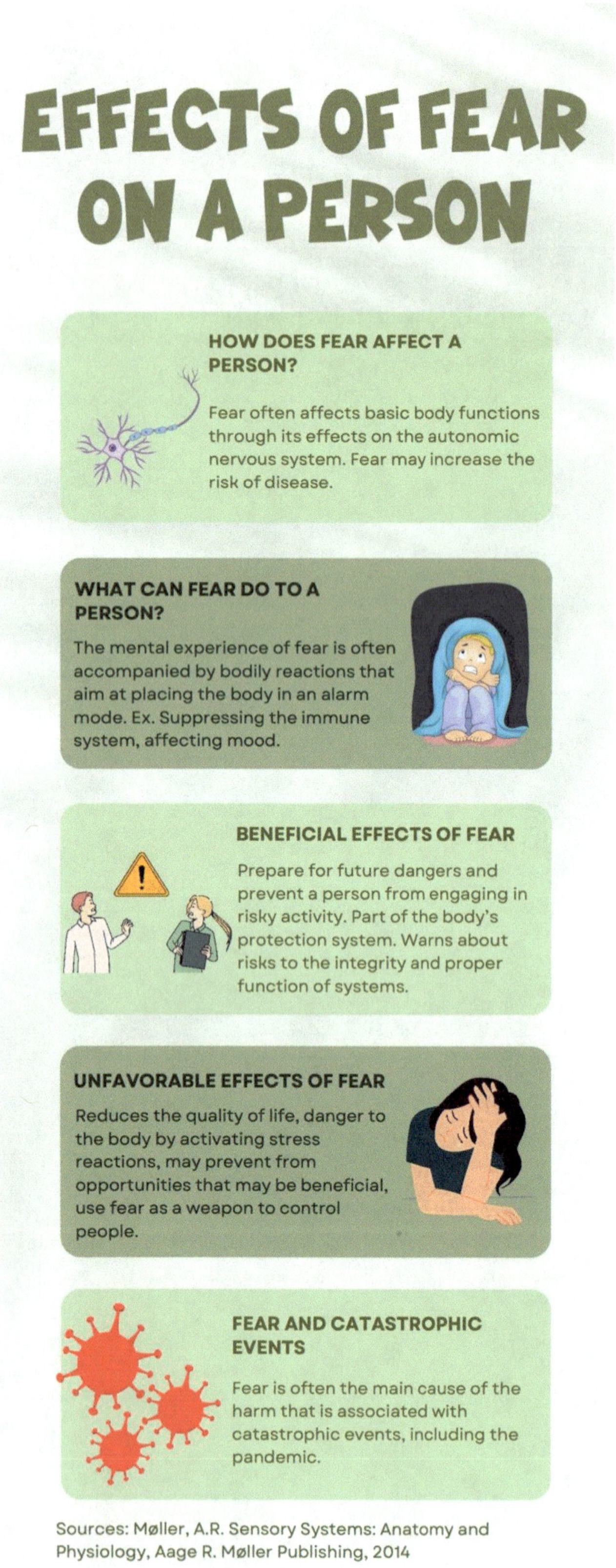

AN INFOGRAPHIC JOURNEY

EFFECTS OF FEAR ON A PERSON

HOW DOES FEAR AFFECT A PERSON?

Fear often affects basic body functions through its effects on the autonomic nervous system. Fear may increase the risk of disease.

WHAT CAN FEAR DO TO A PERSON?

The mental experience of fear is often accompanied by bodily reactions that aim at placing the body in an alarm mode. Ex. Suppressing the immune system, affecting mood.

BENEFICIAL EFFECTS OF FEAR

Prepare for future dangers and prevent a person from engaging in risky activity. Part of the body's protection system. Warns about risks to the integrity and proper function of systems.

UNFAVORABLE EFFECTS OF FEAR

Reduces the quality of life, danger to the body by activating stress reactions, may prevent from opportunities that may be beneficial, use fear as a weapon to control people.

FEAR AND CATASTROPHIC EVENTS

Fear is often the main cause of the harm that is associated with catastrophic events, including the pandemic.

Sources: Møller, A.R. Sensory Systems: Anatomy and Physiology, Aage R. Møller Publishing, 2014

Sarvani Ganapavarapu, Fall 2023

The Benefits and Drawbacks of Fear

Fear is a basic human emotion that is evoked as a response to a perceived threat. It often affects basic bodily functions through the activation of the sympathetic part of the autonomic system. The mental and physical reactions of fear can be both beneficial and detrimental which is explained below.

Depletes Energy ✗

Fear takes up both mental and physical energy which can interfere with sleep and concentration.

Susceptibility to Disease ✗

Fear suppress a person's immune system. This suppression can place them at higher risk of developing a physical illness or disease.

Danger Warning ✓

Fear can accurately warn a person of any dangers to their body systems and prevent them from performing risky activity

Stress Reponse ✓

Fear can place the body in a state of alarm and prepare for a "fight or flight" response.

Damage to Body ✗

Fear can cause damage to a persons body through the activation of stress reactions.

Influence preventive actions ✓

Fear can influence people to take safe preventative actions such as getting vaccinated, following a health lifestyle, using safety belts, etc.

Protective Mechanisms ✓

Similar to pain, fear is a part of the body's protection system. The brain uses different systems to perceive and respond to threats. Both fast direct actions through the non-classical sensory system and refined responses through the classical sensory system protect the body from perceieved harm.

Citations:

AHANGIRI, F. (2022).Neurobiology of EmotionsFear and Anxiety Chapter 5:Part 1:- Fear and Life of a Person ; PowerPoint Presentation.

Gauri Surendran, Fall 2023

AN INFOGRAPHIC JOURNEY

Effect of Fear and Threat
By Syed Naqvi

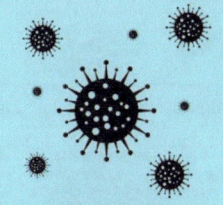

Affect of Fear
- Alter the quality of life
- Activation of the autonomic nervous system
- Increase disease risk

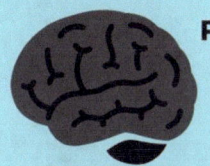

Psychological affect of fear
- Activate the autonomic nervous system
- Suppress the Immune system
- Mood alteration
- Time consumtion

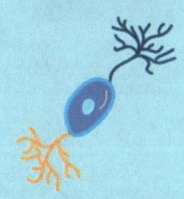

Activation of the Autonomic System
- Supression of digestion
- Decrease blood supply to certain organs
- Increase blood supply to brain and muscles

Beneficial effects of Fear
- Risk aversion
- Self-preservation
- Future planning

Actions that could be based on fear
- Vaccination
- Healthy lifestyle
- Safety belts
- Insurance

NSC 4382
All information from the powerpoint

Syed Naqvi, Fall 2023

Effects of Fear on a Person

The Autonomic Nervous System

Increased Activity of the Sympathetic Portion
- Causes increased blood pressure, heart rate, and sweating

Reduced Activity of the Parasympathetic Portion
- Causes suppression of digestive function, decreased blood supply to digestive organs, and increased blood supply to the muscles and the brain

Benefits

Protective Mechanisms

Provide Warnings for Danger:
- From outside the body
- From inside the body (diseases)
- Puts the body in an alarm condition
- Prepares the body for "flight or fight"

Preventative Actions

Examples:
- Regarding diseases: vaccinations + maintenance of a healthy lifestyle
- Regarding accidents: usage of safety belts
- Regarding loss of property: insurance

Drawbacks

Harm to the Body
- Fear can cause damage to the body by activating stress reactions
- Fear can change the function of many organs in a person's body
- Fear may promote diseases

Other Effects
- Reduces a person's quality of life
- Absorbs mental and physical energy
- Difficulty concentrating + sleeping
- May lead to one making unfavorable decisions

NSC 4382.0W1: Chapter 5, Part 1

Sara Hasan, Fall 2023

AN INFOGRAPHIC JOURNEY

EFFECTS OF FEAR

PHYSICAL EFFECTS

Fear activates the autonomic nervous system, causing effects like increased blood pressure, heart rate, and sweating.

MENTAL EFFECTS

Fear can affect someone's mood, give them unwanted emotions, reduce their quality of life, and take up their time.

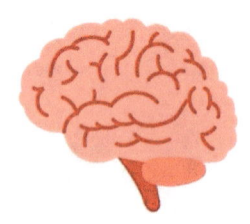

BENEFICIAL EFFECTS

Being afraid helps prepare a person for future dangers and prevents a person from engaging in risky behaviors. It helps warn the body about risks to bodily integrity.

PROTECTIVE MECHANISMS

There are two pathways which responses to fear can take: the fast and dirty one, an immediate reaction, or the slow and accurate one, which is more refined and occurs through the classical sensory system.

HARMFUL EFFECTS

Being afraid may activate stress responses in excess, which would harm the body, and may prevent a person from beneficial opportunities or be used to control them.

Chloe Tee, Spring 2024

Risks of Fear..
Effects of Fear of a Person

Risks of medication

Acetaminophen have many side effects including liver failure. Might increase risk of asthma, Blunting responses to stimuli

Deaths from preventable disease

Influenza Kills 5,000 to 80,000 yearly. More people get the COVID vaccine compared to the Influenza vaccine.

Fear as a manipulator

- Fear can be utilized as a weapon to terrorize people.
- Fear most efficient of all manipulators.

Diagnosis of plasticity disorders

Diagnosis of plasticity is mostly based on exam. MRI are no effective form of studying. Biochemical studies do not reveal function abnormalities/

Three forms of pain.

- Physiological pain: stimulation of pain receptors in normal tissue.
- Pathological pain: stimulation of receptors in pathological tissue. Changes in the function of the nervous system.
- Inflammatory pain: may be regarded as a 3rd form of pain.

Physiological pain

Afferent spinal pathway, including the spinothalamic pathway, carry information from pain receptors to the thalamus. Nociceptive information from the thalamus is projected to the primary somatosensory cortex/

REALLYGREATSITE.COM

Alaina Chenault, Spring 2023

AN INFOGRAPHIC JOURNEY

Effects of Fear

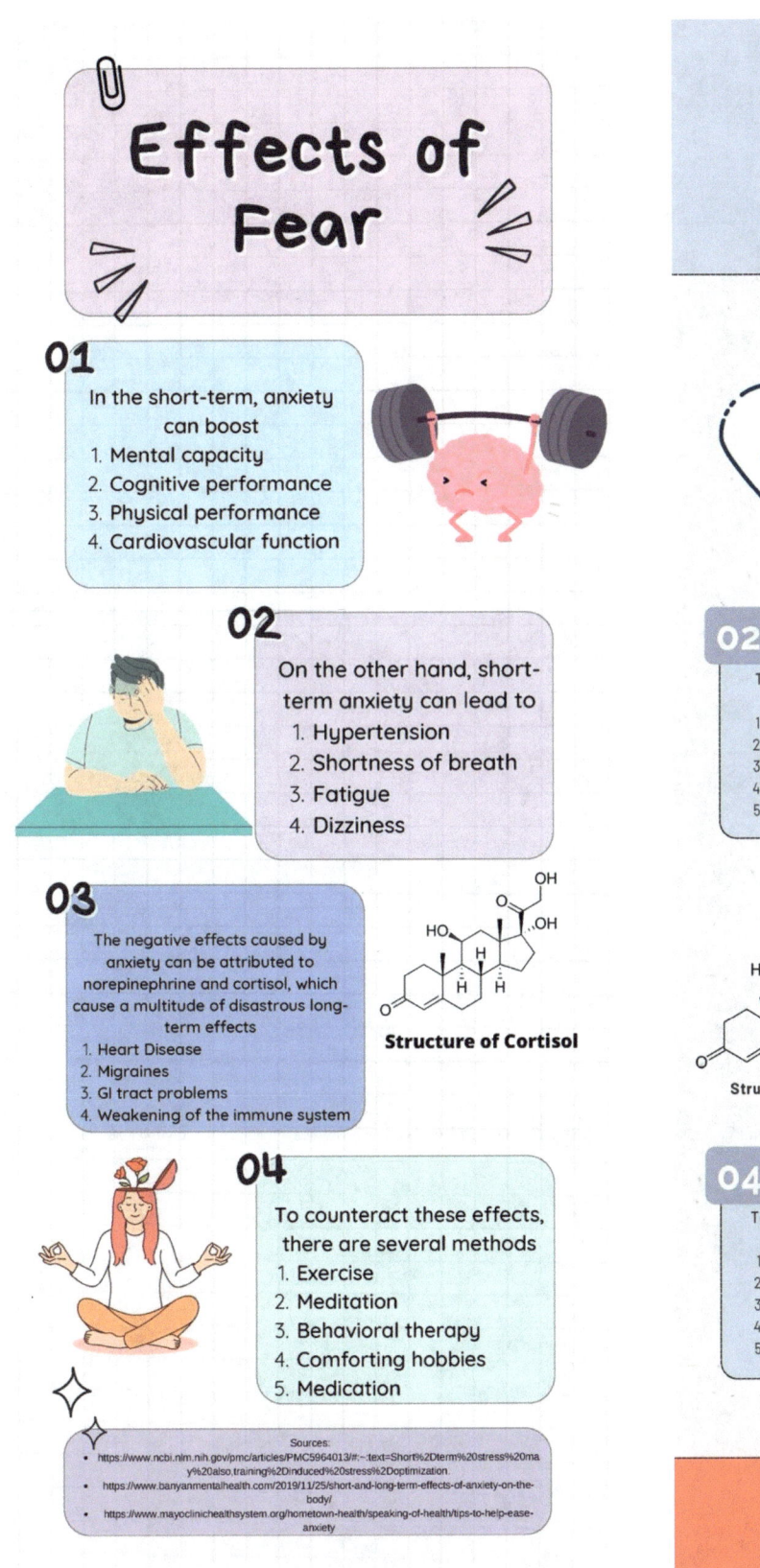

01 In the short-term, anxiety can boost
1. Mental capacity
2. Cognitive performance
3. Physical performance
4. Cardiovascular function

02 On the other hand, short-term anxiety can lead to
1. Hypertension
2. Shortness of breath
3. Fatigue
4. Dizziness

03 The negative effects caused by anxiety can be attributed to norepinephrine and cortisol, which cause a multitude of disastrous long-term effects
1. Heart Disease
2. Migraines
3. GI tract problems
4. Weakening of the immune system

Structure of Cortisol

04 To counteract these effects, there are several methods
1. Exercise
2. Meditation
3. Behavioral therapy
4. Comforting hobbies
5. Medication

Sources:
- https://www.ncbi.nlm.nih.gov/pmc/articles/PMC5964013/#:~:text=Short%2Dterm%20stress%20may%20also,training%2Dinduced%20stress%2Doptimization.
- https://www.banyanmentalhealth.com/2019/11/25/short-and-long-term-effects-of-anxiety-on-the-body/
- https://www.mayoclinichealthsystem.org/hometown-health/speaking-of-health/tips-to-help-ease-anxiety

Allen Liang, Spring 2024

EFFECTS OF FEAR

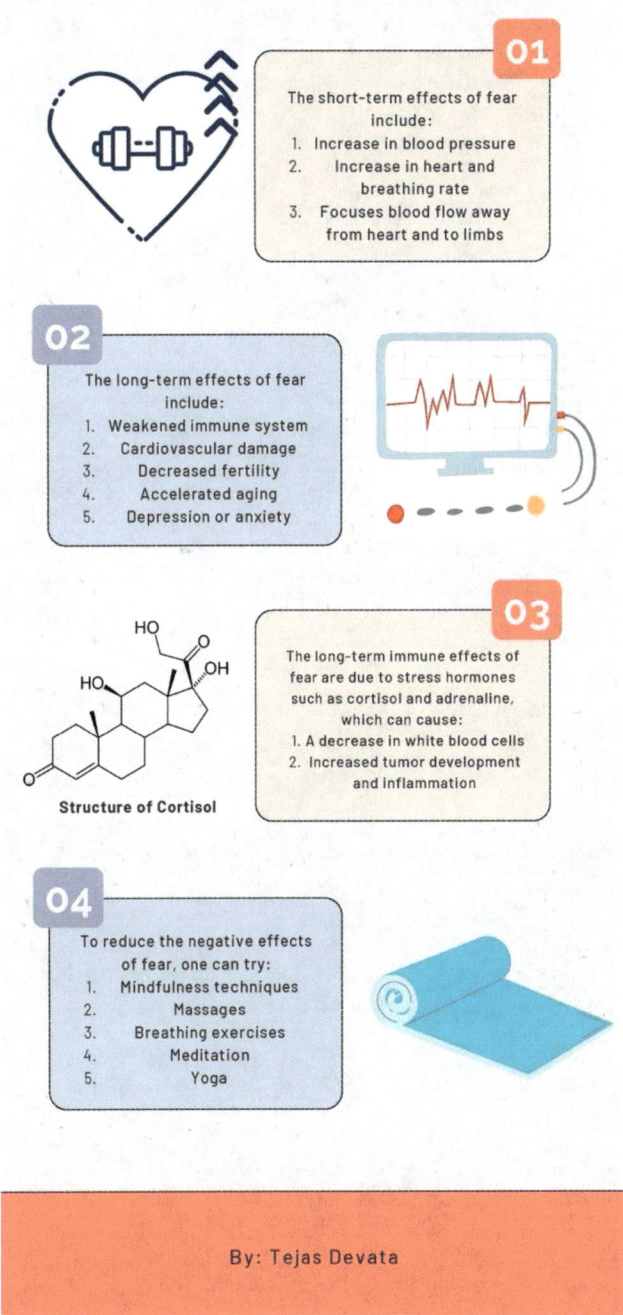

01 The short-term effects of fear include:
1. Increase in blood pressure
2. Increase in heart and breathing rate
3. Focuses blood flow away from heart and to limbs

02 The long-term effects of fear include:
1. Weakened immune system
2. Cardiovascular damage
3. Decreased fertility
4. Accelerated aging
5. Depression or anxiety

03 The long-term immune effects of fear are due to stress hormones such as cortisol and adrenaline, which can cause:
1. A decrease in white blood cells
2. Increased tumor development and inflammation

Structure of Cortisol

04 To reduce the negative effects of fear, one can try:
1. Mindfulness techniques
2. Massages
3. Breathing exercises
4. Meditation
5. Yoga

By: Tejas Devata

Tejas Devata, Spring 2024

AN INFOGRAPHIC JOURNEY

The Effects of Fear

Overlooked Risks

The use of Acetaminophen, also more commonly known as Tylenol, is one of the largest causes of acute liver failure in the US. This is despite the largely held belief that there are little to no side effects from taking it.

Underlooked Risks

In the 2017-18 influenza season, it was documented that 79,400 individuals passed away from the flu. This depicts how some are ill-informed on the importance of receiving the annual flu shot, a free and effective vaccination.

As a Manipulator

Fear is one of the most efficient manipulators. The government may use it to collect taxes. The police may use fear to enforce laws. Fear has a ubiquitous influence in our day-to-day lives.

Effects on the Brain

Sustained threat perception is accompanied by the prolonged activation of threat-related neural circuitry, including the hypothalamicpituitary-adrenal axis, the autonomic nervous system (ANS), and inflammatory response.

Prolonged Fear

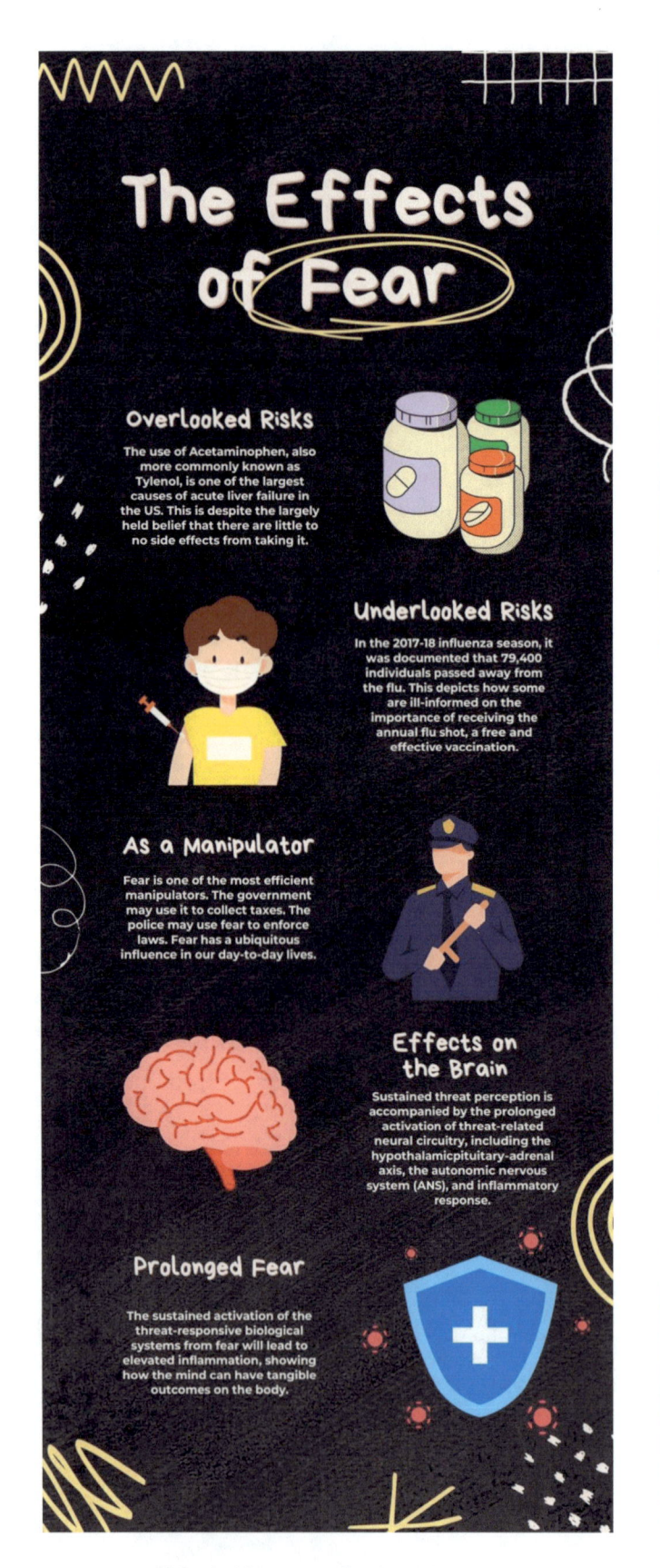

The sustained activation of the threat-responsive biological systems from fear will lead to elevated inflammation, showing how the mind can have tangible outcomes on the body.

Mark Nguyen, Spring 2024

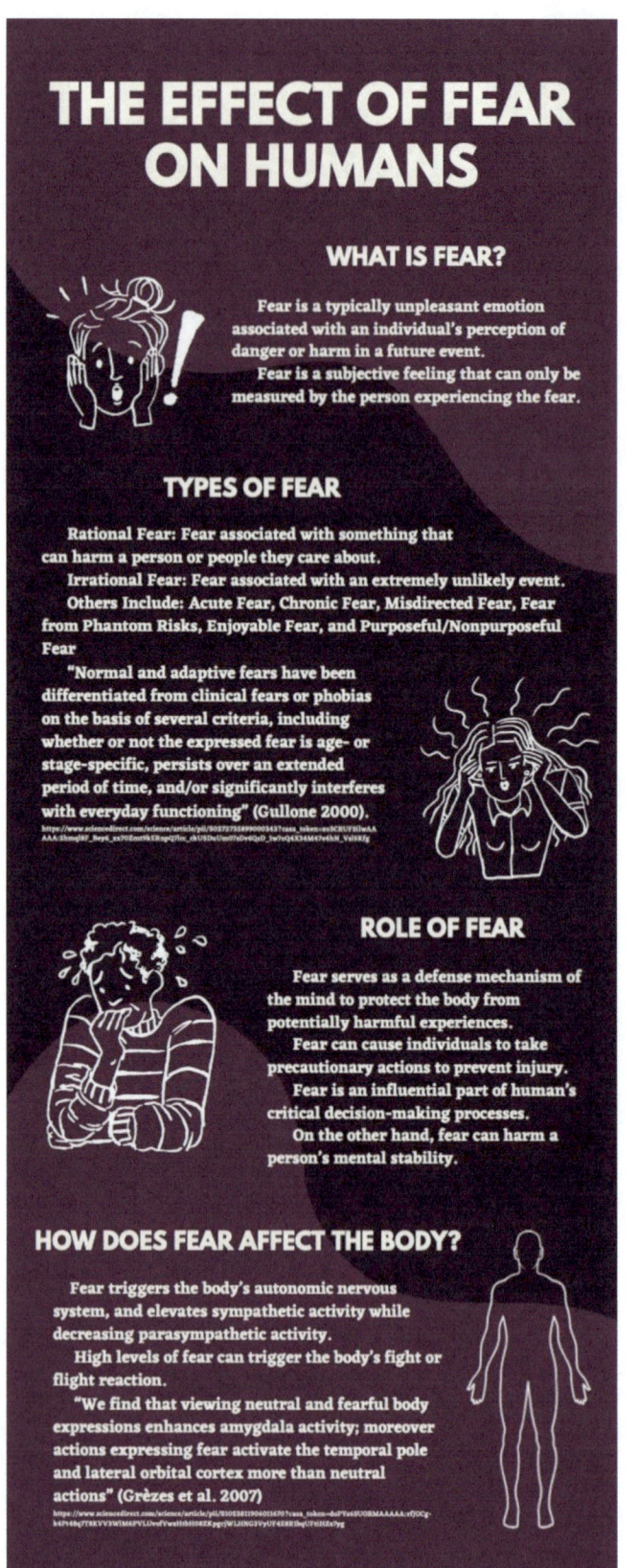

THE EFFECT OF FEAR ON HUMANS

WHAT IS FEAR?

Fear is a typically unpleasant emotion associated with an individual's perception of danger or harm in a future event.
Fear is a subjective feeling that can only be measured by the person experiencing the fear.

TYPES OF FEAR

Rational Fear: Fear associated with something that can harm a person or people they care about.
Irrational Fear: Fear associated with an extremely unlikely event.
Others Include: Acute Fear, Chronic Fear, Misdirected Fear, Fear from Phantom Risks, Enjoyable Fear, and Purposeful/Nonpurposeful Fear
"Normal and adaptive fears have been differentiated from clinical fears or phobias on the basis of several criteria, including whether or not the expressed fear is age- or stage-specific, persists over an extended period of time, and/or significantly interferes with everyday functioning" (Gullone 2000).

ROLE OF FEAR

Fear serves as a defense mechanism of the mind to protect the body from potentially harmful experiences.
Fear can cause individuals to take precautionary actions to prevent injury.
Fear is an influential part of human's critical decision-making processes.
On the other hand, fear can harm a person's mental stability.

HOW DOES FEAR AFFECT THE BODY?

Fear triggers the body's autonomic nervous system, and elevates sympathetic activity while decreasing parasympathetic activity.
High levels of fear can trigger the body's fight or flight reaction.
"We find that viewing neutral and fearful body expressions enhances amygdala activity; moreover actions expressing fear activate the temporal pole and lateral orbital cortex more than neutral actions" (Grèzes et al. 2007)

Armaan Sood, Fall 2023

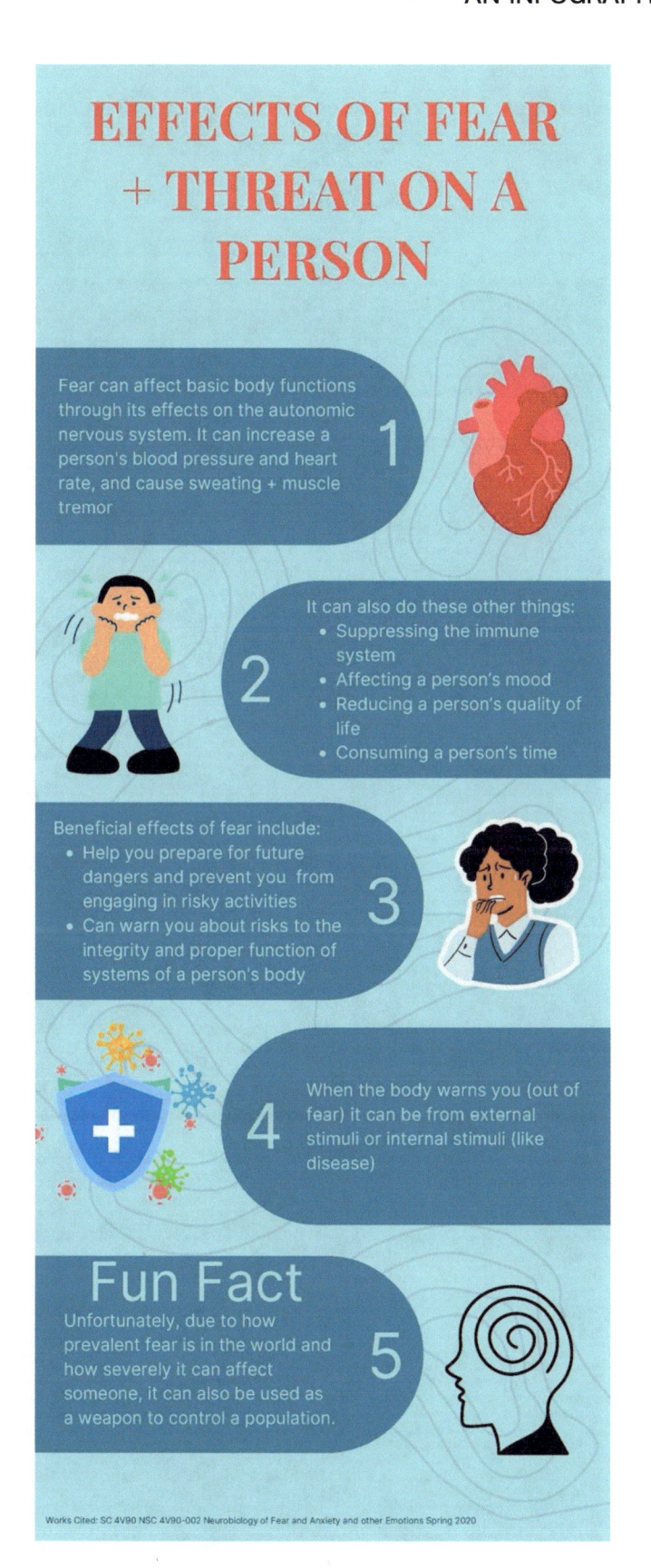

AN INFOGRAPHIC JOURNEY

EFFECTS OF FEAR + THREAT ON A PERSON

1. Fear can affect basic body functions through its effects on the autonomic nervous system. It can increase a person's blood pressure and heart rate, and cause sweating + muscle tremor

2. It can also do these other things:
   - Suppressing the immune system
   - Affecting a person's mood
   - Reducing a person's quality of life
   - Consuming a person's time

3. Beneficial effects of fear include:
   - Help you prepare for future dangers and prevent you from engaging in risky activities
   - Can warn you about risks to the integrity and proper function of systems of a person's body

4. When the body warns you (out of fear) it can be from external stimuli or internal stimuli (like disease)

5. **Fun Fact**
   Unfortunately, due to how prevalent fear is in the world and how severely it can affect someone, it can also be used as a weapon to control a population.

Works Cited: SC 4V90 NSC 4V90-002 Neurobiology of Fear and Anxiety and other Emotions Spring 2020

Ananya Bommakanti, Spring 2024

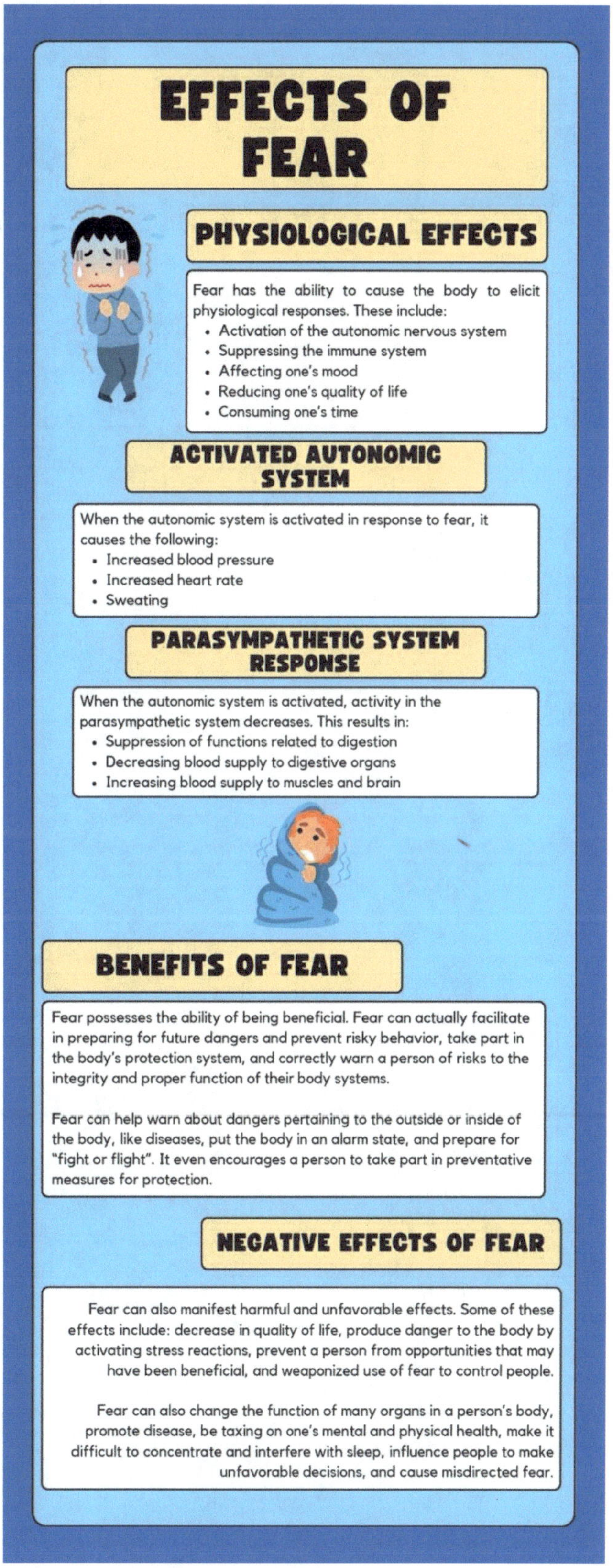

EFFECTS OF FEAR

PHYSIOLOGICAL EFFECTS

Fear has the ability to cause the body to elicit physiological responses. These include:
- Activation of the autonomic nervous system
- Suppressing the immune system
- Affecting one's mood
- Reducing one's quality of life
- Consuming one's time

ACTIVATED AUTONOMIC SYSTEM

When the autonomic system is activated in response to fear, it causes the following:
- Increased blood pressure
- Increased heart rate
- Sweating

PARASYMPATHETIC SYSTEM RESPONSE

When the autonomic system is activated, activity in the parasympathetic system decreases. This results in:
- Suppression of functions related to digestion
- Decreasing blood supply to digestive organs
- Increasing blood supply to muscles and brain

BENEFITS OF FEAR

Fear possesses the ability of being beneficial. Fear can actually facilitate in preparing for future dangers and prevent risky behavior, take part in the body's protection system, and correctly warn a person of risks to the integrity and proper function of their body systems.

Fear can help warn about dangers pertaining to the outside or inside of the body, like diseases, put the body in an alarm state, and prepare for "fight or flight". It even encourages a person to take part in preventative measures for protection.

NEGATIVE EFFECTS OF FEAR

Fear can also manifest harmful and unfavorable effects. Some of these effects include: decrease in quality of life, produce danger to the body by activating stress reactions, prevent a person from opportunities that may have been beneficial, and weaponized use of fear to control people.

Fear can also change the function of many organs in a person's body, promote disease, be taxing on one's mental and physical health, make it difficult to concentrate and interfere with sleep, influence people to make unfavorable decisions, and cause misdirected fear.

Dannah Bagcal, Spring 2024

AN INFOGRAPHIC JOURNEY

Infographic #9: Taha Ahmed
The Effects of Fear & Threat on a Person

How does fear affect a person's life?
Similar to other emotions, fear can affect a person's quality of life. It affects basic body functions via effects on the autonomic nervous system, which can increase BP and heart rate, as well as other symptoms. It also may increase the risk of some diseases.

What are the beneficial effects of fear?
It prepares for future dangers and prevents a person from engaging in risky activity. It is part of the body's protection system, and warns about risks to the integrity and proper function of systems of a person's body.

What are the harmful effects from fear?
Fear typically reduces the quality of life and brings danger to the body by activating stress reactions. It may prevent a person from opportunities that could've been beneficial, and many people can use fear as a weapon to control people.

The negative effects of fear on people
Negative effects can carry from different life experiences. Fear is often the main cause of the harm that is associated with catastrophic events i.e. Covid-19 pandemic. Harmful effects of it are caused by the fear it induced, not the number of deaths it caused.

The protective mechanisms of the body
There are multiple systems in the brain that serve the purpose of survival and actions. A fast direct action is initiated through the non-classical sensory system "fast and dirty." Refined responses to fear occur through the classical sensory system, "slow and accurate."

Taha Ahmed, Spring 2024

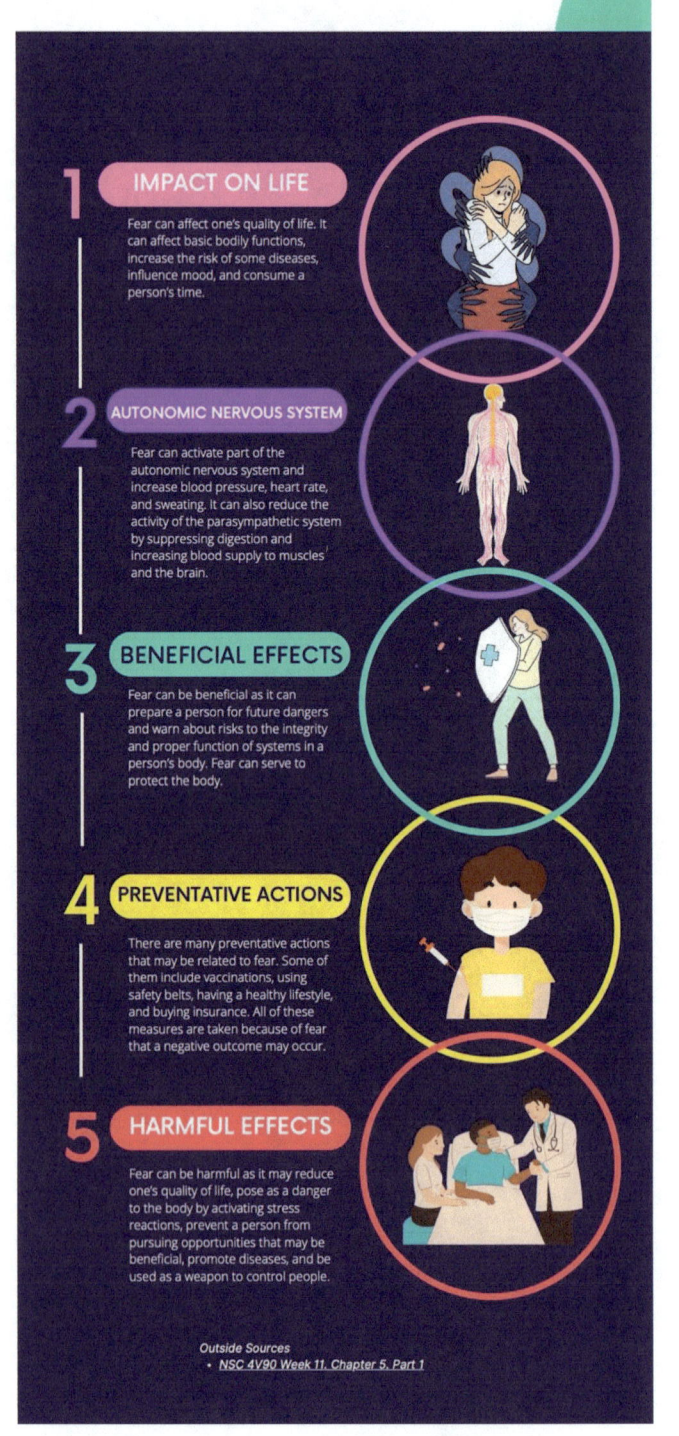

EFFECTS OF FEAR

1 IMPACT ON LIFE
Fear can affect one's quality of life. It can affect basic bodily functions, increase the risk of some diseases, influence mood, and consume a person's time.

2 AUTONOMIC NERVOUS SYSTEM
Fear can activate part of the autonomic nervous system and increase blood pressure, heart rate, and sweating. It can also reduce the activity of the parasympathetic system by suppressing digestion and increasing blood supply to muscles and the brain.

3 BENEFICIAL EFFECTS
Fear can be beneficial as it can prepare a person for future dangers and warn about risks to the integrity and proper function of systems in a person's body. Fear can serve to protect the body.

4 PREVENTATIVE ACTIONS
There are many preventative actions that may be related to fear. Some of them include vaccinations, using safety belts, having a healthy lifestyle, and buying insurance. All of these measures are taken because of fear that a negative outcome may occur.

5 HARMFUL EFFECTS
Fear can be harmful as it may reduce one's quality of life, pose as a danger to the body by activating stress reactions, prevent a person from pursuing opportunities that may be beneficial, promote diseases, and be used as a weapon to control people.

Outside Sources
- NSC 4V90 Week 11, Chapter 5, Part 1

Judith James, Fall 2023

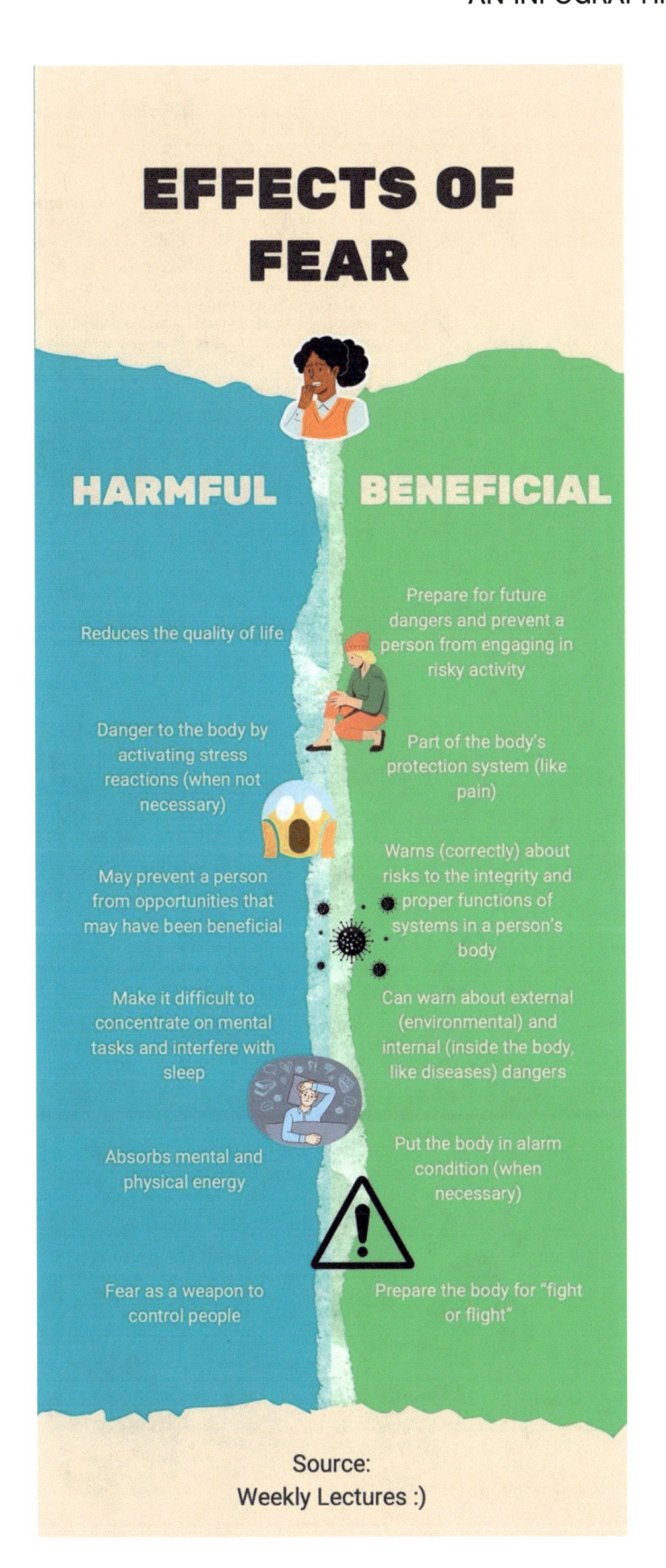

EFFECTS OF FEAR

HARMFUL

- Reduces the quality of life
- Danger to the body by activating stress reactions (when not necessary)
- May prevent a person from opportunities that may have been beneficial
- Make it difficult to concentrate on mental tasks and interfere with sleep
- Absorbs mental and physical energy
- Fear as a weapon to control people

BENEFICIAL

- Prepare for future dangers and prevent a person from engaging in risky activity
- Part of the body's protection system (like pain)
- Warns (correctly) about risks to the integrity and proper functions of systems in a person's body
- Can warn about external (environmental) and internal (inside the body, like diseases) dangers
- Put the body in alarm condition (when necessary)
- Prepare the body for "fight or flight"

Source: Weekly Lectures :)

Audrey Villanueva, Fall 2023

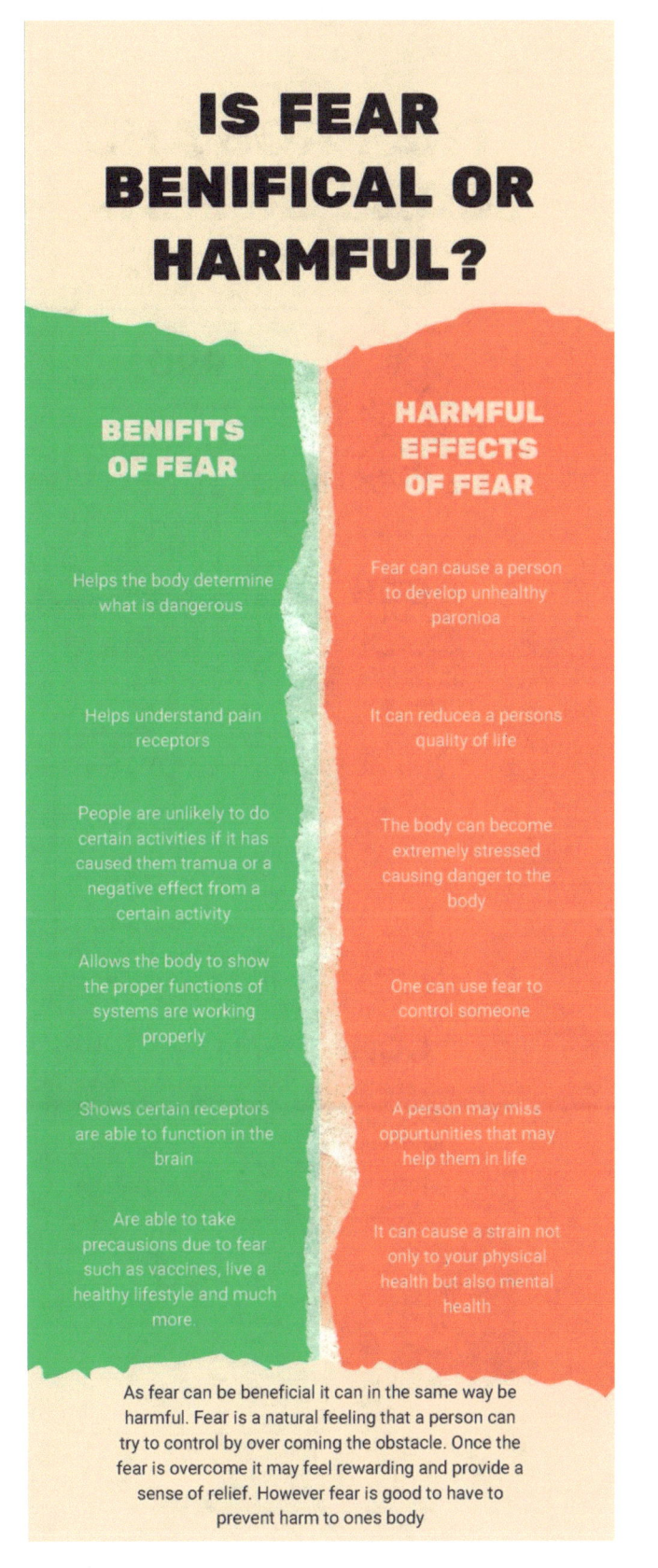

IS FEAR BENIFICAL OR HARMFUL?

BENIFITS OF FEAR

- Helps the body determine what is dangerous
- Helps understand pain receptors
- People are unlikely to do certain activities if it has caused them tramua or a negative effect from a certain activity
- Allows the body to show the proper functions of systems are working properly
- Shows certain receptors are able to function in the brain
- Are able to take precautions due to fear such as vaccines, live a healthy lifestyle and much more.

HARMFUL EFFECTS OF FEAR

- Fear can cause a person to develop unhealthy paronioa
- It can reducea a persons quality of life
- The body can become extremely stressed causing danger to the body
- One can use fear to control someone
- A person may miss oppurtunities that may help them in life
- It can cause a strain not only to your physical health but also mental health

As fear can be beneficial it can in the same way be harmful. Fear is a natural feeling that a person can try to control by over coming the obstacle. Once the fear is overcome it may feel rewarding and provide a sense of relief. However fear is good to have to prevent harm to ones body

Falisha Leava, Spring 2024

AN INFOGRAPHIC JOURNEY

THE PROS AND CONS OF FEAR

Fear often affects the autonomic system causing physiological changes that prepare the body for a possible danger.

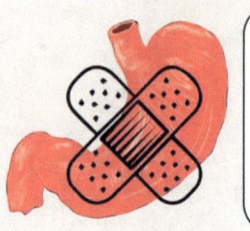

PRO
Fear can accurately warn about risks to the integrity and functionality of the body. This can prevent body systems from becoming damaged or compromised.

CON
Since fear activates the sympathetic system which increases heart rate, muscle tension, breathing, etc. it can quickly deplete energy. This can cause fatigue, compromised sleep and concentration.

PRO
In a dangerous situation, activation of the sympathetic system causes the "flight or fight response." This prepares the body to challenge or flee the danger, thus preserving integrity and functionality.

CON
Chronic or prolonged fear can be detrimental to the body by preventing risk taking as well as causing problems like compromised immunity and insomnia.

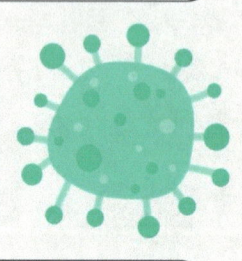

PRO
Fear can be an impetus for preventative behavior. For instance, fear of an upcoming test can cause the person to study in advance.

Source
Jahanghiri, Faisal R. "Fear and Life of a Person." PowerPoint.

Jagannath Ravindran, Fall 2023

BENEFICIAL AND HARMFUL EFFECTS OF FEAR

BY OLIVE ROEDE

PROTECTION
Fear is part of the body's protection systems. Fear allows a person to prepare for future dangers and prevents a person from engaging in risky activity. Fear also warns (correctly) about risks to the integrity and proper function of systems of a person's body.

SURVIVAL
There are several systems in the brain that serve the purpose of ensuring survival. These systems take action when a threat of one kind or another occurs. Fear is one of these survival systems.

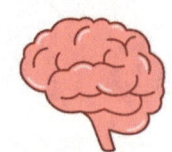

TWO PATHS
A fast direct action is initiated through the nonclassical sensory system "fast and dirty"; a more refined response to various forms of fear may occur through the classical sensory system, "slow and accurate"

FEAR'S BENEFIT
Fear warns a person about dangers from outside or inside the body (such as disease) and prepares the body for fight or flight.

PREVENTATIVE MEASURES
Fear may cause a person to take preventative measures for their safety, including getting vaccinated, using their seatbelt, or getting insurance.

HARMFUL EFFECTS
Fear can greatly reduce a person's quality of life. Fear can pose danger to the body by activating stress reactions. Fear may also prevent a person from opportunities that may have been beneficial.

FEAR AND THE BODY
Fear activates stress reactions, and chronic stress is known to have harmful effects on the body. Stress can cause damage to vital organs and promote disease.

QUALITY OF LIFE
As stated previously, fear has a negative effect on quality of life. To be fearful is unpleasant, and absorbs both mental and physical energy. Fear can also affect concentration and sleep.

SOURCED FROM CHAPTER 5 OF "NEUROBIOLOGY OF FEAR, ANXIETY AND OTHER EMOTIONS" BY A.R. MØLLER

Olive Roede, Fall 2023

AN INFOGRAPHIC JOURNEY

BENEFITS AND HARMFULNESS OF FEAR

There are several advantages and disadvantages of being fearful. Let's discuss the differences on how it can benefit or harm us!

BENEFITS

Warn
Being fearful keeps us alert by warning us about internal or external dangers. Internal dangers include bodily diseases while external dangers include imminent threats.

Alarm
Being in a fearful state can also alarm us from potential threats and save us by initiating decisions on how to relieve ourselves from threatening stimuli.

Flight or Fight
Depending on this stimulus and the level of fear, our body enters a flight or fight mode to prevent us from harm or to immediately remove ourselves from a particular situation.

Examples
Some actions that can prevent rational fears such as catching a disease would be to get vaccinated and to maintain a healthy lifestyle.

HARMFUL EFFECTS

Stress
Reactions to fearful stimuli can signal the body that it is in danger. Sometimes, being overly fearful can activate stress reactions in the body which can harm your body. Some common examples are heart disease, strokes, sleep problems, weight gain, etc.

Weapon
Fear can be used as a weapon to control people such as in an armed robbery.

Quality of Life
Fear can reduce a person's quality of life and may prevent a person from participating in opportunities that may have been beneficial to them.

Examples
After the COVID-19 pandemic, many people started becoming more aware of their surroundings to ensure that they won't get sick. Nowadays, people tend to keep a distance even when someone briefly coughs or sneezes

References
Neurobiology of Fear and Other Emotions, Aage R. Moller

Devapriya Baiju, Fall 2023

PROS VS. CONS OF THE EFFECTS OF FEAR

PRO 1 Prepare for future dangers and prevent a person from engaging in risky activity

CON 1 Being fearful is an unpleasant state that reduces a person's quality of life

PRO 2 Part of the body's protection systems to external stimuli

CON 2 Excess fear releases many stress hormones into the bloodstream

PRO 3 Correctly warns about risks to the proper function of a person's bodily systems

CON 3 Fear can change the function of many organs therefore promoting diseases

PRO 4 Put the body in an alarm condition, preparing the body for fight or flight mode

CON 4 Fear costs mental and physical energy making it difficult to concentrate on different tasks

PRO 5 Heightens your senses and awareness; keeps you alert in situations

CON 5 Misdirected fear may prevent a person from opportunities that could have been beneficial

PRO 6 Can encourage one to take preventative actions such as vaccines and safety belts

CON 6 Fear can be used as a weapon to control people as they are in vulnerable states of mind

Works Cited
Dr. Jahangiri's Slides
https://www.thriveyard.com/the-positive-side-of-fear-15-benefits-of-fear/
https://www.everydayhealth.com/emotional-health/all-about-fear/

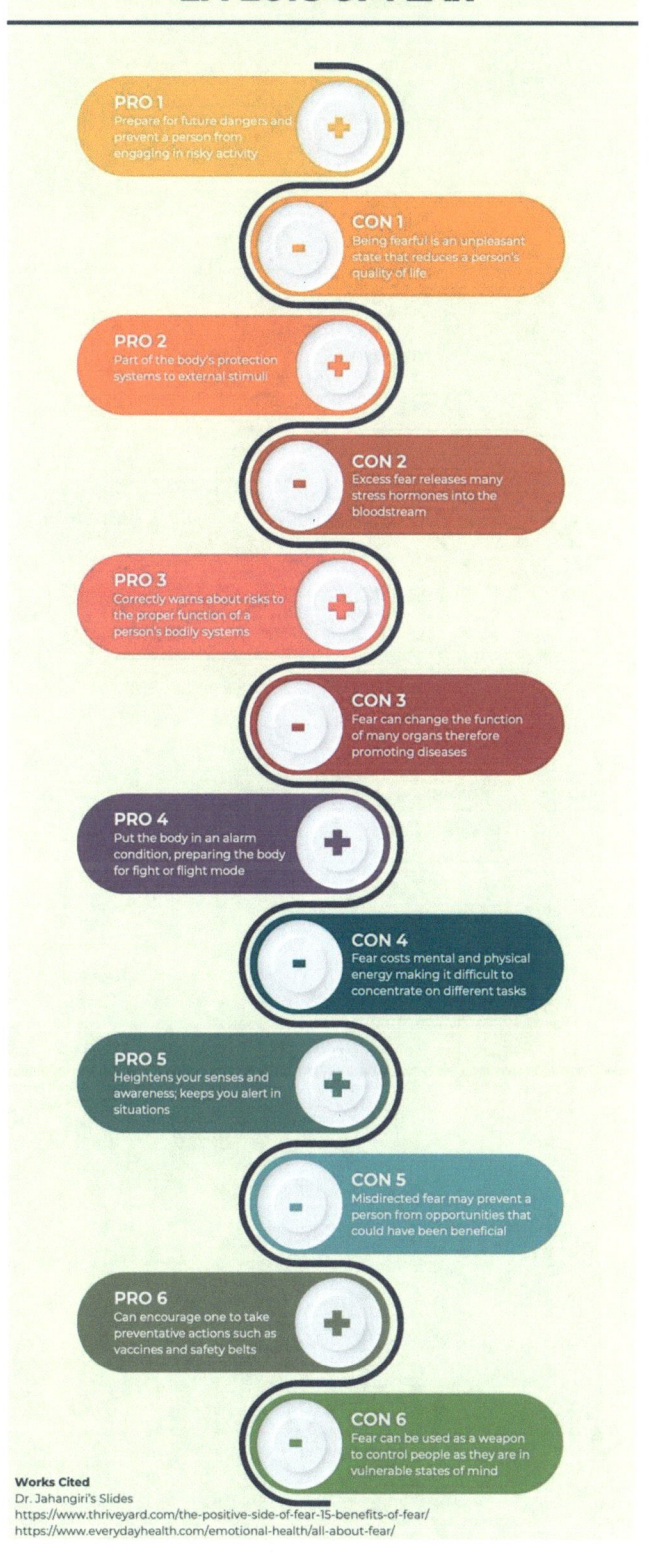

Rohita Arjarapu, Fall 2023

AN INFOGRAPHIC JOURNEY

The Benefits and Detriments of Fear

Protects and Keeps you Safe
1. Fear allows you to be wary of the threats and dangers around you. This is an evolutionary advantage that allows you to survive!

Allows you to Feel Closer to Other People
2. The fear response involves the secretion of oxytocin which is considered to be a hormone associated with prosocial behavior.

Judgment can be Impaired
3. The amygdala senses fear and the cerebral cortex (which helps with reasoning) will then become impaired. This makes it difficult to engage in decision-making.

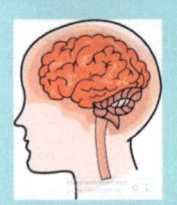

Association with Mood Disorders
4. Fear is often associated with anxiety and depression. Fear can also exacerbate or give rise to these disorders.

Interference with Life
5. Fear can be healthy in small doses but if it prevents you from doing the things you love it is harmful. It is useful to have caution but not more than needed to stay safe.

Anonymous, Spring 2023

The Power and Abuse of Fear

Fear is a natural emotion that is generally helpful for survival and making the best decisions in life. However, sometimes people can have too little or too much fear, both of which can be detrimental for an individual's well-being. People, specifically the masses, can be convinced to fear something and therefore be controlled by it.

Fear is actually one of the most efficient 'weapons' in a modern-day society where online or word-of-mouth information dominates over all other sources of truth. It follows, therefore, that some interest groups will be willing to manipulate the masses using fear.

For isntance, governments can use fear to control people from learning hidden secrets that could overthrow them, or they could use fear for something as simple as enforcing laws or taxes. A good portion of the time, the things people fear are either made-up or misleading.

Nevertheless, when the seed is planted, it will relentlessly grow and will be extremely difficult to unroot, since people tend to not modify their beliefs, especially those involving fear. Thus, you should watch out for fear-mongering attempts, and follow Winston Churchill's advice: "the only thing we have to fear is fear itself."

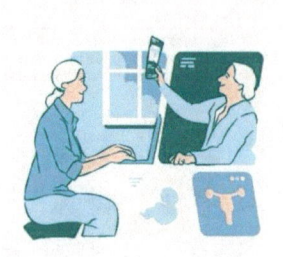

Ibrahim Khalilullah, Spring 2024

AN INFOGRAPHIC JOURNEY

WHY IS FEAR GOOD?
By: Akash Sivakumar

WHAT IS FEAR?
Fear is an unpleasant emotion that occurs due to a perceived danger that may occur in the future.

FEAR IS A FORM OF PROTECTION FOR OUR BODY!

1. PHYSICAL BENEFITS
Fear helps us protect our physical body by preventing us from participating in dangerous situations. Fear can help us improve our physical body by making us more active and boosting our survival instinct.

2. MENTAL BENEFITS
Fear can keep our brains focused in dangerous situations. Fear can also help us remember more details in risky events.

3. SHORT TERM BENEFITS
Fear can trigger the sympathetic system and enhance physical abilities like agility, and enhanced endurance.

4. LONG TERM BENEFITS
Fear helps prolong our lifespan. Fear can be a motivator to maintain our mental and physical lifestyle.

Akash Sivakumar, Fall 2023

FEAR IS A USEFUL EMOTION

Encourages Planning Ahead
Fear is characterized by worry about a future event that may occur. In response to fear, people may take more time to prepare for these future events.

Motivates Behavior
Fear encourages us to take action. For those with a busy schedule, fear may be the deciding factor in whether or not one goes to the doctor about a new symptom.

Improves Performance
One's fear of public performance may actually improve their abilities, to some extent. The Yerkes-Dodson Law states that one's performance is actually best with a intermediate level of stress.

Protects from Pain
Fear activates the sympathetic nervous system, triggering our "fight or flight" response. This response causes elevation of heart rate, increased blood glucose levels, and cessation of unnecessary processes like digestion. These changes prepare us to respond to danger.

Transcends Language
Fear is one of the six basic emotions that are universally recognized. Other animals also appear to experience fear.

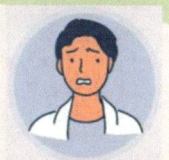

Fear can become irrational
When fear arises without reason or persists once the threat is gone, it is no longer useful. Mental health professionals can help manage this issue.

Vijaya Dutt, Fall 2023

AN INFOGRAPHIC JOURNEY

How to LOVE FEAR
Nicole K.

BENEFITS OF FEAR
- Prepares you for future danger
- Protects your body from harm
- Warns you to avoid risks
- Keeps you safe!

BE GENTLE WITH YOURSELF

BE KIND TO YOUR MIND
It can be scary, fear can affect quality of life if you let it. It can decrease digestion, increase blood pressure and heart rate, cause sweats, and increase risk for diseases.

BE GENTLE
It's okay to feel the way you do when you're afraid. Here are some common reactions to fear:
- Activation of ANS (autonomic nervous system)
- Suppression of immune system
- Mood affected

SELF LOVE CLUB

THE BEST TIPS
Fear can be healthy if it exists in balanced amounts. Too much can be too stressful, and too little can lead to avoidable accidents. A tip, to not let fear control you do your research! Sometimes fear comes from too little knowledge and believing another person's lies.

- Love what you do
- Treat yourself
- Stay positive
- Exercise
- Healthy lifestyle

ASK FOR HELP
IT'S OKAY TO ASK FOR HELP

Beware of confirmation bias and only listening/reading information that affirms your fear or denies the opposing view. If you need more information and help getting over a fear ask someone for help!

Nicole Kumanova, Spring 2023

The Power of Fear

1. Fear as a manipulator
Fear can be used as a powerful weapon in order to get people to do something completely irrational. It is used by countries on a large scale but also by individuals in our daily lives. Typically fear has been used by people holding positions of power.

2. Fear mongering
This is " the action of deliberately arousing public fear or alarm about a particular issue." Fear mongering is fear being used as a tool in the most malicious and dangerous manner. It is typically used by governments, but can also be used at an individual level.

3. Fear mongering examples
Fear mongering has been used as a tool in some of the worst atrocities history has ever seen. Nazi Germany, the U.S.S.R, and North Korea are some instances in which fear mongering has been used to kill and manipulate millions.

4. Believing
Believing is the basis of why fear mongering is so powerful in the first place. Humans have a very strong resistance to changing their mind, particularly when it would require them to accept that their belief could have caused harm. So once you get someone to believe something, they are likely to ignore even rational arguments against it.

Austin Sprouse, Spring 2024

The Power and Usage of Fear
Rakshak Ravichandran

1. Fear as a Manipulator
- Most efficient of all great manipulators
- Can be used as a weapon for terrorization
- Used for personal gain
- Can be evident in certain laws

2. Uses of Fear as a Manipulator
- Government
- Oher people
- Spouse
- Employees
- Police

3. The Power of Fear
- One of the oldest and most effective ways to dominate orther people
- Can be used at any level
  - Creating fear of jail
  - Political oppression
- Used by modern politicians to support their agenda

4. Purposes of Inducing Fear
- To ensure people follow the law
- Using risks that may not exist may serve interest of society
- Incorrect information may be spread for monetary gain

5. Sources
- Møller, A.R. "Neurobiology of Fear, Anxiety and other Emotions"
- Week 11. Chapter 5. Part 2. Effect of Fear on a Person

Rakshak Ravichandran, Fall 2023

Fear. It's nicer than you think
By: Asif Lakhani

What is fear?
Fear is defined as a feeling, usually an unpleasant one, derived from the belief of something dangerous, potentially causing harm. Fear can only be measured by the one feeling it.

Types of fear
Rational: When our fear has a basis, a reasoning behind it. True potential, eminent danger which may harm our body.

Irrational: A baseless fear, an imaginary or non-harmful stimuli which triggers fear.

Why do we have fear?
Fear can be good, it often servs as a warning signal to our bodies that a harmful stimulus may occur and takes proper precautions to avoid it, hence activating our body's alarm system.

Uses of fear
Fear is commonly, and unfortunately, used to control people. Fear is often employed as dominance in many social relationships: marriage, children, workplace, politics, etc.

Can we control fear?
Yes and No. While we can't stop ourselves from feeling fear, we can elicit it. Fear-mongering is known as purposely causing fear in a public on a certain issue. A common example is the influence the stock market by a rumor.

Asif Lakhani, Spring 2024

AN INFOGRAPHIC JOURNEY

The importance of FEAR

FEAR as an alarm system

FEAR can warn us about future and immediate dangers
-> We then take precaution!
- by driving properly
- by avoiding unhealthy food
- by avoiding going near wild animals
- by keeping proper hygiene

FEAR activates the autonomic nervous system

Fear prepares the body for a proper and protective action
How?
- Fight or Flight reaction
  - elevate sympathetic activity
  - lower parasympathetic activity
- Fight: nutrients redirected to the muscles
- Flight: run away from danger!
- + "freezing" can sometimes be safer than running away

There are RATIONAL FEARS

Although too much fear can decrease quality of life, there are still benefits associated with this emotion

- Fear of illness
  - Causes us to take precaution in avoiding getting sick
    - eg. vaccination
    - eg. notice pain
    - eg. eating healthier
- Fear of falling
  - forces us to take precaution
    - eg. put a rug on the bathroom floor

Jasha Dela Cruz, Spring 2024

How People Benefit from Fear

1. Fear can act as a warning which can prevent people from getting involved in harmful situations

2. It not only alerts someone's brain to potential harm but prepares the body for possible threat or injury.

3. When a potential threat is suspected a fast action is initiated through the non-classical sensorry system

4. Once fear has warned the body of danger, it can cause the body to be on high alert and prepare for "figth or flight".

Emily Lopez, Spring 2024

AN INFOGRAPHIC JOURNEY

3 WAYS FEAR IS UNFAVORABLE
Made by: Kaeli Nguyen

WHAT REALLY IS FEAR?
Conscious feeling/awareness that one is either in harms way or about to be in harms way.

1. MENTAL HEALTH
Fear can take a huge toll on the human body and mind. Being overly fearful can lead to mental health deterioration and mental disorders like anxiety disorder. These can cause one's mindset and health to drastically decrease

2. REDUCE QUALITY OF LIFE
Fear can lead to things such as isolation which affects a persons quality of life limiting them from the opportunities life may offer for the worse.

3. RASH/BAD DECISIONS
Lastly, fear can cause irrational decisions that can be more harmful to the individual than the initial stimuli for the fear reaction.

CONCLUSION:
Fear can have its advantages, but it still has many disadvantages that can be much more harmful and dangerous than what is causing the fear.

Kaeli Nguyen, Spring 2024

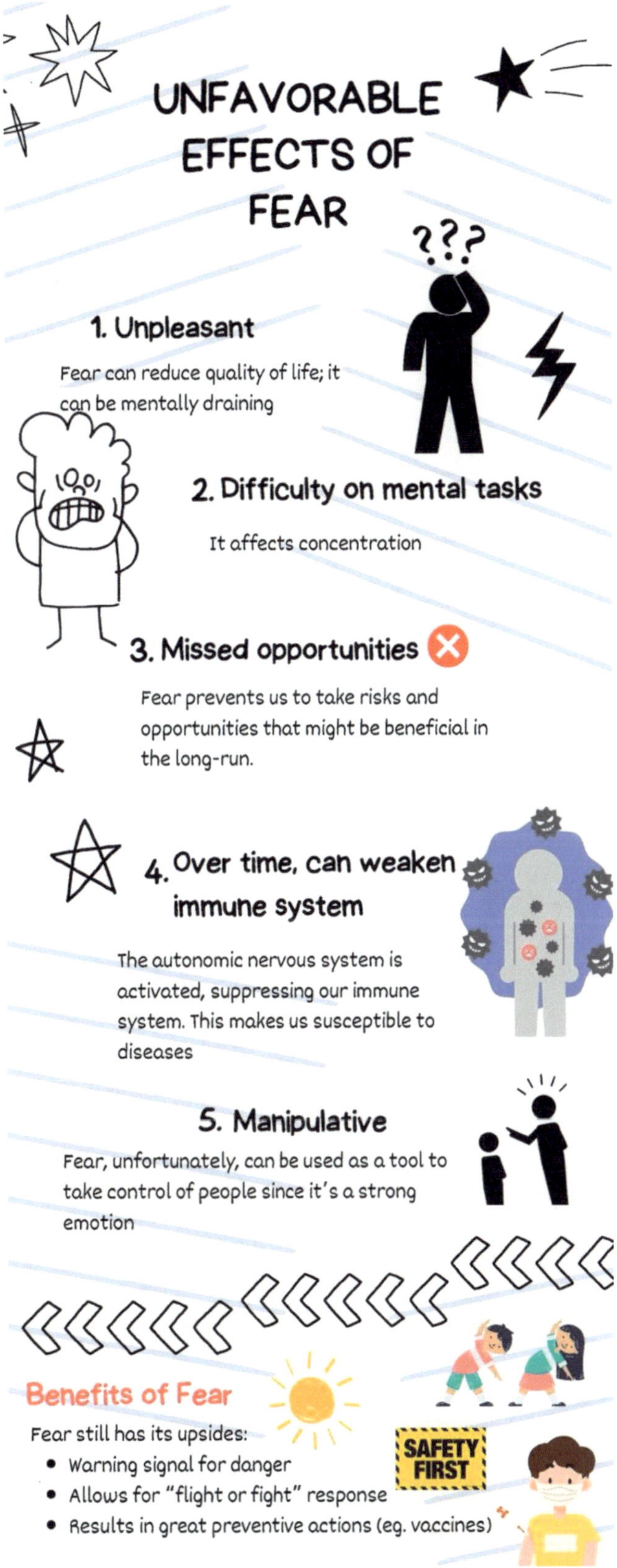

UNFAVORABLE EFFECTS OF FEAR

1. Unpleasant
Fear can reduce quality of life; it can be mentally draining

2. Difficulty on mental tasks
It affects concentration

3. Missed opportunities
Fear prevents us to take risks and opportunities that might be beneficial in the long-run.

4. Over time, can weaken immune system
The autonomic nervous system is activated, suppressing our immune system. This makes us susceptible to diseases

5. Manipulative
Fear, unfortunately, can be used as a tool to take control of people since it's a strong emotion

Benefits of Fear
Fear still has its upsides:
- Warning signal for danger
- Allows for "flight or fight" response
- Results in great preventive actions (eg. vaccines)

Jasha Dela Cruz, Spring 2024

AN INFOGRAPHIC JOURNEY

AN INFOGRAPHIC JOURNEY

CHAPTER 4

The Body on Fear

The Hidden Impact: How Fear Alters the Body and Mind

By Arya Kolte, Spring 2024

Have you ever been so scared that you start shaking, sweating, and cannot think anymore? This would all be caused by fear and anxiety. Fear is an evolutionary survival mechanism that is deeply ingrained in our minds which has great influence over our bodies as well. It is natural to feel fear in response to threats, but it can be detrimental to have chronic or intense fear. In this blog post, we will expand on how fear causes these symptoms and how our body reacts, shedding light on how this emotion can impact our health. Fear is a protective measure, but chronic fear can often lead to negative physiological and psychological issues which can be prevented by small tasks in our daily lives.

To understand the effects of fear, let's first understand what fear itself is. Fear is a complex emotion that triggers a cascade of physiological responses that is designed for us to protect from any potential danger. When we are faced with a threat, our brain's amygdala, which is the hub of our emotional processing, sends signals to the hypothalamus which initiates our body's fight-or-flight response. This sets off a series of reactions involving the nervous, endocrine, and immune systems. All these systems help the body to confront the danger or run away from it.

The physical symptoms of fear and anxiety appear as an increase in stress hormones, muscle tension, digestive issues, and immune suppression. Fear causes the release of stress hormones like adrenaline and cortisol, which elevate the heart rate, increase blood pressure, and boost energy levels. These responses are needed for survival, but if you have too many stress hormones for an extended period, then it can lead to chronic conditions like diabetes, heart disease, and hypertension. When we are scared, our bodies tense up to prepare for physical action. These muscular tensions can cause aches and pains. Fear also triggers a decrease in blood flow to the digestive stomach, leading to nausea or diarrhea. Chronic fear can also lead to irritable bowel syndrome or ulcers. The gut-brain axis connects the gut and the brain. Fear and stress can disrupt this pathway, which leads to abdominal symptoms. Prolonged exposure to fear can cause the immune system to weaken, making the body more susceptible to infections or illnesses. Fear can also cause a lot of brain fog. Brain fog is when you cannot concentrate or think straight, and your mind automatically goes into panic mode. Chronic fear can also cause changes in brain structure and function, affecting neuroplasticity. This can affect memory processing, learning abilities, and emotional regulation.

There are also psychological impacts of fear that can be seen as anxiety disorders, depression, social isolation, and sleep disturbances. Fear can often escalate into anxiety disorders like generalized anxiety disorder (GAD), panic disorder, and post-traumatic stress disorder (PTSD). These disorders can impair day-to-day lives and significantly affect an individual's quality of life. Chronic fear and anxiety are often correlated with depression. The constant feeling of having to worry can ruin a person's willingness to fight for themselves and cause feelings of helplessness and hatred towards themselves. Fear can cause people to have limited social interactions because they are scared that others will judge or reject them. Isolating yourself can increase mental health issues and create an extreme feeling of loneliness. Another psychological impact of fear is sleeping disturbances. Fear interrupts sleep patterns, which leads to insomnia, nightmares, and restless nights. Sleep deprivation increases physiological and psychological issues, which causes even more distress in the body. Therefore, fear has a great variety of physiological effects on our bodies.

Fear can also impact various systems in our bodies. For example, our cardiovascular health can be impacted by adrenaline, as mentioned above. When experiencing fear, our breathing patterns change by becoming shallow and rapid. This can lead to asthma or panic attacks. Another big role fear plays is dealing with pain perception. Fear can change how we perceive pain because we may process fear more than pain in a threatening situation. Ignoring pain can lead to heightened pain tolerance, but on the other hand, chronic fear can sensitize the nervous system and make pain more apparent. Skin issues like hives, acne, or eczema may appear during a stressful time. Challenging childhood experiences, including trauma and neglect, can increase the risk of mental health disorders. In addition, the cumulative impact of fear on the mind and body can take a significant toll on overall well-being, leading to feelings of fatigue, irritability, and diminished quality of life. Hence, fear can impact our bodies negatively psychologically and physiologically.

So, how do we deal with this fear lurking inside of us? We can practice mindfulness. Mindfulness meditation is like hitting a reset button for your brain, which helps you focus on the calmness in your life. Another beneficial habit in dealing with fear is moving your body. Exercise is not just good for your body, but it also helps to reduce fear. A little physical activity can go a long way to decrease stress levels. Having good habits like earring light, getting enough sleep, and avoiding toxic substances can create a more manageable stress response and reduce physical symptoms of fear. Do not be afraid to lean on friends, family, or a therapist when fear gets the best of you. Many people are scared to talk about their emotions, like fear, but after you start talking about it, you realize that you are not alone. Sometimes all it takes is a listening ear to feel relaxed and hear. Talking out your problems with someone you trust can be beneficial.

Even though fear is needed for survival, it can take a heavy toll on the body and mind when it is not appropriately managed. Understanding the physiological and psychological mechanisms of fear can help us understand a better way to manage stress, fear, and anxiety. By prioritizing self-care, seeking support, and fostering a sense of inner calm, we can manage our stressful situations to help our bodies. Fear is inevitable, but it should not have control over us. With mindful awareness and good habits, we can manage our daily stresses in a healthy way. Knowing the adverse effects of fear, we should try to manage our daily habits to learn how to deal with stressful situations, so our bodies are not harmed in the long run. Recognizing the adverse effects of this emotion can motivate us to have self-care, strong determination, and create good practices.

References

1. "Impact of Fear and Anxiety." *Taking Charge of Your Wellbeing*, www.takingcharge.csh.umn.edu/impact-fear-and-anxiety. Accessed 8 Apr. 2024.
2. Keifer, Orion P, et al. "The Physiology of Fear: Reconceptualizing the Role of the Central Amygdala in Fear Learning." *Physiology (Bethesda, Md.)*, U.S. National Library of Medicine, Sept. 2015, www.ncbi.nlm.nih.gov/pmc/articles/PMC4556826/.
3. Ropeik, David. "The Consequences of Fear." *EMBO Reports*, U.S. National Library of Medicine, Oct. 2004, www.ncbi.nlm.nih.gov/pmc/articles/PMC1299209/.
4. Steimer, Thierry. "The Biology of Fear- and Anxiety-Related Behaviors." *Dialogues in Clinical Neuroscience*, U.S. National Library of Medicine, Sept. 2002, www.ncbi.nlm.nih.gov/pmc/articles/PMC3181681/.

AN INFOGRAPHIC JOURNEY

PHYSIOLOGICAL EFFECTS OF FEAR

What occurs when your body is exposed to a threat?

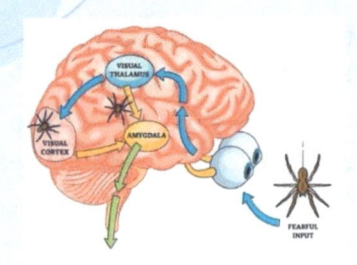

IN THE BRAIN

A threat stimulus triggers a fear response in the amygdala, which activates the sympathetic nervous system, kicking our body into a "fight or flight" response.

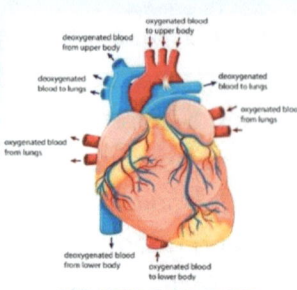

01

HEART & BLOOD

When a person is perceived to be in danger, the brain triggers a rush of adrenaline, which makes the heart beat faster and pushes the body into "fight-or-flight" mode. Our blood flow also changes in a state of fear. Blood flows away from the heart and into our muscles and limbs, making it easier for our body to react to any threat.

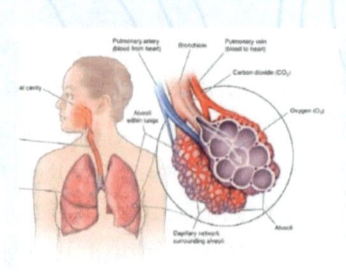

02

RESPIRATION

The release of adrenaline causes our rate of breathing to increase. The dilation of our airways allows more oxygen to travel into our bloodstream, making our bodies ready for action. The additional oxygen goes to our brain and makes our senses sharper in preparation for defensive action.

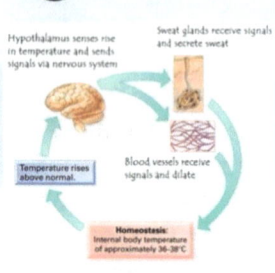

03

SKIN

When in a state of fear, our sweat glands can be stimulated from the sympathetic nervous system. Sweating is a stress response that helps cool our body down so we don't overheat internally. You can also begin to feel flushed or have cold hands when you're afraid. This is due to blood flowing away from the edges of the body toward the interior muscles.

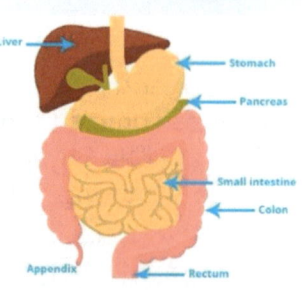

04

DIGESTIVE SYSTEM

Reduced activity in the stomach and intestines. Overall blood flow is decreased and redirected to our brain and muscles. Therefore digestion slows or even halts so that the body can divert all its internal energy to facing a perceived threat.

05

Zaineb Ali, Spring 2024

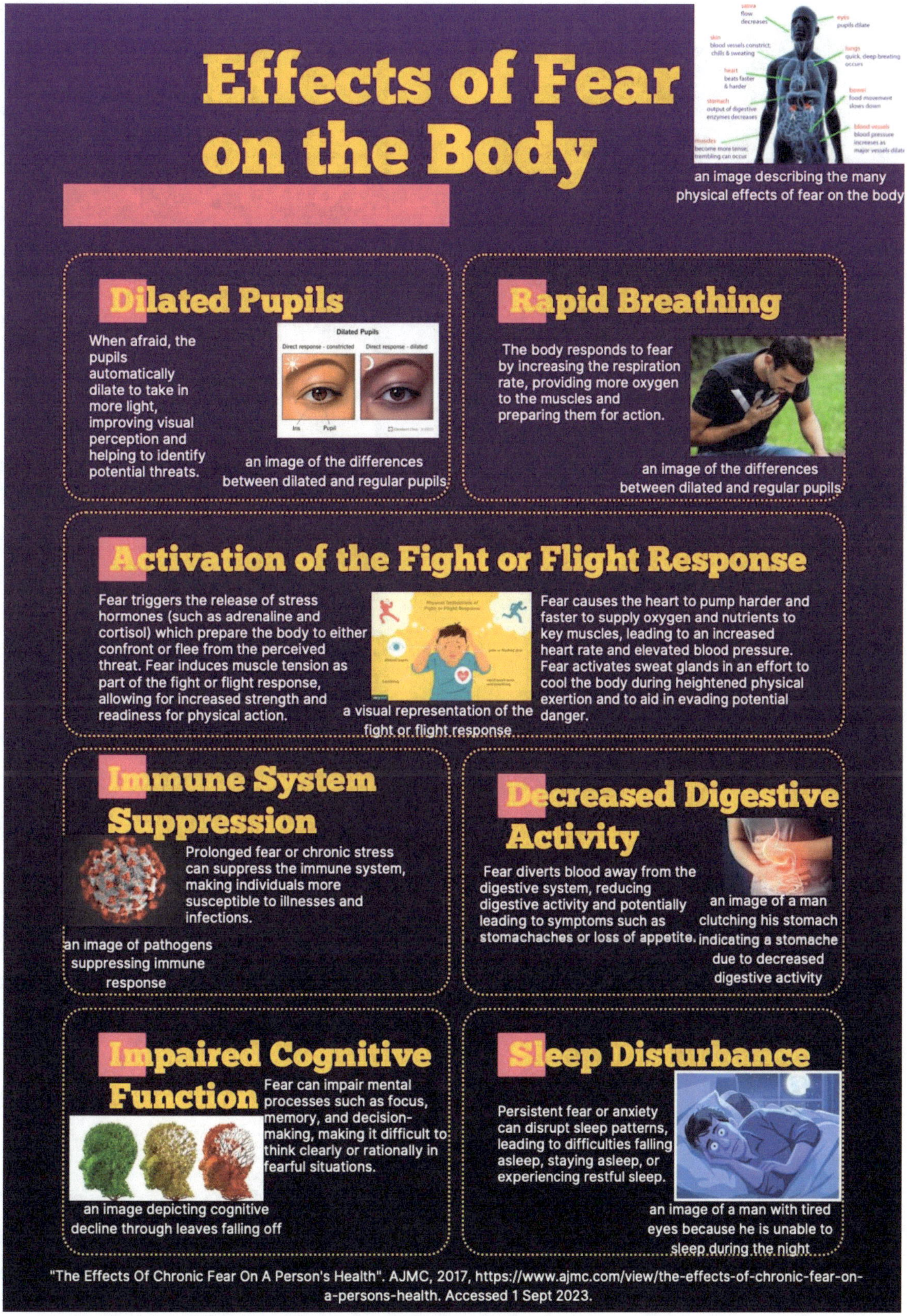

AN INFOGRAPHIC JOURNEY

Effects of Fear on the Body

an image describing the many physical effects of fear on the body

Dilated Pupils

When afraid, the pupils automatically dilate to take in more light, improving visual perception and helping to identify potential threats.

an image of the differences between dilated and regular pupils

Rapid Breathing

The body responds to fear by increasing the respiration rate, providing more oxygen to the muscles and preparing them for action.

an image of the differences between dilated and regular pupils

Activation of the Fight or Flight Response

Fear triggers the release of stress hormones (such as adrenaline and cortisol) which prepare the body to either confront or flee from the perceived threat. Fear induces muscle tension as part of the fight or flight response, allowing for increased strength and readiness for physical action.

a visual representation of the fight or flight response

Fear causes the heart to pump harder and faster to supply oxygen and nutrients to key muscles, leading to an increased heart rate and elevated blood pressure. Fear activates sweat glands in an effort to cool the body during heightened physical exertion and to aid in evading potential danger.

Immune System Suppression

Prolonged fear or chronic stress can suppress the immune system, making individuals more susceptible to illnesses and infections.

an image of pathogens suppressing immune response

Decreased Digestive Activity

Fear diverts blood away from the digestive system, reducing digestive activity and potentially leading to symptoms such as stomachaches or loss of appetite.

an image of a man clutching his stomach indicating a stomache due to decreased digestive activity

Impaired Cognitive Function

Fear can impair mental processes such as focus, memory, and decision-making, making it difficult to think clearly or rationally in fearful situations.

an image depicting cognitive decline through leaves falling off

Sleep Disturbance

Persistent fear or anxiety can disrupt sleep patterns, leading to difficulties falling asleep, staying asleep, or experiencing restful sleep.

an image of a man with tired eyes because he is unable to sleep during the night

"The Effects Of Chronic Fear On A Person's Health". AJMC, 2017, https://www.ajmc.com/view/the-effects-of-chronic-fear-on-a-persons-health. Accessed 1 Sept 2023.

Anisha Reedy, Fall 2023

AN INFOGRAPHIC JOURNEY

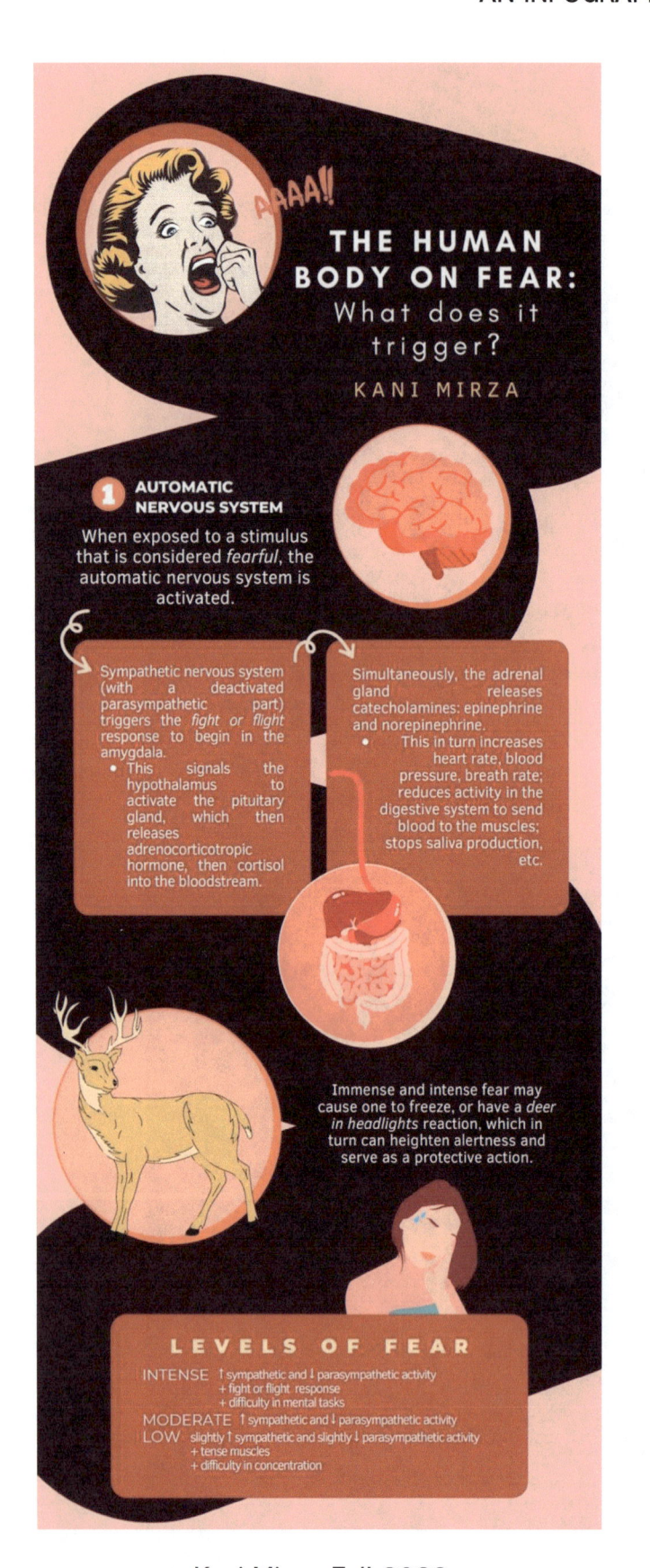

Kani Mirza, Fall 2022

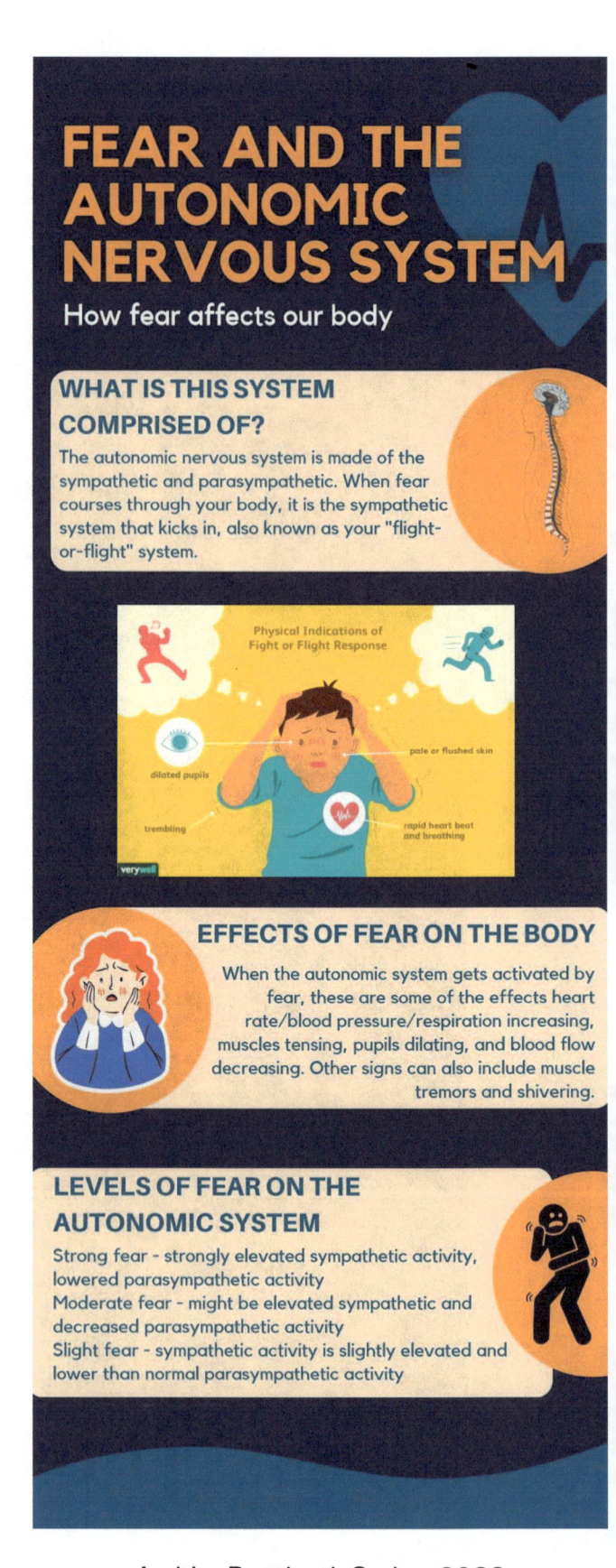

Amitha Prattipati, Spring 2023

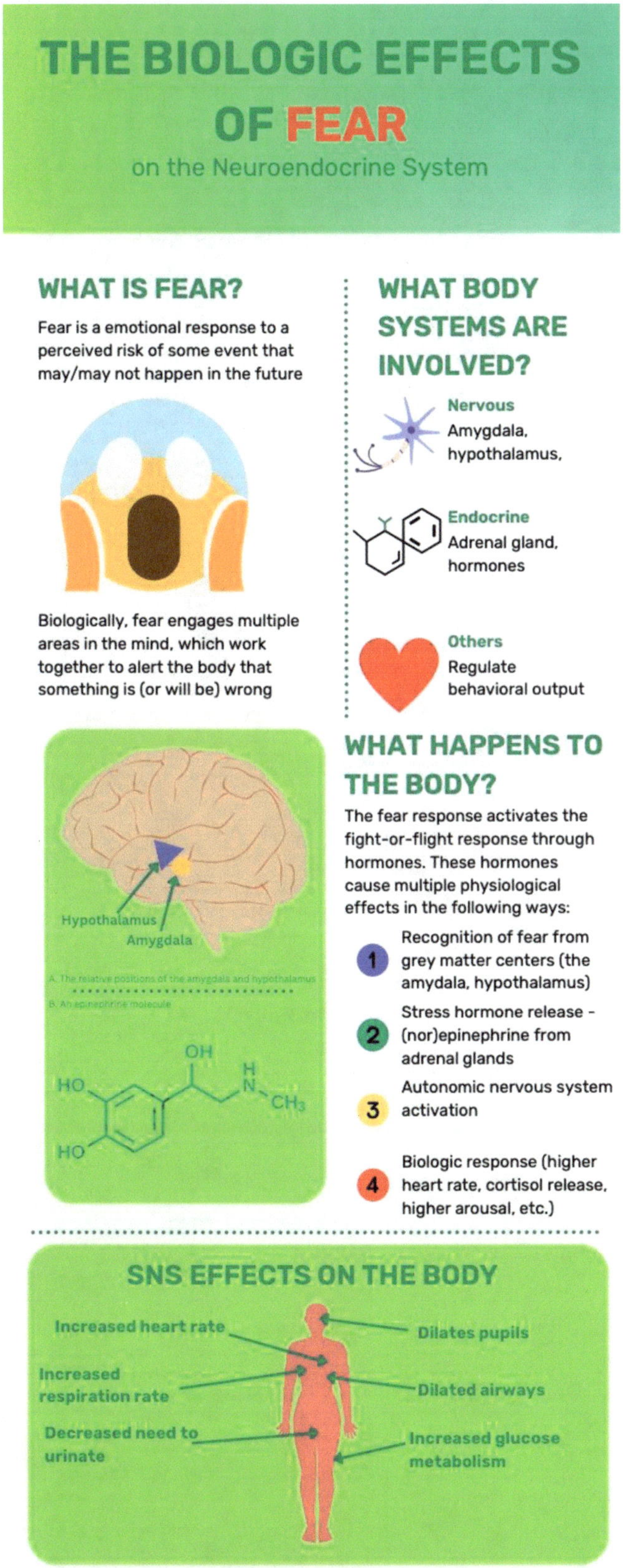

AN INFOGRAPHIC JOURNEY

THE BIOLOGIC EFFECTS OF FEAR
on the Neuroendocrine System

WHAT IS FEAR?

Fear is a emotional response to a perceived risk of some event that may/may not happen in the future

Biologically, fear engages multiple areas in the mind, which work together to alert the body that something is (or will be) wrong

WHAT BODY SYSTEMS ARE INVOLVED?

- **Nervous** — Amygdala, hypothalamus,
- **Endocrine** — Adrenal gland, hormones
- **Others** — Regulate behavioral output

WHAT HAPPENS TO THE BODY?

The fear response activates the fight-or-flight response through hormones. These hormones cause multiple physiological effects in the following ways:

1. Recognition of fear from grey matter centers (the amydala, hypothalamus)
2. Stress hormone release - (nor)epinephrine from adrenal glands
3. Autonomic nervous system activation
4. Biologic response (higher heart rate, cortisol release, higher arousal, etc.)

Hypothalamus, Amygdala
A. The relative positions of the amygdala and hypothalamus
B. An epinephrine molecule

SNS EFFECTS ON THE BODY

- Increased heart rate
- Increased respiration rate
- Decreased need to urinate
- Dilates pupils
- Dilated airways
- Increased glucose metabolism

Hussam Asim, Fall 2023

WEEK 1

The Effect of Fear on the Sympathetic Nervous System

Hanah Kim

01 Epinephrine and Norepinephrine

When a person feels fear, activity of their sympathetic nervous system is elevated, causing the adrenal glands to release the epinephrine (EPI) and norepinephrine (NE). EPI and NE bind to adrenergic α and β receptors throughout the body, stimulating the common responses to fear.

02 Blood Pressure

EPI and NE bind to receptors in blood vessels, causing vasoconstriction and increasing blood pressure. Blood vessels supplying skeletal muscles, however, dilate. EPI can be used to treat hypotension.

03 Heart Rate

Elevated levels of EPI and NE cause increased heart contractility, raising heart rate. This increases cardiac output in order to increase blood and oxygen supply to the body.

04 Pupil Dilation

When the sympathetic nervous system is activated, radial muscles of the pupil contract, causing pupil dilation. This allows more light to enter the eye and improve vision.

05 Bronchodilation

EPI is a bronchodilator, meaning it causes dilation of bronchi by relaxing smooth muscles in the airway. This allows more air to enter the lungs. Bronchodilators may be used to treat patients with respiratory problems like asthma and wheezing.

Hanah Kim, Spring 2023

AN INFOGRAPHIC JOURNEY

THE BIOLOGICAL EXTENT OF FEAR

THE FEAR REACTION

The fear reaction begins in an area of the brain known as the Amygdala. This segment of the brain activates when a human face with emotion is in our presence and elevates based on the emotion of the person such as anger, sadness, etc. If a threat stimulus is detected, the hippocampus aids the amygdala to interpret the threat in order to process contextual information.

THE NEUTROTRANSMITTER ASSOCIATED WITH FEAR REACTION

Based on the biological perspective, GABA is involved in the motivation for fear & anxiety. GABA is a transmitter inhibitor that maintains the most ideal flow of stimulation in order to reduce neural transmission.

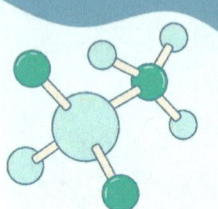

GABA RECEPTOR SITES AND ANXIETY DRUGS

GABA receptors are present in order for GABA to bind so that neural transmission can be reduced. The manner in which GABA binds is dependent on benzodiazepines which are anti-anxiety drugs. These drugs include Valium, Librum, and Alprazolam and they regulate neural transmission by increasing the effects of GABA

TRIGGERS OF ANXIETY

1. **Overstimulation**
   a. when an individual is bombarded with information.
2. **Cognitive Incongruity**
   a. when an individual has difficulty adapting to a situation.
3. **Response Unavailability**
   a. when an individual doesn't know how to handle a difficult situation.

Mahwish Quadri, Spring 2023

Effects of Fear On Body Functions

Fear On Autonomic Nervous System

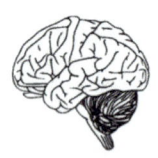

The autonomic nervous system consists of the sympathetic system and parasympathetic system. Theses two systems have opposite effects regarding blood pressure, heart rate, and digestive system.

Strong Fear

When the body deals with strong fear, the following will occur:
- flight or fright reaction
- elevated sympathetic
- low parasympathtic
- difficulty performing mental tasks

Moderate Fear

When the body deals with moderate fear, the following will occur:
- elevated sympathetic
- decreased parasympathtic

Slight Fear

When the body deals with slight fear, the following will occur:
- somewhat elevated sympathetic
- lower than normal parasympathetic
- tense muscles
- distractions

Freedom of Fear

When the body deals with freedom of fear, the following will occur:
- regular sympathtic activity
- regular parasympathetic activity
- relaxed muscles
- concentration

Aisha Ali, Spring 2024

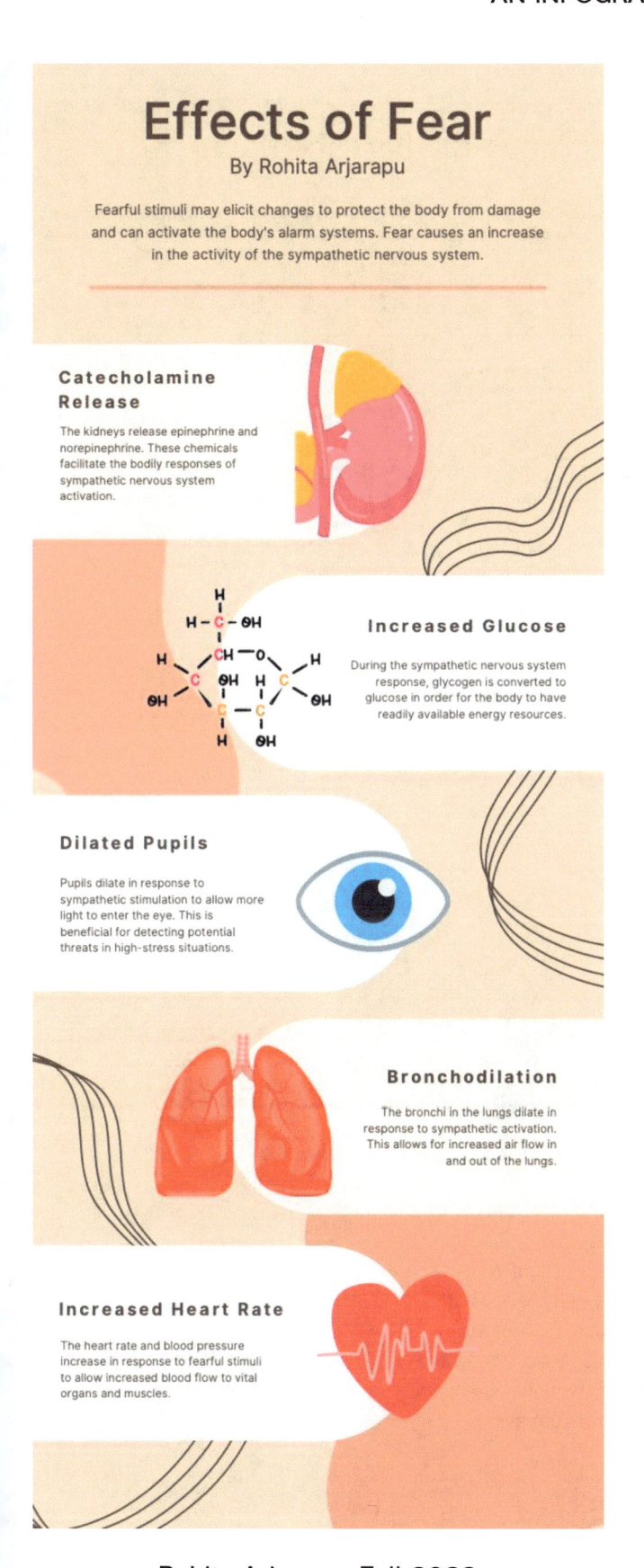

AN INFOGRAPHIC JOURNEY

Effects of Fear
By Rohita Arjarapu

Fearful stimuli may elicit changes to protect the body from damage and can activate the body's alarm systems. Fear causes an increase in the activity of the sympathetic nervous system.

Catecholamine Release
The kidneys release epinephrine and norepinephrine. These chemicals facilitate the bodily responses of sympathetic nervous system activation.

Increased Glucose
During the sympathetic nervous system response, glycogen is converted to glucose in order for the body to have readily available energy resources.

Dilated Pupils
Pupils dilate in response to sympathetic stimulation to allow more light to enter the eye. This is beneficial for detecting potential threats in high-stress situations.

Bronchodilation
The bronchi in the lungs dilate in response to sympathetic activation. This allows for increased air flow in and out of the lungs.

Increased Heart Rate
The heart rate and blood pressure increase in response to fearful stimuli to allow increased blood flow to vital organs and muscles.

Fear Response In the Brain

Thalamus
Acts as a relay station receiving input from sight, sound, and touch senses, directing that information to the appropriate brain areas for processing.

Hypothalamus
Triggers physiologiccal changes such as increased sweating, heart rate, and alertness. Regulates bodily responses through release of adrenaline and cortisol stress hormones as well as activation of the autonomic nervous system

Hippocampus + Amygdala
The amygdala helps determine if the stimulus is indeed a threat while the hippocampus helps in forming memories surrounding the fear-inducing stimuli. Together work to form memory consolidation and fear conditioning.

Frontal + Temporal Lobes
The frontal lobe helps to assess threat levels and control emotional reactions. The temporal lobe processes sensory input related to the threats.

Sneha Sharma

Rohita Arjarapu, Fall 2023 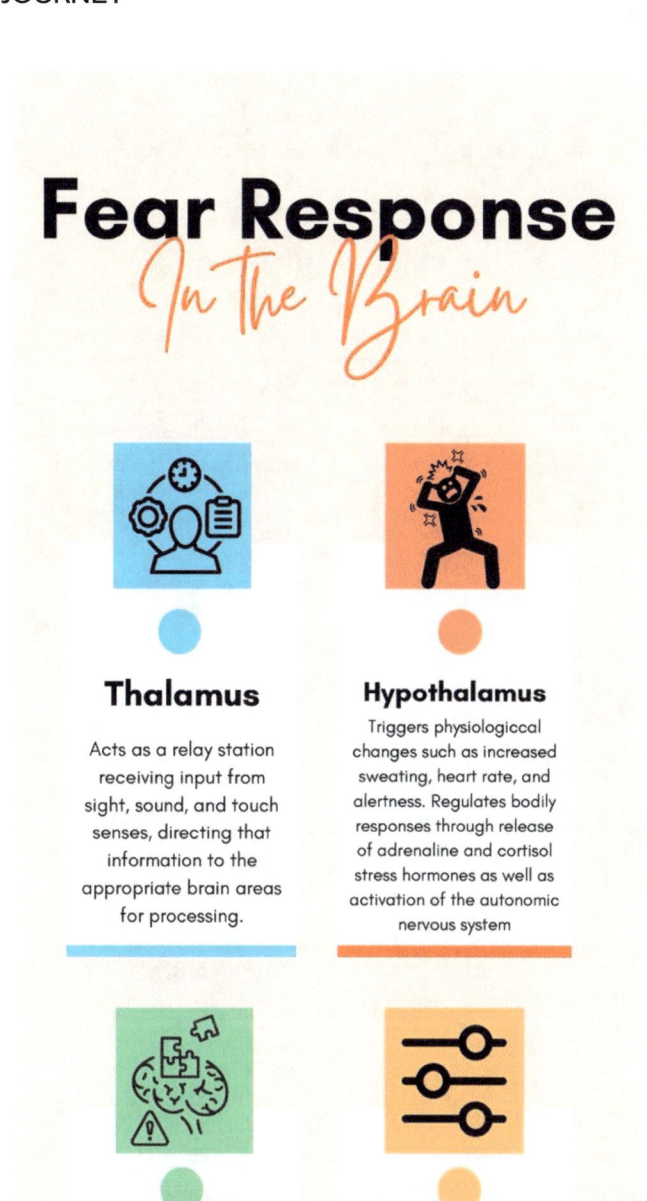 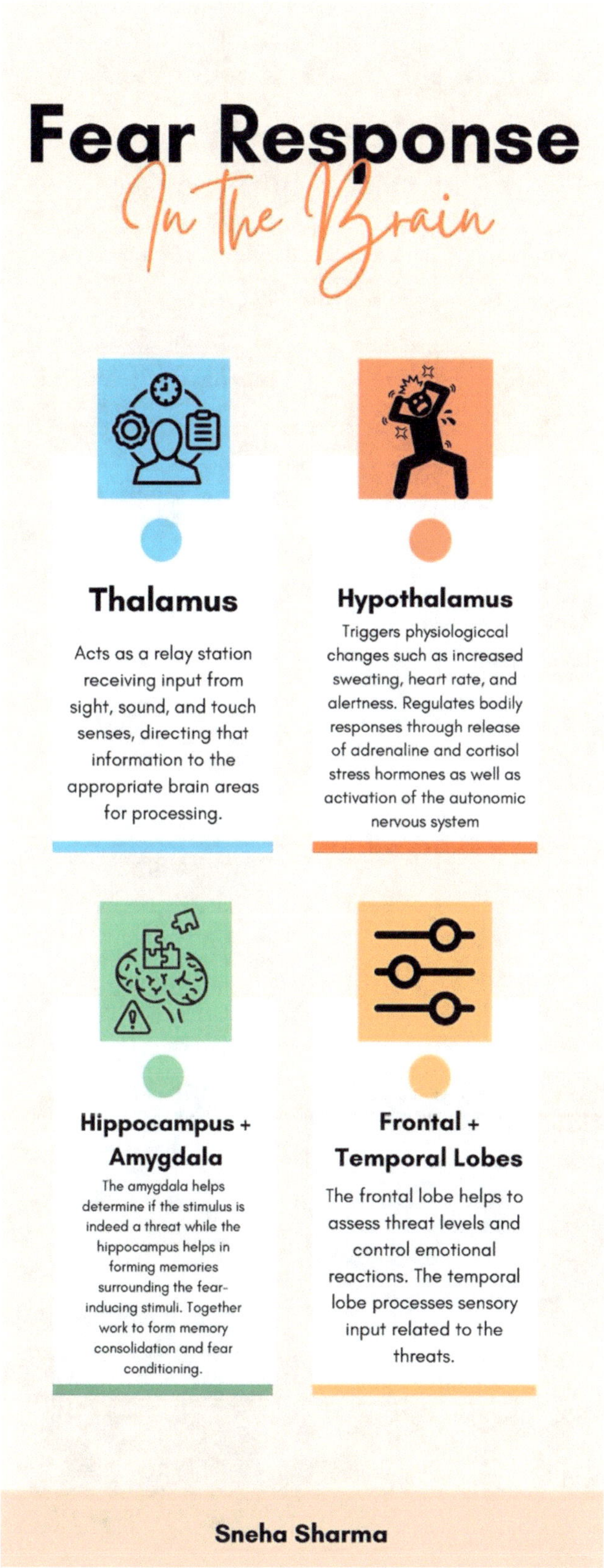   Sneha Sharma, Spring 2024

AN INFOGRAPHIC JOURNEY

Effects of Fear on the Body
By Sahiti Pydimarri

The evolutionary role of fear is to activate the body's alarm system and protect the body from damage. Fearful stimuli is processed by the **amygdala** and activates various arousal processes. This includes elevated **sympathetic nervous system** responses such as:

Increased heart rate
The heart rate and blood pressure increases in response to fear and stress in order to pump more blood to muscles and vital organs. Blood is redirected away from the skin and the digestive system

Bronchodilation
The breathing rate increases as well in order to deliver more oxygen to the muscles in order to support physical exertion. Hyperventilation can lead to a panic attack.

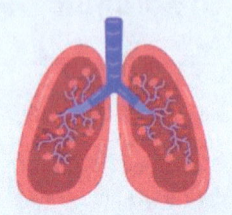

Dilation of pupils
During the sympathetic nervous system response, pupils dilate to allow more light to enter the eye which is beneficial for detecting potential threats in high stress situations

Suppression of non-essential functions
Functions like digestion and immune responses are temporarily suppressed so that the body can divert enerergy elsewhere such as making the brain stay more alert and focused

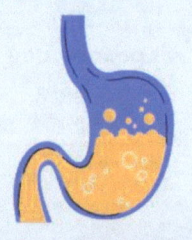

Release of adrenaline
The adrenal glands release adrenaline or epinephrine which is a stress hormone that amplifies the fight or flight repsponse. It also leads to enhanced sensory perception

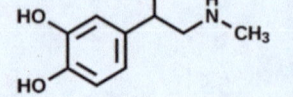

Sahiti Pydimarri, Fall 2023

By: Bernice David
Fear - Influence on the Brain

THALAMUS
Essentially a giant switchboard that directs information to other parts of the brain.

HYPOTHALAMUS
Where the flight-or-flight response is activated. Messages are sent to the kidneys' adrenal glands, which release stress hormones.

HIPPOCAMPUS
Sensory cortex and amygdala areas of the brain that establish situational and emotional context and officially deem the situation a fearful.

FRONTAL AND TEMPORAL LOBES
Higher cortical areas where experiences of dread occur, release chemicals like dopamine that can cause panicked, irrational behavior.

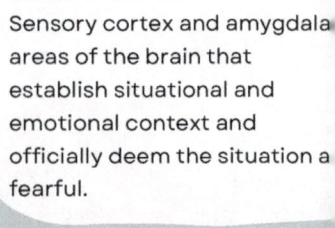

Bernice David, Spring 2024

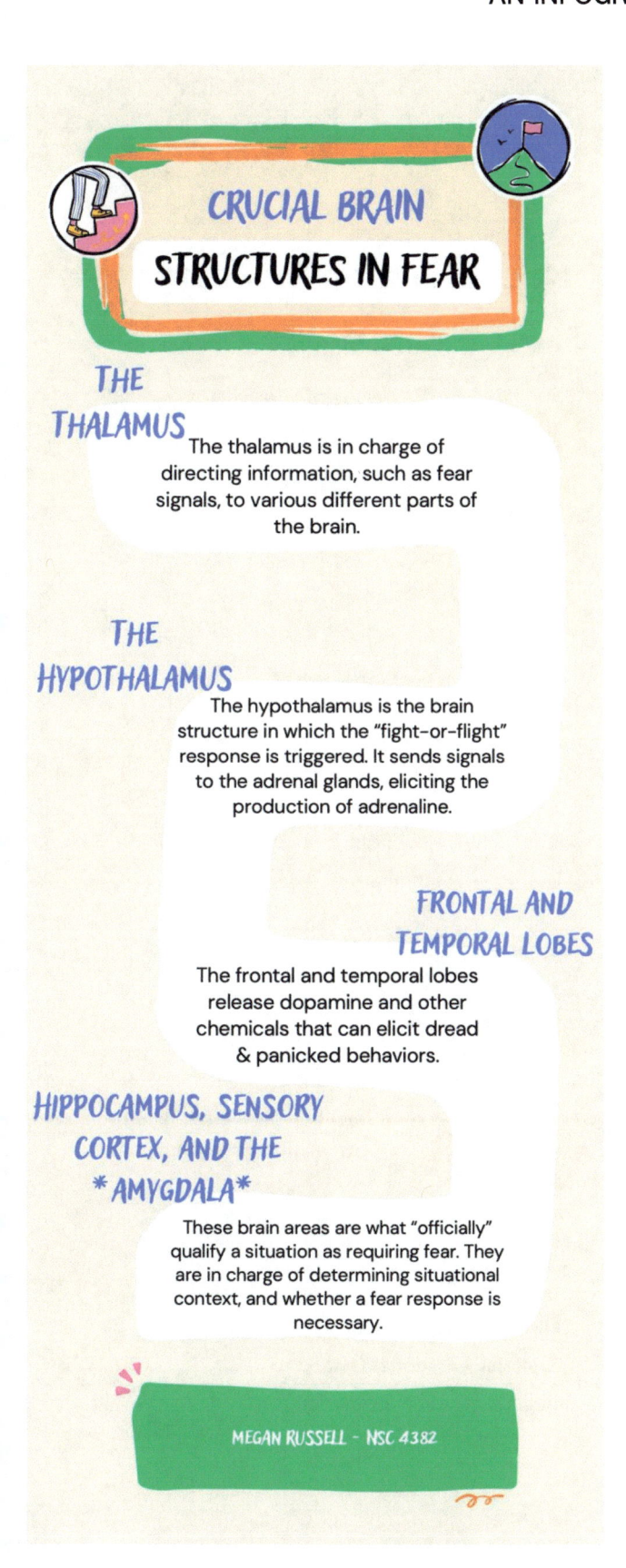

AN INFOGRAPHIC JOURNEY

CRUCIAL BRAIN STRUCTURES IN FEAR

THE THALAMUS
The thalamus is in charge of directing information, such as fear signals, to various different parts of the brain.

THE HYPOTHALAMUS
The hypothalamus is the brain structure in which the "fight-or-flight" response is triggered. It sends signals to the adrenal glands, eliciting the production of adrenaline.

FRONTAL AND TEMPORAL LOBES
The frontal and temporal lobes release dopamine and other chemicals that can elicit dread & panicked behaviors.

HIPPOCAMPUS, SENSORY CORTEX, AND THE *AMYGDALA*
These brain areas are what "officially" qualify a situation as requiring fear. They are in charge of determining situational context, and whether a fear response is necessary.

MEGAN RUSSELL - NSC 4382

Megan Russell, Fall 2023

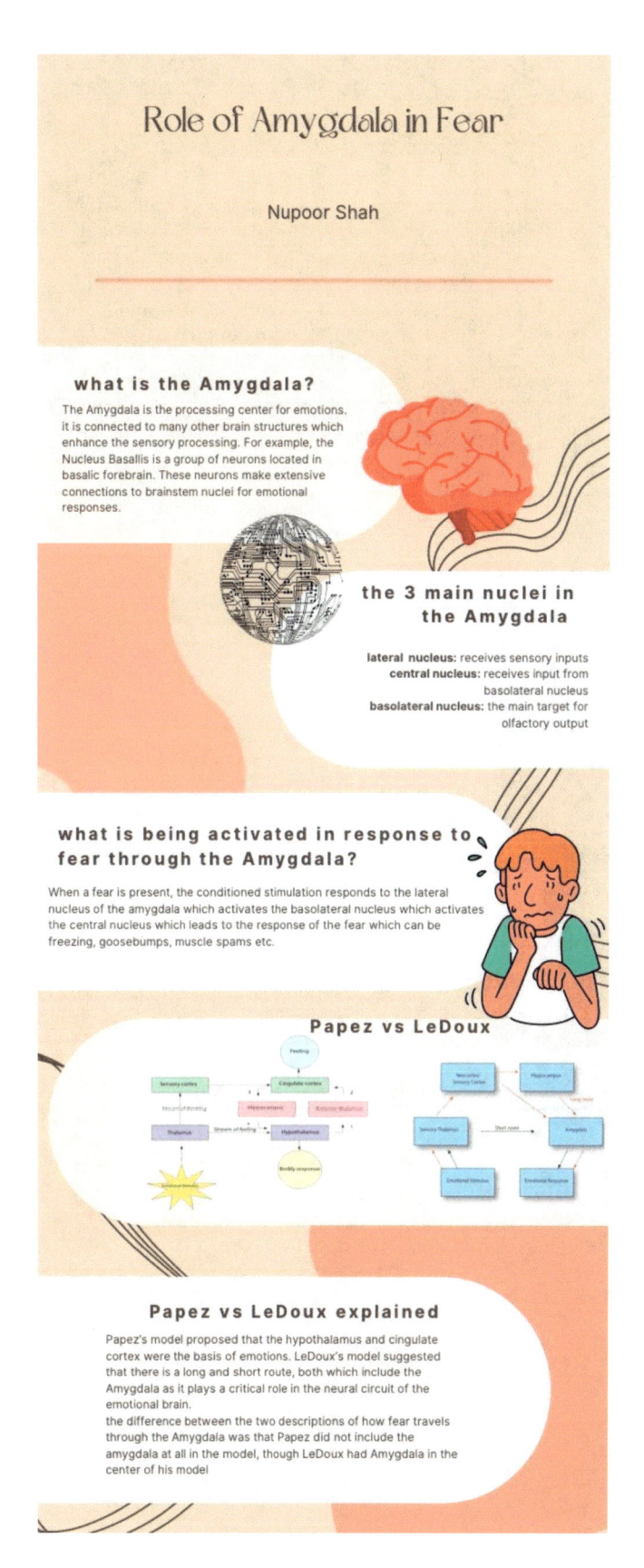

Role of Amygdala in Fear

Nupoor Shah

what is the Amygdala?
The Amygdala is the processing center for emotions. It is connected to many other brain structures which enhance the sensory processing. For example, the Nucleus Basallis is a group of neurons located in basalic forebrain. These neurons make extensive connections to brainstem nuclei for emotional responses.

the 3 main nuclei in the Amygdala
lateral nucleus: receives sensory inputs
central nucleus: receives input from basolateral nucleus
basolateral nucleus: the main target for olfactory output

what is being activated in response to fear through the Amygdala?
When a fear is present, the conditioned stimulation responds to the lateral nucleus of the amygdala which activates the basolateral nucleus which activates the central nucleus which leads to the response of the fear which can be freezing, goosebumps, muscle spams etc.

Papez vs LeDoux

Papez vs LeDoux explained
Papez's model proposed that the hypothalamus and cingulate cortex were the basis of emotions. LeDoux's model suggested that there is a long and short route, both which include the Amygdala as it plays a critical role in the neural circuit of the emotional brain.
the difference between the two descriptions of how fear travels through the Amygdala was that Papez did not include the amygdala at all in the model, though LeDoux had Amygdala in the center of his model

Nupoor Shah, Fall 2023

AN INFOGRAPHIC JOURNEY

STRUCTURES INVOLVED IN FEAR REACTION

Sensory information is gathered from the stimulus and relayed to different areas of the brain. All of these structures generate a response which allows us to react to fearful and threatening stimuli. Let's dive into the major structures responsible for this!

Source: Neurobiology of Fear and Other Emotions, Aage R. Moller

Hypothalamus
This structure is responsible in generating your FIGHT OR FLIGHT RESPONSE! The hypothalamus signals the adrenal glands to release stress hormones.

Stress hormones: Adrenaline and Cortisol.

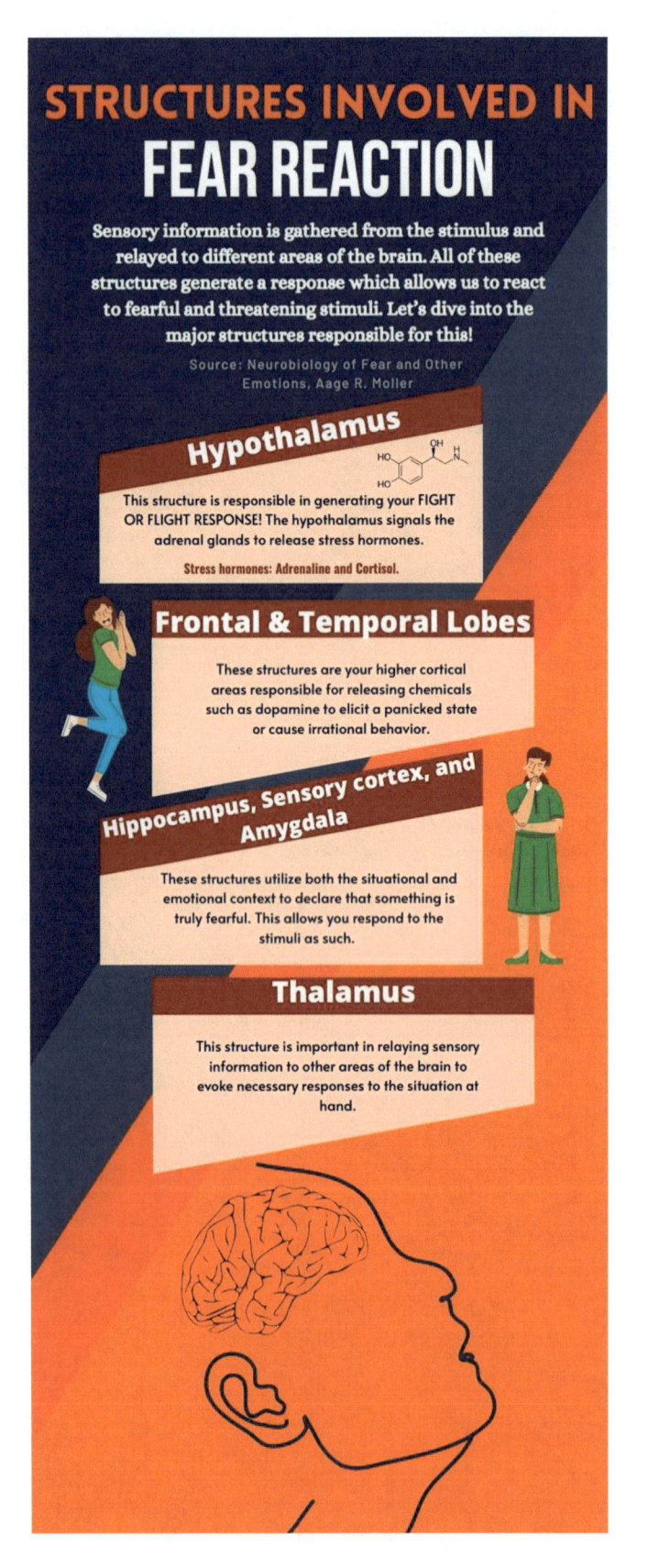

Frontal & Temporal Lobes
These structures are your higher cortical areas responsible for releasing chemicals such as dopamine to elicit a panicked state or cause irrational behavior.

Hippocampus, Sensory cortex, and Amygdala
These structures utilize both the situational and emotional context to declare that something is truly fearful. This allows you respond to the stimuli as such.

Thalamus
This structure is important in relaying sensory information to other areas of the brain to evoke necessary responses to the situation at hand.

Devapriya Baiju, Fall 2023

Neural Centers of Fear in the Brain

Thalamus is considered the switchboard of the brain and the main relay center

Hypothalamus sends messages to the adrenal glands that activate the fight for flight response.

Frontal and Temporal Lobes can release dopamine which stimulates a panic response.

Hippocampus and Amygdala establish emotional context to help us assess if a situation is fearful or not.

Chenghao Liu, Spring 2023

CHAPTER 5

Anxiety

Fear & Anxiety Unveiled

By Masa Jallad & Daka Rashed, Spring 2024

Have you ever woken up in the morning with a knot in your stomach or your heart racing at 100 mph? Welcome to the world of fear and anxiety. Despite their subtle yet substantial differences in how they impact our lives, fear and anxiety are often used interchangeably. This blog post will encompass the main differences between these two emotions and how one can understand the nature of an individual's perception of fear and anxiety.

It's significant to understand that both anxiety and fear are emotions brought on by the conviction that an unpleasant, hazardous, or dangerous occurrence could happen in the future and that it might harm the individual. These risks can originate from the outside of the body, or they can manifest inwardly. Although they are similar in this specific way, they also differ in other consequential forms. To begin, "Fear is one of the six innate emotions: anger, disgust, fear, happiness, sadness, and surprise." (Moller). Fear is one of the fundamental emotions that can significantly alter a person's quality of life. Although fear affects most people at some point in their lives, there are significant differences in the frequency and intensity of fear. A person's perception and reaction to fear can be influenced by various variables such as personality traits, genetics, previous experiences, and present conditions. On the other hand, anxiety is a form of worry or fear from actual or imaginary threats. There are many different anxiety disorders, such as post-traumatic stress disorder (PTSD), phobias- also known as social anxiety disorder (SAD), and panic disorders. According to an article by the National Institute of Mental Health (NIH) in 2023, it has been revealed that about 31.1% of adults in the United States have experienced any anxiety disorder at some point in their lifetime. Anxiety is a common occurrence for individuals, with some experiencing it more frequently than others and varying in how it affects them.

Fear is often triggered by a response to perceived threats, which can be real or imaginary. Real risks include things such as an accident, the death of a loved one, the loss of property, money, or one's job. If one perceives that something may be hazardous in the future, this also leads to the rise of fear. Imagination is a fascinating topic that correlates heavily with fear. Fear often stems from an individual's imagination. The capacity of the mind to generate and organize ideas or pictures in the brain that are not physically visible to the senses. A person's imagination regarding what could be dangerous is frequently unrelated to actuality, such as the history of what has induced threats and danger (Jahangiri). Fear, like other emotions, can impact a person's quality of life and frequently interfere with numerous vital physiological processes, including autonomic functions. These autonomic processes can impact an individual's heart rate, blood pressure, sweating, and muscle tremor. Fear can influence several body systems, including the endocrine, circulatory, and immunological systems (Moller). An individual's mood and overall quality of life are impacted by fear, and the body may go into fight-or-flight mode when faced with extreme terror.

Many people don't seem to realize how common anxiety disorder truly is. According to the World Health Organization, "anxiety disorders are the world's most common mental disorders, affecting 301 million people in 2019." (2023). Phobias are considered irrational types of fear which are correlated to certain circumstances or events. It is characterized by an anxiety disorder that targets objects or occasions that commonly present little risk. Acute flight responses and anticipatory anxiety are two characteristics of phobias. Furthermore, phobias are frequently linked to stimuli like snakes or spiders. Phobias consist of fears such as acrophobia (fear of heights), claustrophobia (fear of tight spaces), and social phobia. People will travel far lengths to avoid their biggest phobia.

Now that you know a little bit more about phobias, take a moment to think about yours if you have any. Oftentimes, we tend to believe that we would do the most for a fortune, but would you ever consider facing your greatest fear for a shot at glory? In the show "Fear Factor" contestants are brought to face their deepest phobias for a chance to win $50,000. However, you will be eliminated if you fail or refuse to complete a challenge. As thrilling as it sounds, many people were at risk of death from shock from coming face to face with their phobias. One episode from this show that is engraved in my mind was a claustrophobic episode about couples being tied with rope to an underground cage while getting buried alive in cement. The objective was to untie the rope from the cage as soon as possible before the cement filled up to the top.

The cement flowed into the cage at an extremely rapid speed while also adding a heavy amount of weight on top of the contestants. Ultimately, many of the contestants couldn't untie the rope and were getting crushed against the metal cage, where they were forced to forfeit. The contestant's terrified escape from the confined area in the deadly silence of defeat represents an unsettling reminder of the phobias' unwavering power, displaying how even the strongest individuals may become trapped by the overpowering grip of anxiety in its most restrictive form.

In conclusion, fear and anxiety are extremely powerful factors that can completely shape and alter the lives of all human beings. Both emotions influence the quality of life from a young age and continue to take part in the future. Furthermore, being able to separate and identify the main differences between anxiety and fear can be immensely helpful for people as it would help develop coping strategies, reduce misinterpretation, and assist with prevention.

Understanding certain symptoms of anxiety, such as dizziness, heart-racing palpitations, and sweating, while also acknowledging how complex our emotions are regarding fear helps people navigate through the difficulties that come along with fear and anxiety with ease and strength.

References

1. Jahangiri, Faisal. "Neurobiology of Emotions Fear and Anxiety." Week 1. Chapter 1. Part 2. Fear & Anxiety. Apr. 2024.
2. Jahangiri, Faisal. "Neurobiology of Emotions Fear and Anxiety." Week 2. Chapter 1. Part 2. Causes of Fear. Apr. 2024.
3. Moller, Aage. "Neurobiology of Fear, Anxiety and Other Emotions." *Neurobiology of Fear, Anxiety and Other Emotions | Amazon.Com.Br*, 2019, www.amazon.com.br/Neurobiology-Fear-Anxiety-other-Emotions/dp/1081392193. Accessed 14 Apr. 2024.
4. National Institute of Mental Health. "Any Anxiety Disorder." *National Institute of Mental Health*, U.S. Department of Health and Human Services, 2017, www.nimh.nih.gov/health/statistics/any-anxietydisorder#:~:text=Prevalence%20of%20Any%20Anxiety%20Disorder%20Among%20Adults,Based%20on%20diagnostic&text=An%20estimated%2031.1%25%20of%20U.S.,some%20time%20in%20their%20lives. Accessed 14 Apr. 2024.
5. World Health Organization. "Anxiety Disorders." World Health Organization, Sept. 2023, www.who.int/news-room/fact-sheets/detail/anxiety disorders#:~:text=Anxiety%20disorders%20are%20the%20world's,effective%20treatments%20for%20anxiety%20disorders. Accessed 14 Apr. 2024.

AN INFOGRAPHIC JOURNEY

Anxiety, What is it?

constant feeling of worry, nervousness, or unease about an event with an unpredictable outcome. The emotional state of worry affects the physiological state of your body.

01 Fear vs Anxiety

Fear is temporarily rooted in confrontation with a potential threatful stimulus. While anxiety is a tonic state connected to prediction. Thus, anxiety has unknown causes that initiate a deep state of worry.

02 Fear is a Emotion

Fundamentally, fear is an emotion to cause worry, which is used to describe a concerned nervous state. Anxiety negatively impacts our spatial & verbal working memory. Spatial memory is more easily affected by an anxious stimulus.

03 Effects of Anxiety

Anxiety aids in sustaining a readiness state to facilitate threat processing and preparing defense mechanisms. Anxiety disrupts our cognitive performance.

04 Anxiety Disorders

Symptoms:
- Irritability
- Muscle tension
- Difficulty sleeping & fatigue
- Lasting, excessive worry (at least 6 months)

Treatments for Anxiety Disorders

Anxiety disorders are very common and treatable using Cognitive Behavioral Therapy and other techniques like: meditation, relaxation techniques, and biofeedback

Dhruv Patel, Spring 2023

An Overview of Anxiety

Maryam Imam

Definition of Anxiety

Anxiety is defined as a general feeling of unease or worry about real or imaginary future events which usually pose little risk.

Anxiety Disorders
- Post-Traumatic stress disorder (PTSD)
- Social Anxiety Disorder
- Panic Disorders
- Specific Phobias

Physical effects of anxiety on the body
- Feeling your heart racing
- Sweating or shivering
- Feeling lighthearted or dizzy
- Feeling your body trembling

Benefits of Anxiety
- Some anxiety may increase performance
- Anxiety enhances memory
- Anxiety drives creativity
- Anxiety leads to faster detection of threats

Harmful Effects of Anxiety
- Anxiety can result in a loss of appetite
- Anxiety may lead to sleep disturbances
- Anxiety is associated with higher risk of getting diseases

How to reduce Anxiety
- Taking anxiolytic drugs
- Doing regular physical exercise
- Practicing meditation
- Using deep breathing techniques

Maryam Imam, Fall 2023

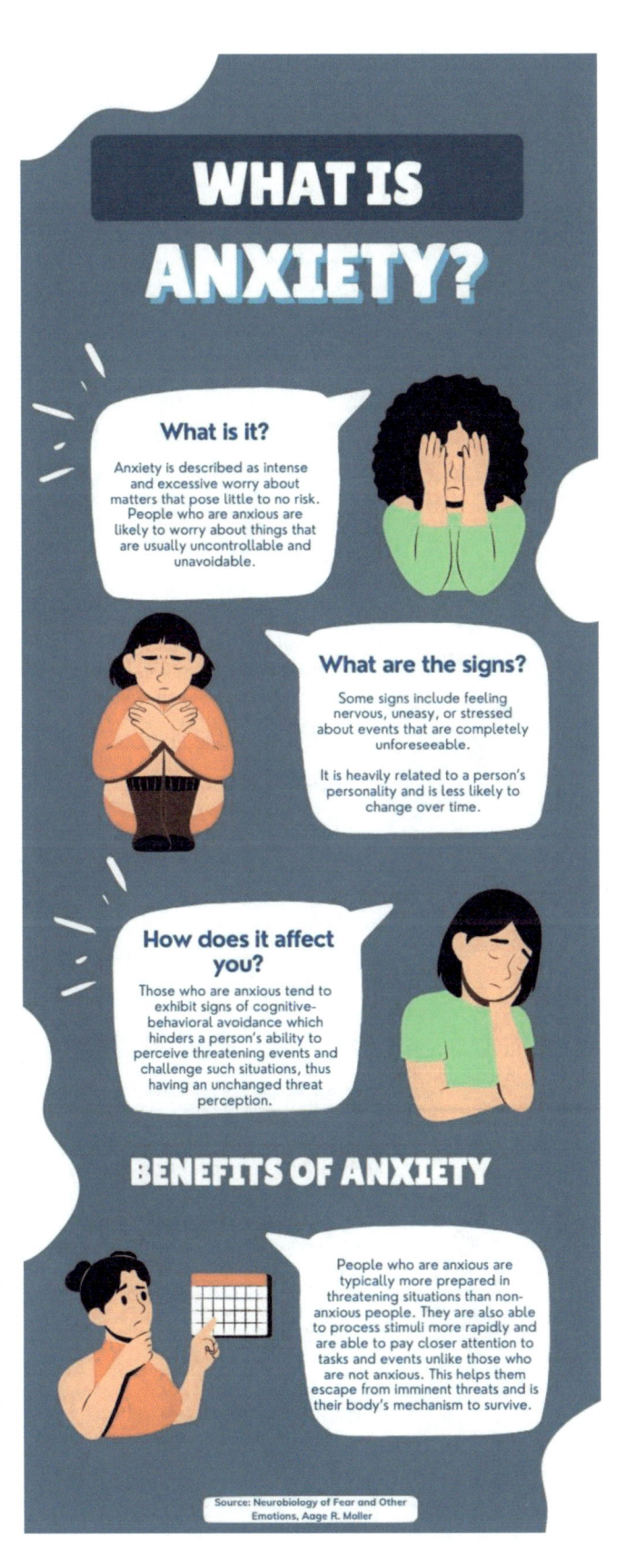

AN INFOGRAPHIC JOURNEY

WHAT IS ANXIETY?

What is it?
Anxiety is described as intense and excessive worry about matters that pose little to no risk. People who are anxious are likely to worry about things that are usually uncontrollable and unavoidable.

What are the signs?
Some signs include feeling nervous, uneasy, or stressed about events that are completely unforeseeable.

It is heavily related to a person's personality and is less likely to change over time.

How does it affect you?
Those who are anxious tend to exhibit signs of cognitive-behavioral avoidance which hinders a person's ability to perceive threatening events and challenge such situations, thus having an unchanged threat perception.

BENEFITS OF ANXIETY

People who are anxious are typically more prepared in threatening situations than non-anxious people. They are also able to process stimuli more rapidly and are able to pay closer attention to tasks and events unlike those who are not anxious. This helps them escape from imminent threats and is their body's mechanism to survive.

Source: Neurobiology of Fear and Other Emotions, Aage R. Moller

Devapriya Baiju, Fall 2023

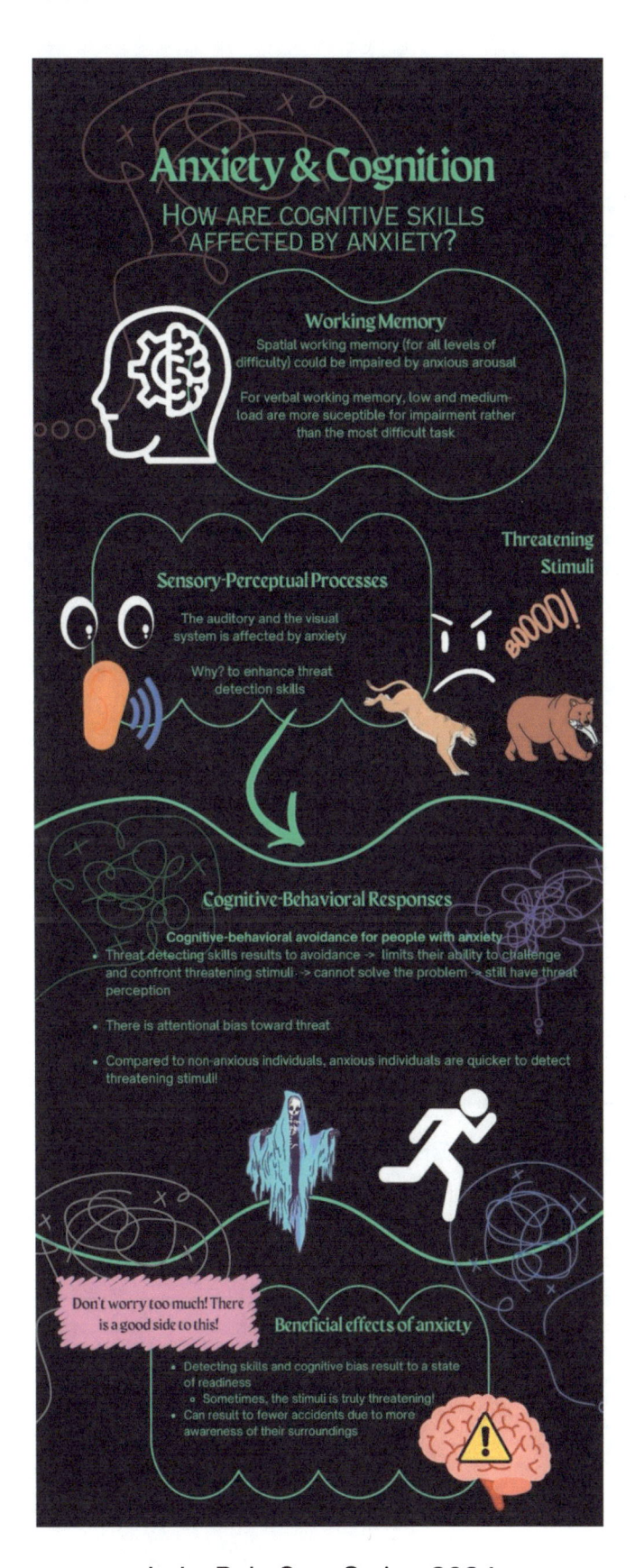

Anxiety & Cognition
HOW ARE COGNITIVE SKILLS AFFECTED BY ANXIETY?

Working Memory
Spatial working memory (for all levels of difficulty) could be impaired by anxious arousal

For verbal working memory, low and medium-load are more suceptible for impairment rather than the most difficult task

Sensory-Perceptual Processes
The auditory and the visual system is affected by anxiety

Why? to enhance threat detection skills

Threatening Stimuli

Cognitive-Behavioral Responses
Cognitive-behavioral avoidance for people with anxiety
- Threat detecting skills results to avoidance -> limits their ability to challenge and confront threatening stimuli -> cannot solve the problem -> still have threat perception
- There is attentional bias toward threat
- Compared to non-anxious individuals, anxious individuals are quicker to detect threatening stimuli

Don't worry too much! There is a good side to this!

Beneficial effects of anxiety
- Detecting skills and cognitive bias result to a state of readiness
- Sometimes, the stimuli is truly threatening!
- Can result to fewer accidents due to more awareness of their surroundings

Jasha Dela Cruz, Spring 2024

AN INFOGRAPHIC JOURNEY

ANXIETY UNVEILED
By: Masa Jallad

What is Anxiety?
- Anxieties are forms of worry or fear from real or imaginary threats.
- Anxiety can be illustrated by feelings of worry and hyperarousal along with a more generalized state of distress.
- People are affected by anxiety more frequently and differently than others.

Signs of Anxiety
- A general feeling of worry or unease.
- Nervousness, worry, or uneasiness in anticipation of an upcoming event with an unpredictable outcome.
- EX: Experiencing anxiety in anticipation of a hospital visit and waiting for test results.

U.S. Prevalence: 31.1%

According to the National Institute of Mental Health (NIH), it has been revealed that about 31.1% of adults in the United States have experienced any type of anxiety disorder at some point in their lifetime (2023).

Types of anxiety disorders:
- Post-traumatic stress disorder (Estimated prevalence of 6.8%)
- Phobias, also known as social anxiety disorder (SAD) (prevalence of 12.1%)
- Panic disorders (prevalence of 4.7%).

What are the types of treatment?
Drugs such as anxiolytics are standard. Physical exercise also effectively relieves anxiety and stress. Having a variety of treatment options is beneficial as it lowers the likelihood of developing these disorders.

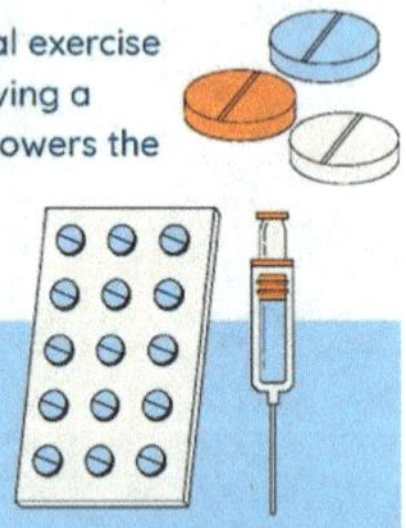

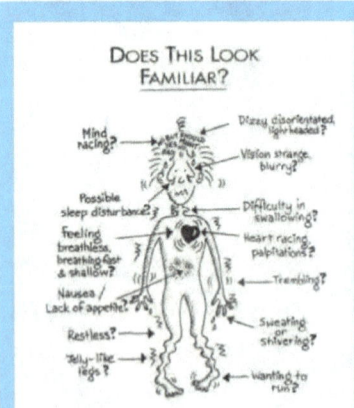

Does This Look Familiar?
- Mind racing?
- Dizzy disoriented lightheaded?
- Vision strange blurry?
- Possible sleep disturbance?
- Difficulty in swallowing?
- Feeling breathless, breathing fast & shallow?
- Heart racing palpitations?
- Nausea / Lack of appetite?
- Trembling?
- Restless?
- Sweating or shivering?
- Jelly-like legs?
- Wanting to run?

Benefits of Anxiety:
- Enhancing effect on memory
- Anxious people often see the worst in circumstances- Can be advantageous in particular situations and at certain times.
- Have fewer accidents- They often worry about what's going on around them.
- Helps retain a form of readiness- Enhances defensive reaction and danger processing.

Masa Jallad, Spring 2024

Anxiety and its Symptoms

01 What is anxiety?
Anxiety is an **emotion** that spurs from the feeling of worry, nervousness, or unease about an event.

if prolonged, it could be diagnosed as a **disease**

02 Anxiety as a Disease:
General anxiety disorder (GAD) can cause a person an excessive amount of anxiety for an extended period of time

~40 million American adults have an anxiety disorder

03 Symptoms of Anxiety:
Physical symptoms: racing heart, dry mouth, upset stomach, tension, sweating, trembling
- overall cause a negative affect on physical health

Other common symptoms: feeling weak or tired, sense of doom, trouble concentrating

Source: https://www.mayoclinic.org/diseases-conditions/anxiety/symptoms-causes/syc-20350961

04 Are fear and anxiety different?
Yes! anxiety is a **general** term for conditions that cause nervousness, worrying, and **fear**

Fear involves perceiving danger while anxiety is an emotion due to perceiving uncontrollable threats

Fun fact: the amygdala plays an important role in both fear and anxiety!

Alyssa Tran, Fall 2023

AN INFOGRAPHIC JOURNEY

ANXIETY

WHAT IS ANXIETY?
Anxiety is a normal reaction to stress, but can become chronic and disruptive. There are many types of anxiety disorders such as Generalized Anxiety Disorder (GAD), Social Anxiety Disorder, Panic Disorder, etc.

This image outlines the signs of an anxiety disorder

"Visualize yourself not falling off the wall."
This image depicts past trauma which can be a cause of anxiety

CAUSES AND RISK FACTORS
Genetics: Family history of anxiety disorders.
Brain chemistry: Imbalances in neurotransmitters.
Traumatic experiences: Past trauma or significant life events.
Chronic stress: Ongoing stressors in life.
Substance abuse: Alcohol, drugs, or caffeine can worsen anxiety.

COMMON SYMPTOMS
Physical symptoms: Elevated HR, sweating, trembling, muscle tension.
Cognitive symptoms: Excessive worry, intrusive thoughts, fear.
Emotional symptoms: Irritability, restlessness, a sense of impending doom.
Behavioral symptoms: Avoidance, seeking reassurance, compulsive behaviors.

a sense of impending doom

EXAMPLES OF ANXIOUS BEHAVIORS
Avoidance: Avoiding places, people, or situations that trigger anxiety.
Safety behaviors: Relying on habits or rituals to reduce anxiety.
Perfectionism: Setting unrealistic standards and fearing failure.
Catastrophizing: Imagining the worst possible outcomes.

IMPACT ON DAILY LIFE
Impaired social relationships: Difficulty in forming and maintaining connections.
Occupational challenges: Reduced productivity and job performance.
Physical health issues: Insomnia, digestive problems, headaches.
Substance abuse: Self-medication with alcohol or drugs.

anxiety self medicated with substance abuse

COPING STRATEGIES
Lifestyle changes: Exercise, a balanced diet, and adequate sleep.
Relaxation techniques: Deep breathing, meditation, progressive muscle relaxation.
Therapy: Cognitive-Behavioral Therapy (CBT), Exposure Therapy, etc.
Medication: Antidepressants or anti-anxiety medications
Support networks: Family and friends can provide emotional support.

deep breathing can temporarily reduce some anxiety symptoms

HOW TO MINIMIZE ANXIETY
Recognize triggers: Identify what causes your anxiety.
Mindfulness: Focus on the present moment and reduce rumination.
Time management: Prioritize tasks and avoid overwhelming yourself.
Seek professional help: Consult a therapist or psychiatrist.
Self-care: Practice self-compassion and engage in hobbies you enjoy.

focusing on the present can help minimize anxiety

PREVENTION
Early intervention: Address anxiety symptoms promptly.
Stress management: Develop healthy coping mechanisms.
Healthy lifestyle: Regular exercise, balanced diet, and adequate sleep.

examples of healthy coping strategies to prevent anxiety

"ANXIETY." MEDLINEPLUS, U.S. NATIONAL LIBRARY OF MEDICINE, MEDLINEPLUS.GOV/ANXIETY.HTML. ACCESSED 4 SEPT. 2023.

Anxiety

What is anxiety?
The constant feeling of worry, nervousness, or unease typically about something with an uncertain outcome. It is an emotion characterized by the feelings of tension.

The general effects of anxiety

nervousness, panic attacks, rapid heart rate, sweating, shaking, fatigue, dizziness, chest pain (MedicalNewsToday)

Low and medium load verbal working memory is more susceptible to anxiety relation disruption relative to high load. Spatial working memory is disrupted regardless of task difficulty

People exposed to chronic stress age rapidly

The telomeres in their cells of all types shorten faster. Inflammation is another important feature of stress and anxiety that, along with aging, accounts for the phenomenon of inflammaging. (PubMed Central)

Aging

Sustained threat perception is accompanied by prolonged activation of threat related neural circuitry and threat response biological systems including the:
- hypothalamic pituitary adrenal axis
- autonomic nervous system
- inflammatory response

Anxiety vs Fear

What are the differences between anxiety and fear?

Anxiety:
- tonic state related to prediction
- a general term used for several conditions that cause nervousness, fear, apprehension, and worrying
- similarities with fear but often it concerns unspecific causes
- anxiety is an emotion that occurs due to the perception of uncontrollable threats of circumstances

Fear:
- transient state based on confrontation with threatening stimuli
- related to specific perceived dangers

Anisha Reddy, Fall 2023 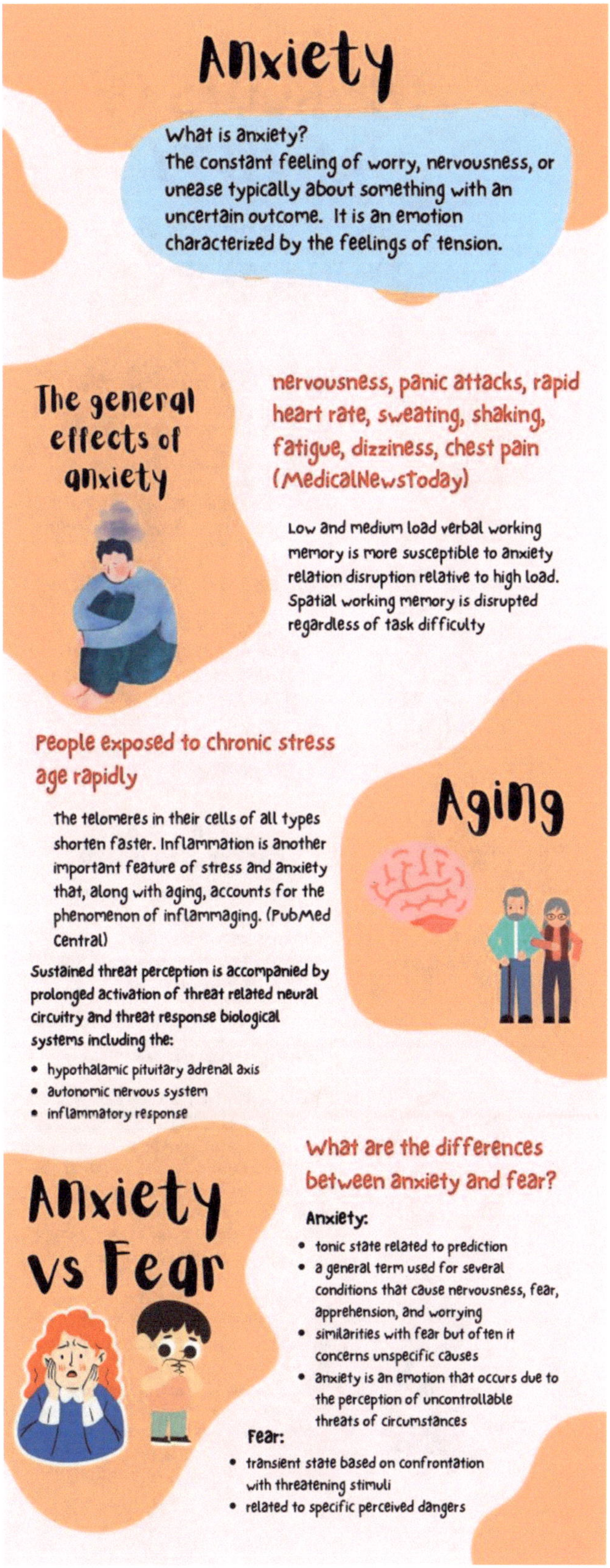   Samiksha Sivajumar, Fall 2023

AN INFOGRAPHIC JOURNEY

THE ROOTS OF ANXIETY
INFOGRAPHIC #4
BY JAVERIA AHMED

WHAT IS SOCIAL ANXIETY?
ANXIETY IS A FORM OF PHOBIA THAT CAN BE CHARACTERIZED BY OVERWHELMING SELF-CONSCIOUSNESS DURING COMMON SOCIAL SITUATIONS AND CAN STEM FROM THE WORRY OF BEING JUDGED OR BEHAVING IN A WAY THAT CAN CAUSE EMBARRASSMENT.

WHERE DOES THE TERM COME FROM?
"SOCIAL ANXIETY," COINED BY JANET (1903), WAS MEANT TO DESCRIBE PEOPLE WHO FEARED BEING OBSERVED, HOWEVER NOWADAYS, IT IS USED TO DESCRIBE EXCESSIVE FEAR OR NERVOUSNESS DURING SOCIAL INTERACTIONS.

WHAT IS A SPECIFIC PHOBIA?
SPECIFIC PHOBIAS ARE MARKED BY PERSISTENT, EXCESSIVE FEAR OF A SPECIFIC OBJECT OR SITUATION. THESE PHOBIA MAY INCLUDE PANIC DISORDERS, PTSD, OR SOCIAL ANXIETY DISORDER.

ROLE OF DEFICITS IN SOCIAL INTERACTIONS
SOME PEOPLE HAVE MENTAL DISORDERS THAT ARE OFTEN ASSOCIATED WITH DEFICITS IN SOCIAL INTERACTIONS SUCH AS AUTISM, SOCIAL ANXIETY DISORDER, AND BORDERLINE PERSONALITY DISORDER. INDIVIDUALS WITH SUCH DEFICIENCIES OFTEN BENEFIT FROM PSYCHOBIOLOGICAL THERAPIES.

WHAT IS WORRY?
"WORRY" IS A TERM USED TO DESCRIBE GIVING AWAY TO ANXIETY AND CAN BE GOOD OR BAD. IT IS AN INTERNAL REACTION THAT MAY BE USEFUL, HOWEVER, IT CAN ALSO CAUSE HARM AND STRESS, DECREASING THE OVERALL QUALITY OF LIFE.

Javeria Ahmed, Spring 2024

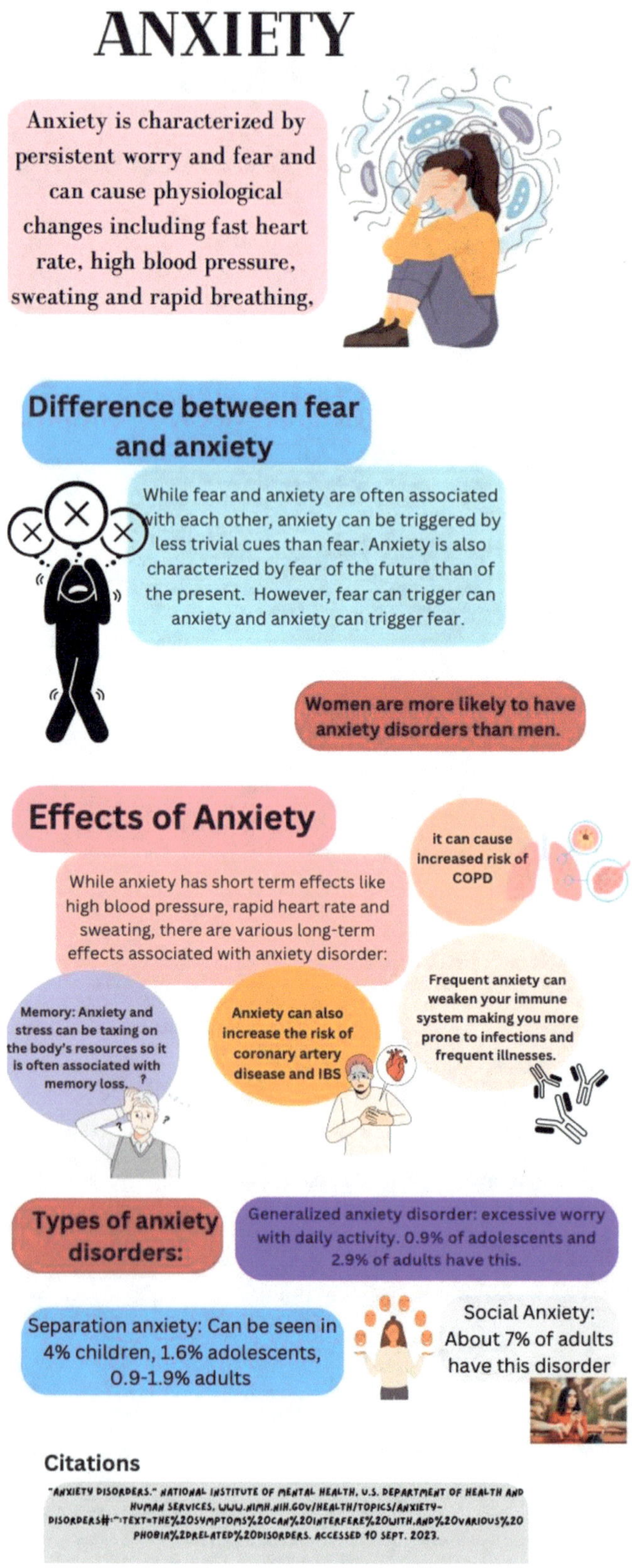

ANXIETY

Anxiety is characterized by persistent worry and fear and can cause physiological changes including fast heart rate, high blood pressure, sweating and rapid breathing.

Difference between fear and anxiety

While fear and anxiety are often associated with each other, anxiety can be triggered by less trivial cues than fear. Anxiety is also characterized by fear of the future than of the present. However, fear can trigger can anxiety and anxiety can trigger fear.

Women are more likely to have anxiety disorders than men.

Effects of Anxiety

While anxiety has short term effects like high blood pressure, rapid heart rate and sweating, there are various long-term effects associated with anxiety disorder:

it can cause increased risk of COPD

Memory: Anxiety and stress can be taxing on the body's resources so it is often associated with memory loss.

Anxiety can also increase the risk of coronary artery disease and IBS

Frequent anxiety can weaken your immune system making you more prone to infections and frequent illnesses.

Types of anxiety disorders:

Generalized anxiety disorder: excessive worry with daily activity. 0.9% of adolescents and 2.9% of adults have this.

Separation anxiety: Can be seen in 4% children, 1.6% adolescents, 0.9-1.9% adults

Social Anxiety: About 7% of adults have this disorder

Citations
"ANXIETY DISORDERS." NATIONAL INSTITUTE OF MENTAL HEALTH, U.S. DEPARTMENT OF HEALTH AND HUMAN SERVICES. WWW.NIMH.NIH.GOV/HEALTH/TOPICS/ANXIETY-DISORDERS#:~:TEXT=THE%20SYMPTOMS%20CAN%20INTERFERE%20WITH.AND%20VARIOUS%20PHOBIA%2DRELATED%20DISORDERS. ACCESSED 10 SEPT. 2023.

Diya Thapa, Fall 2023

AN INFOGRAPHIC JOURNEY

Angst and Anxiety
Helen Nguyen

Perceived threats

Anxious individuals show cognitive biases toward threatening information, which leads them to detect threatening stimuli more quickly than non-anxious individuals and appraise both ambiguous and threatening stimuli as more threatening

The ultimate result of this process is failure to achieve resolution of perceived threats, resulting in sustained threat perception

Anxiety and aging
- Exaggerated neurobiological sensitivity to threat in anxious individuals may lead to cognitive-behavioral threat responses characterized by a pattern of vigilance-avoidance, resulting in sustained threat perception
- Over time, the effects on central and peripheral systems may become chronic through structural changes in the central nervous system (CNS), altered sensitivity of receptors on immune cells, and accelerated cellular aging
- Chronic elevations in inflammation can increase risk for, and accelerate the progression of, diseases of aging

Anxiety disorder symptoms
- Persistent, excessive worry about several different things for at least six months
- Fatigue, difficulty sleeping, or restlessness
- Trouble concentrating
- Irritability
- Muscle tension
- Feeling tense or "on edge"
- racing heart
- dry mouth
- upset stomach

These bodily expressions of anxiety can have a negative effect on physical health

Causes of anxiety
- In modern society, there are numerous events and happenings that can cause anxiety
- The mass media brings news of natural disasters, potential pandemics, terrorist atrocities, and violent crime straight into our homes
- Perhaps it is not surprising that nearly one in four of us will experience a clinical level of anxiety within our lifetimes
- The amygdala plays an important role

Anxiety disorders are common
- Anxiety disorders are among the most common mental illnesses, affecting roughly 40 million American adults each year
- There are alternative treatments for anxiety, such as relaxation techniques, mindfulness meditation, and biofeedback
- CBT helps people recognize when they are misinterpreting events, exaggerating difficulties, or making unnecessarily pessimistic assumptions, and offers new ways to respond to anxiety-provoking situations

ANXIETY
the feeling of fear, dread, and uneasiness

COGNITIVE RESPONSE

Individuals with anxiety show cognitive biases towards threatening info. they detect the stimuli more quickly than a nonanxious person. they then engage in cognitive behavioral avoidance which limits their ability to confront and resolve the issue, thus resulting in failure. the cycle then begans again.

ANXIETY & AGING

Anxiety can result in adverse effects and accelerate the progression of diseases of aging. This is due to chronic inflammation caused by neurobiological alterations.

CAUSES OF ANXIETY

Numerous things trigger anxiety. Nowadays, violent tragedies are brought straight to us through the media. People hate others because of differences. Imagination plays a key role in what people perceive as a threat

ANXIETY DISORDERS

Around 40 million American adults are affected by anxiety disorders every year. those with generalized anxiety disorder tend to worry excessively about simple matters. they worry about something going wrong, missing something, and worrying.

Symptoms:
- Excessive worry
- Restlessness
- Muscle tension
- Feeling on edge

TREATMENT

Individuals with generalized anxiety disorder should seek cognitive behavioral therapy. CBT helps people recognize when they tend to misinterpret things and find ways ti respond to these anxiety-inducing situations

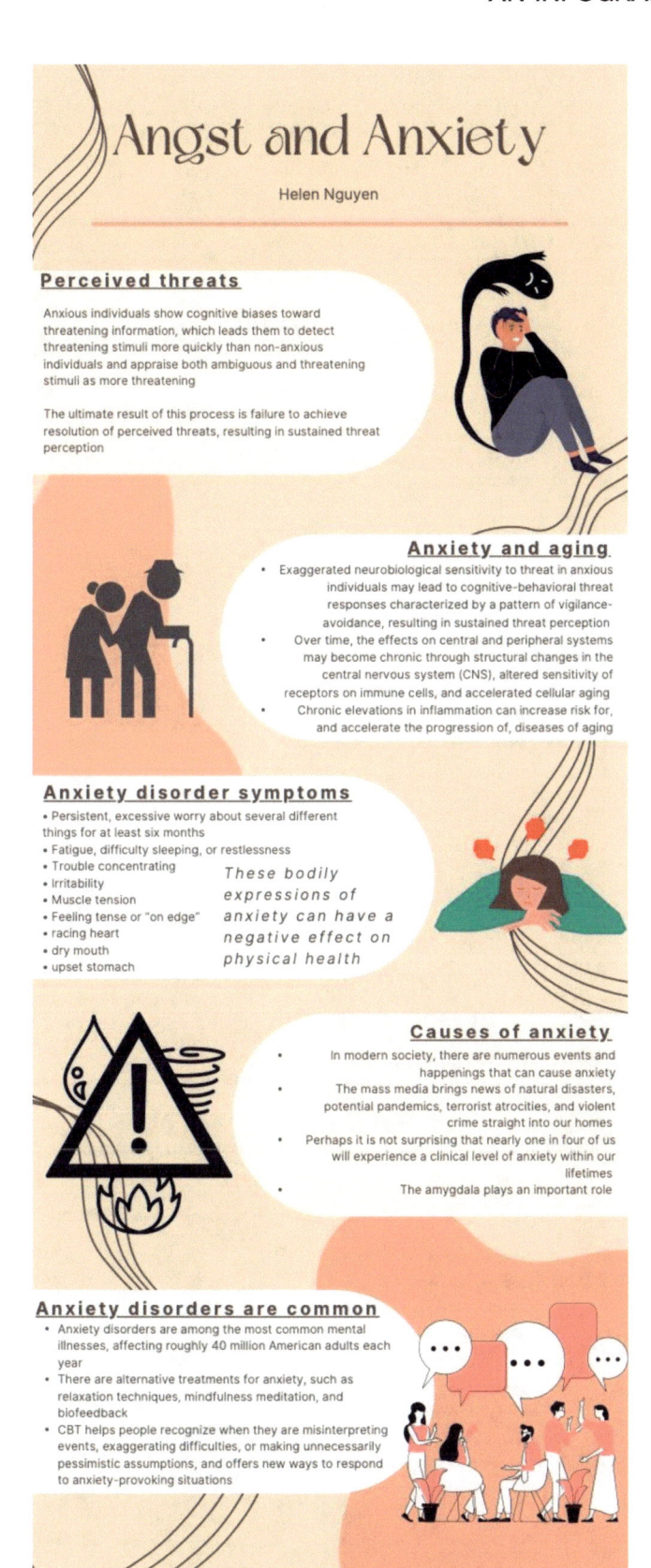

IT'S OKAY TO ASK FOR HELP

people fear the wrong things

Helen Nguyen, Fall 2023   Katelyn Bonvillain, Spring 2023

AN INFOGRAPHIC JOURNEY

ANXIETY

01 WHAT IS ANXIETY?

Anxiety is an emotion that consists of feelings of worry, tension, and physical changes. After a period of time anxiety becomes a prolonged fear that can eventually become a disease.

02 ANXIETY VS. FEAR

Fear is a transient state based on a threat or a perceived danger. Anxiety is a tonic state based on what could occur. Anxiety may be based on unspecific causes.

03 SYMPTOMS OF ANXIETY

- Excessive worry
- Fatigue, sleepiness
- trouble concentrating,
- Irritability
- Muscle tension

04 TREATMENTS

- Relaxation techniques
- Meditation
- Biofeedback

05 CAUSES

- Imagination
- Mass media
- Differences in society such as religion, skin color

Valeria Viveros, Spring 2024

ANXIETY VS FEAR
By: Dhara Sheth

PSYCHOLOGICAL DIFFERENCE

Anxiety:
- Chronic worry or unease
- Negative thoughts
- Difficulty concentrating
- Avoidance of triggers

Fear:
- Immediate response to danger
- Flight or fight response
- Focus on the source of fear

Causes and Triggers

Anxiety:
- Traumatic experiences
- Genetics
- Chronic stress
- Substance abuse

Fear:
- Threatening or dangerous situation
- Memories of traumatic experiences
- Cultural or social conditioning

UNDERSTANDING THE IMPACT ON DAILY LIFE

Anxiety:
- Interference with daily activities
- Impairment of relationships and social life
- Difficulty sleeping or concentrating
- Increased substance abuse

Coping Mechanisms:
- Practice self-care
- Exercise
- Consider therapy
- Meditate
- Focus on present

Both are similar yet different in many ways: anxiety is related to prediction while fear is built on encounters with threatening stimuli.

While worrying too much can be dangerous, a combination of therapy, medication, and lifestyle changes can assist in managing symptoms and improve quality of life.

Fear:
- Avoidance of agonizing experiences
- Impact on personal and professional life
- Difficulty carrying out normal activities
- Increased stress and tension.

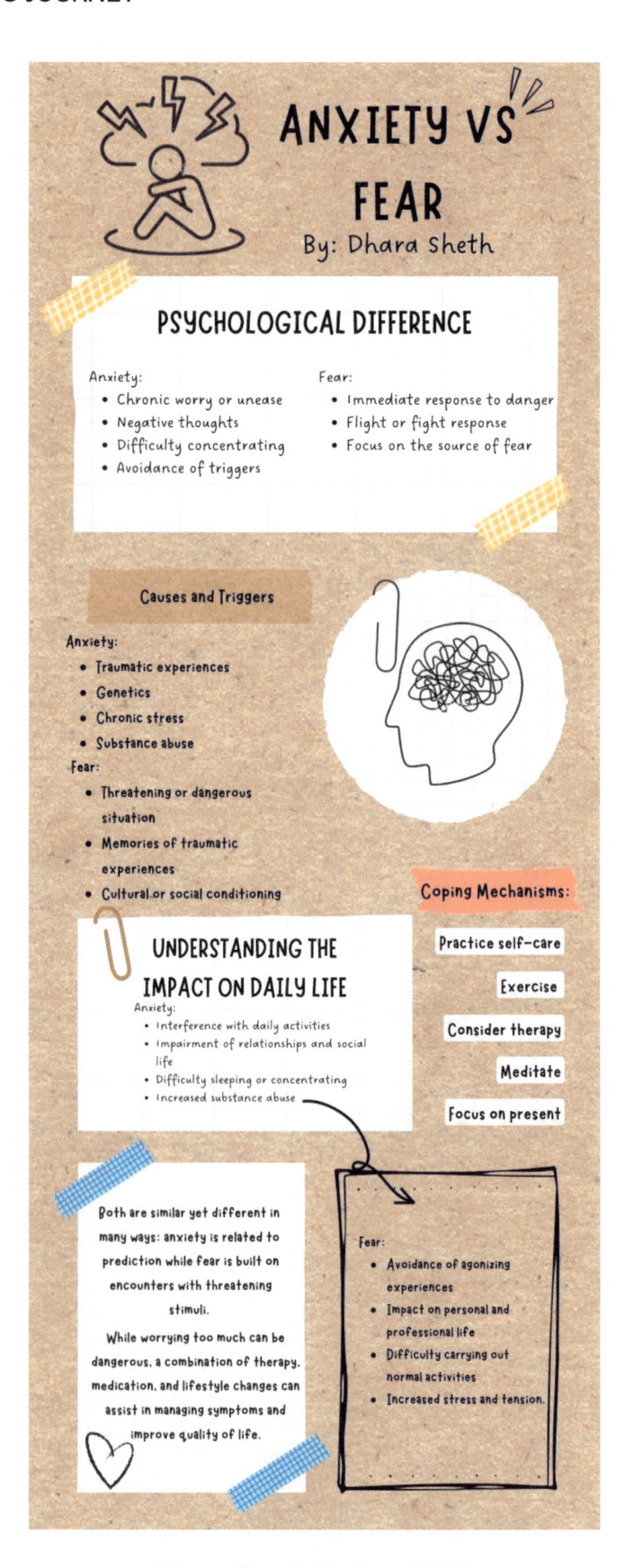

Dhara Sheth, Spring 2023

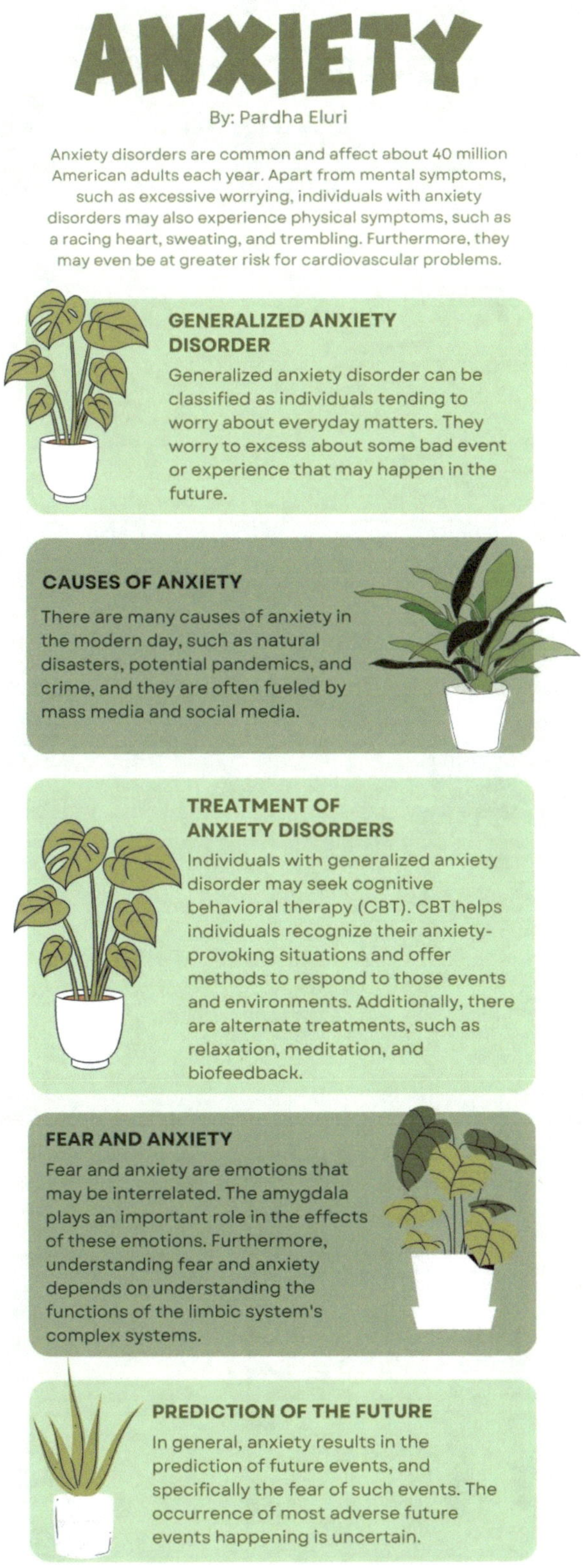

AN INFOGRAPHIC JOURNEY

ANXIETY
By: Pardha Eluri

Anxiety disorders are common and affect about 40 million American adults each year. Apart from mental symptoms, such as excessive worrying, individuals with anxiety disorders may also experience physical symptoms, such as a racing heart, sweating, and trembling. Furthermore, they may even be at greater risk for cardiovascular problems.

GENERALIZED ANXIETY DISORDER
Generalized anxiety disorder can be classified as individuals tending to worry about everyday matters. They worry to excess about some bad event or experience that may happen in the future.

CAUSES OF ANXIETY
There are many causes of anxiety in the modern day, such as natural disasters, potential pandemics, and crime, and they are often fueled by mass media and social media.

TREATMENT OF ANXIETY DISORDERS
Individuals with generalized anxiety disorder may seek cognitive behavioral therapy (CBT). CBT helps individuals recognize their anxiety-provoking situations and offer methods to respond to those events and environments. Additionally, there are alternate treatments, such as relaxation, meditation, and biofeedback.

FEAR AND ANXIETY
Fear and anxiety are emotions that may be interrelated. The amygdala plays an important role in the effects of these emotions. Furthermore, understanding fear and anxiety depends on understanding the functions of the limbic system's complex systems.

PREDICTION OF THE FUTURE
In general, anxiety results in the prediction of future events, and specifically the fear of such events. The occurrence of most adverse future events happening is uncertain.

Angst & Anxiety
Week 4 - Rahil Howlader

ANXIOUS INDIVIDUALS SHOW COGNITIVE BIASES TOWARD THREATENING INFORMATION, WHICH LEADS THEM
1. to detect threatening stimuli more quickly than non-anxious individuals
2. to appraise both ambiguous and threatening stimuli as more threatening

SYMTPOMS OF GENERALIZED ANXIETY DISORDERS
- Persistent, excessive worry about several different things for at least six months
- Fatigue, difficulty sleeping, or restlessness
- Trouble concentrating
- Irritability
- Muscle tension
- Feeling tense or "on edge"

THERAPY OF ANXIETY DISORDERS
If a person has a generalized anxiety disorder, therapy — particularly cognitive behavioral therapy (CBT) — can help

CBT helps people recognize when they are misinterpreting events, exaggerating difficulties, or making unnecessarily pessimistic assumptions, and offers new ways to respond to anxiety-provoking situations

FEAR AND ANXIETY ARE EMOTIONS
Understanding fear and anxiety, depends on understanding the function of some of complex systems in the brain, belonging to the limbic system

The amygdala plays an important role

PEOPLE IN GENERAL FEAR THE WRONG THINGS
Fear is often misdirected
Unjustified fear cause people to make choices that are not beneficial
Too much fear may cause people miss opportunities

Pardha Eluri, Spring 2023 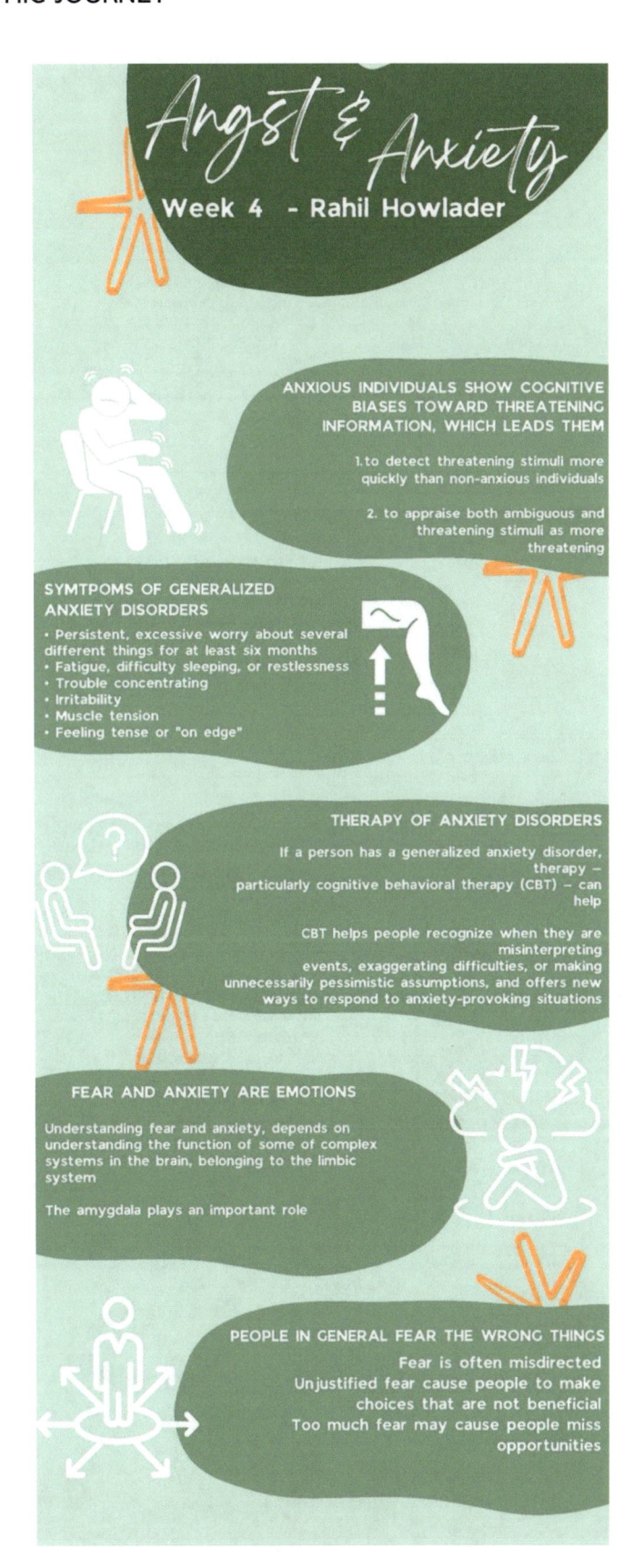   Rahil Howlader, Spring 2024

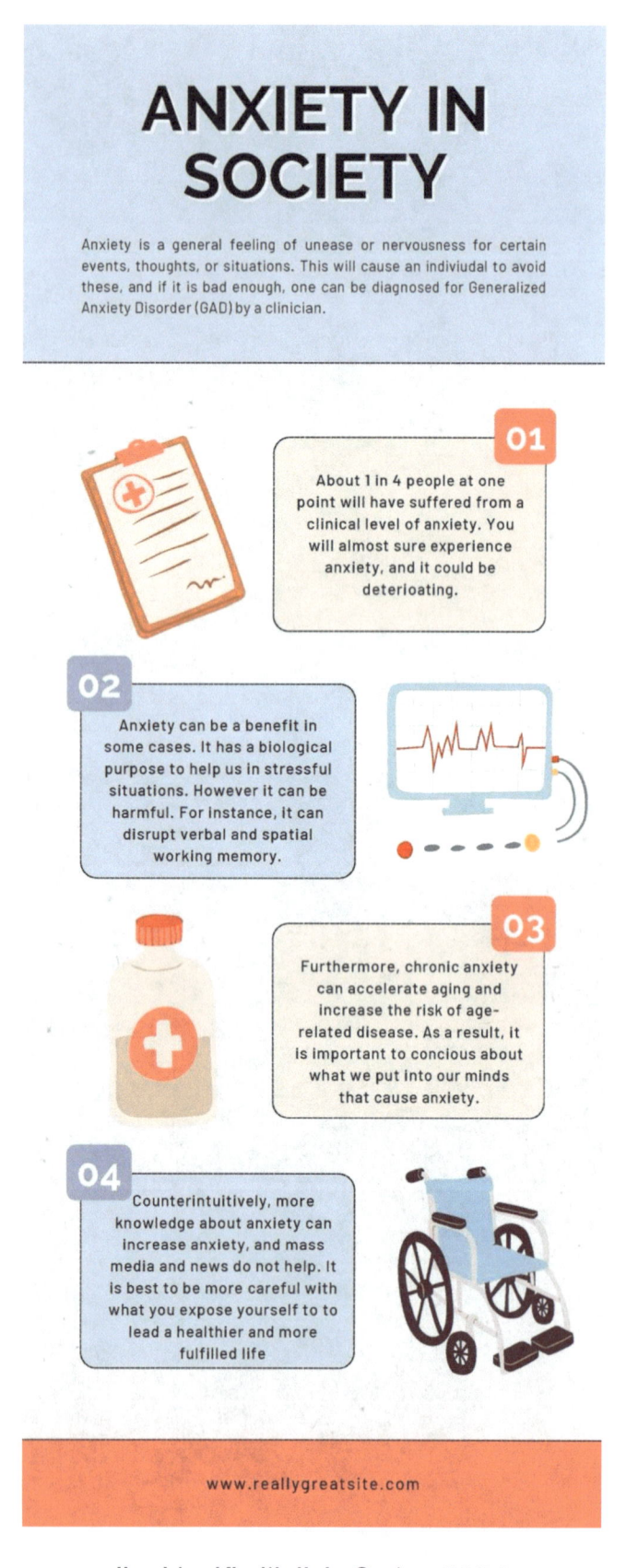

AN INFOGRAPHIC JOURNEY

ANXIETY IN SOCIETY

Anxiety is a general feeling of unease or nervousness for certain events, thoughts, or situations. This will cause an indiviudal to avoid these, and if it is bad enough, one can be diagnosed for Generalized Anxiety Disorder (GAD) by a clinician.

01 About 1 in 4 people at one point will have suffered from a clinical level of anxiety. You will almost sure experience anxiety, and it could be deterioating.

02 Anxiety can be a benefit in some cases. It has a biological purpose to help us in stressful situations. However it can be harmful. For instance, it can disrupt verbal and spatial working memory.

03 Furthermore, chronic anxiety can accelerate aging and increase the risk of age-related disease. As a result, it is important to concious about what we put into our minds that cause anxiety.

04 Counterintuitively, more knowledge about anxiety can increase anxiety, and mass media and news do not help. It is best to be more careful with what you expose yourself to to lead a healthier and more fulfilled life

www.reallygreatsite.com

Ibrahim Khalilullah, Spring 2024

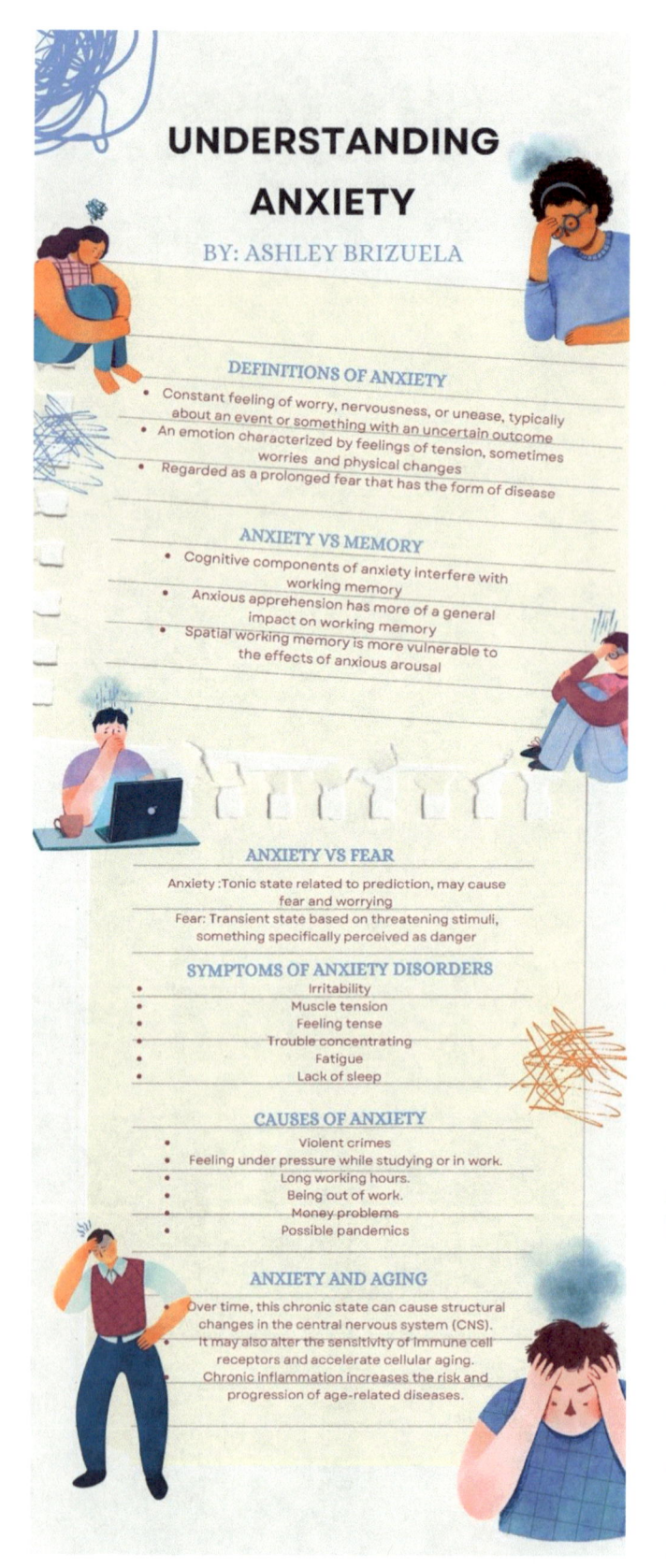

UNDERSTANDING ANXIETY
BY: ASHLEY BRIZUELA

DEFINITIONS OF ANXIETY
- Constant feeling of worry, nervousness, or unease, typically about an event or something with an uncertain outcome
- An emotion characterized by feelings of tension, sometimes worries and physical changes
- Regarded as a prolonged fear that has the form of disease

ANXIETY VS MEMORY
- Cognitive components of anxiety interfere with working memory
- Anxious apprehension has more of a general impact on working memory
- Spatial working memory is more vulnerable to the effects of anxious arousal

ANXIETY VS FEAR
Anxiety: Tonic state related to prediction, may cause fear and worrying
Fear: Transient state based on threatening stimuli, something specifically perceived as danger

SYMPTOMS OF ANXIETY DISORDERS
- Irritability
- Muscle tension
- Feeling tense
- Trouble concentrating
- Fatigue
- Lack of sleep

CAUSES OF ANXIETY
- Violent crimes
- Feeling under pressure while studying or in work.
- Long working hours.
- Being out of work.
- Money problems
- Possible pandemics

ANXIETY AND AGING
- Over time, this chronic state can cause structural changes in the central nervous system (CNS). It may also alter the sensitivity of immune cell receptors and accelerate cellular aging. Chronic inflammation increases the risk and progression of age-related diseases.

Ashley Brizuela, Spring 2024

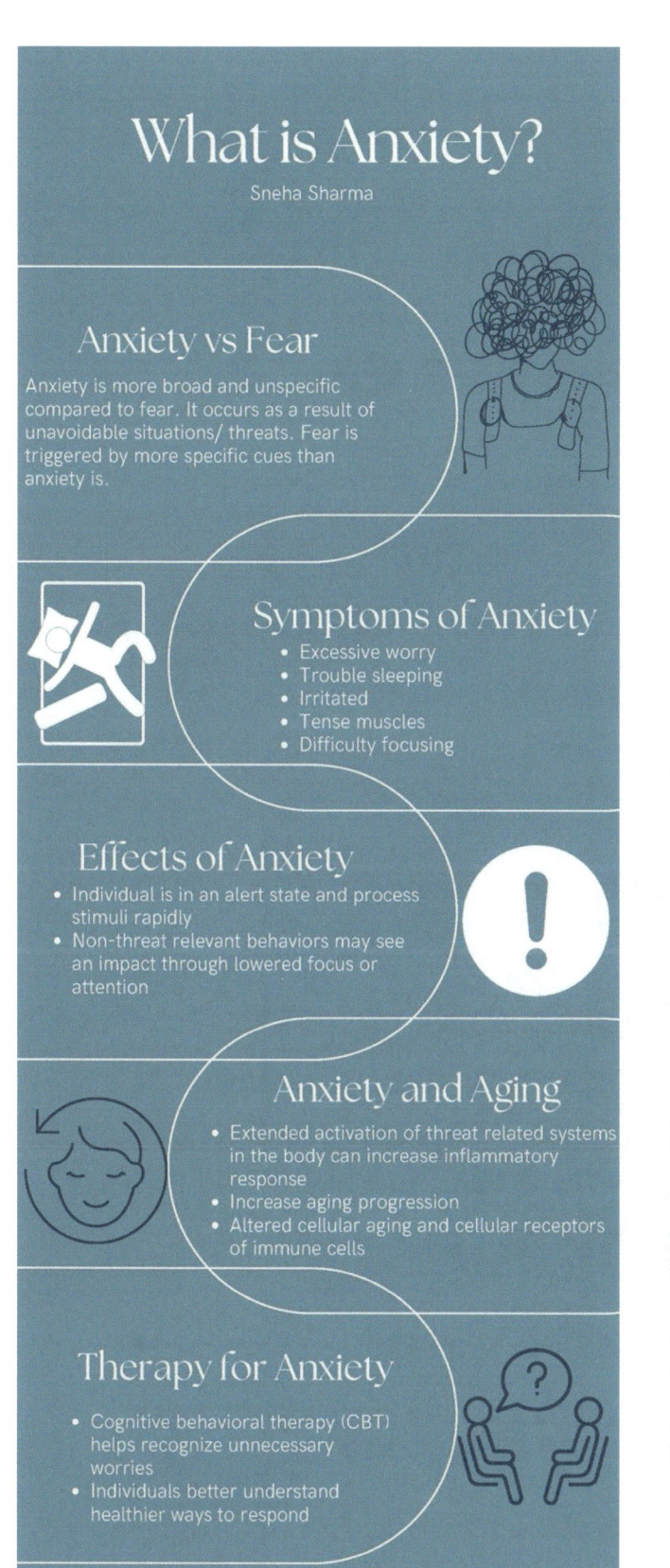

AN INFOGRAPHIC JOURNEY

What is Anxiety?
Sneha Sharma

Anxiety vs Fear
Anxiety is more broad and unspecific compared to fear. It occurs as a result of unavoidable situations/ threats. Fear is triggered by more specific cues than anxiety is.

Symptoms of Anxiety
- Excessive worry
- Trouble sleeping
- Irritated
- Tense muscles
- Difficulty focusing

Effects of Anxiety
- Individual is in an alert state and process stimuli rapidly
- Non-threat relevant behaviors may see an impact through lowered focus or attention

Anxiety and Aging
- Extended activation of threat related systems in the body can increase inflammatory response
- Increase aging progression
- Altered cellular aging and cellular receptors of immune cells

Therapy for Anxiety
- Cognitive behavioral therapy (CBT) helps recognize unnecessary worries
- Individuals better understand healthier ways to respond

Sneha Sharma, Spring 2024

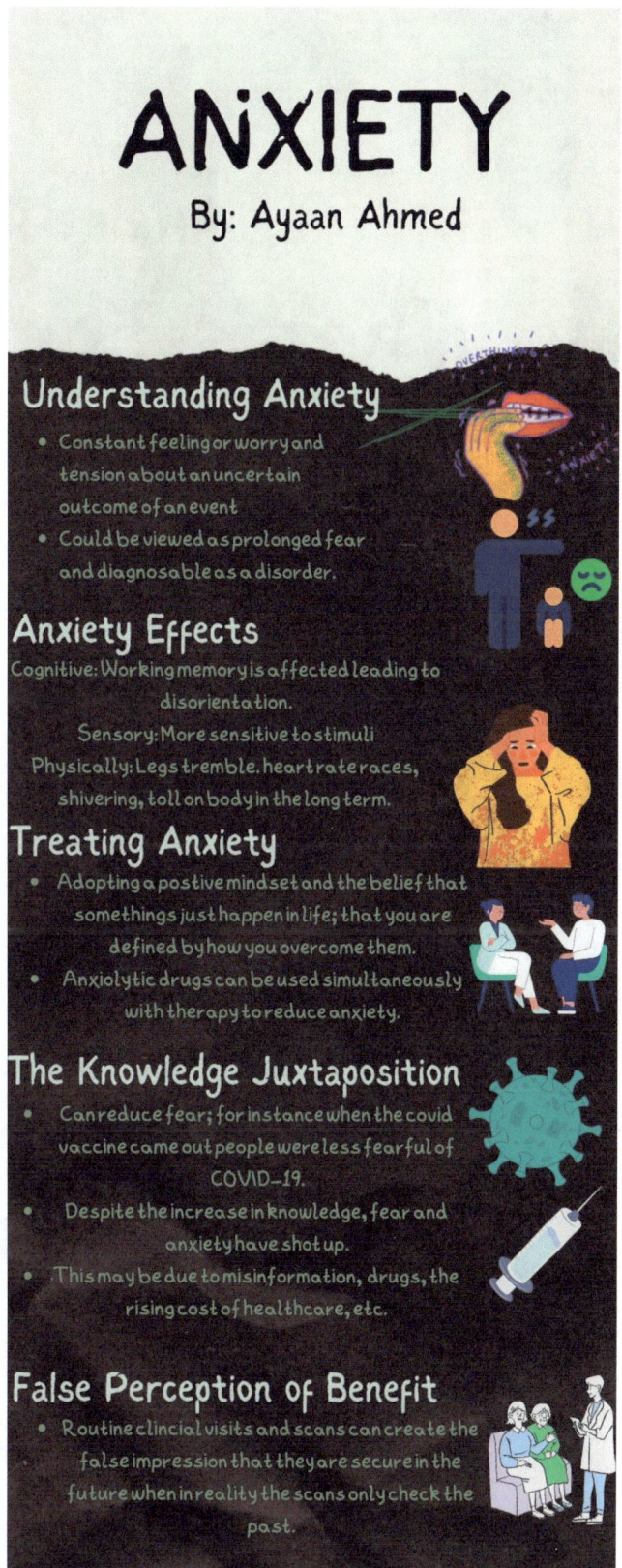

ANXIETY
By: Ayaan Ahmed

Understanding Anxiety
- Constant feeling or worry and tension about an uncertain outcome of an event
- Could be viewed as prolonged fear and diagnosable as a disorder.

Anxiety Effects
Cognitive: Working memory is affected leading to disorientation.
Sensory: More sensitive to stimuli
Physically: Legs tremble, heart rate races, shivering, toll on body in the long term.

Treating Anxiety
- Adopting a postive mindset and the belief that somethings just happen in life; that you are defined by how you overcome them.
- Anxiolytic drugs can be used simultaneously with therapy to reduce anxiety.

The Knowledge Juxtaposition
- Can reduce fear; for instance when the covid vaccine came out people were less fearful of COVID-19.
- Despite the increase in knowledge, fear and anxiety have shot up.
- This may be due to misinformation, drugs, the rising cost of healthcare, etc.

False Perception of Benefit
- Routine clincial visits and scans can create the false impression that they are secure in the future when in reality the scans only check the past.

Ayaan Ahmed, Spring 2023

Anxiety and Fear
What is The Difference?

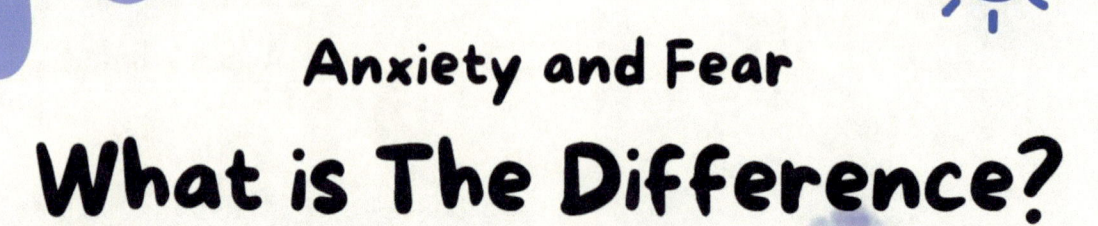

What is Anxiety?
Anxiety is a constant feeling of worry, nervousness, or unease, typically about an event or occurrence with an uncertain outcome.

How are they different?
Fear is transient. It is based on response to threatening stimuli.

However, anxiety is tonic, and is related to predicting the threatening stimuli.

Anxiety can be used as a general term to include fear, but not all fear is anxiety.

While fear is related to specific perceived dangers, anxiety is an emotion that occurs due to uncontrollable threats or circumstances.

What are symptoms of anxiety?
Feeling tense, worried, and having physical changes like elevated blood pressure, and impaired performance on tasks which require attention, maintenance of information, and rapid sensory perception.

Chloe Tee, Spring 2024

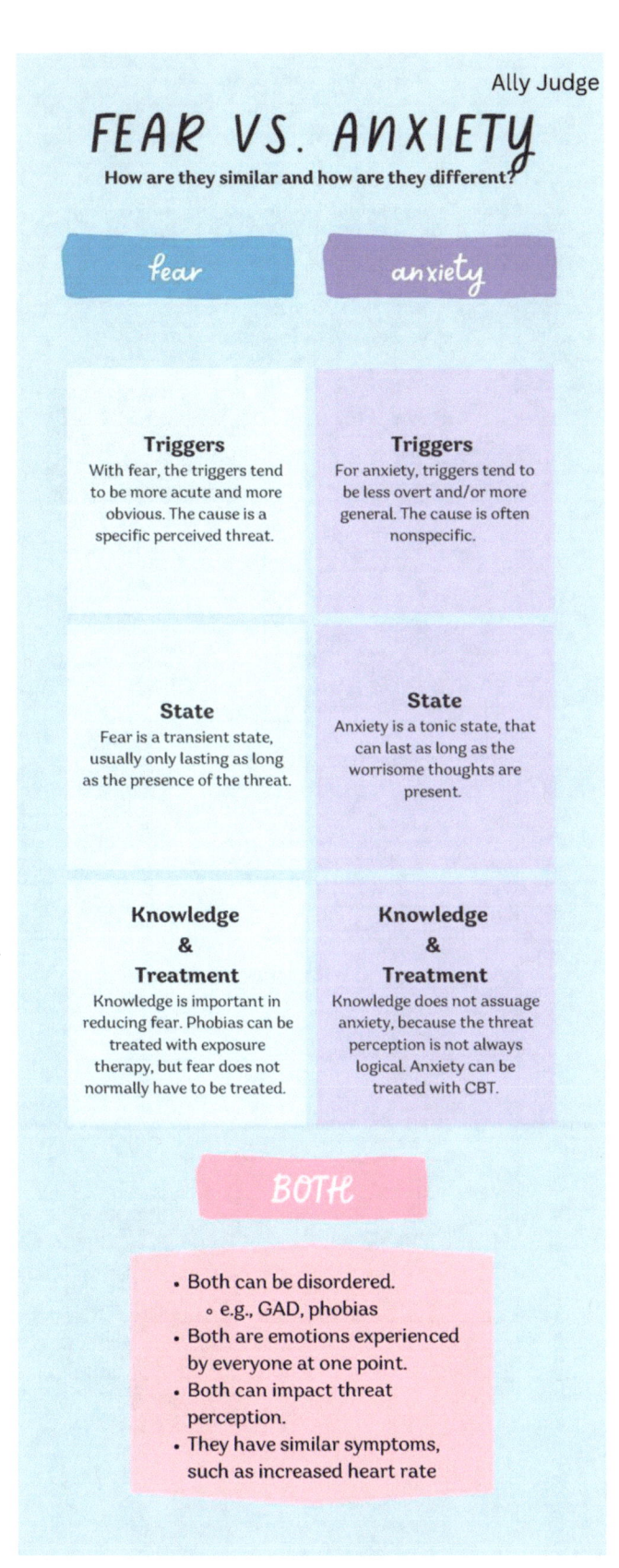

AN INFOGRAPHIC JOURNEY

FEAR VS. ANXIETY
How are they similar and how are they different?

Ally Judge

fear

Triggers
With fear, the triggers tend to be more acute and more obvious. The cause is a specific perceived threat.

State
Fear is a transient state, usually only lasting as long as the presence of the threat.

Knowledge & Treatment
Knowledge is important in reducing fear. Phobias can be treated with exposure therapy, but fear does not normally have to be treated.

anxiety

Triggers
For anxiety, triggers tend to be less overt and/or more general. The cause is often nonspecific.

State
Anxiety is a tonic state, that can last as long as the worrisome thoughts are present.

Knowledge & Treatment
Knowledge does not assuage anxiety, because the threat perception is not always logical. Anxiety can be treated with CBT.

BOTH
- Both can be disordered.
  - e.g., GAD, phobias
- Both are emotions experienced by everyone at one point.
- Both can impact threat perception.
- They have similar symptoms, such as increased heart rate

Allyson Judge, Spring 2024

The Relationship Between Fear and Anxiety

Fear vs Anxiety

Specificity
- Fear: Specific, directed toward the possibility of one risk occurring
- Anxiety: General feeling of unease caused by the belief that *something* negative will happen

Time Course
- Fear: Generally reduces and disappears after the specific risk that was causing it is removed
- Anxiety: Usually persists as a mental state of heightened vigilance and apprehension

Causes
- Fear: Similar stimuli in most individuals, since the majority of people judge the same things to be dangerous
- Anxiety: Varies more between individuals due to differences in genetics, personality, etc., but relatively constant within individuals

How Fear and Anxiety are Related

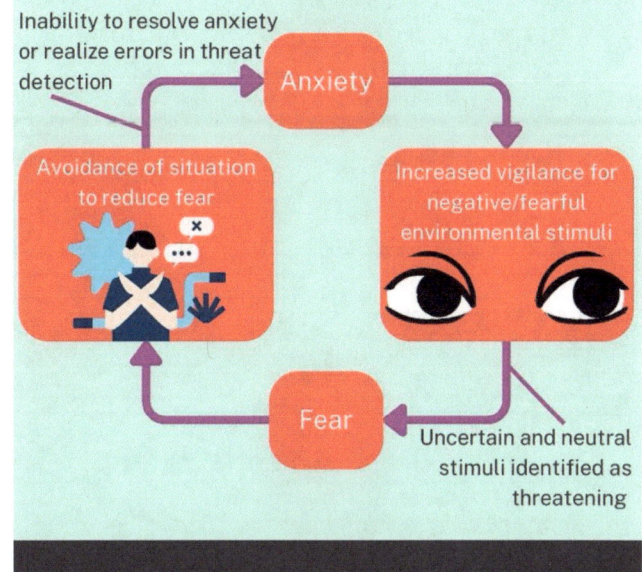

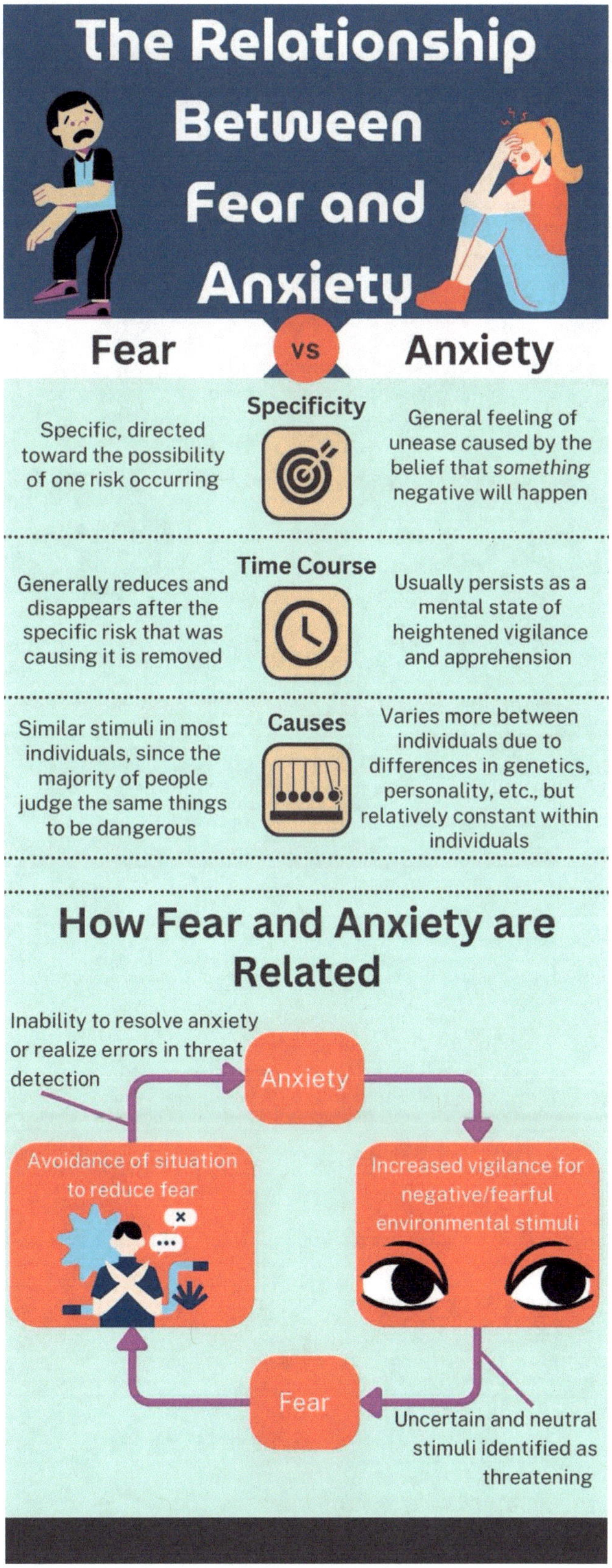

- Inability to resolve anxiety or realize errors in threat detection → Anxiety
- Anxiety → Increased vigilance for negative/fearful environmental stimuli
- Increased vigilance → Uncertain and neutral stimuli identified as threatening → Fear
- Fear → Avoidance of situation to reduce fear
- Avoidance → (back to Anxiety)

Allyson Macfee, Spring 2024

AN INFOGRAPHIC JOURNEY

FEAR AND ANXIETY

HOW FEAR IS DEFINED

Fear is characterized as an unpleasant sensation that can't be objective measurability and is solely evaluated by the individual undergoing the feeling of fear. Fear is the unwanted experience that may happen in the future.

KINDS OF FEAR

1. Chronic
2. Acute
3. Irrational fear
4. Rational Fear
5. Misdirected fear
6. Fear from phantom risks
7. Fear that is enjoyable
8. Fear that is purposeful and fear that is not purposeful

THE EFFECTS OF FEAR ON A PERSON

Strong fear: Evoke a flight of or fight reaction which elevates the sympathetic activity and lowers the parasympathetic activity. This can cause difficulty performing mental tasks and muscle tremors.

Moderate fear: Elevate sympathetic acitivty and decrease parasympathetic activity

Slight fear: Somewhat elevates sympathetic activity and lowers than normal parasympathetic acitivity.

Fear and anxiety also create diseases

FEAR AS A DEFESNE SYSTEM

Fear has a person take precautions to reduce of getting sick or create trauma. This is done in our day to day lives.

1. Seatbelts
2. Exercising to keep a healthy lifestyle
3. Vaccination

RATIONAL V.S IRRATIONAL FEAR

Rational fear is the potential dangerous where one has to protect themselves.
Examples of rational fear: Victim of a crime, loss of a child, Undergoing a harmful accident or traffic accident.

Irrational fear is a often a threat that never occurs
Examples of irrational fear: Ghosts, bugs, animals and foods.

ADDITONAL FUN FACT

Animals show fear conditioning but react threats which is similar to how humans react to expected dangers.

SO DONT' WORRY AND CARRY ON!

Emily Gutierrez, Fall 2023

FEAR & ANXIETY

"Fear and anxiety are emotions that are caused by a person's belief that some unpleasant, harmful, or dangerous event may occur in the future and that it may affect the person in adverse ways." – Aage R. Møller, PhD

RATIONAL FEAR

Fear is considered rational when there is a real, imminent threat to a person. For example, a parent may experience the fear of losing their child in a very crowded shopping center. This fear is labeled as rational because if the child wanders off they could be kidnapped or get themselves hurt.

IRRATIONAL FEAR

Fear is considered irrational when there is no possibility of harm or inconvenience to a person. For example, darkness is a common fear that people experience at nighttime. This fear is irrational because no harm can come from the darkness that occurs in one's bedroom when the sun goes down and the lights are off.

PERCEPTIONS OF FEAR

Different people describe fear differently. Deciding how to react to a danger is often based on an individual's perception of the potential for harm, and not the actual possibility that something harmful would happen to them. Factors that influence perceptions of fear include education, occupation, and professional background. For example, an infectious disease physician may fear getting sick due to their knowledge of various diseases.

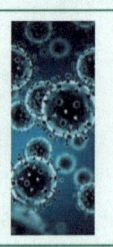

ANXIETY DISORDERS

There are several types of anxiety disorders, including post-traumatic stress disorder, obsessive-compulsive disorder, panic disorder, and social anxiety disorder. Anxiety disorders differ from occasional anxiety in that the feeling of fear or anxiety is constant and overwhelming for those with a disorder. Whether one's trigger is internal or external, the feelings of fear and anxiety that stem from an anxiety disorder can be managed.

ANGST

Angst is a feeling directly related to anxiety. It can be described as an intense feeling of apprehension, anxiety, or inner turmoil which is often unfocused. One way to visualize the feeling of angst is through the famous painting "The Scream" by Edvard Munich, whose goal was to represent "an infinite scream passing through nature".

Stefanie Favaro, Spring 2023

AN INFOGRAPHIC JOURNEY

FEAR AND ANXIETY EXPLAINED

WHAT IS FEAR?
Fear is the complex feeling of being afraid. Fear can be described in numerous terms hence making it apparent that individuals experience different forms of fear and anxiety.

SOURCES OF FEAR
Fear is more based on belief rather than facts. Fear is caused by the belief that danger may occur. The cause of fear can be external or internal. Some sources include genetics and unfamiliarity.

EFFECTS OF FEAR
Fear causes one to take precautions and be aware of situations hence reducing risks of trauma and being ill. The overall effects of both fear and anxiety are underestimated since people respond differently.

RATIONAL FEAR
Rational fear is a fear that is justified. Sources include financial stability, family situation, a victim of crime or accident, or illnesses.

IRRATIONAL FEAR
Irrational fear includes fear of situations that cannot cause harm or damage to a person. It is pure imagination and exaggerated beyond reality. The prediction about the danger is usually incorrect.

WHAT TO FEAR ABOUT?
The choice to fear is usually based on the perception of the risk of harm and not the actual risk. Perception of fear is based on belief therefore for survival, it requires one to limit fear to not be too high or low.

ANXIETY
Anxiety is a form of worry or fear that comes from real or imaginary threats. The frequency of anxiety can be higher or lower for some but most people have encountered this. Anxiety is similar to fear but anxiety is characterized as a mental state that has no specific stimuli.

DISORDERS
PTSD, postpartum depression and anxiety, panic disorder, social anxiety disorders, hypochondriasis, and Munchausen syndrome.

Seema Arjuna, Fall 2023

FEAR & ANXIETY
SARAH PADANI

WHAT is FEAR?
A primary emotion that is characterized by an unpleasant experience or emotion caused by the belief that something dangerous is going to occur resulting in pain or bodily injury. It can only be measured by the person who experiences it.

TYPES of FEAR
- Rational or justified fear
- Irrational or unjustified fear
- Acute fear
- Chronic fear
- Misdirected fear
- Fear from phantom risks
- Enjoyable fear
- Purposeful and not purposeful fear

WHY are FEAR & ANXIETY important?
Fear is part of the body's alarm system that signals and warns about immediate and future dangers respectively. It activates the body's alarm system and induces actions to protect the body from harm.

Do ANIMALS experience FEAR & ANXIETY?
Fear developed as a protective mechanism during evolution. Animals show fear conditioning and display reactionary behavior to protect against danger but whether animals can experince fear is unknown since only animal ractions can be observed.

EFFECTS of FEAR & ANXIETY
- Influence a person to circumvent the risks of injury or sickness
- Fear and anxiety play a role in creating diseases
- Activation of the autonomic nervous system resulting in an increase in sympathetic acitivity and a decrease in parasympathetic activity.

DID you KNOW...
According to a study published in the journal Psychological Science on November 5th, humans can smell fear from the sweat of other people!

Sarah Padani, Fall 2023

AN INFOGRAPHIC JOURNEY

Alana Simpson, Spring 2023

Alifiya Shaikh, Fall 2023

88

AN INFOGRAPHIC JOURNEY

Saad Tanwir, Spring 2024

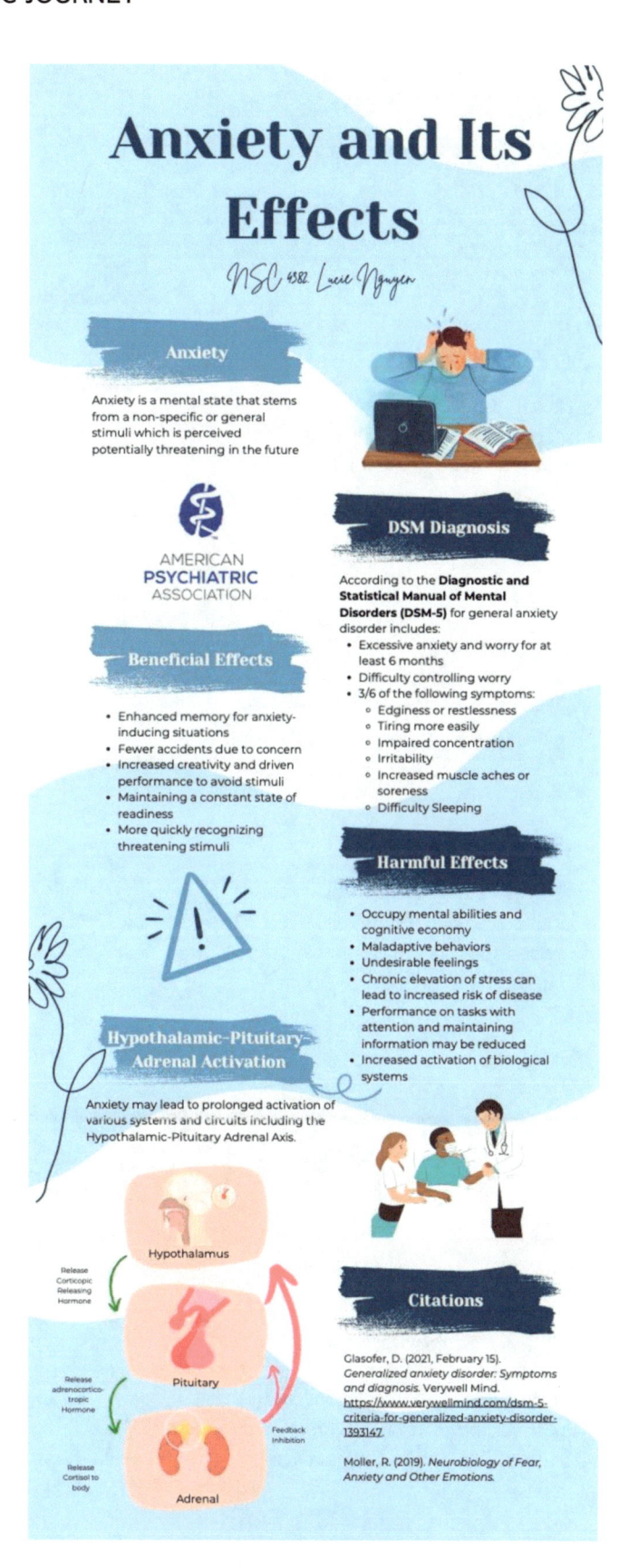

Lucie Nguyen, Fall 2023

AN INFOGRAPHIC JOURNEY

GENERAL EFFECTS OF ANXIETY

1. Readiness
Anxiety helps maintain a state of readiness. It facilitates threat processing and defensive responding, but also prompts cognitive changes.

2. Biases
The gathering of resources extends cognitive-affective biases that are manifested in behavior.

3. Processing
There are examples of these biases found in studies where negatively valued stimuli are processed more rapidly under anxious conditions.

4. Behaviors
These biases may decrease other goal-directed behaviors that are not threat-relevant.

5. Performance
Performance on tasks that involve attention, maintenance of information, and rapid sensory perception may be imparied.

Audrey Villanueva, Fall 2023

How does anxiety affect the body?
By Katelin Tran

What is anxiety?
Anxiety is categorized as general and unspecific fear. While fear is related to specific stimuli, anxiety involves fear about unspecific causes for an extended period of time. The disorder tends to occur with other conditions, such as substance abuse, depression, etc.

Inflammation response
The threat of fear activates many biological systems to produce the fear response, such as the HPA axis and autonomic nervous system, which increase inflammatory responses. The response can be measured through inflammation and coagulation markers, such as C-reactive protein, interleukin-6 and tumor-necrosis factor alpha. These markers are known to be involved in both inflammation and inflammation response.

Chronic inflammation
Because anxiety is unspecified and can last an extended period of time, this means the threat perception and inflammatory response is sustained. In many studies, an elevated level of inflammatory markers were found in participants with anxiety disorders. These results point to a chronic level of inflammation and are still being further studied.

Cellular aging
Chronic inflammation can change the structure of the central nervous system, resulting in modified sensitivity of immune receptors. This causes cells to age faster, as chronic inflammation exhausts the cell's defense system and can weaken cellular structures.

Treatment of anxiety disorders
- Medication and pharmaceuticals are preferred by physicians.
- Physical exercise has also helped treat anxiety. Physical exercise can increase brain-derived neurotrophic factor and recycling of cell organelles.
- Different cognitive-behavior therapies are also employed to overcome anxiety.

Katelin Tran, Fall 2022

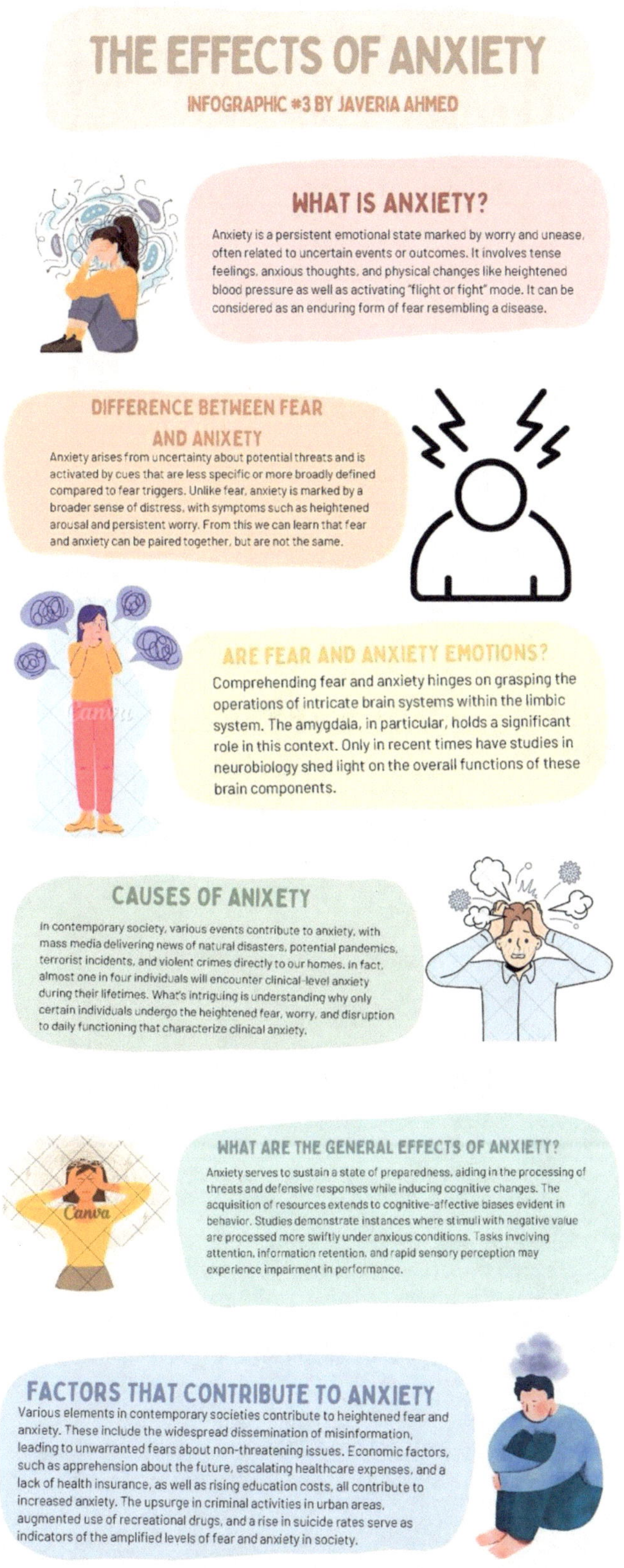

AN INFOGRAPHIC JOURNEY

THE EFFECTS OF ANXIETY
INFOGRAPHIC #3 BY JAVERIA AHMED

WHAT IS ANXIETY?
Anxiety is a persistent emotional state marked by worry and unease, often related to uncertain events or outcomes. It involves tense feelings, anxious thoughts, and physical changes like heightened blood pressure as well as activating "flight or fight" mode. It can be considered as an enduring form of fear resembling a disease.

DIFFERENCE BETWEEN FEAR AND ANIXETY
Anxiety arises from uncertainty about potential threats and is activated by cues that are less specific or more broadly defined compared to fear triggers. Unlike fear, anxiety is marked by a broader sense of distress, with symptoms such as heightened arousal and persistent worry. From this we can learn that fear and anxiety can be paired together, but are not the same.

ARE FEAR AND ANXIETY EMOTIONS?
Comprehending fear and anxiety hinges on grasping the operations of intricate brain systems within the limbic system. The amygdala, in particular, holds a significant role in this context. Only in recent times have studies in neurobiology shed light on the overall functions of these brain components.

CAUSES OF ANIXETY
In contemporary society, various events contribute to anxiety, with mass media delivering news of natural disasters, potential pandemics, terrorist incidents, and violent crimes directly to our homes. In fact, almost one in four individuals will encounter clinical-level anxiety during their lifetimes. What's intriguing is understanding why only certain individuals undergo the heightened fear, worry, and disruption to daily functioning that characterize clinical anxiety.

WHAT ARE THE GENERAL EFFECTS OF ANXIETY?
Anxiety serves to sustain a state of preparedness, aiding in the processing of threats and defensive responses while inducing cognitive changes. The acquisition of resources extends to cognitive-affective biases evident in behavior. Studies demonstrate instances where stimuli with negative value are processed more swiftly under anxious conditions. Tasks involving attention, information retention, and rapid sensory perception may experience impairment in performance.

FACTORS THAT CONTRIBUTE TO ANXIETY
Various elements in contemporary societies contribute to heightened fear and anxiety. These include the widespread dissemination of misinformation, leading to unwarranted fears about non-threatening issues. Economic factors, such as apprehension about the future, escalating healthcare expenses, and a lack of health insurance, as well as rising education costs, all contribute to increased anxiety. The upsurge in criminal activities in urban areas, augmented use of recreational drugs, and a rise in suicide rates serve as indicators of the amplified levels of fear and anxiety in society.

ANXIETY and its effects

WHAT DOES ANXIETY MEAN?
Anxiety is a constant feeling of *worry*, *nervousness*, or *unease*, typically about an event or something with an uncertain outcome. Anxiety may be regarded as a prolonged fear that has a form of a disease.

WHAT IS THE DIFFERENCE BETWEEN ANXIETY AND FEAR?
Anxiety involves uncertainty as to the expectancy of a threat and is triggered by less explicit or more generalized cues than fear.

ANXIETY & MEMORY
Results from several studies demonstrate that anxiety differentially impacts verbal and spatial working memory. Low and medium-load verbal working memory is more susceptible to anxiety-related disruption relative to high-load

ANXIETY & COGNITION
Anxiety alters early sensory-perceptual processes in the auditory and visual system. This may serve to promote threat detection (e.g. detection of auditory tones or visual cues).

PHYSICAL EFFECTS
Anxiety affects the function of many body systems. Some effects may include mind racing, blurry vision, nausea, sweating, restless, and difficulty breathing.

Javeria Ahmed, Spring 2024 　　　　　　　　　　Khadeeja Moosa, Spring 2023

Beneficial effects of anxiety

Enhancement of Performance:
A certain degree of anxiety can act as a motivator, pushing individuals to perform better in tasks. This is often seen in situations like public speaking, exams, or sports, where a moderate level of anxiety can heighten focus and energy levels.

Memory Enhancement
Anxiety can lead to heightened awareness and increased attention to detail, which in turn can enhance memory. This might be particularly true for memories associated with emotionally charged events or information.

Depth of Thinking:
People with a degree of anxiety might ponder over situations more thoroughly than their less anxious counterparts. This deep thinking can lead to more considered and well-thought-out decisions.

Creativity
Following Kierkegaard's thoughts, anxiety can be a powerful driver for creativity. The tension and unease of anxiety can push individuals to think outside the box, leading to creative breakthroughs.

Readiness and Threat Processing:
Anxiety helps in maintaining a state of readiness and facilitates the processing of threats. This can be beneficial in scenarios where quick response and alertness to danger are critical.

Zahra Khan, Spring 2024

AN INFOGRAPHIC JOURNEY

IMPORTANCE OF ANXIETY
By: Rashed Daka

DEFINITION OF ANXIETY

Anxiety is a persistent state of worry, nervousness, or discomfort, often about something with an unpredictable result. It manifests through emotional stress, anxious thinking, and physical symptoms like higher blood pressure. Considered an extended form of fear, anxiety can develop into a disorder. Those affected may experience ongoing troubling thoughts and frequently avoid situations that cause them anxiety.

ANXIETY RELATIONS AND (GAD)

Anxiety can arise from particular issues like upcoming exams, or it might be a broad worry without a direct cause. Individuals with Generalized Anxiety Disorder (GAD) experience intense anxiety frequently and over extended periods.

ANXIETY COMPARED TO FEAR

Anxiety is linked to the uncertainty surrounding potential threats, often set off by vague or wide-ranging signals, unlike fear, which is more specific. It manifests as a widespread state of distress, marked by heightened alertness and concern, differing from the more focused sensation of fear.

GENERAL EFFECTS OF ANXIETY

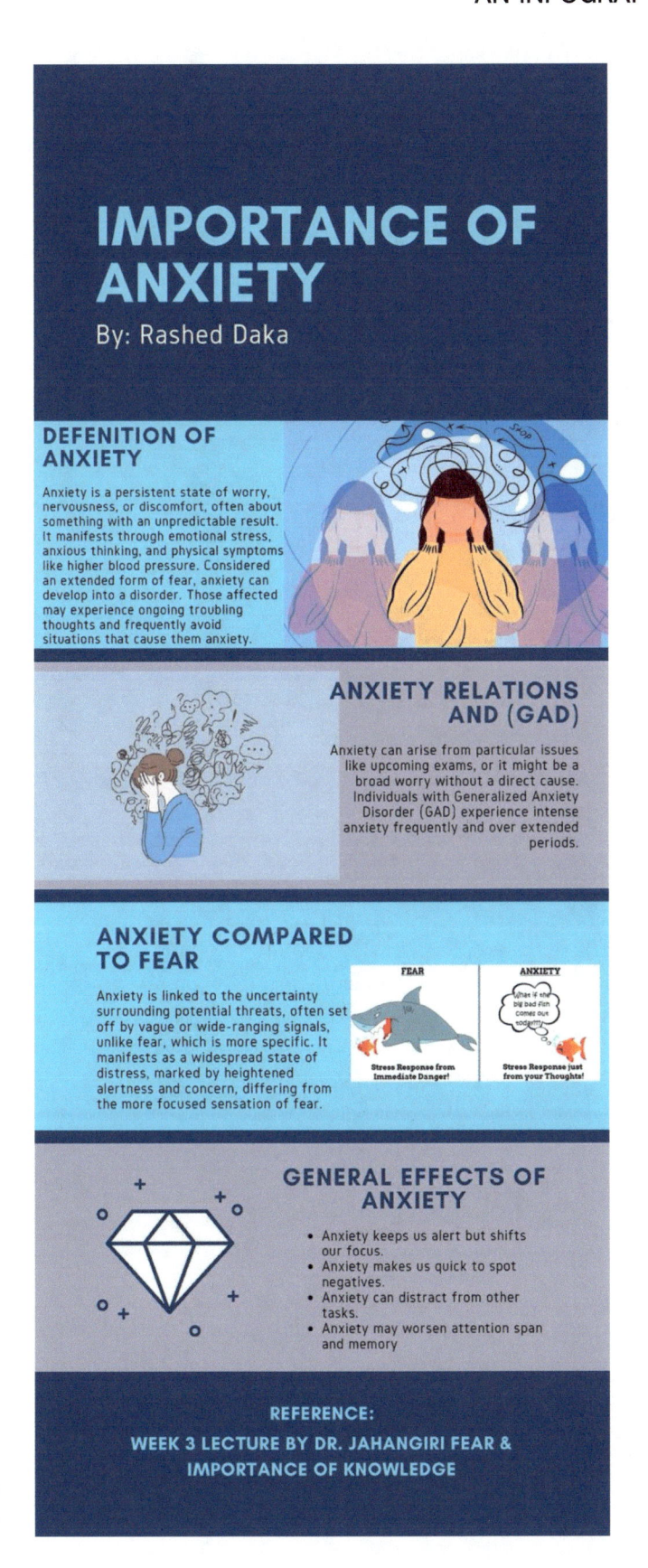

- Anxiety keeps us alert but shifts our focus.
- Anxiety makes us quick to spot negatives.
- Anxiety can distract from other tasks.
- Anxiety may worsen attention span and memory

REFERENCE:
WEEK 3 LECTURE BY DR. JAHANGIRI FEAR & IMPORTANCE OF KNOWLEDGE

Rashed Daka, Spring 2024

---

3 WAYS ANXIETY IS HELPFUL
Made by: Kaeli Nguyen

WHAT IS ANXIETY?

A worrisome or uneasy feeling that is usually attached to inevitable event or circumstance.

1. ALERTNESS

With decent managements, "enough" anxiety can help individuals stay alert and aware of their surrounding decreasing likelihood of harm.
- ie. Being alert in an uneasy/unknown area in case of harm

2. PREPARED OR PREPERTAION

Being anxious over a specific situation can cause one to overprepare or make sure to be prepared ahead of time to reduce anxiety/worry.
- ie. Preparing for presentation

3. MOTIVATION

Anxiety can bring an individual a lot of stress yet it can also provide motivation to persevere in order to feel relieved.

THE 333 RULE

If one is still dealing with severe anxiety preventing them from utilizing it as a helpful tool, one can try the 333 rule: Identify 3 objects, 3 sounds, then move 3 body parts.

Kaeli Nguyen, Spring 2024

AN INFOGRAPHIC JOURNEY

CHAPTER 6

Anxiety Disorders

Different Anxiety Disorders and their Implications

By Tejas Devata & Allen Liang, Spring 2024

Anxiety is a normal human emotion. It is our brain's natural way of responding to stress or alerting us to possible dangers. Everyone feels anxious, be it due to an upcoming exam, job interview, or when making a life decision, and this is okay. Occasional anxiety is, again, normal. However, anxiety disorders are different. Anxiety disorders are a form of mental illness that involves constant anxiety, possibly presenting due to some form of trigger that can worsen an individual's symptoms. Anxiety disorders can lead to implications in a person's daily life, causing them to be more reclusive from family and avoid social settings. However, treatment is available and can often effectively mitigate or manage symptoms.

Generalized Anxiety Disorder (GAD) is a prevalent disorder that affects roughly 6.8 million people in the United States, or about 3.1% of the population. The risk of developing GAD has risen from 2-3% to 5% over the last few years. This increase may be due to increased social media usage, lack of proper sleep, genetics, and environmental factors. However, this percentage is not evenly distributed among all genders, races, and social classes. Women are afflicted by this condition twice as much as men, according to the NIH. There are a variety of chemical factors that also play a role in the neurological and physiological basis of the disorder. Neurotransmitters such as gamma-aminobutyric acid (GABA), serotonin, and dopamine may lead to abnormalities in function and behavior.

To be diagnosed with GAD, an individual must have excessive anxiety and worry for more days than not over a period of 6 months. Additionally, they must find it difficult to control the worry, with it not being attached to a medical condition or substance use. Lastly, they must express at least three symptoms: restlessness (feeling on edge), easily fatigued, difficulty concentrating, irritability, muscle tension, and sleep disturbance. Hope is not all lost, as treatment for GAD is effective compared to other mental disorders. However, only 43.2% of those suffering from GAD is receiving treatment, which does not even include those that have yet to be diagnosed. Various treatments aid in recovery. These include pharmaceuticals such as selective serotonin reuptake inhibitors (SSRIs) and psychotherapy such as cognitive behavioral therapy (CBT). The former targets the chemical basis behind the symptoms, while the latter targets the psychological basis.

Panic Disorder is a common disorder that affects about 2.7% of adults in the United States. According to the NIH, females are disproportionately affected compared to males, citing a prevalence of 3.8% compared to males at 1.6%. However, nearly 4.7% of adults in the United States have experienced a panic disorder at one point in their lives. The disorder presents itself as recurring, frequent, and unexpected panic attacks. These attacks can be characterized as waves of fear, discomfort, or a sense of losing control, with or without the presence of a significant trigger. Panic attacks can also involve physical symptoms that may mirror those of a heart attack, such as chest pain, rapid heart rate, tingling, or tremors. Panic attacks can occur at varying frequencies and vary from individual to individual. Attacks can occur multiple times a day to a few times a year, and attacks can occur with no warning, leading to many individuals being forced to change their lifestyles as a result. Different risk factors for panic disorders can include a familial history of panic disorders or attacks, a traumatic event, excessive stress, overuse of caffeine, or a history of smoking. Various treatments can aid in coping or recovering from a panic disorder and panic attacks. These include medications such as SSRIs and psychotherapy such as CBT or talk therapy.

Agoraphobia is an uncommon disorder that affects about 1.3% of adults in their lifetime within the United States. It is marked by fear and anxiety in a crowded place or environment. The yearly prevalence rate is about 0.9%, similar for males and females. Each age group also has a similar incidence rate. It has recently diverged from the classification of panic disorder, which may lead to an underestimation in terms of the actual raw numbers. Moreover, the severity also has a roughly even distribution, with 40.6% classifying under severe, 30.7% under moderate, and 28.7% under mild. The mean age of diagnosis hovers around the mid to late 20s, with most coming before age 35. Several risk factors have been explored regarding this disorder. These include parental overprotectiveness, presence of night terrors and/or childhood trauma, experience of fear, and genetics, which the DSM-5, the manual for all psychological disorders, has stratified into categories.

To be diagnosed with agoraphobia, these criteria must be met. There must be a marked fear or anxiety about at least two of the following five situations: using public transportation, being in open spaces, being in enclosed spaces such as shops, theaters, or cinemas, standing in line or being in a crowd, or being outside the home alone. Additionally, these situations are actively avoided, provoking disproportionate fear or anxiety in the context. These symptoms must be distressing enough to impact daily life and social functioning for at least six months. However, when it comes to treatment, some factors must be assessed, such as the severity of the disease and the patient's choices. Once again, there are options for both psychotherapy and pharmacotherapy. CBT targets the thought patterns, behaviors, and emotions that are tied to the disorder and is often used for less severe cases, with drugs such as SSRIs, tricyclic antidepressants (TCAs), and benzodiazepines being used for more severe cases.

Illness Anxiety Disorder (IAD), previously known as hypochondriasis, is an extremely rare disorder that affects around 0.1% of people in the United States per year, and often develops during early adulthood, and is typically a chronic condition. There are conflicting studies regarding IAD's prevalence among different genders. However, anxiety disorders are generally more prevalent in women. There are two categories of IAD: care-seeking and care-avoidant. True to their name, care-seeking means individuals are obsessive regarding medical tests and going to doctors, often worrying excessively about being sick and persisting despite normal test results. They may also take normal signs such as sweating or indigestion as serious medical conditions. Care-avoidant is when individuals avoid medical professionals and do not believe they take their care or concern for symptoms seriously, leading to an equal amount of fear and anxiety that adversely affects the individual's daily life. Childhood trauma/abuse, excessive and chronic stress, family history of illness, and other mental health disorders are all possible causes of IAD. Medications such as antidepressants and psychotherapy such as CBT are both used to combat the physical and psychological aspects of the condition and help individuals cope. However, there is no known treatment for IAD.

All in all, it is crucial to be aware of the symptoms of these various anxiety disorders and be mindful of those who may suffer from them. Public education and information on mental disorders are grossly underrepresented. Additionally, it is imperative to receive constant check-ups to ensure that these afflictions do not creep into our daily lives. This allows medical professionals to address the issues as early as possible. Lastly, support systems and treatment are critical to recovery from these disorders.

References

1. Balaram, K., & Marwaha, R. (2023, February 13). *Agoraphobia*. StatPearls [Internet]. https://www.ncbi.nlm.nih.gov/books/NBK554387/.
2. Cleveland Clinic. (n.d.). *Illness anxiety disorder (hypochondria): Symptoms & treatments*. Illness Anxiety Disorder (Hypochondria, Hypochondriasis). https://my.clevelandclinic.org/health/diseases/9886-illness-anxiety-disorder-hypochondria-hypochondriasis.
3. French, J. H., & Hameed, S. (2023, July 16). *Illness anxiety disorder*. StatPearls [Internet]. https://www.ncbi.nlm.nih.gov/books/NBK554399/.
4. *Generalized anxiety disorder (GAD): Anxiety and depression association of america, ADAA*. Generalized Anxiety Disorder (GAD) | Anxiety and Depression Association of America, ADAA. (n.d.). https://adaa.org/understanding-anxiety/generalized-anxiety-disorder-gad.
5. Hernandez, J., & Kellner, R. (1992, September). *Hypochondriacal concerns and attitudes toward illness in males and females*. SageJournals. https://journals.sagepub.com/doi/10.2190/W9KG-6HU9-5QJX-NW76?icid=int.sj-abstract.similar-articles.
6. Mishra, A. K., & Varma, A. R. (2023, September 28). *A comprehensive review of the Generalized Anxiety Disorder*. Cureus. https://www.ncbi.nlm.nih.gov/pmc/articles/PMC10612137/.
7. Substance Abuse and Mental Health Services Administration. (2016a, June). *Table 3.10, panic disorder and agoraphobia criteria changes from DSM-IV to DSM-5 - impact of the DSM-IV to DSM-5 changes on the National Survey on Drug Use and health - NCBI bookshelf*. Impact of the DSM-IV to DSM-5 Changes on the National Survey on Drug Use and Health [Internet]. https://www.ncbi.nlm.nih.gov/books/NBK519704/table/ch3.t10/.
8. Substance Abuse and Mental Health Services Administration. (2016b, June). *Table 3.15, DSM-IV to DSM-5 generalized anxiety disorder comparison - impact of the DSM-IV to DSM-5 changes on the National Survey on Drug Use and health - NCBI bookshelf*.
9. Impact of the DSM-IV to DSM-5 Changes on the National Survey on Drug Use and Health [Internet]. https://www.ncbi.nlm.nih.gov/books/NBK519704/table/ch3.t15/.
10. U.S. Department of Health and Human Services. (n.d.-a). *Agoraphobia*. National Institute of Mental Health. https://www.nimh.nih.gov/health/statistics/agoraphobia.
11. U.S. Department of Health and Human Services. (n.d.-b). *Anxiety disorders*. National Institute of Mental Health. https://www.nimh.nih.gov/health/topics/anxiety-disorders.
12. U.S. Department of Health and Human Services. (n.d.-c). *Panic disorder*. National Institute of Mental Health. https://www.nimh.nih.gov/health/statistics/panic-disorder.
13. U.S. Department of Health and Human Services. (n.d.-d). *Panic disorder: When fear overwhelms*. National Institute of Mental Health. https://www.nimh.nih.gov/health/publications/panic-disorder-when-fear-overwhelms.

AN INFOGRAPHIC JOURNEY

ANXIETY DISORDERS

These feelings of anxiety and panic interfere with daily activities, are difficult to control, are out of proportion to the actual danger and can last a long time. You may avoid places or situations to prevent these feelings. Symptoms may start during childhood or the teen years and continue into adulthood.

01 Symptoms of Anxiety Disorders
- Sweating
- Trembling
- Hyperventilating
- Nervousness or resltssness

02 Anxiety disorders are among the most common mental illnesses, affecting roughly 40 million American adults each year

03 Examples of anxiety disorders include generalized anxiety disorder, social anxiety disorder (social phobia), specific phobias and separation anxiety disorder. You can have more than one anxiety disorder. Sometimes anxiety results from a medical condition that needs treatment.

04 Your worries may not go away on their own, and they may get worse over time if you don't seek help. See your doctor or a mental health provider before your anxiety gets worse. It's easier to treat if you get help early.

https://www.mayoclinic.org/diseases-conditions/anxiety/symptoms-causes/syc-20350961

Ashley Kiser, Fall 2023

Anxiety Disorder
Nupoor Shah

Anxiety disorders
A person with anxiety disorder tend to worry about everyday matters such as losing a job, car accidents, etc. They fear that they will not be prepared enough when the time of disaster arrives.

Symptoms
- trouble concentrating
- muscle tension
- fatigue
- feeling tense
- dry mouth
- sweating

Cognitive Behavior Therapy
Cognitive behavior therapy is a form of therapy for those who have anxiety or depression. It allows people to change their way of thinking and behavior when they are feeling anxious.

Causes of anxiety
Anxiety can be caused by life disrupting events such as pandemics, violence, crimes, illnesses.

What part of the brain does anxiety affect?
Anxiety disrupts the emotional processing center. This is within the limbic system and affects the amygdala. The Amygdala plays a major role in the processing center and is connected to other brain structures which is responsible for making extensive connections to brainstem for emotional responses

citations:
https://www.nm.org/healthbeat/healthy-tips/emotional-health/the-science-of-anxiety
https://www.healthline.com/health/cognitive-behavioral-therapy

Nupoor Shah, Fall 2023

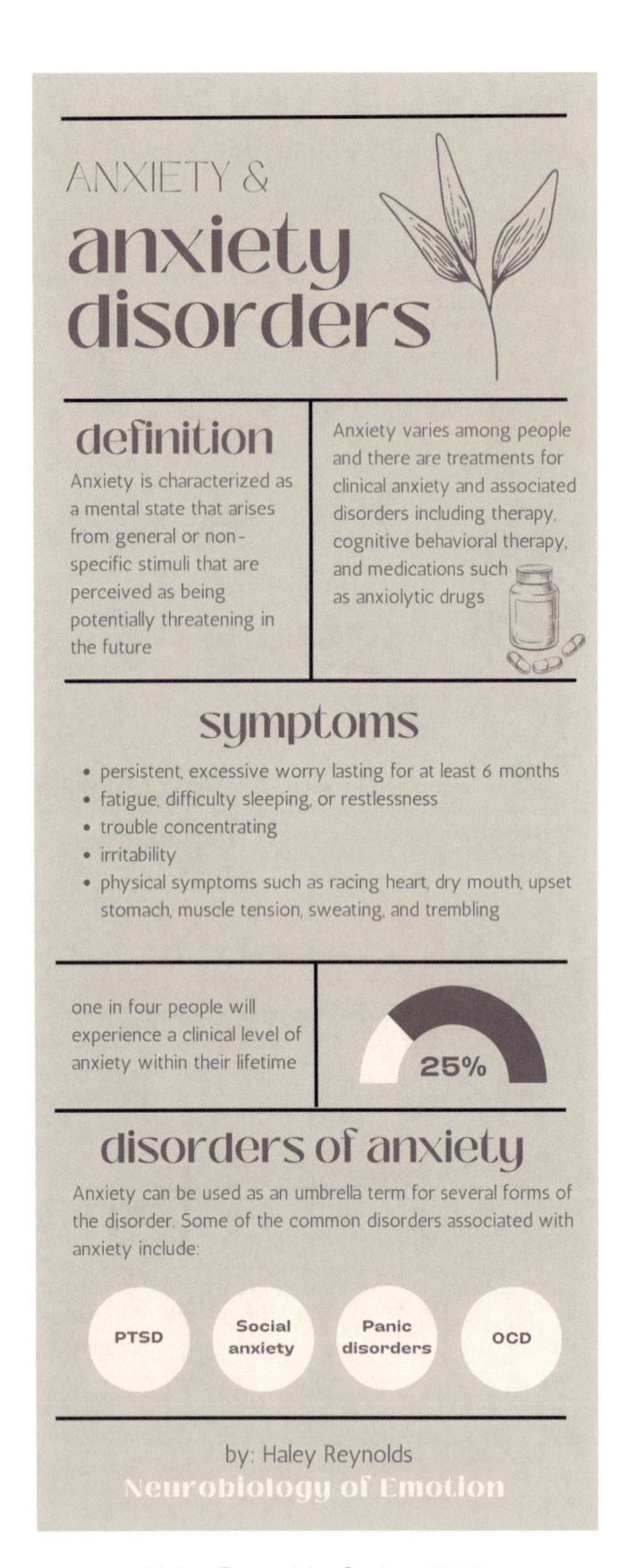

AN INFOGRAPHIC JOURNEY

ANXIETY & anxiety disorders

definition

Anxiety is characterized as a mental state that arises from general or non-specific stimuli that are perceived as being potentially threatening in the future

Anxiety varies among people and there are treatments for clinical anxiety and associated disorders including therapy, cognitive behavioral therapy, and medications such as anxiolytic drugs

symptoms

- persistent, excessive worry lasting for at least 6 months
- fatigue, difficulty sleeping, or restlessness
- trouble concentrating
- irritability
- physical symptoms such as racing heart, dry mouth, upset stomach, muscle tension, sweating, and trembling

one in four people will experience a clinical level of anxiety within their lifetime — 25%

disorders of anxiety

Anxiety can be used as an umbrella term for several forms of the disorder. Some of the common disorders associated with anxiety include:

- PTSD
- Social anxiety
- Panic disorders
- OCD

by: Haley Reynolds
Neurobiology of Emotion

Haley Reynolds, Spring 2023

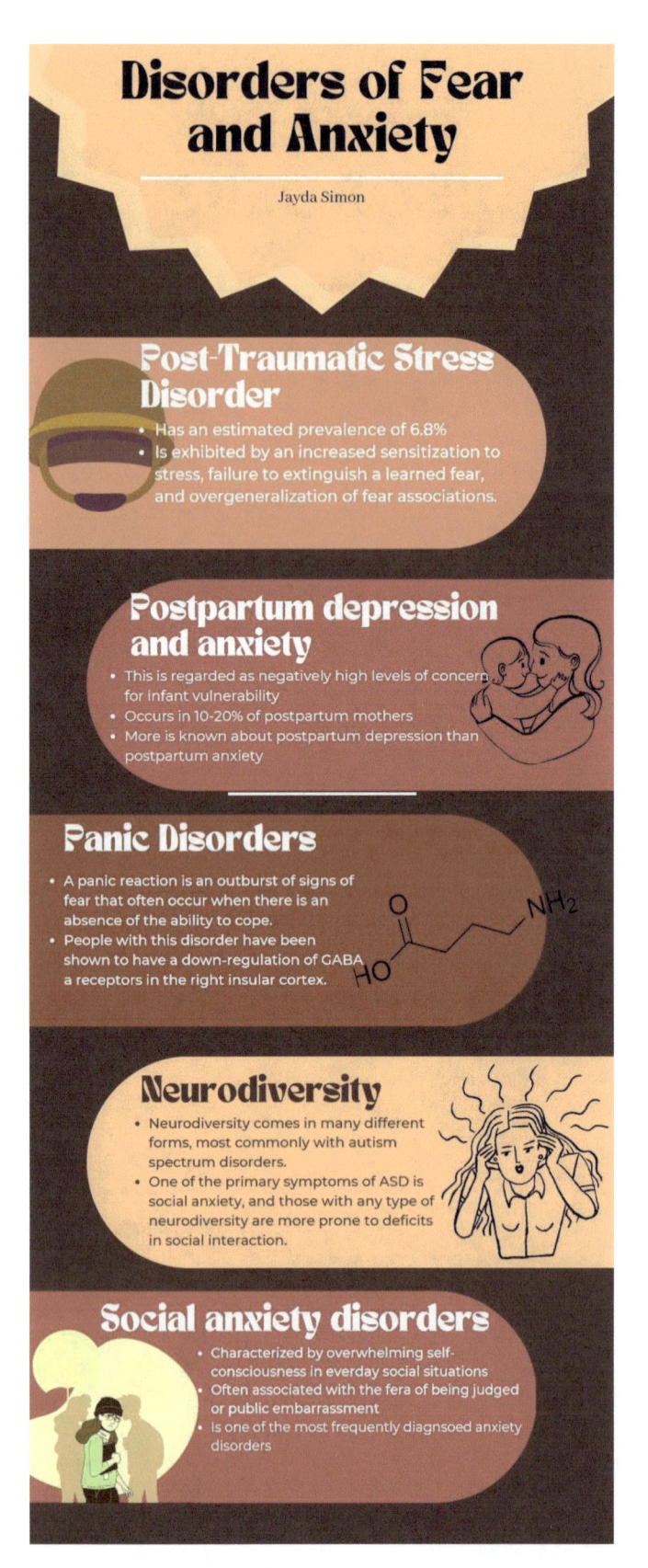

Disorders of Fear and Anxiety

Jayda Simon

Post-Traumatic Stress Disorder
- Has an estimated prevalence of 6.8%
- Is exhibited by an increased sensitization to stress, failure to extinguish a learned fear, and overgeneralization of fear associations.

Postpartum depression and anxiety
- This is regarded as negatively high levels of concern for infant vulnerability
- Occurs in 10-20% of postpartum mothers
- More is known about postpartum depression than postpartum anxiety

Panic Disorders
- A panic reaction is an outburst of signs of fear that often occur when there is an absence of the ability to cope.
- People with this disorder have been shown to have a down-regulation of GABA a receptors in the right insular cortex.

Neurodiversity
- Neurodiversity comes in many different forms, most commonly with autism spectrum disorders.
- One of the primary symptoms of ASD is social anxiety, and those with any type of neurodiversity are more prone to deficits in social interaction.

Social anxiety disorders
- Characterized by overwhelming self-consciousness in everday social situations
- Often associated with the fera of being judged or public embarrassment
- Is one of the most frequently diagnsoed anxiety disorders

Jayda Simon, Spring 2023

DISORDERS OF FEAR AND ANXIETY !!!

Post-traumatic stress disorder
Fear that is associated with specific traumatic events cues that can trigger a fear-related disorder.

Postpartum depression and anxiety
Excessive worrying from mothers about the infant's vulnerability and safety after giving birth. Presented in 10-20% of postpartum mothers.

Panic disorders
This disorder shows an outburst of signs of fear that results from a severe and acute scare in the absence of an ability to cope with fearful sensations.

Social Anxiety Disroders
A form of phobia that is characterized by an overwhelming self-consciousness. It is caused by the worry of being judged or being embarrassed in front of others.

Hypochondriasis
A form of anxiety with the strong belief of having a severe disease or illness without any signs or other objective indications of something being wrong with the person's health.

Munchausen syndrome
A mental illness which characterized by repeated false claims of having a physical or mental disorder without having any disease to draw attention and sympathy.

Hyeonji Lee, Fall 2023

DISEASES CAUSED BY ANXIETY

01 Cardiovascular Problems
Long-term anxiety can contribute to high blood pressure, increased heart rate, and a higher risk of cardiovascular issues.

02 Digestive Disorders
Anxiety may lead to digestive problems such as irritable bowel syndrome, indigestion, or other gastrointestinal issues.

03 Respiratory Issues
Anxiety may contribute to respiratory problems such as shortness of breath or exacerbation of preexisting respiratory conditions like asthma.

04 Muscle Tension and Pain
Anxiety can cause muscle tension and contribute to conditions such as tension headaches, migraines, and chronic pain.

Neha Gannapaneni, Spring 2024

AN INFOGRAPHIC JOURNEY

THE DEVELOPMENT OF FEAR DISORDERS IN FOUR STEPS
Victor Onuorah Jr

01 PRE-EXISTING SENSITIVITY
- A combination of genetics and the environment one is raised in
- This will determine a person's predisposition to certain fears

02 LEARNING OF FEAR
- The initial traumatic event that inspires a fear

03 CONSOLIDATION OF FEAR
- After experience a traumatic event, the memory of the experience consolidates over the next few hours or days

04 EXPRESSION OF FEAR
- The memory leads to the development of unpleasant flashbacks, nightmares and desire to avoid whatever triggered the trauma

Social Anxiety Disorder Risk Factors
- Early traumatic event
- Parenting style
- Isolated upbringing
- Observing others with SAD
- Brain structure
- Genetics
- Societal expectations

Victor Onuorak Jr, Fall 2022

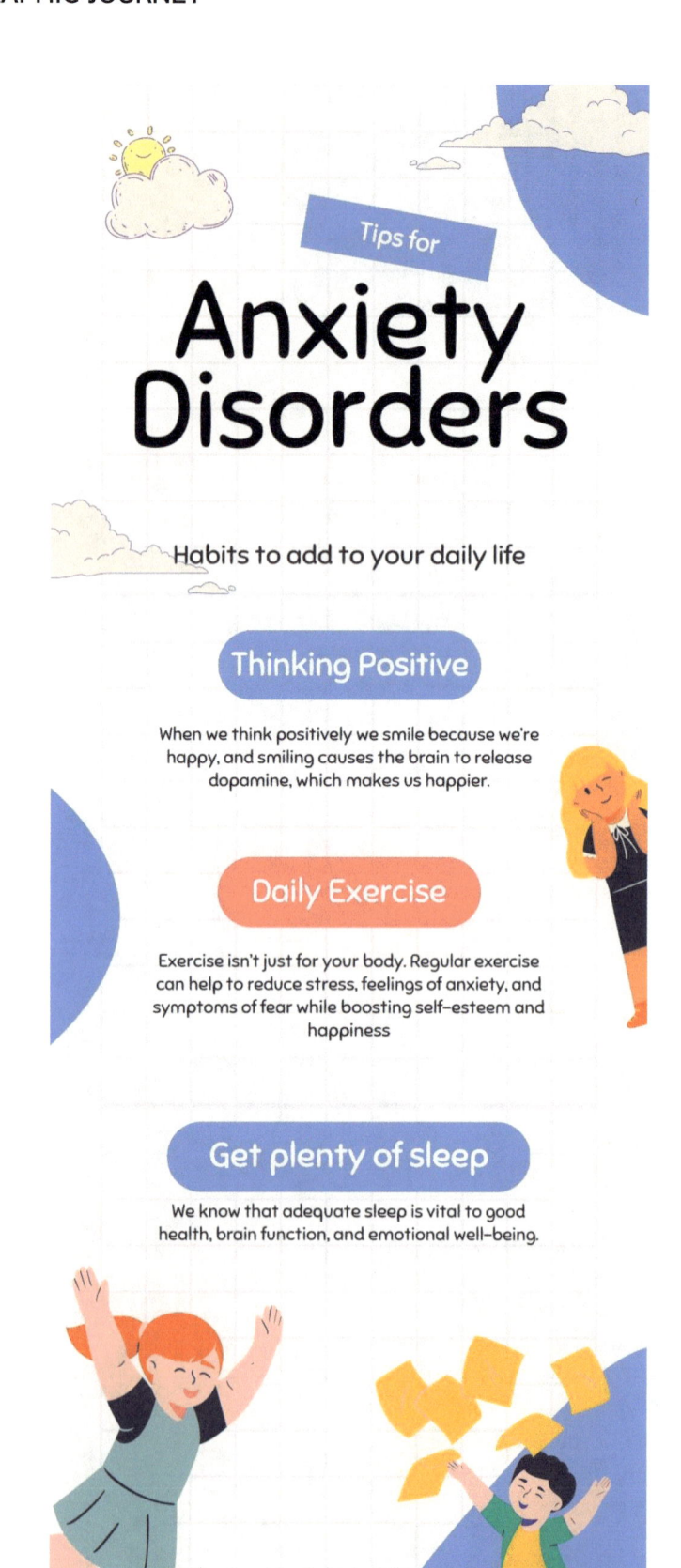

Tips for Anxiety Disorders
Habits to add to your daily life

Thinking Positive
When we think positively we smile because we're happy, and smiling causes the brain to release dopamine, which makes us happier.

Daily Exercise
Exercise isn't just for your body. Regular exercise can help to reduce stress, feelings of anxiety, and symptoms of fear while boosting self-esteem and happiness

Get plenty of sleep
We know that adequate sleep is vital to good health, brain function, and emotional well-being.

Tamjeed Islam, Spring 2023

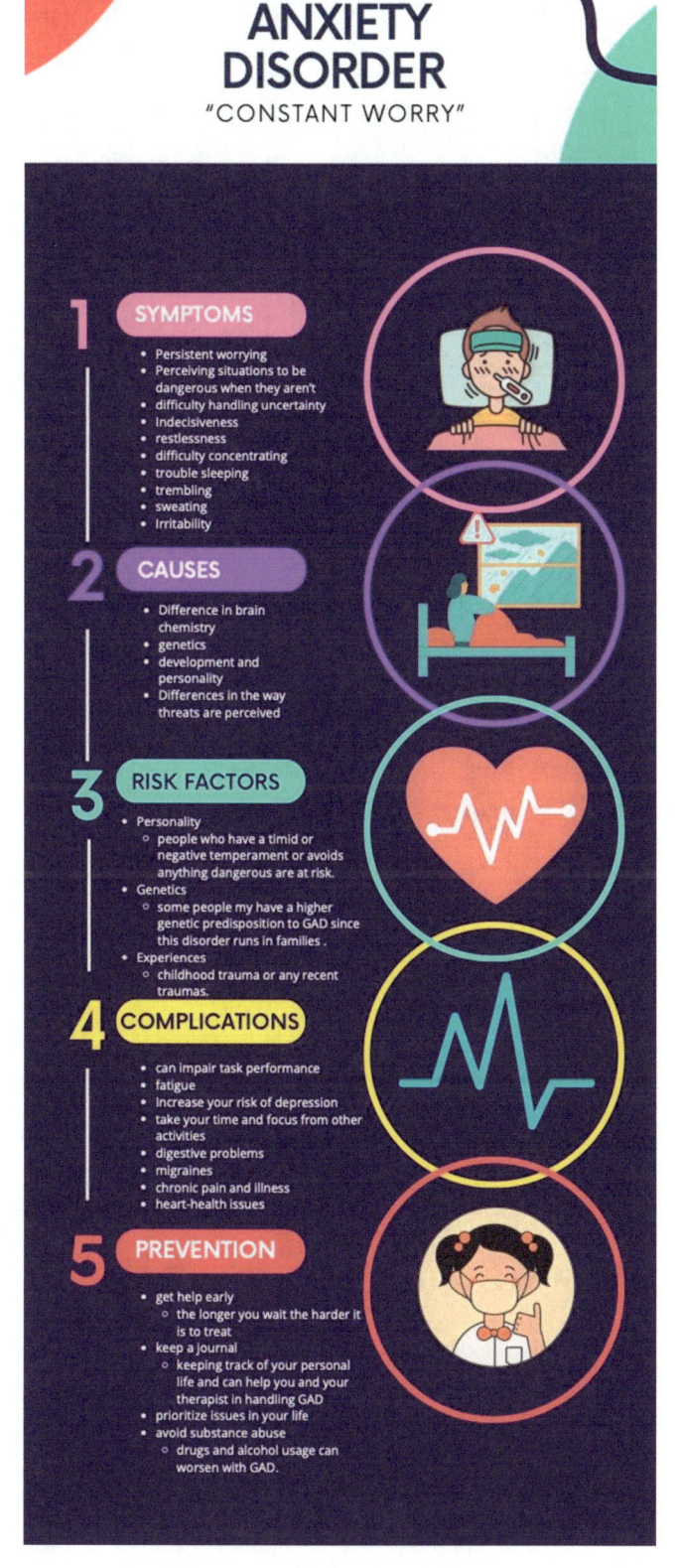

AN INFOGRAPHIC JOURNEY

GENERALIZED ANXIETY DISORDER
"CONSTANT WORRY"

1 SYMPTOMS
- Persistent worrying
- Perceiving situations to be dangerous when they aren't
- difficulty handling uncertainty
- Indecisiveness
- restlessness
- difficulty concentrating
- trouble sleeping
- trembling
- sweating
- Irritability

2 CAUSES
- Difference in brain chemistry
- genetics
- development and personality
- Differences in the way threats are perceived

3 RISK FACTORS
- Personality
  - people who have a timid or negative temperament or avoids anything dangerous are at risk.
- Genetics
  - some people my have a higher genetic predisposition to GAD since this disorder runs in families.
- Experiences
  - childhood trauma or any recent traumas.

4 COMPLICATIONS
- can impair task performance
- fatigue
- Increase your risk of depression
- take your time and focus from other activities
- digestive problems
- migraines
- chronic pain and illness
- heart-health issues

5 PREVENTION
- get help early
  - the longer you wait the harder it is to treat
- keep a journal
  - keeping track of your personal life and can help you and your therapist in handling GAD
- prioritize issues in your life
- avoid substance abuse
  - drugs and alcohol usage can worsen with GAD.

Jesse Idemudia, Fall 2023

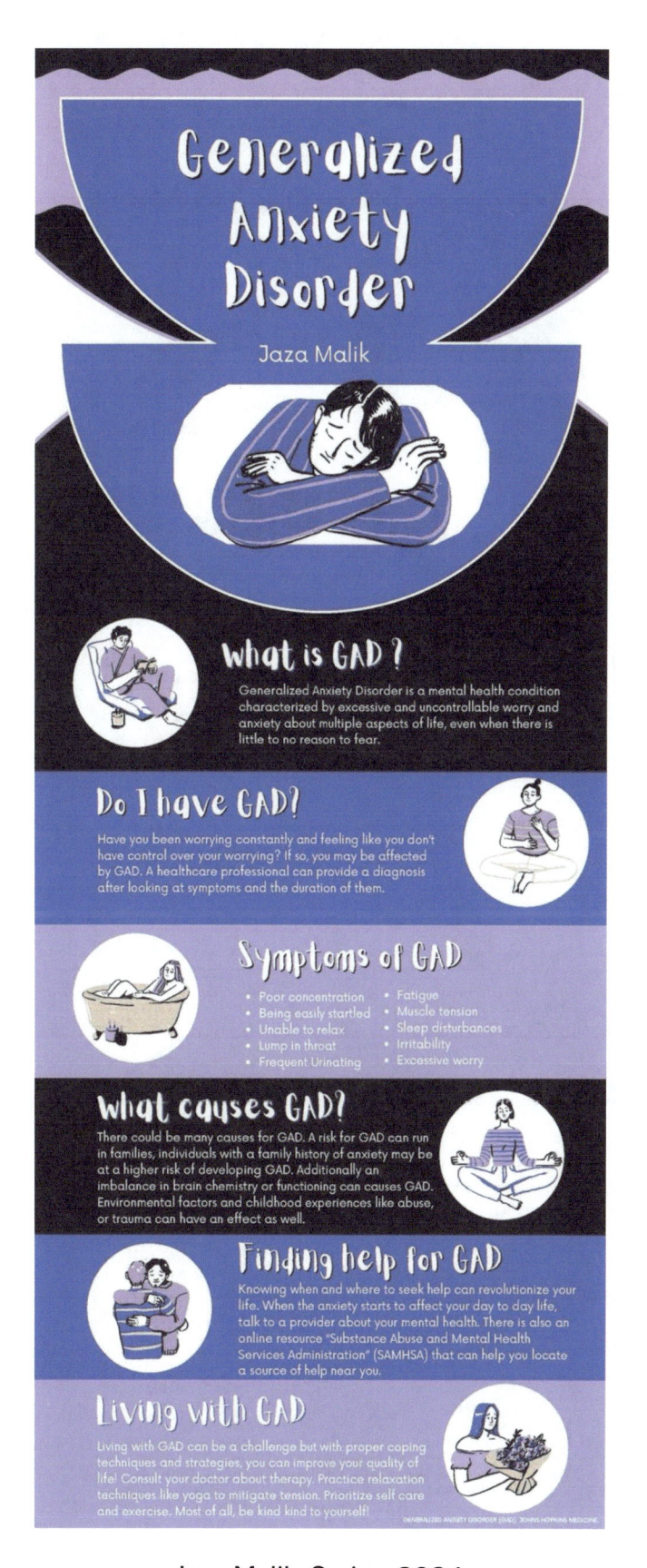

Generalized Anxiety Disorder
Jaza Malik

What is GAD?
Generalized Anxiety Disorder is a mental health condition characterized by excessive and uncontrollable worry and anxiety about multiple aspects of life, even when there is little to no reason to fear.

Do I have GAD?
Have you been worrying constantly and feeling like you don't have control over your worrying? If so, you may be affected by GAD. A healthcare professional can provide a diagnosis after looking at symptoms and the duration of them.

Symptoms of GAD
- Poor concentration
- Being easily startled
- Unable to relax
- Lump in throat
- Frequent Urinating
- Fatigue
- Muscle tension
- Sleep disturbances
- Irritability
- Excessive worry

What causes GAD?
There could be many causes for GAD. A risk for GAD can run in families, individuals with a family history of anxiety may be at a higher risk of developing GAD. Additionally an imbalance in brain chemistry or functioning can causes GAD. Environmental factors and childhood experiences like abuse, or trauma can have an effect as well.

Finding help for GAD
Knowing when and where to seek help can revolutionize your life. When the anxiety starts to affect your day to day life, talk to a provider about your mental health. There is also an online resource "Substance Abuse and Mental Health Services Administration" (SAMHSA) that can help you locate a source of help near you.

Living with GAD
Living with GAD can be a challenge but with proper coping techniques and strategies, you can improve your quality of life! Consult your doctor about therapy. Practice relaxation techniques like yoga to mitigate tension. Prioritize self care and exercise. Most of all, be kind kind to yourself!

Jaza Malik, Spring 2024

103

AN INFOGRAPHIC JOURNEY

more about Generalized Anxiety Disorder

Definition

A condition of excessive worry about everyday issues and situations. Usually diagnosed when worrying happens for more than 4 days out of the week for at least 6 months.

Prevalence

GAD affects 6.8 million adults, or 3.1% of the US population. However, only 43.2% are receiving treatment.

Symptoms

- Trouble falling or staying asleep
- Irritability
- Hot Flashes
- Nausea
- Sweating
- Fatigue
- Poor Concentration
- Unable to relax

Co-morbidities

Mood and anxiety disorders as well as chronic pain and sleep conditions are common disorders seen in relation to GAD.

Treatment

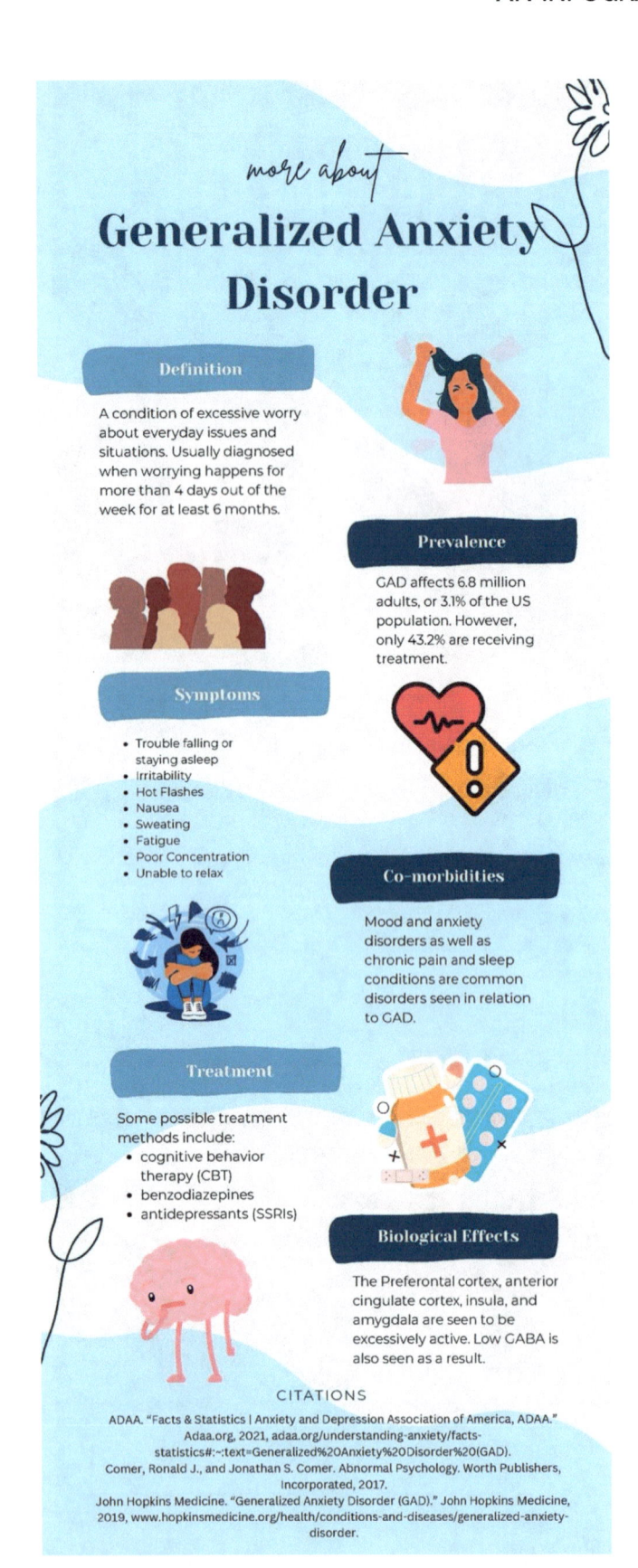

Some possible treatment methods include:
- cognitive behavior therapy (CBT)
- benzodiazepines
- antidepressants (SSRIs)

Biological Effects

The Preferontal cortex, anterior cingulate cortex, insula, and amygdala are seen to be excessively active. Low GABA is also seen as a result.

CITATIONS
ADAA. "Facts & Statistics | Anxiety and Depression Association of America, ADAA." Adaa.org, 2021, adaa.org/understanding-anxiety/facts-statistics#:~:text=Generalized%20Anxiety%20Disorder%20(GAD).
Comer, Ronald J., and Jonathan S. Comer. Abnormal Psychology. Worth Publishers, Incorporated, 2017.
John Hopkins Medicine. "Generalized Anxiety Disorder (GAD)." John Hopkins Medicine, 2019, www.hopkinsmedicine.org/health/conditions-and-diseases/generalized-anxiety-disorder.

Zaara Siddiki, Spring 2024

GENERALIZED ANXIETY DISORDER

People with generalized anxiety disorder tend to worry about everyday matters and feel tension about generalized cues.

SYMPTOMS

A diagnosis of generalized anxiety disorder (GAD) results from persistent, excessive worry that lasts for at least 6 months. Other symptoms include fatigue, difficulty sleeping, restlessness, irritability, hindered concentration, and muscle tension.

TREATMENT

Cognitive behavioral therapy helps people with GAD be more conscious of their thoughts and recognize when they are misinterpreting cues and offer methods to respond to anxiety-provoking stimuli. Other treatments include relaxation techniques, meditation, and biofeedback.

PHYSICAL SYMPTOMS

Physical symptoms of GAD include elevated heart rate, dry mouth, upset stomach, muscle tension, sweating, trembling, and irritability. These physical symptoms can also cause greater risk for cardiovascular problems and cause prolonged activatation of the autonomic nervous sysytem, leading to increased inflammation.

CAUSES

People worry about everyday matters such as work. Imagination also plays an important role in forming mental concepts about possible dangers. The mass media can also cause anxiety by reporting on natural disasters, pandemics, and violence.

Kajal Patel, Spring 2024

AN INFOGRAPHIC JOURNEY

SOCIAL ANXIETY DISORDER

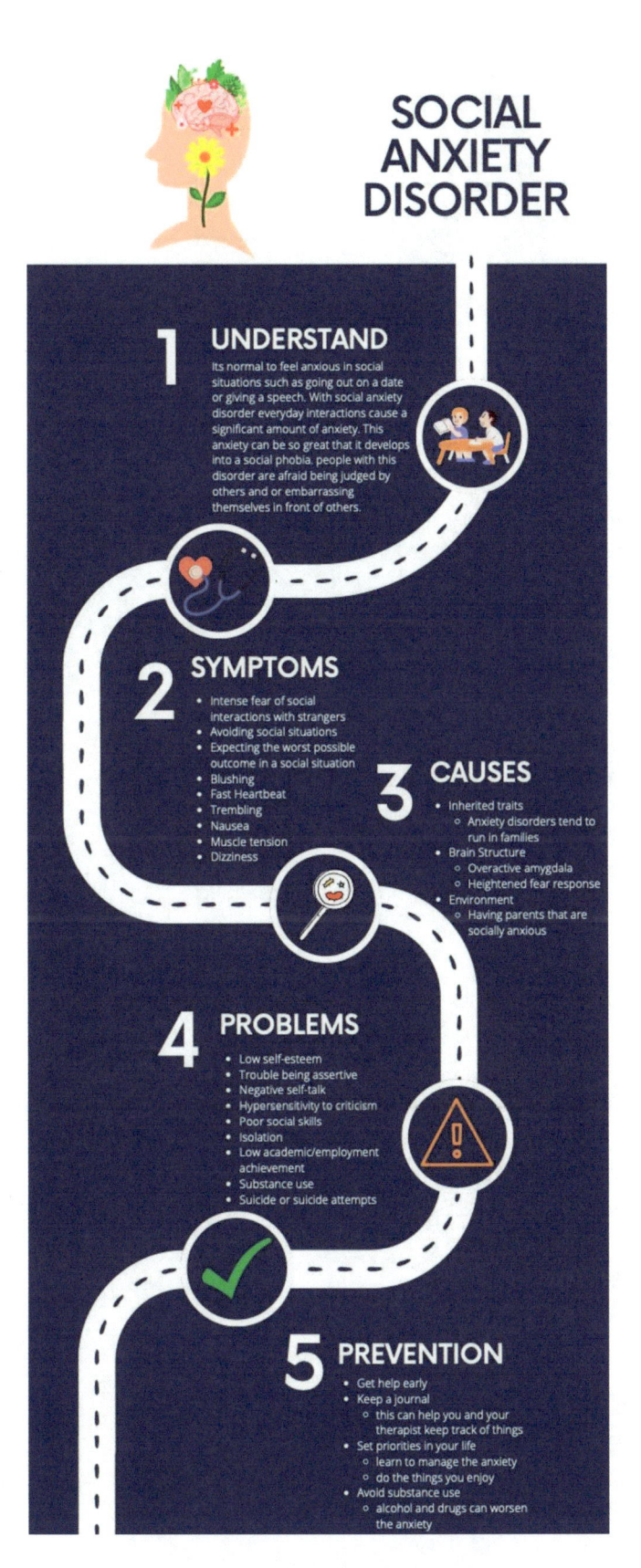

1 UNDERSTAND
It's normal to feel anxious in social situations such as going out on a date or giving a speech. With social anxiety disorder everyday interactions cause a significant amount of anxiety. This anxiety can be so great that it develops into a social phobia. people with this disorder are afraid being judged by others and or embarrassing themselves in front of others.

2 SYMPTOMS
- Intense fear of social interactions with strangers
- Avoiding social situations
- Expecting the worst possible outcome in a social situation
- Blushing
- Fast Heartbeat
- Trembling
- Nausea
- Muscle tension
- Dizziness

3 CAUSES
- Inherited traits
  - Anxiety disorders tend to run in families
- Brain Structure
  - Overactive amygdala
  - Heightened fear response
- Environment
  - Having parents that are socially anxious

4 PROBLEMS
- Low self-esteem
- Trouble being assertive
- Negative self-talk
- Hypersensitivity to criticism
- Poor social skills
- Isolation
- Low academic/employment achievement
- Substance use
- Suicide or suicide attempts

5 PREVENTION
- Get help early
- Keep a journal
  - this can help you and your therapist keep track of things
- Set priorities in your life
  - learn to manage the anxiety
  - do the things you enjoy
- Avoid substance use
  - alcohol and drugs can worsen the anxiety

Jesse Idemudia, Fall 2023

Social Anxiety and Emotions

Sources: Week 4 part 1 and 2 Lecture Slides

SOCIAL ANXIETY
Social Anxiety is a form of phobia that is characterized by overwhelming self-consciousness during common social situations. This is caused by worries of being judged and avoiding embarrassment

WORRIES
Worry is an internal reaction that may be useful. But that is if it leads to a person taking appropriate precautions or resolving a problem. Worry about matters that may be real may happen. But over situations where there is no control is not beneficial

EMOTION THEORY
Different career fields define emotion differently. There are 6 main emotions that include: Happy, surprise, fear, disgust, anger, and sad. The body's reactions to emotions can be regarded as an expression of various kinds of emotions. This can cause various reactions.

Seema Arjuna, Fall 2023

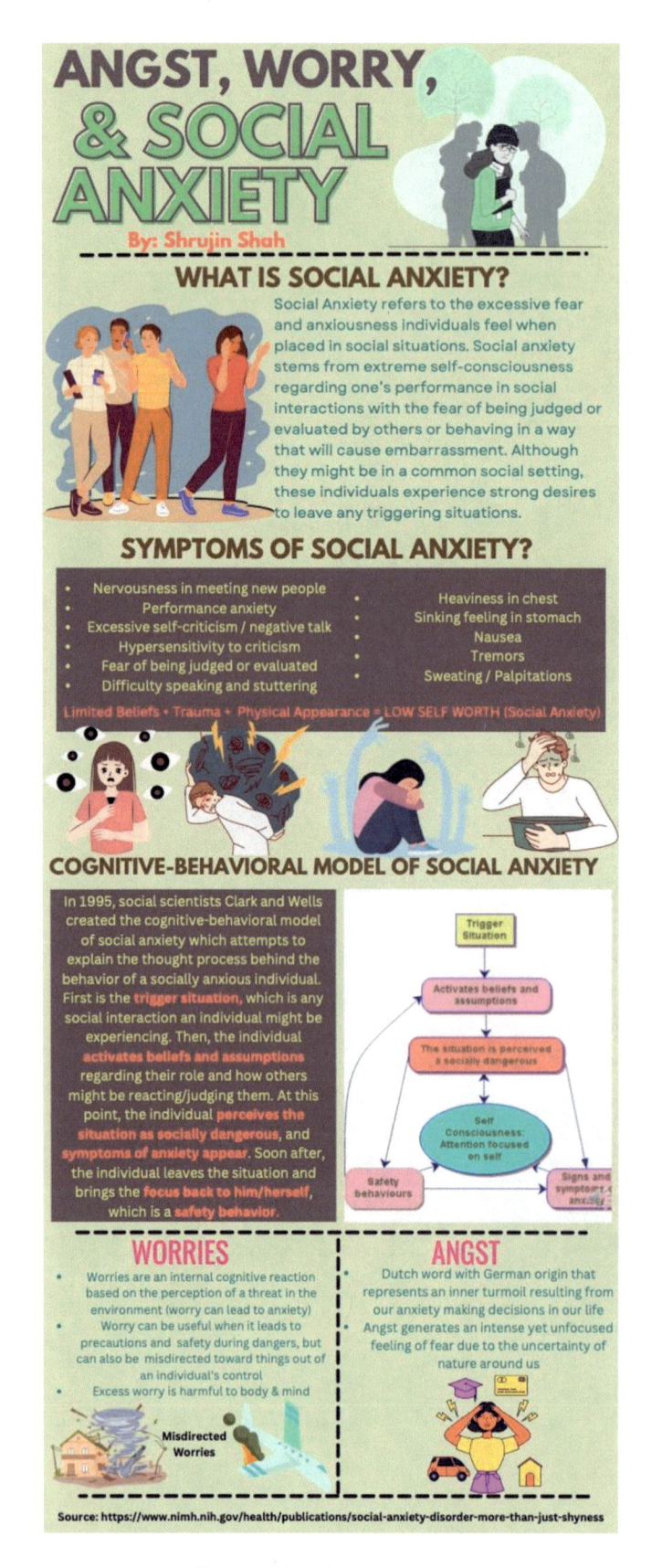

Shrujin Shah, Fall 2023

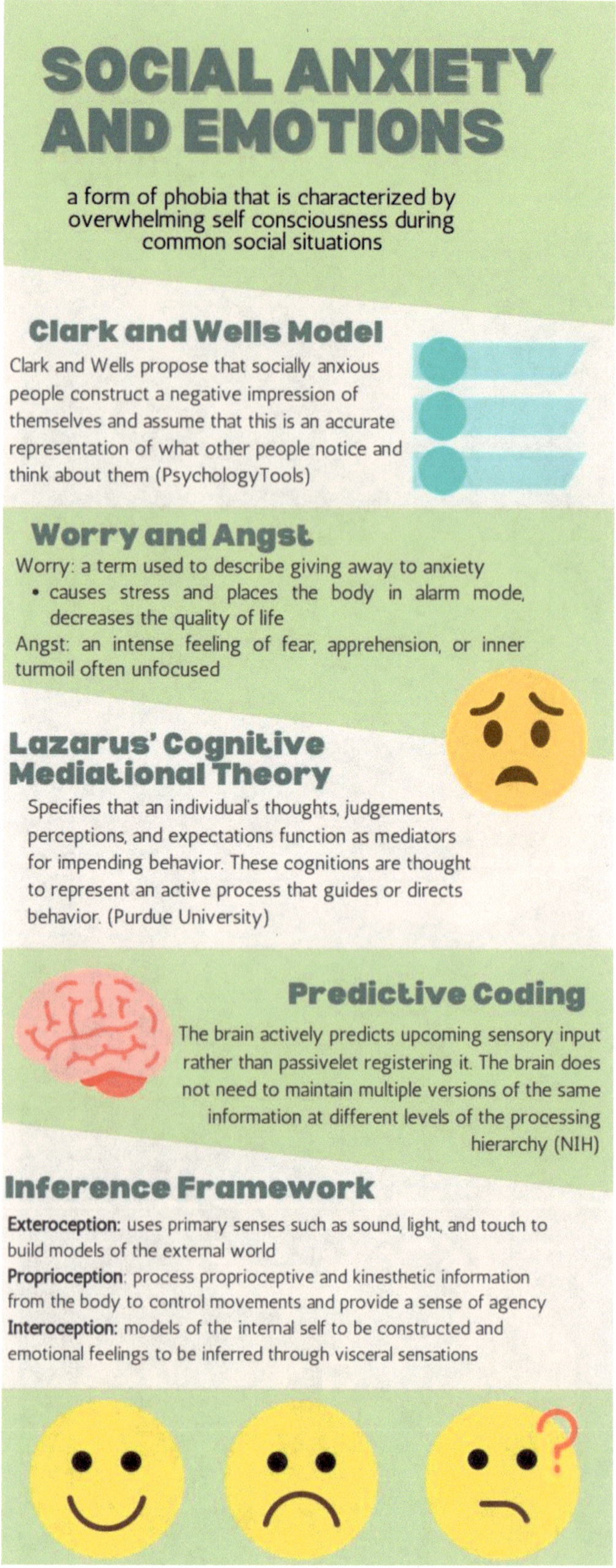

Samiksha Sivakumar, Fall 2023

Sneha Sharma, Spring 2024

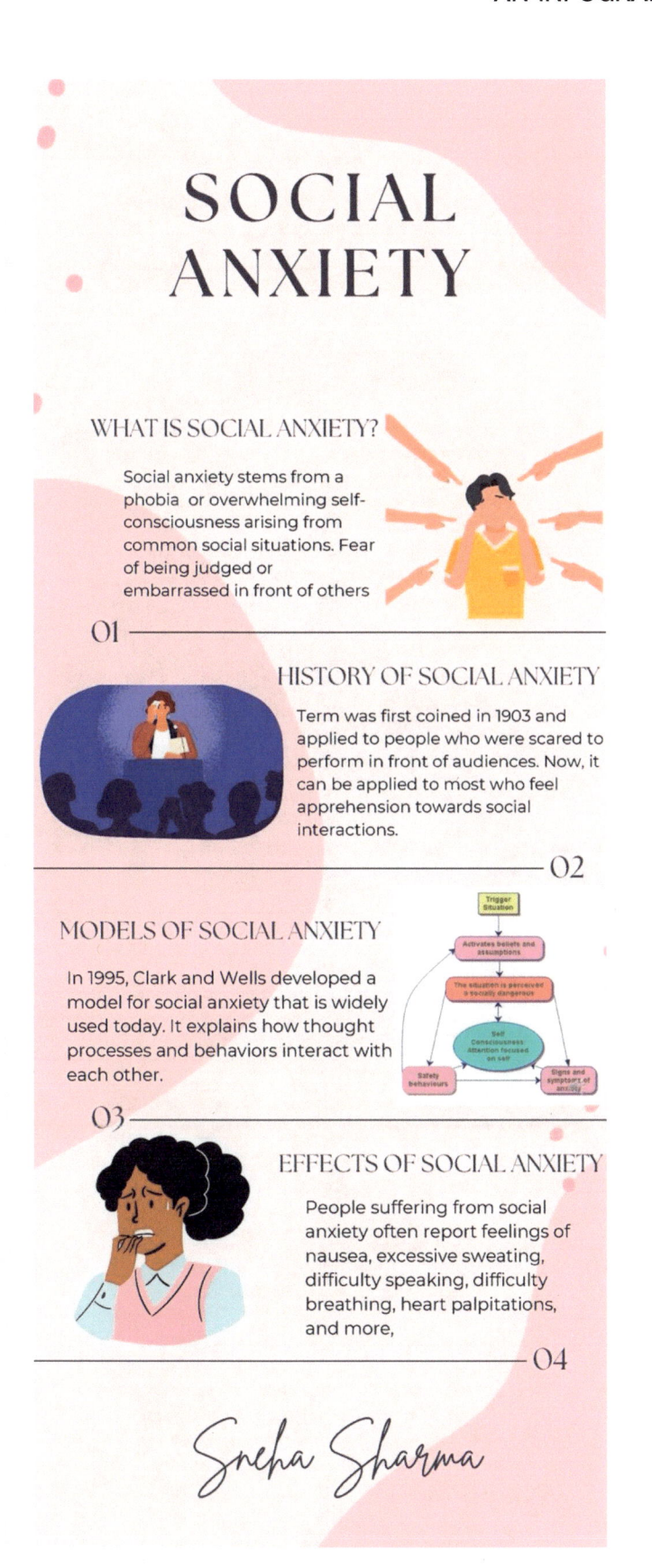

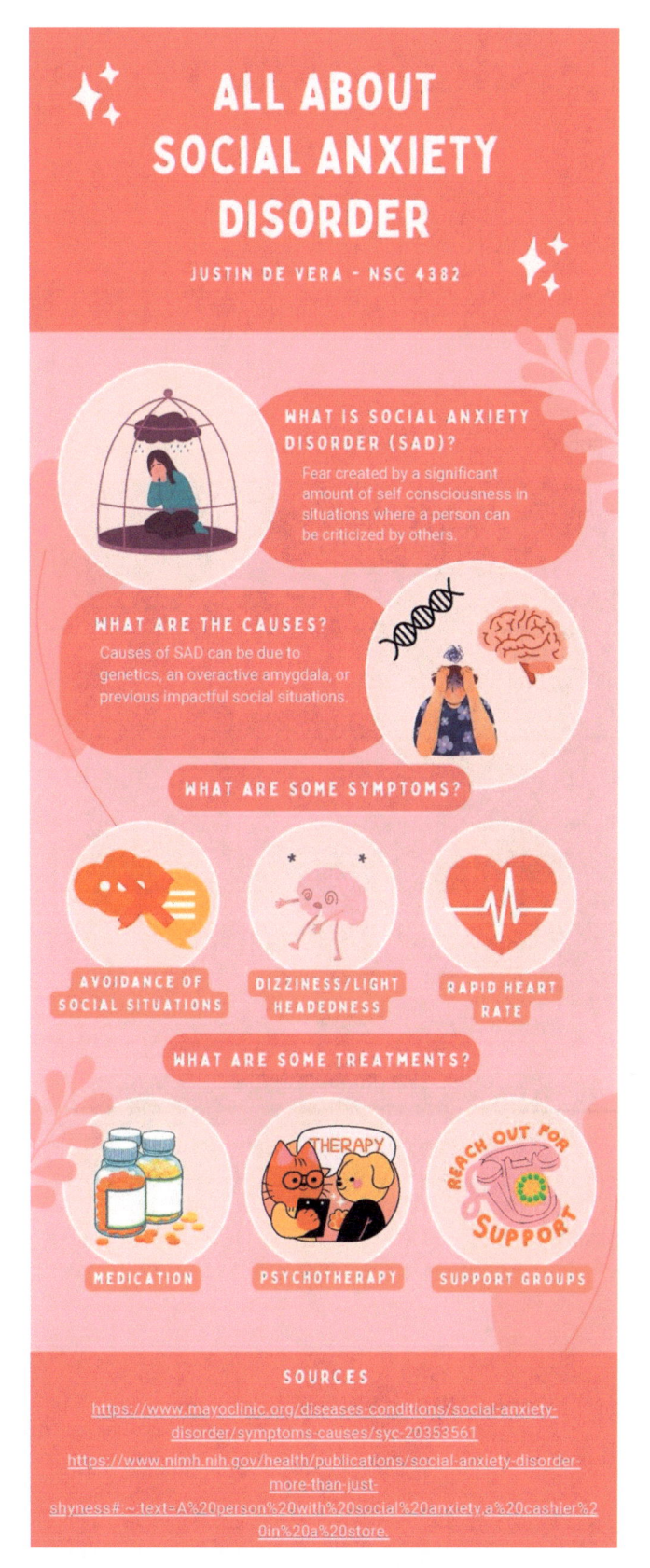

Justin De Vera, Spring 2024

AN INFOGRAPHIC JOURNEY

SOCIAL ANXIETY
By: Karina Slobodkin

WHAT IS SOCIAL ANXIETY?
It is a type of phobia characterized by the excessive fear of being judged and embarrassed in social interactions. It is a from of overwhelming self-consciousness that can decrease a person's quality of life.

FACTORS OF SOCIAL ANXIETY
- Nervousness in front of others (Performance Anxiety)
- Heaviness in chest, sweating, shaking, nausea, etc.
- Difficulty in speaking clearly and loudly
- Feeling of self-consciousness, fear of being judged by others
- Excessive self criticism, negative self-talk, lack of confidence and self esteem

COGNITIVE BEHAVIORAL MODEL
A certain trigger that is perceived to be dangerous can lead to feelings of self-consciousness and cause a fear of judgement and embarrassment. This contributes to feelings of anxiety in social settings.

TRIGGER → Activate Belief & Assumptions → Situation Thought To Be Dangerous → Become Self-Consciousness → Safety Behaviors / Symptoms of Anxiety

Safety behaviors are coping mechanisms to reduce feelings of anxiety and fear. Ex: avoiding eye contact, speaking softly, touching face, etc

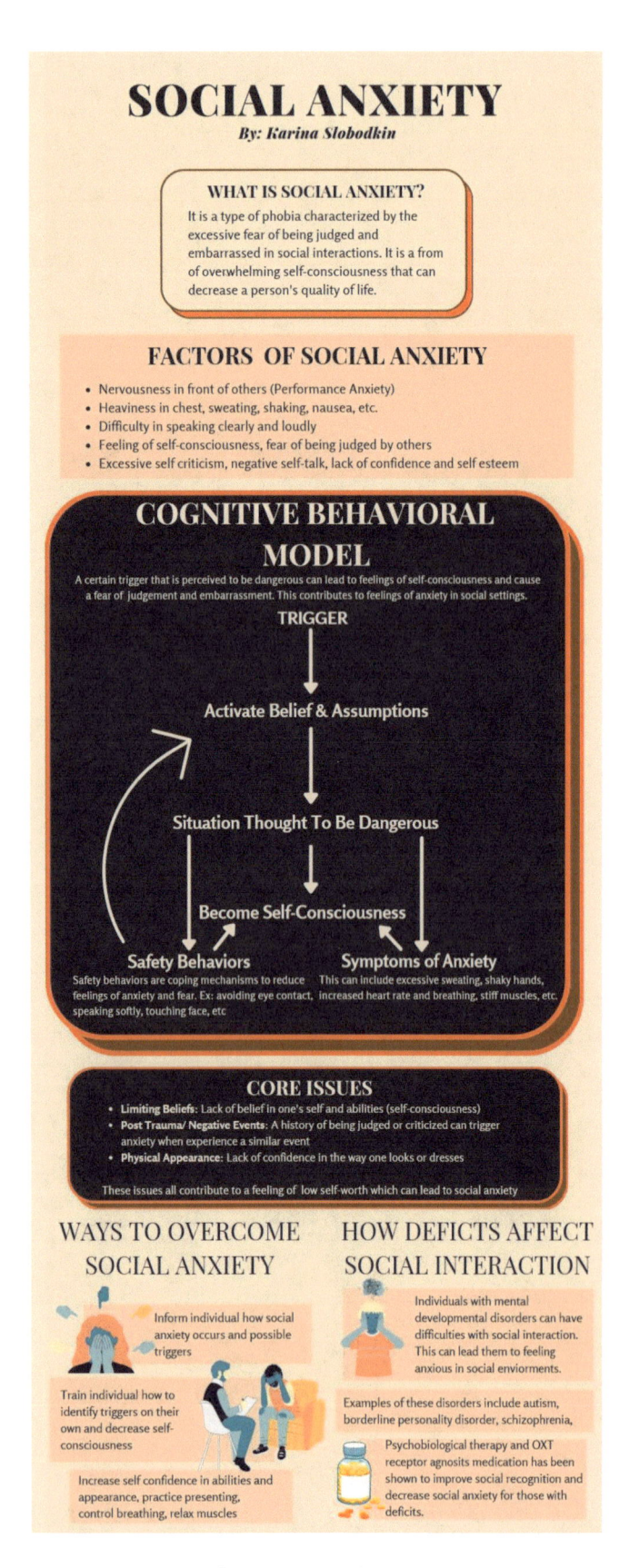

Symptoms of Anxiety: This can include excessive sweating, shaky hands, increased heart rate and breathing, stiff muscles, etc.

CORE ISSUES
- **Limiting Beliefs**: Lack of belief in one's self and abilities (self-consciousness)
- **Post Trauma/ Negative Events**: A history of being judged or criticized can trigger anxiety when experience a similar event
- **Physical Appearance**: Lack of confidence in the way one looks or dresses

These issues all contribute to a feeling of low self-worth which can lead to social anxiety

WAYS TO OVERCOME SOCIAL ANXIETY
- Inform individual how social anxiety occurs and possible triggers
- Train individual how to identify triggers on their own and decrease self-consciousness
- Increase self confidence in abilities and appearance, practice presenting, control breathing, relax muscles

HOW DEFICTS AFFECT SOCIAL INTERACTION
- Individuals with mental developmental disorders can have difficulties with social interaction. This can lead them to feeling anxious in social enviorments.
- Examples of these disorders include autism, borderline personality disorder, schizophrenia,
- Psychobiological therapy and OXT receptor agonists medication has been shown to improve social recognition and decrease social anxiety for those with deficits.

Karina Slobodkin, Spring 2023

Clark and Wells
SOCIAL ANXIETY MODEL

What is social anxiety?

Social anxiety is used to describe the excessive fear, nervousness, and apprehension that people experience in social interactions. It's a form of phobia characterized by overwhelming self-consciousness during ordinary social situations. The anxiety generally stems from the worry of being judged or behaving in a way that would cause embarrassment in front of others.

The Cognitive-Behavioral Model of Social Anxiety

Social situation → Activates beliefs and assumptions → Perceived social danger ↔ Self-consciousness: attention focused on self → Safety behaviors → Somatic and cognitive symptoms

What is the Clark and Wells model of social anxiety?

The Clark and Wells model, shown above, was devised in 1995 and is one of the most common and well supported models of social anxiety. The cognitive behavioral solution to social anxiety is generally based around this model, showing the thought processes, behaviors, and their interactions with one another.

Arshad Manzar, Spring 2024

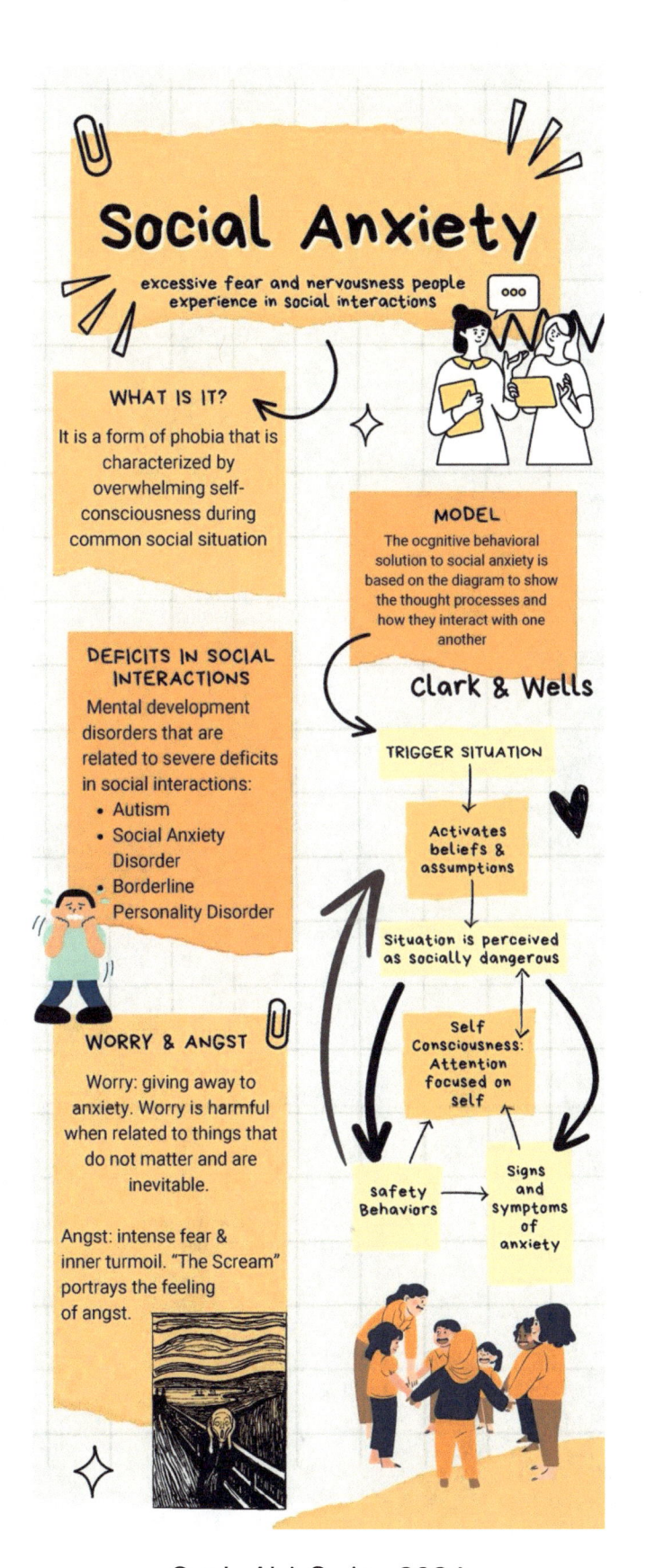

AN INFOGRAPHIC JOURNEY

Social Anxiety

excessive fear and nervousness people experience in social interactions

WHAT IS IT?
It is a form of phobia that is characterized by overwhelming self-consciousness during common social situation

MODEL
The cognitive behavioral solution to social anxiety is based on the diagram to show the thought processes and how they interact with one another

DEFICITS IN SOCIAL INTERACTIONS
Mental development disorders that are related to severe deficits in social interactions:
- Autism
- Social Anxiety Disorder
- Borderline Personality Disorder

Clark & Wells

TRIGGER SITUATION → Activates beliefs & assumptions → Situation is perceived as socially dangerous → Self Consciousness: Attention focused on self → safety Behaviors → Signs and symptoms of anxiety

WORRY & ANGST
Worry: giving away to anxiety. Worry is harmful when related to things that do not matter and are inevitable.

Angst: intense fear & inner turmoil. "The Scream" portrays the feeling of angst.

Syeda Alvi, Spring 2024

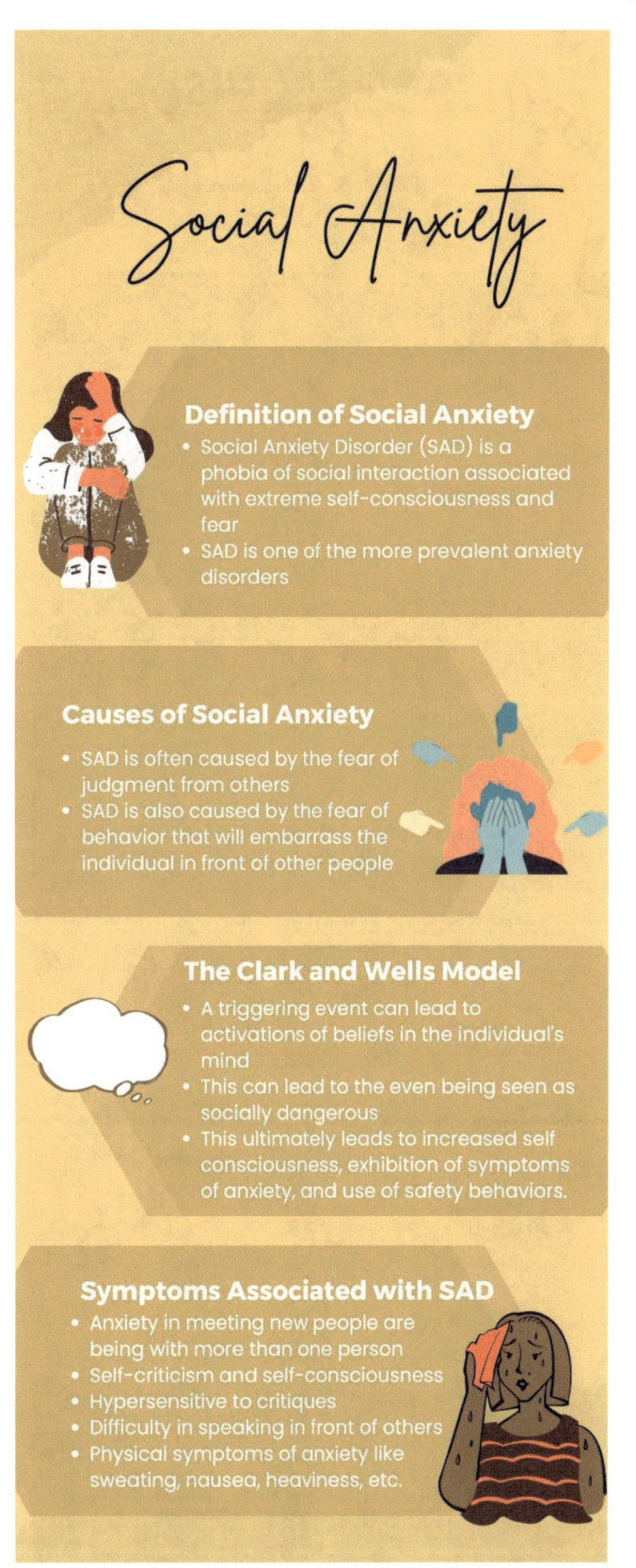

Social Anxiety

Definition of Social Anxiety
- Social Anxiety Disorder (SAD) is a phobia of social interaction associated with extreme self-consciousness and fear
- SAD is one of the more prevalent anxiety disorders

Causes of Social Anxiety
- SAD is often caused by the fear of judgment from others
- SAD is also caused by the fear of behavior that will embarrass the individual in front of other people

The Clark and Wells Model
- A triggering event can lead to activations of beliefs in the individual's mind
- This can lead to the even being seen as socially dangerous
- This ultimately leads to increased self consciousness, exhibition of symptoms of anxiety, and use of safety behaviors.

Symptoms Associated with SAD
- Anxiety in meeting new people are being with more than one person
- Self-criticism and self-consciousness
- Hypersensitive to critiques
- Difficulty in speaking in front of others
- Physical symptoms of anxiety like sweating, nausea, heaviness, etc.

Katelyn Bonvillain, Sping 2023

AN INFOGRAPHIC JOURNEY

SOCIAL ANXIETY DISORDER

What is Social Anxiety Disorder?

Definition

Persistent, excessive fear of being judged by other people or acting in an embarrassing manner in front of them

Symptoms
- Intense anxiety when in social situations
- Hypersensitivity to criticism and excessive self-criticism
- Elevated heart rate, sweating, or nausea when around others
- Difficulty speaking when being watched
- Avoidance of social situations

Statistics

- **12.1%** People with Social Anxiety Disorder
- **8%** Females with Social Anxiety Disorder
- **6.1%** Males with Social Anxiety Disorder
- **29.9%** People with Social Anxiety Disorder that are seriously impaired by the condition

Mechanism of Social Anxiety Disorder

Trigger Situation → Beliefs and Assumptions → Perception of Situation as Dangerous → Signs of Anxiety / Self Consciousness / Safety Behaviors

Statistics from the National Comorbidity Survey Replication. U.S. Department of Health and Human Services. Social Anxiety Disorder. National Institute of Mental Health.

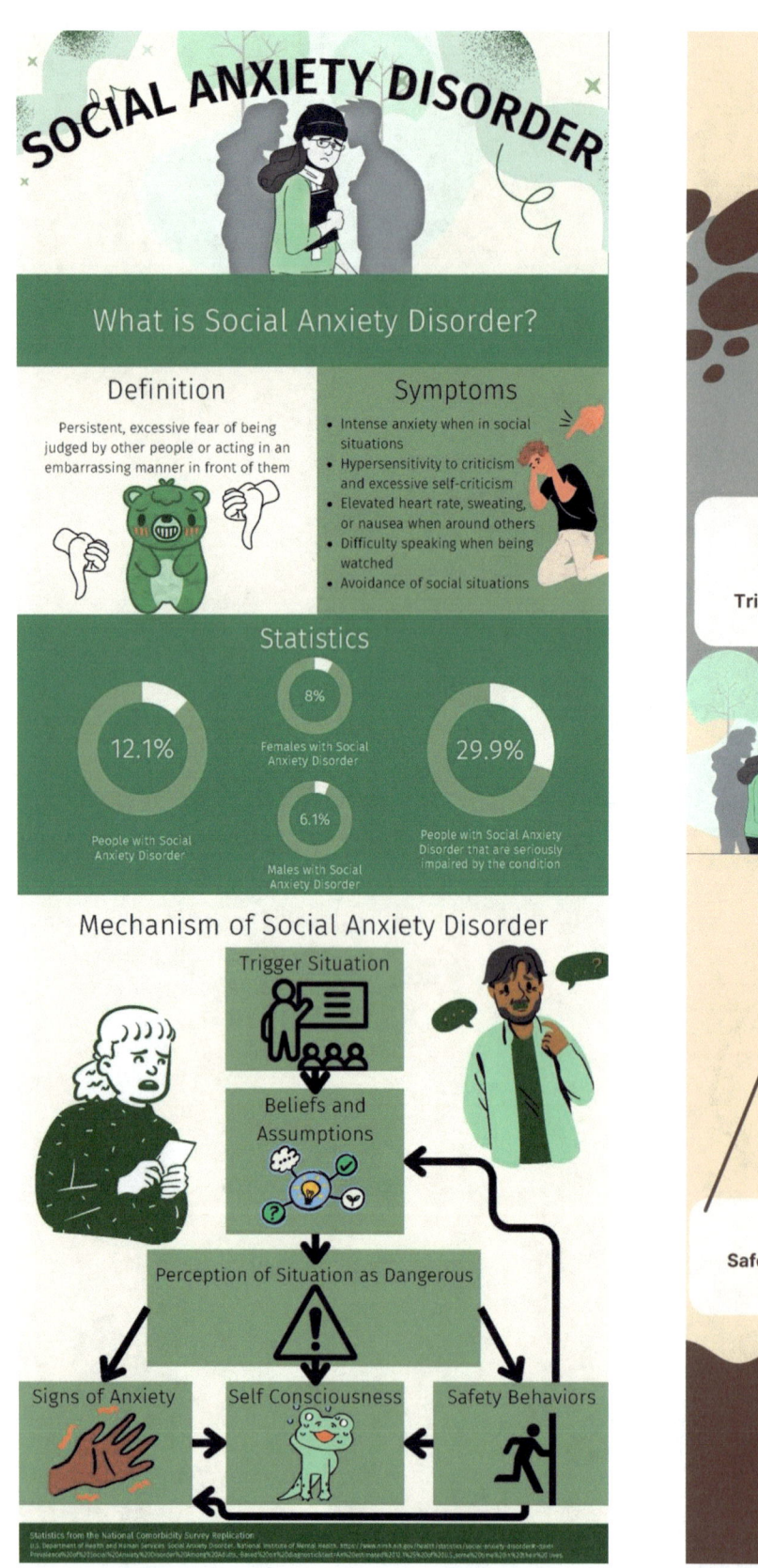

Allyson Macfee, Spring 2024

Social Anxiety

Form of a phobia during social situations causing overwhelming self-consciousness

Symptoms
- Worry of being judged, embarrassed
- Heaviness in chest
- Heart palpitations
- Anxiety about meeting new people
- Excessive self-criticism
- Difficulty in speaking

Trigger situation → Activate beliefs and Assumptions → Social situation perceived as dangerous → Self Consciousness → Safety Behaviors / Signs and Symptoms of Social Anxiety

Clark and Wells Cognitive Behavioral Model 1995

Avalon De Curtis, Spring 2023

AN INFOGRAPHIC JOURNEY

DISSECTING SOCIAL ANXIETY

HUMBLE BEGINNINGS
Social anxiety was first defined as a fear of public speaking, playing the piano, or even just writing (Moller).

WHERE WE ARE NOW
Social anxiety is now described as the excessive, fear experienced by some during social interactions.

WHAT EXACTY IS SOCIAL ANXIETY?
Social anxiety is categorized as a *phobia*. In particular, it is the fear of *embarrassing oneself* during a social interaction. It involves extreme levels of self-consciousness.

TREATMENTS
Cognitive Behavioral Therapy: Working with a therapist to teach you different reactions to situations to help you feel less anxious and fearful (Social)

Medication: Antidepressants and beta blockers can also be helpful in reducing the anxiety felt from social situations, especially when used in conjunction with cognitive behavioral therapy (Social)!

SOURCES
Moller, Aage R. Neurobiology of Fear and Other Emotions. AAGE R MOLLER PUBLISHING, 2019.

"Social Anxiety Disorder: More than Just Shyness." National Institute of Mental Health, U.S. Department of Health and Human Services, www.nimh.nih.gov/health/publications/social-anxiety-disorder-more-than-just-shyness#:~:text=Social%20anxiety%20disorder%20is%20generally,the%20best%20treatment%20for%20you. Accessed 17 Sept. 2023.

Abhi Patel, Fall 2023

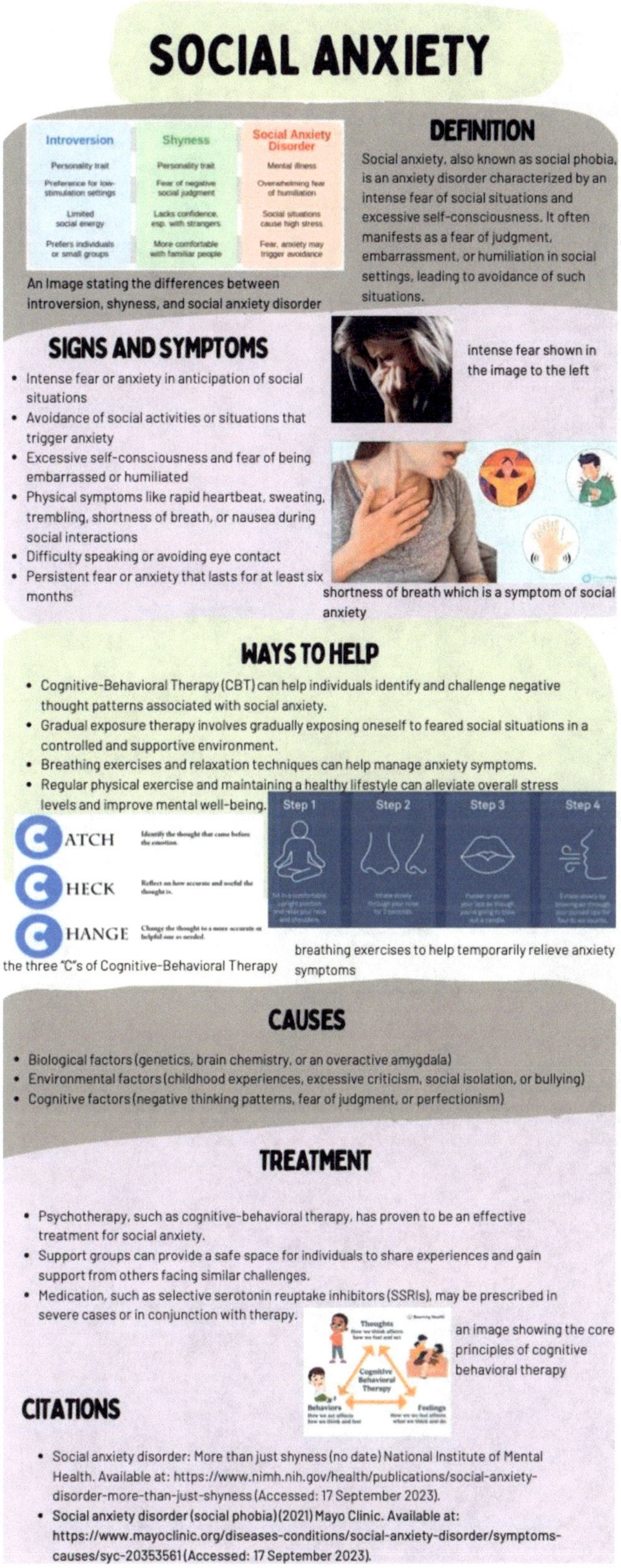

SOCIAL ANXIETY

DEFINITION
Social anxiety, also known as social phobia, is an anxiety disorder characterized by an intense fear of social situations and excessive self-consciousness. It often manifests as a fear of judgment, embarrassment, or humiliation in social settings, leading to avoidance of such situations.

An Image stating the differences between introversion, shyness, and social anxiety disorder

SIGNS AND SYMPTOMS
- Intense fear or anxiety in anticipation of social situations
- Avoidance of social activities or situations that trigger anxiety
- Excessive self-consciousness and fear of being embarrassed or humiliated
- Physical symptoms like rapid heartbeat, sweating, trembling, shortness of breath, or nausea during social interactions
- Difficulty speaking or avoiding eye contact
- Persistent fear or anxiety that lasts for at least six months

intense fear shown in the image to the left

shortness of breath which is a symptom of social anxiety

WAYS TO HELP
- Cognitive-Behavioral Therapy (CBT) can help individuals identify and challenge negative thought patterns associated with social anxiety.
- Gradual exposure therapy involves gradually exposing oneself to feared social situations in a controlled and supportive environment.
- Breathing exercises and relaxation techniques can help manage anxiety symptoms.
- Regular physical exercise and maintaining a healthy lifestyle can alleviate overall stress levels and improve mental well-being.

the three "C"s of Cognitive-Behavioral Therapy

breathing exercises to help temporarily relieve anxiety symptoms

CAUSES
- Biological factors (genetics, brain chemistry, or an overactive amygdala)
- Environmental factors (childhood experiences, excessive criticism, social isolation, or bullying)
- Cognitive factors (negative thinking patterns, fear of judgment, or perfectionism)

TREATMENT
- Psychotherapy, such as cognitive-behavioral therapy, has proven to be an effective treatment for social anxiety.
- Support groups can provide a safe space for individuals to share experiences and gain support from others facing similar challenges.
- Medication, such as selective serotonin reuptake inhibitors (SSRIs), may be prescribed in severe cases or in conjunction with therapy.

an image showing the core principles of cognitive behavioral therapy

CITATIONS
- Social anxiety disorder: More than just shyness (no date) National Institute of Mental Health. Available at: https://www.nimh.nih.gov/health/publications/social-anxiety-disorder-more-than-just-shyness (Accessed: 17 September 2023).
- Social anxiety disorder (social phobia) (2021) Mayo Clinic. Available at: https://www.mayoclinic.org/diseases-conditions/social-anxiety-disorder/symptoms-causes/syc-20353561 (Accessed: 17 September 2023).

Anisha Reddy, Fall 2023

AN INFOGRAPHIC JOURNEY

Life With Social Anxiety

Social Anxiety Defined
A phobia that is defined by the extreme self-consciousness during common social interactions. The worry of being judged or embarrassed in front of peers or friends.

The Trigger
Many individuals with social anxiety have distinct social situations that cause the triggering of the overwhelming anxiety. Such triggers could include public presentation, meeting new people, or being the center of attention.

Signs and Symptoms
Heaviness in the chest, sweating, stuttering over words, nausea, and an uncomfortable feeling in the stomach. In extreme cases, heart palpitations and low blood pressure can be observed.

Fighting Social Anxiety
Most importantly is first recognizing the problem and deciding to address it. As with other anxiety disorders, avoiding the problem only makes it worse. Restructuring the confidence of one's self and ability in combination with exposure therapy can have a beneficial effect.

Austin Sprouse, Spring 2024

SOCIAL ANXIETY 101

1 WHAT IS SOCIAL ANXIETY?
A type of phobia characterized by excessive self-consciousness in everyday social situations. Social anxiety is typically caused by a fear of being judged by friends or peers or behaving in a way that would cause embarrassment in front of others.

2 IS SOCIAL ANXIETY A TYPE OF FEAR?
Anxiety has many similarities with fear, but they are, in fact, two independent entities with their own definitions. Anxiety is characterized as a mental state that arises from general and non-specific stimuli that are perceived as potentially threatening in the future. This perception often results in an anxious mood accompanied by an increased level of arousal and vigilance which persist for an extended time when taken to an extreme.

3 SOCIAL GENETICS?
Some anxiety disorders have been associated with the stress of various kinds. Many studies have provided substantial evidence that stress affecting epigenetics creates anxiety diseases, especially regarding the effect on the HPA axis. Anxiety can have many causes, including genetic or environmental stimuli or circumstances, but it also occurs without any known cause.

4 SOCIAL ANXIETY, KNOW THE SIGNS
Social anxiety can be recognized by symptoms such as excessive self-criticism after social interactions and apprehension in the presence of more than one person: sinking feeling, heart palpitations, sweating, nausea, difficulty speaking, and stuttering in social engagements. Social anxiety core issues have reportedly been linked to self-image, limiting beliefs, and past traumatic experiences.

Nicolas Gambardella, Spring 2023

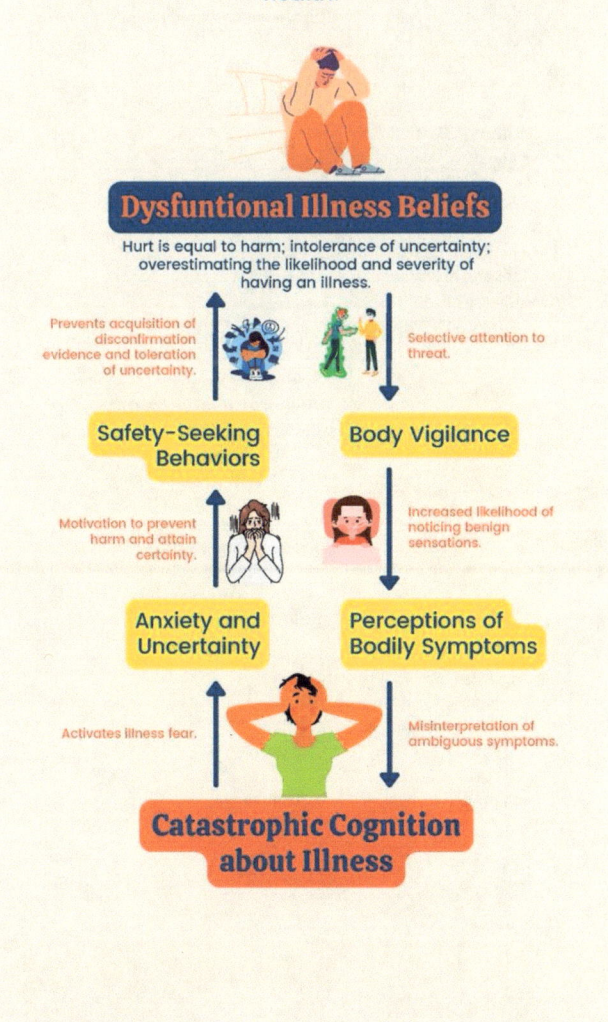

Hypochondriasis

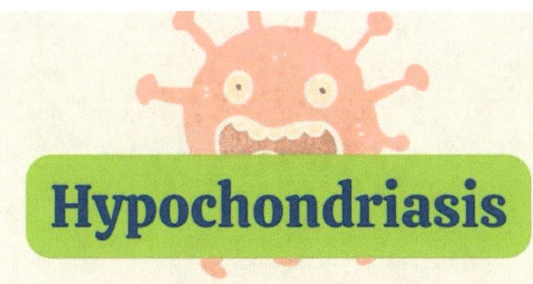

Hypochondriasis is a form of anxiety.

It is the unrealistic fear of having a severe medical condition that can last a long time, involving excessive worrying about having a severe illness without any signs or objective indications of something being wrong with the person's health.

Dysfuntional Illness Beliefs

Hurt is equal to harm; intolerance of uncertainty; overestimating the likelihood and severity of having an illness.

- Prevents acquisition of disconfirmation evidence and toleration of uncertainty.
- Selective attention to threat.

Safety-Seeking Behaviors
Motivation to prevent harm and attain certainty.

Body Vigilance
Increased likelihood of noticing benign sensations.

Anxiety and Uncertainty
Activates illness fear.

Perceptions of Bodily Symptoms
Misinterpretation of ambiguous symptoms.

Catastrophic Cognition about Illness

Arshad Manzar, Spring 2024

ILLNESS ANXIETY DISORDER
(HYPOCHONDRIASIS)

WHAT IS IT?
A long-term condition marked by the strong belief or excessive worry of having a severe illness, despite an absence of signs or physical symptoms.

SYMPTOMS
Preoccupation with having a severe illness based on normal body sensation, body vigilance, avoidance of places and people for fear of health risks, finding no reassurance from doctors or negative tests, excess distress that impairs function

POSSIBLE CAUSES
history of severe illness in childhood, having a family that may worry too much about health, beliefs or difficulty tolerating uncertainty of body sensation driving evidence-seeking behaviors

TREATMENT
Cognitive behavioral therapy, medications such as SSRIs, lifestyle changes or stress management techniques

Minaal Atif, Spring 2024

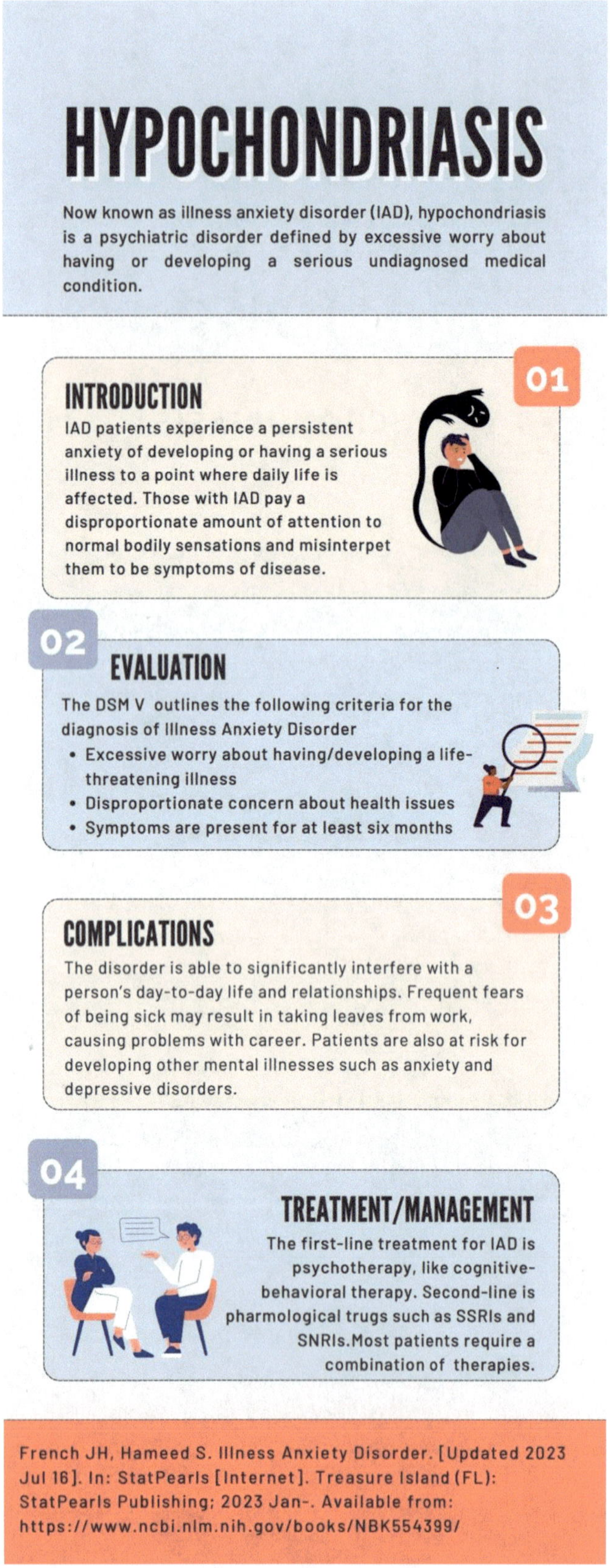

HYPOCHONDRIASIS

Now known as illness anxiety disorder (IAD), hypochondriasis is a psychiatric disorder defined by excessive worry about having or developing a serious undiagnosed medical condition.

01 INTRODUCTION
IAD patients experience a persistent anxiety of developing or having a serious illness to a point where daily life is affected. Those with IAD pay a disproportionate amount of attention to normal bodily sensations and misinterpet them to be symptoms of disease.

02 EVALUATION
The DSM V outlines the following criteria for the diagnosis of Illness Anxiety Disorder
- Excessive worry about having/developing a life-threatening illness
- Disproportionate concern about health issues
- Symptoms are present for at least six months

03 COMPLICATIONS
The disorder is able to significantly interfere with a person's day-to-day life and relationships. Frequent fears of being sick may result in taking leaves from work, causing problems with career. Patients are also at risk for developing other mental illnesses such as anxiety and depressive disorders.

04 TREATMENT/MANAGEMENT
The first-line treatment for IAD is psychotherapy, like cognitive-behavioral therapy. Second-line is pharmological trugs such as SSRIs and SNRIs. Most patients require a combination of therapies.

French JH, Hameed S. Illness Anxiety Disorder. [Updated 2023 Jul 16]. In: StatPearls [Internet]. Treasure Island (FL): StatPearls Publishing; 2023 Jan-. Available from: https://www.ncbi.nlm.nih.gov/books/NBK554399/

Ashley Tran, Fall 2023

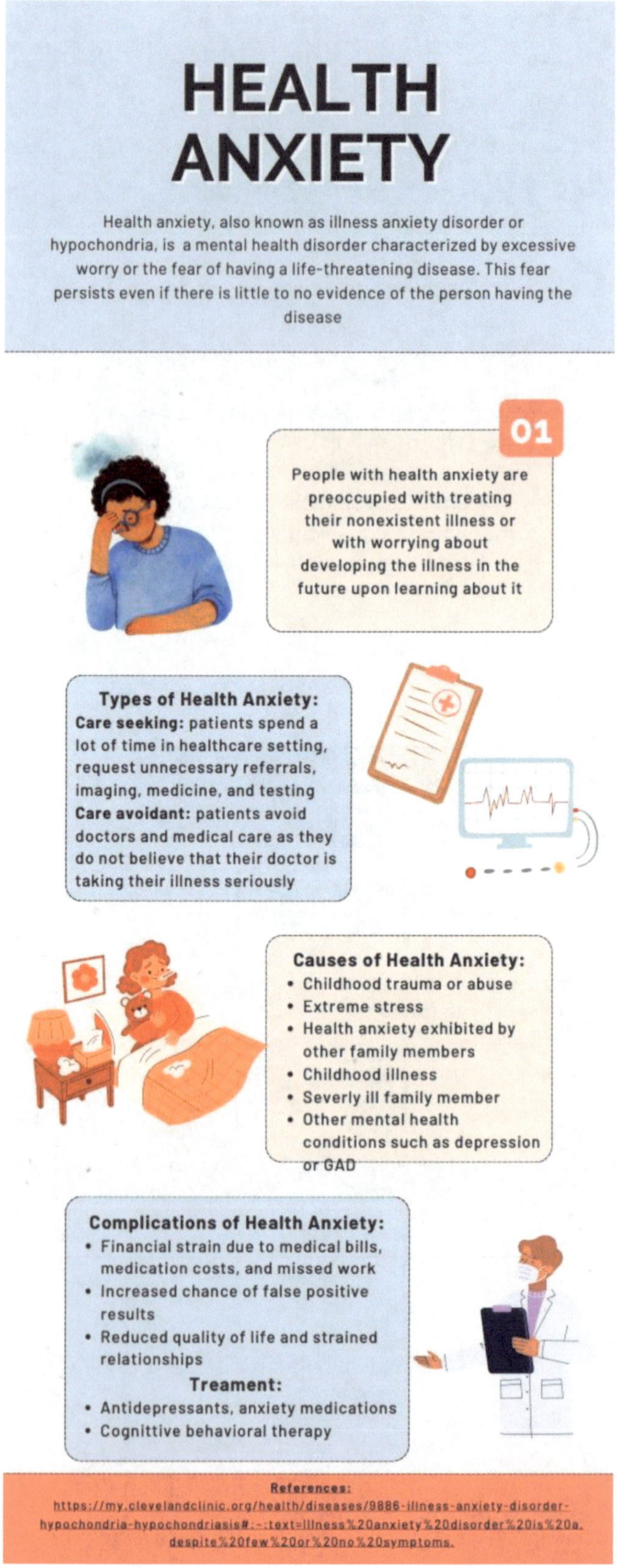

HEALTH ANXIETY

Health anxiety, also known as illness anxiety disorder or hypochondria, is a mental health disorder characterized by excessive worry or the fear of having a life-threatening disease. This fear persists even if there is little to no evidence of the person having the disease

01
People with health anxiety are preoccupied with treating their nonexistent illness or with worrying about developing the illness in the future upon learning about it

Types of Health Anxiety:
Care seeking: patients spend a lot of time in healthcare setting, request unnecessary referrals, imaging, medicine, and testing
Care avoidant: patients avoid doctors and medical care as they do not believe that their doctor is taking their illness seriously

Causes of Health Anxiety:
- Childhood trauma or abuse
- Extreme stress
- Health anxiety exhibited by other family members
- Childhood illness
- Severly ill family member
- Other mental health conditions such as depression or GAD

Complications of Health Anxiety:
- Financial strain due to medical bills, medication costs, and missed work
- Increased chance of false positive results
- Reduced quality of life and strained relationships

Treament:
- Antidepressants, anxiety medications
- Cognittive behavioral therapy

References:
https://my.clevelandclinic.org/health/diseases/9886-illness-anxiety-disorder-hypochondria-hypochondriasis#:~:text=Illness%20anxiety%20disorder%20is%20a.despite%20few%20or%20no%20symptoms.

Sahiti Pydimarri, Fall 2023

AN INFOGRAPHIC JOURNEY

MYSOPHOBIA
FEAR OF GERMS

Mysophobia is the extreme fear of germs and contamination. "Germaphobes" have mysophobia.

ABOUT MYSOPHOBIA

Mysophobia commonly affects individuals with OCD due to a nature of **repetitive and irrational thoughts**. People with mysophobia may also be affected by: ataxophobia (fear of untidiness), microphobia (fear of small things) and more.

CAUSES OF MYSOPHOBIA

Genetics can make people predisposed to having certain phobias. Environmental stimuli of an emotional trauma or physical encounter can also trigger it.

DO YOU HAVE MYSOPHOBIA?

If you experience **discomfort and a sense of worry** about coming into contact with: other people's body fluids, dust, dirt, mold, contaminated food, unclean surfaces and objects.... you may be affected.

SYMPTOMS AND BEHAVIORS
- Excessive handwashing
- Wearing gloves to prevent contact with germs
- Avoiding social interactions
- Taking multiple showers a day
- Experiencing brain fog, irritability, restlessness, sweating and shaking

YOU CAN OVERCOME YOUR FEARS!

If you feel affected by Mysophobia, there is no need to let fear dictate your life. There are ways to overcome these worries. Talk to your doctor about **exposure therapy**, to find the underlying reasons behind your fears. **Medication** and **stress reduction** such as yoga or meditation can also help deal with symptoms.

FOR MORE INFORMATION VISIT:
https://my.clevelandclinic.org/health/diseases/22436-mysophobia-germophobia

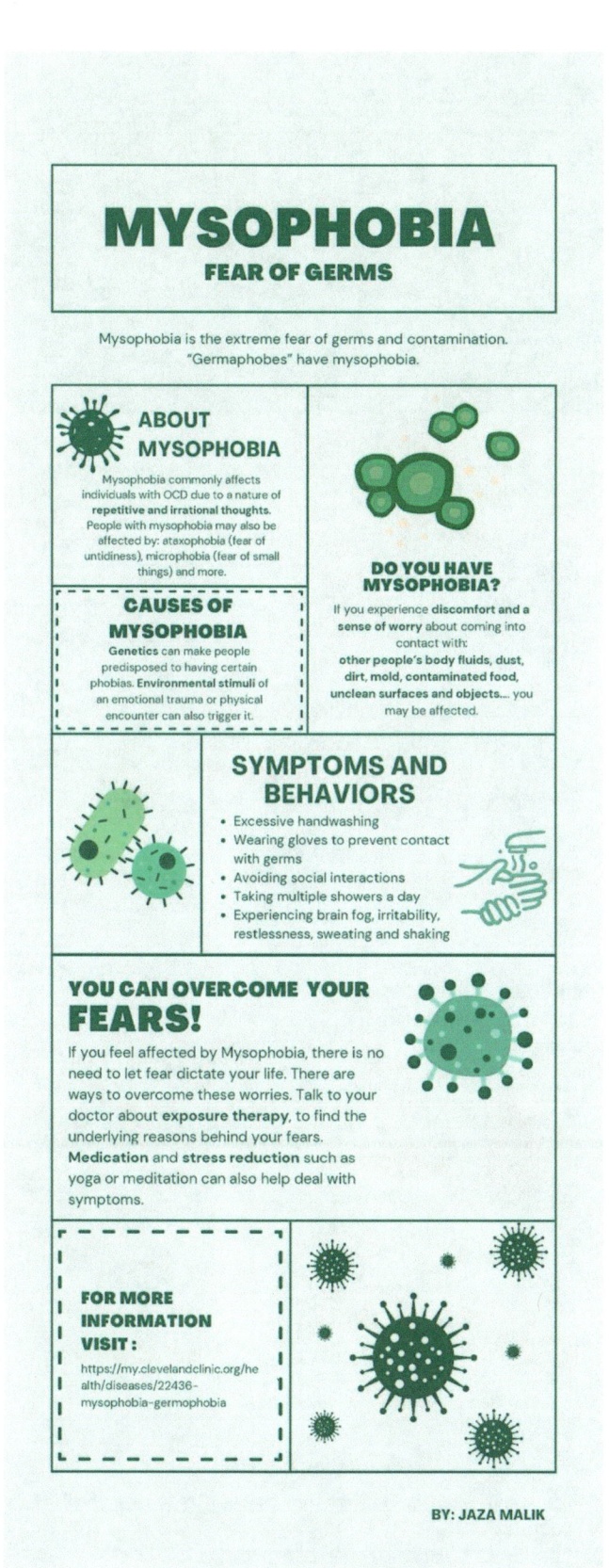

BY: JAZA MALIK

Jaza Malik, Spring 2024

Pranavi Maddipatla

Types of Phobias

ACCORDING TO THE DSM-5

What is a phobia?

Phobias are a type of anxiety disorders characterized by persistent, irrational fear that is commonly excessive and overwhelming.

Specific phobias:

Specific phobias are associated with a particular object or situation, such as clusters of small holes (trypophobia) or small spaces (claustrophobia).

Social phobia:

Social phobia is also known as social anxiety disorder and is often caused by a fear of being negatively scrutinized by others in any social situation.

Agoraphobia:

Agoraphobia is the fear of entering situations that may induce a panic attack, and is normally developed after having experienced panic attacks previously. It often results in people choosing to stay at home to remain "safe" rather than risk going outside.

References
Digital, A. (2022). Fear vs. Phobia. The Recovery Village Drug and Alcohol Rehab. https://www.therecoveryvillage.com/mental-health/phobias/fear-vs-phobia/

Pranavi Maddipatla, Fall 2023

AN INFOGRAPHIC JOURNEY

PHOBIAS
THE FEAR OF MATTERS THAT CAN'T CAUSE ANY HARM

1. ARACHNOPHOBIA
Arachnophobia is an intense and irrational fear of spiders. People with this type of phobia avoid places or situations in which they might experience a spider, a spider web or see pictures of them.

2. TRYPANOPHOBIA
Trypanophobia is the extreme fear of needles in the medical setting. Injection phobia may prevent people from seeking medical care or avoiding medical procedures.

3. ACROPHOBIA
People with acrophobia experience intense and unreasonable fear when they think of tall heights or are positioned at a significant height.

4. PTEROMERHANOPHOBIA
Aerophobia is an extreme fear of flying in an airplane. An aerophobic may have a fear of different aspects of flying, such as takeoff, landing, or being stuck in the plane.

5. MYSOPHOBIA
Mysophobia is an extreme fear of germs. It causes an overwhelming obsession with contamination. People with mysophobia may also suffer from obsessive-compulsive disorder (OCD).

6. CYNOPHOBIA
Cynophobia is the overwhelming fear of dogs. People with this anxiety disorder feel intense fear and anxiety when they think about, see or encounter a dog.

7. ORNITHOPHOBIA
Cynophobia is the extreme fear of dogs. Those who suffer from this phobia may feel as though birds are threatening them and fear for their safety when they see birds.

ALL ABOUT MYSOPHOBIA
JUSTIN DE VERA – NSC 4382

What is Mysophobia?
Mysophobia is the fear of germs. It can change a person's routine to the point where they try to actively avoid contact with germs.

What disorders/conditions is it connected to?
- Obsessive Compulsive Disorder (OCD)
- Anxiety
- Past impactful events involving germs

What symptoms are associated with it?
- Rapid heart beat (tachycardia)
- Sweating
- Irritable mood
- Excessive washing of hands

How is it treated?
- Therapy (cognitive behavioral, exposure)
- Relaxation techniques (such as yoga)

Sources Used
https://my.clevelandclinic.org/health/diseases/22436-mysophobia-germophobia
https://www.osmosis.org/answers/mysophobia

Valentina Grijalba, Spring 2024    Justin De Vera, Spring 2024

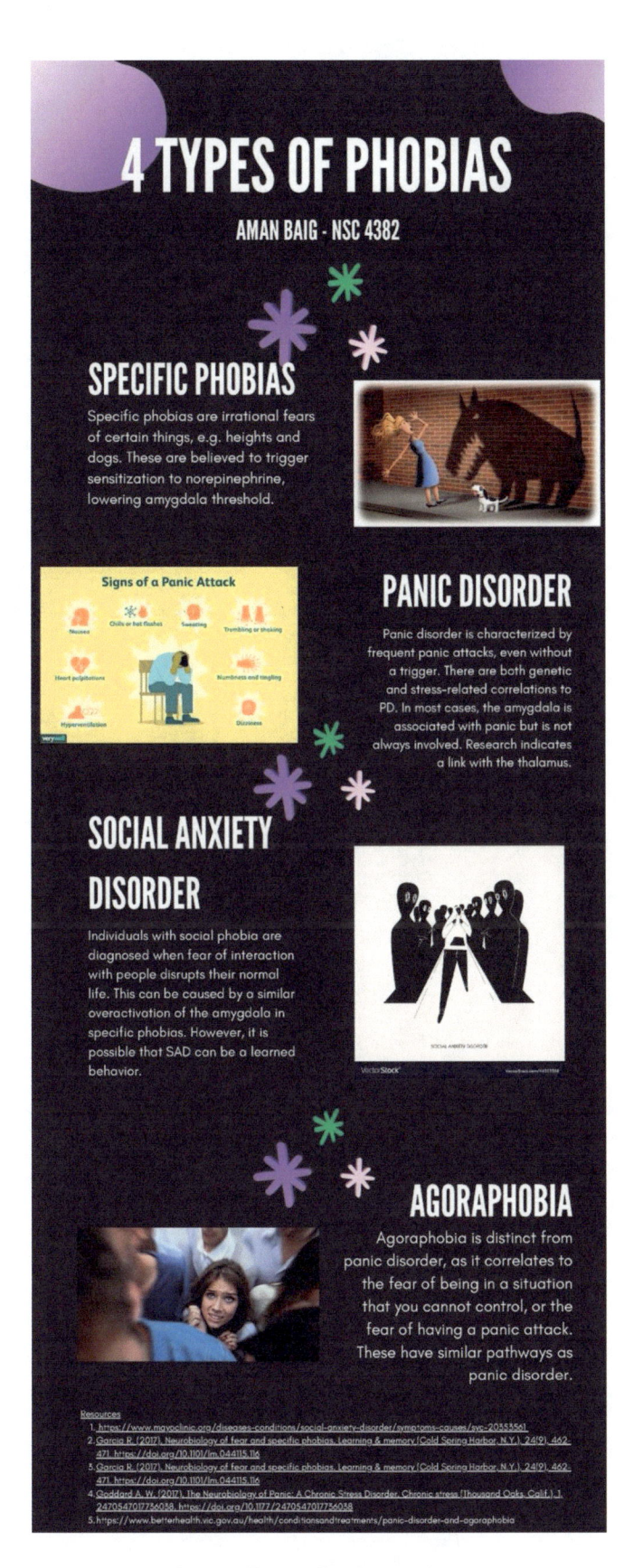

4 TYPES OF PHOBIAS
AMAN BAIG - NSC 4382

SPECIFIC PHOBIAS
Specific phobias are irrational fears of certain things, e.g. heights and dogs. These are believed to trigger sensitization to norepinephrine, lowering amygdala threshold.

PANIC DISORDER
Panic disorder is characterized by frequent panic attacks, even without a trigger. There are both genetic and stress-related correlations to PD. In most cases, the amygdala is associated with panic but is not always involved. Research indicates a link with the thalamus.

SOCIAL ANXIETY DISORDER
Individuals with social phobia are diagnosed when fear of interaction with people disrupts their normal life. This can be caused by a similar overactivation of the amygdala in specific phobias. However, it is possible that SAD can be a learned behavior.

AGORAPHOBIA
Agoraphobia is distinct from panic disorder, as it correlates to the fear of being in a situation that you cannot control, or the fear of having a panic attack. These have similar pathways as panic disorder.

Aman Baig, Spring 2024

HANA AHMAD - SEPTEMBER 2023
Common Phobias

Arachnophobia
- This is a fear of spiders
- Someone afraid of spiders might avoid doing outdoor activities or going outside

Mysophobia
- This is a fear of germs
- Especially during and after the COVID-19 pandemic, this fear is not irrational
- Can cause excessive hand-washing and avoidance of places perceived as "dirty"

Agoraphobia
- This is a fear of being in situations that cause anxiety or panic
- People with this fear may avoid new or unfamiliar situations or crowded places where escape isn't easy

Acrophobia
- This is a fear of heights
- People with this fear may avoid doing activities like ziplining, flying in planes, rock climbing, or mountain hiking

Treating phobias
- As you can see, severe phobias can prevent someone from enjoying life and trying new experiences
- Exposure therapy is one of the most effective treatments, involving gradual exposure to feared object which reduces the fear response over time

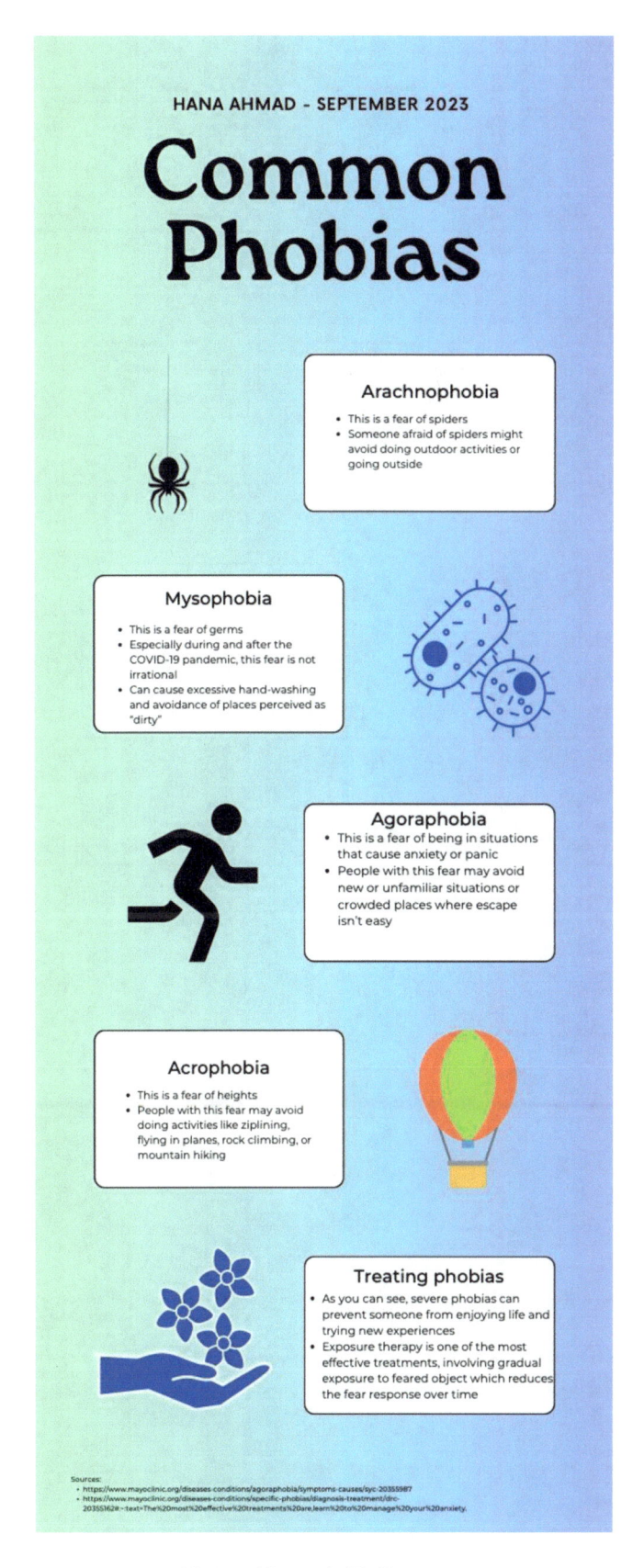

Hana Ahmad, Fall 2023

AN INFOGRAPHIC JOURNEY

CHAPTER 7

Emotions

Theory of Emotions

By Naomi Kurian & Madhav Bhatt, Spring 2024

The six universal emotions, surprise, anger, fear, sadness, and disgust, are experienced by about 90% of the population, according to the National Institutes of Health (NIH). These emotions, also known as "archetypical emotions," are not bound by cultural or national boundaries. They are a shared human experience connecting us all. However, how exactly are these emotions formed? How does our biological body prompt such an emotional response to life events? Since the late 1800s, psychologists have been aiming to find answers to these questions with four notable theories: James-Lange theory, Cannon-Bard theory, Lazarus Appraisal theory, and Schacter-Singer's Two-Factor theory. Each of these theories has various similarities and differences in their perspectives. However, each one strives to hypothesize potential pathways our minds and bodies use to turn stimuli into neural reactions.

The James-Lange theory was the first theory of emotion proposed independently by psychologist William James in 1884 and physiologist Carl Lange in 1888. In summary, this theory states that emotions occur due to physiological reactions to an event. For example, imagine you are hiking through the woods when a big brown bear suddenly encounters you. The James-Lange theory suggests that the next event would be that your body would physically react to seeing the bear through increased heart rate, increased breathing, sweating profusely, and tensing of muscles. Following these physical responses, your brain interprets and experiences these reactions as an emotion. In this case, that emotion is expressed as extreme and intense fear. So, the James-Lange theory suggests that if your body could not switch to fight or flight mode upon seeing the threat, it would be unable to produce fear as an emotion as the unconscious physical reaction needs to be interpreted first. This theory aligns with bottom-up processing, focusing on our peripheral perspective to form a concept and express the feeling.

On the other hand, the Cannon-Bard theory was formed cooperatively by Walter Cannon and Philip Bard several decades later with a different perspective on the formation of emotions. The theory is different in that emotions co-occur with physical responses. For example, an emotion-inducing stimulus, such as hearing a loud noise, is sent to the brain for processing. As mentioned earlier, this event triggers two processes: the autonomic nervous system produces bodily reactions, and the sensory signal is relayed to form an emotion. The theory suggests that two processes occur parallelly rather than following one after the other, meaning that one does not necessarily influence the other. This differs from the James-Lange theory, which views bodily arousal as happening first, leading to the experience of the emotion from interpreting those physiological changes. On the contrary, the Cannon-Bard theory suggests that emotions could arise from cognitive factors and brain activity alone, even without physiological arousal as a reaction to events.

Developed in the 1960s by psychologist Richard Lazarus, Lazarus' Appraisal Theory promotes a cognitive approach to understanding emotions, emphasizing that they stem not merely from physical reactions but from our mental interpretations and evaluations. This theory illustrates that different people can experience various emotions in response to the same event depending on their interpretations. For example, if two individuals encounter a snake while walking in a forest, one might react with fear, while the other finds it harmless or intriguing, feeling curious instead. Lazarus' Appraisal Theory attributes this variance to past personal experiences, cultural backgrounds, and individual personality traits. Essentially, there is an interplay between all these experiences and events, which leads to the assessment of perceived threats, causing an emotional response along with a physiological one. This theory underscores the significance of personal meaning in emotional experiences and highlights how closely our emotions are linked to our cognitive processes.

Psychologists Stanley Schachter and Jerome E. Singer proposed the Schachter-Singer Two-Factor Theory in 1962. According to this model, emotions are experienced only when a physiological response is cognitively interpreted in the context of the environment. For instance, if your heart pounds and your palms sweat during a job interview, you will most likely label the physiological arousal as anxiety. However, the same physiological responses experienced on a date might be interpreted as excitement. Cognition is a crucial component of the Schachter-Singer Two Factor Theory and the Lazarus Theory, but there is a distinction between the two theories. Like in the name, the Two-factor theory suggests that two factors elicit an emotional response. The cognitive processing of a physiological stimulus leads to an emotion. This differs from Lazarus' Appraisal Theory because cognition completely dominates this theory, where cognition decides an emotional response and a physiological reaction. The Schachter-Singer Theory essentially suggests that the same physiological states can be distinguished into different emotions based on cognitive context, emphasizing the complexity of how emotions are formed.

In conclusion, human emotions require a nuanced exploration of various theories that portray the complex interplay between physiological responses, cognitive methods, and emotional studies. The James-Lange theory shows that emotions derive from physiological responses to stimuli, emphasizing the significance of physiological reactions in shaping our emotional states. In comparison, the Cannon-Bard Theory argues that emotional studies and physiological reactions occur concurrently, highlighting the mind's position in triggering emotions independently of physical responses. In a cognitive approach, Lazarus' Appraisal Theory shows that emotions are shaped by our opinions and interpretations of occasions, underscoring the effect of personal judgments on emotional responses. Similarly, the Schachter-Singer Two-Factor Theory integrates physiological and cognitive aspects, explaining that emotions result from each physical arousal and the contextual interpretation of these reactions. Overall, these theories provide a comprehensive understanding of the causes of emotions. Together, they show that feelings are not simply universal experiences but are shaped through individual factors. Each principle contributes crucial insights, advocating a holistic understanding of human feelings.

References

1. Møller, A., & Moller, A.R. (2019). Neurobiology of Fear, Anxiety and Other Emotions. Independently Published.
2. Trampe, D., Quoidbach, J., & Taquet, M. (2015). Emotions in Everyday Life. *PloS one*, *10*(12), e0145450. https://doi.org/10.1371/journal.pone.0145450.

AN INFOGRAPHIC JOURNEY

WHAT IS EMOTION?

Emotions can be described as a strong feeling, or a complex experience and affective state of consciousness that also influences bodily sensation and behavior.

01 Archetypical Emotions
The archetypical emotions, or the primary emotions, are surprise, happiness, sadness, afraid (fear), anger, and disgust.

02 Bodily Expressions of Emotions
Emotions can be triggered by signals in the environment and therefore affect many different bodily functions. For example, we may experience butterflies in our stomach, quicker breathing, and feel jittery when we are excited or anxious; light and energized when we are happy; heavy, tired, and slow when we are sad; and tense and energized when we are angry.

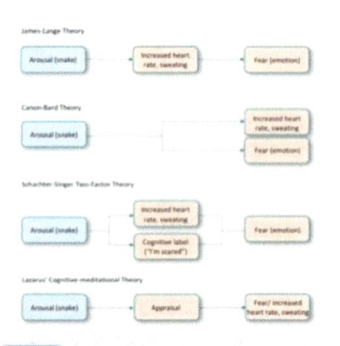

03 Theories of Emotions
The oldest theory of emotion is the James-Lange Theory. This theory states that emotions are created after an event causes arousal and interpretation. On the other hand, the Cannon-Bard Theory assumes that the event simultaneously creates arousal and emotions. In the Schachter-Singer Two-Factor Theory, it states that emotions are based off physiological arousal and a cognitive label. As for the Lazarus' Cognitive-meditational Theory, it states that upon encountering an event, a person will go through appraisal to determine if it is a potential threat, and if they are able to manage and mitigate the situation. After this appraisal, emotions occur.

04 Love and Hate
Love and hate can be regarded as kinds of emotions. Love is a passionate relationship, while hate is a passionate and robust form of aversion or dislike. Not everyone loves or hates the same things. Hate can be related to fear, and can be regarded as different forms of phobia.

Sources:
Free design tool: Presentations, video, social media | CANVA. Canva. (n.d.). https://www.canva.com/
Møller, A. R. (2019). Neurobiology of Fear and other Emotions. Aage R Møller Publishing.

Tiffany Nouanesengsy, Fall 2023

EMOTIONS

WHAT ARE EMOTIONS?

Emotion: an affective state of consciousness. Different professionals may define this word differently. For example, a **psychologist** might focus on *feelings*, while a **neuroscientist** might focus on the *areas of the brain* responsible for emotion.

EXPRESSIONS OF EMOTIONS

When we feel:

Happy:
- light
- energized

Sad:
- slow
- tired

Anxious/Excited:
- jittery
- quicker breaths

Angry:
- tense
- energized

When emotions are triggered, the body can express these emotions through various functions/systems. Many bodily reactions can have adverse effects if over-triggered.

ARCHETYPAL EMOTIONS

Happy | Sad | Disgust
Angry | Afraid | Surprise

Archetypal emotions refer to the six universally agreed upon primary/basic emotions.

Infographic by Myan Lam

Myan Lam, Spring 2023

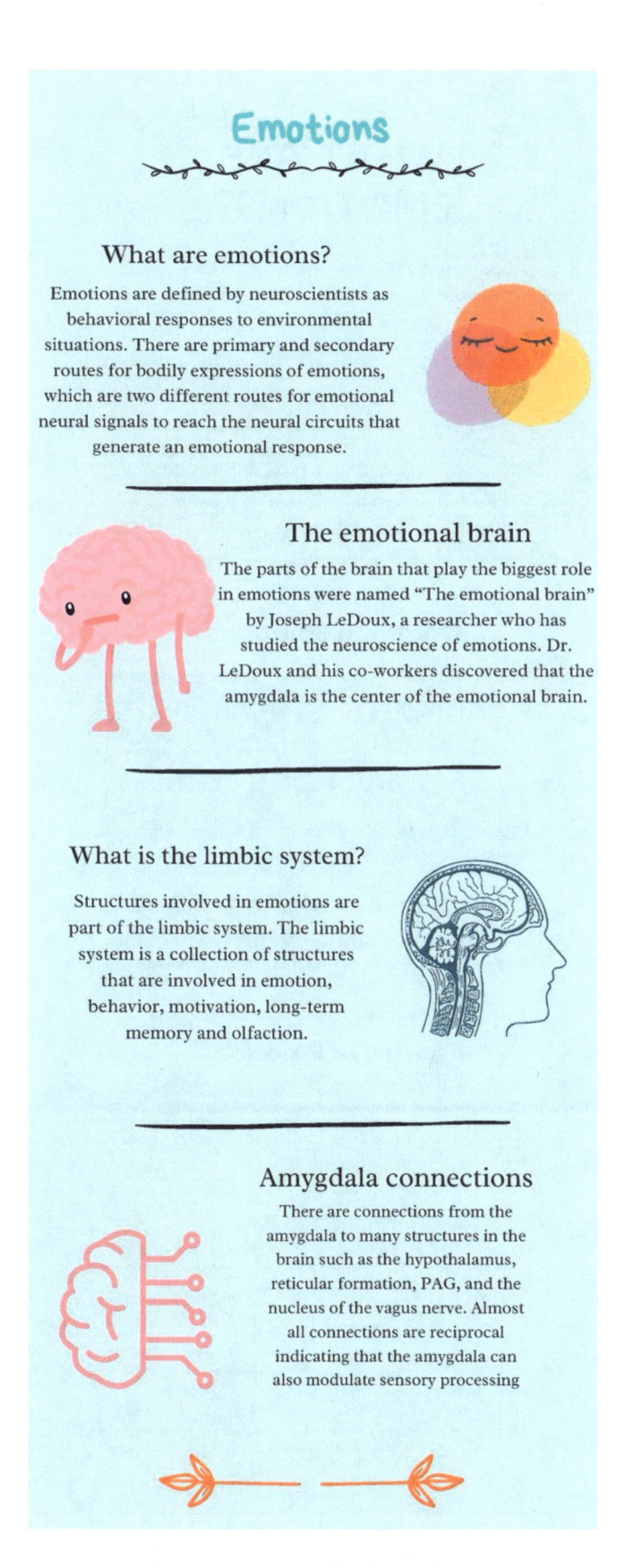

AN INFOGRAPHIC JOURNEY

Emotions

What are emotions?
Emotions are defined by neuroscientists as behavioral responses to environmental situations. There are primary and secondary routes for bodily expressions of emotions, which are two different routes for emotional neural signals to reach the neural circuits that generate an emotional response.

The emotional brain
The parts of the brain that play the biggest role in emotions were named "The emotional brain" by Joseph LeDoux, a researcher who has studied the neuroscience of emotions. Dr. LeDoux and his co-workers discovered that the amygdala is the center of the emotional brain.

What is the limbic system?
Structures involved in emotions are part of the limbic system. The limbic system is a collection of structures that are involved in emotion, behavior, motivation, long-term memory and olfaction.

Amygdala connections
There are connections from the amygdala to many structures in the brain such as the hypothalamus, reticular formation, PAG, and the nucleus of the vagus nerve. Almost all connections are reciprocal indicating that the amygdala can also modulate sensory processing

Seth Abraham, Spring 2024

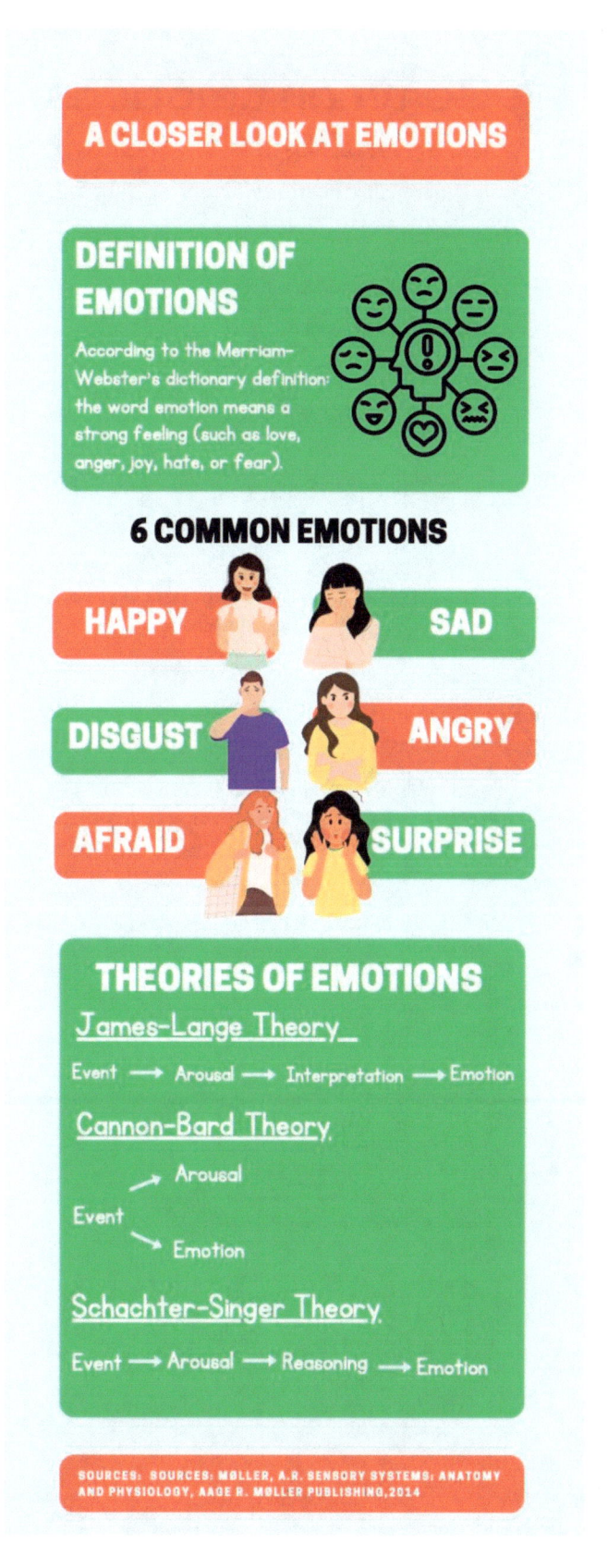

A CLOSER LOOK AT EMOTIONS

DEFINITION OF EMOTIONS
According to the Merriam-Webster's dictionary definition: the word emotion means a strong feeling (such as love, anger, joy, hate, or fear).

6 COMMON EMOTIONS
- HAPPY
- SAD
- DISGUST
- ANGRY
- AFRAID
- SURPRISE

THEORIES OF EMOTIONS

James-Lange Theory
Event → Arousal → Interpretation → Emotion

Cannon-Bard Theory
Event → Arousal
Event → Emotion

Schachter-Singer Theory
Event → Arousal → Reasoning → Emotion

SOURCES: SOURCES: MØLLER, A.R. SENSORY SYSTEMS: ANATOMY AND PHYSIOLOGY, AAGE R. MØLLER PUBLISHING, 2014

Sarvani Ganapavarapu, Fall 2023

6 Common Emotions

A widely accepted theory that details our common basic emotions.

Happiness
Happiness is a positive emotional response composed of feelings of joy and satisfaction. Happiness can cause people to smile or appear to be cheerful.

Sadness
Sadness is an emotional state characterized by grief, disappointment or hopelessness. Sadness can lead to crying or seclusion.

Fear
Fear is a result of a perceived danger. It triggers your fight or flight reponse to combat the perceived danger or threat.

Anger
Anger can be characterized by powerful feelings of irritation, frustration and hostility. It occurs in response to perceived threats.

Surprise
Surprise is an unexpected and sudden response to an unforeseen event. Surprise can be experienced in both positive and negative instances.

Disgust
Disgust is a reponse to stimuli that may be offensive, unpleasant or repulsive. This can cause feelings of aversion and discomfort.

By: Jaza Malik

Jaza Malik, Spring 2024

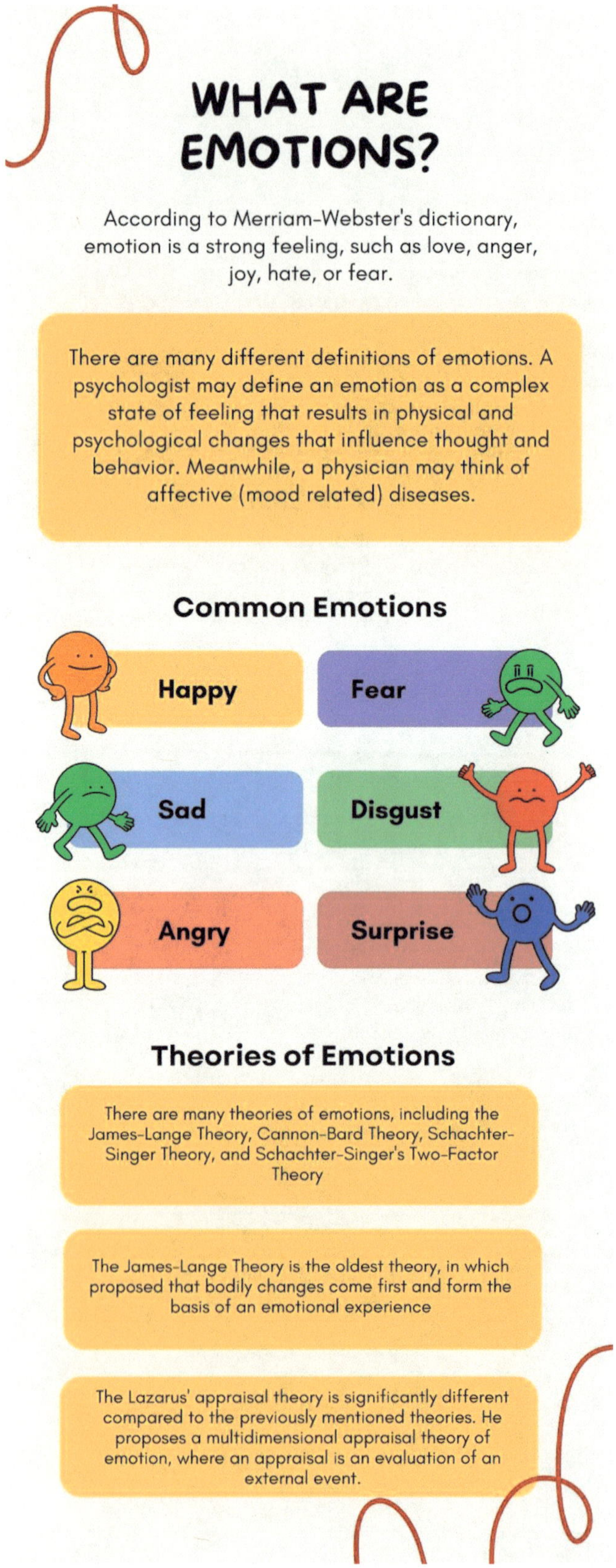

WHAT ARE EMOTIONS?

According to Merriam-Webster's dictionary, emotion is a strong feeling, such as love, anger, joy, hate, or fear.

There are many different definitions of emotions. A psychologist may define an emotion as a complex state of feeling that results in physical and psychological changes that influence thought and behavior. Meanwhile, a physician may think of affective (mood related) diseases.

Common Emotions

- Happy
- Fear
- Sad
- Disgust
- Angry
- Surprise

Theories of Emotions

There are many theories of emotions, including the James-Lange Theory, Cannon-Bard Theory, Schachter-Singer Theory, and Schachter-Singer's Two-Factor Theory

The James-Lange Theory is the oldest theory, in which proposed that bodily changes come first and form the basis of an emotional experience

The Lazarus' appraisal theory is significantly different compared to the previously mentioned theories. He proposes a multidimensional appraisal theory of emotion, where an appraisal is an evaluation of an external event.

Khadeeja Moosa, Spring 2023

AN INFOGRAPHIC JOURNEY

EMOTIONS
BY: VIVIAN WANG

Different definitions of emotions

- A clinical psychologist could associate emotions with behavioral problems.
- A physician could think about affective (mood related) diseases.
- A psychologist could define emotion as a complex state of feeling that results in physical and psychological changes that influence thought and behavior.
- A neuroscientist could define emotion as something that engage specific parts of the brain such the emotional brain especially the amygdala.

Common Emotions

Happy — Description: Fulfilled, Contented, Glad, Complete, Satisfied, Optimistic, Pleased

Excited — Description: Ecstatic, Energetic, Aroused, Bouncy, Nervous, Perky, Antsy

Sad — Description: Down, blue, mopey, grieved, dejected, depressed, heartbroken

Angry — Description: Irritated, resentful, miffed, upset, mad, furious, raging

Scared — Description: Tense, nervous, anxious, jittery, frightened, panic-stricken, terrified

Tender — Description: Intimate, loving, warm-hearted, sympathetic, touched, kind, soft

Bodily expressions to emotions

Anger: Body can feel tense and energized.
Excited: Body can feel jittery, butterflies in our stomach, and can experience quicker breathing.
Sad: Body can feel heavy, tired, and slow.
Anxious: Body can feel jittery, butterflies in our stomach, and can experience quicker breathing
Happy: Our body feels light and energized.

EMOTION

What is Emotion?
Emotion is an experienced state of consciousness, distinguished from cognitive thought and expression

What Emotions exist?
There are considered to be 6 primary emotions. These basic emotions are referred to as archetypical emotions

- **ANGER** — A strong feeling of hostility
- **FEAR** — Unpleasant feeling caused by fear
- **HAPPINESS** — Positive feeling of joy and well being
- **SADNESS** — A feeling of sorrow or unhappiness
- **DISGUST** — A strong feeling of revulsion or disapproval
- **SURPRISE** — An unexpected feeling of shock or amazement

What is the purpose of Emotion?
Emotions are not always logical, they can appear to come and go. So what is their purpose? One potential purpose of emotion may be to help regulate decision-making. A certain memory associated with a particular memory may be a critical part of an individual's decision-making for future events.

Emotion may also be used as a form of interoception, or sense of self. Emotions play an essential role in creating models of internal self and allow individuals to utilize visceral senses, such as hunger and thirst more effectively

Body reactions to Emotion
External stimuli can trigger certain emotions and create a physical response in the body. For example, when someone shows feelings of anxiousness, they may physically appear jittery.

Works Referenced
Jahangiri, Faisal R. "Chap 2. Emotions: Theory of Emotion." Neurobiology of Emotions. 17 Sept. 2023, University of Texas at Dallas, University of Texas at Dallas, https://tinyurl.com/297v8efy. Accessed 17 Sept. 2023.

Vivian Wang, Spring 2024

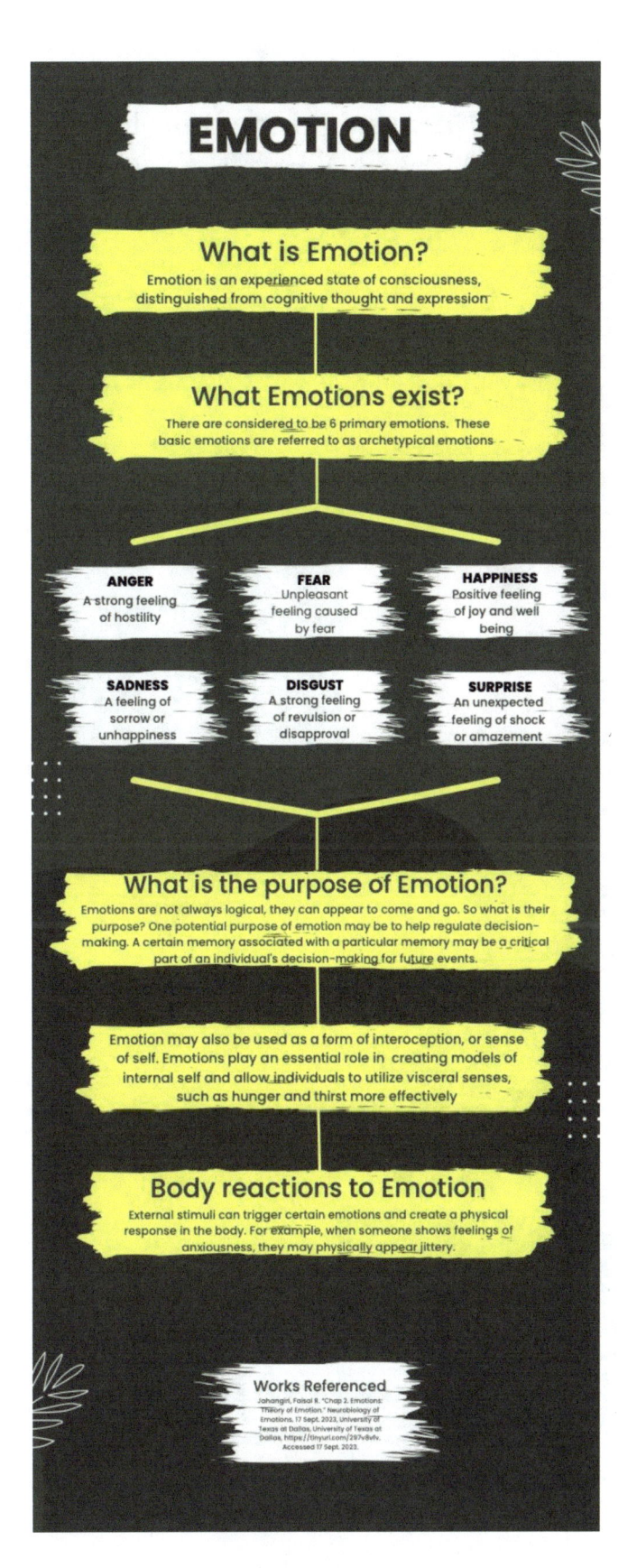

Ani Sharma, Fall 2023

AN INFOGRAPHIC JOURNEY

5 Different interactions to EMOTIONS

1 GENETICS
The genetic theory of the emotions is thus that excitement, the undifferentiated emotion present at birth, becomes differentiated and associated with certain situations and certain motor responses to form the separate emotions of later life.

2 EPIGENETICS
The effect of early life stress and a gene-environment interaction may play a role in the development of stress vulnerability as a risk factor for depression.

3 LEARNING AND MEMORY
Emotions and learning are inseparable. Emotions can both enhance and interfere with learning depending on which ones are driving or colouring the experience.

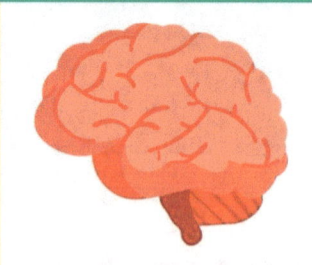

4 SOCIAL BEHAVIOR
Social-emotional skills are essential for connecting with others! They help us manage our emotions, build healthy relationships, and feel empathy.

5 STRESS
When stress becomes overwhelming and prolonged, the risks for mental health problems and medical problems increase. Long-term stress increases the risk of mental health problems such as anxiety and depression, substance use problems, sleep problems, etc.

BY ELSA CHITTET

Elsa Chittet, Spring 2024

SIX COMMON ARCHETYPICAL EMOTIONS
BY ELSA CHITTET

1 HAPPY
When one is happy, they can describe their emotion as "fulfilled" or "contented"; this can cause the body to feel light and energized during the day.

2 SURPRISE
Also known as "ecstatic" or "energetic"; it can cause the body to feel jittery, quicker breathing, or something we describe as "butterflies in our stomach"

3 SAD
Often described as depressed or "blue"; it can cause the body to feel heavy, slow, and tired.

4 AFRAID
Also described as "tense" or "anxious"; this causes the body to feel our racing heart, faster breathing, and sweaty hands.

5 ANGRY
Also described as "irritated" or "resentful"; it can cause the body to feel tense and energized, but this time in preparation for threats the mind may perceive.

6 DISGUST
Also described as "aversion" or "distaste"; it can cause the body to feel revulsion in the mouth, throat, and/or stomach; nausea; or physical repulsion (i.e. vomiting). These are seen in major cases of disgust, but most of the time it does not cause physical arousal.

Elsa Chittet, Spring 2024

AN INFOGRAPHIC JOURNEY

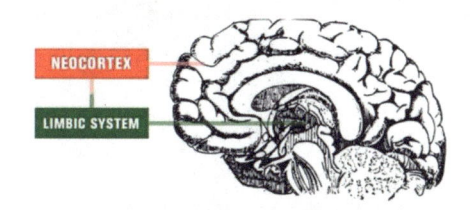

6 COMMON EMOTIONS

Emotion
- Emotion is derived from a Latin word *"emovere"* which means *"stirred up"* or *"to excite"*.
- So emotion is the excited state or stirred up state of an individual and it is purely a private experience.
- An **emotion** is a full body/mind/behavior response to a situation.

The 6 common emotions, often referred to as archetypical emotions, include: surprise, happy, sad, afraid, angry, and disgust. The dictionary definition for emotion means experiencing a strong feeling (joy, sorrow, fear, like, hate, etc). Our emotions are not always logical and can be very volatile at times.

There are several definitions of emotions in the science field depending on who is giving you the definition of it. Physicians would consider affective, mood related, diseases. A psychologist might characterize it as a complex state of feeling leading to both physical and psychological alterations, which in turn affect cognition and actions. Neuroscientists would look at it in terms of what specific parts of the brain are activated when feeling certain emotion. Clinical neurpsychologists might link it to behavioral issues.

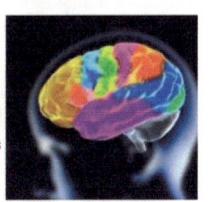

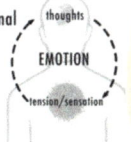

When taking you look at emotions and our awareness of emotions, we wonder the experience and awareness of emotions like fear akin to sensory experiences such as those evoked by sounds, light, and odors or taste that individuals perceive? How do sensations like hunger, thirst, and illness, which also come into awareness but aren't typically considered sensory qualities, compare? Furthermore, how do emotions such as anger, pleasure, love, and hate fit into this comparison? Some researchers even include stress and anger within the realm of emotions.

Two very strong and related emotions are love and hate. There's the saying "there's a thin line between love and hate," which does hold some truth. Love can be seen as an intense bond, often viewed as an emotion. Hate, conversely, is a strong and vehement form of dislike or aversion, also categorized as an emotion. Individuals may harbor hatred towards various entities, and what elicits hatred in one person may differ from another. Similarly, what one person loves may contrast with another's preferences.

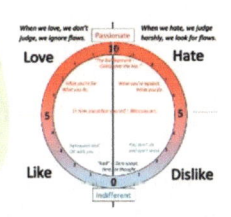

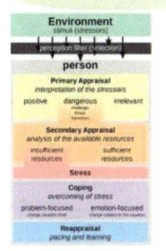

Since emotions are still something we don't fully understand, there are several theories surrounding them. Lazarus' cognitive-mediational theory says that when faced with a stressor, an individual first assesses its potential threat through primary appraisal, followed by evaluating the availability of effective coping options to manage the situation via secondary appraisal.

On the other hand, according to Prinz's somatic feedback theory, fear is the mental condition resulting from the body's feedback, specifically the perception of bodily changes. For example, stress tends to occur when a stressor is perceived as threatening and there are limited or no effective coping mechanisms available.

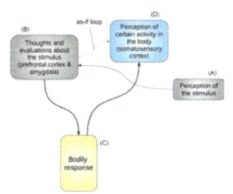

Kailyn Endres, Spring 2024

HOW EMOTIONS REVEAL IN THE BODY
BY AFROSA ISLAM

EMOTIONS AND US

People may associate emotions with starting in the human mind and then having some physical side effects, like how feeling sadness can cause someone to cry. However, it is important to recognize that emotions are also bodily experiences. What happens in our body can directly influence the cognitive aspects of our emotions.

SADNESS

Advanced sadness can lead to disruptions in sleep whether it's too little sleep (staying up due to insomnia), poor quality sleep (fewer REM cycles), or too much sleep (oversleeping). Extreme sadness can also lead people to experience pain more strongly. Sadness can also be connected to vitamin deficiencies, such as how a lack of vitamin D is a contributor to seasonal depression in the winter.

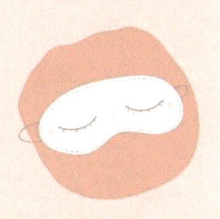

ANXIETY

Long-lasting anxiety can lead to people experiencing headaches and migraines more often. Some of the most noticeable physical symptoms of anxiety are sweating, quicker heart rate, and rapid breathing. Anxiety can also negatively affect the enteric system and digestive system, leading to upset stomach, diarrhea, etc.

LOVE

The feeling of love can have a widespread effect on the body. Having healthy, loving relationships in one's life can lead to beneficial effects like better physical health, improved immune system function, etc. The body also releases hormones like dopamine, which engage the reward pathway in the brain, when you see a person you love. Oxytocin can also be released, and this hormone facilitates feelings of bonding and affection.

Afrosa Islam, Spring 2023

AN INFOGRAPHIC JOURNEY

Theories of Emotion

Tarik Ehsan

WHAT ARE EMOTIONS?

Emotions are difficult to define. Although they have a connotation with feelings, different professionals each have their own methods of defining them. One dictionary, Merriam-Webster, defines emotion as a strong feeling. Another, Dictionary.com, defines it as an affective state of consciousness deparate from cognitive states of consciousness.

WHAT ARE THE MAIN EMOTIONS?

The primary (archetypal) emotions are six in number. They include:
- disgust
- happiness
- surprise
- anger
- fear
- sadness

JAMES-LANGE THEORY

This is the oldest know theory of emotion, created by two American psychologists. It proposes that:
- an event causes arousal
- the individual interprets this arousal
- an emotion is created

CANNON-BARD THEORY

This theory assumes that the event that causes emotion has two parallel processes:
- arousal
- creation of feeling of emotion

These two processes occur simultaneously.

THE BIOLOGY OF EMOTION

Environmental signals can cause emotions which in turn alter homeostatic functions in the body. This can happen, for example, in the form of the activation of the sympathetic nervous system. This can increase the risk of disease.

HATE

Hate is a special kind of emotions. It is a passionate dislike of something. This could stem from a desire for revenge or simply the fact that one may find something or someone else distasteful. Examples include hatred of another ethnicity/religion/skin color.

SOURCES CITED:
MØLLER, A.R. "NEUROBIOLOGY OF FEAR, ANXIETY AND OTHER EMOTIONS"

Tarik Ehsan, Fall 2023

AN INFOGRAPHIC JOURNEY

THEORIES OF EMOTIONS
Helen Nguyen

DEFINITION OF "EMOTION"
- Merriam-Webster's dictionary has the word emotion meaning a strong feeling (such as love, anger, joy, hate, or fear)
- A neuroscientist may define emotion as something that engages specific parts of the brain such as the emotional brain, especially the amygdala
- A physician may think about affective (mood-related) diseases

COMMON EMOTIONS
The primary or basic emotions are referred to as archetypical emotions:
- happy
- sad
- disgust
- surprised
- afraid
- angry

THEORIES OF EMOTIONS
1. James-Lange Theory
   - event -> arousal -> interpretation -> emotion
2. Cannon-Bard theory
   - event -> arousal -> emotion
3. Schachter-Singer Theory
   - event -> arousal -> reasoning -> emotion
4. Schachter-Singer's two-factor Theory
   - event -> arousal -> cognitive labels -> emotion

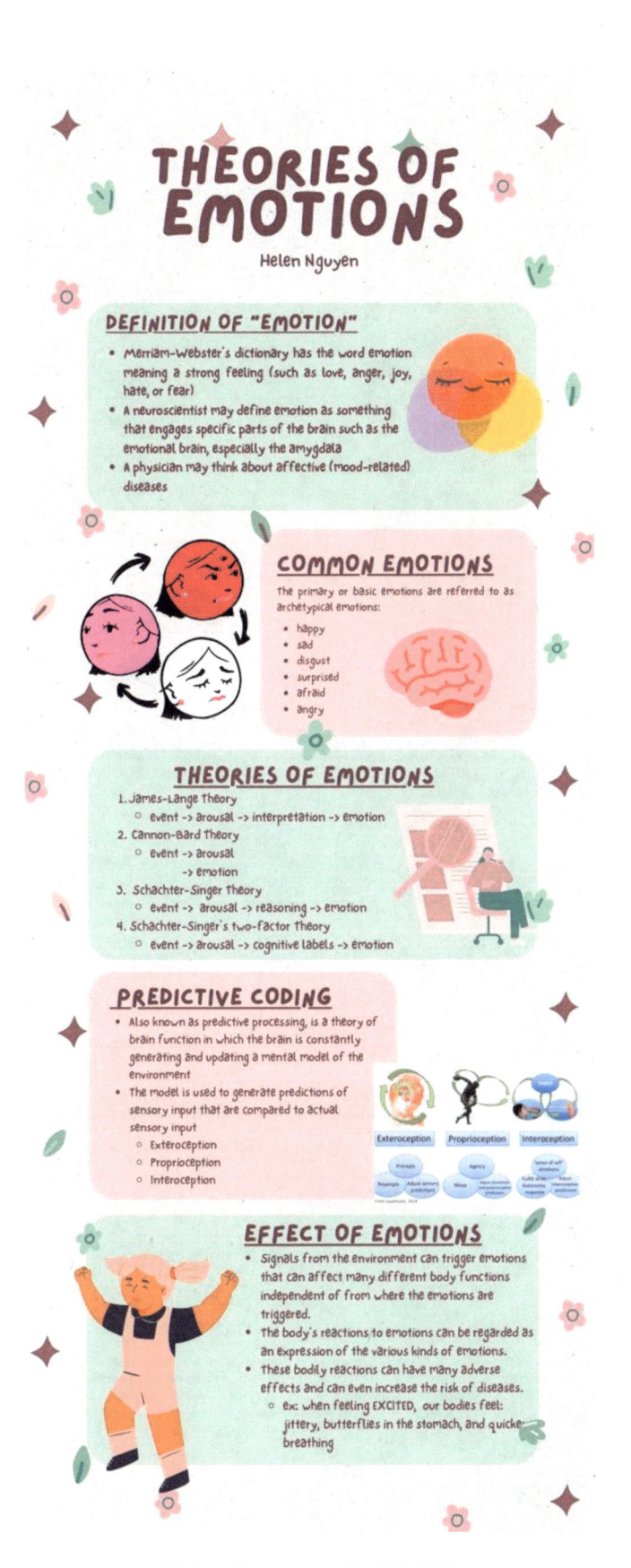

PREDICTIVE CODING
- Also known as predictive processing, is a theory of brain function in which the brain is constantly generating and updating a mental model of the environment
- The model is used to generate predictions of sensory input that are compared to actual sensory input
  - Exteroception
  - Proprioception
  - Interoception

EFFECT OF EMOTIONS
- Signals from the environment can trigger emotions that can affect many different body functions independent of from where the emotions are triggered.
- The body's reactions to emotions can be regarded as an expression of the various kinds of emotions.
- These bodily reactions can have many adverse effects and can even increase the risk of diseases.
  - ex: when feeling EXCITED, our bodies feel: jittery, butterflies in the stomach, and quicker breathing

Helen Nguyen, Fall 2023

Theories of Emotion

What is an emotion?
According to the Merriam-Webster's dictionary, emotion is a **strong feeling**. Examples of basic or primary emotions are anger, fear, happiness, surprised, disgust, and sadness.

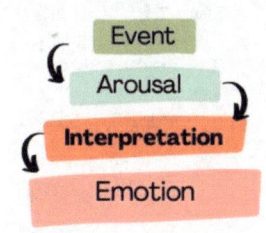

James-Lange Theory
Event → Arousal → Interpretation → Emotion

Oldest and most well known theory about emotion.

An event causes an arousal or activity in the brain. After **interpretation**, an emotion is created.

Example: An individual sees a snake, which results in the activation of the sympathetic system. After interpretation of the event, the individual may feel afraid.

Cannon-Brad Theory
An event leads to activation of the brain (arousal) and the creation of an emotion, at the same time.

No interpretation occurs.

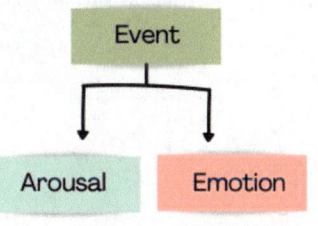

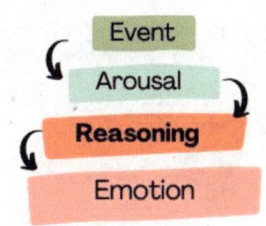

Event → Arousal / Emotion

Schachter-Singer Theory
Event → Arousal → Reasoning → Emotion

An event causes activation of the brain. After **reasoning**, an emotion is created.

Example: An individual sees a snake. Next, they experience increased heart rate and **recognize** that they are scared. Lastly, the feel the emotion of fear.

Schachter-Singer's Two Factor Theory
Similar to the Schachter-Singer Theory, but assumes that **cognitive labels** preceded the creation of an emotion rather than recognition.

Resource: All information is from Week 4 Lecture by Dr. Jahangiri & Neurobiology of Fear and other Emotions by Dr. Moller

Haniya Qavi, Fall 2023

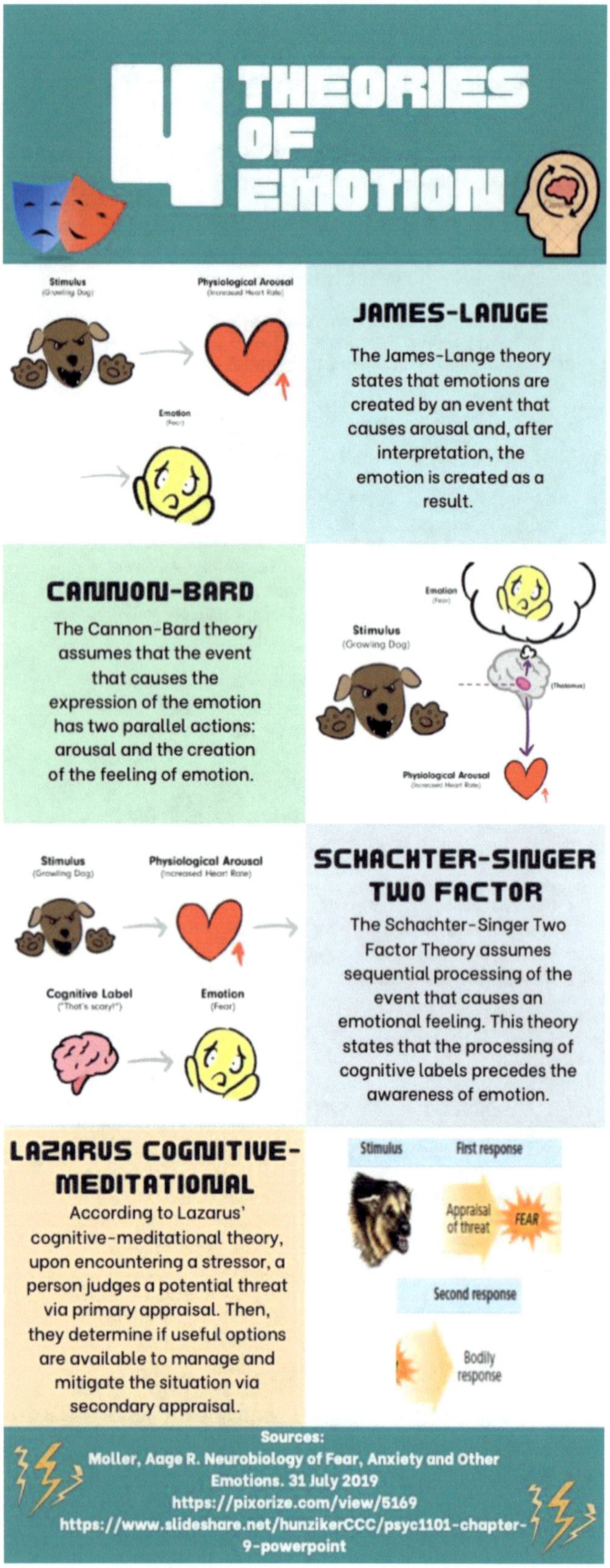

AN INFOGRAPHIC JOURNEY

Megha Akkineni, Fall 2023

Saad Tanwir, Spring 2024

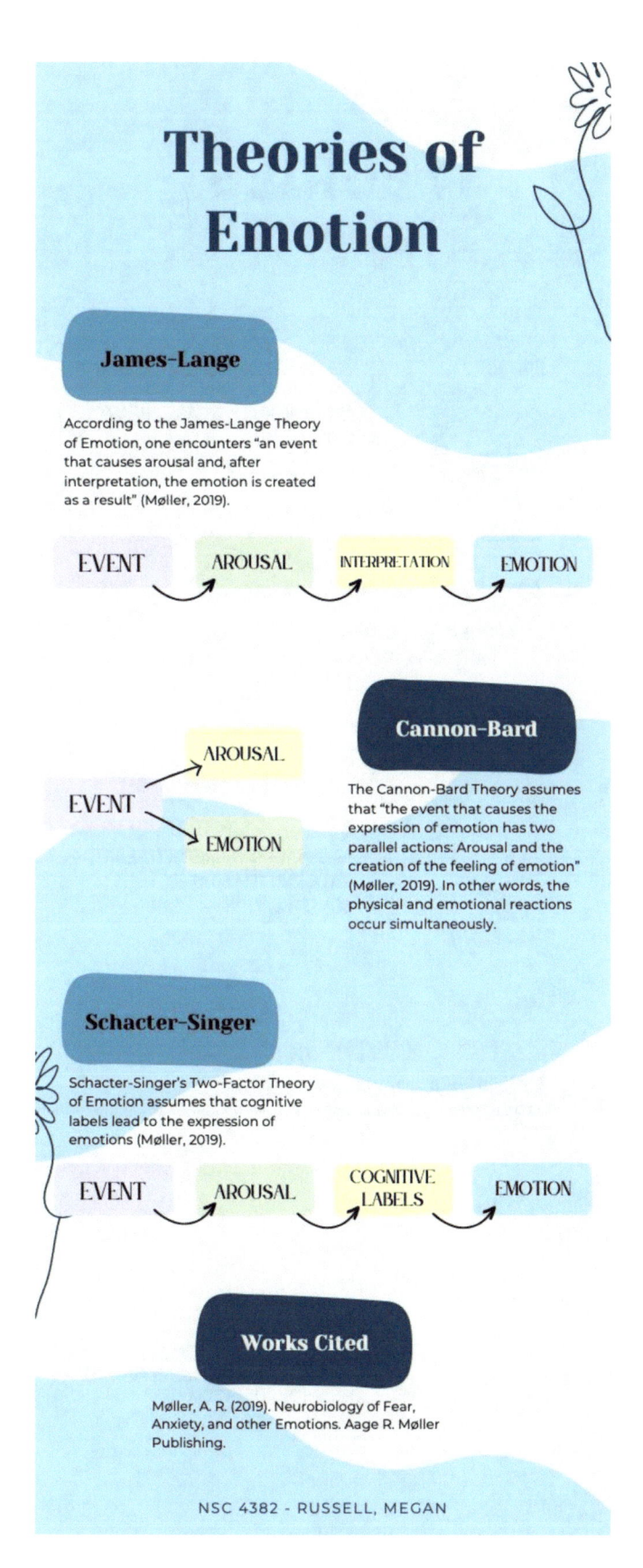

Theories of Emotion

James-Lange
According to the James-Lange Theory of Emotion, one encounters "an event that causes arousal and, after interpretation, the emotion is created as a result" (Møller, 2019).

EVENT → AROUSAL → INTERPRETATION → EMOTION

Cannon-Bard
The Cannon-Bard Theory assumes that "the event that causes the expression of emotion has two parallel actions: Arousal and the creation of the feeling of emotion" (Møller, 2019). In other words, the physical and emotional reactions occur simultaneously.

EVENT → AROUSAL / EMOTION

Schacter-Singer
Schacter-Singer's Two-Factor Theory of Emotion assumes that cognitive labels lead to the expression of emotions (Møller, 2019).

EVENT → AROUSAL → COGNITIVE LABELS → EMOTION

Works Cited
Møller, A. R. (2019). Neurobiology of Fear, Anxiety, and other Emotions. Aage R. Møller Publishing.

NSC 4382 - RUSSELL, MEGAN

Megan Russell, Fall 2023

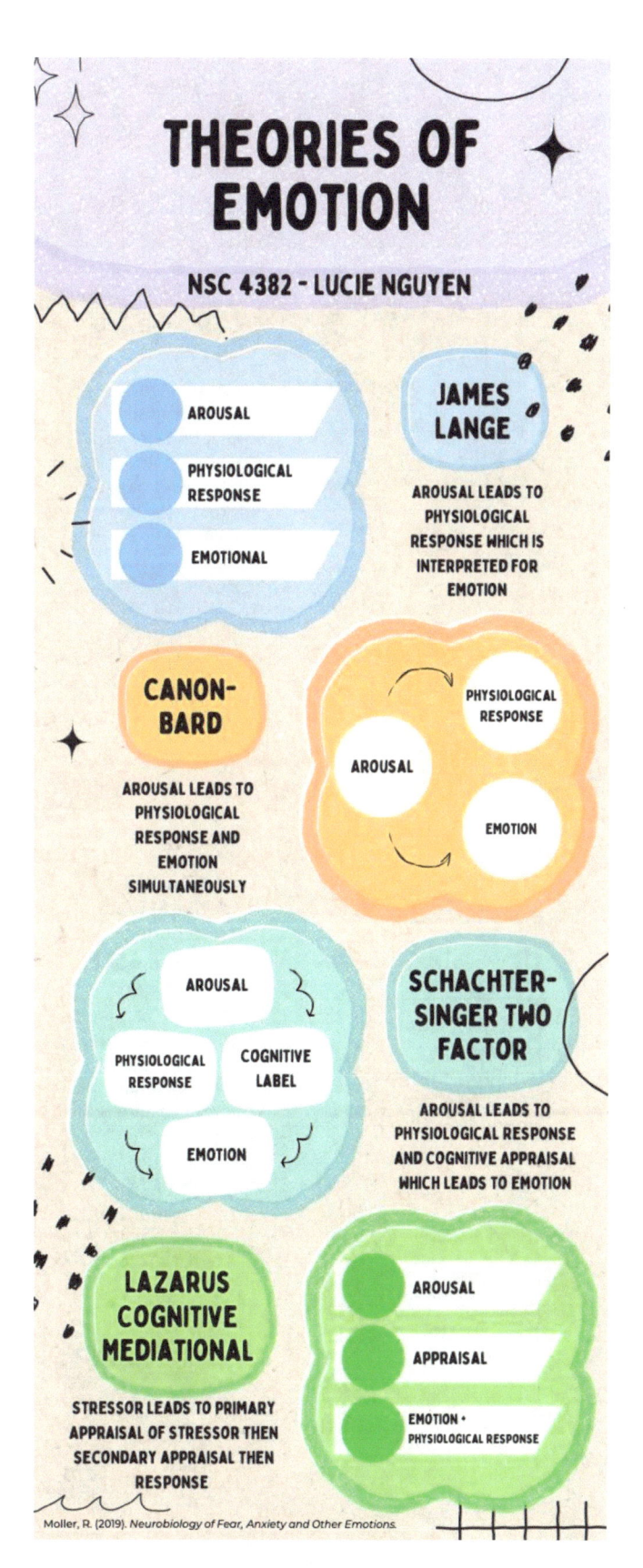

THEORIES OF EMOTION

NSC 4382 - LUCIE NGUYEN

JAMES LANGE
- AROUSAL
- PHYSIOLOGICAL RESPONSE
- EMOTIONAL

AROUSAL LEADS TO PHYSIOLOGICAL RESPONSE WHICH IS INTERPRETED FOR EMOTION

CANON-BARD
AROUSAL → PHYSIOLOGICAL RESPONSE / EMOTION

AROUSAL LEADS TO PHYSIOLOGICAL RESPONSE AND EMOTION SIMULTANEOUSLY

SCHACHTER-SINGER TWO FACTOR
AROUSAL, PHYSIOLOGICAL RESPONSE, COGNITIVE LABEL, EMOTION

AROUSAL LEADS TO PHYSIOLOGICAL RESPONSE AND COGNITIVE APPRAISAL WHICH LEADS TO EMOTION

LAZARUS COGNITIVE MEDIATIONAL
- AROUSAL
- APPRAISAL
- EMOTION + PHYSIOLOGICAL RESPONSE

STRESSOR LEADS TO PRIMARY APPRAISAL OF STRESSOR THEN SECONDARY APPRAISAL THEN RESPONSE

Moller, R. (2019). Neurobiology of Fear, Anxiety and Other Emotions.

Lucie Nguyen, Fall 2023

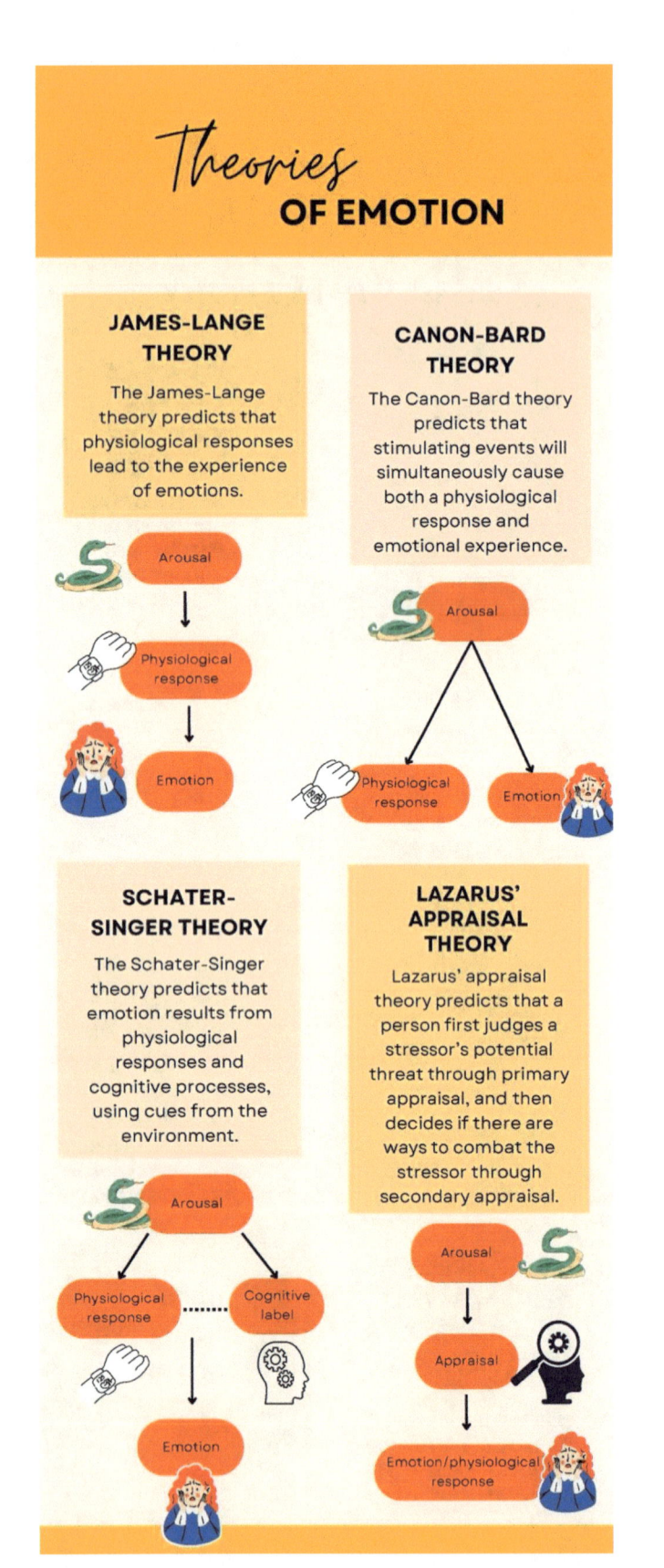

AN INFOGRAPHIC JOURNEY

Theories of Emotion

JAMES-LANGE THEORY
The James-Lange theory predicts that physiological responses lead to the experience of emotions.

Arousal → Physiological response → Emotion

CANON-BARD THEORY
The Canon-Bard theory predicts that stimulating events will simultaneously cause both a physiological response and emotional experience.

Arousal → Physiological response / Emotion

SCHATER-SINGER THEORY
The Schater-Singer theory predicts that emotion results from physiological responses and cognitive processes, using cues from the environment.

Arousal → Physiological response / Cognitive label → Emotion

LAZARUS' APPRAISAL THEORY
Lazarus' appraisal theory predicts that a person first judges a stressor's potential threat through primary appraisal, and then decides if there are ways to combat the stressor through secondary appraisal.

Arousal → Appraisal → Emotion/physiological response

Kajal Patel, Spring 2024

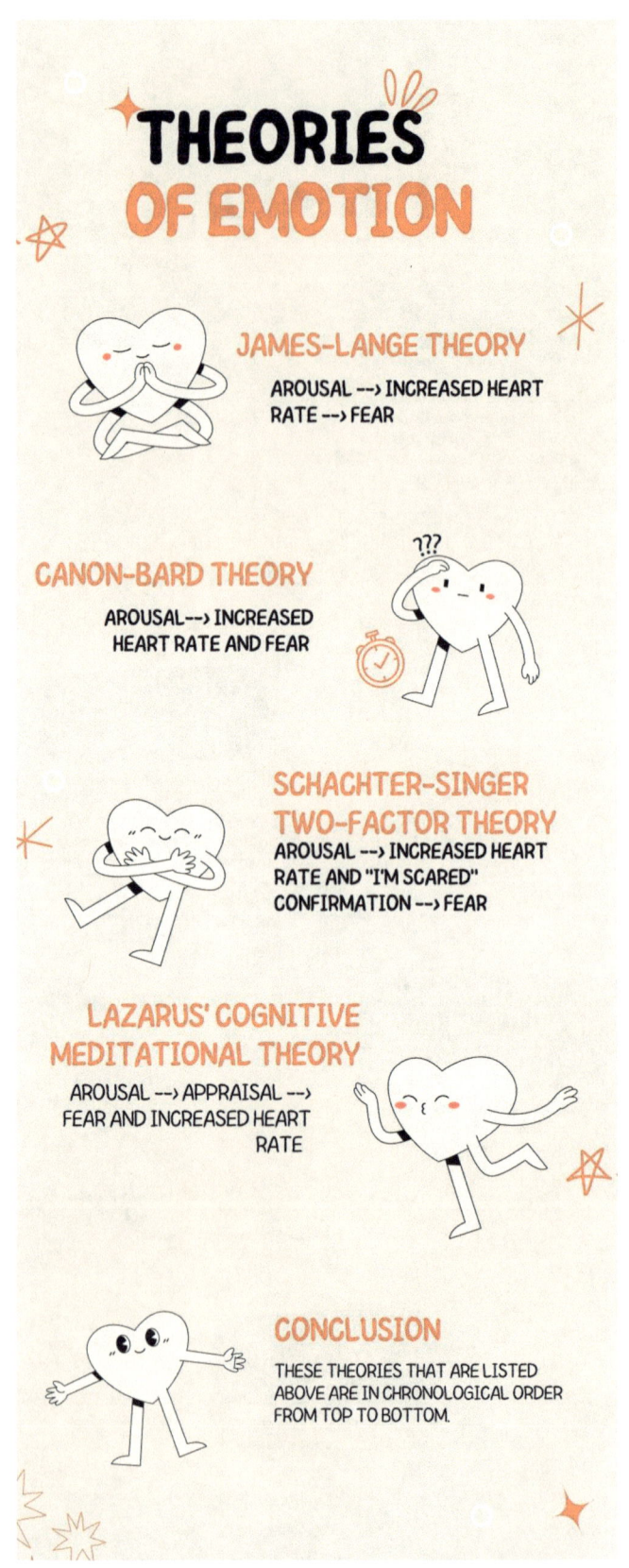

THEORIES OF EMOTION

JAMES-LANGE THEORY
AROUSAL --> INCREASED HEART RATE --> FEAR

CANON-BARD THEORY
AROUSAL --> INCREASED HEART RATE AND FEAR

SCHACHTER-SINGER TWO-FACTOR THEORY
AROUSAL --> INCREASED HEART RATE AND "I'M SCARED" CONFIRMATION --> FEAR

LAZARUS' COGNITIVE MEDITATIONAL THEORY
AROUSAL --> APPRAISAL --> FEAR AND INCREASED HEART RATE

CONCLUSION
THESE THEORIES THAT ARE LISTED ABOVE ARE IN CHRONOLOGICAL ORDER FROM TOP TO BOTTOM.

Priya Upadhyaya, Spring 2023

AN INFOGRAPHIC JOURNEY

Emotions and their Theories
By: Asif Lakhani

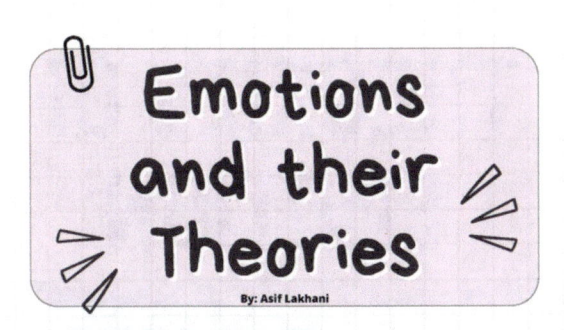

01 What are Emotions?
While the definition of emotion varies based on the context and application; emotion can be described as the fluid state of feeling which causes changes in physical, physiological, and mental states, ultimately altering behavior. Emotions are often accompanied with engagement with parts of the brain, usually the amygdala.

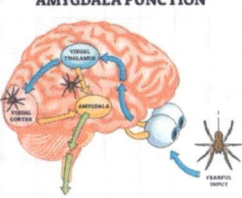

AMYGDALA FUNCTION

02 Common Emotions
There are 6 main, common emotions: Surprise, Happy, Sad, Afraid, Angry, Disgust. All emotions are characterized with feelings, activation of the visceral motor system, and facial expression. These emotions are also often known as archetypical emotions.

03 Emotion Theories
Three Main theories exist which aim to explain how emotions are processed and interpreted.
James-Lange: An event leads to arousal, which when interpreted leads to an emotion
Cannon-Bard: An event leads to emotions and arousal, at the same time.
Schachter-Singer: An event leads to arousal, causing reasoning leading to an emotion

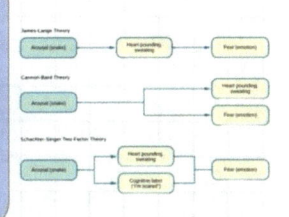

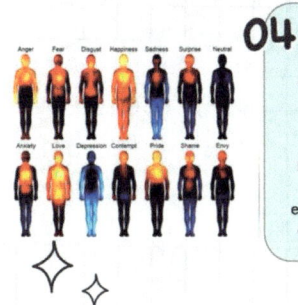

04 Physiological Effects
A large part of emotions is the accompaniment with physiological changes. Some fears target our Sympathetic NS, while others activate our Parasympathetic NS. Feelings of excitement and anxiety may cause a jittery feeling, for example. While feelings of happiness and anger cause energetic effects.

Asif Lakhani, Spring 2024

Infographic #4: Taha Ahmed

THEORIES OF EMOTIONS

What are the different definitions of "emotion?"
- a **psychologist** sees emotion as a complex state of feeling
- **neuroscientists** see it as a thing that engages different parts of the brain
- a **physician** may think about affective (mood-related) diseases
- a **clinical neurophysiologist** may associate emotions with behavioral problems

What are the six common emotions?
The primary or basic emotions that are referred to as archetypical emotions include **happiness, sadness, disgust, anger, afraid, and surprise**

What are the different theories on emotion?
- According to the **Lazarus theory**, a person who encounters a stressor judges the threat and decides if there are useful options available to manage the situation
- According to **Prinz's theory**, fear is a mental state caused by feedback from the body
- Stress is likely to result if a stressor is perceived as a threat and few or no effective coping options are available

What is predictive coding?
Also known as **predictive processing**, is a theory of brain function in which the brain is constantly making and updating a mental model of the environment
- used to generate predictions of sensory input that are compared to actual sensory input

What are different bodily expressions of emotion?
Different signals from the environment can trigger emotions which can affect many body functions independent of from where the emotions are triggered
- **Ex:** when we are **happy**, our body feels **light and energized**

Taha Ahmed, Spring 2024

EMOTION THEORIES

How are they similar and how are they different?

JAMES-LANGE THEORY
Lange proposed that emotions were preceded by a three-step process, starting with the event, then arousal, and finally interpretation of the arousal.

Event → Arousal → Interpretation → Emotion

SCHACTER-SINGER THEORY (1)
Theorized by the same scientists, this theory is slightly different in that they proposed reasoning, rather than interpretation, followed the event and arousal.

Event → Arousal → Reasoning → Emotion

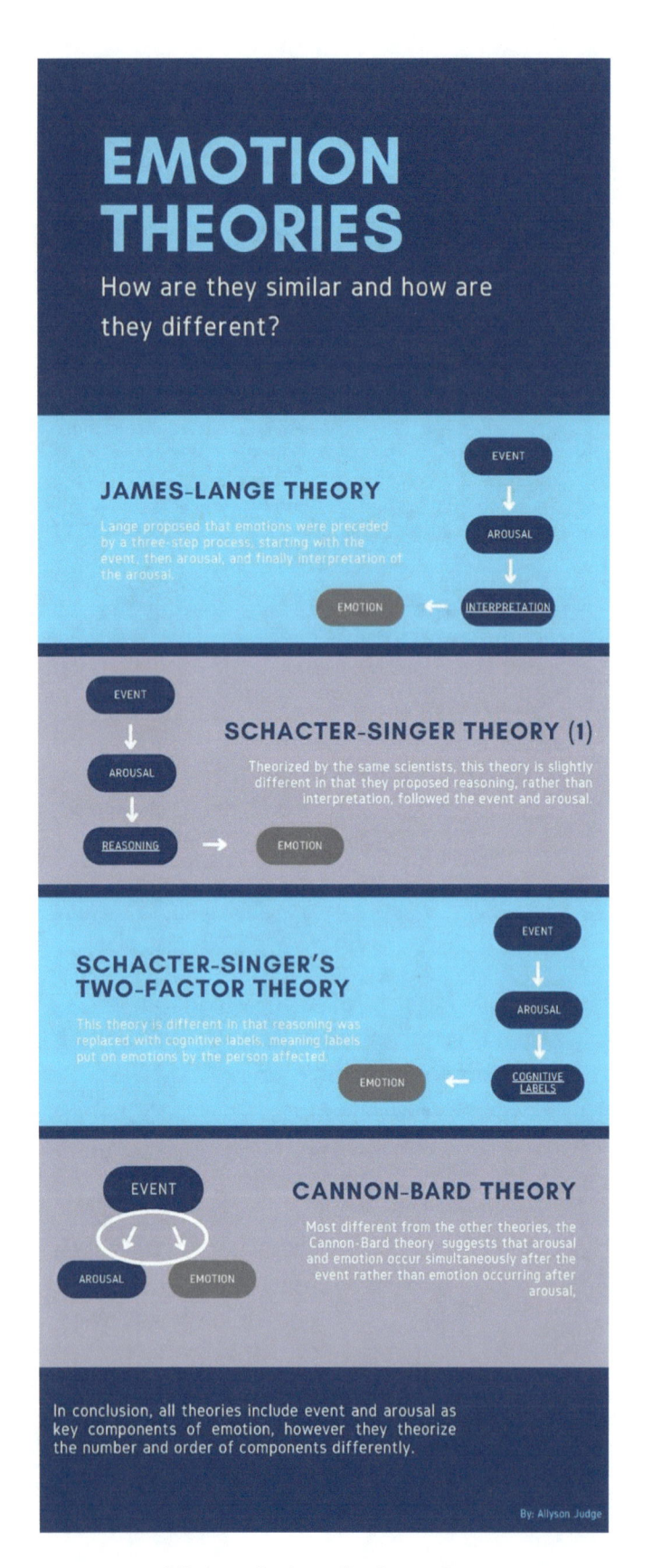

SCHACTER-SINGER'S TWO-FACTOR THEORY
This theory is different in that reasoning was replaced with cognitive labels, meaning labels put on emotions by the person affected.

Event → Arousal → Cognitive Labels → Emotion

CANNON-BARD THEORY
Most different from the other theories, the Cannon-Bard theory suggests that arousal and emotion occur simultaneously after the event rather than emotion occurring arousal.

Event → Arousal / Emotion

In conclusion, all theories include event and arousal as key components of emotion, however they theorize the number and order of components differently.

By: Allyson Judge

Allyson Judge, Spring 2024

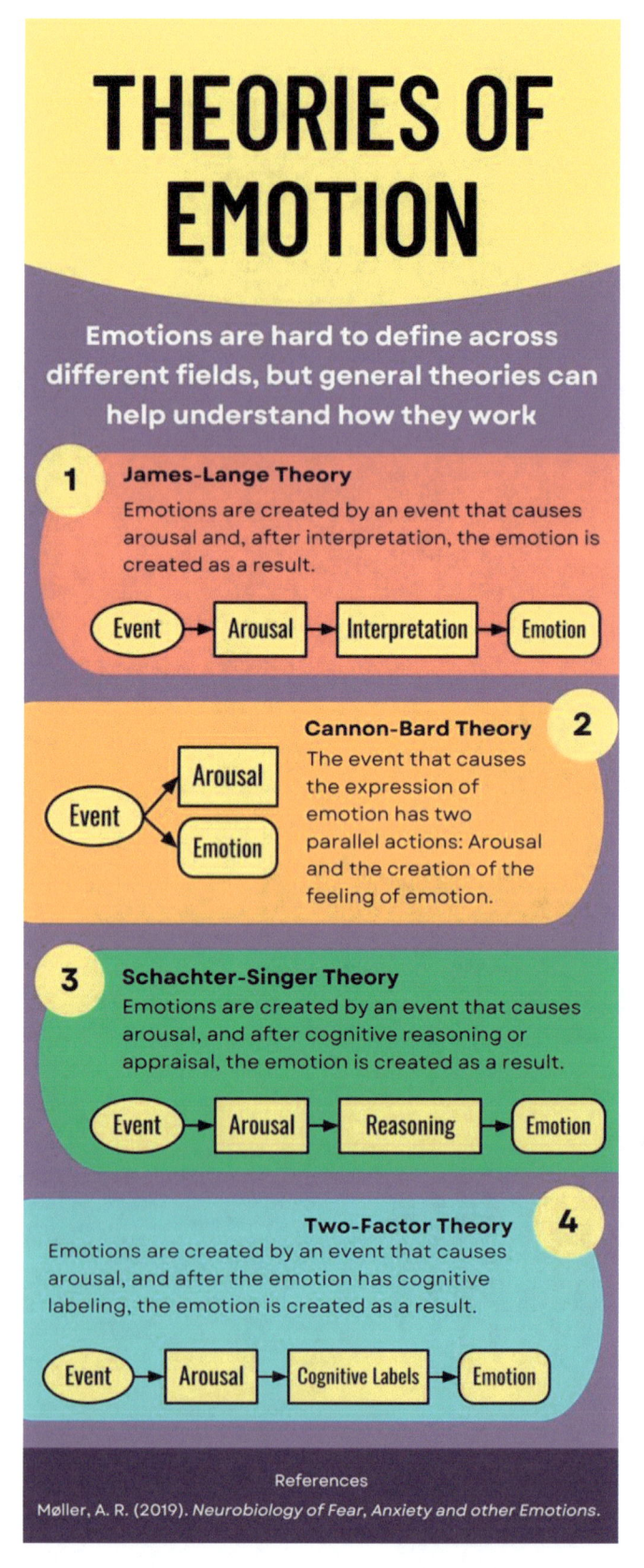

THEORIES OF EMOTION

Emotions are hard to define across different fields, but general theories can help understand how they work

1. James-Lange Theory
Emotions are created by an event that causes arousal and, after interpretation, the emotion is created as a result.

Event → Arousal → Interpretation → Emotion

2. Cannon-Bard Theory
The event that causes the expression of emotion has two parallel actions: Arousal and the creation of the feeling of emotion.

Event → Arousal / Emotion

3. Schachter-Singer Theory
Emotions are created by an event that causes arousal, and after cognitive reasoning or appraisal, the emotion is created as a result.

Event → Arousal → Reasoning → Emotion

4. Two-Factor Theory
Emotions are created by an event that causes arousal, and after the emotion has cognitive labeling, the emotion is created as a result.

Event → Arousal → Cognitive Labels → Emotion

References
Møller, A. R. (2019). *Neurobiology of Fear, Anxiety and other Emotions.*

Natalie Laguer Torres, Fall 2023

AN INFOGRAPHIC JOURNEY

THEORIES OF EMOTION

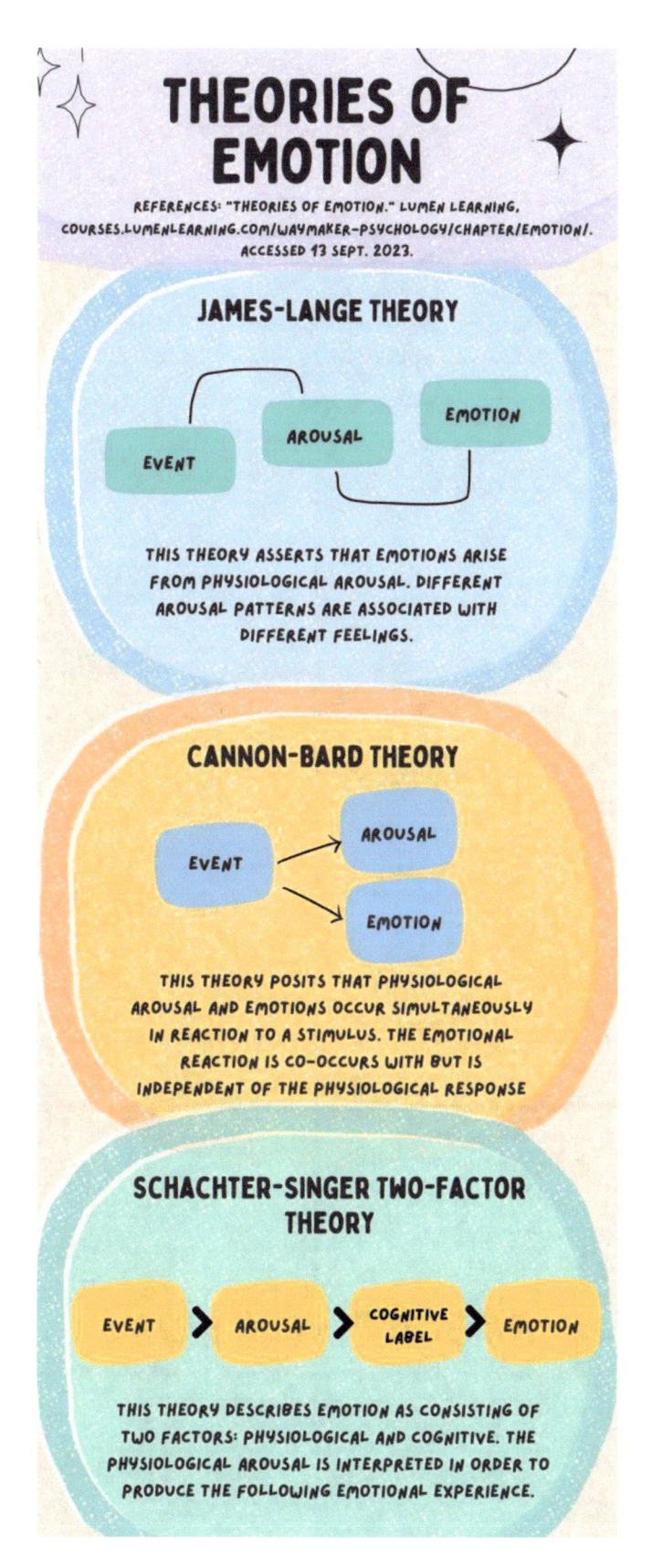

REFERENCES: "THEORIES OF EMOTION." LUMEN LEARNING. COURSES.LUMENLEARNING.COM/WAYMAKER-PSYCHOLOGY/CHAPTER/EMOTION/. ACCESSED 13 SEPT. 2023.

JAMES-LANGE THEORY

EVENT → AROUSAL → EMOTION

THIS THEORY ASSERTS THAT EMOTIONS ARISE FROM PHYSIOLOGICAL AROUSAL. DIFFERENT AROUSAL PATTERNS ARE ASSOCIATED WITH DIFFERENT FEELINGS.

CANNON-BARD THEORY

EVENT → AROUSAL
EVENT → EMOTION

THIS THEORY POSITS THAT PHYSIOLOGICAL AROUSAL AND EMOTIONS OCCUR SIMULTANEOUSLY IN REACTION TO A STIMULUS. THE EMOTIONAL REACTION IS CO-OCCURS WITH BUT IS INDEPENDENT OF THE PHYSIOLOGICAL RESPONSE

SCHACHTER-SINGER TWO-FACTOR THEORY

EVENT → AROUSAL → COGNITIVE LABEL → EMOTION

THIS THEORY DESCRIBES EMOTION AS CONSISTING OF TWO FACTORS: PHYSIOLOGICAL AND COGNITIVE. THE PHYSIOLOGICAL AROUSAL IS INTERPRETED IN ORDER TO PRODUCE THE FOLLOWING EMOTIONAL EXPERIENCE.

Ashley Tran, Fall 2023

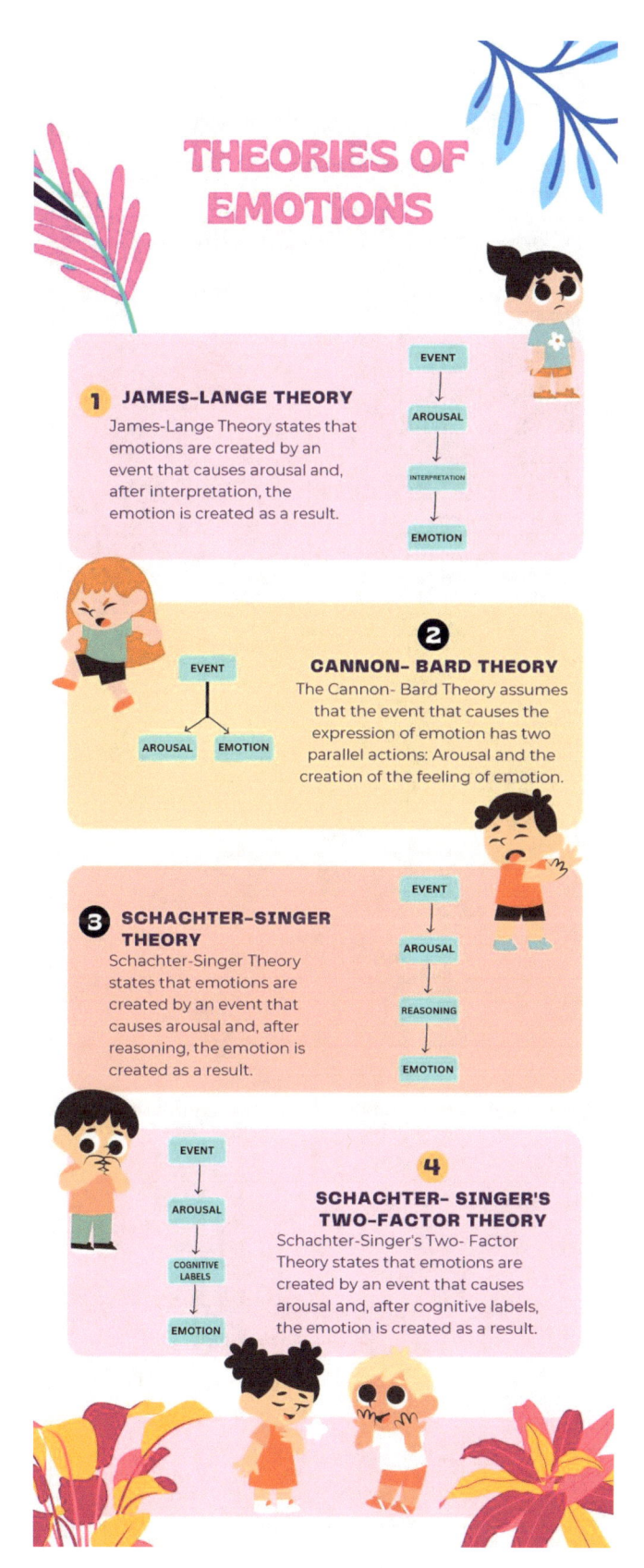

THEORIES OF EMOTIONS

1 JAMES-LANGE THEORY
James-Lange Theory states that emotions are created by an event that causes arousal and, after interpretation, the emotion is created as a result.

EVENT → AROUSAL → INTERPRETATION → EMOTION

2 CANNON-BARD THEORY
The Cannon-Bard Theory assumes that the event that causes the expression of emotion has two parallel actions: Arousal and the creation of the feeling of emotion.

EVENT → AROUSAL / EMOTION

3 SCHACHTER-SINGER THEORY
Schachter-Singer Theory states that emotions are created by an event that causes arousal and, after reasoning, the emotion is created as a result.

EVENT → AROUSAL → REASONING → EMOTION

4 SCHACHTER-SINGER'S TWO-FACTOR THEORY
Schachter-Singer's Two-Factor Theory states that emotions are created by an event that causes arousal and, after cognitive labels, the emotion is created as a result.

EVENT → AROUSAL → COGNITIVE LABELS → EMOTION

Preena Desai, Spring 2023

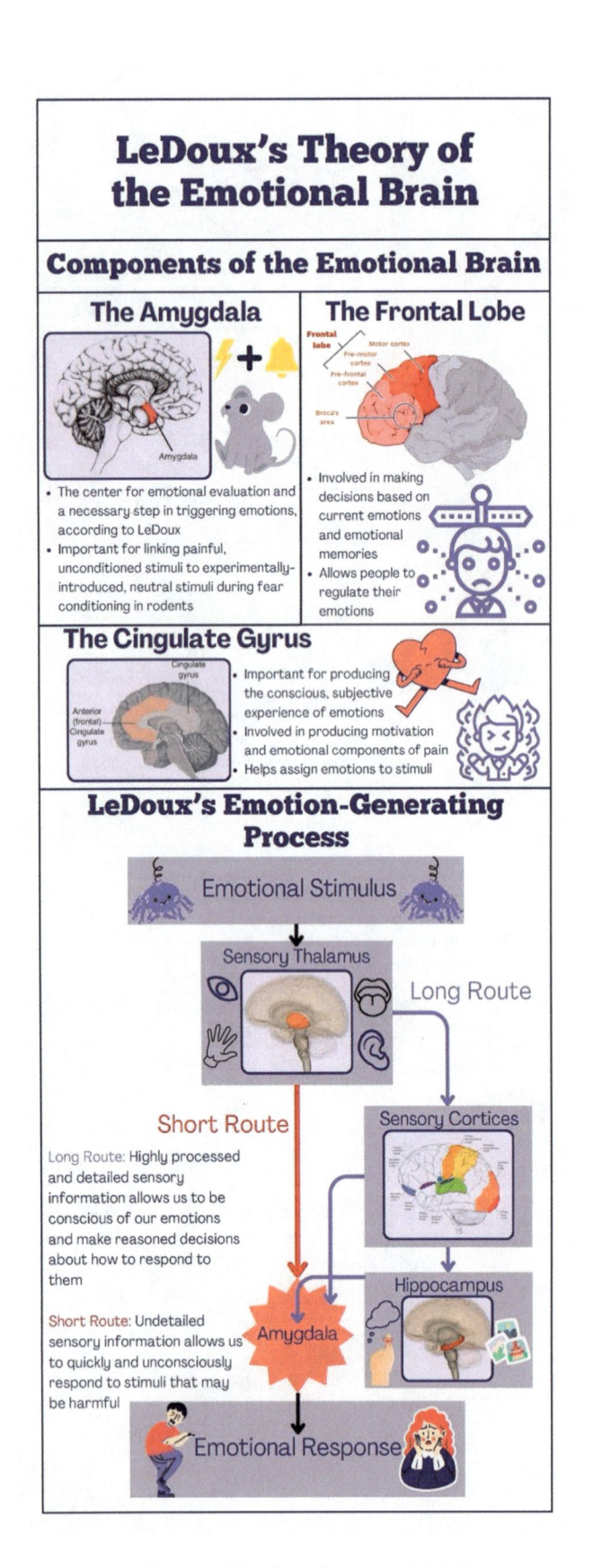

An Infographic Journey

LeDoux's Theory of the Emotional Brain

Components of the Emotional Brain

The Amygdala
- The center for emotional evaluation and a necessary step in triggering emotions, according to LeDoux
- Important for linking painful, unconditioned stimuli to experimentally-introduced, neutral stimuli during fear conditioning in rodents

The Frontal Lobe
- Involved in making decisions based on current emotions and emotional memories
- Allows people to regulate their emotions

The Cingulate Gyrus
- Important for producing the conscious, subjective experience of emotions
- Involved in producing motivation and emotional components of pain
- Helps assign emotions to stimuli

LeDoux's Emotion-Generating Process

Emotional Stimulus → Sensory Thalamus → (Long Route) Sensory Cortices → Hippocampus → Amygdala → Emotional Response
Sensory Thalamus → (Short Route) Amygdala → Emotional Response

Long Route: Highly processed and detailed sensory information allows us to be conscious of our emotions and make reasoned decisions about how to respond to them

Short Route: Undetailed sensory information allows us to quickly and unconsciously respond to stimuli that may be harmful

Allyson Macfee, Spring 2024

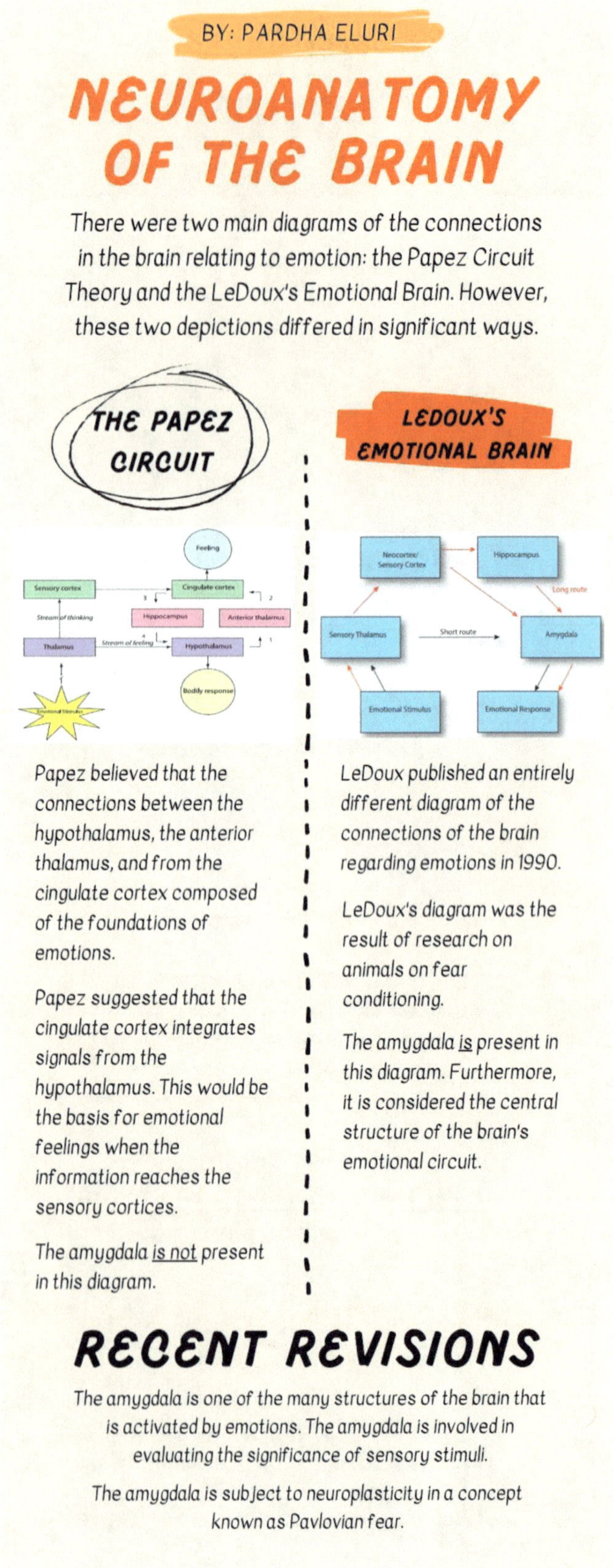

BY: PARDHA ELURI

NEUROANATOMY OF THE BRAIN

There were two main diagrams of the connections in the brain relating to emotion: the Papez Circuit Theory and the LeDoux's Emotional Brain. However, these two depictions differed in significant ways.

THE PAPEZ CIRCUIT

Papez believed that the connections between the hypothalamus, the anterior thalamus, and from the cingulate cortex composed of the foundations of emotions.

Papez suggested that the cingulate cortex integrates signals from the hypothalamus. This would be the basis for emotional feelings when the information reaches the sensory cortices.

The amygdala _is not_ present in this diagram.

LEDOUX'S EMOTIONAL BRAIN

LeDoux published an entirely different diagram of the connections of the brain regarding emotions in 1990.

LeDoux's diagram was the result of research on animals on fear conditioning.

The amygdala _is_ present in this diagram. Furthermore, it is considered the central structure of the brain's emotional circuit.

RECENT REVISIONS

The amygdala is one of the many structures of the brain that is activated by emotions. The amygdala is involved in evaluating the significance of sensory stimuli.

The amygdala is subject to neuroplasticity in a concept known as Pavlovian fear.

Pardha Eluri, Spring 2023

AN INFOGRAPHIC JOURNEY

Theories for the Neural Basis of Emotion: Papez vs. LeDoux

01 PAPEZ
Papez suggested that emotions stem from connections between the cingulate cortex and the anterior thalamus. Following a top-down structure, signals from the cingulate cortex go to the hippocampus and then to the hypothalamus, producing both a bodily response as well as continuing back to the cingulate cortex where it's coded as a feeling

02 LEDOUX
LeDoux believed that there are two ways to trigger a fear response from the amygdala. There is a fast "low road", which extends from the thalamus to the amygdala, and a slow "high road" that goes from the thalamus to the neocortex to the amygdala.

amygdala

03 THE DIFFERENCE
The main difference between the Papez and LeDoux theories is the role of the amygdala. In the LeDoux theory, the amygdala plays a central role in managing fear whereas in the Papez theory the amygdala is not included.

04 CONTEMPORARY REVISIONS
Modern-day research has highlighted the role of other structures, such as cortical or midline thalamic neurons, in affecting the integration and coding of emotion.

Sources: https://www.apa.org/monitor/nov02/synaptic#:~:text=Studies%20have%20shown%20that%20there,to%20the%20amygdala%2C%20said%20LeDoux.

Isha Rojanala, Fall 2023

The Papez Circle

THE OLD DESCRIPTION OF THE EMOTIONAL BRAIN

01 BASIS
Papez proposed that connections between the hypothalamus and the anterior thalamus and from the cingulate cortex were the basis for emotions.

02 INTEGRATION
Papez also suggested that the cingulate cortex integrates these signals from the hypothalamus that would be the basis for emotional experiences or feelings when the information reaches the sensory cortices.

03 "FEELING"
Papez assumed that signals from the cingulate cortex reach the hippocampus and then the hypothalamus allowing a top-down cortical control of emotional responses, and back to the cortex, where a trace of the emotional response to the particular situation is coded and stored as a "feeling"

PAPEZ CIRCUIT THEORY

Emotional Stimulus → Thalamus
- Stream of Thinking → Anterior Thalamus → Hypothalamus → Bodily Response
- → Hippocampus
- Stream of Feeling → Cingulate Cortex → Feeling
Sensory Cortex

Notice that the amygdala is not present in this description

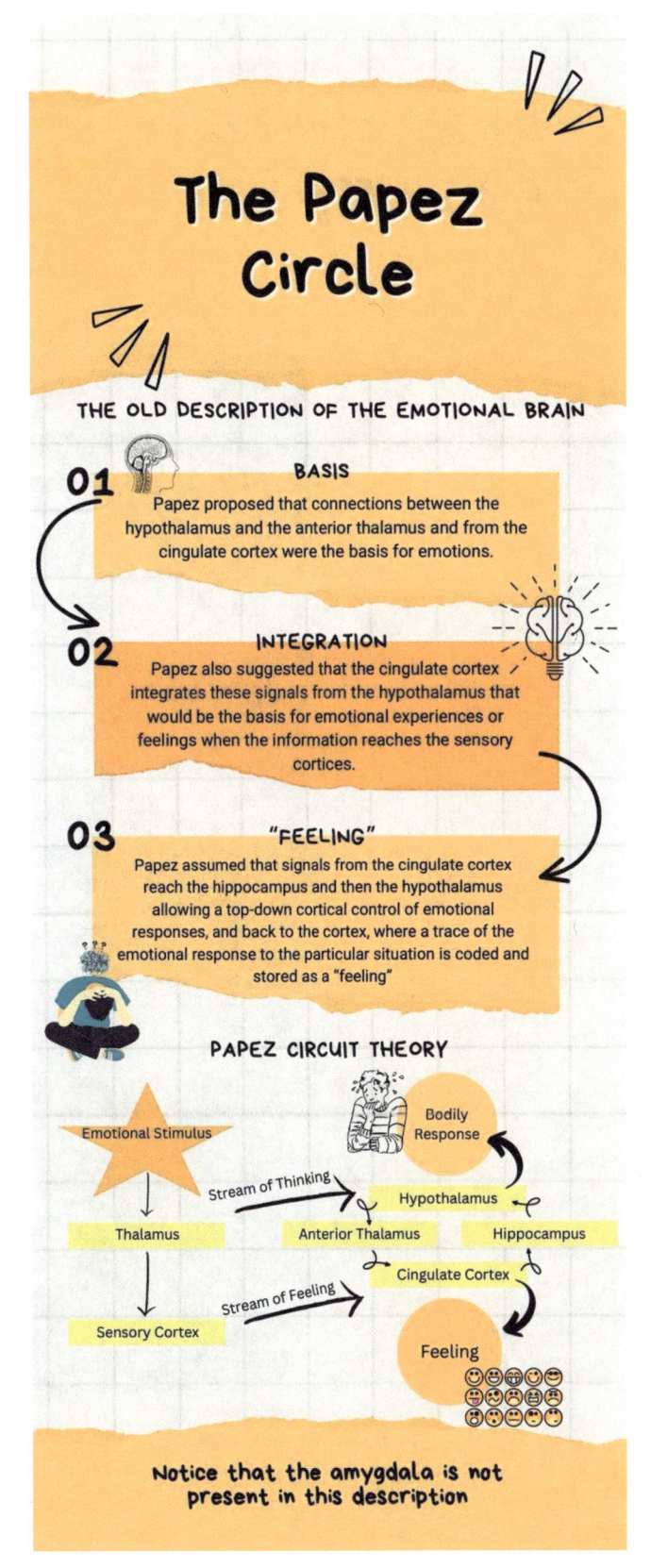

Audrey Villanueva, Fall 2023

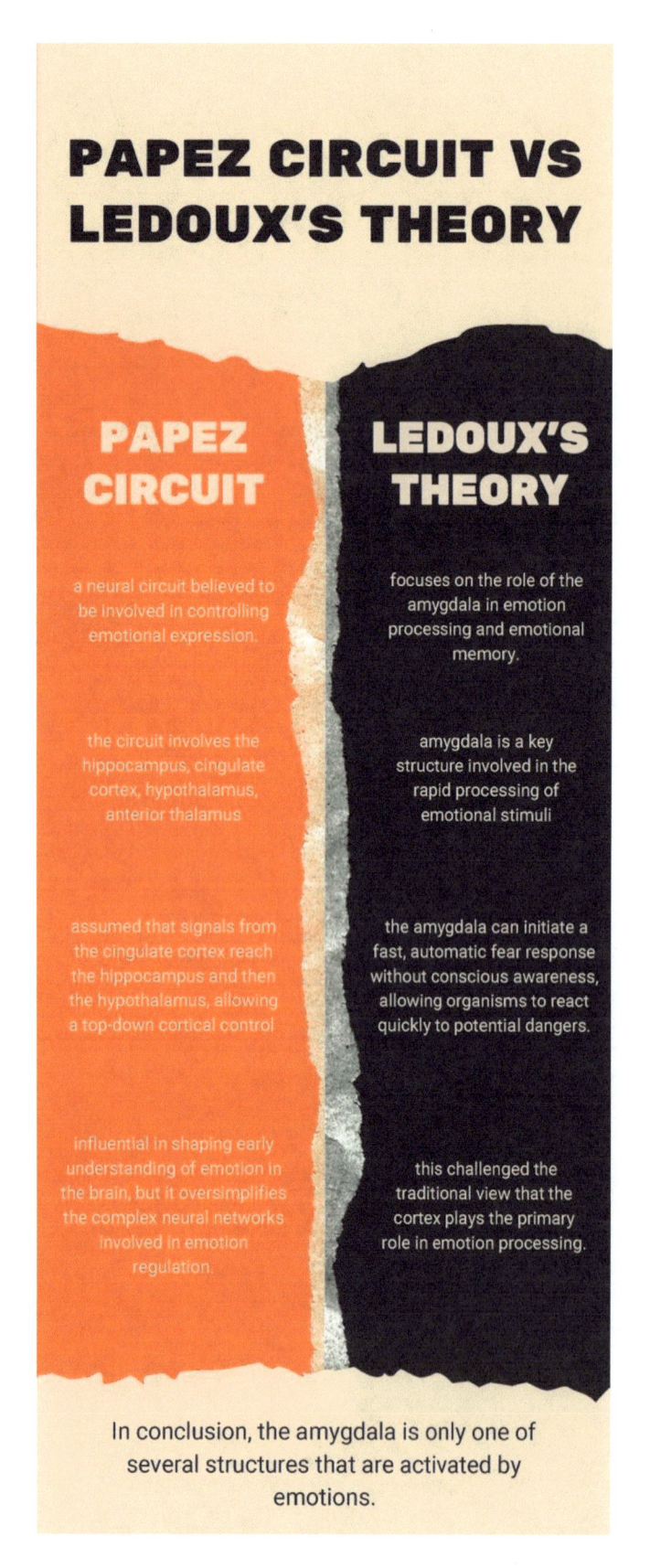

PAPEZ CIRCUIT VS LEDOUX'S THEORY

PAPEZ CIRCUIT

a neural circuit believed to be involved in controlling emotional expression.

the circuit involves the hippocampus, cingulate cortex, hypothalamus, anterior thalamus

assumed that signals from the cingulate cortex reach the hippocampus and then the hypothalamus, allowing a top-down cortical control

influential in shaping early understanding of emotion in the brain, but it oversimplifies the complex neural networks involved in emotion regulation.

LEDOUX'S THEORY

focuses on the role of the amygdala in emotion processing and emotional memory.

amygdala is a key structure involved in the rapid processing of emotional stimuli

the amygdala can initiate a fast, automatic fear response without conscious awareness, allowing organisms to react quickly to potential dangers.

this challenged the traditional view that the cortex plays the primary role in emotion processing.

In conclusion, the amygdala is only one of several structures that are activated by emotions.

Akshara Rao, Spring 2024

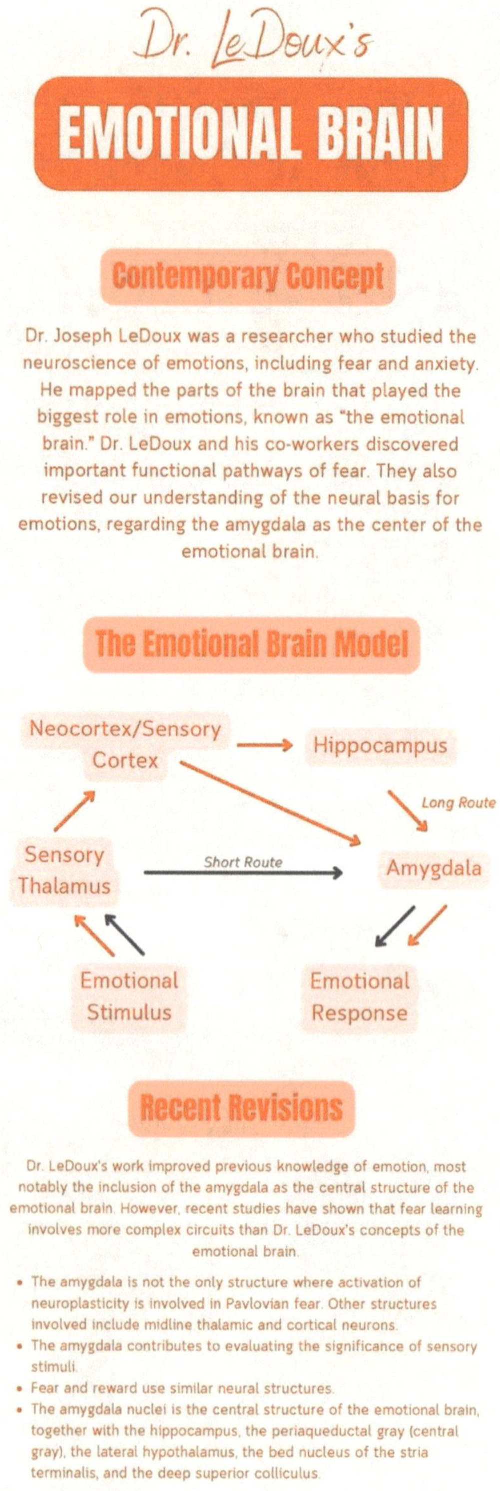

Dr. LeDoux's EMOTIONAL BRAIN

Contemporary Concept

Dr. Joseph LeDoux was a researcher who studied the neuroscience of emotions, including fear and anxiety. He mapped the parts of the brain that played the biggest role in emotions, known as "the emotional brain." Dr. LeDoux and his co-workers discovered important functional pathways of fear. They also revised our understanding of the neural basis for emotions, regarding the amygdala as the center of the emotional brain.

The Emotional Brain Model

Neocortex/Sensory Cortex → Hippocampus
Sensory Thalamus — Short Route → Amygdala (Long Route via Hippocampus)
Emotional Stimulus → Sensory Thalamus
Amygdala → Emotional Response

Recent Revisions

Dr. LeDoux's work improved previous knowledge of emotion, most notably the inclusion of the amygdala as the central structure of the emotional brain. However, recent studies have shown that fear learning involves more complex circuits than Dr. LeDoux's concepts of the emotional brain.

- The amygdala is not the only structure where activation of neuroplasticity is involved in Pavlovian fear. Other structures involved include midline thalamic and cortical neurons.
- The amygdala contributes to evaluating the significance of sensory stimuli.
- Fear and reward use similar neural structures.
- The amygdala nuclei is the central structure of the emotional brain, together with the hippocampus, the periaqueductal gray (central gray), the lateral hypothalamus, the bed nucleus of the stria terminalis, and the deep superior colliculus.

Arshad Manzar, Spring 2024

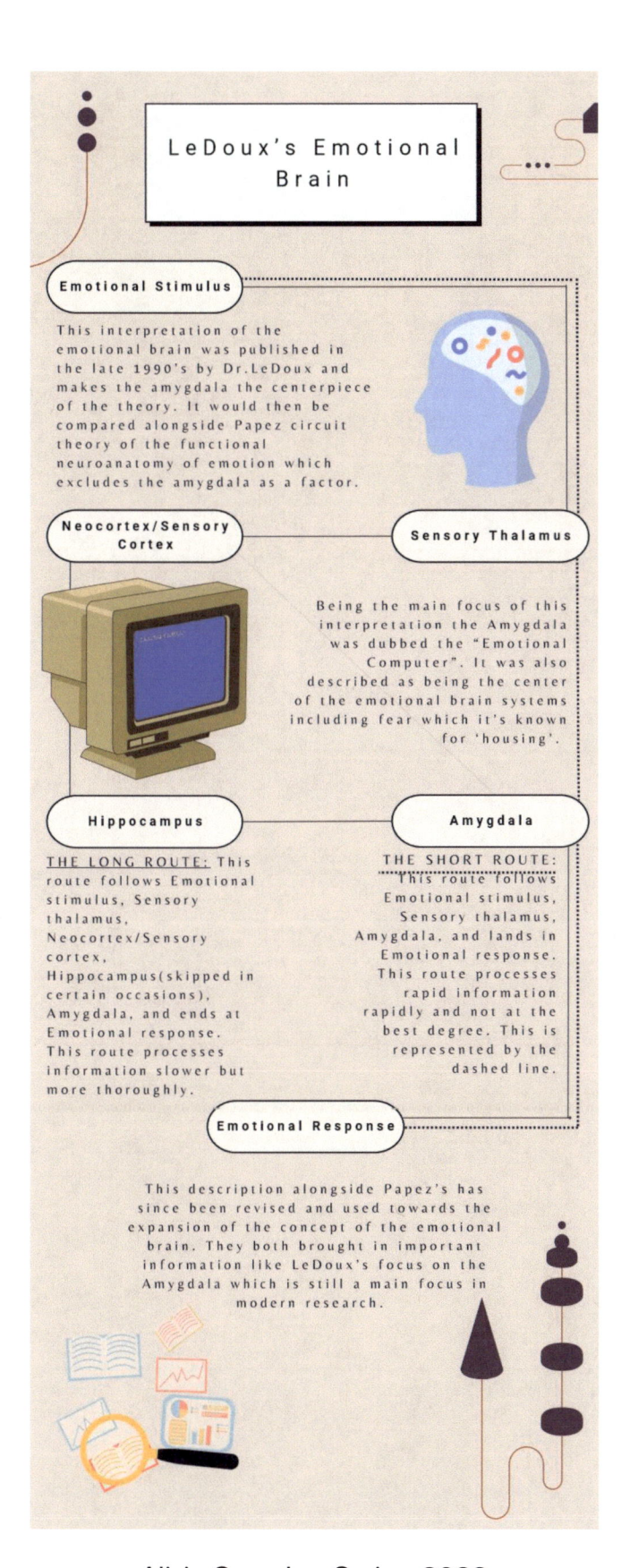

AN INFOGRAPHIC JOURNEY

LeDoux's Emotional Brain

Emotional Stimulus

This interpretation of the emotional brain was published in the late 1990's by Dr. LeDoux and makes the amygdala the centerpiece of the theory. It would then be compared alongside Papez circuit theory of the functional neuroanatomy of emotion which excludes the amygdala as a factor.

Neocortex/Sensory Cortex

Sensory Thalamus

Being the main focus of this interpretation the Amygdala was dubbed the "Emotional Computer". It was also described as being the center of the emotional brain systems including fear which it's known for 'housing'.

Hippocampus

Amygdala

THE LONG ROUTE: This route follows Emotional stimulus, Sensory thalamus, Neocortex/Sensory cortex, Hippocampus (skipped in certain occasions), Amygdala, and ends at Emotional response. This route processes information slower but more thoroughly.

THE SHORT ROUTE: This route follows Emotional stimulus, Sensory thalamus, Amygdala, and lands in Emotional response. This route processes rapid information rapidly and not at the best degree. This is represented by the dashed line.

Emotional Response

This description alongside Papez's has since been revised and used towards the expansion of the concept of the emotional brain. They both brought in important information like LeDoux's focus on the Amygdala which is still a main focus in modern research.

Alicia Gonzalez, Spring 2023

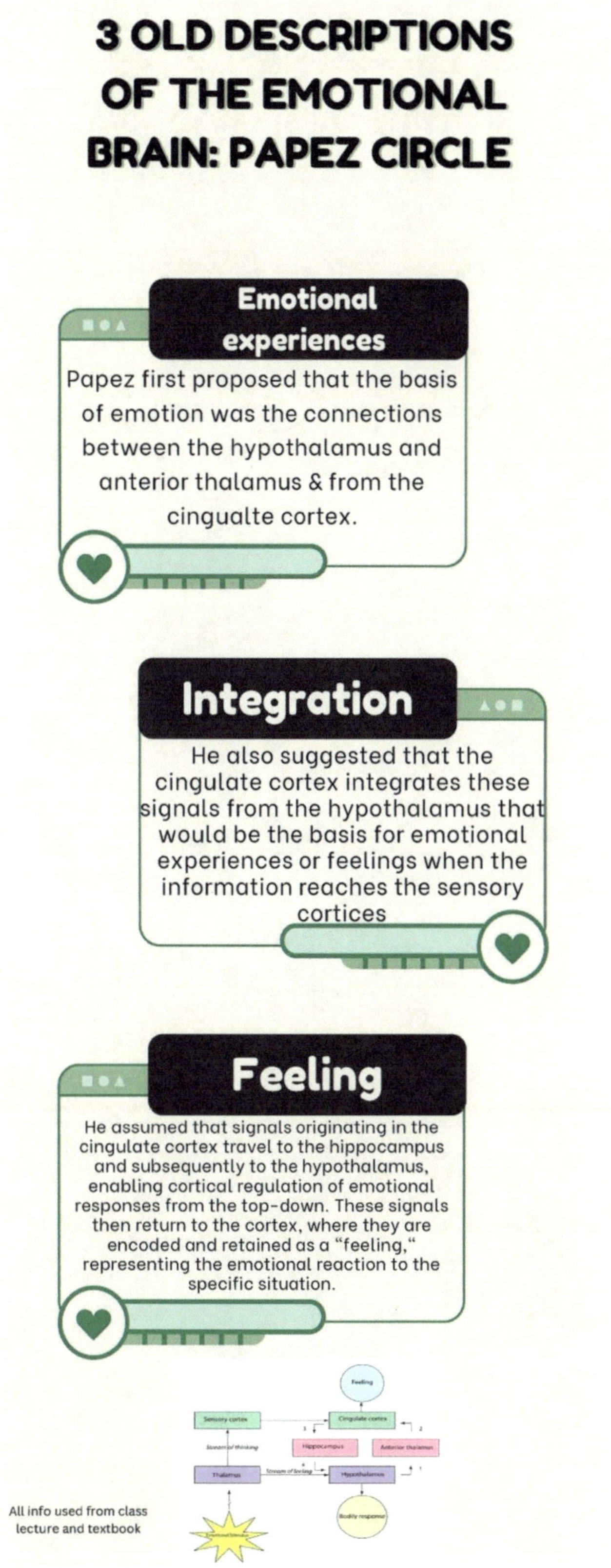

3 OLD DESCRIPTIONS OF THE EMOTIONAL BRAIN: PAPEZ CIRCLE

Emotional experiences

Papez first proposed that the basis of emotion was the connections between the hypothalamus and anterior thalamus & from the cingualte cortex.

Integration

He also suggested that the cingulate cortex integrates these signals from the hypothalamus that would be the basis for emotional experiences or feelings when the information reaches the sensory cortices

Feeling

He assumed that signals originating in the cingulate cortex travel to the hippocampus and subsequently to the hypothalamus, enabling cortical regulation of emotional responses from the top-down. These signals then return to the cortex, where they are encoded and retained as a "feeling," representing the emotional reaction to the specific situation.

All info used from class lecture and textbook

Susana Kudsi, Spring 2024

AN INFOGRAPHIC JOURNEY

CHAPTER 8

Emotion, Memory, and Prediction

Relationship of Emotion and Memory

By Jasha Dela Cruz, Spring 2024

Memories are not screen recordings of one's vision; Emotions are attached to them. Research on autobiographical memory in humans suggests that emotional memories are the ones people perceive to be more vivid (Farmer, 2018). Unfortunately, emotions can be negative feelings, and they can be attached to a memory. This results in fear and anxiety. People could develop trauma and PTSD from events that seared a mark in their minds. The relationship between emotion and memory could be explained by the role of emotion-related brain parts, such as the amygdala, and hormones, such as adrenergic substances (Moller, 2019). This blog will dive into emotional memory.

Research on flashbulb memories was strengthened after research was done around when the 9/11 tragedy struck (Farmer, 2018; Hen, 2020). Flashbulb memories are the memories that humans perceive to be very vivid and detailed. This is due to the powerful emotions attached to the memory. The 9/11 tragedy was very heartbreaking, considering that it was an unexpected event with many innocent lives lost. With this, people developed flashbulb memories. They vividly recall what they were doing when the tragedy happened. For example, a person could remember sitting at a corner of a restaurant eating a hash brown while wearing a green checkered shirt, and the background music was Dixie Chicks when they saw the news that a plane went through the Twin Towers on the television. However, they could not remember what they ate for breakfast the day before. Although flashbulb memories do not immediately indicate accuracy, people still have a strong vision of the specific memory. According to Columbia professor Rene Hen, selectively storing memories is for our good; it is a learning experience (2020). This is when fear learning becomes essential. Seeing a plane hit the buildings resulted in several people canceling their plane trips. Memory and fear became a defense mechanism to increase chances of survival by avoiding the things known to be dangerous (Moller, 2019). In a more experimental set-up, another experiment has shown how emotions contribute to a more memorable memory. A study by Richards and Gross (1999) had participants watch images of injured people. The independent variable in this experiment is whether the participant is allowed to show emotions upon seeing injured people. Those who had to suppress showing emotions were worse in memory tasks than the control group who were free to show emotions. This shows that emotions do play a role in making events more memorable.

The phenomenon of having memorable emotional memories is explained by the amygdala, the part of the brain that controls emotions and regulates memory. When it comes to negative emotions, basolateral amygdala results in the release of stress hormones via the hypothalamic-pituitary-adrenal (HPA) axis, which helps in the consolidation of memory or processing memories to be part of our long-term memory (Moller, 2019; Roozendaal et al., 2018). These stress hormones, such as epinephrine and glucocorticoids, are secreted from the adrenal glands, and they help consolidate memories for the long term (Roozendaal et al., 2008). Norepinephrine strengthens the connection between the amygdala and the hippocampus (Bahtiyar et al., 2020). The hippocampus primarily transfers short-term memory to long-term memory. However, only certain hormones and neurotransmitters can help with memory. Memory retrieval is more difficult once it reaches a maximum amount (Moller, 2019). Unfortunately, chronic stress and mental exhaustion negatively affect memory (Tyng et al., 2017).

Another piece of evidence that shows the relationship between emotions and memory is using beta-adrenergic blockers to blunt negative emotions. Beta-adrenergic blockers such as Propranolol block the effects of androgenic substances and are used to lessen symptoms of anxiety and severe fear. In a mice study, memory traces of fear in the amygdala were reduced in those administered with Propranolol compared to the control group (Leal Santos et al., 2021). This explains why beta-adrenergic blockers are currently used to treat PTSD or post-traumatic stress disorder (Leal Santos et al., 2021). Propranolol helps in decreasing intrusive traumatic memories, startling, and nightmares for people suffering from PTSD. In fact, with propanol, forcing one to recall traumatic experiences actively results in fewer PTSD symptoms (Gore, 2024). Problematic psychiatric disorders such as PTSD show how memories and emotions are interconnected. Unfortunately, the constant interaction between maladaptive emotions and memories could become brain plasticity. Plasticity occurs when there are changes in the brain, such as new synaptic connections. When a person is in a fearful and stressful state, specific circuits in the brain change, leading to memory formation specific to fear (Bronston, 2022). This occurs in people with PTSD. Since plasticity increases arousal, negative memories eventually become unforgettable and intrusive (Bronston, 2022). Those who are resilient or have recovered from PTSD show to have the capability to eliminate fear memories that were traumatizing (Moller, 2019).

Aside from the neurotransmitters and hormones the amygdala produces, the amygdala also has connections to parts of the brain that deal with memory (Moller, 2019). For example, the amygdala has neural connections to parts of the brain that deal with working memory (conscious current short-term memory), declarative memory (recollection of facts and events), and nondeclarative memory (procedural memory, usually unconscious). The amygdala directly connects with the medial temporal lobe memory system, including the hippocampus. It also has direct and indirect connections with the ventral prefrontal cortex, which deals with retrieval of personal episodic memory and semantic memory; and the dorsal prefrontal cortex, which deals with working memory and prospective memory, which is memory for the future. These connections show the possible neural mechanisms that illustrate how the amygdala, the part of the brain that deals with emotions, influences memory (Moller, 2019).

To survive, there are certain things that we must remember and keep in mind. Although fear could be a temporary feeling, attaching such emotions to memory could be helpful for our well-being. Some events warn us about what to avoid. Hence, fear learning (Izquierdo et al., 2016). The connection between emotion and memory in the brain made sense to protect us from our environment. Forgetting a memory of cutting yourself with a knife might lead you to more danger if you eventually choose to use the knife carelessly. Emotional memory seems to be purposefully memorable for this reason.

References

1. Bahtiyar, S., Karaca, K. G., Henckens, M. J., & Roozendaal, B. (2020). Norepinephrine and glucocorticoid effects on the brain mechanisms underlying memory accuracy and generalization. *Molecular and Cellular Neuroscience*, *108*, 103537.
2. Bronston, B. (2022). *Study examines why memory of fear is seared into our brains.* Tulane University. https://news.tulane.edu/pr/study-examines-why-memory-fear-seared-our-brains Farmer, T. (2018). *Cognition*.
3. Wiley Hen, R. (2020). *Why are memories attached to emotions so strong.* https://www.cuimc.columbia.edu/news/why-are-memories-attached-emotions-so-strong.
4. Izquierdo, I., Furini, C. R., & Myskiw, J. C. (2016). Fear memory. *Physiological reviews*, *96*(2), 695-750.
5. Leal Santos, S., Stackmann, M., Muñoz Zamora, A., Mastrodonato, A., De Landri, A. V., Vaughan, N., Chen, B. K., Lanio, M., & Denny, C. A. (2021). Propranolol Decreases Fear Expression by Modulating Fear Memory Traces. *Biological psychiatry*, *89*(12), 1150–1161. https://doi.org/10.1016/j.biopsych.2021.01.005

6. Moller, A. (2019). Neurobiology of Fear and other Emotions.

7. Richards, J. M., & Gross, J. J. (1999). Composure at Any Cost? The Cognitive Consequences of Emotion Suppression. Personality and Social Psychology Bulletin, 25(8), 1033-1044. https://doi.org/10.1177/01461672992511010

8. Roozendaal, B., Barsegyan, A., & Lee, S. (2008). Adrenal stress hormones, amygdala activation, and memory for emotionally arousing experiences. *Progress in brain research*, *167*, 79–97. https://doi.org/10.1016/S0079-6123(07)67006-X

9. Roozendaal, B., McEwen, B. S., & Chattarji, S. (2009). Stress, memory and the amygdala. *Nature Reviews Neuroscience*, *10*(6), 423-433.

10. T Allen Gore, M. (2024). *Posttraumatic stress disorder medication*. Selective serotonin reuptake inhibitors, Beta-blockers, Alpha-1 Receptor Antagonists, Alpha-2 Adrenergic Agonists. https://emedicine.medscape.com/article/288154-medication?form=fpf.

11. Tyng, C. M., Amin, H. U., Saad, M. N. M., & Malik, A. S. (2017). The Influences of Emotion on Learning and Memory. *Frontiers in psychology*, *8*, 1454. https://doi.org/10.3389/fpsyg.2017.01454.

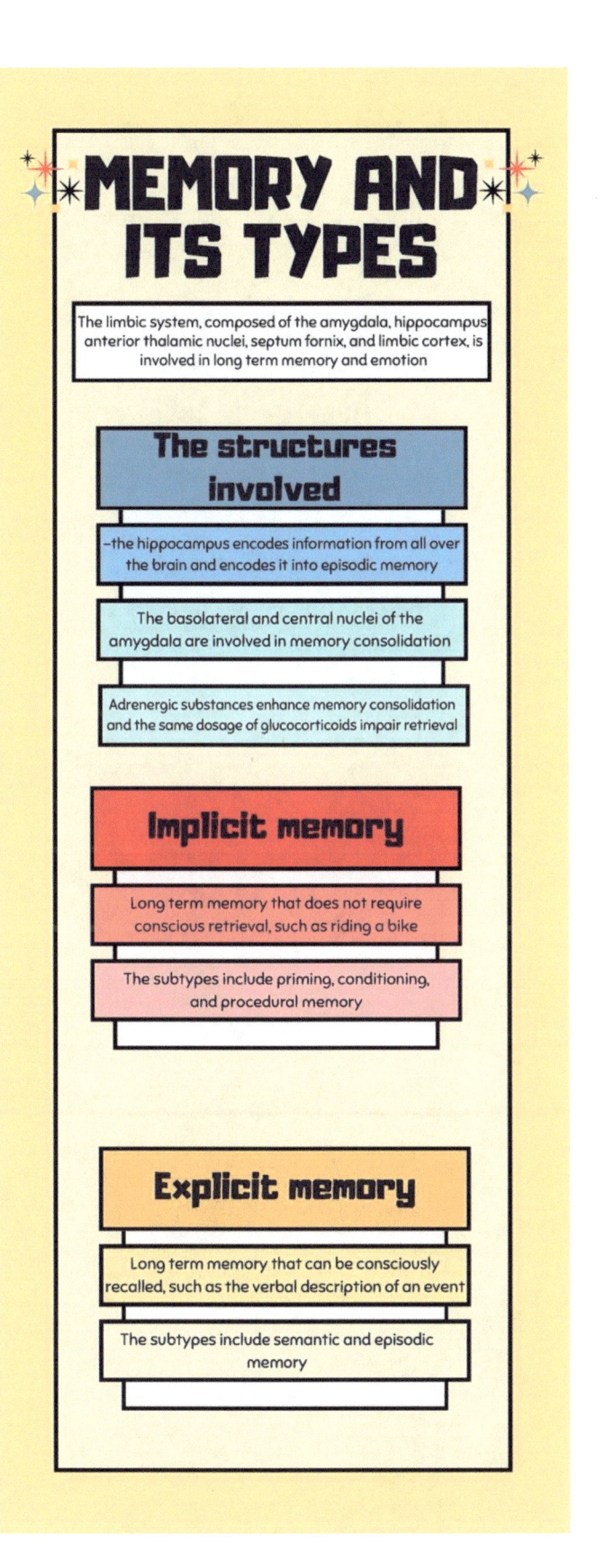

AN INFOGRAPHIC JOURNEY

MEMORY AND ITS TYPES

The limbic system, composed of the amygdala, hippocampus anterior thalamic nuclei, septum fornix, and limbic cortex, is involved in long term memory and emotion

The structures involved

- the hippocampus encodes information from all over the brain and encodes it into episodic memory

The basolateral and central nuclei of the amygdala are involved in memory consolidation

Adrenergic substances enhance memory consolidation and the same dosage of glucocorticoids impair retrieval

Implicit memory

Long term memory that does not require conscious retrieval, such as riding a bike

The subtypes include priming, conditioning, and procedural memory

Explicit memory

Long term memory that can be consciously recalled, such as the verbal description of an event

The subtypes include semantic and episodic memory

Minaal Atif, Spring 2024

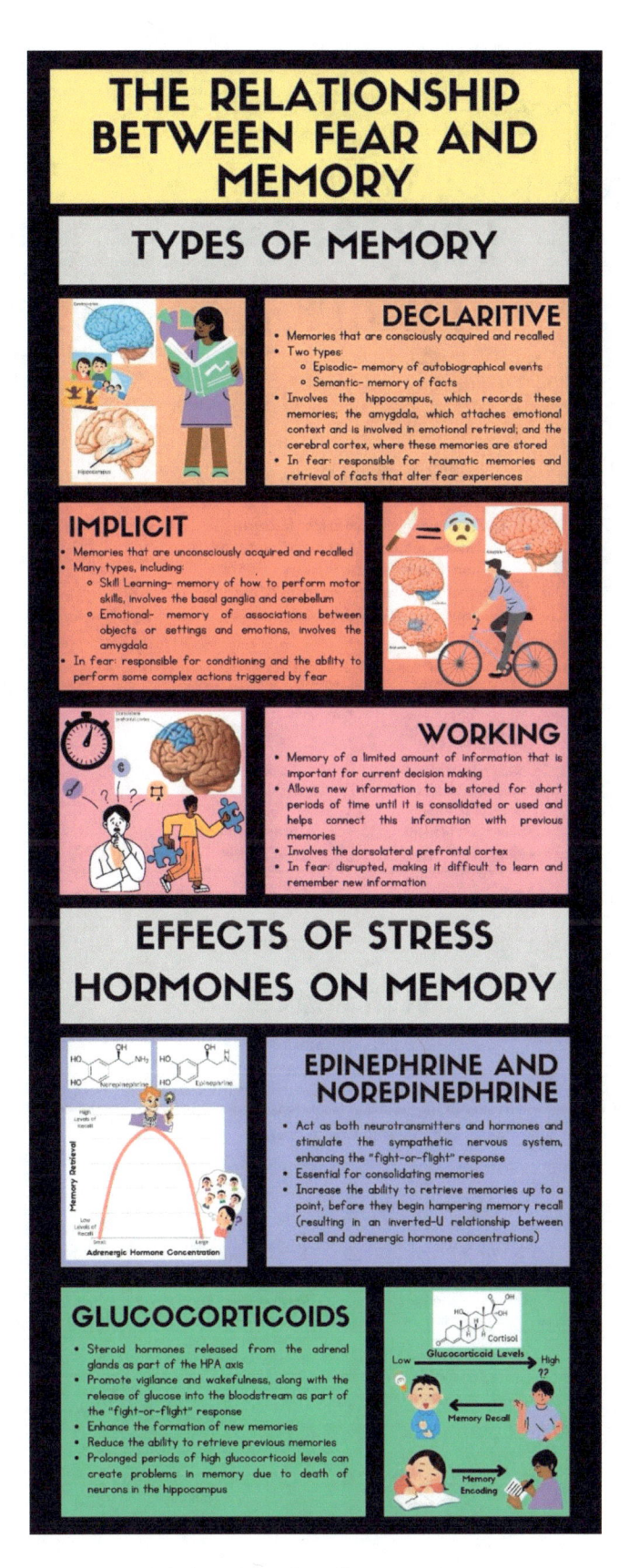

THE RELATIONSHIP BETWEEN FEAR AND MEMORY

TYPES OF MEMORY

DECLARITIVE
- Memories that are consciously acquired and recalled
- Two types:
  - Episodic- memory of autobiographical events
  - Semantic- memory of facts
- Involves the hippocampus, which records these memories; the amygdala, which attaches emotional context and is involved in emotional retrieval; and the cerebral cortex, where these memories are stored
- In fear: responsible for traumatic memories and retrieval of facts that alter fear experiences

IMPLICIT
- Memories that are unconsciously acquired and recalled
- Many types, including:
  - Skill Learning- memory of how to perform motor skills, involves the basal ganglia and cerebellum
  - Emotional- memory of associations between objects or settings and emotions, involves the amygdala
- In fear: responsible for conditioning and the ability to perform some complex actions triggered by fear

WORKING
- Memory of a limited amount of information that is important for current decision making
- Allows new information to be stored for short periods of time until it is consolidated or used and helps connect this information with previous memories
- Involves the dorsolateral prefrontal cortex
- In fear: disrupted, making it difficult to learn and remember new information

EFFECTS OF STRESS HORMONES ON MEMORY

EPINEPHRINE AND NOREPINEPHRINE
- Act as both neurotransmitters and hormones and stimulate the sympathetic nervous system, enhancing the "fight-or-flight" response
- Essential for consolidating memories
- Increase the ability to retrieve memories up to a point, before they begin hampering memory recall (resulting in an inverted-U relationship between recall and adrenergic hormone concentrations)

GLUCOCORTICOIDS
- Steroid hormones released from the adrenal glands as part of the HPA axis
- Promote vigilance and wakefulness, along with the release of glucose into the bloodstream as part of the "fight-or-flight" response
- Enhance the formation of new memories
- Reduce the ability to retrieve previous memories
- Prolonged periods of high glucocorticoid levels can create problems in memory due to death of neurons in the hippocampus

Allyson Macfee, Spring 2024

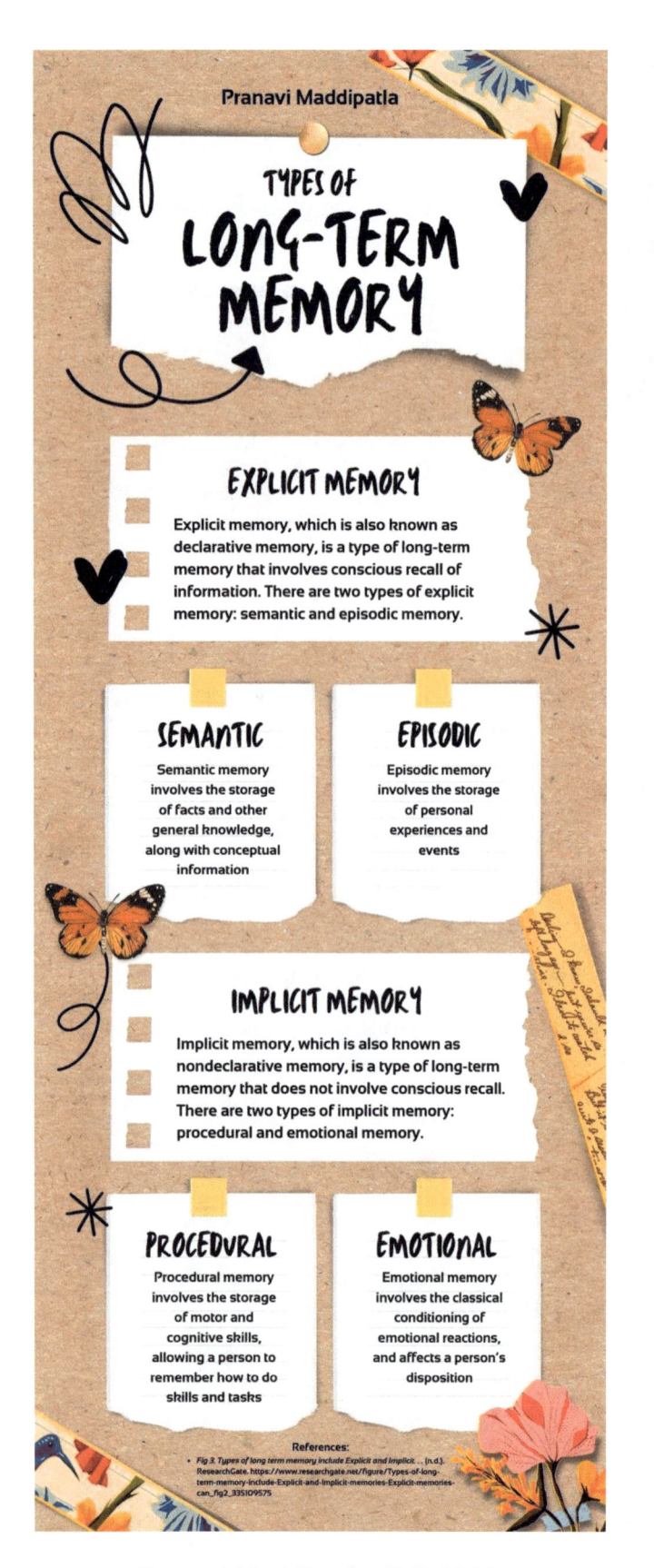

AN INFOGRAPHIC JOURNEY

Types of Long-Term Memory

Pranavi Maddipatla

EXPLICIT MEMORY
Explicit memory, which is also known as declarative memory, is a type of long-term memory that involves conscious recall of information. There are two types of explicit memory: semantic and episodic memory.

SEMANTIC
Semantic memory involves the storage of facts and other general knowledge, along with conceptual information

EPISODIC
Episodic memory involves the storage of personal experiences and events

IMPLICIT MEMORY
Implicit memory, which is also known as nondeclarative memory, is a type of long-term memory that does not involve conscious recall. There are two types of implicit memory: procedural and emotional memory.

PROCEDURAL
Procedural memory involves the storage of motor and cognitive skills, allowing a person to remember how to do skills and tasks

EMOTIONAL
Emotional memory involves the classical conditioning of emotional reactions, and affects a person's disposition

References:
Fig 3. Types of long term memory include Explicit and Implicit... (n.d.). ResearchGate. https://www.researchgate.net/figure/Types-of-long-term-memory-include-Explicit-and-Implicit-memories-Explicit-memories-can_fig2_335109575

Pranavi Maddipatla, Fall 2023

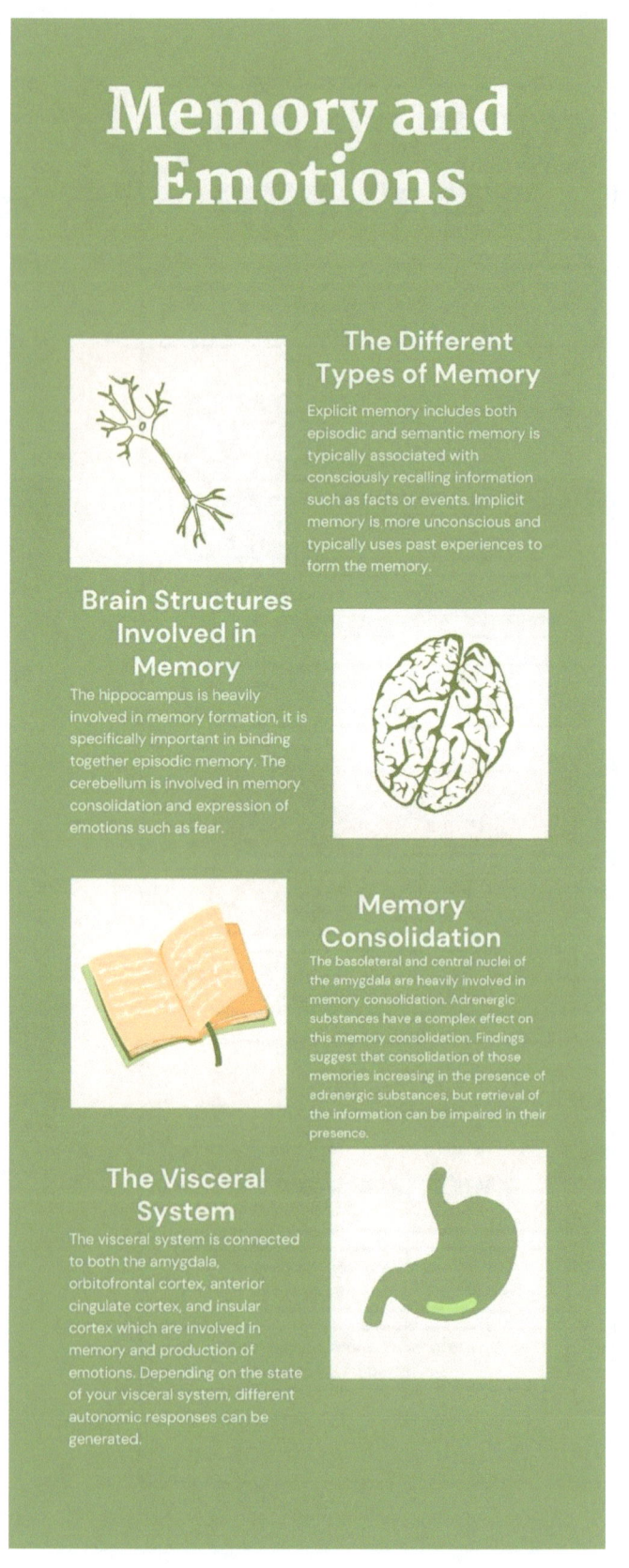

Memory and Emotions

The Different Types of Memory
Explicit memory includes both episodic and semantic memory is typically associated with consciously recalling information such as facts or events. Implicit memory is more unconscious and typically uses past experiences to form the memory.

Brain Structures Involved in Memory
The hippocampus is heavily involved in memory formation, it is specifically important in binding together episodic memory. The cerebellum is involved in memory consolidation and expression of emotions such as fear.

Memory Consolidation
The basolateral and central nuclei of the amygdala are heavily involved in memory consolidation. Adrenergic substances have a complex effect on this memory consolidation. Findings suggest that consolidation of those memories increasing in the presence of adrenergic substances, but retrieval of the information can be impaired in their presence.

The Visceral System
The visceral system is connected to both the amygdala, orbitofrontal cortex, anterior cingulate cortex, and insular cortex which are involved in memory and production of emotions. Depending on the state of your visceral system, different autonomic responses can be generated.

Austin Sprouse, Spring 2024

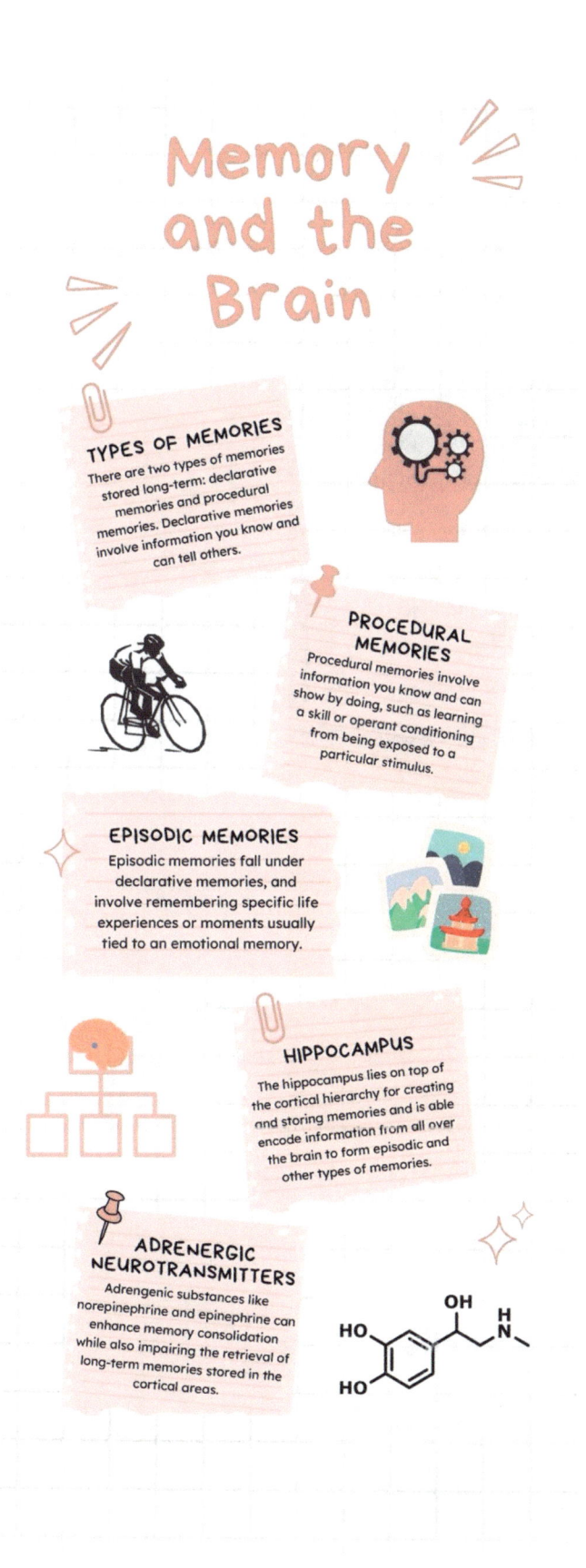

Memory and the Brain

TYPES OF MEMORIES
There are two types of memories stored long-term: declarative memories and procedural memories. Declarative memories involve information you know and can tell others.

PROCEDURAL MEMORIES
Procedural memories involve information you know and can show by doing, such as learning a skill or operant conditioning from being exposed to a particular stimulus.

EPISODIC MEMORIES
Episodic memories fall under declarative memories, and involve remembering specific life experiences or moments usually tied to an emotional memory.

HIPPOCAMPUS
The hippocampus lies on top of the cortical hierarchy for creating and storing memories and is able encode information from all over the brain to form episodic and other types of memories.

ADRENERGIC NEUROTRANSMITTERS
Adrenergic substances like norepinephrine and epinephrine can enhance memory consolidation while also impairing the retrieval of long-term memories stored in the cortical areas.

Shreya Jupelly, Spring 2024

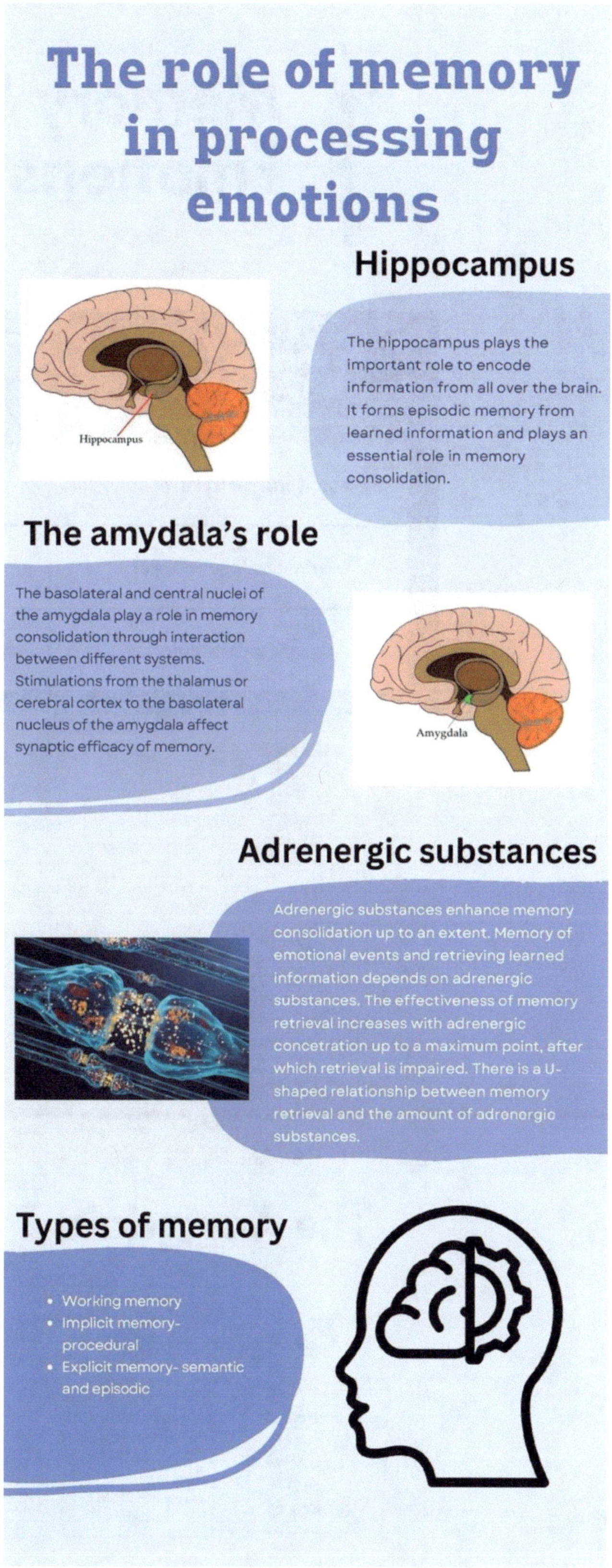

The role of memory in processing emotions

Hippocampus
The hippocampus plays the important role to encode information from all over the brain. It forms episodic memory from learned information and plays an essential role in memory consolidation.

The amydala's role
The basolateral and central nuclei of the amygdala play a role in memory consolidation through interaction between different systems. Stimulations from the thalamus or cerebral cortex to the basolateral nucleus of the amygdala affect synaptic efficacy of memory.

Adrenergic substances
Adrenergic substances enhance memory consolidation up to an extent. Memory of emotional events and retrieving learned information depends on adrenergic substances. The effectiveness of memory retrieval increases with adrenergic concetration up to a maximum point, after which retrieval is impaired. There is a U-shaped relationship between memory retrieval and the amount of adrenergic substances.

Types of memory
- Working memory
- Implicit memory- procedural
- Explicit memory- semantic and episodic

Kajal Patel, Spring 2024

Memory & Emotions

Two complex systems influencing one another

Components of Emotion Affect Memory

basolateral and central n. of amygdala	involved in memory consolidation
adrenergic substances	enhance consolidation and affect retrieval
glucocorticoids	enhance consolidation or impair retrieval

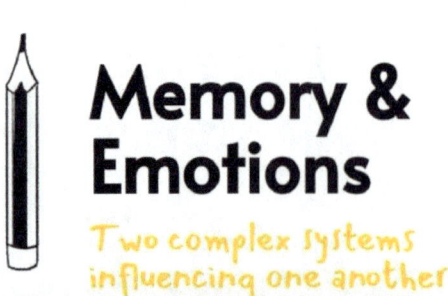

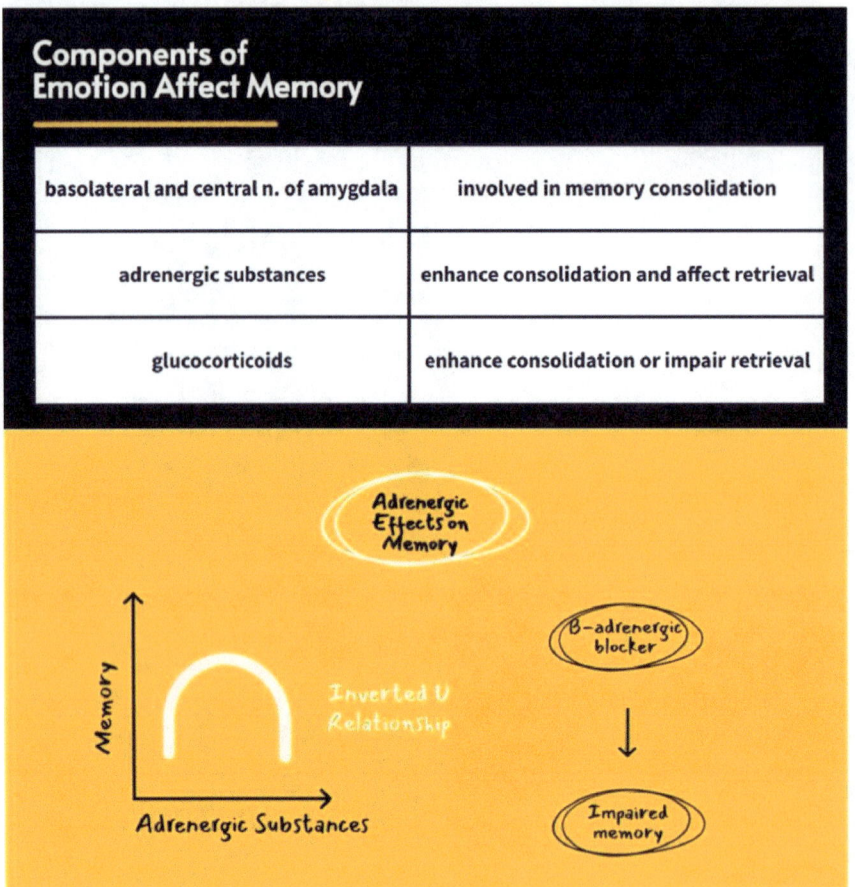

Adrenergic Effects on Memory

Inverted U Relationship — Memory vs. Adrenergic Substances

β-adrenergic blocker → Impaired memory

The Amygdala & Memory
Modulatory Effects

- Amygdala triggers release of stress hormones
- Amygdala signals areas involved with working, declarative, and non-declarative memory
- Amygdala mediates influence of emotional arousal on memory
- Amygdala facilitates neural plasticity

Dominique Ortiz, Fall 2022

AN INFOGRAPHIC JOURNEY

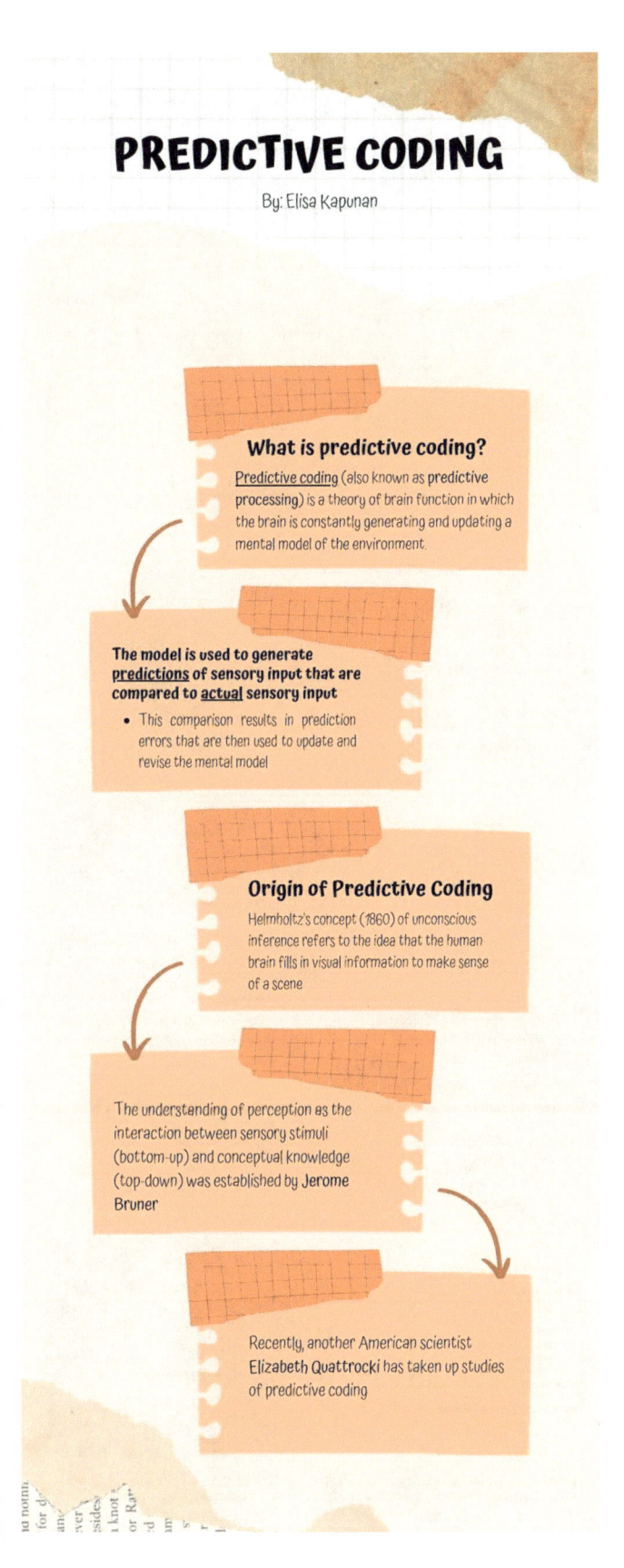

Elisa Kapunan, Spring 2023

Emily Leung, Fall 2023

PREDICTIVE CODING

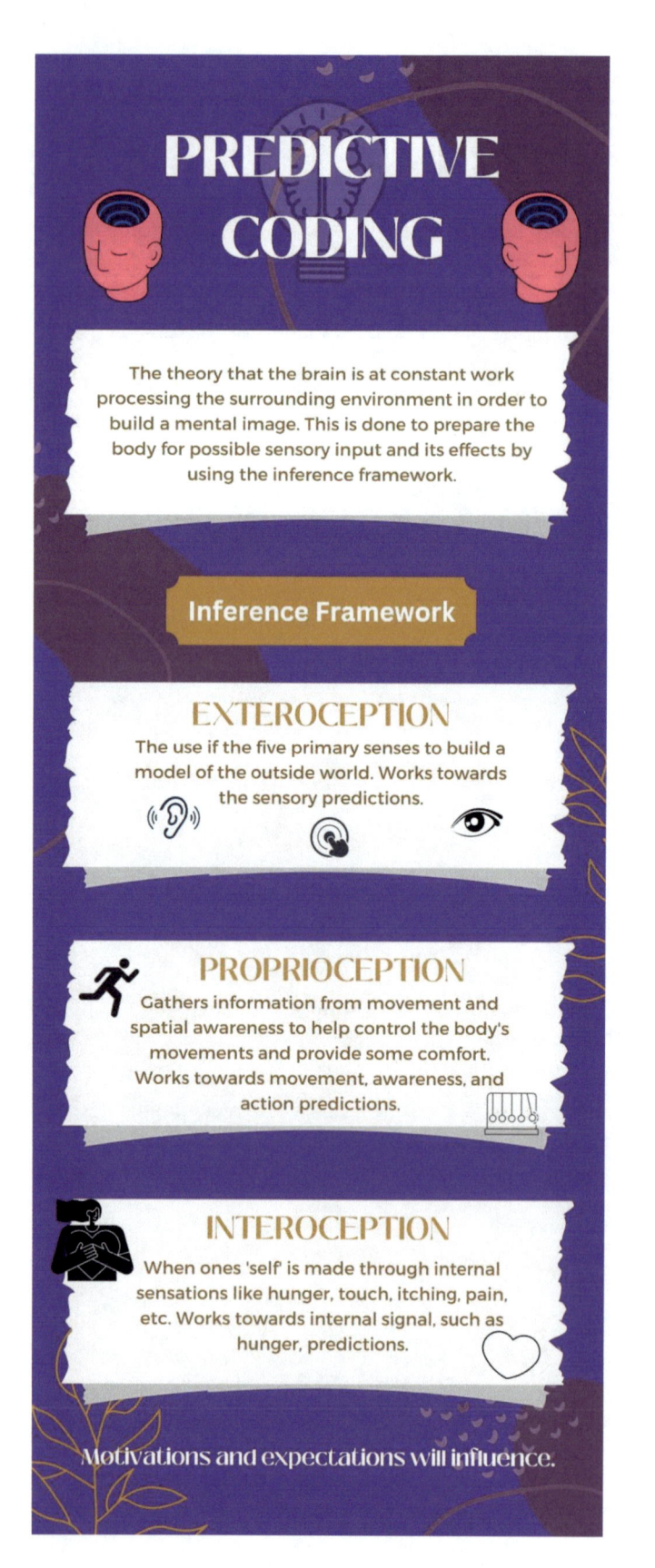

The theory that the brain is at constant work processing the surrounding environment in order to build a mental image. This is done to prepare the body for possible sensory input and its effects by using the inference framework.

Inference Framework

EXTEROCEPTION
The use if the five primary senses to build a model of the outside world. Works towards the sensory predictions.

PROPRIOCEPTION
Gathers information from movement and spatial awareness to help control the body's movements and provide some comfort. Works towards movement, awareness, and action predictions.

INTEROCEPTION
When ones 'self' is made through internal sensations like hunger, touch, itching, pain, etc. Works towards internal signal, such as hunger, predictions.

Motivations and expectations will influence.

Alicia Gonzalez, Spring 2023

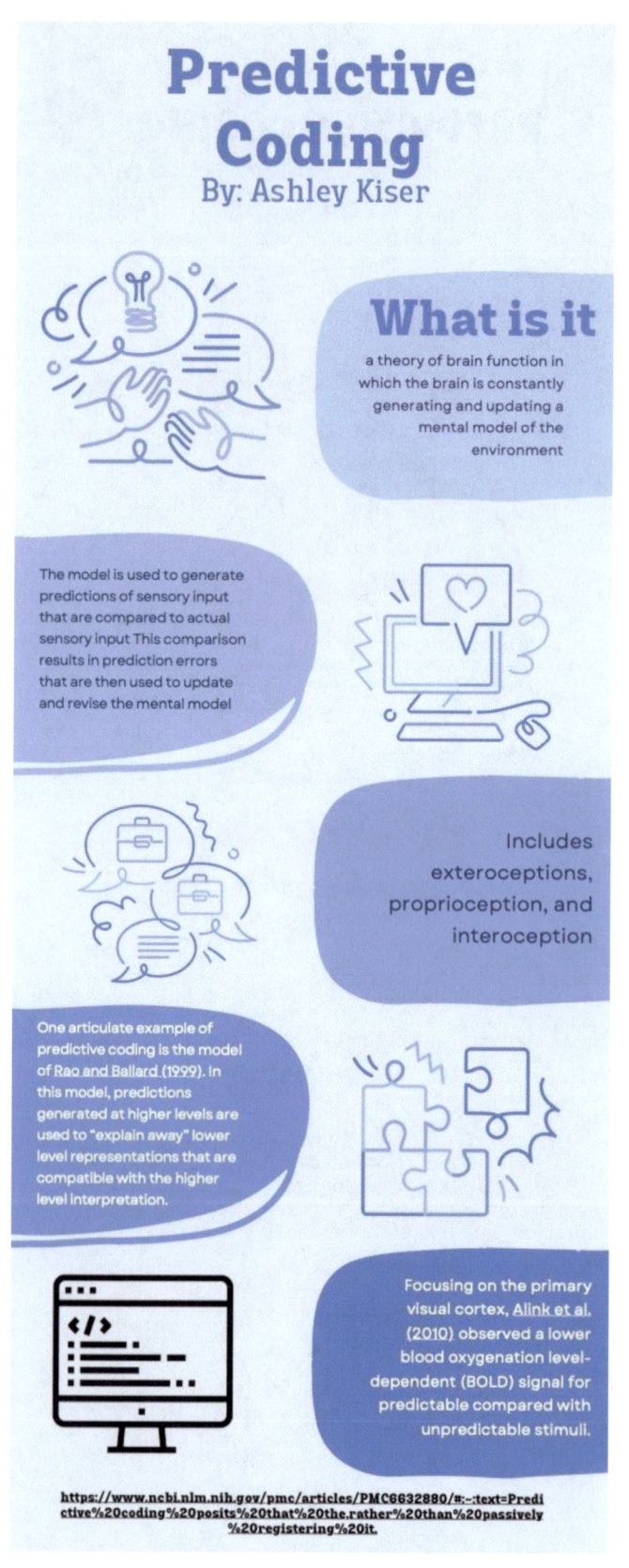

Predictive Coding
By: Ashley Kiser

What is it
a theory of brain function in which the brain is constantly generating and updating a mental model of the environment

The model is used to generate predictions of sensory input that are compared to actual sensory input This comparison results in prediction errors that are then used to update and revise the mental model

Includes exteroceptions, proprioception, and interoception

One articulate example of predictive coding is the model of Rao and Ballard (1999). In this model, predictions generated at higher levels are used to "explain away" lower level representations that are compatible with the higher level interpretation.

Focusing on the primary visual cortex, Alink et al. (2010) observed a lower blood oxygenation level-dependent (BOLD) signal for predictable compared with unpredictable stimuli.

https://www.ncbi.nlm.nih.gov/pmc/articles/PMC6632880/#:~:text=Predictive%20coding%20posits%20that%20the,rather%20than%20passively%20registering%20it.

Ashley Kiser, Fall 2023

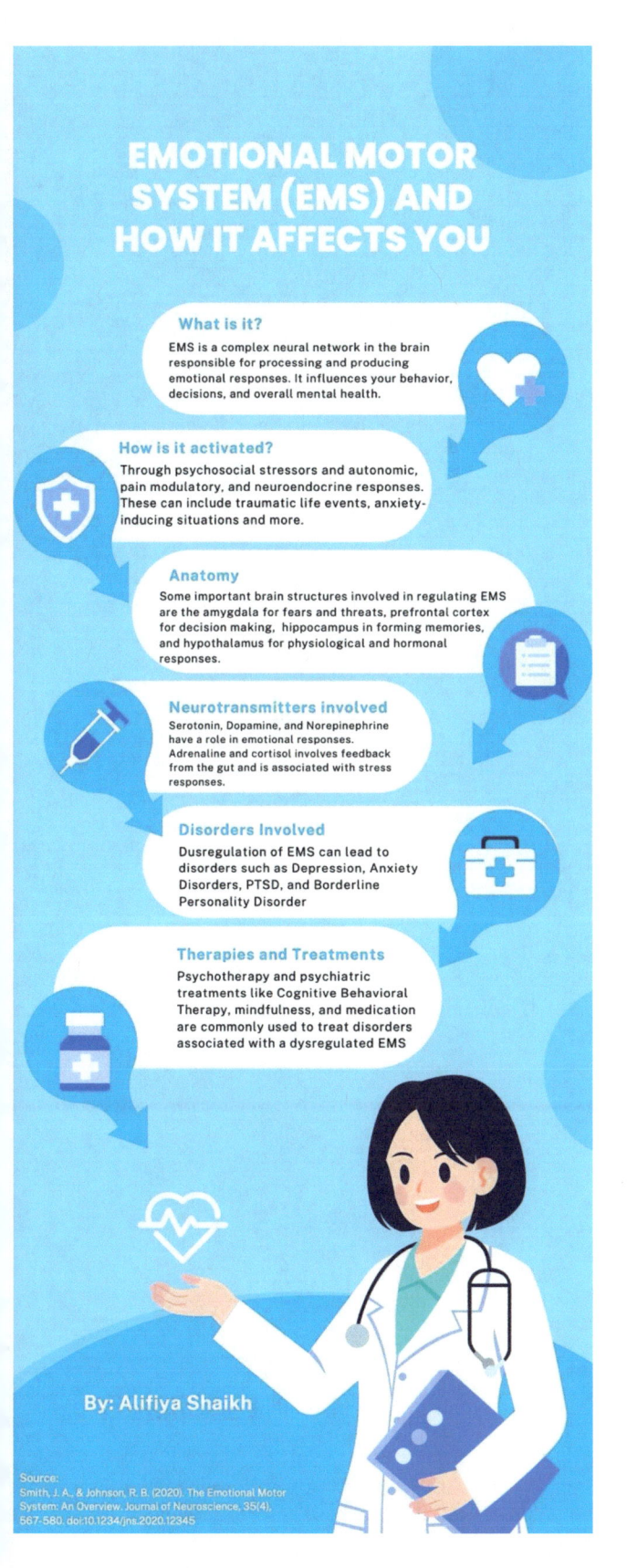

AN INFOGRAPHIC JOURNEY

EMOTIONAL MOTOR SYSTEM (EMS) AND HOW IT AFFECTS YOU

What is it?
EMS is a complex neural network in the brain responsible for processing and producing emotional responses. It influences your behavior, decisions, and overall mental health.

How is it activated?
Through psychosocial stressors and autonomic, pain modulatory, and neuroendocrine responses. These can include traumatic life events, anxiety-inducing situations and more.

Anatomy
Some important brain structures involved in regulating EMS are the amygdala for fears and threats, prefrontal cortex for decision making, hippocampus in forming memories, and hypothalamus for physiological and hormonal responses.

Neurotransmitters involved
Serotonin, Dopamine, and Norepinephrine have a role in emotional responses. Adrenaline and cortisol involves feedback from the gut and is associated with stress responses.

Disorders Involved
Dysregulation of EMS can lead to disorders such as Depression, Anxiety Disorders, PTSD, and Borderline Personality Disorder

Therapies and Treatments
Psychotherapy and psychiatric treatments like Cognitive Behavioral Therapy, mindfulness, and medication are commonly used to treat disorders associated with a dysregulated EMS

By: Alifiya Shaikh

Source: Smith, J. A., & Johnson, R. B. (2020). The Emotional Motor System: An Overview. Journal of Neuroscience, 35(4), 567-580. doi:10.1234/jns.2020.12345

Alifiya Shaikh, Fall 2023

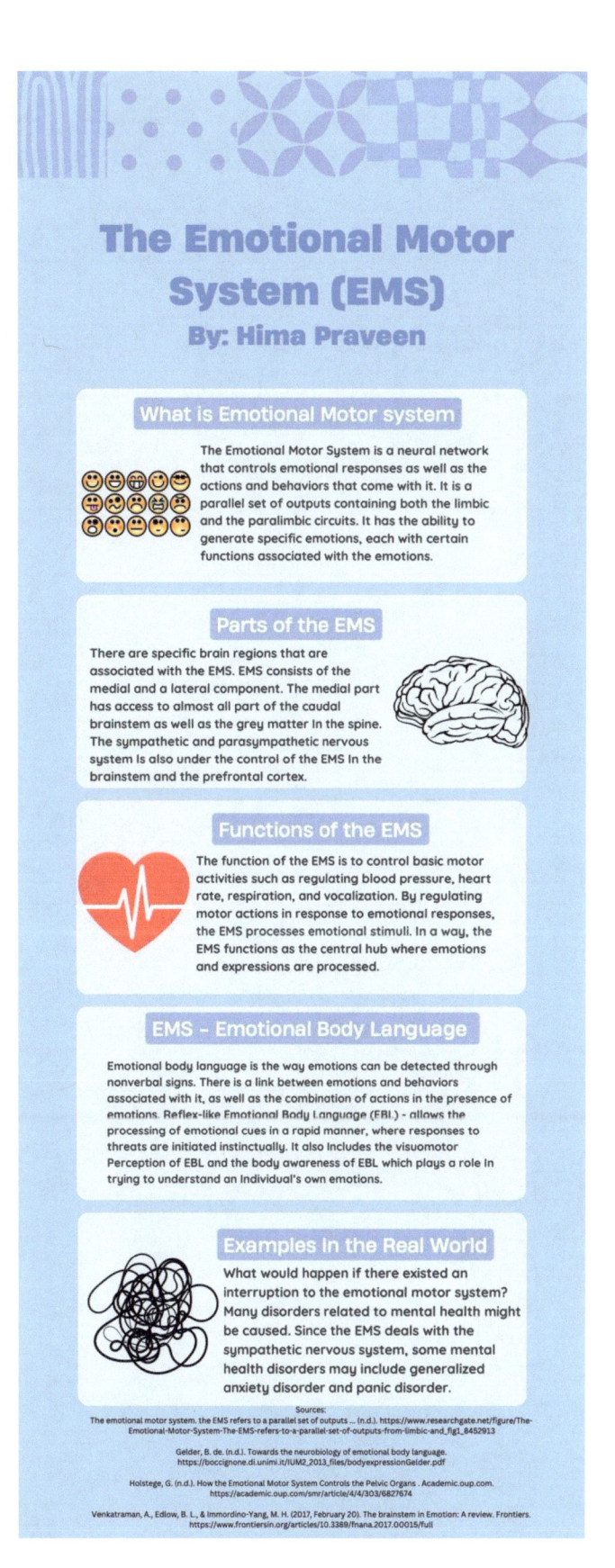

The Emotional Motor System (EMS)
By: Hima Praveen

What is Emotional Motor system
The Emotional Motor System is a neural network that controls emotional responses as well as the actions and behaviors that come with it. It is a parallel set of outputs containing both the limbic and the paralimbic circuits. It has the ability to generate specific emotions, each with certain functions associated with the emotions.

Parts of the EMS
There are specific brain regions that are associated with the EMS. EMS consists of the medial and a lateral component. The medial part has access to almost all part of the caudal brainstem as well as the grey matter in the spine. The sympathetic and parasympathetic nervous system is also under the control of the EMS in the brainstem and the prefrontal cortex.

Functions of the EMS
The function of the EMS is to control basic motor activities such as regulating blood pressure, heart rate, respiration, and vocalization. By regulating motor actions in response to emotional responses, the EMS processes emotional stimuli. In a way, the EMS functions as the central hub where emotions and expressions are processed.

EMS - Emotional Body Language
Emotional body language is the way emotions can be detected through nonverbal signs. There is a link between emotions and behaviors associated with it, as well as the combination of actions in the presence of emotions. Reflex-like Emotional Body Language (EBL) - allows the processing of emotional cues in a rapid manner, where responses to threats are initiated instinctually. It also includes the visuomotor Perception of EBL and the body awareness of EBL which plays a role in trying to understand an individual's own emotions.

Examples In the Real World
What would happen if there existed an interruption to the emotional motor system? Many disorders related to mental health might be caused. Since the EMS deals with the sympathetic nervous system, some mental health disorders may include generalized anxiety disorder and panic disorder.

Sources:
The emotional motor system. the EMS refers to a parallel set of outputs ... (n.d.). https://www.researchgate.net/figure/The-Emotional-Motor-System-The-EMS-refers-to-a-parallel-set-of-outputs-from-limbic-and_fig1_8452913

Gelder, B. de. (n.d.). Towards the neurobiology of emotional body language. https://boccignone.di.unimi.it/IUM2_2013_files/bodyexpressionGelder.pdf

Holstege, G. (n.d.). How the Emotional Motor System Controls the Pelvic Organs . Academic.oup.com. https://academic.oup.com/smr/article/4/4/303/6827674

Venkatraman, A., Edlow, B. L., & Immordino-Yang, M. H. (2017, February 20). The brainstem in Emotion: A review. Frontiers. https://www.frontiersin.org/articles/10.3389/fnana.2017.00015/full

Hima Praveen, Fall 2023

AN INFOGRAPHIC JOURNEY

AN INFOGRAPHIC JOURNEY

CHAPTER 9

The Nervous System

AN INFOGRAPHIC JOURNEY

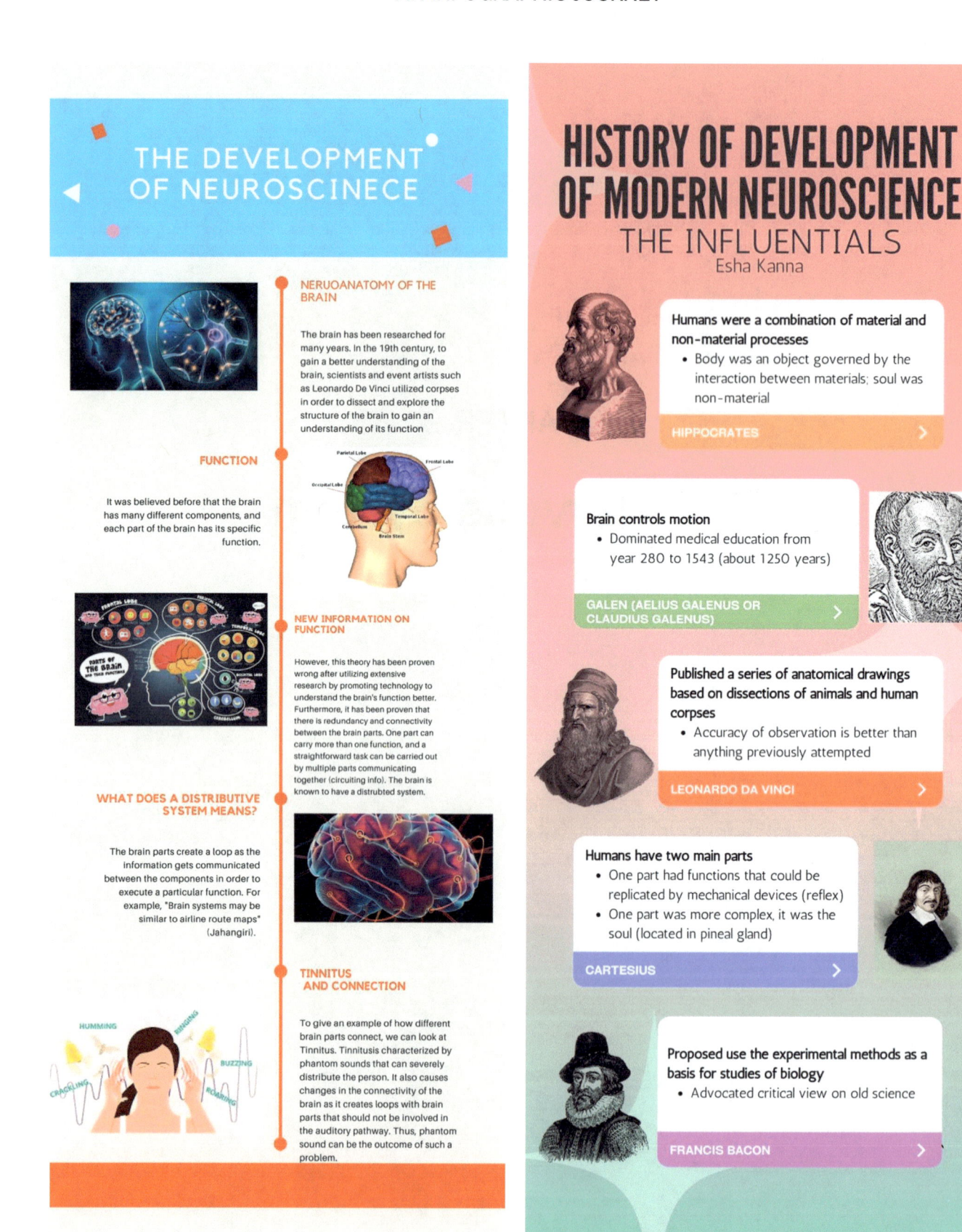

THE DEVELOPMENT OF NEUROSCINECE

NERUOANATOMY OF THE BRAIN

The brain has been researched for many years. In the 19th century, to gain a better understanding of the brain, scientists and event artists such as Leonardo De Vinci utilized corpses in order to dissect and explore the structure of the brain to gain an understanding of its function

FUNCTION

It was believed before that the brain has many different components, and each part of the brain has its specific function.

NEW INFORMATION ON FUNCTION

However, this theory has been proven wrong after utilizing extensive research by promoting technology to understand the brain's function better. Furthermore, it has been proven that there is redundancy and connectivity between the brain parts. One part can carry more than one function, and a straightforward task can be carried out by multiple parts communicating together (circuiting info). The brain is known to have a distrubted system.

WHAT DOES A DISTRIBUTIVE SYSTEM MEANS?

The brain parts create a loop as the information gets communicated between the components in order to execute a particular function. For example, "Brain systems may be similar to airline route maps" (Jahangiri).

TINNITUS AND CONNECTION

To give an example of how different brain parts connect, we can look at Tinnitus. Tinnitusis characterized by phantom sounds that can severely distribute the person. It also causes changes in the connectivity of the brain as it creates loops with brain parts that should not be involved in the auditory pathway. Thus, phantom sound can be the outcome of such a problem.

HISTORY OF DEVELOPMENT OF MODERN NEUROSCIENCE
THE INFLUENTIALS
Esha Kanna

Humans were a combination of material and non-material processes
- Body was an object governed by the interaction between materials; soul was non-material

HIPPOCRATES

Brain controls motion
- Dominated medical education from year 280 to 1543 (about 1250 years)

GALEN (AELIUS GALENUS OR CLAUDIUS GALENUS)

Published a series of anatomical drawings based on dissections of animals and human corpses
- Accuracy of observation is better than anything previously attempted

LEONARDO DA VINCI

Humans have two main parts
- One part had functions that could be replicated by mechanical devices (reflex)
- One part was more complex, it was the soul (located in pineal gland)

CARTESIUS

Proposed use the experimental methods as a basis for studies of biology
- Advocated critical view on old science

FRANCIS BACON

Rola Mukhtar, Fall 2022   Esha Kanna, Fall 2022

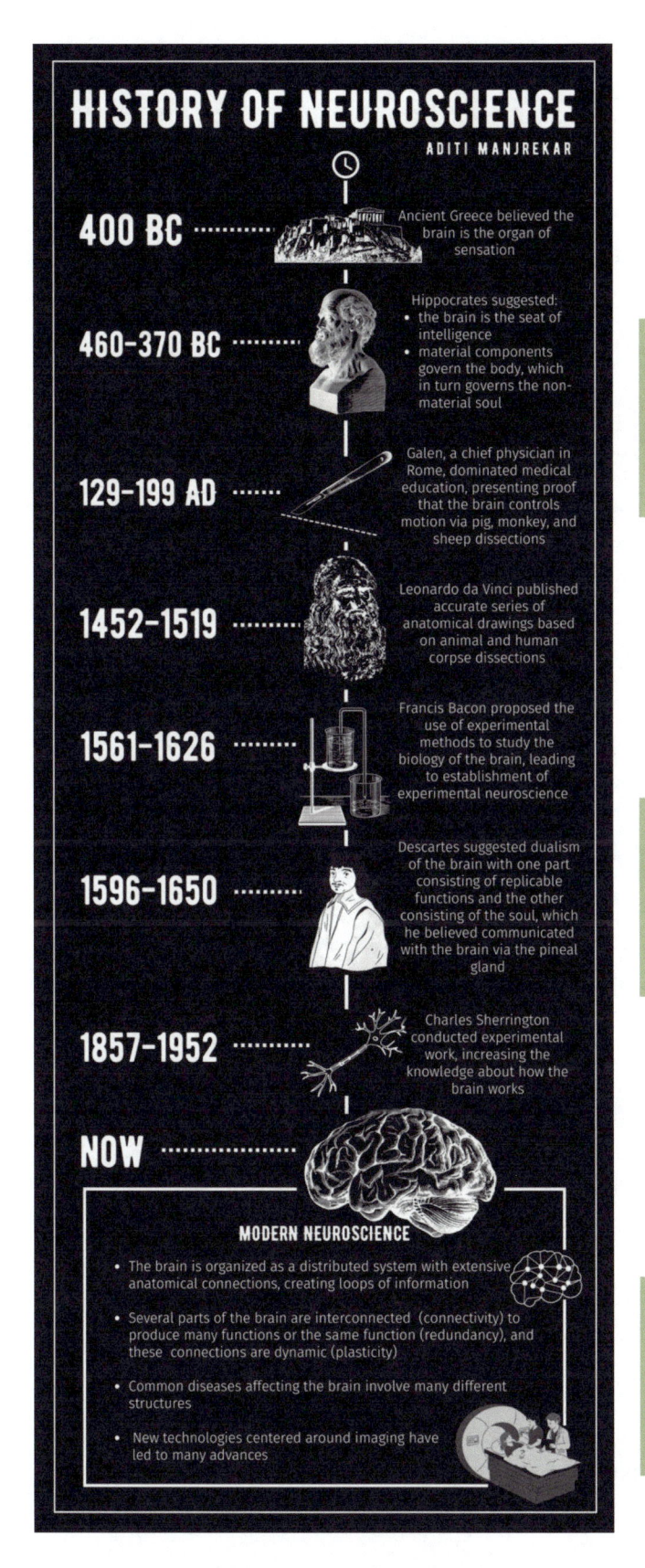

AN INFOGRAPHIC JOURNEY

HISTORY OF NEUROSCIENCE
ADITI MANJREKAR

400 BC — Ancient Greece believed the brain is the organ of sensation

460-370 BC — Hippocrates suggested:
- the brain is the seat of intelligence
- material components govern the body, which in turn governs the non-material soul

129-199 AD — Galen, a chief physician in Rome, dominated medical education, presenting proof that the brain controls motion via pig, monkey, and sheep dissections

1452-1519 — Leonardo da Vinci published accurate series of anatomical drawings based on animal and human corpse dissections

1561-1626 — Francis Bacon proposed the use of experimental methods to study the biology of the brain, leading to establishment of experimental neuroscience

1596-1650 — Descartes suggested dualism of the brain with one part consisting of replicable functions and the other consisting of the soul, which he believed communicated with the brain via the pineal gland

1857-1952 — Charles Sherrington conducted experimental work, increasing the knowledge about how the brain works

NOW

MODERN NEUROSCIENCE
- The brain is organized as a distributed system with extensive anatomical connections, creating loops of information
- Several parts of the brain are interconnected (connectivity) to produce many functions or the same function (redundancy), and these connections are dynamic (plasticity)
- Common diseases affecting the brain involve many different structures
- New technologies centered around imaging have led to many advances

Aditi Manjrekar, Fall 2022

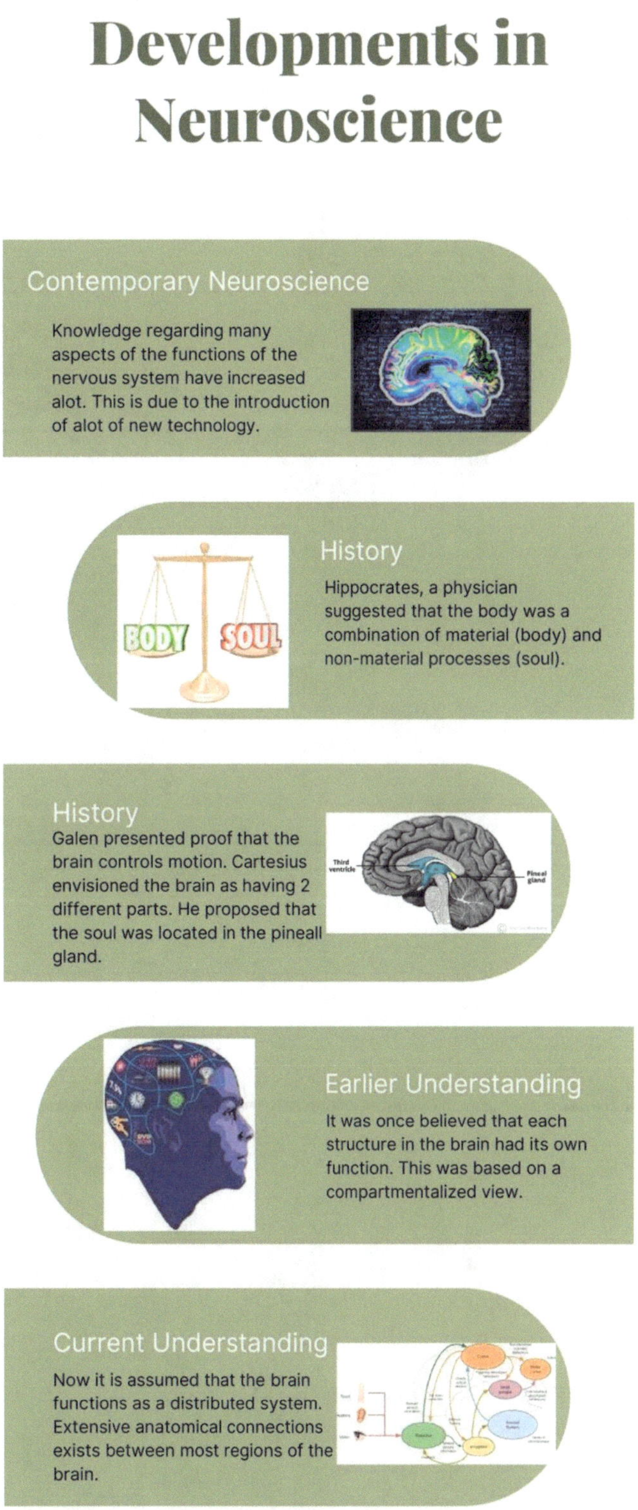

Developments in Neuroscience

Contemporary Neuroscience
Knowledge regarding many aspects of the functions of the nervous system have increased alot. This is due to the introduction of alot of new technology.

History
Hippocrates, a physician suggested that the body was a combination of material (body) and non-material processes (soul).

History
Galen presented proof that the brain controls motion. Cartesius envisioned the brain as having 2 different parts. He proposed that the soul was located in the pineall gland.

Earlier Understanding
It was once believed that each structure in the brain had its own function. This was based on a compartmentalized view.

Current Understanding
Now it is assumed that the brain functions as a distributed system. Extensive anatomical connections exists between most regions of the brain.

Shani Hibbert, Fall 2022

AN INFOGRAPHIC JOURNEY

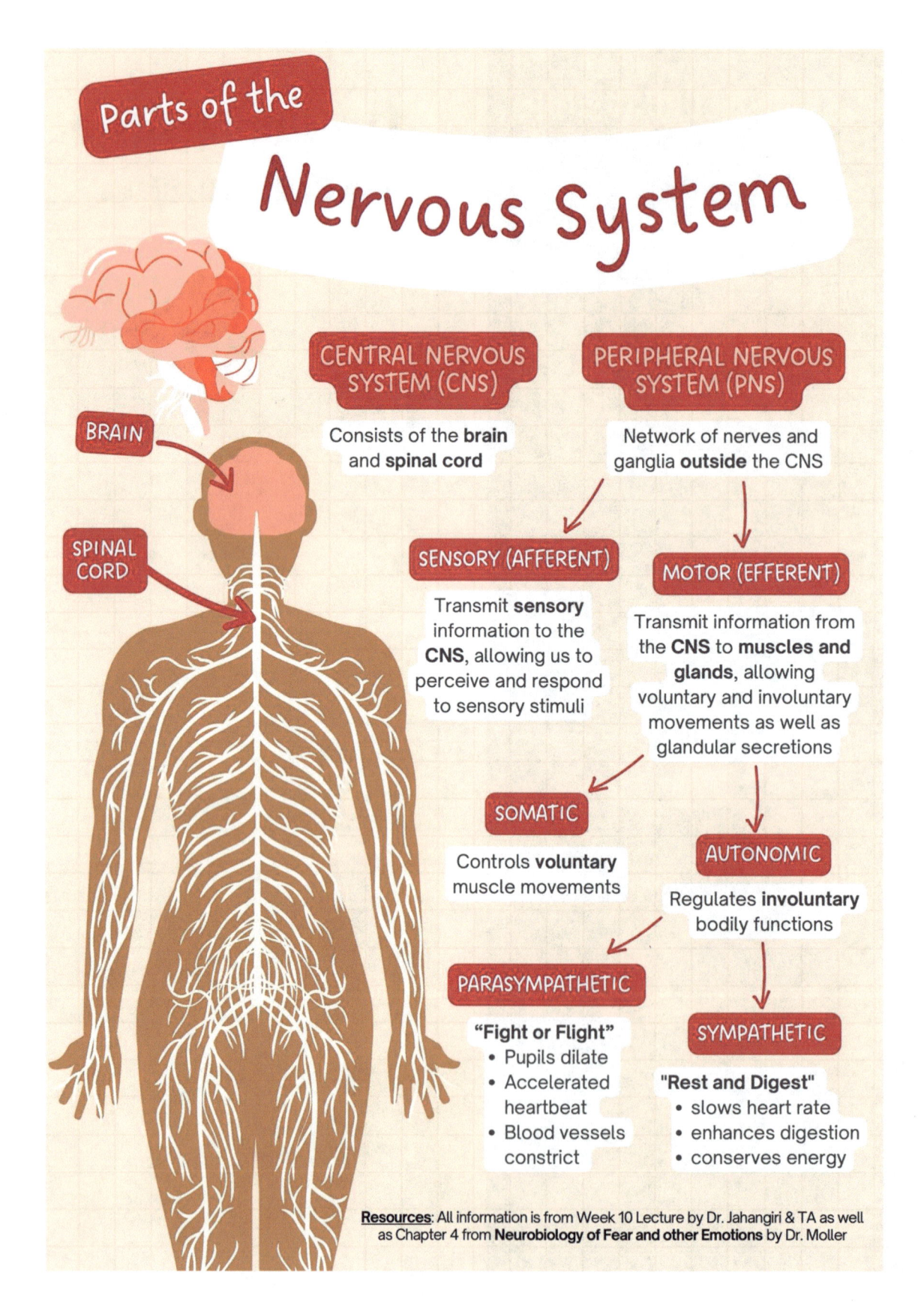

Parts of the Nervous System

BRAIN

SPINAL CORD

CENTRAL NERVOUS SYSTEM (CNS)
Consists of the **brain** and **spinal cord**

PERIPHERAL NERVOUS SYSTEM (PNS)
Network of nerves and ganglia **outside** the CNS

SENSORY (AFFERENT)
Transmit **sensory** information to the **CNS**, allowing us to perceive and respond to sensory stimuli

MOTOR (EFFERENT)
Transmit information from the **CNS** to **muscles and glands**, allowing voluntary and involuntary movements as well as glandular secretions

SOMATIC
Controls **voluntary** muscle movements

AUTONOMIC
Regulates **involuntary** bodily functions

PARASYMPATHETIC
"Fight or Flight"
- Pupils dilate
- Accelerated heartbeat
- Blood vessels constrict

SYMPATHETIC
"Rest and Digest"
- slows heart rate
- enhances digestion
- conserves energy

<u>Resources</u>: All information is from Week 10 Lecture by Dr. Jahangiri & TA as well as Chapter 4 from **Neurobiology of Fear and other Emotions** by Dr. Moller

Haniya Qavi, Fall 2023

AN INFOGRAPHIC JOURNEY

The Autonomic Nervous System

The autonomic nervous system
- It is important in maintaining the body's homeostasis.
- The autonomic nervous system has 2 divisions: the sympathetic & parasympathetic systems.
- It includes neurons that innervate smooth muscle, cardiac muscles, and glands.

Sympathetic nervous system
- The fight or flight system.
- It includes the thoracic and lumbar portions of the spinal cord.
- This system is activated by negative emotions, such as fear.

Parasympathetic nervous system
- The rest and digest system.
- It includes the cranial and sacral portions of the spinal cord.
- Its autonomic ganglia is close to target organs.
- Has short postganglionic axons.

Adrenal Medulla
- The adrenal medulla is the inner part of adrenal gland.
- It produces epinephrine and norepinephrine.
- Prolonged stress can deplete its stores causing brain fog, low energy, and lightheadedness.

Reference:
"Neurobiology of Fear, Anxiety, and Other Emotions" Møller, A.R

Maryam Imam, Fall 2023

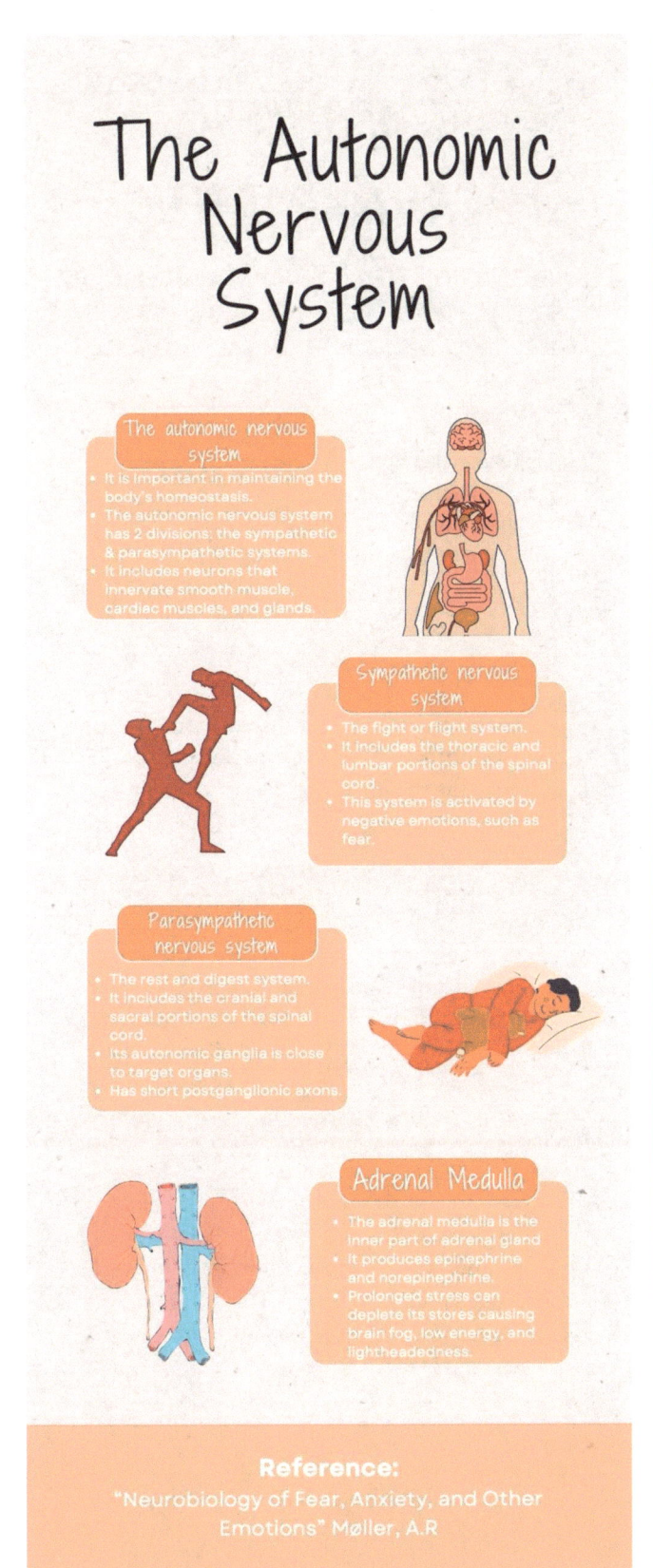

AUTONOMIC NERVOUS SYSTEM

NSC 4382. Lucie Nguyen.

SYMPATHETIC | PARASYMPATHETIC

Anatomical Differences

- From Thoracolumbar region of CNS
- Ganglia close to spinal cord
- Long postganglionic fibers
- Lots of branching

- From Craniosacral region
- Ganglia close to target organs
- Short postganglionic fibers
- Very little branching

Other Differences

HPA-AXIS
Hypothalamus-Pituitary-Adrenal
- System that controls Hormones
- Fear Signaling Activates
- Estrogen can regulate and HPA can inhibit estrogen secretion

Hypothalamus → Anterior Pituitary → Adrenal Cortex → Cortisol to Body
Corticotropin Releasing Hormone / Adrenocorticotropic Hormone

VAGUS NERVE
- Serves as a connection from the brain to other parts of the body
- Descending - parasympathetic control of abdominal organs
- Ascending - abdomen and chest influence emotional brain
  - Reach basal nucleus and facilitates neuroplasticity
- Involved in inflammatory reflex
- Increasingly important in reversing maladaptive plasticity in diseases

Function

FIGHT OR FLIGHT
- Use Energy
- Prepare the body for danger
- Some functions include dilate pupils, relax airways, inhibit digestion

REST AND DIGEST
- Make Energy
- Some functions include constrict pupils, constrict airways, stimulate digestion, slow heartbeat

ADDITIONAL FACTS
- Prolonged activation of HPA Axis and Autonomic Nervous System can lead to inflammation that increases risk of disease
- Both the Parasympathetic and Sympathetic Nervous System work to maintain homeostasis in the body

REFERENCES
Moller, A. (2019). Neurobiology of Fear, Anxiety and Other Emotions.

Lucie Nguyen, Fall 2023

AN INFOGRAPHIC JOURNEY

Autonomic Nervous System

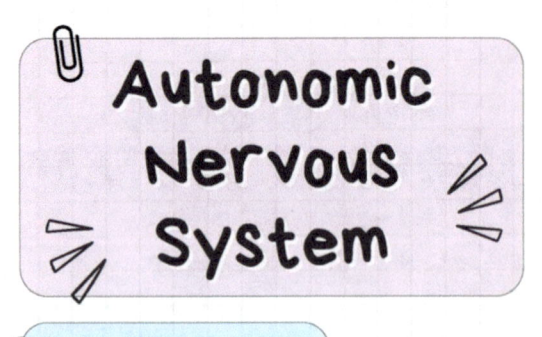

01 The autonomic nervous system is a division of the nervous system that controls most involuntary actions of the body, such as smooth muscle innervation. It is often thought of as the complement to the somatic nervous system, which controls voluntary movement, such as skeletal muscle.

02 The autonomic nervous system is divided into two broad categories: the sympathetic nervous system and the parasympathetic nervous system. The sympathetic nervous system is often thought of as flight or flight while parasympathetic is rest and digest.

03 Important functions of the sympathetic nervous system include dilating the pupils, dilating bronchioles, increasing heart rate, secreting adrenaline, and more. These functions are associated with responses the body has to high stress.

04 Important functions of the parasympathetic nervous system include constricting the pupils, constricting the bronchioles, slowing the heartbeat, and more. These functions are associated with low stress situations when the body has time to carry out non fight or flight functions.

Varun Thavanampalli

Sympathetic vs Parasympathetic

FIGHT, FLIGHT, FREEZE — Sympathetic
REST + DIGEST — Parasympathetic

Sympathetic	Parasympathetic
Region of the CNS — From the thoracolumbar region.	**Region of the CNS** — From the craniosacral region.
Location of Ganglia — Close to the spinal cord in a chain.	**Location of Ganglia** — Close to target organs.
Length of Postganglionic Fiber — Long	**Length of Postganglionic Fiber** — Short
Postganglionic Branching — Lots, so that multiple organs can be mobilized at once.	**Postganglionic Branching** — Very little branching.

Sources
Week 9 Lectures :)

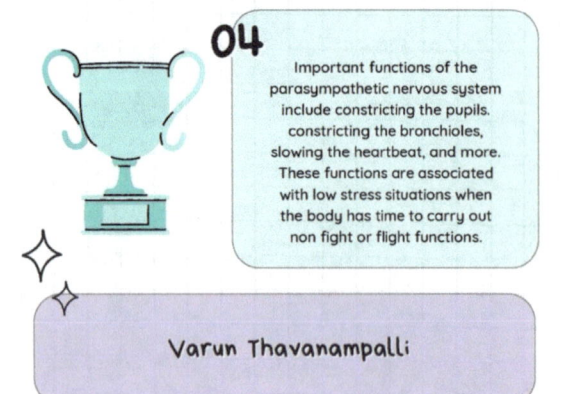

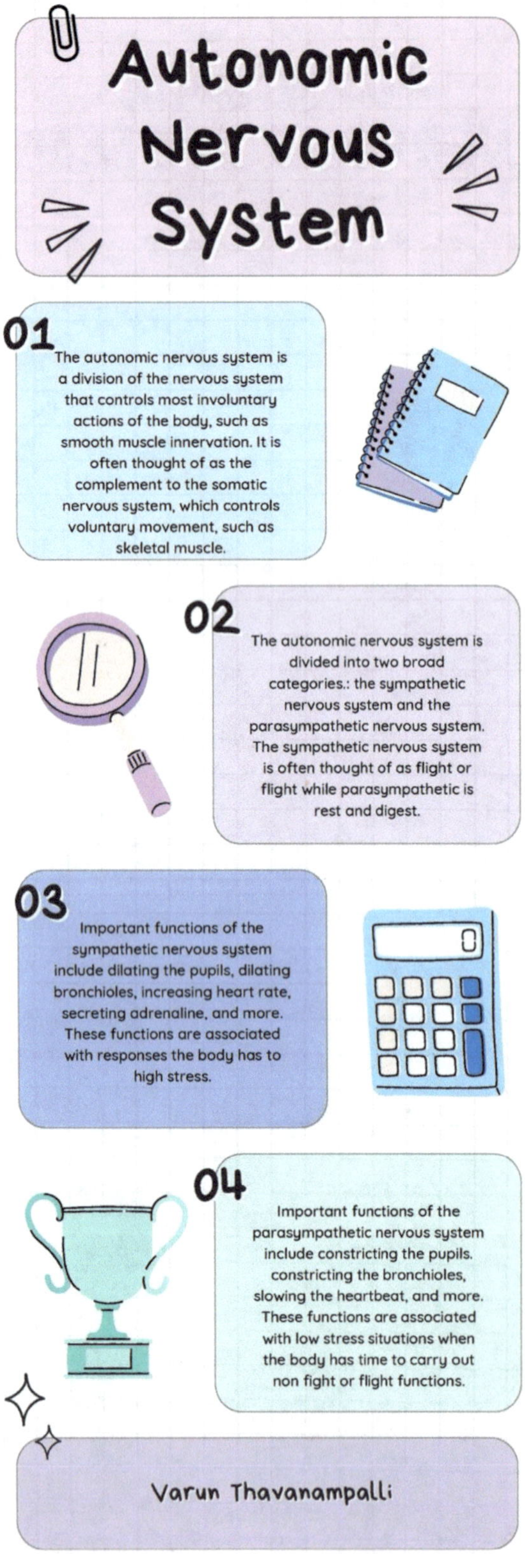

Varun Thavanampalli, Spring 2024 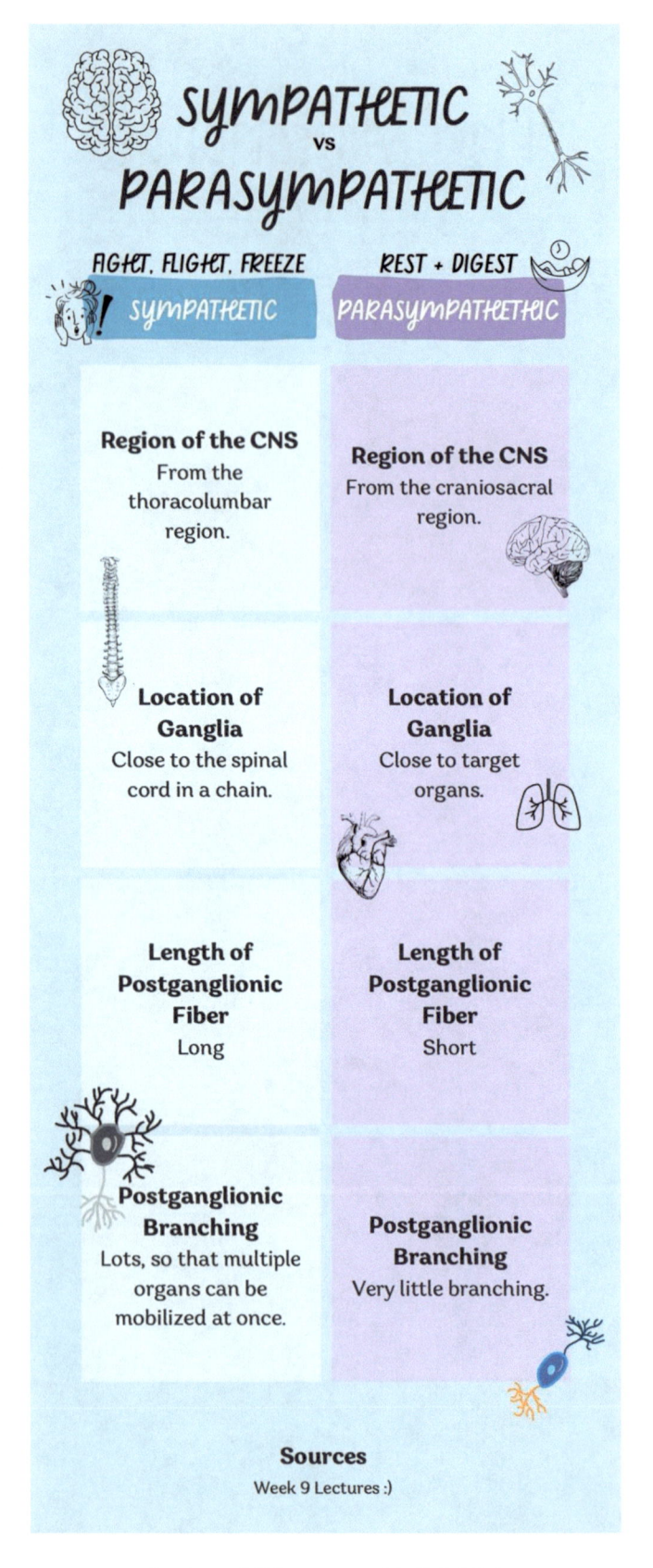   Audrey Villanueva, Fall 2023

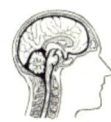

AN INFOGRAPHIC JOURNEY

Sympathetic Nervous System

What does it do?

Sympathetic Nervous system is a part of the autonomic Nervous system that controls fight and flight response in the body. Any type of dangerous or stressful situation can increase the activity of SNS. The increase in secretion of hormones like corticotropin or cortisol released during stress coordinates the activities of SNS.

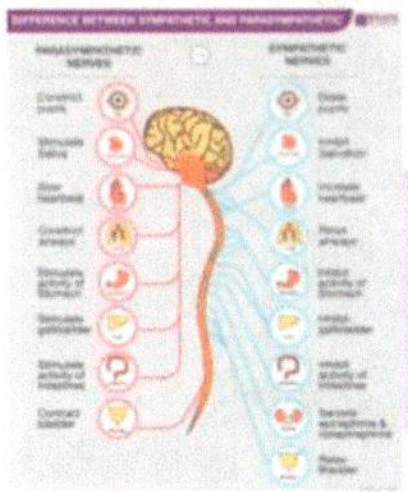

Effects on organs

sympathetic Nervous system has different effects on various organs: pupil dilation, increased heart rate, bronchodilation in lung, decreased contraction and motility in the abdomen, increased in endocrine and exocrine functions including enzyme and insulin secretion

Structure

The sympathetic nervous system consists of preganglionic and postganglionic neurons and fibers as well as the sympathetic chain ganglion. It has shorter preganglionic fibers and longer post-ganglionic fibers and is found within the T1-T12 and L1-L3.

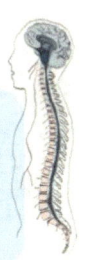

Overactivity and it's effects

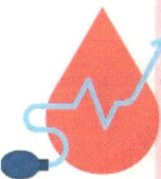

The overactivation of the sympathetic nervous system has far-reaching implications for various physiological processes and health conditions. Its role in hypertension (HTN) is well established as it leads to vasoconstriction, increased heart rate, and elevated blood pressure. Still, it has various other effects, including vascular hypertrophy, atherosclerosis, glomerulosclerosis, and insulin resistance. The increase in activities of stress hormones like cortisol on organs can lead to other physiological consequences like hyperglycemia, bowel disease, anxiety, and depression.

Neurotransmitters and receptor

the major neurotransmitters used by the sympathetic nervous system (SNS) to communicate include norepinephrine, epinephrine and acetycholine. The receptors of SNS includes alpha-1, alpha-2, beta-1, beta-2 and beta-3 receptors

Citation:
Hamilton, Lucinda. "Sympathetic Nervous System." Physiopedia, www.physio-pedia.com/Sympathetic_Nervous_System. Accessed 27 Aug. 2023.

Diya Thapa, Fall 2023

COMPARING SYMPATHETIC AND PARASYMPATHETIC SYSTEMS

BY AFROSA ISLAM

SIMILARITIES

ACTION:

BOTH SYMPATHETIC AND PARASYMPATHETIC SYSTEMS REGULATE KEY PHYSIOLOGICAL RESPONSES TO EMOTIONAL AND INTERNAL STIMULI. CONSIDER HOW YOUR HEART RACES WHEN YOU FEEL FEAR OR HOW MAY FEEL TIRED WHEN YOU EAT A LOT OF FOOD AND ARE DIGESTING.

METHOD:

BOTH SYSTEMS UTILIZE HORMONAL SIGNALING AND OCCASIONALLY NEURONAL CONNECTIONS TO COMMUNICATE WITH OTHER ORGAN SYSTEMS.

DIFFERENCES

FUNCTION:

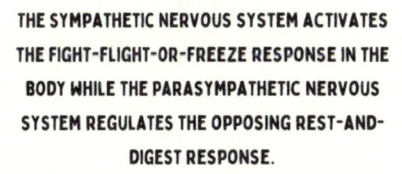

THE SYMPATHETIC NERVOUS SYSTEM ACTIVATES THE FIGHT-FLIGHT-OR-FREEZE RESPONSE IN THE BODY WHILE THE PARASYMPATHETIC NERVOUS SYSTEM REGULATES THE OPPOSING REST-AND-DIGEST RESPONSE.

ANATOMY:

THE SYMPATHETIC SYSTEM'S GANGLIA ARE LOCATED CLOSE TO AND ALONG THE SPINAL CORD. MEANWHILE, THE PARASYMPATHETIC SYSTEM'S GANGLIA ARE LOCATED CLOSER TO VITAL ORGANS AND TO THE BRAIN STEM.

Afrosa Islam, Spring 2023

AN INFOGRAPHIC JOURNEY

THE CEREBRAL CORTEX

THE CEREBRAL CORTEX PLAYS A SIGNIFICANT ROLE IN EMOTION REGULATION AND PROCESSING, PRIMARILY THROUGH CONNECTIONS WITH SUBCORTICAL STRUCTURES LIKE THE AMYGDALA AND HYPOTHALAMUS

PLAYS A PART IN CREATING EMOTIONAL RESPONSE

THE CEREBRAL CORTEX PLAYS A ROLE IN SOME FORMS OF DISCRIMINATION OF SENSORY STIMULI SUCH AS DISCRIMINATION OF OBJECTS THAT MAY BE DANGEROUS

THE CEREBRAL CORTEX DOES NOT PLAY A ROLE IN FEAR CONDITIONING

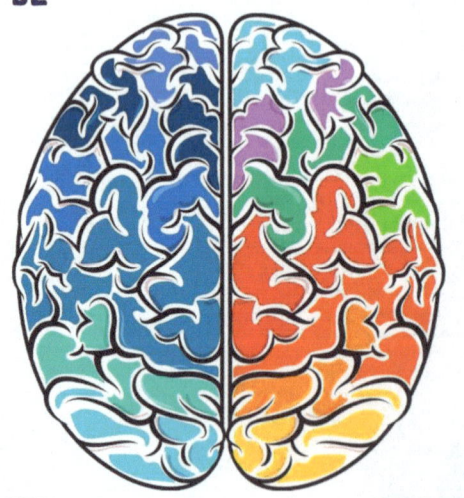

LEFT
- LOGICAL
- FOCUSED ON FACTS
- REALISM PREDOMINATES
- PLANNED AND ORDERLY
- MATH AND SCIENCE-MINDED
- PREFERS NON-FICTION

RIGHT
- EMOTIONAL
- ART AND CREATIVITY
- DREAMS AND IMAGINATION
- OCCASIONALLY ABSENTMINDED
- PREFERS FICTION
- CREATIVE STORYTELLING

Nhi Nguyen, Spring 2024

AN INFOGRAPHIC JOURNEY

LEFT VS RIGHT SIDE OF CEREBRAL CORTEX

BY: AMBERLYN HAQUE

LEFT CEREBRAL CORTEX

1. It is more logical and focuses more on facts.
2. Realism takes over this side of the cerebral cortex.
3. This side is much more orderly and planned.
4. This side prefers to deal with more science and math subjects. It also enjoys more non-fiction.

RIGHT CEREBRAL CORTEX

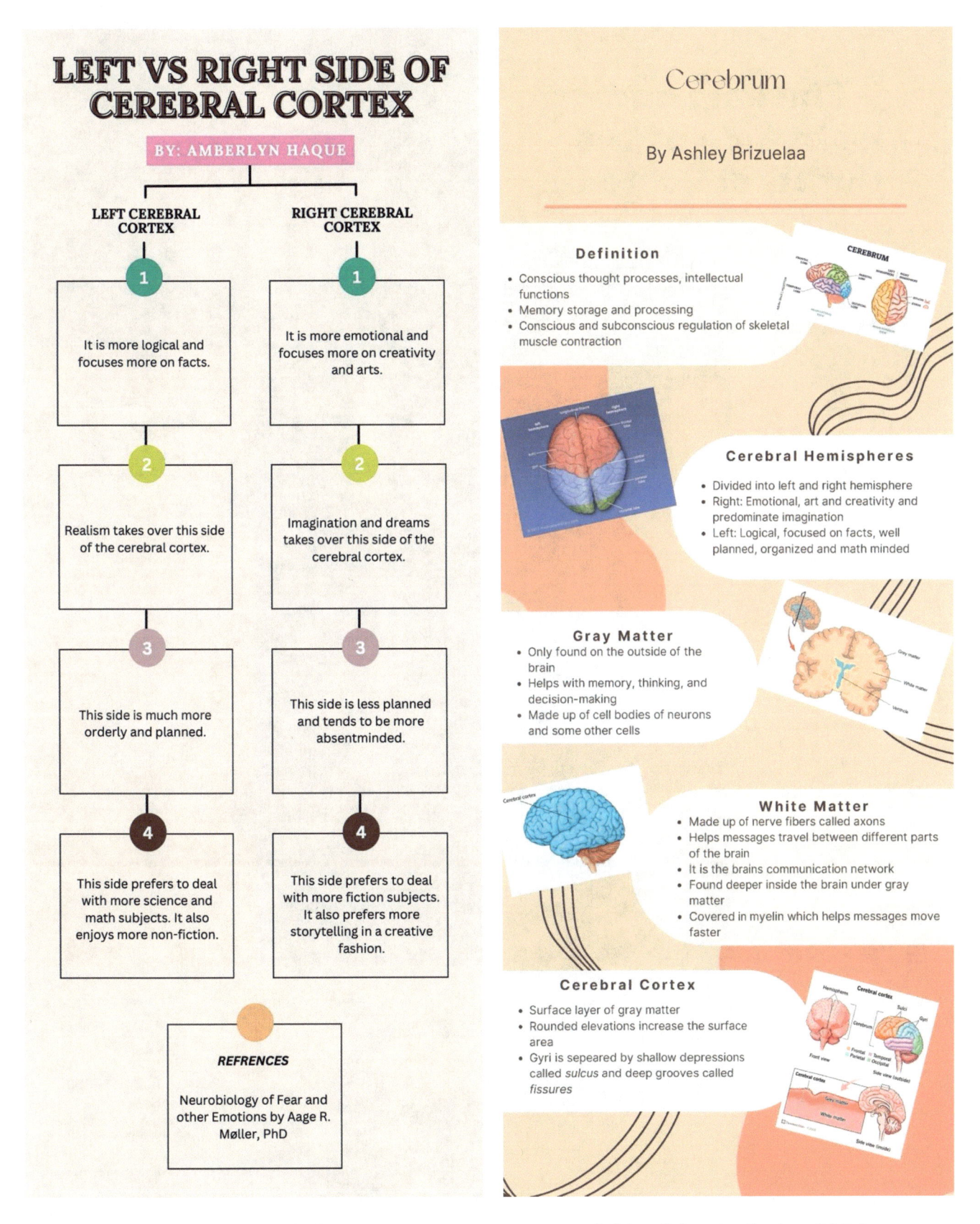

1. It is more emotional and focuses more on creativity and arts.
2. Imagination and dreams takes over this side of the cerebral cortex.
3. This side is less planned and tends to be more absentminded.
4. This side prefers to deal with more fiction subjects. It also prefers more storytelling in a creative fashion.

REFRENCES

Neurobiology of Fear and other Emotions by Aage R. Møller, PhD

Amberlyn Haque, Fall 2023

Cerebrum

By Ashley Brizuelaa

Definition
- Conscious thought processes, intellectual functions
- Memory storage and processing
- Conscious and subconscious regulation of skeletal muscle contraction

Cerebral Hemispheres
- Divided into left and right hemisphere
- Right: Emotional, art and creativity and predominate imagination
- Left: Logical, focused on facts, well planned, organized and math minded

Gray Matter
- Only found on the outside of the brain
- Helps with memory, thinking, and decision-making
- Made up of cell bodies of neurons and some other cells

White Matter
- Made up of nerve fibers called axons
- Helps messages travel between different parts of the brain
- It is the brains communication network
- Found deeper inside the brain under gray matter
- Covered in myelin which helps messages move faster

Cerebral Cortex
- Surface layer of gray matter
- Rounded elevations increase the surface area
- Gyri is sepeared by shallow depressions called *sulcus* and deep grooves called *fissures*

Ashley Brizuela, Spring 2024

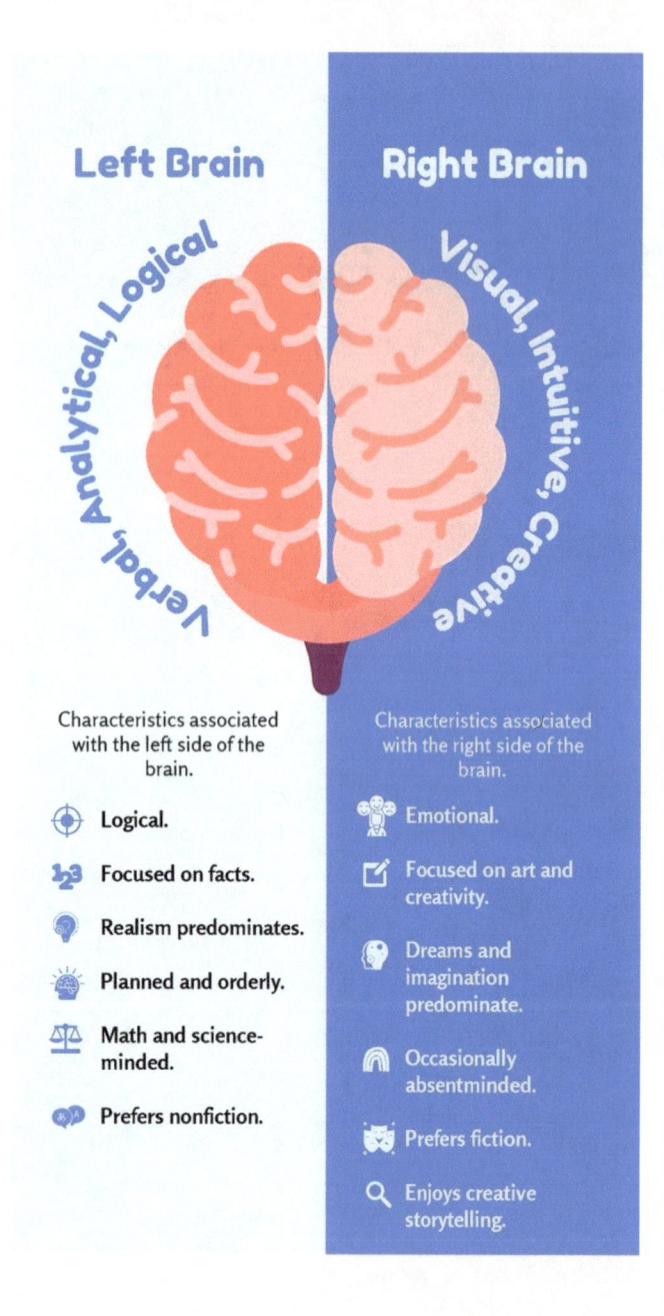

AN INFOGRAPHIC JOURNEY

The Left and Right Side of the Cerebral Cortex

Left Brain — Verbal, Analytical, Logical

Right Brain — Visual, Intuitive, Creative

Characteristics associated with the left side of the brain.
- Logical.
- Focused on facts.
- Realism predominates.
- Planned and orderly.
- Math and science-minded.
- Prefers nonfiction.

Characteristics associated with the right side of the brain.
- Emotional.
- Focused on art and creativity.
- Dreams and imagination predominate.
- Occasionally absentminded.
- Prefers fiction.
- Enjoys creative storytelling.

Arshad Manzar, Spring 2024

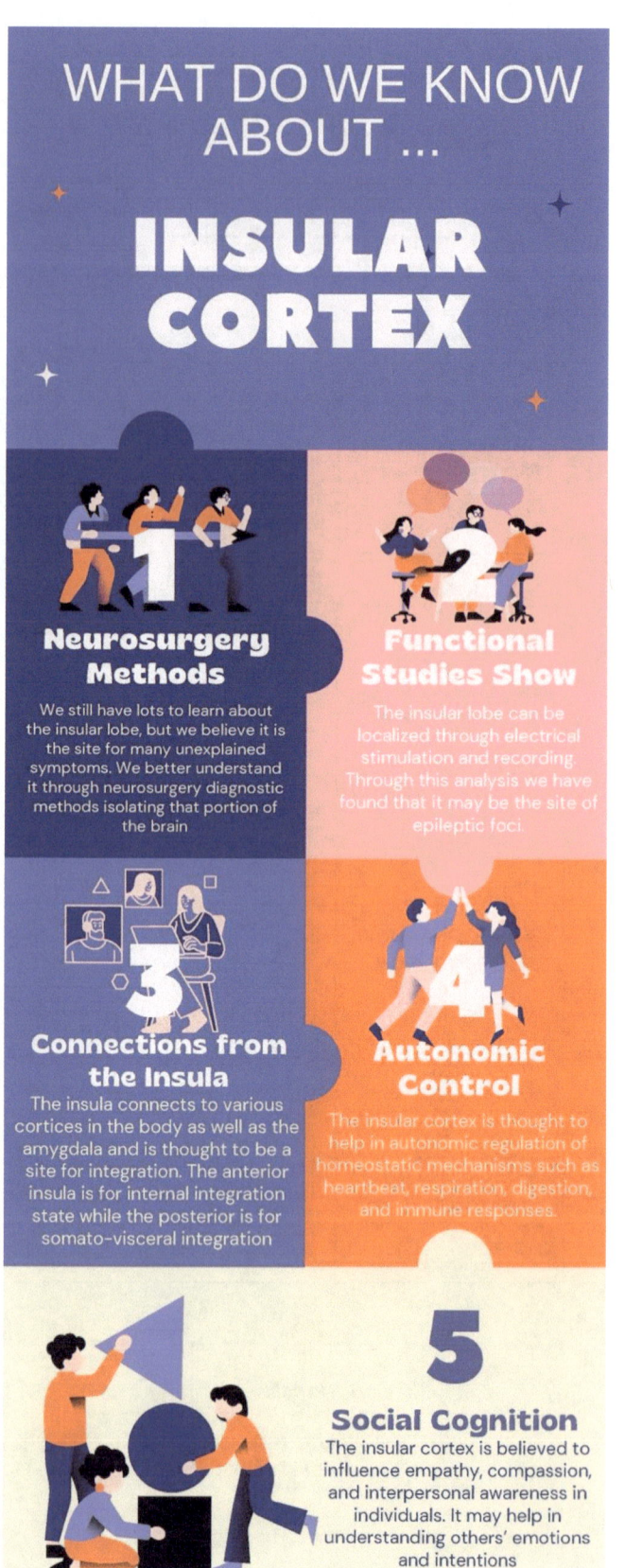

WHAT DO WE KNOW ABOUT … INSULAR CORTEX

1. Neurosurgery Methods
We still have lots to learn about the insular lobe, but we believe it is the site for many unexplained symptoms. We better understand it through neurosurgery diagnostic methods isolating that portion of the brain

2. Functional Studies Show
The insular lobe can be localized through electrical stimulation and recording. Through this analysis we have found that it may be the site of epileptic foci.

3. Connections from the Insula
The insula connects to various cortices in the body as well as the amygdala and is thought to be a site for integration. The anterior insula is for internal integration state while the posterior is for somato-visceral integration

4. Autonomic Control
The insular cortex is thought to help in autonomic regulation of homeostatic mechanisms such as heartbeat, respiration, digestion, and immune responses.

5. Social Cognition
The insular cortex is believed to influence empathy, compassion, and interpersonal awareness in individuals. It may help in understanding others' emotions and intentions

Sneha Sharma, Spring 2024

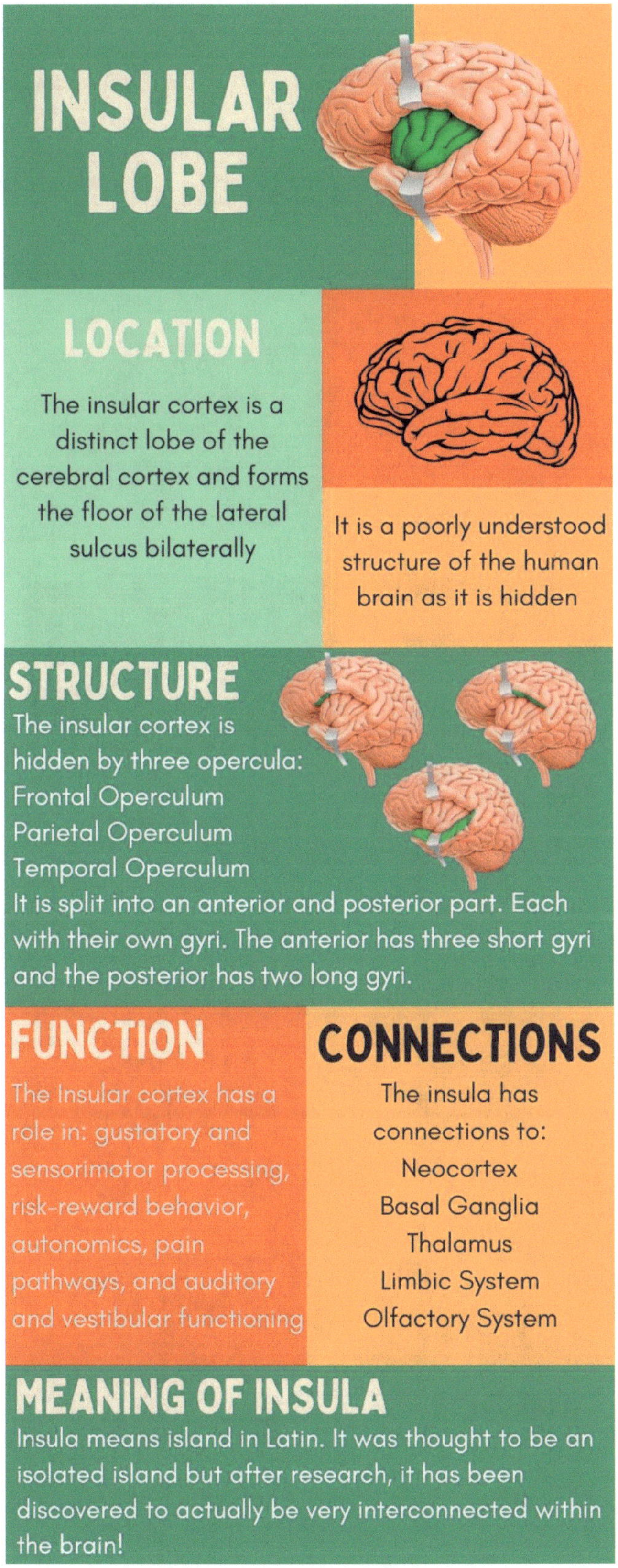

AN INFOGRAPHIC JOURNEY

INSULAR LOBE

LOCATION
The insular cortex is a distinct lobe of the cerebral cortex and forms the floor of the lateral sulcus bilaterally

It is a poorly understood structure of the human brain as it is hidden

STRUCTURE
The insular cortex is hidden by three opercula:
Frontal Operculum
Parietal Operculum
Temporal Operculum
It is split into an anterior and posterior part. Each with their own gyri. The anterior has three short gyri and the posterior has two long gyri.

FUNCTION
The Insular cortex has a role in: gustatory and sensorimotor processing, risk-reward behavior, autonomics, pain pathways, and auditory and vestibular functioning

CONNECTIONS
The insula has connections to:
Neocortex
Basal Ganglia
Thalamus
Limbic System
Olfactory System

MEANING OF INSULA
Insula means island in Latin. It was thought to be an isolated island but after research, it has been discovered to actually be very interconnected within the brain!

Zaynah Bawa, Spring 2023

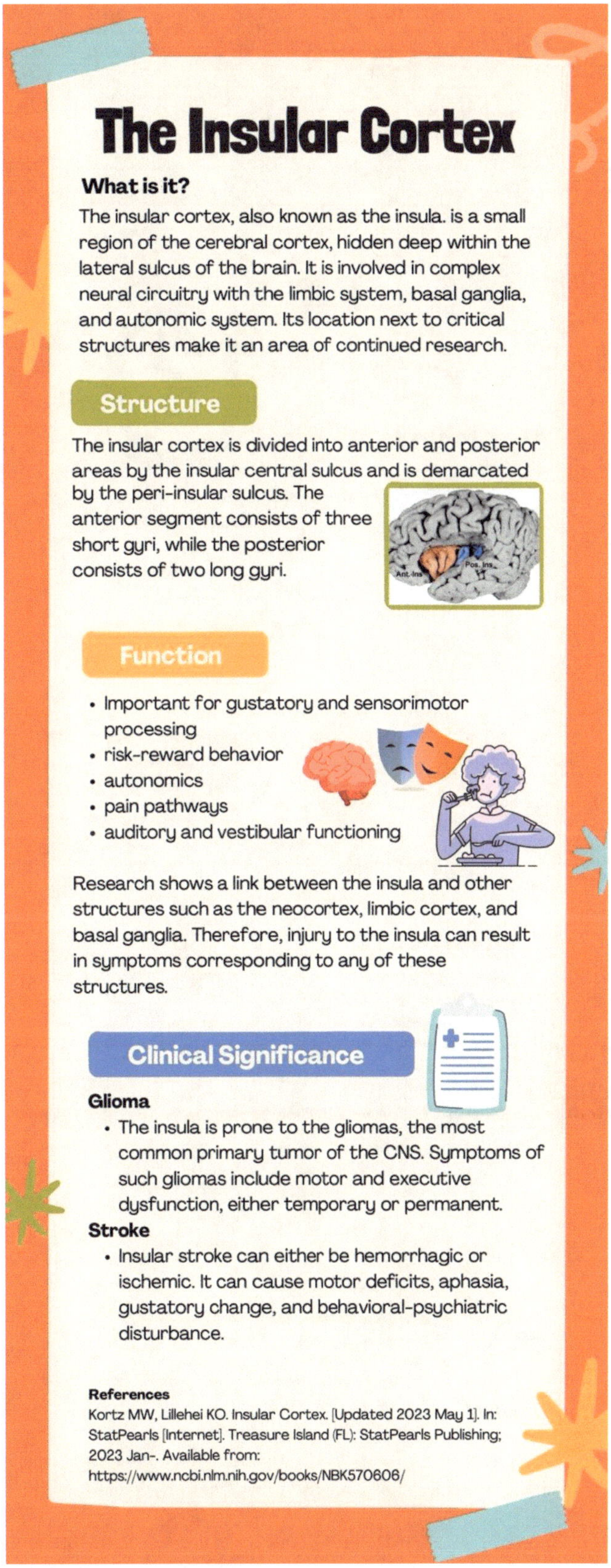

The Insular Cortex

What is it?
The insular cortex, also known as the insula, is a small region of the cerebral cortex, hidden deep within the lateral sulcus of the brain. It is involved in complex neural circuitry with the limbic system, basal ganglia, and autonomic system. Its location next to critical structures make it an area of continued research.

Structure
The insular cortex is divided into anterior and posterior areas by the insular central sulcus and is demarcated by the peri-insular sulcus. The anterior segment consists of three short gyri, while the posterior consists of two long gyri.

Function
- Important for gustatory and sensorimotor processing
- risk-reward behavior
- autonomics
- pain pathways
- auditory and vestibular functioning

Research shows a link between the insula and other structures such as the neocortex, limbic cortex, and basal ganglia. Therefore, injury to the insula can result in symptoms corresponding to any of these structures.

Clinical Significance

Glioma
- The insula is prone to the gliomas, the most common primary tumor of the CNS. Symptoms of such gliomas include motor and executive dysfunction, either temporary or permanent.

Stroke
- Insular stroke can either be hemorrhagic or ischemic. It can cause motor deficits, aphasia, gustatory change, and behavioral-psychiatric disturbance.

References
Kortz MW, Lillehei KO. Insular Cortex. [Updated 2023 May 1]. In: StatPearls [Internet]. Treasure Island (FL): StatPearls Publishing; 2023 Jan-. Available from: https://www.ncbi.nlm.nih.gov/books/NBK570606/

Ashley Tran, Fall 2023

AN INFOGRAPHIC JOURNEY

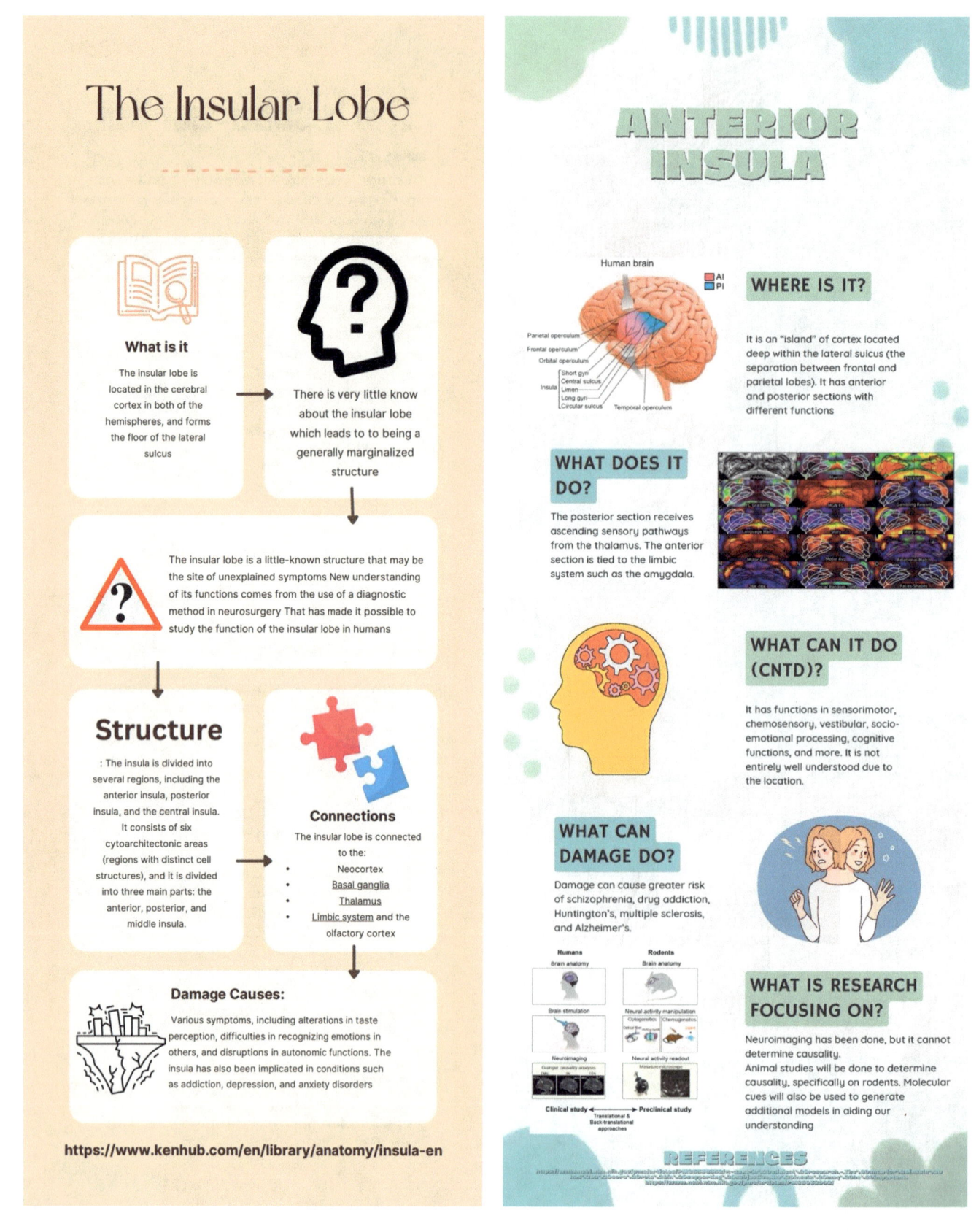

Ashley Kiser, Fall 2023

Allen Liang, Spring 2024

AN INFOGRAPHIC JOURNEY

NUCLEUS BASALIS (NUCLEUS OF MEYNERT)

WHAT DOES IT DO

Output pathways from the central nucleus of the amygdala make extensive connections with brain stem nuclei for emotional responses

First described by Theodor Meynert in 1872

WHAT IS IT MADE OF

It is a collection of cholinergic neurons in the basal forebrain. It provides most of the cholinergic innervations from the cerebral cortex

IMPORTANCE?

control of attention and maintenance of arousal, both key functions for appropriate learning and memory formation

ALZEIHMER'S

Has been targeted in various studies with the disease

Projections from the nucleus basalis to the cortex can arouse the cerebral cortex and promote plastic changes in other parts of the brain

brought to you by:
HTTPS://WWW.SCIENCEDIRECT.COM/TOPICS/NEUROSCIENCE/NUCLEUS-BASALIS-OF-MEYNERT

Ashley Kiser, Fall 2023

OTHER BRAIN SYSTEMS

CEREBRAL CORTEX

Plays a role in some forms of discrimination of objects that may be dangerous.

The hippocampus sits on "top" of the cortical hierarchy from all over the brain, binding it together into episodic memory.

ROLES OF VISCERAL BRAIN...

Emotional stimuli can activate the visceral system through three different routes...
1. One using the amygdala
2. Another uses the orbitofrontal cortex and
3. using the anterior cingulate cortex and insular cortex
4. Activation of the visceral system produces different kinds of autonomic responses.

WHAT FEAR CAN DO TO A PERSON.

- Activation of the autonomic nervous system
- Suppressing the immune system
- Affecting a person's mood
- Reducing a person's quality of life
- Consuming a person's time

BENEFITS OF FEAR...
- Prepare for future dangers and prevent a person from engaging in risky activity

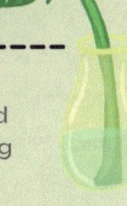

brought to you by:
REALLYGREATSITE.COM

Alaina Chenault, Spring 2023

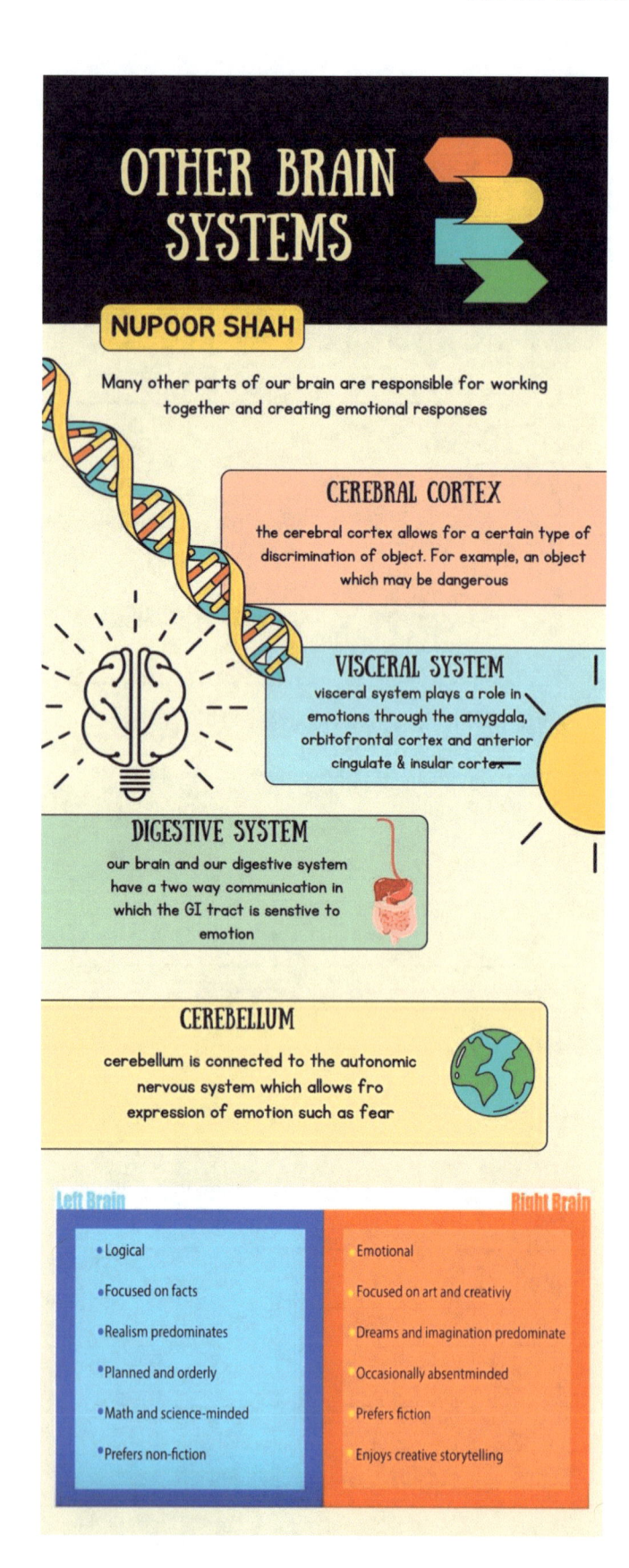

AN INFOGRAPHIC JOURNEY

OTHER BRAIN SYSTEMS
NUPOOR SHAH

Many other parts of our brain are responsible for working together and creating emotional responses

CEREBRAL CORTEX
the cerebral cortex allows for a certain type of discrimination of object. For example, an object which may be dangerous

VISCERAL SYSTEM
visceral system plays a role in emotions through the amygdala, orbitofrontal cortex and anterior cingulate & insular cortex

DIGESTIVE SYSTEM
our brain and our digestive system have a two way communication in which the GI tract is sensitive to emotion

CEREBELLUM
cerebellum is connected to the autonomic nervous system which allows fro expression of emotion such as fear

Left Brain
- Logical
- Focused on facts
- Realism predominates
- Planned and orderly
- Math and science-minded
- Prefers non-fiction

Right Brain
- Emotional
- Focused on art and creativiy
- Dreams and imagination predominate
- Occasionally absentminded
- Prefers fiction
- Enjoys creative storytelling

Nupoor Shah, Fall 2023

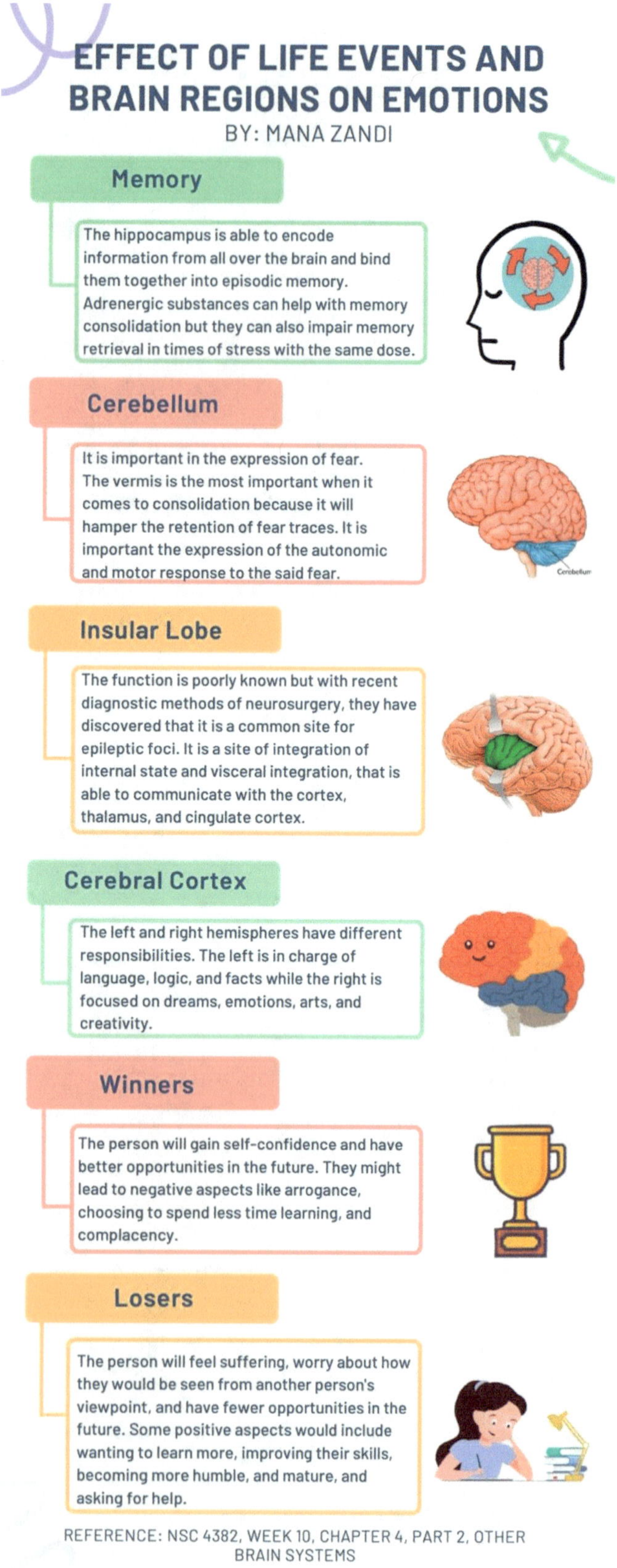

EFFECT OF LIFE EVENTS AND BRAIN REGIONS ON EMOTIONS
BY: MANA ZANDI

Memory
The hippocampus is able to encode information from all over the brain and bind them together into episodic memory. Adrenergic substances can help with memory consolidation but they can also impair memory retrieval in times of stress with the same dose.

Cerebellum
It is important in the expression of fear. The vermis is the most important when it comes to consolidation because it will hamper the retention of fear traces. It is important the expression of the autonomic and motor response to the said fear.

Insular Lobe
The function is poorly known but with recent diagnostic methods of neurosurgery, they have discovered that it is a common site for epileptic foci. It is a site of integration of internal state and visceral integration, that is able to communicate with the cortex, thalamus, and cingulate cortex.

Cerebral Cortex
The left and right hemispheres have different responsibilities. The left is in charge of language, logic, and facts while the right is focused on dreams, emotions, arts, and creativity.

Winners
The person will gain self-confidence and have better opportunities in the future. They might lead to negative aspects like arrogance, choosing to spend less time learning, and complacency.

Losers
The person will feel suffering, worry about how they would be seen from another person's viewpoint, and have fewer opportunities in the future. Some positive aspects would include wanting to learn more, improving their skills, becoming more humble, and mature, and asking for help.

REFERENCE: NSC 4382, WEEK 10, CHAPTER 4, PART 2, OTHER BRAIN SYSTEMS

Mana Zandi, Fall 2023

AN INFOGRAPHIC JOURNEY

STRUCTURES OF THE EMOTIONAL BRAIN

1. THE CEREBRAL
The cerebral cortex plays a role in some forms of discrimination of sensory stimuli such as discrimination of objects that may be dangerous.

2. CEREBELLUM
The cerebellum plays an important role in the expression of emotions such as fear, related to its connections to the autonomic nervous system. Inactivation of the cerebella vermis during the consolidation or the reconsolidation period hampers the retention of fear memory traces

3. HIPPOCAMPUS
The hippocampus sits on "top" of the cortical hierarchy and can encode information from all over the brain, binding it together into episodic memory.

4. MEMORY
The basolateral and central nuclei of the amygdala are involved in memory consolidation in a complicated way through interaction between many different systems.

5. MEMORY PT.2
Stimulation that reaches the basolateral nucleus of the amygdala either from the thalamus (the subcortical or low route) or the cerebral cortex (the cortical or high route) can change synaptic efficacy as an expression of "learning".

6. MEMORY PT.3
Adrenergic substances enhance memory consolidation, but it is remarkable that the same dose of glucocorticoids, (a stress hormone) that enhances consolidation of memory, can impair retrieval of memory

7. VISCERAL SYSTEM
Emotional stimuli can activate the visceral system through three different routes, one using the amygdala, another using orbitofrontal cortex and a third route using the anterior cingulate cortex and insular cortex.

8. INSULAR LOBE
The insular lobe is a little-known structure that may be the site of unexplained symptoms. New understanding of its functions comes from the use of a diagnostic method in neurosurgery. That have made it possible study the function of the insular lobe in humans.

Jesse Idemudia, Fall 2023

Reticular Formation
by Allen Liang

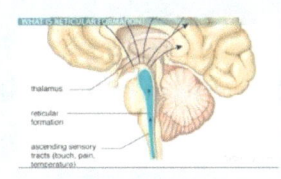

WHAT IS IT?
The reticular formation is a network of brainstem nuclei and neurons located between the spinal cord and brain.

WHAT IS THE FUNCTION?
The reticular formation has two systems, ascending and descending. The former deals with consciousness, arousal, and senses. The latter deals with movement, balance, and coordination.

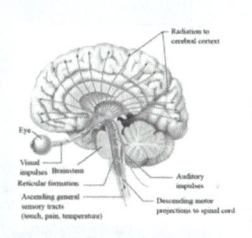

WHAT HAPPENS IF IT'S DAMAGED?
There may be issues such as
- Periods of unconsciousness
- Lack of habituation
- Pain
- Coma
- Death

DOES IT EXIST IN OTHER ANIMALS?
In fact, they do! Mammals share morphology with reptiles and elasmobranchs (sharks). It is phylogenetically one of the oldest parts of the brain, as it controls many important functions in more complex organisms.

SOURCES
- https://study.com/academy/lesson/reticular-formation-definition-functions-quiz.html
- https://www.physio-pedia.com/Reticular_Formation
- https://pubmed.ncbi.nlm.nih.gov/3077010
- https://kids.britannica.com/students/article/reptiles/276696
- https://en.wikipedia.org/wiki/Shark#/media/File:Carl0207_(28225976491).jpg

Allen Liang, Spring 2024

AN INFOGRAPHIC JOURNEY

CHAPTER 10

The Amygdala

The Complex Role and Neural Circuitry of the Amygdala in Fear and Emotion

By Nhi Nguyen & Zahra Khan, Spring 2024

When understanding our emotions, the amygdala takes center stage in the brain. The amygdala is a tiny, almond-shaped cluster of nuclei located deep within the temporal lobes, which significantly impacts how we perceive and respond to emotions such as fear and pleasure. Given its profound impact on our emotional experiences, the amygdala is a focal point of research into the intricacies of emotional and cognitive processes. This essay examines the amygdala's role in fear-related learning and emotional regulation and its neuronal inputs, internal structure, and the intricate network of connections that sustain its functions.

The amygdala's primary function is processing and encoding memories of emotional responses. It plays a crucial role in regulating a person's reaction to stimuli according to the emotional context in which they are presented. It is primarily engaged in the creation of fear-related memories. The amygdala's function in survival strategies is reinforced by its ability to affect both the autonomic and endocrine responses, guiding innate and learned responses to threats.

Understanding the diverse inputs that feed into the amygdala provides information on how it executes its central functions in emotional processing and memory encoding. Different brain regions send information to the amygdala (Phelps & LeDoux, 2005). These include processed data from the prefrontal cortex, which contains higher-order processing that helps control amygdala reactions depending on learned experiences, contextual information from the hippocampus, and direct sensory inputs from the thalamus and sensory cortex. Thanks to this array of inputs, the amygdala can carry out its functions.

The lateral nucleus, basolateral nucleus, and central nucleus are the three primary nuclei that serve different but essential roles inside the amygdala. As the input nucleus, the lateral nucleus is mainly responsible for taking in sensory data and starting the processing of emotional reactions. When integrating sensory experiences with higher-order cognitive processes like memory and decision-making, the basolateral nucleus (BLA) is essential for emotion-related cognitive processing. Finally, linking to brainstem regions that regulate these manifestations, the central nucleus primarily serves as the amygdala's output nucleus, triggering the body's physical reactions to emotional cues (Papez, 1937).

Establishing the distinct functions of the lateral, basolateral, and central nuclei within the amygdala sets the stage for exploring how these interconnected regions collaborate to regulate emotional responses. The amygdala's intrinsic connections between its nuclei enable a complex information flow that enables advanced processing of emotional reactions. After being processed and sent by the lateral nucleus, the basolateral nucleus integrates information with cognitive functions, which then transmits signals to the central nucleus. This circuit emphasizes how the amygdala produces synchronized reactions to emotional cues.

Applying acquired emotional reactions to novel circumstances depends on the connections between the prefrontal cortex and other brain regions, especially the basolateral nucleus. These links guarantee that emotional information permeates cognitive processes, influencing behavior based on memories and projected future outcomes (LeDoux, 2000).

The amygdala's circuitry is built to effectively condition and recall fear-related behaviors relevant to fear learning. This is made possible by the direct connections between the amygdala and thalamic sensory inputs emphasized in LeDoux's model, highlighting the amygdala's function in the quick processing of fear (LeDoux, 1996). The conditioned and immediate fear responses are vital for life, and these connections are crucial for them.

The amygdala's ability to evaluate the importance of sensory inputs is essential for both short-term and long-term reactions to environmental risks and possibilities. The amygdala supports complex behavioral strategies by combining sensory data with contextual and cognitive information, allowing for subtle emotional reactions. Understanding these systems will help explain the biological foundations of emotion and cognition and offer potential options for treating emotional disorders. More research and understanding of this brain circuitry could lead to the development of new techniques for treating emotional and fear-related disorders, which can enhance overall mental and physical health.

The amygdala can be activated by external and internal sources within the body. External stimuli include sensory inputs such as auditory, visual, somatosensory, and taste information, which can enter the amygdala via its lateral nucleus. Olfaction is another external source that can reach the amygdala via the central nucleus. On the other hand, information from internal sources, such as thoughts, imagination, and memories, can access the amygdala, along with input from the Vagus nerve system and the cerebral cortex. At the center of its function, interoception and exteroception are part of the broader framework of internal and external sources. Exteroception is the processing of external sensory information that can influence emotional responses and behaviors. In contrast, interoception involves perceiving internal stimuli, such as bodily sensations, which also influence the amygdala's emotional processing and regulatory functions.

Moreover, there are two distinct pathways for processing sensory information, mainly related to fear and emotional responses that lead to the amygdala, known as the high and low routes. In the high route, the ventral thalamus projects to the primary and secondary cerebral cortices, which then project to the association cortices and finally to the lateral nucleus of the amygdala, where the processed sensory information contributes to the generation of emotional responses and behaviors. Then, there is the low route, where the dorsal and medial thalamus are projected to the lateral nucleus of the amygdala and other subcortical structures.

In conclusion, given all of the information provided, we understand how vital the amygdala is for emotional and cognitive processing, particularly in the perception and response to fear-inducing stimuli; now consider what happens if it is damaged. Damage to the amygdala can lead to a condition known as Klüver–Bucy syndrome. This syndrome is characterized by a variety of behavioral changes and symptoms, including: "psychic blindness", hyper-sexuality, altered emotional behavior, hyperorality, the tendency to react to every visual stimulus, and memory deficits. According to Dr. Adolphs and colleagues, observations of patients with damaged amygdala revealed that "data showed that bilateral, but not unilateral, damage to the amygdala impairs judgments of the intensity of expression of fear, and of expressions normally judged to be very similar to fear, such as surprise" (Adolphs, 1994). Avoiding damage to the amygdala is vital to ensure good emotional regulation, cognitive functioning, appropriate behavioral responses, and overall well-being. Without the amygdala, our ability to navigate the complex landscape of human emotions would be severely compromised.

References

1. https://neuro.psychiatryonline.org/doi/full/10.1176/jnp.10.3.354
2. https://www.open.edu/openlearn/health-sports-psychology/health/emotions-and-emotional-disorders/cont ent-section-2.4
3. https://pubmed.ncbi.nlm.nih.gov/7666173/
4. Neurobiology of Fear and other Emotions by Aage R. Møller, PhD (DMedSci)
5. NEUROPLASTICITY its DARK SIDES: Disorders of the Nervous System Second Edition by Aage R. Møller, PhD (DMedSci)
6. SENSORY SYSTEMS: Anatomy and physiology Second Edition Aage R. Møller, PhD (DMedSci)
7. LeDoux, J. (1996). The Emotional Brain: The Mysterious Underpinnings of Emotional Life. LeDoux, J. (2000). Emotion circuits in the brain. Annual Review of Neuroscience, 23, 155-184. LeDoux, J. (2007). The amygdala. Current Biology, 17(20), R868-R874.
8. Papez J.W. A proposed mechanism of emotion. Arch. Neurol. Psychiatry. 1937;38:725. doi: 10.1001/archneurpsyc.1937.02260220069003.

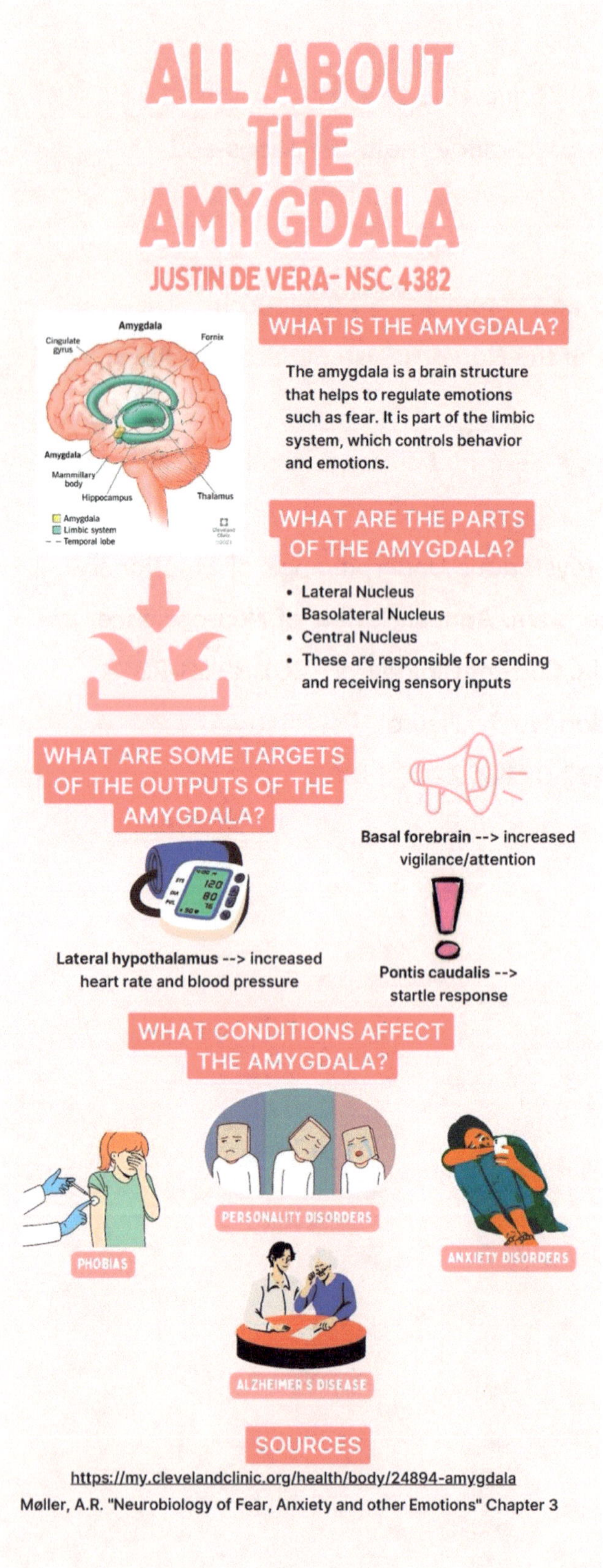

AN INFOGRAPHIC JOURNEY

ALL ABOUT THE AMYGDALA
JUSTIN DE VERA- NSC 4382

WHAT IS THE AMYGDALA?
The amygdala is a brain structure that helps to regulate emotions such as fear. It is part of the limbic system, which controls behavior and emotions.

WHAT ARE THE PARTS OF THE AMYGDALA?
- Lateral Nucleus
- Basolateral Nucleus
- Central Nucleus
- These are responsible for sending and receiving sensory inputs

WHAT ARE SOME TARGETS OF THE OUTPUTS OF THE AMYGDALA?
- Basal forebrain --> increased vigilance/attention
- Lateral hypothalamus --> increased heart rate and blood pressure
- Pontis caudalis --> startle response

WHAT CONDITIONS AFFECT THE AMYGDALA?
- PHOBIAS
- PERSONALITY DISORDERS
- ANXIETY DISORDERS
- ALZHEIMER'S DISEASE

SOURCES
https://my.clevelandclinic.org/health/body/24894-amygdala
Møller, A.R. "Neurobiology of Fear, Anxiety and other Emotions" Chapter 3

Justin De Vera, Spring 2024

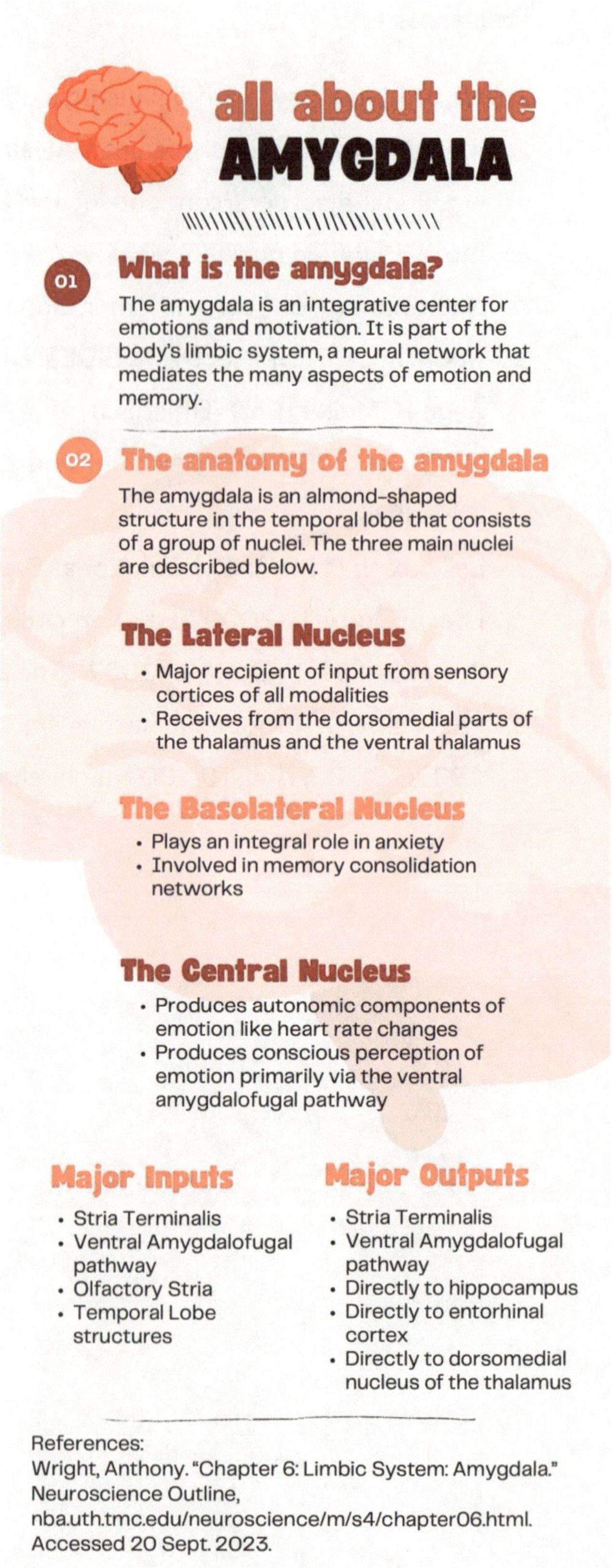

---

all about the AMYGDALA

01 What is the amygdala?
The amygdala is an integrative center for emotions and motivation. It is part of the body's limbic system, a neural network that mediates the many aspects of emotion and memory.

02 The anatomy of the amygdala
The amygdala is an almond-shaped structure in the temporal lobe that consists of a group of nuclei. The three main nuclei are described below.

The Lateral Nucleus
- Major recipient of input from sensory cortices of all modalities
- Receives from the dorsomedial parts of the thalamus and the ventral thalamus

The Basolateral Nucleus
- Plays an integral role in anxiety
- Involved in memory consolidation networks

The Central Nucleus
- Produces autonomic components of emotion like heart rate changes
- Produces conscious perception of emotion primarily via the ventral amygdalofugal pathway

Major Inputs
- Stria Terminalis
- Ventral Amygdalofugal pathway
- Olfactory Stria
- Temporal Lobe structures

Major Outputs
- Stria Terminalis
- Ventral Amygdalofugal pathway
- Directly to hippocampus
- Directly to entorhinal cortex
- Directly to dorsomedial nucleus of the thalamus

References:
Wright, Anthony. "Chapter 6: Limbic System: Amygdala." Neuroscience Outline, nba.uth.tmc.edu/neuroscience/m/s4/chapter06.html. Accessed 20 Sept. 2023.

Ashley Tran, Fall 2023

AN INFOGRAPHIC JOURNEY

THE AMYGDALA

THE EMOTIONAL BRAIN
The parts of the brain that play the biggest role in emotions were coined "the emotional brain" by researcher Joseph LeDoux. The amygdala plays an important role in processing fear and emotion and is the center of the emotional brain.

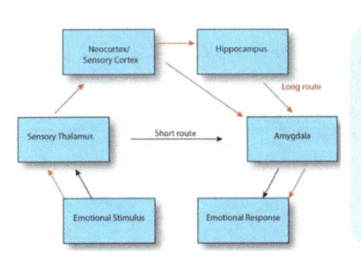

LEDOUX'S EMOTIONAL BRAIN
In the late 1990s Dr. LeDoux, his students, and his coworkers published a radical revision of understanding of the neural basis for emotions. The amygdala was defined as the center for emotional evaluation, specifically involved in fear conditions. Red arrows are shown with the black arrows, and the short routes are shown with the red arrows.

AMYGDALA ANATOMY
The amygdala consists of three main nuclei: the lateral nucleus, the basolateral nucleus, and the central nucleus. The lateral nucleus projects to the basolateral nucleus and receives sensory inputs, except olfactory, directly from the dorsomedial parts of the thalamus and from the ventral thalamus through the primary, secondary, and association sensory cortices. The central nucleus is the main output nucleus and connects to the endocrine, behavioral, and autonomic centers of the brain. The central nucleus receives input from the basolateral nucleus, which is the main target of olfactory input.

INPUT TO THE AMYGDALA
The amygdala can be activated from both exteroceptive and interoceptive sources. It receives input from many structures of the brain including the frontal cortex, the limbic system, the olfactory system, and the hippocampus. It also receives input from the sensory systems through the dorsomedial thalamus; the association cortex of the temporal lobe; the orbitofrontal cortex; the cingulate gyrus; and the nucleus of the solitary tract (NST).

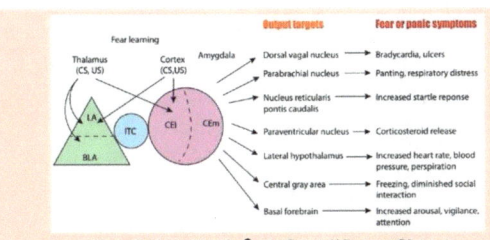

CONNECTIONS TO & FROM THE AMYGDALA
This image shows the inputs and output targets of the amygdala, as well as the fear or panic symptoms that arise based on the target output. The central nucleus (CE) mediates the output of the amygdala nuclei to other parts of the brain.

SOURCES:
Free design tool: Presentations, video, social media | CANVA. Canva. (n.d.). https://www.canva.com/ Møller, A. R. (2019). Neurobiology of Fear and other Emotions. Aage R Møller Publishing.

Tiffany Nouanesengsy, Fall 2023

Amygdala in Humans

The Role of the Amygdala
The amygdala has the ability to process and evaluate stimuli.

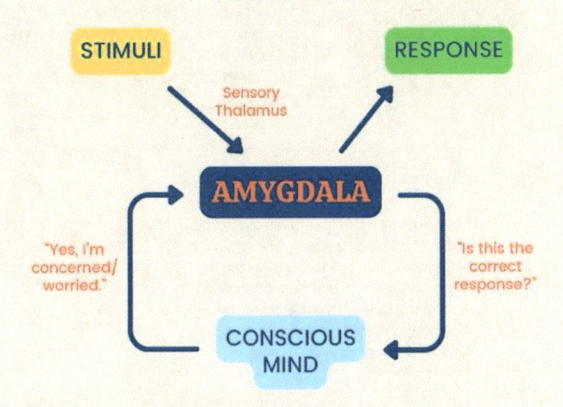

The Kluver-Bucy Syndrome
Dr. Hayman and his co-workers reported the following effects caused by the isolated symmetric damage to the amygdala and their cortical connections in a patient:

- "Psychic blindness" - the inability to recognize the emotional importance of events.
- Hyper-sexuality, often directed indiscriminately.
- Altered emotional behavior.
- Hyperorality - the excessive preoccupation with oral sensations and behaviors.
- Tendency to react to every visual stimuli.
- Memory deficits.

Effects of Amygdala Damage
Dr. Adolphs and his colleagues observed patients with a damaged amygdala and found that the "human amygdala is indispensable to:

1. recognize fear in facial expressions
2. recognize multiple emotions in a single facial expression; but
3. it is NOT required for recognizing personal identity from faces."

Arshad Manzar, Spring 2024

AN INFOGRAPHIC JOURNEY

The Amygdala's Purpose
By Rida Hamid

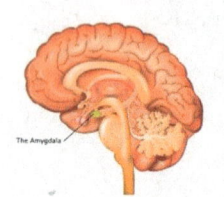

What is The Amygdala?
The amygdala is the brain's emotion-processing center. This was discovered by LeDoux and his colleagues, who also discovered that there are multiple fear pathways.

The Amygdala's Connections
The limbic system consists of the structures involved in emotion-processing. The amygdala interacts with brain regions such as the hypothalamus, the reticular formation, and more. Most of these connections are reciprocal, meaning they receive sensory input and send out sensory outputs as well.

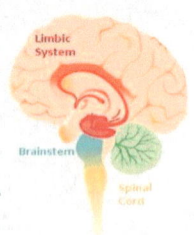

Schematics of Amygdala in Fear learning
There are specific symptoms that arise when specific areas in the amygdala are targeted. For example, when the amygdala targets the parabrachial nucleus, this results in panting or respiratory distress; similarly, targeting the central grey area would result in freezing. Even small things such as grinding your teeth in your sleep are controlled by the amygdala!

Fear Conditioning
Auditory fear conditioning leads to brain plasticity, as seen in animals that have been tested in this area. The lateral amygdala can communicate with the basal nucleus, the central nucleus, and more - all producing different responses to the stimulus.

Main Parts of the Amygdala
The **lateral nucleus** receives sensory information (excluding olfactory); the **basolateral nucleus** connects with the **central nucleus**, and gives input to the CN. The hypothalamus also plays a role in emotional responses alongside the amygdala.

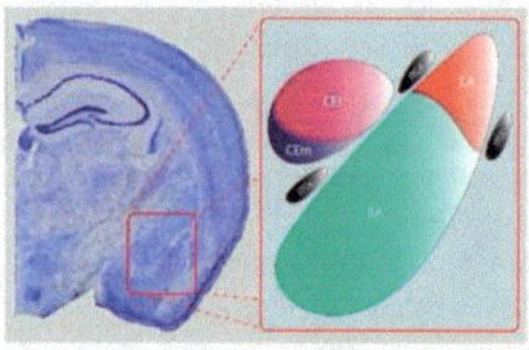

The Basolateral Nuclei
The BLN of the amygdala is connected with regions that regulate cognition, stress responses, and motivation. Essentially, it plays a big role in emotional arousal.

Rida Hamid, Fall 2023

Amygdala
By: Mana Zandi

Amygdala
Receives input from the thalamus, the cortexes, the cingulate gyrus, the hippocampus, and the hypothalamus and incorporates all of these to create an emotional response. The lateral nucleus receives sensory input, the central nucleus receives input from the olfactory and basolateral nucleus.

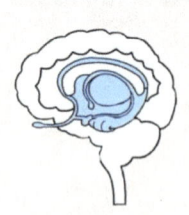

Connections
The amygdala makes connections to many brain structures, including the hypothalamus and the nucleus of the solitary tract. All the connections are mostly double-sided, so the amygdala can influence sensory processing but also the opposite way.

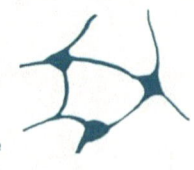

Nucleus Basalis
This is the central nucleus of the Amygdala. It makes connections with the brain stem nuclei, cortical areas, and cortex which will promote plastic changes. The different targets can lead to different fear or panic symptoms.

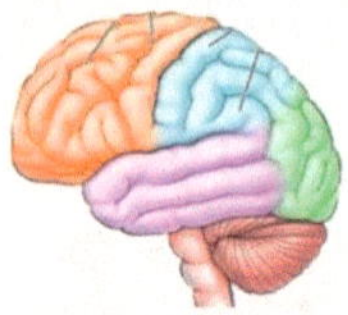

Papez Circuits
The hypothalamus, anterior thalamus, and cingulate cortex are the basis of emotions. The cingulate cortex makes the connections that reach the sensory cortexes. It allows for the top-down control of emotion from the hippocampus to the hypothalamus and back to the cortex and the trace is stored as a "feeling".

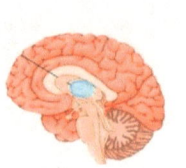

LeDoux Emotional Brain
The amygdala is the center of the emotional brain. The pathway could involve a short or long route. The short route involves the sensory thalamus to the amygdala leading to a response, while the longer route also involves the neocortex and the hippocampus.

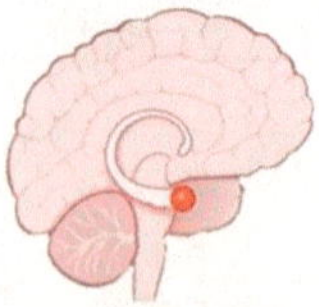

Auditory Fear Conditioning and Revisions
Animals fear a tone, a tone, and a shock are paired to lead to defensive reactions like freezing. They converge in the Lateral Amygdala which will communicate with the Central Nucleus to lead to the freezing behavior. It has been found that fear and reward use similar neuronal structures.

Reference - NSC 4382 Week 5 Chapter 3 Part 1 and Part 2

Mana Zandi, Fall 2023

AN INFOGRAPHIC JOURNEY

THE AMYGDALA AND THE BRAIN

Citation: MØLLER, Aage, and Moller Phd, Aage R. Neurobiology of Fear, Anxiety and Other Emotions. N.p., Independently Published, 2019.

THE WAY EMOTIONS WORK IN THE BRAIN RELIES ON INTERACTIONS BETWEEN:
1. Epigenetics
2. Genetics
3. Social behavior
4. Stress
5. Learning and memory

EXTROCEPTION
- Sensing the external enviroment
- Using the five senses

INTEROCEPTION
- Perception of sensations from inside the body
- Heart beat, respiration

THERE ARE TWO DISTINCT PATHWAYS FOR EMOTIONAL NEURAL SIGNALS TO REACH THE NEURAL CIRCUITS RESPONSIBLE FOR GENERATING AN EMOTIONAL REACTION.

Event → Appraisal → Emotional response (Zajonc/ LeDoux; Lazarus/ Schachter-slnger)

SYSTEMS THAT PLAY A ROLE IN OUR EMOTIONS
1. The amygdala (biggest role)
2. The limbic system (processing our emotions)

ADDITIONAAL INFORMATION OF THE AMYGDALA
1. The amygdala has 3 main nuclei, the lateral nucleus, the basolateral, and the central nucleus
2. The lateral nucleus of the amygdala gets sensory inputs, excluding smell, directly from certain areas in the thalamus and through sensory processing areas in the brain.
3. The central nucleus of the amygdala gets signals from the basolateral nucleus, which is the primary recipient of olfactory input.
4. The amygdala nuclei also get input from the frontal cortex and the orbitofrontal cortex.

THE SPECIFIC DESTINATIONS OF CELLS IN THE MIDDLE PART OF THE CENTRAL NUCLEUS OF THE AMYGDALA.
Output targets:
- Nucleus reticularis
- Parabrachial nucleus

-**Fear or panic syndrome**: Panting, respiratory distress
- Pontis caudalis

-**Fear or panic syndrome**: Increased startled response
- Dorsal vagus nucleus

-**Fear or panic syndrome**: Bradycardia, ulcers
- Basal forebrain attention

-**Fear or panic syndrome**: increased arousal, vigilance
- Lateral hypothalamus pressure, perspiration

-**Fear or panic syndrome**: increased heart rate, blood
- Central gray area

-**Fear or panic syndrome**: Freezing, diminish social interaction
- Paraventricular nucleus

-**Fear or panic syndrome**: Corticosteroid release

5. Other parts of the brain also play a role in creating emotional responses, such as the hypothalamus

Emily Gutierrez, Fall 2023

The Amygdala

- The center of the emotional brain
- Almost all connections are reciprocal
- Hypothalamus plays an essential role in emotional responses and output

RECEIVES INPUT FROM:
- Sensory systems through the dorsomedial thalamus
- The association cortex of the temporal lobe
- The frontal cortex, the limbic system, and the olfactory system;
- The orbitofrontal cortex, whose inputs come from the other regions of the frontal lobes, temporal pole, amygdala, and limbic system
- The cingulate gyrus, and projects to the limbic system and the frontal cortex

3 MAIN NUCLEI:
- Lateral, Basolateral, and Central nucleus
- Lateral nucleus
  - receives sensory inputs, except olfactory, directly from the dorsomedial parts of the thalamus and from the ventral thalamus through the primary, secondary, and association sensory cortices.
- Central nucleus
  - receives input from the Basolateral nucleus, which is the main target of olfactory input.

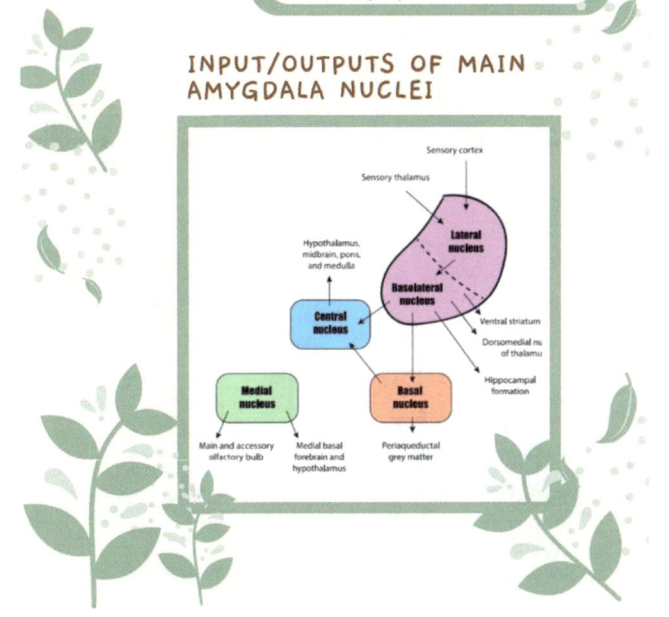

INPUT/OUTPUTS OF MAIN AMYGDALA NUCLEI

Avalon De Curtis, Spring 2023

AN INFOGRAPHIC JOURNEY

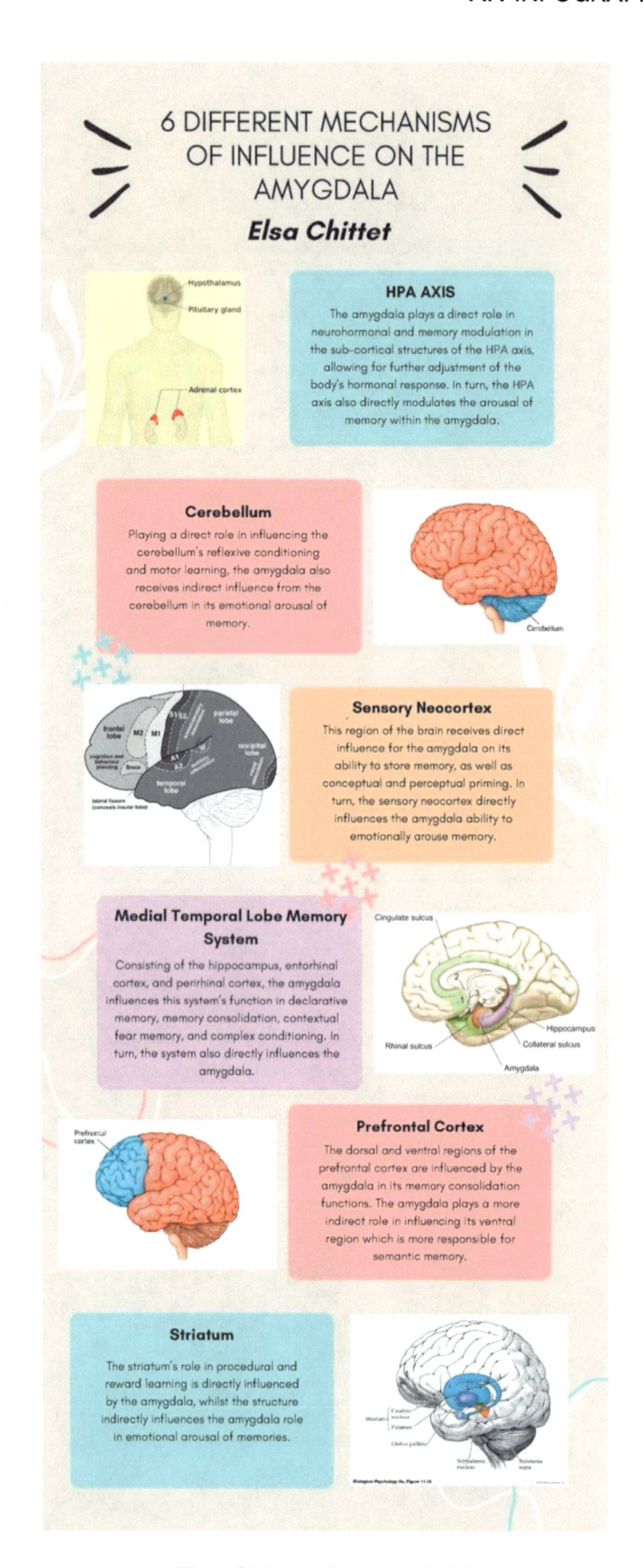

6 DIFFERENT MECHANISMS OF INFLUENCE ON THE AMYGDALA
Elsa Chittet

HPA AXIS
The amygdala plays a direct role in neurohormonal and memory modulation in the sub-cortical structures of the HPA axis, allowing for further adjustment of the body's hormonal response. In turn, the HPA axis also directly modulates the arousal of memory within the amygdala.

Cerebellum
Playing a direct role in influencing the cerebellum's reflexive conditioning and motor learning, the amygdala also receives indirect influence from the cerebellum in its emotional arousal of memory.

Sensory Neocortex
This region of the brain receives direct influence for the amygdala on its ability to store memory, as well as conceptual and perceptual priming. In turn, the sensory neocortex directly influences the amygdala ability to emotionally arouse memory.

Medial Temporal Lobe Memory System
Consisting of the hippocampus, entorhinal cortex, and perirhinal cortex, the amygdala influences this system's function in declarative memory, memory consolidation, contextual fear memory, and complex conditioning. In turn, the system also directly influences the amygdala.

Prefrontal Cortex
The dorsal and ventral regions of the prefrontal cortex are influenced by the amygdala in its memory consolidation functions. The amygdala plays a more indirect role in influencing its ventral region which is more responsible for semantic memory.

Striatum
The striatum's role in procedural and reward learning is directly influenced by the amygdala, whilst the structure indirectly influences the amygdala role in emotional arousal of memories.

Elsa Chittet, Spring 2024

ACTIVATION OF THE AMYGDALA

THE AMYGDALA CAN BE ACTIVATED FROM:

→ **External Sources**
- Sensory information for hearing, vision, somatosensory and taste can reach the amygdala through its lateral nucleus
- Central nucleus for olfactory information

→ **Internal Sources**
- Information from thinking, imagining memory, vagus nerve, and cerebral cortex can reach the amygdala

DORSAL-MEDIAL THALAMUS
Establishes a direct route from sensory systems to the amygdala. Little-processed information can reach the amygdala nuclei and have negative effects.

SENSORY ROUTES TO AMYGDALA
All sensory systems, except the olfactory nerve, project to the lateral nucleus of the amygdala.

TWO ASCENDING SENSORY PATHWAYS

High Route:
Ventral thalamus → Primary, secondary cerebral cortices → Association cortices → Amygdala lateral nucleus

Low Route:
Dorsal and medial thalamus → lateral nucleus of the amygdala and other subcortical structure

Sources: Møller, A.R. Sensory Systems: Anatomy and Physiology, Aage R. Møller Publishing, 20

Sarvani Ganapavarapu, Fall 2023

AN INFOGRAPHIC JOURNEY

The Activation of the Amygdala
By: Karina Slobodkin

External & Internal Sources
1. **External** - Sensory information such as hearing, taste, and smell.
   a. All senses except olfaction reaches the amygdala through the lateral nucleus
   b. Olfaction uses the central nucleus
2. **Internal** - Information from thinking, imagining, and memory
   a. Reaches the amygdala through the vagus nerve and cerebral cortex.

Exteroception sensing the outside Ex: sight, sound, smell, taste

Interception sensing the inside Ex: headache, hunger, thirst

The Thalamus & Amygdala
- Pathways from the thalamus to the amygdala is crucial for emotional learning.
- The dorsal medial thalamus establishes a direct connection between sensory info and the amygdala
- This connection allows for fast, poorly processed information to reach the amygdala and negatively affect body functions

Locations of Sensory Processing
- Olfactory pathways project to the olfactory cortex
- Equilibrium pathways project to the cerebellum
- Majority of sensory pathways project to thalamus which modifies and relays information to cortices

Fig. 10-4

Sensory Pathways Leading to the Amygdala

High Route: Ventral Thalamus -> Primary and Secondary Cerebral Cortices -> Association Cortices -> Lateral Nucleus (Amygdala)
- Highly processed information
- "Classical" ascending pathway
- Slower processing of sensory information, however, it is more accurate
- Receives input from the Central Nucleus and the Inferior Colliculus

Low Route: Dorsal and Medial Thalamus -> Lateral Nucleus of Amygdala and other subcortical areas
- Less processed information
- "Non-Classical" ascending pathway
- Faster processing of sensory information, however, it is less accurately interpreted
- Receives input from the External Nucleus and Dorsal Cortex of the Inferior Colliculus

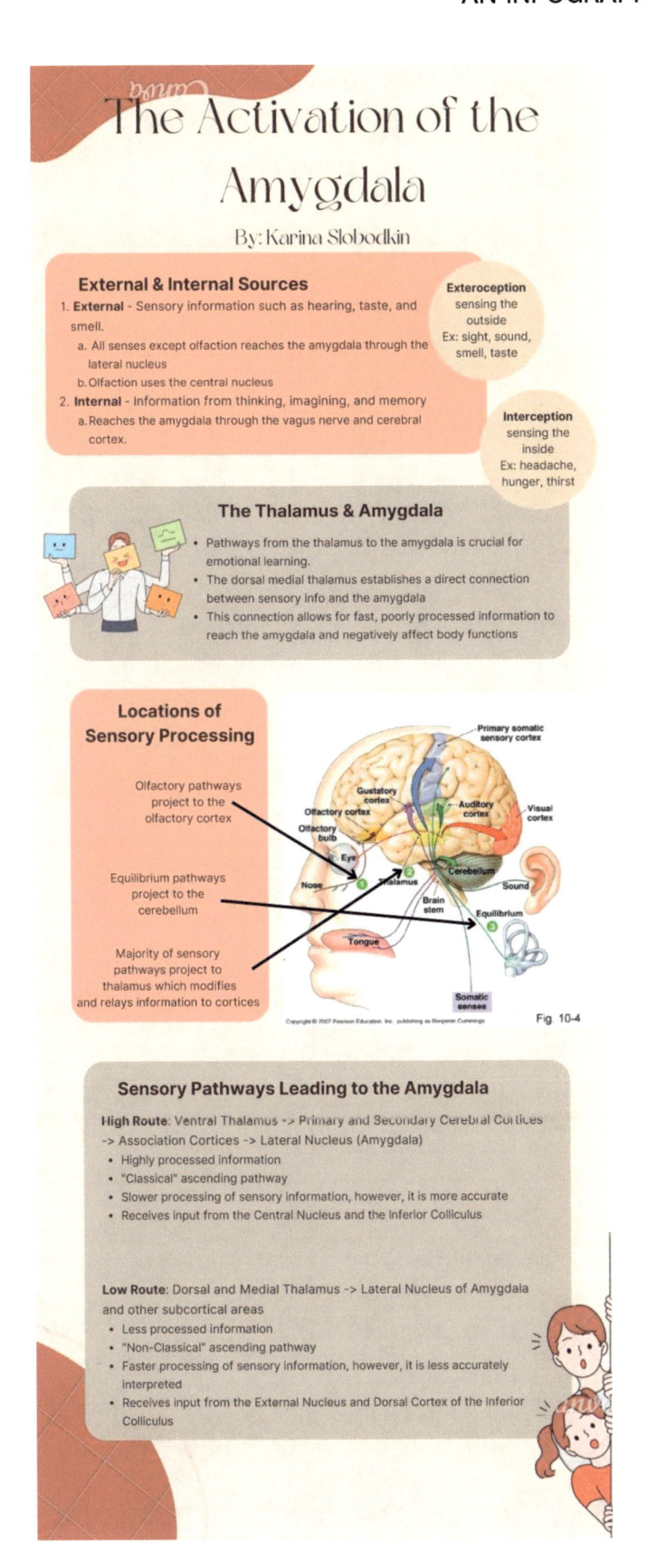

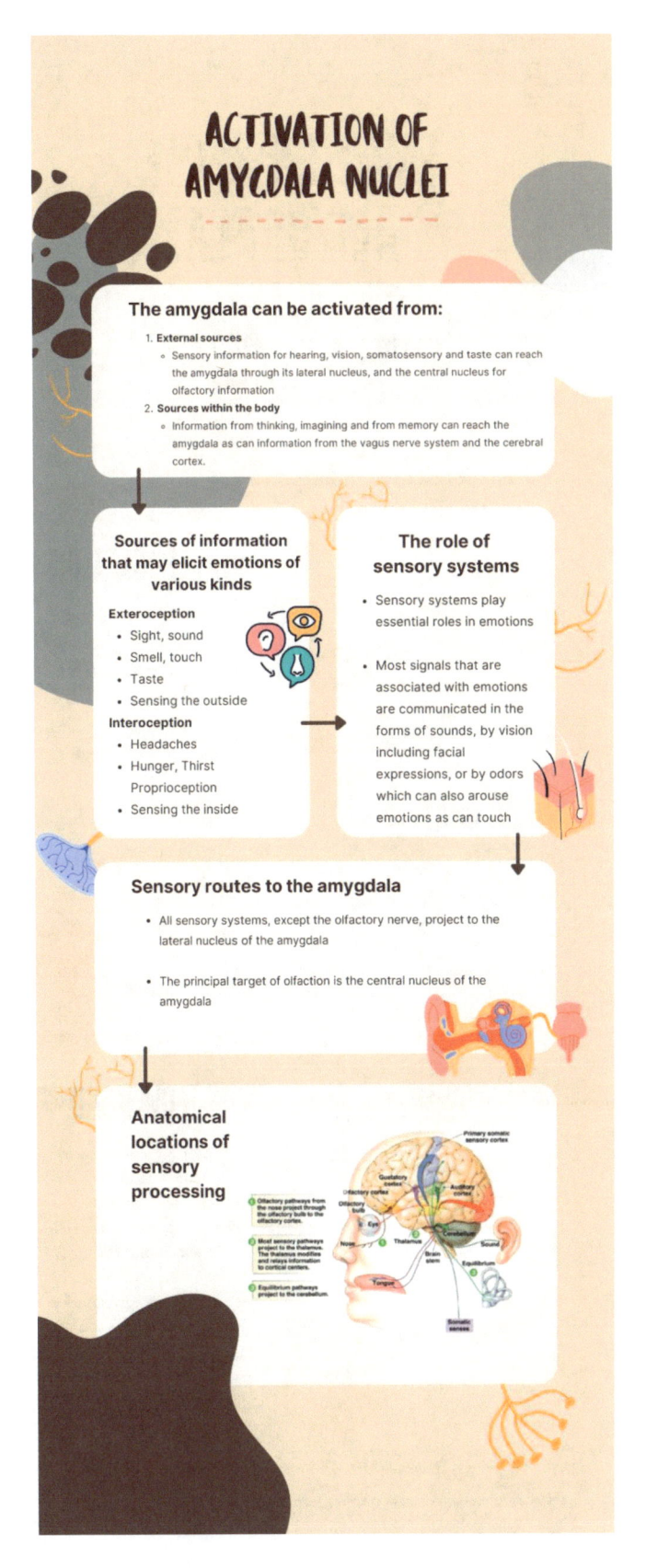

Karina Slobodkin, Spring 2023

ACTIVATION OF AMYGDALA NUCLEI

The amygdala can be activated from:
1. **External sources**
   - Sensory information for hearing, vision, somatosensory and taste can reach the amygdala through its lateral nucleus, and the central nucleus for olfactory information
2. **Sources within the body**
   - Information from thinking, imagining and from memory can reach the amygdala as can information from the vagus nerve system and the cerebral cortex.

Sources of information that may elicit emotions of various kinds
Exteroception
- Sight, sound
- Smell, touch
- Taste
- Sensing the outside

Interoception
- Headaches
- Hunger, Thirst
- Proprioception
- Sensing the inside

The role of sensory systems
- Sensory systems play essential roles in emotions
- Most signals that are associated with emotions are communicated in the forms of sounds, by vision including facial expressions, or by odors which can also arouse emotions as can touch

Sensory routes to the amygdala
- All sensory systems, except the olfactory nerve, project to the lateral nucleus of the amygdala
- The principal target of olfaction is the central nucleus of the amygdala

Anatomical locations of sensory processing
- Olfactory pathways from the nose project through the olfactory bulb to the olfactory cortex.
- Most sensory pathways project to the thalamus. The thalamus modifies and relays information to cortical cortex.
- Equilibrium pathways project to the cerebellum.

Khadeeja Moosa, Spring 2023

AN INFOGRAPHIC JOURNEY

EMOTION & THE AMYGDALA

EXTEROCEPTION
The amygdala can be activated by external stimuli. Experiences dealing with the senses, such as touch, taste, sight, smell, and sound can elicit a variety of emotions.

INTEROCEPTION
The amygdala can also be triggered via internal sources. These include stimuli from the body's own systems, like visceral pain and proprioception.

HIGH ROAD
The high road pathway is one of two sensory pathways to the amygdala. In this pathway, stimuli ascends up the spinal cord to the ventral thalamus. Then to cerebral cortices before finally ending at the amygdala. Since incoming information goes to the cortex before the amygdala (and thus information is synthesized and processed before reaching the amygdala), the high road response is a more measured, thoughtful, and slower fear response.

LOW ROAD
In the low road pathway, information goes from the dorsal-medial thalamus to the lateral nucleus of the amygdala and other subcortical structures. By skipping the primary sensory cortices, information is processed faster making the fear response more rash and instinctive.

Dorsal-medial thalamus → Lateral nucleus of amygala

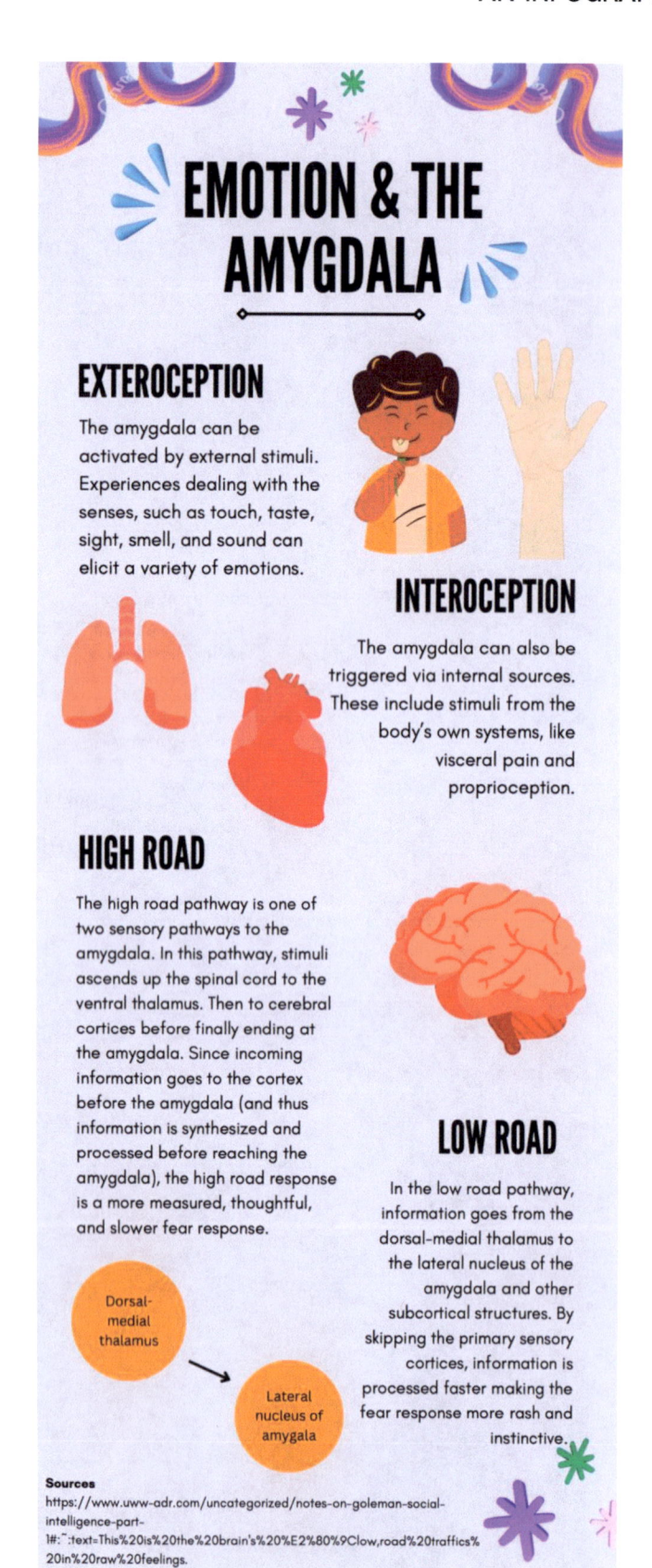

Sources
https://www.uww-adr.com/uncategorized/notes-on-goleman-social-intelligence-part-1#:~:text=This%20is%20the%20brain's%20%E2%80%9Clow,road%20traffics%20in%20raw%20feelings.

Isha Rojanala, Fall 2023

AMYGDALA AND EMOTION
Alifiya Shaikh

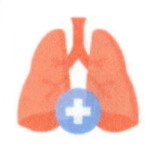

What is the amygdala?
It is a small almond shaped structure in the brain connected to the limbic system. It also plays a role in emotions (especially anxiety and fear), behavior, and even danger.

ANATOMY
It is part of the temporal lobe, and there are two on each side of the brain. It is close to structures that process smell, and structures that process vision and hearing as well.

COMPOSITION
Amygdala is made up of neurons that send electrical and chemical signals as well as glial cells that support the neuron.

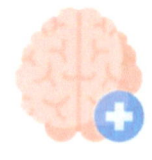

Conditions associated with the amygdala
Anxiety disorder, panic disorder, PTSD, personality disorders, phobias, autism spectrum disorder, Alzheimer's etc.

Physical Symptoms
Some physical symptoms relating to the amygdala are faster heart rate (tachycardia), fast breathing (tachypnea), and sweating

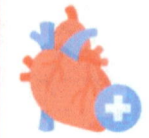

How to take care of your amygdala
Maintain a healthy weight, eat a balanced diet, protect yourself from head injuries (such as wearing a helmet), manage any chronic conditions

professional, C. C. medical. (n.d.). The amygdala: A small part of your Brain's biggest abilities. Cleveland Clinic. https://my.clevelandclinic.org/health/body/24894-amygdala

Alifiyah Shaikh, Fall 2023

AN INFOGRAPHIC JOURNEY

Elicitation of Various Emotions!

Know how the amygdala can be activated from different stimuli.

EXTEROCEPTION | **INTEROCEPTION**

Sight, Sound
These 2 body systems work together in order to determine what external stimuli looks like and how it sounds like. Processing this information can help us figure out how to react.

Smell, Touch
Olfaction can be reached through the central nucleus of amygdala deciphering what the smell is and how we should react to it.

Taste
Gustatory system allows the processing of taste to elicit emotions such as disgust or pleasure.

Sensing the Outside
External stimuli can activate a series of emotions. Without these senses, we would not be properly able to react appropriately.

Headaches
This is the body's way of letting us know that there may be some internal issues that needs to be regulated.

Hunger, Thirst
This is especially important for survival allowing us to know when it is time for us to provide our body with much-needed fuel.

Proprioception
Having a good sense of where your body is and producing movement based on what is needed.

Sensing the Inside
Our body does not lie when it comes to telling us if we feel under the weather or overly stressed.

Skyla Lopez, Spring 2023

Sources of Emotion

Certain aspects of the environment around us can elicit specific emotional responses. These sources in our environment can be both internal and external and are primarily identified into two main categories: Interception and Exteroception

Exteroception
Exteroception can be defined as the sensory receptors in our body's response to external stimuli in our environment. These can cause a wide array of emotions that could involve nostalgia and memory from the limbic system as well.

"Sensing the Outside"
Exteroception is like sensing the outside; some main sources include sound, touch, taste, and sight. All senses that allow us to acclimatize to our environment and understand where we are and how that might make us feel.

Interception
Interception refers to stimuli found internally that may provoke an emotional response. Once again, this response can encompass a wide range of emotions, depending on how we perceive the internal stimuli our brain is receiving.

"Sensing the Inside"
Interception can be looked at as sensing the inside, and this may include headaches we experience during the day, hunger, and even proprioception which is our body's internal awareness of the position of our muscles in the body.

Cheng Hao, Spring 2023

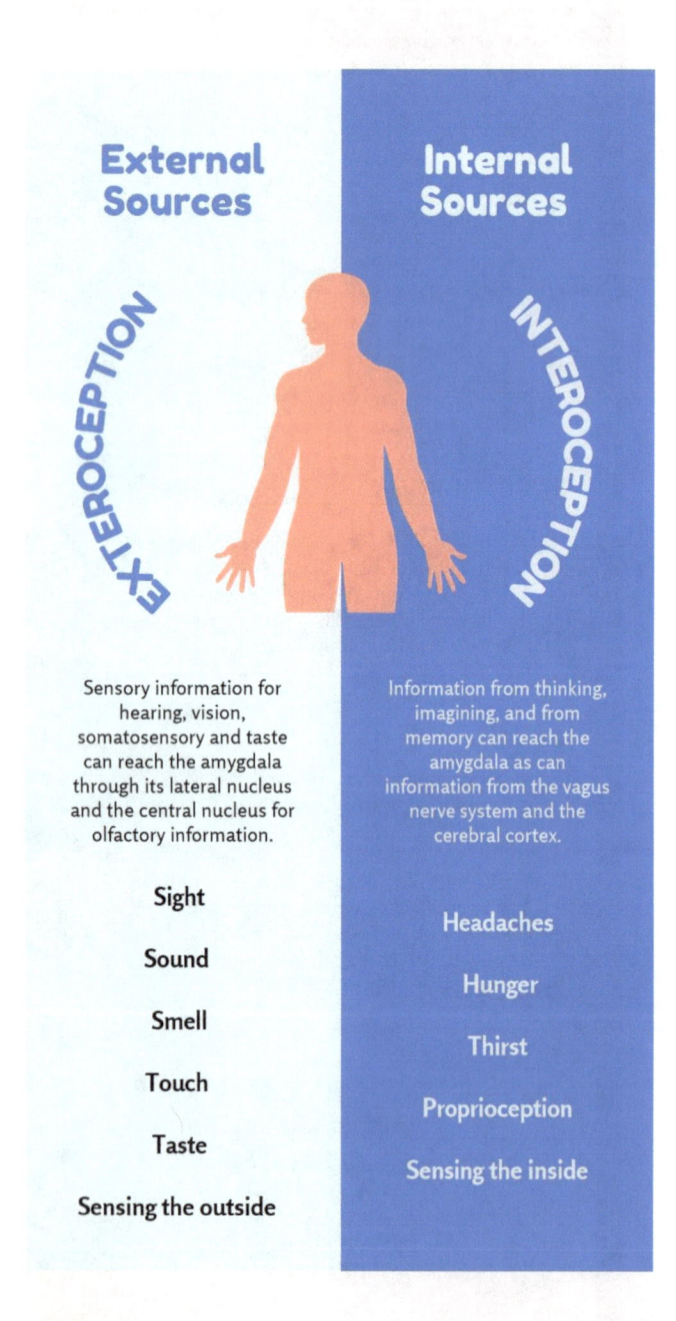

AN INFOGRAPHIC JOURNEY

How Can The Amygdala Be Activated?

External Sources — EXTEROCEPTION

Sensory information for hearing, vision, somatosensory and taste can reach the amygdala through its lateral nucleus and the central nucleus for olfactory information.

- Sight
- Sound
- Smell
- Touch
- Taste
- Sensing the outside

Internal Sources — INTEROCEPTION

Information from thinking, imagining, and from memory can reach the amygdala as can information from the vagus nerve system and the cerebral cortex.

- Headaches
- Hunger
- Thirst
- Proprioception
- Sensing the inside

Preena Desai, Spring 2023

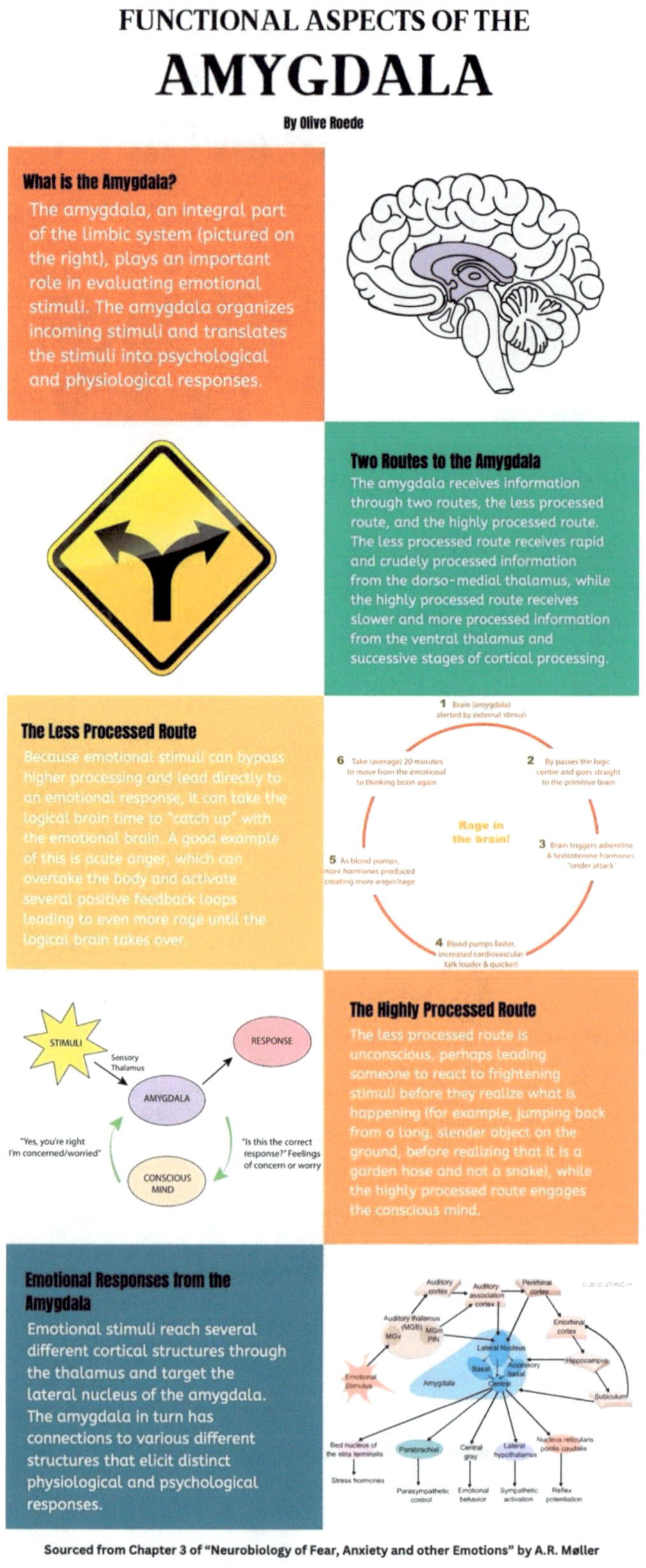

FUNCTIONAL ASPECTS OF THE AMYGDALA
By Olive Roede

What is the Amygdala?
The amygdala, an integral part of the limbic system (pictured on the right), plays an important role in evaluating emotional stimuli. The amygdala organizes incoming stimuli and translates the stimuli into psychological and physiological responses.

Two Routes to the Amygdala
The amygdala receives information through two routes, the less processed route, and the highly processed route. The less processed route receives rapid and crudely processed information from the dorso-medial thalamus, while the highly processed route receives slower and more processed information from the ventral thalamus and successive stages of cortical processing.

The Less Processed Route
Because emotional stimuli can bypass higher processing and lead directly to an emotional response, it can take the logical brain time to "catch up" with the emotional brain. A good example of this is acute anger, which can overtake the body and activate several positive feedback loops leading to even more rage until the logical brain takes over.

The Highly Processed Route
The less processed route is unconscious, perhaps leading someone to react to frightening stimuli before they realize what is happening (for example, jumping back from a long, slender object on the ground, before realizing that it is a garden hose and not a snake), while the highly processed route engages the conscious mind.

Emotional Responses from the Amygdala
Emotional stimuli reach several different cortical structures through the thalamus and target the lateral nucleus of the amygdala. The amygdala in turn has connections to various different structures that elicit distinct physiological and psychological responses.

Sourced from Chapter 3 of "Neurobiology of Fear, Anxiety and other Emotions" by A.R. Møller

Olive Roede, Fall 2023

AN INFOGRAPHIC JOURNEY

Functional Aspects of the Amygdala

The amygdala plays an important role in evaluating emotional stimuli
The amygdala and orbitofrontal cortex help **organize** emotional response and translate it into **actions**

Amygdala receiving input:
The amygdala receives input from two main sensory systems:
1. Rapid and crudely processes info from the **dorso-medial thalamus** (non-classical sensory pathways) and the nucleus of the solitary tract (NTS)
2. slower and more processed info from the **central thalamus** and successive stages of cortical processing (classical sensory pathways)

The amygdala evaluating stimuli:
This diagram shows the processing and evaluating ability of the amygdala when given stimuli

Expression of emotional response:
- Cerebral cortex pathways relay detailed and accurate representations of the environment
  - BUT the multiple neural links cause the pathway to be **slow** in comparison

Expression of different emotional responses of the amygdala:
There are a variety of connections from emotional stimuli that involve the main nuclei of the amygdala to other brain structures (as seen in diagram)

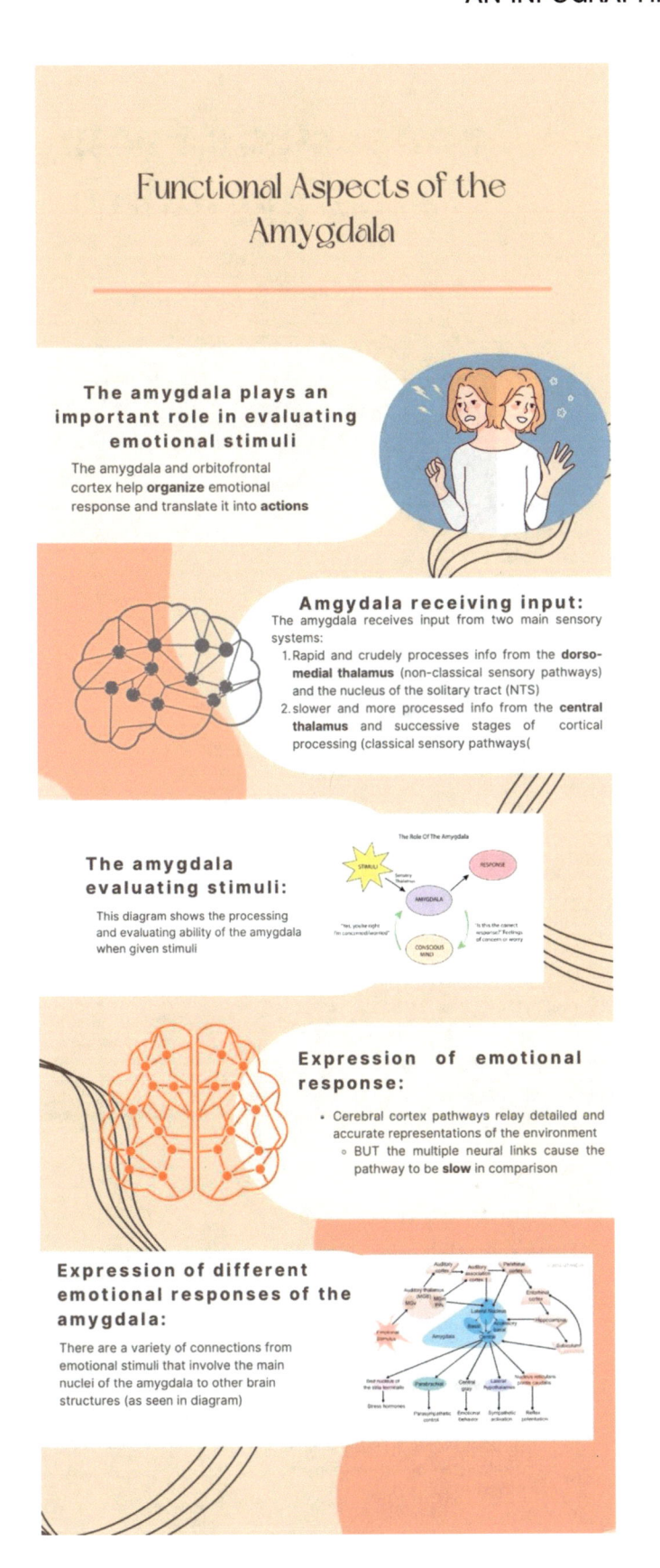

Alyssa Tran, Fall 2023

FUNCTIONAL ASPECTS OF THE AMYGDALA

Function of Amygdala
The amygdala evaluates emotional stimuli. With the orbitofrontal cortex, it plays essential roles in organizing emotional responses and triggering responses based on stimuli.

Definition by LeDoux
LeDoux defines the amygdala as a "center for emotional evaluation." (Ledoux, 1987)

Importance
The amygdala functions to recognize multiple emotions in facial expressions. Damage to the amygdala results in altered emotional behavior and an inability to recognize emotional significance.

Inputs into the Amygdala
1. The amygdala receives rapid inputs from the dorso-medial thalamus and the nucleus of the solitary tract (NTS). This constitutes the non-classical sensory pathway through which information is quickly processed.
2. The amygdala receives slower inputs from the ventral thalamus and successive stages of cortical processing. This constitutes the classical sensory pathway through which information is more processed.

Role of the Amygdala

Stimuli → Sensory Thalamus → Amygdala → Response
"Yes, you're right to feel this way." / "Is this the correct response to the stimuli?"
Conscious mind

Kajal Patel, Spring 2024

181

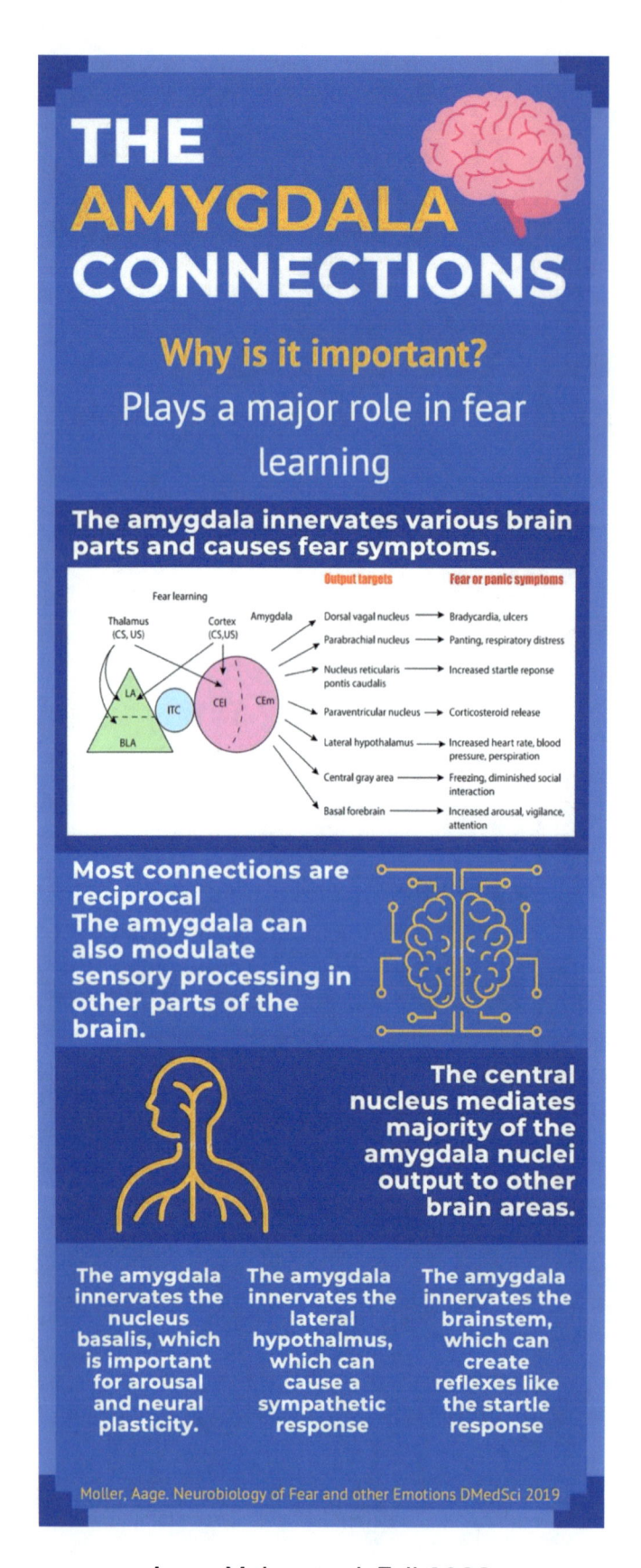

AN INFOGRAPHIC JOURNEY

THE AMYGDALA CONNECTIONS

Why is it important?
Plays a major role in fear learning

The amygdala innervates various brain parts and causes fear symptoms.

Most connections are reciprocal. The amygdala can also modulate sensory processing in other parts of the brain.

The central nucleus mediates majority of the amygdala nuclei output to other brain areas.

The amygdala innervates the nucleus basalis, which is important for arousal and neural plasticity.

The amygdala innervates the lateral hypothalmus, which can cause a sympathetic response.

The amygdala innervates the brainstem, which can create reflexes like the startle response.

Moller, Aage. Neurobiology of Fear and other Emotions DMedSci 2019

Aman Mohammad, Fall 2023

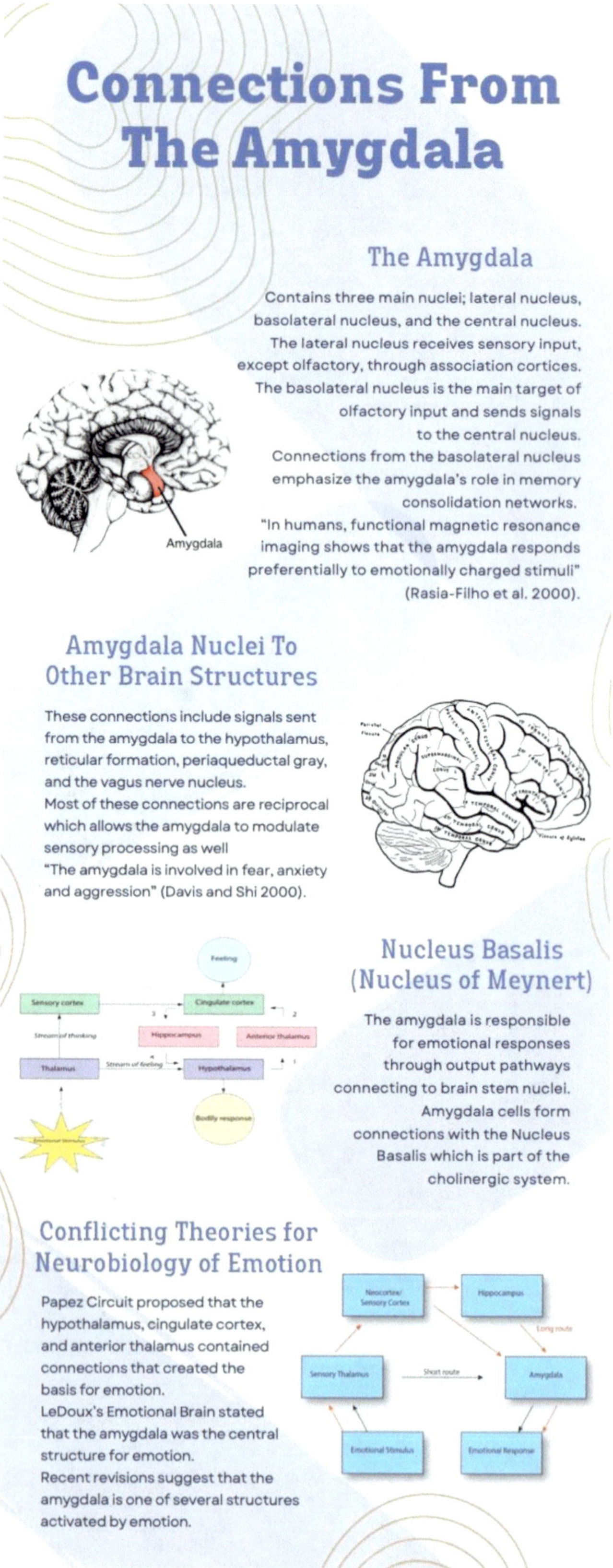

Connections From The Amygdala

The Amygdala
Contains three main nuclei; lateral nucleus, basolateral nucleus, and the central nucleus. The lateral nucleus receives sensory input, except olfactory, through association cortices. The basolateral nucleus is the main target of olfactory input and sends signals to the central nucleus. Connections from the basolateral nucleus emphasize the amygdala's role in memory consolidation networks.
"In humans, functional magnetic resonance imaging shows that the amygdala responds preferentially to emotionally charged stimuli" (Rasia-Filho et al. 2000).

Amygdala Nuclei To Other Brain Structures
These connections include signals sent from the amygdala to the hypothalamus, reticular formation, periaqueductal gray, and the vagus nerve nucleus.
Most of these connections are reciprocal which allows the amygdala to modulate sensory processing as well.
"The amygdala is involved in fear, anxiety and aggression" (Davis and Shi 2000).

Nucleus Basalis (Nucleus of Meynert)
The amygdala is responsible for emotional responses through output pathways connecting to brain stem nuclei. Amygdala cells form connections with the Nucleus Basalis which is part of the cholinergic system.

Conflicting Theories for Neurobiology of Emotion
Papez Circuit proposed that the hypothalamus, cingulate cortex, and anterior thalamus contained connections that created the basis for emotion.
LeDoux's Emotional Brain stated that the amygdala was the central structure for emotion.
Recent revisions suggest that the amygdala is one of several structures activated by emotion.

Armaan Sood, Fall 2023

An Infographic Journey

Routes to the Amygdala

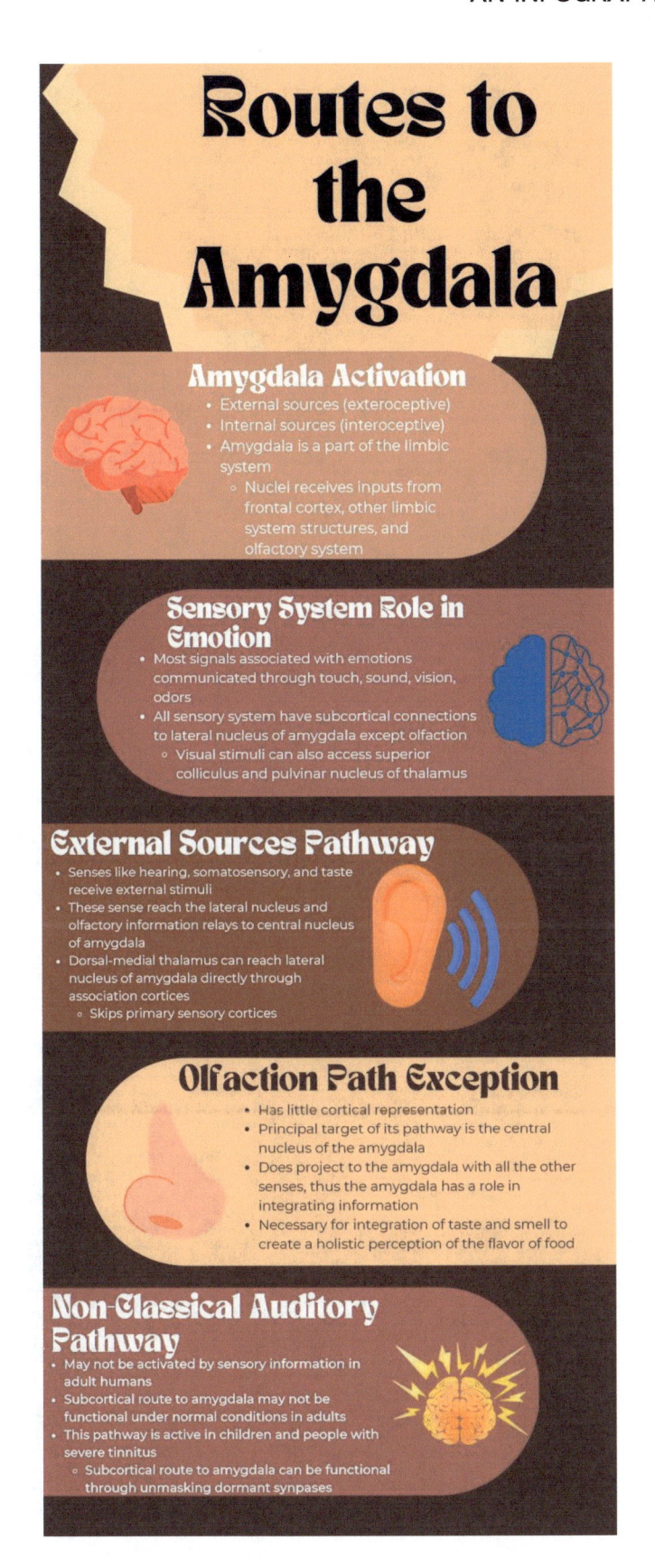

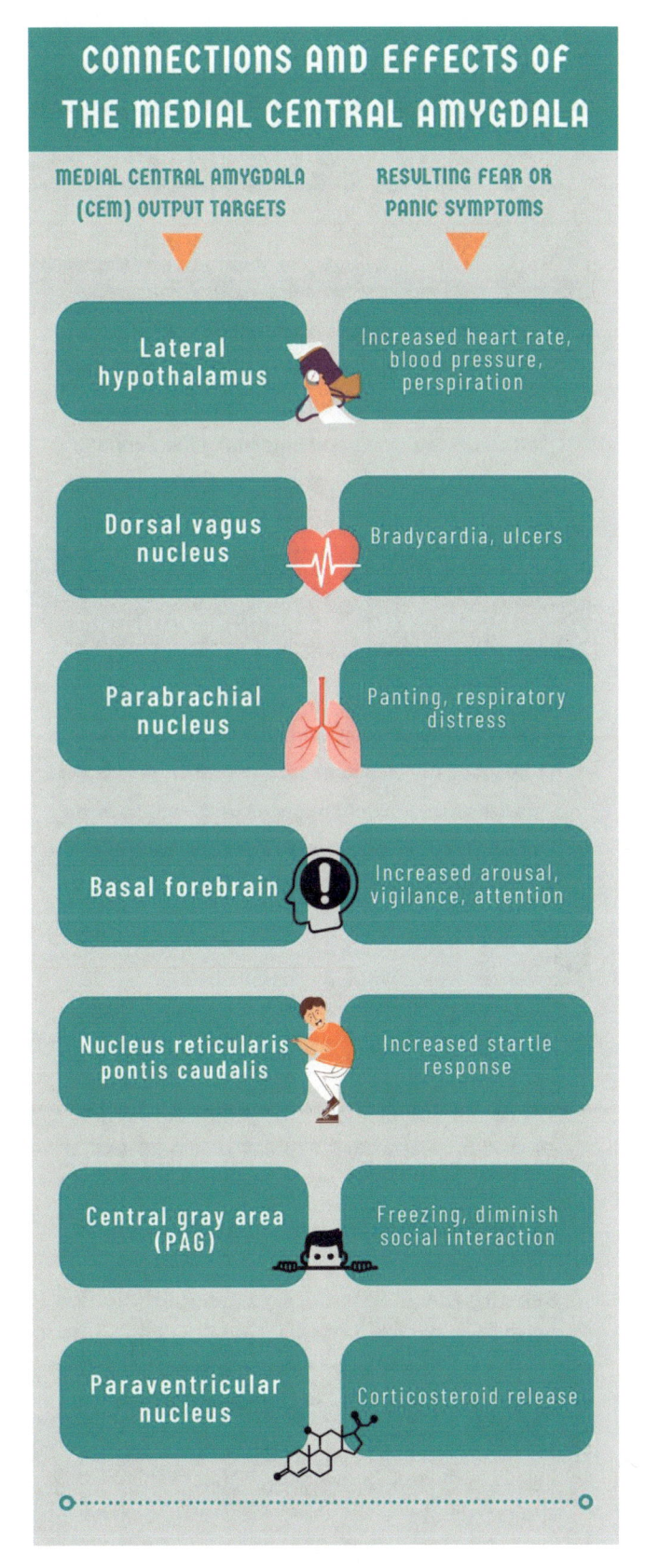

Amygdala Activation
- External sources (exteroceptive)
- Internal sources (interoceptive)
- Amygdala is a part of the limbic system
  - Nuclei receives inputs from frontal cortex, other limbic system structures, and olfactory system

Sensory System Role in Emotion
- Most signals associated with emotions communicated through touch, sound, vision, odors
- All sensory system have subcortical connections to lateral nucleus of amygdala except olfaction
  - Visual stimuli can also access superior colliculus and pulvinar nucleus of thalamus

External Sources Pathway
- Senses like hearing, somatosensory, and taste receive external stimuli
- These sense reach the lateral nucleus and olfactory information relays to central nucleus of amygdala
- Dorsal-medial thalamus can reach lateral nucleus of amygdala directly through association cortices
  - Skips primary sensory cortices

Olfaction Path Exception
- Has little cortical representation
- Principal target of its pathway is the central nucleus of the amygdala
- Does project to the amygdala with all the other senses, thus the amygdala has a role in integrating information
- Necessary for integration of taste and smell to create a holistic perception of the flavor of food

Non-Classical Auditory Pathway
- May not be activated by sensory information in adult humans
- Subcortical route to amygdala may not be functional under normal conditions in adults
- This pathway is active in children and people with severe tinnitus
  - Subcortical route to amygdala can be functional through unmasking dormant synapses

Hannah Nguyen, Spring 2023

Connections and Effects of the Medial Central Amygdala

Medial Central Amygdala (CEM) Output Targets	Resulting Fear or Panic Symptoms
Lateral hypothalamus	Increased heart rate, blood pressure, perspiration
Dorsal vagus nucleus	Bradycardia, ulcers
Parabrachial nucleus	Panting, respiratory distress
Basal forebrain	Increased arousal, vigilance, attention
Nucleus reticularis pontis caudalis	Increased startle response
Central gray area (PAG)	Freezing, diminish social interaction
Paraventricular nucleus	Corticosteroid release

Mohammad Ali, Spring 2023

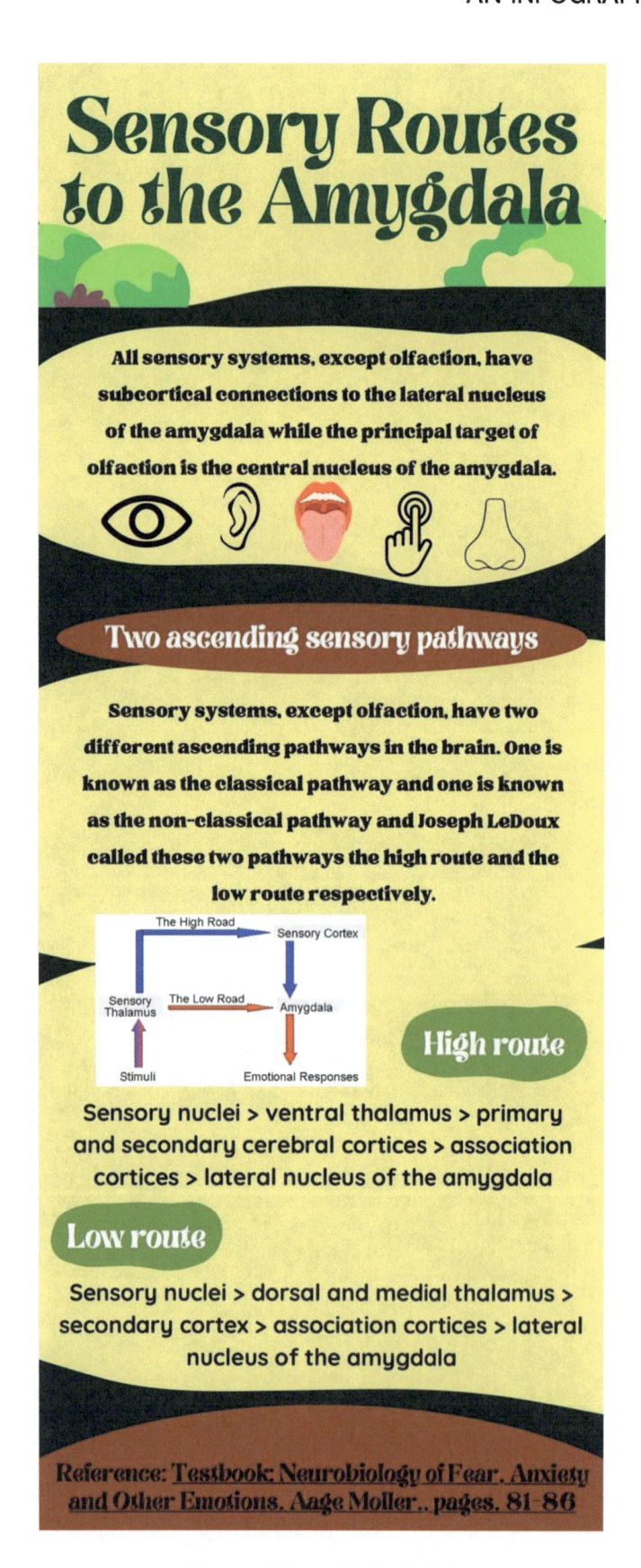

AN INFOGRAPHIC JOURNEY

Sensory Routes to the Amygdala

All sensory systems, except olfaction, have subcortical connections to the lateral nucleus of the amygdala while the principal target of olfaction is the central nucleus of the amygdala.

Two ascending sensory pathways

Sensory systems, except olfaction, have two different ascending pathways in the brain. One is known as the classical pathway and one is known as the non-classical pathway and Joseph LeDoux called these two pathways the high route and the low route respectively.

High route

Sensory nuclei > ventral thalamus > primary and secondary cerebral cortices > association cortices > lateral nucleus of the amygdala

Low route

Sensory nuclei > dorsal and medial thalamus > secondary cortex > association cortices > lateral nucleus of the amygdala

Reference: Textbook: Neurobiology of Fear, Anxiety and Other Emotions. Aage Moller., pages. 81-86

Hyeonji Lee, Fall 2023

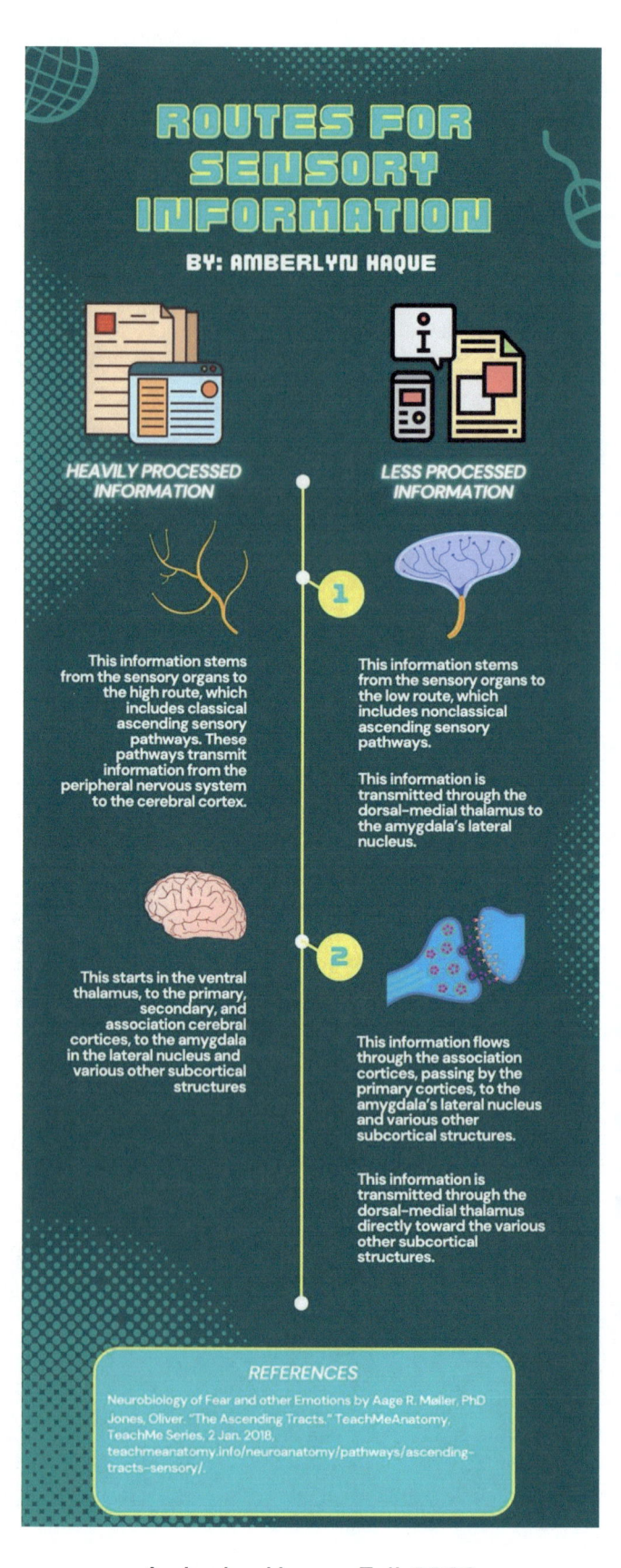

ROUTES FOR SENSORY INFORMATION
BY: AMBERLYN HAQUE

HEAVILY PROCESSED INFORMATION

This information stems from the sensory organs to the high route, which includes classical ascending sensory pathways. These pathways transmit information from the peripheral nervous system to the cerebral cortex.

This starts in the ventral thalamus, to the primary, secondary, and association cerebral cortices, to the amygdala in the lateral nucleus and various other subcortical structures

LESS PROCESSED INFORMATION

This information stems from the sensory organs to the low route, which includes nonclassical ascending sensory pathways.

This information is transmitted through the dorsal-medial thalamus to the amygdala's lateral nucleus.

This information flows through the association cortices, passing by the primary cortices, to the amygdala's lateral nucleus and various other subcortical structures.

This information is transmitted through the dorsal-medial thalamus directly toward the various other subcortical structures.

REFERENCES

Neurobiology of Fear and other Emotions by Aage R. Møller, PhD
Jones, Oliver. "The Ascending Tracts." TeachMeAnatomy, TeachMe Series, 2 Jan. 2018, teachmeanatomy.info/neuroanatomy/pathways/ascending-tracts-sensory/.

Amberlyn Haque, Fall 2023

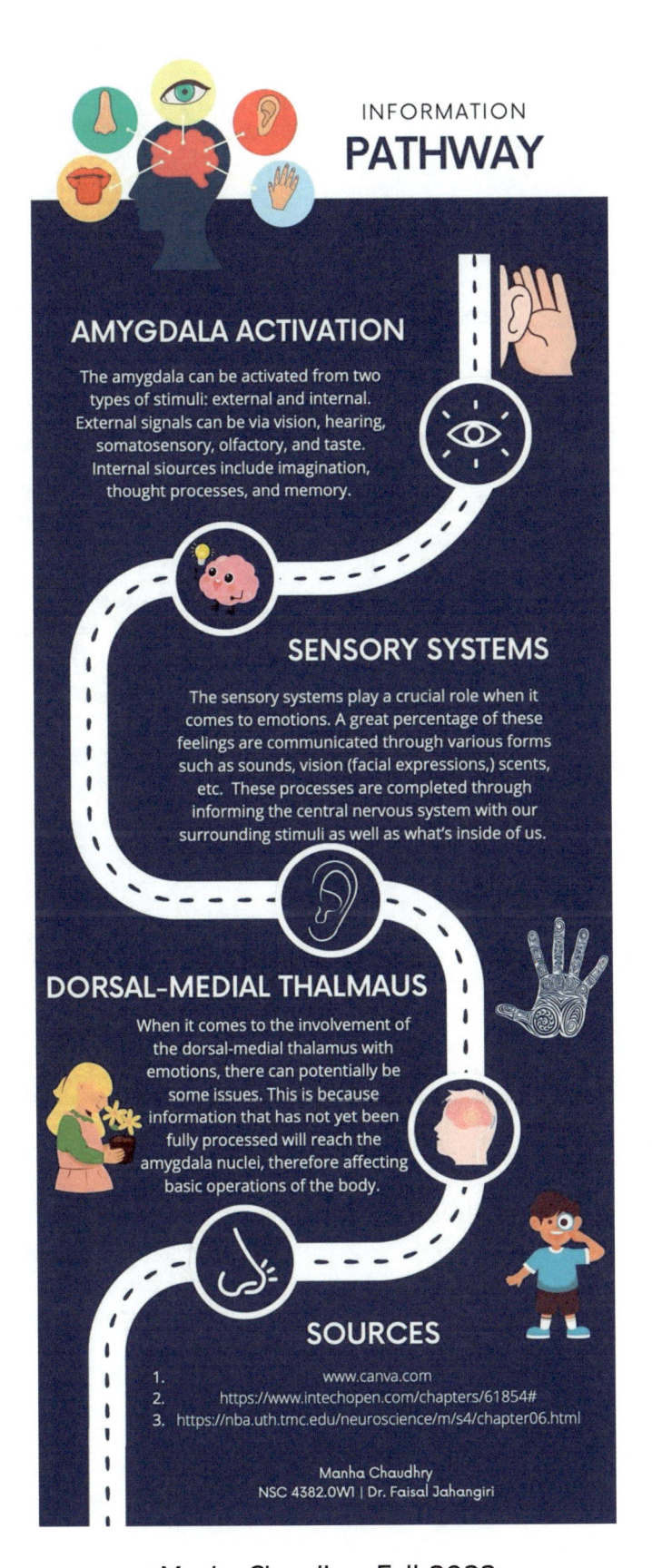

AN INFOGRAPHIC JOURNEY

INFORMATION PATHWAY

AMYGDALA ACTIVATION

The amygdala can be activated from two types of stimuli: external and internal. External signals can be via vision, hearing, somatosensory, olfactory, and taste. Internal siources include imagination, thought processes, and memory.

SENSORY SYSTEMS

The sensory systems play a crucial role when it comes to emotions. A great percentage of these feelings are communicated through various forms such as sounds, vision (facial expressions,) scents, etc. These processes are completed through informing the central nervous system with our surrounding stimuli as well as what's inside of us.

DORSAL-MEDIAL THALMAUS

When it comes to the involvement of the dorsal-medial thalamus with emotions, there can potentially be some issues. This is because information that has not yet been fully processed will reach the amygdala nuclei, therefore affecting basic operations of the body.

SOURCES
1. www.canva.com
2. https://www.intechopen.com/chapters/61854#
3. https://nba.uth.tmc.edu/neuroscience/m/s4/chapter06.html

Manha Chaudhry
NSC 4382.0WI | Dr. Faisal Jahangiri

Manha Chaudhry, Fall 2023

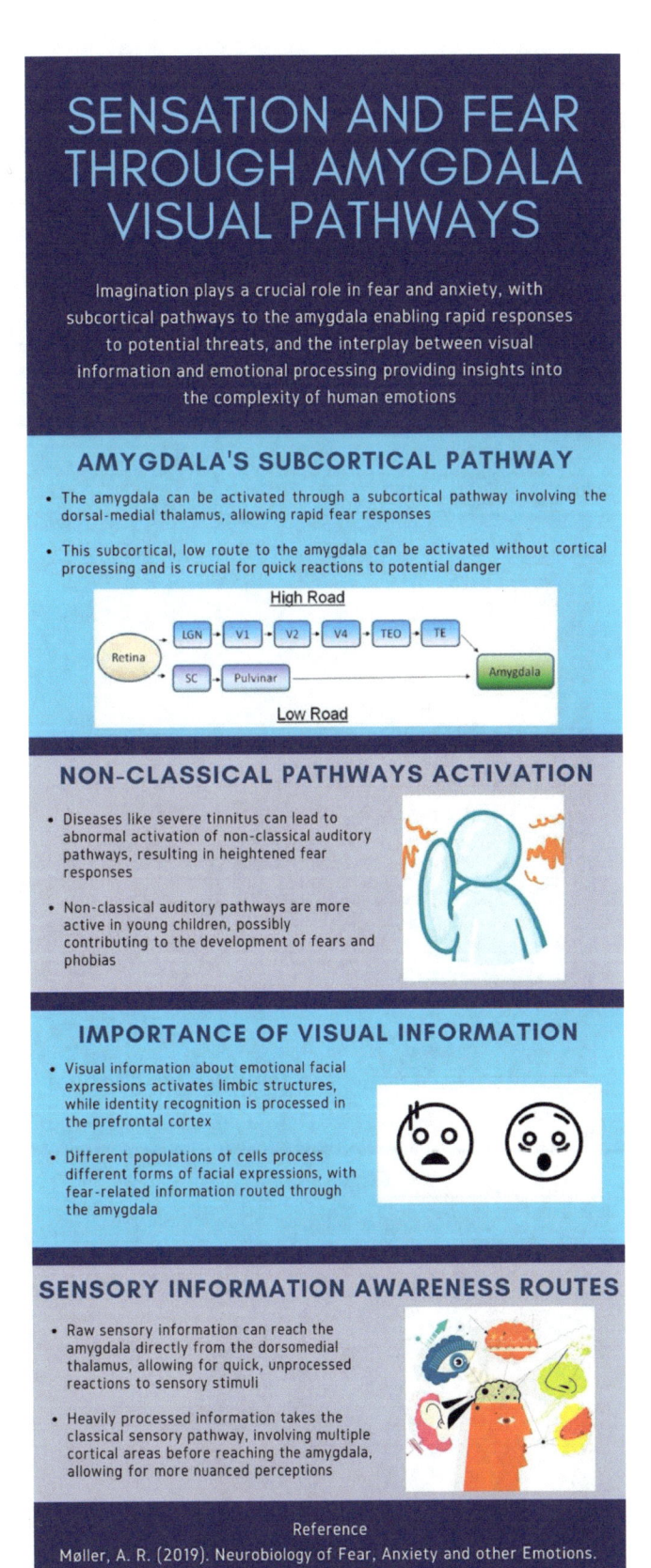

SENSATION AND FEAR THROUGH AMYGDALA VISUAL PATHWAYS

Imagination plays a crucial role in fear and anxiety, with subcortical pathways to the amygdala enabling rapid responses to potential threats, and the interplay between visual information and emotional processing providing insights into the complexity of human emotions

AMYGDALA'S SUBCORTICAL PATHWAY
- The amygdala can be activated through a subcortical pathway involving the dorsal-medial thalamus, allowing rapid fear responses
- This subcortical, low route to the amygdala can be activated without cortical processing and is crucial for quick reactions to potential danger

NON-CLASSICAL PATHWAYS ACTIVATION
- Diseases like severe tinnitus can lead to abnormal activation of non-classical auditory pathways, resulting in heightened fear responses
- Non-classical auditory pathways are more active in young children, possibly contributing to the development of fears and phobias

IMPORTANCE OF VISUAL INFORMATION
- Visual information about emotional facial expressions activates limbic structures, while identity recognition is processed in the prefrontal cortex
- Different populations of cells process different forms of facial expressions, with fear-related information routed through the amygdala

SENSORY INFORMATION AWARENESS ROUTES
- Raw sensory information can reach the amygdala directly from the dorsomedial thalamus, allowing for quick, unprocessed reactions to sensory stimuli
- Heavily processed information takes the classical sensory pathway, involving multiple cortical areas before reaching the amygdala, allowing for more nuanced perceptions

Reference
Møller, A. R. (2019). Neurobiology of Fear, Anxiety and other Emotions.

Natalie Laguer Torres, Fall 2023

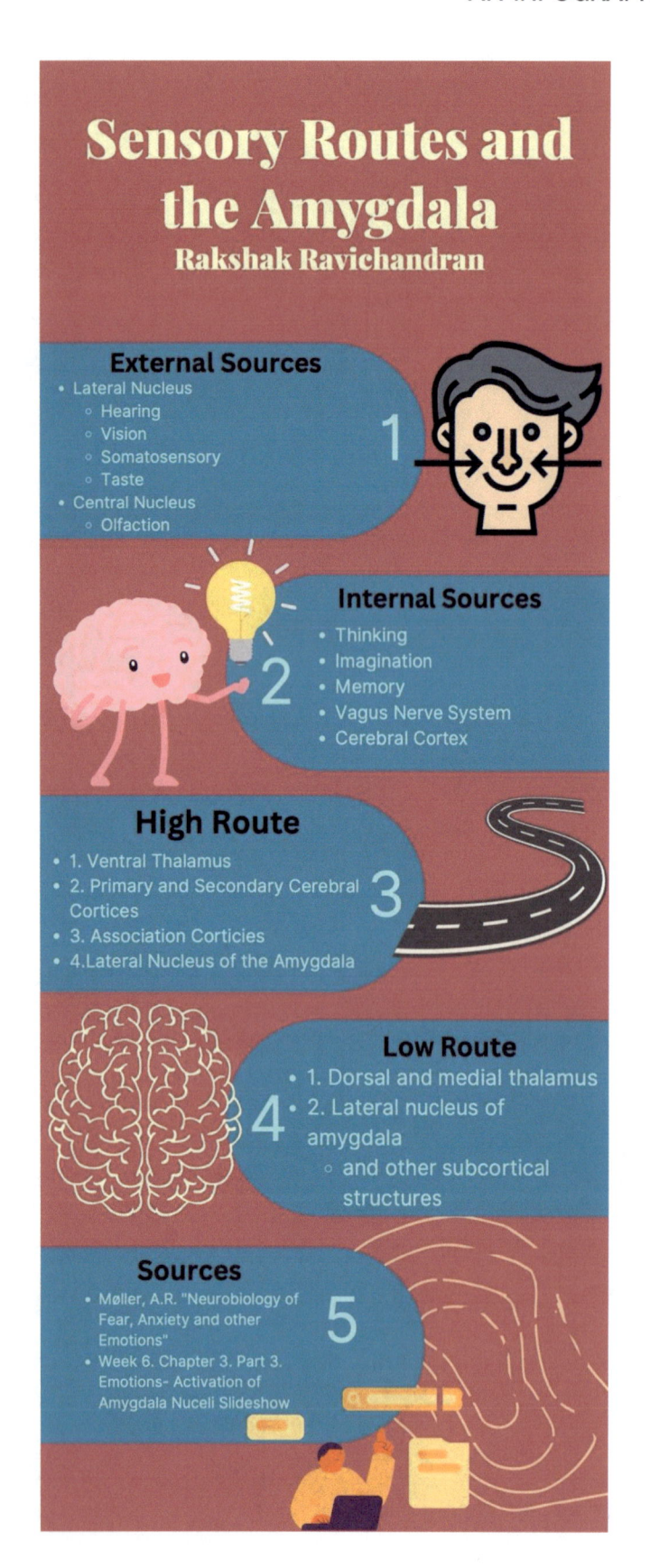

AN INFOGRAPHIC JOURNEY

Sensory Routes and the Amygdala
Rakshak Ravichandran

1. External Sources
- Lateral Nucleus
  - Hearing
  - Vision
  - Somatosensory
  - Taste
- Central Nucleus
  - Olfaction

2. Internal Sources
- Thinking
- Imagination
- Memory
- Vagus Nerve System
- Cerebral Cortex

3. High Route
1. Ventral Thalamus
2. Primary and Secondary Cerebral Cortices
3. Association Corticies
4. Lateral Nucleus of the Amygdala

4. Low Route
1. Dorsal and medial thalamus
2. Lateral nucleus of amygdala
   - and other subcortical structures

5. Sources
- Møller, A.R. "Neurobiology of Fear, Anxiety and other Emotions"
- Week 6. Chapter 3. Part 3. Emotions- Activation of Amygdala Nuceli Slideshow

Rakshak Ravichandran, Fall 2023

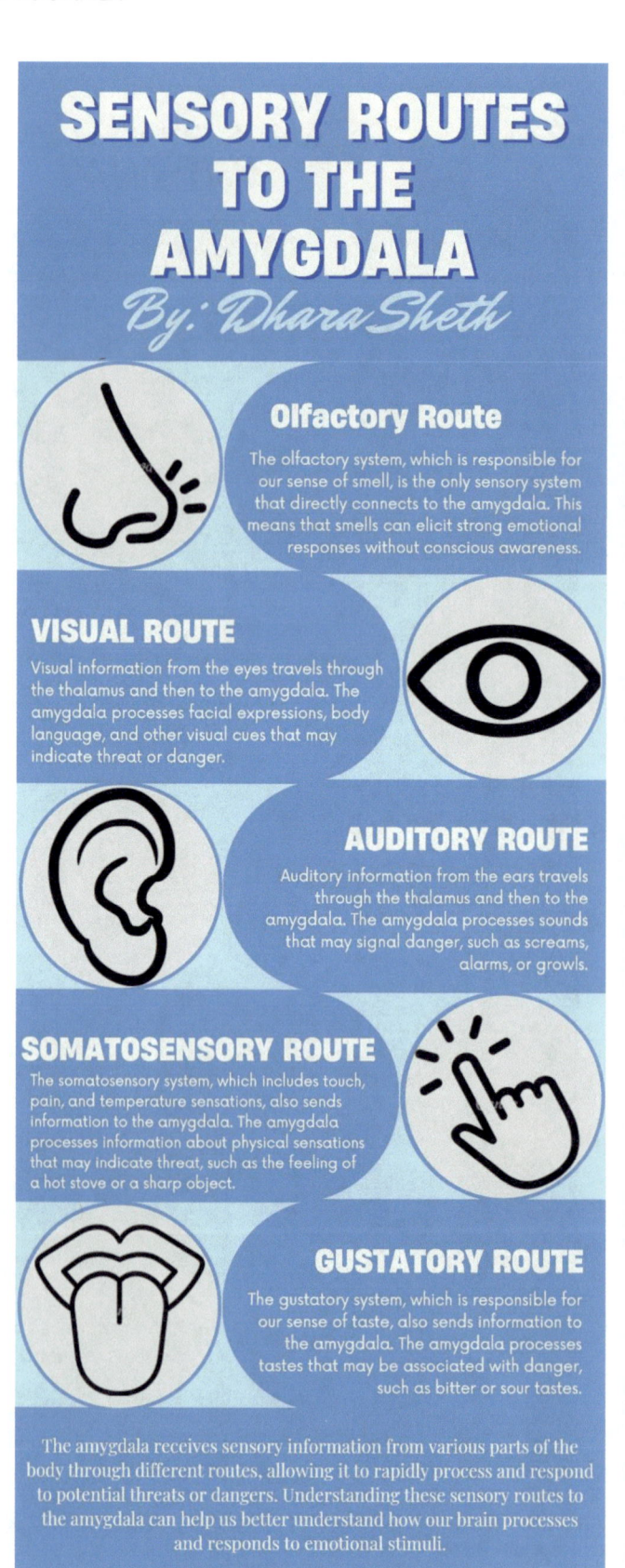

SENSORY ROUTES TO THE AMYGDALA
By: Dhara Sheth

Olfactory Route
The olfactory system, which is responsible for our sense of smell, is the only sensory system that directly connects to the amygdala. This means that smells can elicit strong emotional responses without conscious awareness.

VISUAL ROUTE
Visual information from the eyes travels through the thalamus and then to the amygdala. The amygdala processes facial expressions, body language, and other visual cues that may indicate threat or danger.

AUDITORY ROUTE
Auditory information from the ears travels through the thalamus and then to the amygdala. The amygdala processes sounds that may signal danger, such as screams, alarms, or growls.

SOMATOSENSORY ROUTE
The somatosensory system, which includes touch, pain, and temperature sensations, also sends information to the amygdala. The amygdala processes information about physical sensations that may indicate threat, such as the feeling of a hot stove or a sharp object.

GUSTATORY ROUTE
The gustatory system, which is responsible for our sense of taste, also sends information to the amygdala. The amygdala processes tastes that may be associated with danger, such as bitter or sour tastes.

The amygdala receives sensory information from various parts of the body through different routes, allowing it to rapidly process and respond to potential threats or dangers. Understanding these sensory routes to the amygdala can help us better understand how our brain processes and responds to emotional stimuli.

Dhara Sheth, Spring 2023

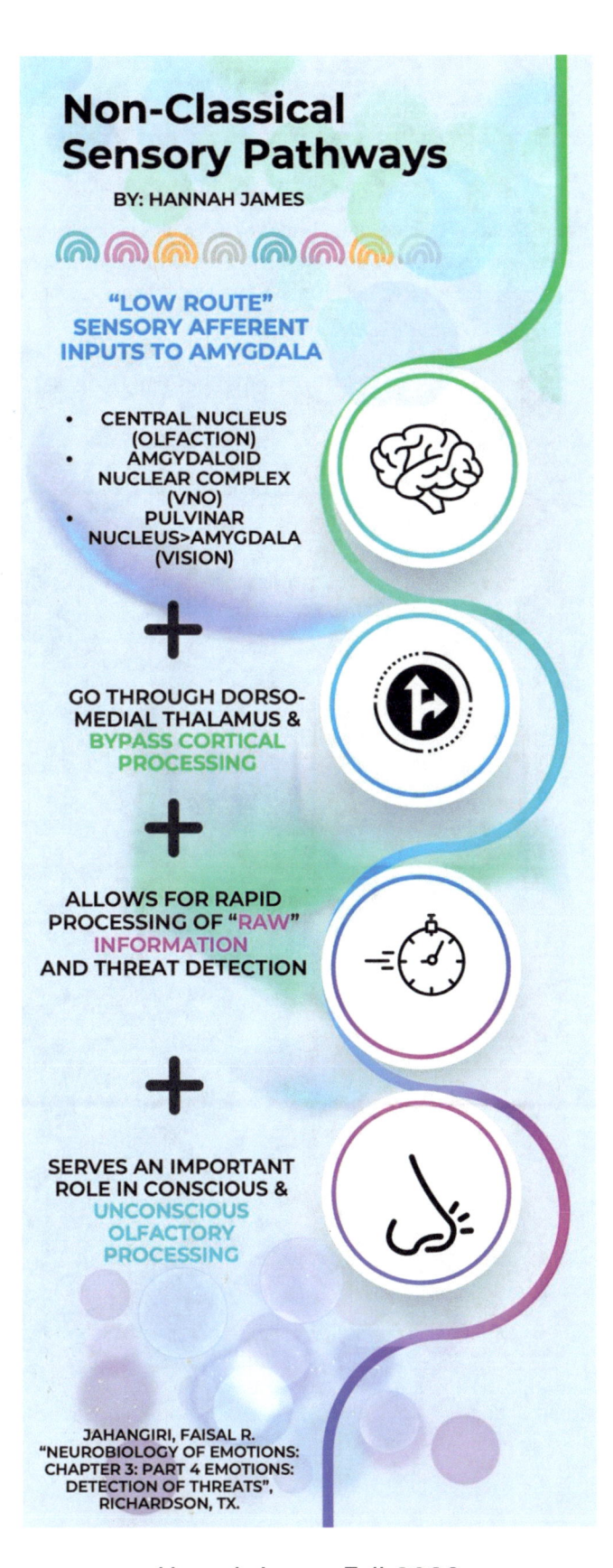

AN INFOGRAPHIC JOURNEY

Non-Classical Sensory Pathways
BY: HANNAH JAMES

"LOW ROUTE" SENSORY AFFERENT INPUTS TO AMYGDALA

- CENTRAL NUCLEUS (OLFACTION)
- AMGYDALOID NUCLEAR COMPLEX (VNO)
- PULVINAR NUCLEUS>AMYGDALA (VISION)

+

GO THROUGH DORSO-MEDIAL THALAMUS & BYPASS CORTICAL PROCESSING

+

ALLOWS FOR RAPID PROCESSING OF "RAW" INFORMATION AND THREAT DETECTION

+

SERVES AN IMPORTANT ROLE IN CONSCIOUS & UNCONSCIOUS OLFACTORY PROCESSING

JAHANGIRI, FAISAL R. "NEUROBIOLOGY OF EMOTIONS: CHAPTER 3: PART 4 EMOTIONS: DETECTION OF THREATS", RICHARDSON, TX.

Hannah James, Fall 2023

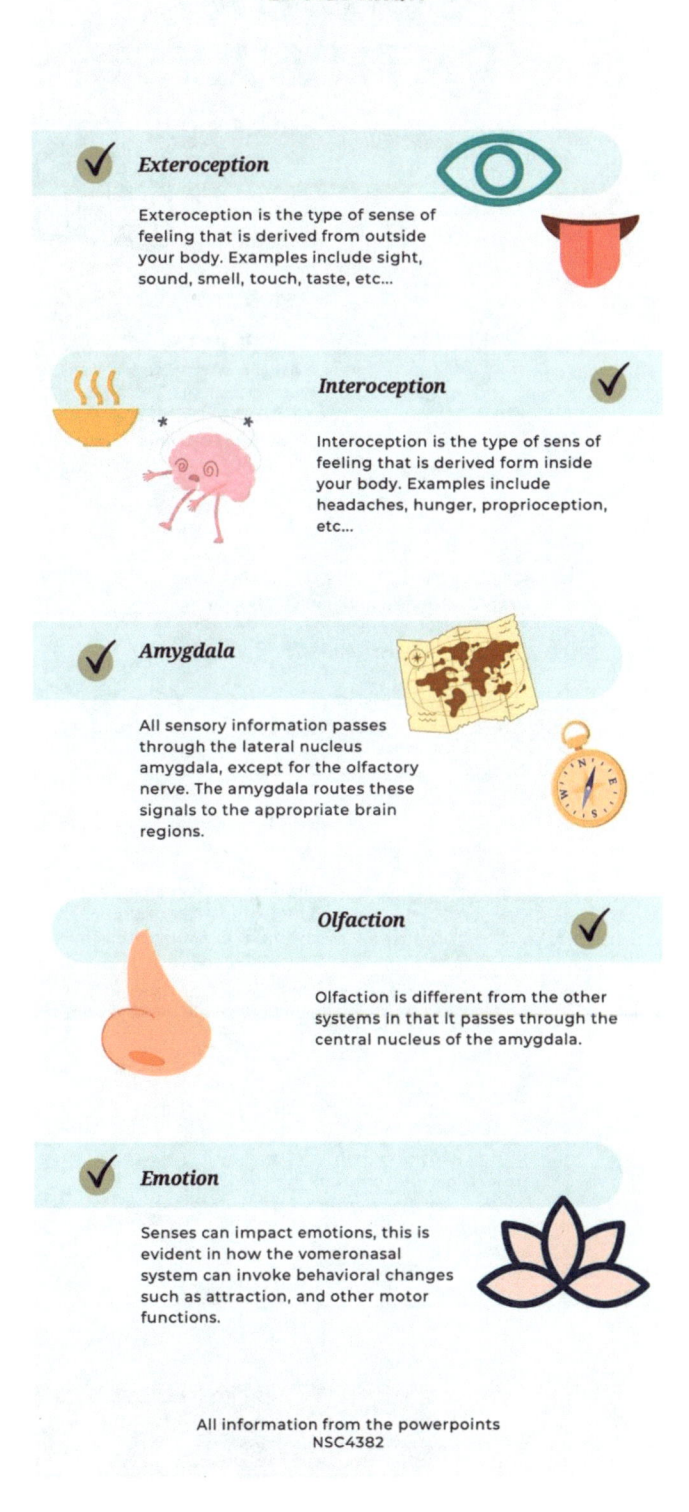

SENSORY AND THE AMYGDALA
BY SYED NAQVI

Exteroception
Exteroception is the type of sense of feeling that is derived from outside your body. Examples include sight, sound, smell, touch, taste, etc...

Interoception
Interoception is the type of sens of feeling that is derived form inside your body. Examples include headaches, hunger, proprioception, etc...

Amygdala
All sensory information passes through the lateral nucleus amygdala, except for the olfactory nerve. The amygdala routes these signals to the appropriate brain regions.

Olfaction
Olfaction is different from the other systems in that it passes through the central nucleus of the amygdala.

Emotion
Senses can impact emotions, this is evident in how the vomeronasal system can invoke behavioral changes such as attraction, and other motor functions.

All information from the powerpoints NSC4382

Syed Naqvi, Fall 2023

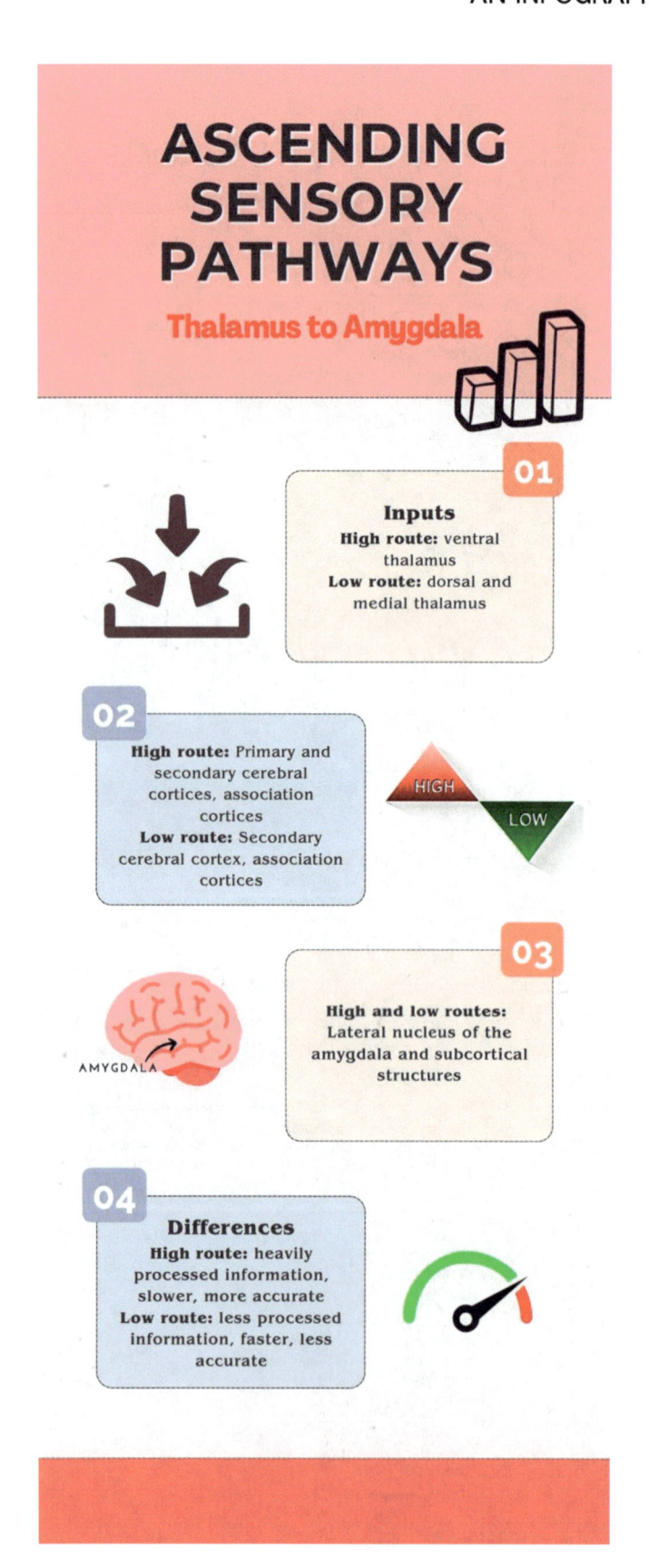

AN INFOGRAPHIC JOURNEY

ASCENDING SENSORY PATHWAYS
Thalamus to Amygdala

01 Inputs
High route: ventral thalamus
Low route: dorsal and medial thalamus

02
High route: Primary and secondary cerebral cortices, association cortices
Low route: Secondary cerebral cortex, association cortices

03
High and low routes: Lateral nucleus of the amygdala and subcortical structures

04 Differences
High route: heavily processed information, slower, more accurate
Low route: less processed information, faster, less accurate

Devaditya Ray, Fall 2023

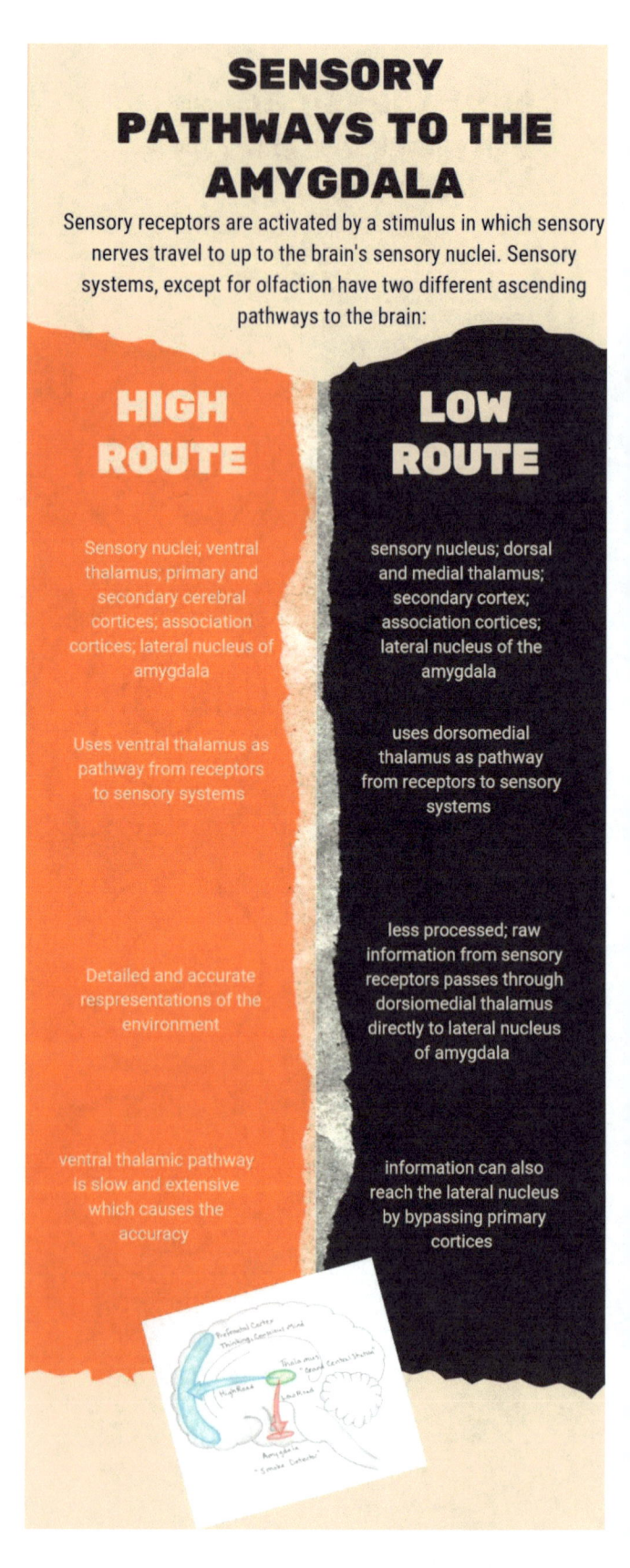

SENSORY PATHWAYS TO THE AMYGDALA

Sensory receptors are activated by a stimulus in which sensory nerves travel to up to the brain's sensory nuclei. Sensory systems, except for olfaction have two different ascending pathways to the brain:

HIGH ROUTE

Sensory nuclei; ventral thalamus; primary and secondary cerebral cortices; association cortices; lateral nucleus of amygdala

Uses ventral thalamus as pathway from receptors to sensory systems

Detailed and accurate respresentations of the environment

ventral thalamic pathway is slow and extensive which causes the accuracy

LOW ROUTE

sensory nucleus; dorsal and medial thalamus; secondary cortex; association cortices; lateral nucleus of the amygdala

uses dorsomedial thalamus as pathway from receptors to sensory systems

less processed; raw information from sensory receptors passes through dorsiomedial thalamus directly to lateral nucleus of amygdala

information can also reach the lateral nucleus by bypassing primary cortices

Natalie Brzezinski, Spring 2023

AN INFOGRAPHIC JOURNEY

The Amygdala in Humans

BY: NAMITHA MARIAM JAIMSON

Damage to the Amygdala can cause:

Kluver-Bucy Syndrome
- Indiscriminate hyper-sexuality
- Ingestion of inappropriate objects
- Deficits in memory
- Psychic blindness: an inability to realize the emotional significance of events

The amygdala is necessary to recognize facial expressions conveying fear and to recognize multiple emotions from a single expression.

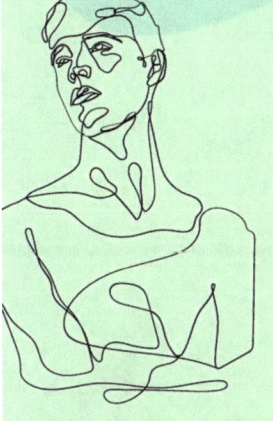

However, according to Dr. Adolphs, the amygdala is NOT necessary for realizing personal identity from people's faces.

Essentially, according to LeDoux, the amygdala is the center for emotional evaluation. It can evaluate stimuli and express various emotional responses like fear.

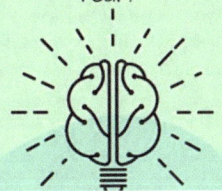

Namitha Mariam Jaimson, Fall 2022

Conditions Associated with Amygdala Disfunction

1. ANXIETY DISORDERS
- As the amygdala plays a crucial role in processing fear and anxiety, dysregulation of these emotions can cause anxiety-related disorders

2. PTSD
- Traumatic experiences can cause alterations in the structure and function of the amygdala, contributing to the development of PTSD symptoms.

3. DEPRESSION
- Although depression is closely related to disturbances in the prefrontal cortex and hippocampus, alterations in the amygdala can also cause mood disorders.

4. PHOBIAS
- The amygdala mediates fear responses, therefore, the majority of the phobias that are caused by fear are caused as a result of dysfunctioning in the amygdala.

5. AUTISM SPECTRUM DISORDER
- Altered amygdala function and connectivity are observed in individuals with ASD, contributing to difficulties in social interaction and emotional processing.

6. KLÜVER-BUCY SYNDROME
- Isolated symmetric damage to amygdala can cause psychic blindness, hyper sexuality, hyperorality, memory deficits, altered emotional behavior, etc.

7. TEMPORAL LOBE EPILEPSY
- As the amygdala is a part of the temporal lobe- epilepsy can affect the amygdala leading to symptoms of altered emotional responses during seizures.

Akshara Rao, Spring 2024

AN INFOGRAPHIC JOURNEY

WHAT HAPPENS IF THE AMYGDALA GETS DAMAGED?

Infographic by Myan Lam

Maladaptive Neuroplasticity

When the brain reorganizes its network of synaptic connections in a detrimental way (i.e. as a response to brain lesions) this maladaptive neuroplasticity can play an important role in many diseases or neurological conditions.

According to a study by Dr. Adolphs...

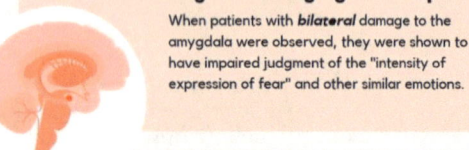

When patients with *bilateral* damage to the amygdala were observed, they were shown to have impaired judgment of the "intensity of expression of fear" and other similar emotions.

Klüver-Bucy Syndrome

Dr. Hayman and colleagues found that *bilateral* damage to the amygdala and its connections induced *Klüver-Bucy Syndrome*, which manifested these symptoms:
1. "Psychic blindness": the inability to recognize the "emotional importance of events"
2. Hypersexuality (indiscriminate)
3. Altered emotional behavior (placidity)
4. Hyperorality (ingestion of inappropriate objects)
5. Hyperreactivity to visual stimuli
6. Memory deficits

These findings suggest...

The amygdala is necessary for:
1. Recognizing fear in facial expressions
2. Recognizing multiple emotions in a single facial expression, but
3. NOT for recognizing personal identity from faces.

This shows how the amygdala is involved in emotion!

Myan Lam, Spring 2023

Effects of Surgical Removal of the Amygdala in a Monkey

Psychic Blindness
Inability to recognize the emotional significance of events

Lack of Fear
The monkey showed a lack of fear from objects that would usually scare a monkey

Appetite Changes
The monkey's appetite changed to develop one for improper foods like rocks

Sexual
The monkey also displayed sexual behavior towards unusual partners, including members of different species

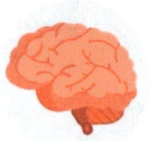

Exploration
Became highly interested in exploring items around them in the environment

Approach
Became placid (calm or not easily excited) when approached

Significance of This Experiment
The results of this expriement by Kluver and Bucy in 1937 indicated which functions were controlled by the amygdala. It was done on primates, who are close to us in ancestry, and this study showed the expansion of the amygdala's role other than emotion.

Mackenzie Park, Fall 2022

AN INFOGRAPHIC JOURNEY

Damage to the Amygdala

Klüver-Bucy syndrome.

- Psychic blindness: inability to recognize the emotional importance of events
- Hypersexuality, often directly indiscriminately
- Altered emotional behavior, often placidity
- Hyperorality and the ingestion of inappropriate objects
- A tendency to react to every visual stimulus
- Memory deficits

Dr. Adolphs

What Dr. Adolphin and his colleagues did was study a lot of different patients with damage to the amygdala and made observations about their behavior.

These observations helped them zero in of the function of the amygdala in relation to emotions, especially fear.

According to Dr. Adolph's Investigation

Bilateral, not unilateral, damage to the amygdala impairs
- Judgment of intensity of expressions of fear
- Judgment of intensity of expressions normally judged to be very similar to fear, such as surprise
- Processing of some facial expressions of emotion, especially the recognition of fear

Thus, we know that

The amygdala is
- Very important in recognizing fear in facial experiments
- Very important in recognizing multiple emotions in single facial expression

But it is actually not required for recognizing personal identity from faces. Hence, there is evidence that the amygdala is involved in emotion from this study.

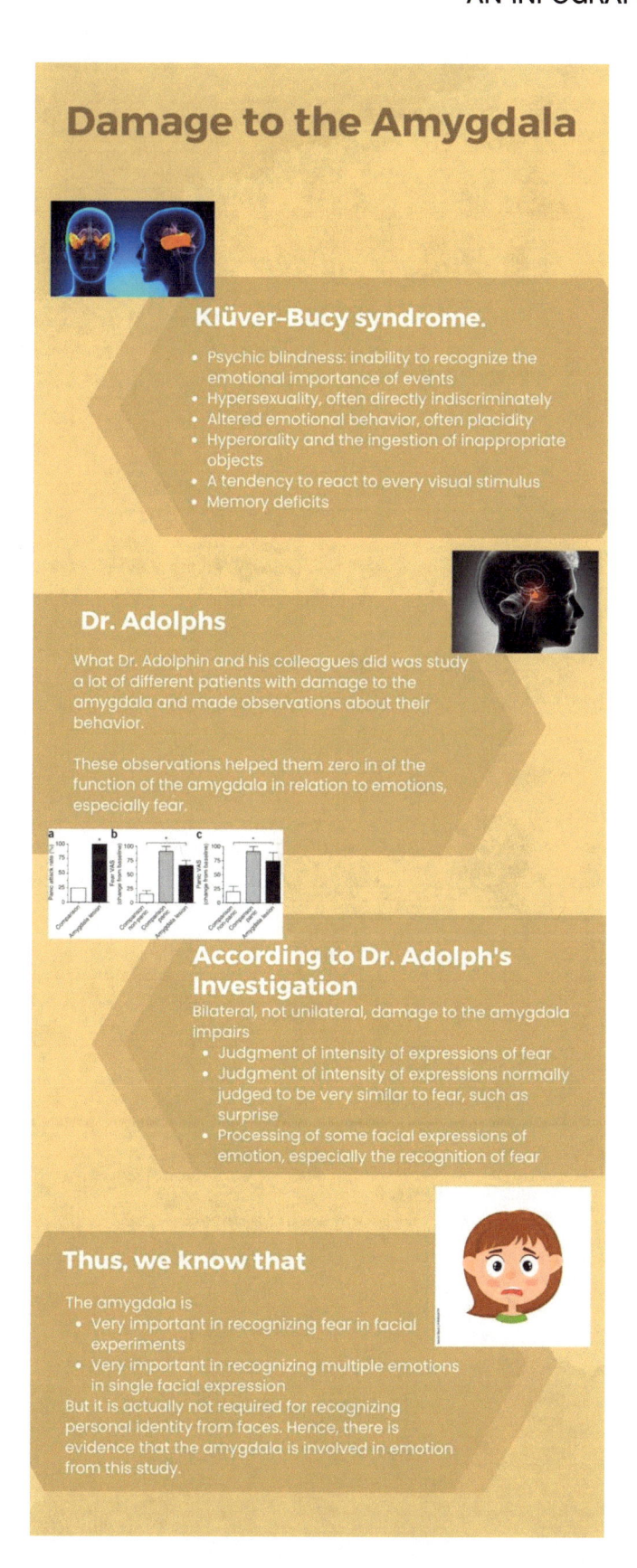

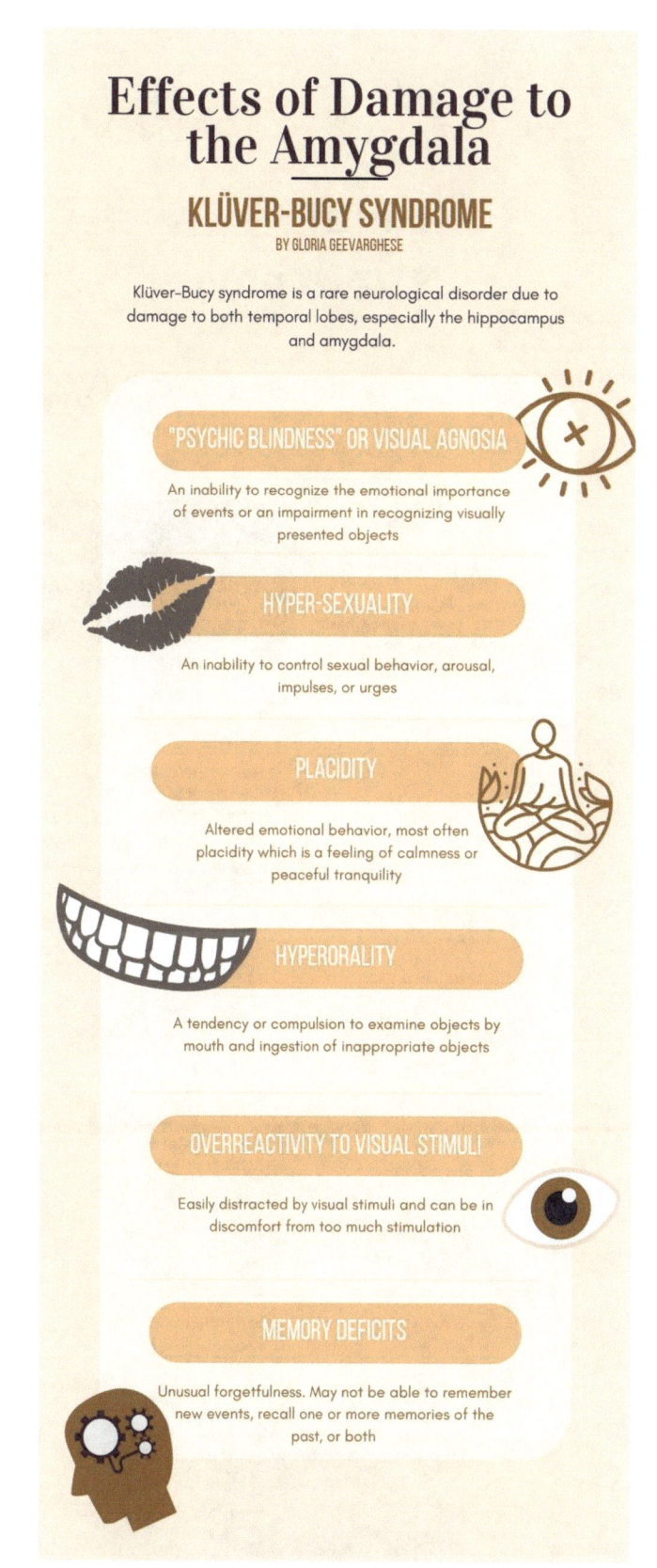

Sanya Bhatt, Fall 2022

Effects of Damage to the Amygdala
KLÜVER-BUCY SYNDROME
BY GLORIA GEEVARGHESE

Klüver-Bucy syndrome is a rare neurological disorder due to damage to both temporal lobes, especially the hippocampus and amygdala.

"PSYCHIC BLINDNESS" OR VISUAL AGNOSIA
An inability to recognize the emotional importance of events or an impairment in recognizing visually presented objects

HYPER-SEXUALITY
An inability to control sexual behavior, arousal, impulses, or urges

PLACIDITY
Altered emotional behavior, most often placidity which is a feeling of calmness or peaceful tranquility

HYPERORALITY
A tendency or compulsion to examine objects by mouth and ingestion of inappropriate objects

OVERREACTIVITY TO VISUAL STIMULI
Easily distracted by visual stimuli and can be in discomfort from too much stimulation

MEMORY DEFICITS
Unusual forgetfulness. May not be able to remember new events, recall one or more memories of the past, or both

Gloria Geevarghese, Spring 2023

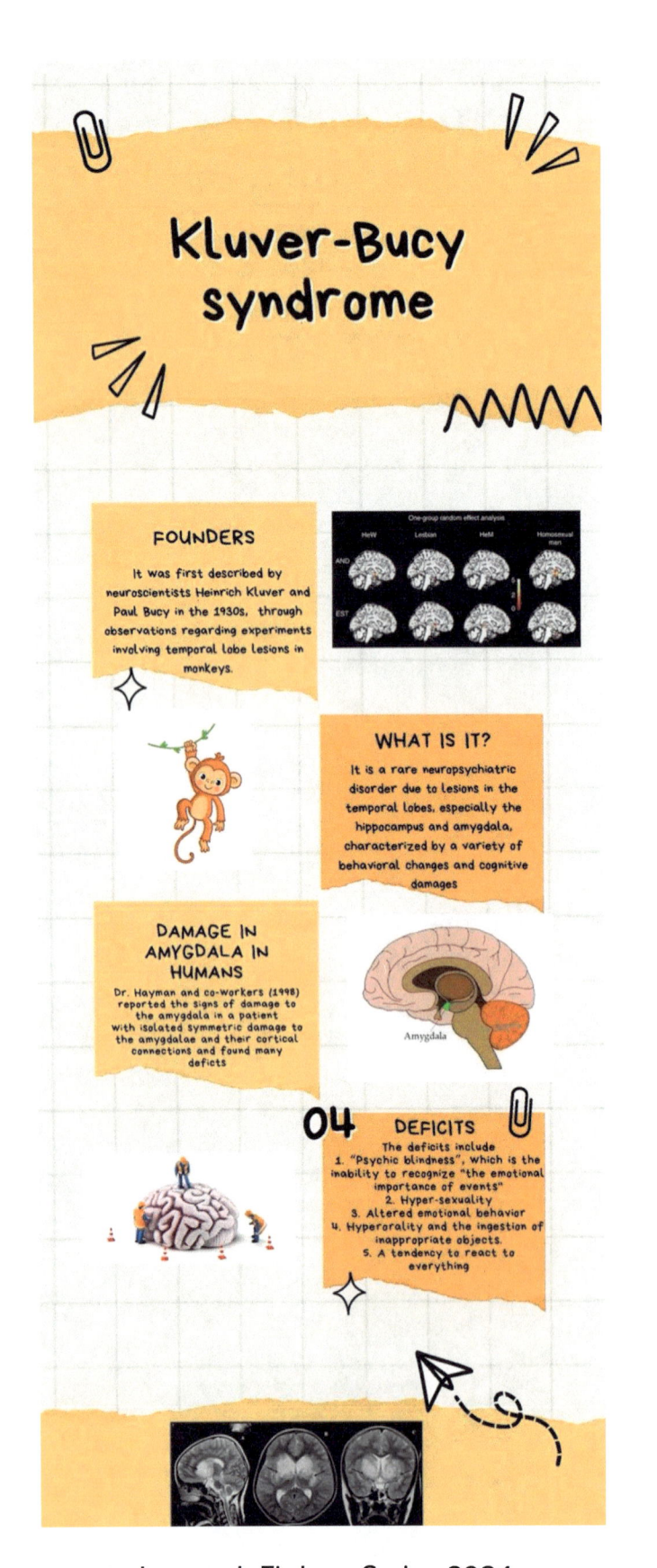

AN INFOGRAPHIC JOURNEY

Kluver-Bucy syndrome

FOUNDERS
It was first described by neuroscientists Heinrich Kluver and Paul Bucy in the 1930s, through observations regarding experiments involving temporal lobe lesions in monkeys.

WHAT IS IT?
It is a rare neuropsychiatric disorder due to lesions in the temporal lobes, especially the hippocampus and amygdala, characterized by a variety of behavioral changes and cognitive damages

DAMAGE IN AMYGDALA IN HUMANS
Dr. Hayman and co-workers (1998) reported the signs of damage to the amygdala in a patient with isolated symmetric damage to the amygdalae and their cortical connections and found many deficits

04 DEFICITS
The deficits include
1. "Psychic blindness", which is the inability to recognize "the emotional importance of events"
2. Hyper-sexuality
3. Altered emotional behavior
4. Hyperorality and the ingestion of inappropriate objects.
5. A tendency to react to everything

Jumeynah Firdaus, Spring 2024

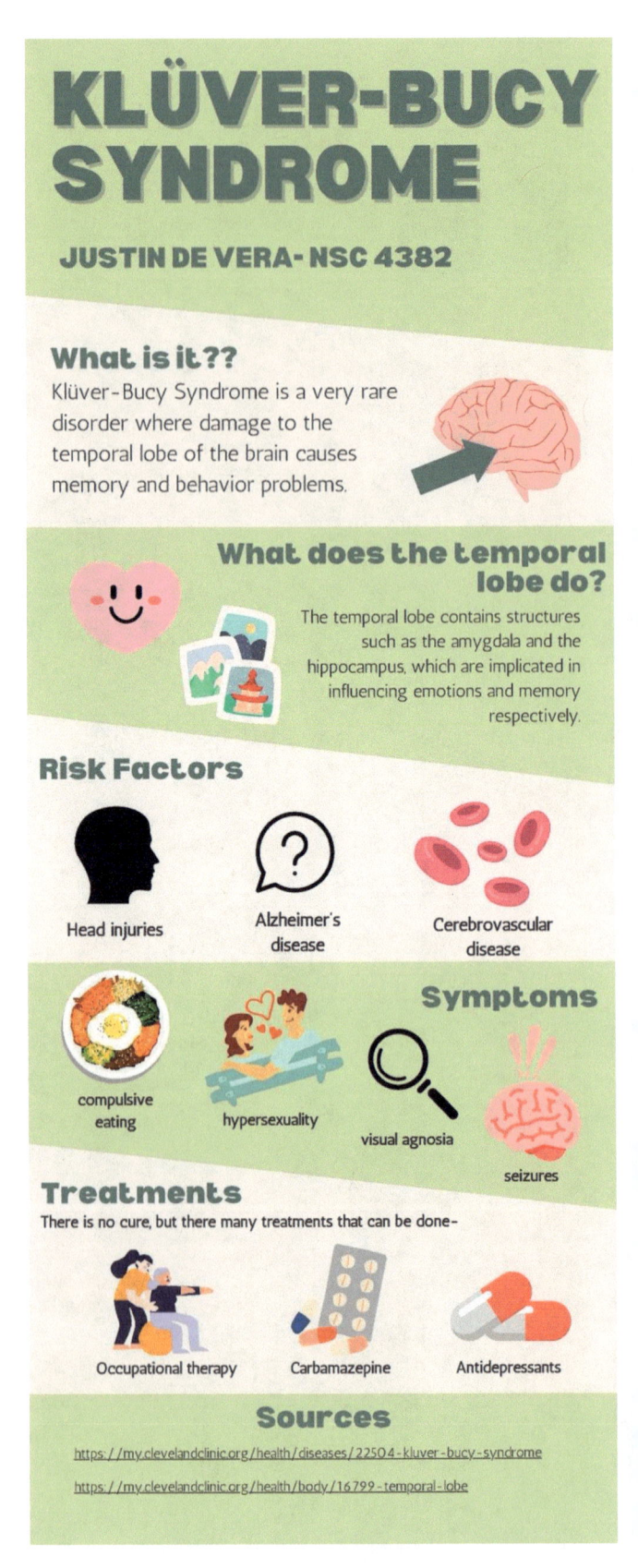

KLÜVER-BUCY SYNDROME

JUSTIN DE VERA - NSC 4382

What is it??
Klüver-Bucy Syndrome is a very rare disorder where damage to the temporal lobe of the brain causes memory and behavior problems.

What does the temporal lobe do?
The temporal lobe contains structures such as the amygdala and the hippocampus, which are implicated in influencing emotions and memory respectively.

Risk Factors
- Head injuries
- Alzheimer's disease
- Cerebrovascular disease

Symptoms
- compulsive eating
- hypersexuality
- visual agnosia
- seizures

Treatments
There is no cure, but there many treatments that can be done-
- Occupational therapy
- Carbamazepine
- Antidepressants

Sources
https://my.clevelandclinic.org/health/diseases/22504-kluver-bucy-syndrome
https://my.clevelandclinic.org/health/body/16799-temporal-lobe

Justin De Vera, Spring 2024

AN INFOGRAPHIC JOURNEY

KLUVER-BUCY
Syndrome

DR. HAYMAN AND CO-WORKERS (1998)

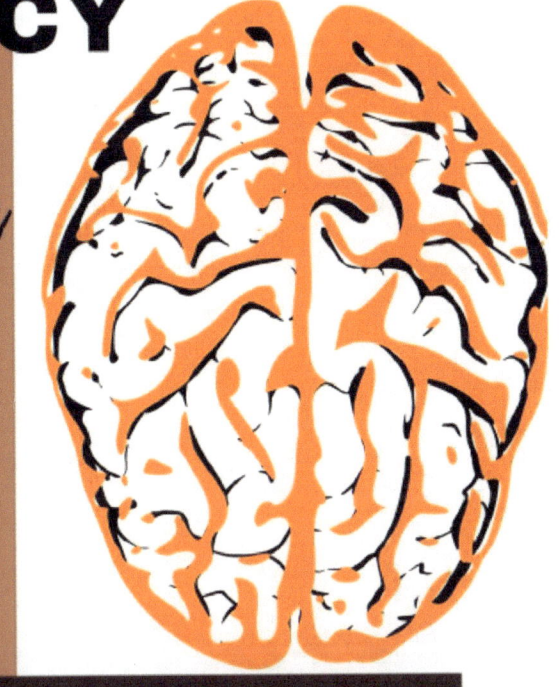

THE SYNDROME IS AS OF A RESULT OF ISOLATED SYMMETRIC DAMAGE TO THE AMYGDALAE AND ITS CORTICAL CONNECTIONS

BY BRIDGET MANU

SIGNS

- PSYCHIC BLINDNESS
- INDISCRIMINATE HYPER-SEXUALITY
- MEMORY DEFICITS
- ALTERED EMOTIONAL BEHAVIOR INCLUDING PLACIDITY
- HYPERORALITY
- A TENDENCY TO REACT TO EVERY VISUAL STIMULUS

Bridget Manu, Fall 2022

AN INFOGRAPHIC JOURNEY

CHAPTER 11

Neurobiology of Emotion

The Neurobiology of Alzheimer's Disease

By Zaineb Ali & Kajal Patel, Spring 2024

Alzheimer's disease is a progressive neurodegenerative disorder characterized by a decline in cognitive abilities, memory loss, and changes in behavior. It is the most common cause of dementia, which is the loss of cognitive functioning. The disease gradually destroys brain cells, particularly those involved in memory and learning. Alzheimer's causes a decline in cognitive function and eventually destroys memory and impairs daily function. While the exact cause of Alzheimer's disease is not fully known, it is believed to involve a combination of genetic, environmental, and lifestyle factors. Maladaptive neuroplasticity also seems to play a role in the onset of the disease, which are changes in the structure and synaptic activity in neurons in the brain that lead to negative impacts for an individual's functioning. As of now, there is no cure for Alzheimer's disease, but treatment options are available to help manage symptoms and slow down its progression.

Causes

Alzheimer's disease is a neurodegenerative disease marked by progressive loss of cognitive function, including memory, thinking, and language abilities. The specific cause of Alzheimer's disease is unknown; however, it is thought to be a combination of hereditary, environmental, and lifestyle factors. While most cases of Alzheimer's disease are not genetic, having a family history of the disease can raise the risk. Certain genes, including the APOE gene, are linked to an increased risk of acquiring Alzheimer's. Advanced age is another major risk factor for Alzheimer's disease. The chance of getting the illness increases with age, with most instances happening in people over 65. Changes in the brain can also potentially cause Alzheimer's disease. The condition is identified by the presence of abnormal protein deposits in the brain. These include beta-amyloid plaques and tau tangles, which disrupt normal brain function and cause cell death. Furthermore, environmental and lifestyle factors such as cardiovascular health, exercise, diet and one's social environment may increase the susceptibility of acquiring Alzheimer's disease.

Diagnosis, Stages, and Symptoms of Disease

Alzheimer's disease is diagnosed through symptoms detected during physical exams, neurological tests, cognitive tests, medical history, and imaging. Physical exams can reveal dementia-like symptoms that are often common causes of Alzheimer's disease which can include depression, sleep apnea, delirium, and thyroid problems. Cognitive exams test for memory, attention, language, and visuospatial skills. Brain imaging can reveal shrinkage in certain brain regions as well as the buildup of amyloid plaques.

Disease progression can be separated into mild, moderate, and severe Alzheimer's disease. During early-stage Alzheimer's, people begin to experience memory lapses and some cognitive difficulties. Moderate Alzheimer's brings more pronounced cognitive decline, behavioral changes, and the need for more outstanding assistance with daily activities. In severe Alzheimer's, individuals face profound cognitive and functional impairment, requiring full-time care and assistance. The progression varies among individuals, influenced by overall health and age.

Symptoms of Alzheimer's disease include:

Mild:
- Memory loss disrupts daily life
- Poor judgement
- Difficulty completing daily tasks
- Difficulty solving problems
- Mood and personality changes
- Increased anxiety or aggression

Moderate:
- Increased confusion and memory loss
- Inability to learn new things
- Changes in sleeping
- Decreased attention
- Hallucinations and paranoia
- Impulsive behavior
- Muscle twitches

Severe:
- Inability to communicate
- Seizures

- No awareness
- Difficulty swallowing and eating
- Loss of bowel control
- Physical decline

Structures Involved

Alzheimer's disease predominantly impacts specific brain regions associated with memory, learning, and cognitive functions. The hippocampus, amygdala, entorhinal cortex, and basal forebrain are key structures affected by Alzheimer's. The hippocampus, crucial for memory formation, is among the first areas affected, causing early symptoms of memory loss and difficulty in forming new memories. The cerebral cortex, responsible for higher cognitive functions like reasoning, language and problem-solving, shrinks significantly due to beta-amyloid plaques and tau tangles accumulation, leading to cognitive impairments. The amygdala, which plays a role in the processing of emoticons, is less affected, however, changes in emotional regulation can manifest with disease progression. The entorhinal cortex, a region of the brain that acts as a bridge between the hippocampus and areas of the cerebral cortex, is vital for memory and spatial navigation. This part of the brain shows early signs of damage in Alzheimer's, contributing to memory decline. Within the basal forebrain, structures like the nucleus basalis of Meynert, which produce acetylcholine crucial for learning and memory, degenerate, reducing acetylcholine levels and worsening memory and cognition. These interconnected brain regions form intricate neural networks crucial for cognitive processes.
Accumulation of abnormal proteins disrupts neuron communication, leading to dysfunction and cell death, culminating in the cognitive decline seen in Alzheimer's disease.

Effects of the Disease

Alzheimer's disease has an immense impact on both individuals diagnosed and their caregivers. Common effects for people diagnosed include memory loss, difficulty communicating, impaired judgment, difficulty problem-solving and making decisions, changes in mood and behavior that can lead to depression or anxiety, inability to perform daily activities, social withdrawal, and physical symptoms like difficulty swallowing and immobility. Alzheimer's also places a significant burden on caregivers, who often experience fatigue, stress, and emotional strain. The disease strongly affects families, relationships, and finances, leading to challenges in managing daily life for both individuals with Alzheimer's and their caregivers.

Prevention and Treatment

Preventing Alzheimer's disease and treating its symptoms are challenging tasks because its underlying causes and mechanisms are not entirely known. However, various techniques can help lower the risk of acquiring Alzheimer's disease and control its symptoms. Healthy lifestyle choices, such as frequent physical exercise, a balanced diet rich in fruits, vegetables, and omega-3 fatty acids, stress management, adequate sleep, and abstaining from smoking and excessive alcohol consumption, may help minimize the risk of Alzheimer's disease. Reading, puzzles, learning new skills, and socializing can all assist in keeping the brain active and lower the risk of cognitive decline. Furthermore, controlling cardiovascular risk factors such as high blood pressure, high cholesterol, diabetes, and obesity may help lower the risk of Alzheimer's disease, as there is evidence linking heart and brain health. Maintaining social relationships and participating in community activities can also help lower the incidence of cognitive decline and Alzheimer's disease. While there is no cure for Alzheimer's disease, several drugs can also help with symptoms and delay the disease's progression. These include cholinesterase inhibitors and memantine, which regulate neurotransmitters involved in memory and cognition. As new scientific and technological discoveries emerge, research into new prevention methods and therapies for Alzheimer's disease continues.

References

1. Alzheimer's Association. (n.d.). *Medications for memory, cognition and dementia-related behaviors*. Alzheimer's Disease and Dementia. https://www.alz.org/alzheimers-dementia/treatments/medications-for-memory

2. *Alzheimer's Disease fact Sheet.* (n.d.). National Institute on Aging. https://www.nia.nih.gov/health/alzheimers-and-dementia/alzheimers-disease-fact-sheet

3. Jahangiri, F. (2024). *Neurobiology of Emotions Chap 6. Minimizing the Risks of Harm Part 1. Diseases of the Nervous System* [Slide show; PowerPoint]. University of Texas at Dallas, Richardson, TX.

4. *Medical tests*. (n.d.). Alzheimer's Disease and Dementia. https://www.alz.org/alzheimers-dementia/diagnosis/medical_tests#:~:text=Physicians%20use%20diagnostic%20tools%20combined,to%20make%20an%20accurate%20diagnosis

5. Moller, A. (2018). *Neuroplasticity and its Dark Sides: Disorders of the Nervous System Second Edition* (2nd ed.). CreateSpace Independent Publishing Platform.

6. *Stages of Alzheimer's*. (n.d.). Alzheimer's Disease and Dementia. https://www.alz.org/alzheimers-dementia/stages

7. *What are the signs of Alzheimer's disease?* (n.d.). National Institute on Aging. https://www.nia.nih.gov/health/alzheimers-symptoms-and-diagnosis/what-are-signs-alzheimers disease#:~:text=Memory%20problems%20are%20typically%20one,the%20early%20stages%20of%20Alzheimer's.

8. *What happens to the brain in Alzheimer's disease?* (n.d.). National Institute on Aging. https://www.nia.nih.gov/health/alzheimers-causes-and-risk-factors/what-happens-brain-alzheimers-disease

AN INFOGRAPHIC JOURNEY

Mana Zandi, Fall 2023

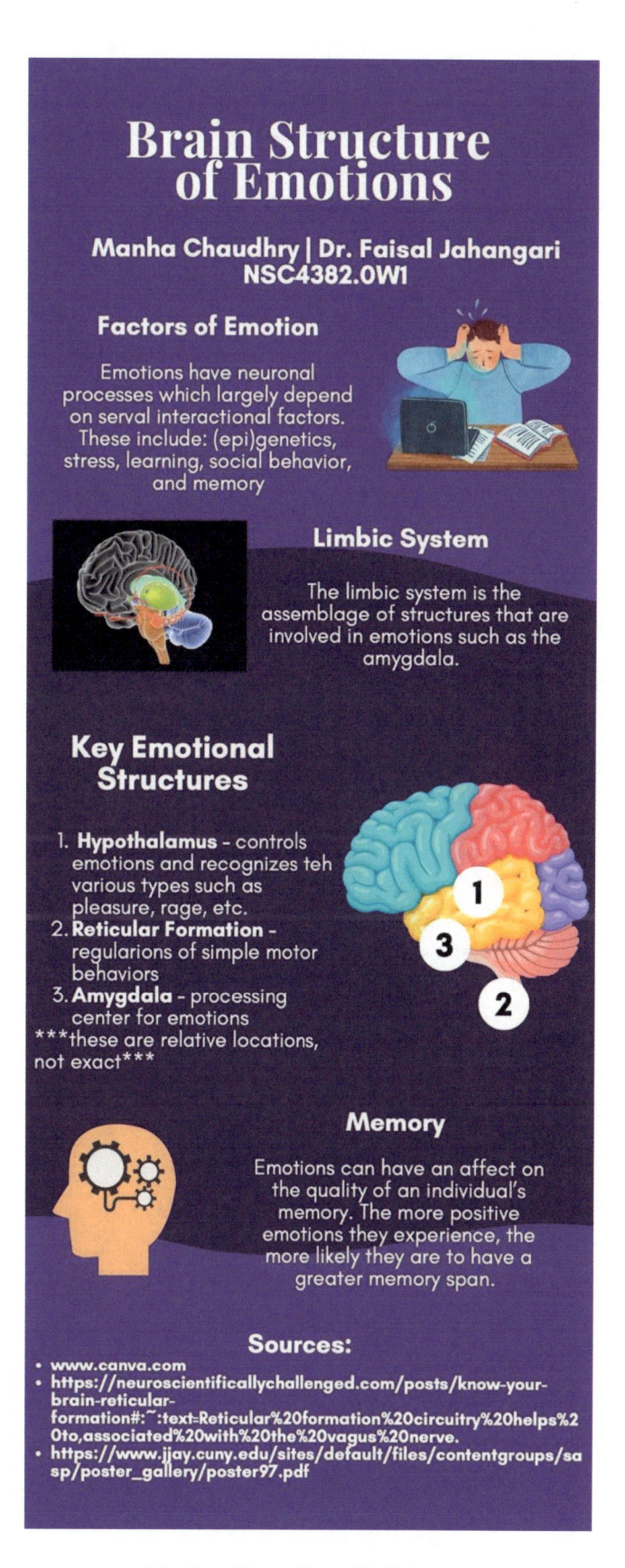

Manha Chaudhry, Fall 2023

AN INFOGRAPHIC JOURNEY

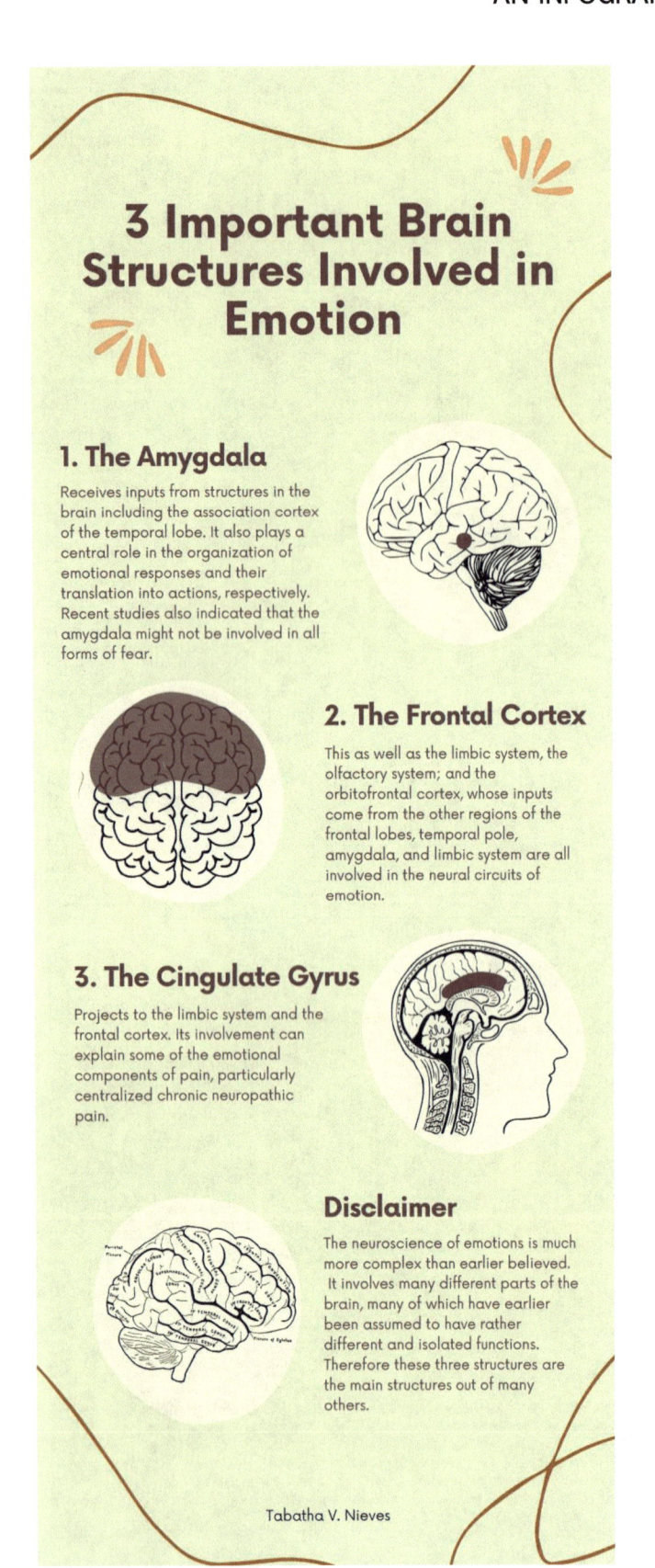

3 Important Brain Structures Involved in Emotion

1. The Amygdala
Receives inputs from structures in the brain including the association cortex of the temporal lobe. It also plays a central role in the organization of emotional responses and their translation into actions, respectively. Recent studies also indicated that the amygdala might not be involved in all forms of fear.

2. The Frontal Cortex
This as well as the limbic system, the olfactory system; and the orbitofrontal cortex, whose inputs come from the other regions of the frontal lobes, temporal pole, amygdala, and limbic system are all involved in the neural circuits of emotion.

3. The Cingulate Gyrus
Projects to the limbic system and the frontal cortex. Its involvement can explain some of the emotional components of pain, particularly centralized chronic neuropathic pain.

Disclaimer
The neuroscience of emotions is much more complex than earlier believed. It involves many different parts of the brain, many of which have earlier been assumed to have rather different and isolated functions. Therefore these three structures are the main structures out of many others.

Tabatha V. Nieves

Tabatha Vaca Nieves, Spring 2023

Brain Circuits Involved with Emotions

Neural Processes of Emotions Depend on:
1. Genetics
2. Epigenetics
3. Learning and memory
4. Social behavior
5. Stress

Emotional Activation
Emotions are defined as behavioral responses to environmental situations. The parts of the brain that play the biggest role in emotions are **the emotional brain** such as the amygdala and **the limbic system**.

Connections from the Amygdala
There are many connections from the amygdala to the brain such as:
- hypothalamus
- reticular formation
- PAG
- nucleus vagus nerve

Emotional Brain
Papez Description (old): the connection between the hypothalamus and anterior thalamus from the cingulate cortex was the basis of emotion
LeDoux Description (new): the amygdala is the center of the neural circuit of the emotional brain

Nuclei that Receive Input from the Brain
1. The amygdala has 3 main nuclei: lateral, basolateral, and central
2. Lateral nucleus receives sensory inputs
3. Central nucleus receives input from the basolateral nucleus
4. Amygdala nuclei receive input from frontal cortex
5. Other parts of the brain play a role in creating emotional

Ranime Goual, Spring 2024

200

AN INFOGRAPHIC JOURNEY

Important Brain Systems Involved With Emotion
Anisah Bakshi

The Autonomic Nervous System
Consists of both the parasympathetic and sympathetic divisions. Negative emotions such as fear and anxiety result in parasympathetic withdrawal and an increase in sympathetic activity. One example is the increase of heartbeat in moments of distress and the decrease in heart beat when the body is resting.

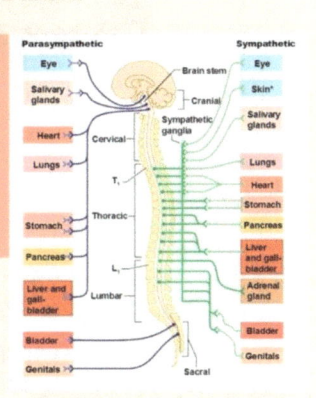

Anatomical Differences
They come from different regions of the CNS:
- Sympathetic: thoracolumbar region
- Parasympathetic: craniosacral region

They come from different locations of the ganglia:
- Sympathetic: close to the spinal cord in a chain
- Parasympathetic: close to target organs

They come from different lengths of postganglionic fibers:
- Sympathetic fibers are long
- Parasympathetic fibers are short

They differ in Postganglionic branching
- Sympathetic has a lot of branching so that multiple organs can be mobilized at once
- Parasympathetic has very little branching

The Autonomic Nervous System, November 29, 2011, By Antranik

Hormones in the Adrenal Medulla
Epinephrine and norepinephrine boost our organ function in response to stress. Prolonged exposures to stress can lead to a low cortisol state. Some symptoms include brain fog, low energy, depressive mood, salt and sweet cravings, and lightheadedness.

The HPA axis
The hypothalamus releases corticotropin releasing hormone (CRH) triggers the release of adrenocorticotropic hormone (ACTH) from the anterior pituitary gland. ACTH then causes the release of cortisol from the adrenal cortex. The release of cortisol initiates that negative feedback loop to prevemnt further release of CRH and ACTH. Signaling from fear-related emotion activates the sympathetic NS and modulates the HPA axis.

The Female HPA-HPG Circuitry
- The HPG axis is differs from the HPA axis. The hypothalamus produces gonadotropin-releasing hormone which triggers the release of luteinizing hormone and follicle-stimulating hormone from the anterior pituitary.
- LH and FSH then stimulates the gonads to release estrogen and progesterone, as well as a small amount of testosterone.
- HPA activity can inhibit estrogen secretion

The Brain on Rage:
1. BRAIN (AMYGDALA) alerted by External Stimuli
2. By passes the LOGIC CENTRE goes straight to the PRIMITIVE BRAIN
3. Brain Triggers ADRENALINE & TESTOSTERONE Hormones "Under Attack"
4. Blood pumps faster, increased CARDIOVASCULAR talk Louder & Quicker!
5. As Blood Pumps, MORE HORMONES Produced creating more Anger/Rage
6. Takes (avg) 20 mins to move from EMOTIONAL to THINKING BRAIN again

RAGE IN THE BRAIN!

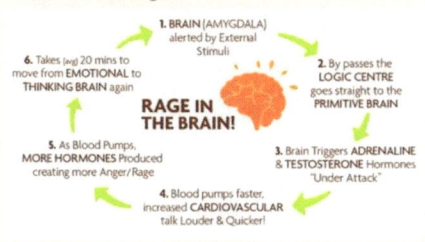

Anisah Bakshi, Fall 2023

The Anatomical & Physiological Aspects of Emotion

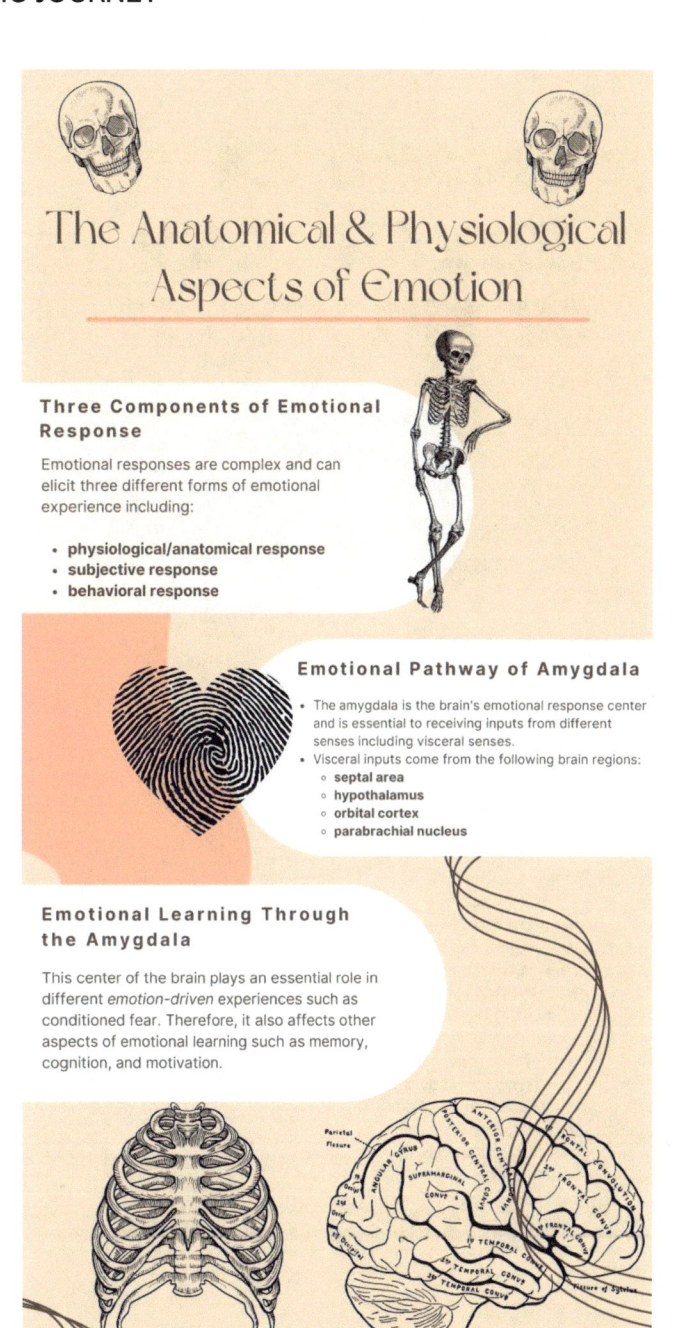

Three Components of Emotional Response
Emotional responses are complex and can elicit three different forms of emotional experience including:
- physiological/anatomical response
- subjective response
- behavioral response

Emotional Pathway of Amygdala
- The amygdala is the brain's emotional response center and is essential to receiving inputs from different senses including visceral senses.
- Visceral inputs come from the following brain regions:
  - septal area
  - hypothalamus
  - orbital cortex
  - parabrachial nucleus

Emotional Learning Through the Amygdala
This center of the brain plays an essential role in different *emotion-driven* experiences such as conditioned fear. Therefore, it also affects other aspects of emotional learning such as memory, cognition, and motivation.

Damage to the Amygdala
- There are a variety of neurological conditions that can damage the structure and function of the amygdala including traumatic brain injury and suffering through a stroke.
- Emotional and behavioral effects persist due to damage to the amygdala including:
  - inability to make decisions
  - anxiety, excessive anger, or fear
  - hypervigilance

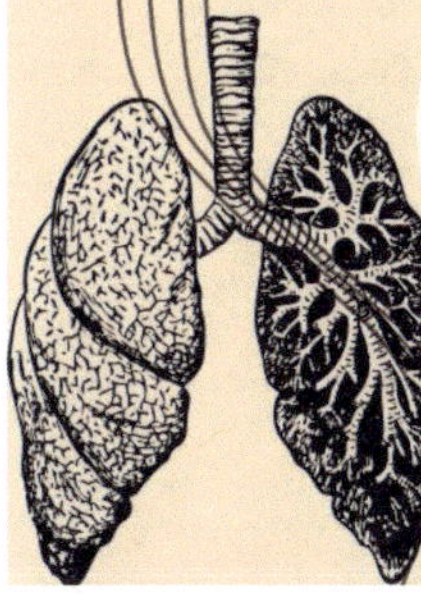

Mahwish Quadri, Spring 2023

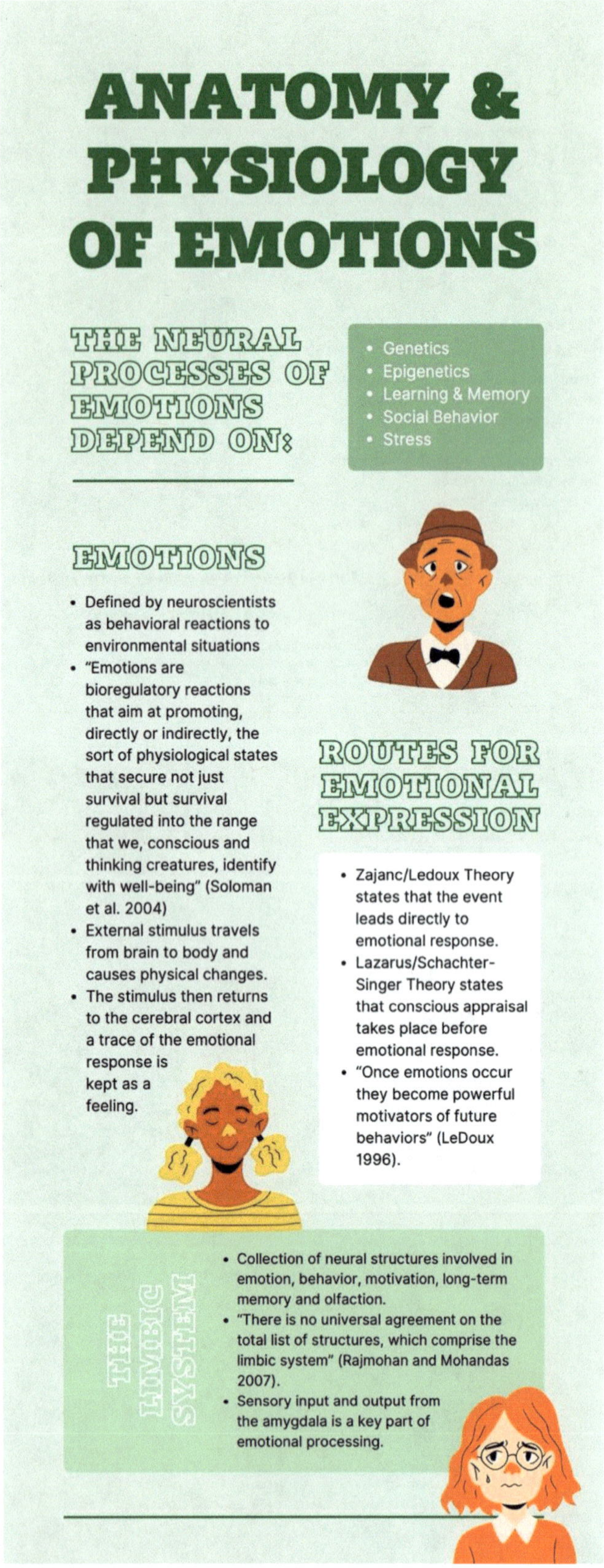

AN INFOGRAPHIC JOURNEY

ANATOMY & PHYSIOLOGY OF EMOTIONS

THE NEURAL PROCESSES OF EMOTIONS DEPEND ON:

- Genetics
- Epigenetics
- Learning & Memory
- Social Behavior
- Stress

EMOTIONS

- Defined by neuroscientists as behavioral reactions to environmental situations
- "Emotions are bioregulatory reactions that aim at promoting, directly or indirectly, the sort of physiological states that secure not just survival but survival regulated into the range that we, conscious and thinking creatures, identify with well-being" (Soloman et al. 2004)
- External stimulus travels from brain to body and causes physical changes.
- The stimulus then returns to the cerebral cortex and a trace of the emotional response is kept as a feeling.

ROUTES FOR EMOTIONAL EXPRESSION

- Zajanc/Ledoux Theory states that the event leads directly to emotional response.
- Lazarus/Schachter-Singer Theory states that conscious appraisal takes place before emotional response.
- "Once emotions occur they become powerful motivators of future behaviors" (LeDoux 1996).

THE LIMBIC SYSTEM

- Collection of neural structures involved in emotion, behavior, motivation, long-term memory and olfaction.
- "There is no universal agreement on the total list of structures, which comprise the limbic system" (Rajmohan and Mohandas 2007).
- Sensory input and output from the amygdala is a key part of emotional processing.

Armaan Sood, Fall 2023

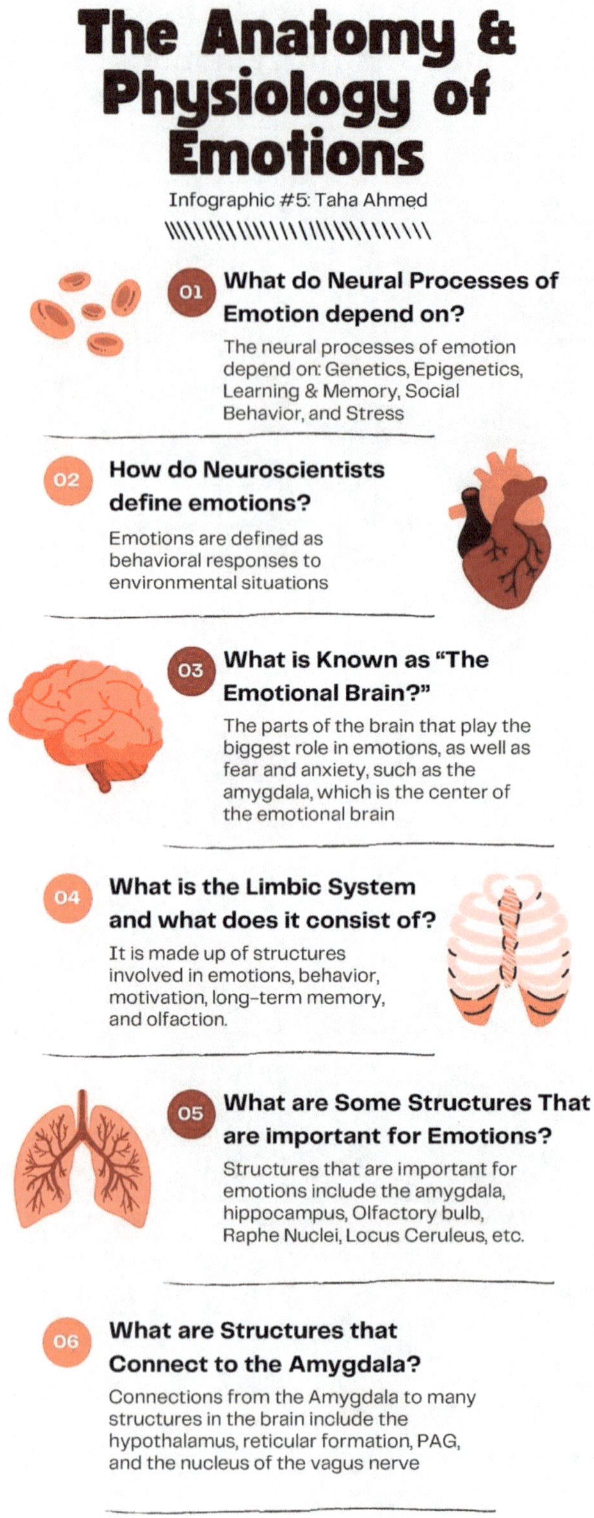

The Anatomy & Physiology of Emotions

Infographic #5: Taha Ahmed

01 What do Neural Processes of Emotion depend on?
The neural processes of emotion depend on: Genetics, Epigenetics, Learning & Memory, Social Behavior, and Stress

02 How do Neuroscientists define emotions?
Emotions are defined as behavioral responses to environmental situations

03 What is Known as "The Emotional Brain?"
The parts of the brain that play the biggest role in emotions, as well as fear and anxiety, such as the amygdala, which is the center of the emotional brain

04 What is the Limbic System and what does it consist of?
It is made up of structures involved in emotions, behavior, motivation, long-term memory, and olfaction.

05 What are Some Structures That are important for Emotions?
Structures that are important for emotions include the amygdala, hippocampus, Olfactory bulb, Raphe Nuclei, Locus Ceruleus, etc.

06 What are Structures that Connect to the Amygdala?
Connections from the Amygdala to many structures in the brain include the hypothalamus, reticular formation, PAG, and the nucleus of the vagus nerve

Taha Ahmed, Spring 2024

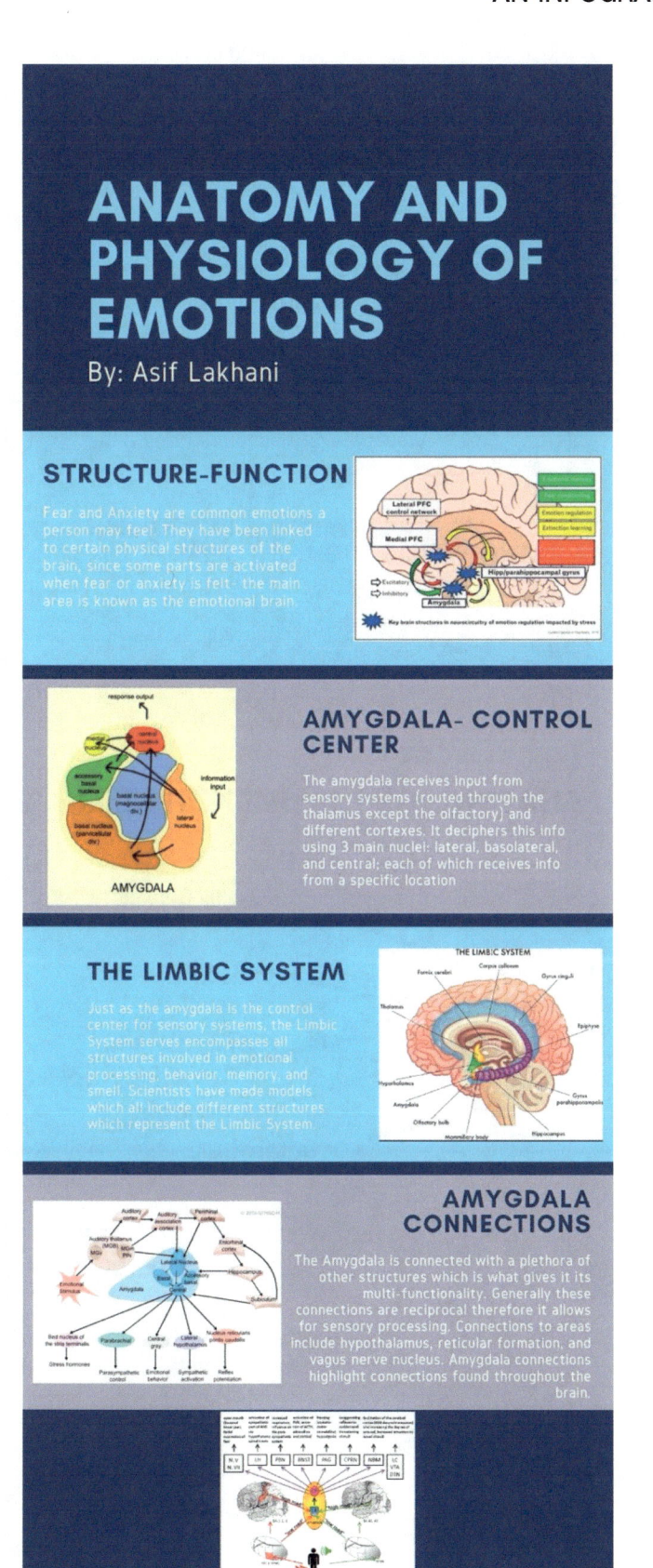

AN INFOGRAPHIC JOURNEY

ANATOMY AND PHYSIOLOGY OF EMOTIONS
By: Asif Lakhani

STRUCTURE-FUNCTION
Fear and Anxiety are common emotions a person may feel. They have been linked to certain physical structures of the brain, since some parts are activated when fear or anxiety is felt- the main area is known as the emotional brain.

AMYGDALA- CONTROL CENTER
The amygdala receives input from sensory systems (routed through the thalamus except the olfactory) and different cortexes. It deciphers this info using 3 main nuclei: lateral, basolateral, and central; each of which receives info from a specific location

THE LIMBIC SYSTEM
Just as the amygdala is the control center for sensory systems, the Limbic System serves encompasses all structures involved in emotional processing, behavior, memory, and smell. Scientists have made models which all include different structures which represent the Limbic System.

AMYGDALA CONNECTIONS
The Amygdala is connected with a plethora of other structures which is what gives it its multi-functionality. Generally these connections are reciprocal therefore it allows for sensory processing. Connections to areas include hypothalamus, reticular formation, and vagus nerve nucleus. Amygdala connections highlight connections found throughout the brain.

Asif Lakhani, Spring 2024

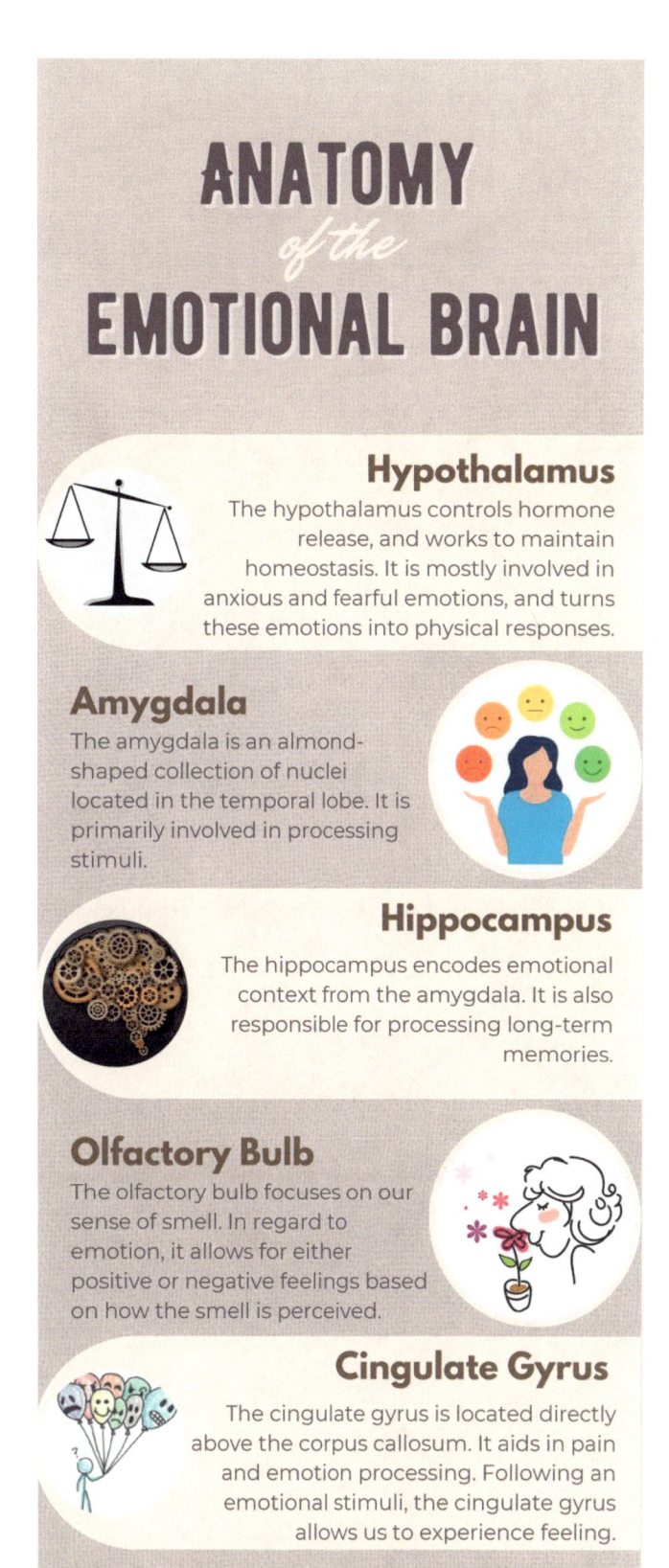

ANATOMY of the EMOTIONAL BRAIN

Hypothalamus
The hypothalamus controls hormone release, and works to maintain homeostasis. It is mostly involved in anxious and fearful emotions, and turns these emotions into physical responses.

Amygdala
The amygdala is an almond-shaped collection of nuclei located in the temporal lobe. It is primarily involved in processing stimuli.

Hippocampus
The hippocampus encodes emotional context from the amygdala. It is also responsible for processing long-term memories.

Olfactory Bulb
The olfactory bulb focuses on our sense of smell. In regard to emotion, it allows for either positive or negative feelings based on how the smell is perceived.

Cingulate Gyrus
The cingulate gyrus is located directly above the corpus callosum. It aids in pain and emotion processing. Following an emotional stimuli, the cingulate gyrus allows us to experience feeling.

Stefanie Favaro, Spring 2023

AN INFOGRAPHIC JOURNEY

HOW THE BRAIN WORKS W/ EMOTION
BY: TOMMY VU

EMOTIONAL ACTIVATION
"Emotions are defined by neuroscientists as behavioral responses to environmental situations". Due to an external stimulus, the brain sends signals out to the body where physical change occurs and back to the cerebral cortex in order to generate a particular feeling. That emotional reaction results in a feeling that pertains to that specific emotion.

LEARNING & MEMORY
After an event that produces a particular emotion/feeling (especially fear), the brain will remember the emotional response due to the interactions with the neural mechanisms. From then, every event that induces fear will create the same physical response such as breaking a sweat or shortness of breath.

THE LIMBIC SYSTEM
The Limbic System is responsible for functions that involve emotion, behavior, motivation, long-term memory, and olfaction. Some different parts of the system include: Fornix, Septum, Frontal cortex, Corpus callosum, Thalamus, Hippocampus, Amygdala, etc. The Limbic System is also involved in fight or flight response.

EXTRO/INTROCEPTION
The body is able to dictate the correct feeling and emotional reaction through the occurrences of extroception and introception. Extroception senses the external environment through the five senses of touch, smell, sight, taste, and hearing. On the other hand, introception is the perception of sensation within the body such as: heart beat and breathing.

SOURCES:
Week 5: Chapter 3. Part 1. What happens in the Brain
https://qbi.uq.edu.au/brain/brain-anatomy/limbic-system#:~:text=The%20limbic%20system%20is%20the,and%20fight%20or%20flight%20responses.

Tommy Vu, Fall 2023

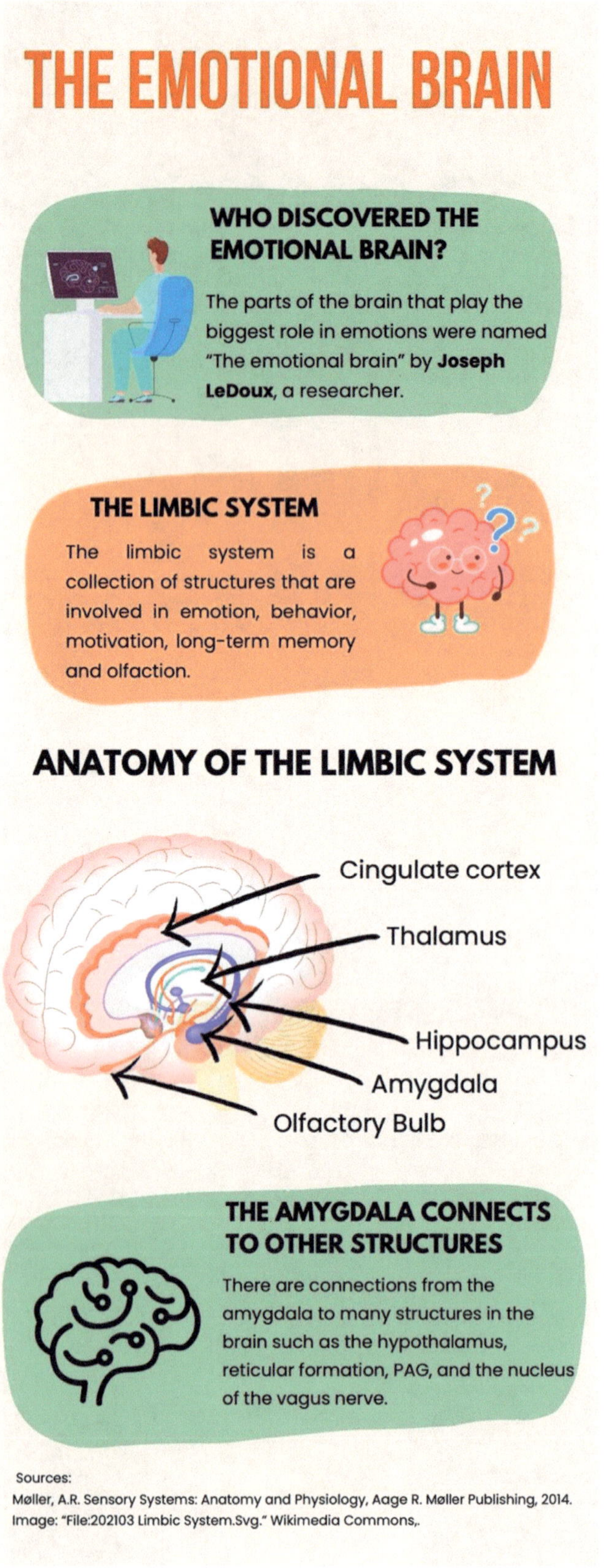

THE EMOTIONAL BRAIN

WHO DISCOVERED THE EMOTIONAL BRAIN?
The parts of the brain that play the biggest role in emotions were named "The emotional brain" by **Joseph LeDoux**, a researcher.

THE LIMBIC SYSTEM
The limbic system is a collection of structures that are involved in emotion, behavior, motivation, long-term memory and olfaction.

ANATOMY OF THE LIMBIC SYSTEM

- Cingulate cortex
- Thalamus
- Hippocampus
- Amygdala
- Olfactory Bulb

THE AMYGDALA CONNECTS TO OTHER STRUCTURES
There are connections from the amygdala to many structures in the brain such as the hypothalamus, reticular formation, PAG, and the nucleus of the vagus nerve.

Sources:
Møller, A.R. Sensory Systems: Anatomy and Physiology, Aage R. Møller Publishing, 2014.
Image: "File:202103 Limbic System.Svg." Wikimedia Commons,.

Sarvani Ganapavarapu, Fall 2023

AN INFOGRAPHIC JOURNEY

THE EMOTIONAL BRAIN

Emily Leung

THE EMOTIONAL BRAIN

American neuroscience researcher, Joseph LeDoux, and his team studied the neuroscience of emotion extensively, discovering important functional pathways of fear. They named the parts of the brain that play the biggest role in emotions "the emotional brain."

THE LIMBIC SYSTEM

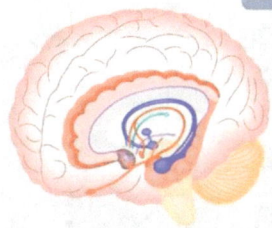

The limbic system is a collection of structures that are involved in emotion, behavior, motivation, long-term memory, and olfaction. Its parts are included in the description of brain structures involved in neural processing of emotion by various researchers.

From Wikimedia Commons

THE AMGYDALA IS THE CENTER OF THE EMOTIONAL BRAIN.

INPUTS

Brainstem, Olfactory Cortex, PAC, NST, Dorsal-Medial Thalamus, Association Sensory Cortex

OUTPUTS

Hypothalamus, Periaqueductal Gray, Reticular Formation, Ventrolateral Medulla, Vagal Nuclei

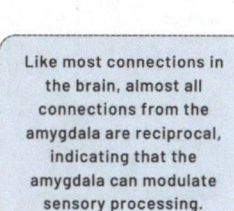

Like most connections in the brain, almost all connections from the amygdala are reciprocal, indicating that the amygdala can modulate sensory processing.

Jahangiri, F.R. (2023). *What Happens in the Brain* [Lecture recording].

Emily Leung, Fall 2023

Understanding the Emotional Brain

Understanding Emotion

This past century has been a growing period for neuroscience and emotions as scientists attempt to understand the biological backings of emotion.

Papez Circle Theory

Papez proposed a neural circuit, connecting the hypothalamus, cingulate cortex, and thalamus for emotions, with the cortex encoding feelings. He believed the Cortex reached the hippocampus and hypothalamus allowing for top-down control of emotions

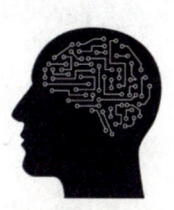

LeDoux's Emotional Brain

Dr. Leboux created a whole new theory that was radically different from previous proposals. Here the amygdala is the center of the neural circuit of processing for the emotional brain. There's short and long pathways of emotional processing.

Differences between the two

There were some huge differences between these two theories of emotion. The biggest was the integration of the amygdala into LeDoux's theory, contrary to Papez's focus on the hypothalamus and thalamus. Differences in speed and pathway as well.

Recent Revisions

However current research has proven the Emotional Brain to be much more complex than believed. In addition to the amygdala, many other structures play a role such as midline thalamic and cortical neurons. Fear and rewards have also been found to use similar structures.

Auditory Fear Conditioning

Auditory fear conditioning enables effective defensive reactions through the Lateral Amygdala pathway. The LA communicates with the Central Nucleus (CE) for fear expression, connecting to Intercalated Cell Masses (ICM) and Basal nucleus (B) for control and contextual processing.

Information from Dr. Faisal R. Jahangiri, Lecture Chapter 3 [Neurobiology of Fear, Anxiety and other Emotions]"

Manuel Jagan, Fall 2023

AN INFOGRAPHIC JOURNEY

EMOTIONS AND HEALTH

The amygdala, neurotransmitters, immunity, and the inflammatory reflex help improve emotional well-being and health.

1. Amygdala's Influence
- The amygdala shapes sensory perception and emotional responses
- It affects issues like hypervigilance and sensory gating

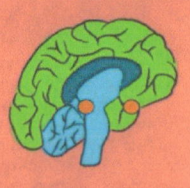

2. Neurotransmitters and Mood
- Dopamine, norepinephrine, and serotonin influence emotions and mood
- They overlap in various emotional functions

3. Emotions and the Immune System
- Emotions, like stress, impact the immune system
- Research focuses on reversing immune system effects

4. Inflammatory Reflex
- Involves vagus nerve and nucleus ambiguus
- Controls immunity and reduces inflammation when activated

References
Møller, A. R. (2019). *Neurobiology of Fear, Anxiety and other Emotions.*

Natalie Laguer Torres, Fall 2023

PROCESSING EMOTIONS

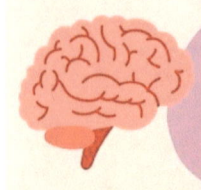

What impacts neural processes of emotions?
Factors such as genetics, epigenetics, learning and memory, social behavior, and stress all impact the neural processes of emotions in a person.

Pathway of Emotion
The general pathway of emotion is initiated by a stimulus or external event. This information is transmitted to the brain, which activates certain responses (ex: hormone release, sympathetic response, movement) and also encodes an emotional response or "feeling" associated with the stimulus.

Old vs. New descriptions of the Emotional Brain
The old description of the emotional brain, proposed by Papez, highlighted that connections between the anterior thalamus and hypothalamus, and the cingulate gyrus were the foundation of emotions in the brain. However, a newer concept, established by LeDoux found the amygdala to be the main link in emotional processing.

The Amygdala
The amygdala was described as the center of the emotional brain by Dr. Joseph LeDoux because it plays a big role in emotions. Specifically, it deals with forming connections between emotions and learning, memories,, and senses.

How Fear Impacts the Emotional Brain Concept
Recent research has shown that fear involves more complex pathways than what LeDoux's research highlighted. Since fear responses often involve learning and conditioning, there are multiple brain structures involved.

References
Clinic, Cleveland. "Amygdala: What It Is and What It Controls - Cleveland Clinic." Cleveland Clinic, 2023, my.clevelandclinic.org

Saara Ahmad, Fall 2023

AN INFOGRAPHIC JOURNEY

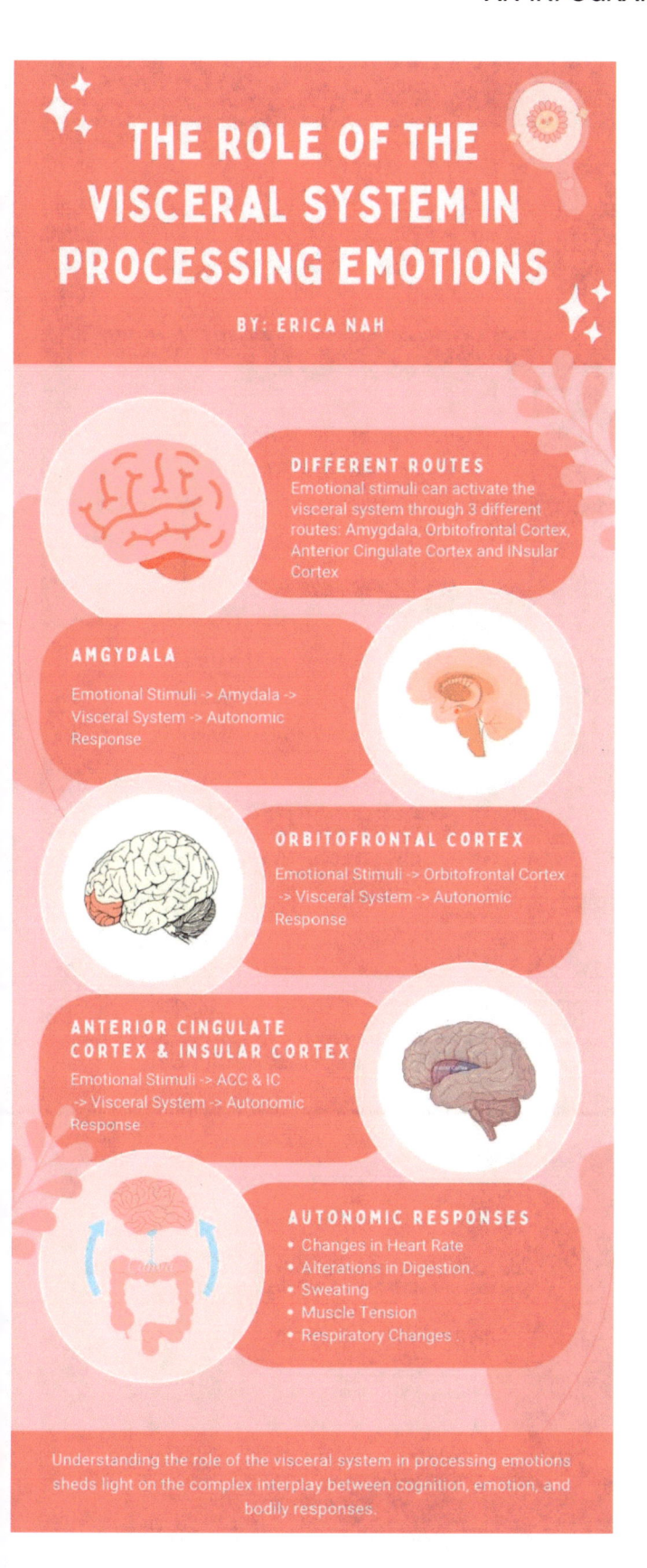

THE ROLE OF THE VISCERAL SYSTEM IN PROCESSING EMOTIONS

BY: ERICA NAH

DIFFERENT ROUTES
Emotional stimuli can activate the visceral system through 3 different routes: Amygdala, Orbitofrontal Cortex, Anterior Cingulate Cortex and INsular Cortex

AMGYDALA
Emotional Stimuli -> Amydala -> Visceral System -> Autonomic Response

ORBITOFRONTAL CORTEX
Emotional Stimuli -> Orbitofrontal Cortex -> Visceral System -> Autonomic Response

ANTERIOR CINGULATE CORTEX & INSULAR CORTEX
Emotional Stimuli -> ACC & IC -> Visceral System -> Autonomic Response

AUTONOMIC RESPONSES
- Changes in Heart Rate
- Alterations in Digestion
- Sweating
- Muscle Tension
- Respiratory Changes

Understanding the role of the visceral system in processing emotions sheds light on the complex interplay between cognition, emotion, and bodily responses.

Erica Nah, Spring 2024

Memory PROCESSING EMOTIONS

Hippocampus
The hippocampus is involed in memory processing of emotions. As it is located at the top of the cortical hierarchy, it encodes sensory input received from all parts of the brain which allows it ro create episodic memory.

Memory is Locational
There are different types of memory. They are all located in different areas of the brain
- working memory - prefrontal cortex
- implicit memory - basal ganglia and cerebellum
- explicit memory - hippocampus, neocortex, and amygdala

Memory Consolidation
The parts of the brain invlved in memory consolidation include the basolateral and central nuclei of the amygdala.. Adrenergic substances can increase the consolidation of memory as well.

Memory Impairment
While there are ways to enhance memory consolidation, such as through adrenergic there substances, there are also ways memory can be impaired. This is through stress hormones, glucocorticoids. These impair the retrieval of memory.

Sources
- https://www.ncbi.nlm.nih.gov/pmc/articles/PMC4605545/#:~:text=Since%20long%20it%20has%20been,working%20memory%20(see%20above).
- https://qbi.uq.edu.au/brain-basics/memory/where-are-memories-stored#:~:text=There%20are%20two%20areas%20of,basal%20ganglia%20and%20the%20cerebellum.
- www.canva. com

Manha Chaudhry | Dr. Faisal Jahangiri | NSC4382.oW1

Manha Chaudhry, Fall 2023

AN INFOGRAPHIC JOURNEY

The Emotional Brain: the Amygdala

Neurobiology of Emotion

01. The system in the brain regulating emotions

The limbic system describes a set of interconnected structures that are involved in behavioral responses, the processing of emotions, long-term memory, and motivation. The amygdala is a key structure of this system due to the high volume of sensory information it recieves from other structures and generates output responses from.

02. Specific function of the Amygdala

The amygdala is involved in responses of aggression and fear to stimuli. Additionally, through reciprocal projections to the hippocampus, it encodes memories associated with strong emotional responses. If one's amygdala were to be removed, they would be unusually trusting and not feel fear.

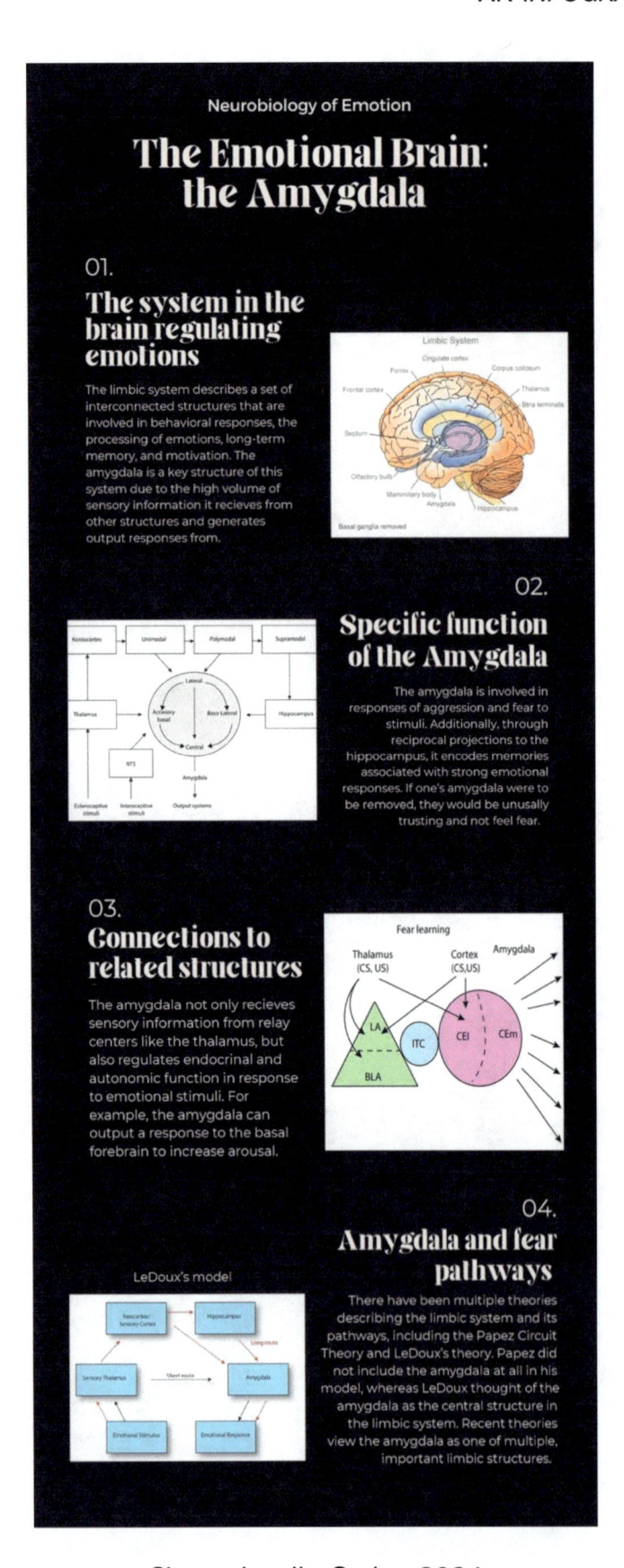

03. Connections to related structures

The amygdala not only recieves sensory information from relay centers like the thalamus, but also regulates endocrinal and autonomic function in response to emotional stimuli. For example, the amygdala can output a response to the basal forebrain to increase arousal.

04. Amygdala and fear pathways

There have been multiple theories describing the limbic system and its pathways, including the Papez Circuit Theory and LeDoux's theory. Papez did not include the amygdala at all in his model, whereas LeDoux thought of the amygdala as the central structure in the limbic system. Recent theories view the amygdala as one of multiple, important limbic structures.

Shreya Jupelly, Spring 2024

Emotions and the Brain

Structures of the brain

The system of the brain responsible for emotions is the limbic system, especially the amygdala.

Functions of the limbic system

The limbic system is involved with emotions, behavior, long-term memory, and olfactory.

Important structures for emotions
- amygdala
- Hippocampus
- Olfactory bulb
- Nucleus basalis of Meynert
- Raphe nuclei
- Locus ceruleus

Connections to the Amygdala

The amygdala is connected to:
- hypothalamus
- Reticular formation
- PAG
- Vagus nerve

Amygdala's main nuclei
1. Lateral nucleus– sensory inputs
2. Basolateral– target of olfactory input
3. Central nucleus

Valeria Viveros, Spring 2024

208

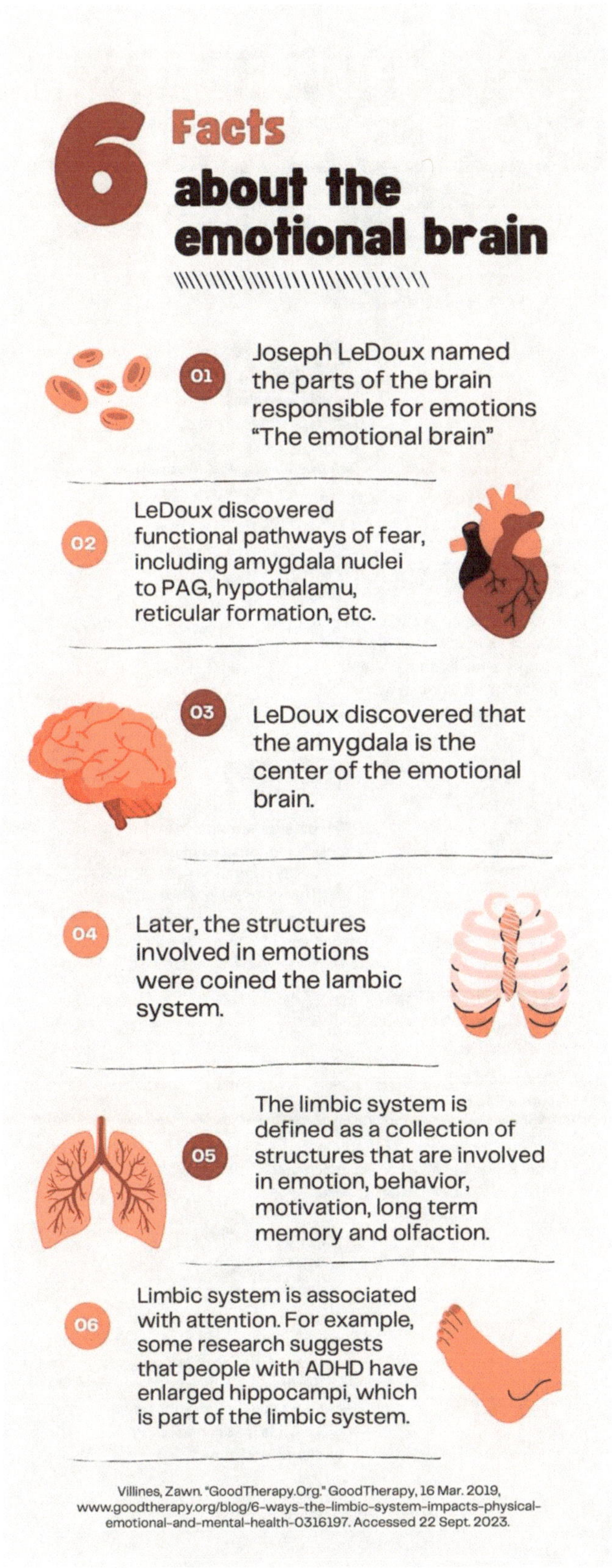

AN INFOGRAPHIC JOURNEY

6 Facts about the emotional brain

01 Joseph LeDoux named the parts of the brain responsible for emotions "The emotional brain"

02 LeDoux discovered functional pathways of fear, including amygdala nuclei to PAG, hypothalamu, reticular formation, etc.

03 LeDoux discovered that the amygdala is the center of the emotional brain.

04 Later, the structures involved in emotions were coined the lambic system.

05 The limbic system is defined as a collection of structures that are involved in emotion, behavior, motivation, long term memory and olfaction.

06 Limbic system is associated with attention. For example, some research suggests that people with ADHD have enlarged hippocampi, which is part of the limbic system.

Villines, Zawn. "GoodTherapy.Org." GoodTherapy, 16 Mar. 2019, www.goodtherapy.org/blog/6-ways-the-limbic-system-impacts-physical-emotional-and-mental-health-0316197. Accessed 22 Sept. 2023.

Vyshnavi Poruri, Fall 2023

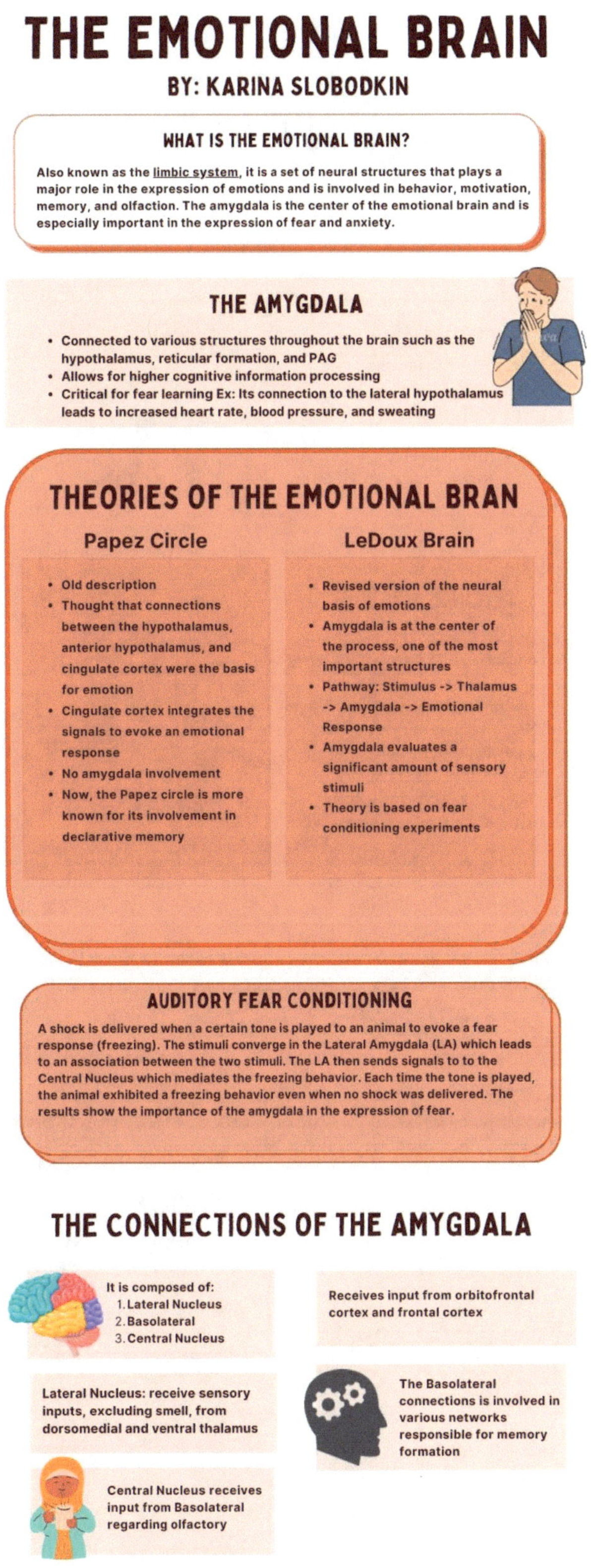

THE EMOTIONAL BRAIN
BY: KARINA SLOBODKIN

WHAT IS THE EMOTIONAL BRAIN?

Also known as the limbic system, it is a set of neural structures that plays a major role in the expression of emotions and is involved in behavior, motivation, memory, and olfaction. The amygdala is the center of the emotional brain and is especially important in the expression of fear and anxiety.

THE AMYGDALA
- Connected to various structures throughout the brain such as the hypothalamus, reticular formation, and PAG
- Allows for higher cognitive information processing
- Critical for fear learning Ex: Its connection to the lateral hypothalamus leads to increased heart rate, blood pressure, and sweating

THEORIES OF THE EMOTIONAL BRAN

Papez Circle
- Old description
- Thought that connections between the hypothalamus, anterior hypothalamus, and cingulate cortex were the basis for emotion
- Cingulate cortex integrates the signals to evoke an emotional response
- No amygdala involvement
- Now, the Papez circle is more known for its involvement in declarative memory

LeDoux Brain
- Revised version of the neural basis of emotions
- Amygdala is at the center of the process, one of the most important structures
- Pathway: Stimulus -> Thalamus -> Amygdala -> Emotional Response
- Amygdala evaluates a significant amount of sensory stimuli
- Theory is based on fear conditioning experiments

AUDITORY FEAR CONDITIONING

A shock is delivered when a certain tone is played to an animal to evoke a fear response (freezing). The stimuli converge in the Lateral Amygdala (LA) which leads to an association between the two stimuli. The LA then sends signals to to the Central Nucleus which mediates the freezing behavior. Each time the tone is played, the animal exhibited a freezing behavior even when no shock was delivered. The results show the importance of the amygdala in the expression of fear.

THE CONNECTIONS OF THE AMYGDALA

It is composed of:
1. Lateral Nucleus
2. Basolateral
3. Central Nucleus

Receives input from orbitofrontal cortex and frontal cortex

Lateral Nucleus: receive sensory inputs, excluding smell, from dorsomedial and ventral thalamus

The Basolateral connections is involved in various networks responsible for memory formation

Central Nucleus receives input from Basolateral regarding olfactory

Karina Slobodkin, Spring 2023

AN INFOGRAPHIC JOURNEY

EMOTIONAL BRAIN

PAPEZ CIRCLE

In 1937, Papez proposed that the basis of emotions arose from connections between
- Cingulate cortex
- Hypothalamus
- Anterior thalamus

"FEELINGS" (PAPEZ)

According to Papex, when the emotional reaches the cingulate cortex, it...
1. Reaches the hippocampus then to
2. Hypothalamus sends a bodily response signal (top-down)
3. Passes the anterior thalamus back to the cortex, where it's stored as a "feeling" (bottom-up)

LEDOUX'S DEFINITION

In 1998, LeDoux and his students proposed a model that, along with the structures in Papez's model, included and was centered around the amygdala.

AMYGDALA

The amygdala is a pair of almond shaped clusters of nuclei located deep within the temporal lobe.
- Receives sensory inputs (except olfactory)
- Activated by emotions
- Play a role in memory consolidation

HOW OUR BRAIN CREATES EMOTIONAL REACTIONS
A GENERAL OVERVIEW

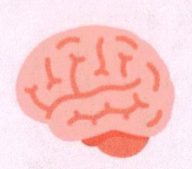

1. ENVIRONMENTAL TRIGGERS

Different things in our surroundings can trigger an emotional response, whether it's physical touch, something we see, or even something we hear

EMOTIONAL ACTIVATION

Once something in our environment stimulates our senses, our brain interprets the information and decides what emotion we our body should react with.

2. MUSCLES

The brain sends signals to the muscles to cause us to move or physically react to the stimuli. If our brain wants to react with fear for example, this might include making you jump.

3. AUTONOMIC NERVOUS SYSTEM

Signals are also sent to our autonomic nervous system which controls basic functions of the body like our heartbeat and breathing rate. For example, when reacting to fear, your heart will start to race.

4. ENDOCRINE SYSTEM

Finally, you brain sends the response signals to your endocrine system which handles hormones. Using hormones, this system controls your mood, your sleep-wake cycle, regulating blood pressure, and more.

CREATED BY KHYRA WHITE

Kathy Nguyen, Spring 2023

Khyra White, Spring 2024

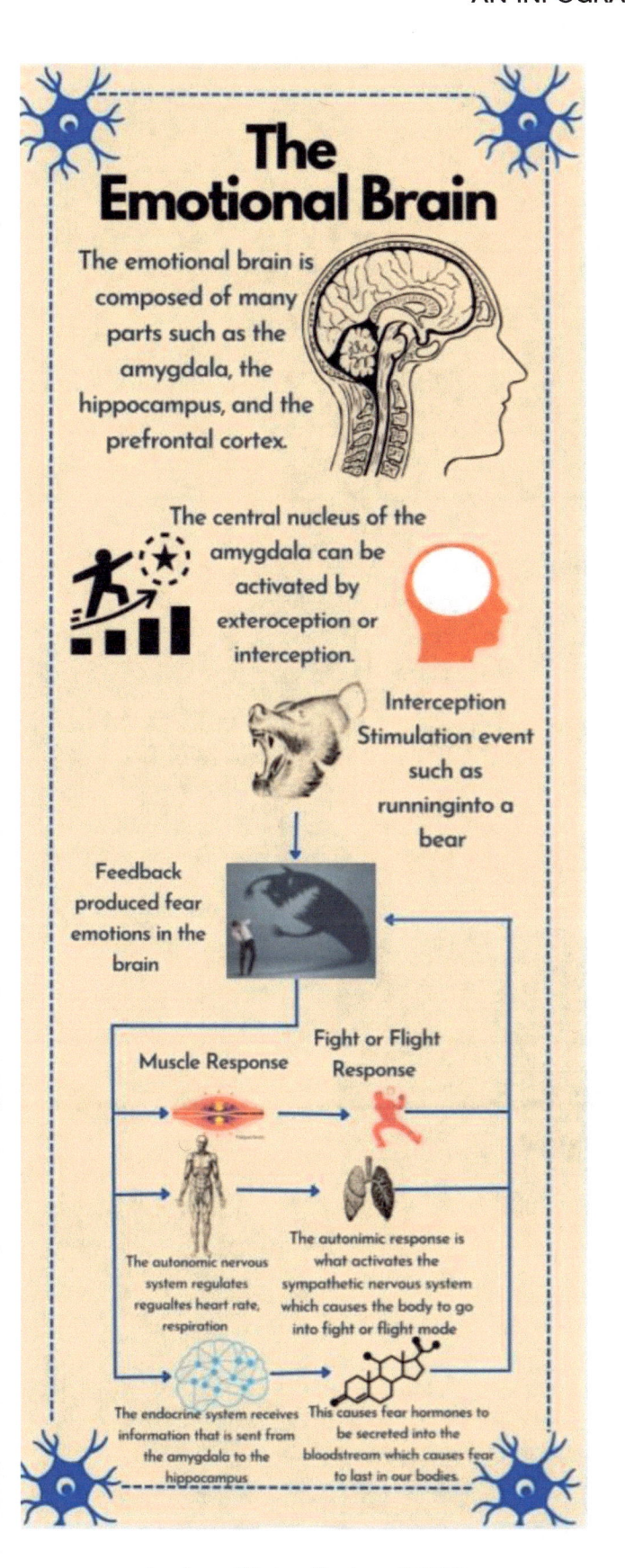

AN INFOGRAPHIC JOURNEY

The Emotional Brain

The emotional brain is composed of many parts such as the amygdala, the hippocampus, and the prefrontal cortex.

The central nucleus of the amygdala can be activated by exteroception or interception.

Interception Stimulation event such as running into a bear

Feedback produced fear emotions in the brain

Muscle Response

The autonomic nervous system regulates regualtes heart rate, respiration

Fight or Flight Response

The autonimic response is what activates the sympathetic nervous system which causes the body to go into fight or flight mode

The endocrine system receives information that is sent from the amygdala to the hippocampus

This causes fear hormones to be secreted into the bloodstream which causes fear to last in our bodies

Andrea Pinto, Spring 2023

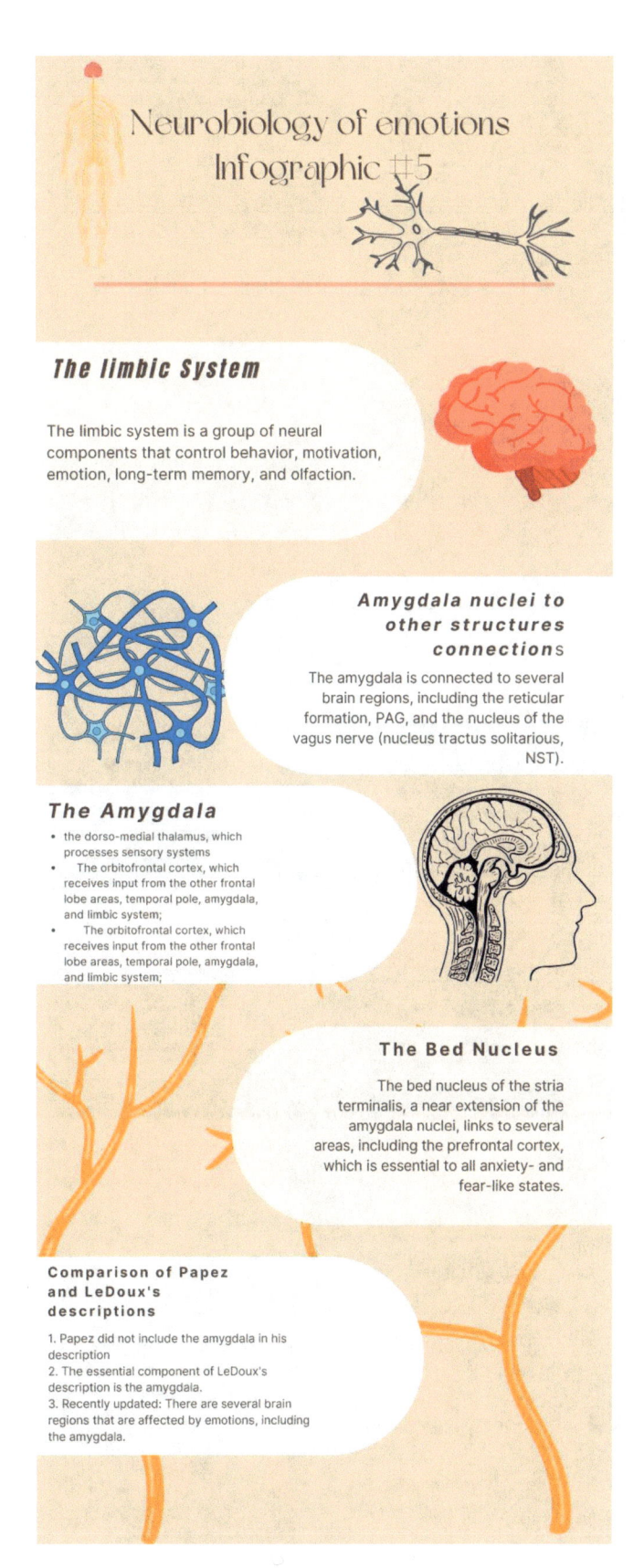

Neurobiology of emotions Infographic #5

The limbic System

The limbic system is a group of neural components that control behavior, motivation, emotion, long-term memory, and olfaction.

Amygdala nuclei to other structures connections

The amygdala is connected to several brain regions, including the reticular formation, PAG, and the nucleus of the vagus nerve (nucleus tractus solitarious, NST).

The Amygdala

- the dorso-medial thalamus, which processes sensory systems
- The orbitofrontal cortex, which receives input from the other frontal lobe areas, temporal pole, amygdala, and limbic system;
- The orbitofrontal cortex, which receives input from the other frontal lobe areas, temporal pole, amygdala, and limbic system;

The Bed Nucleus

The bed nucleus of the stria terminalis, a near extension of the amygdala nuclei, links to several areas, including the prefrontal cortex, which is essential to all anxiety- and fear-like states.

Comparison of Papez and LeDoux's descriptions

1. Papez did not include the amygdala in his description
2. The essential component of LeDoux's description is the amygdala.
3. Recently updated: There are several brain regions that are affected by emotions, including the amygdala.

Anonymous, Spring 2023

AN INFOGRAPHIC JOURNEY

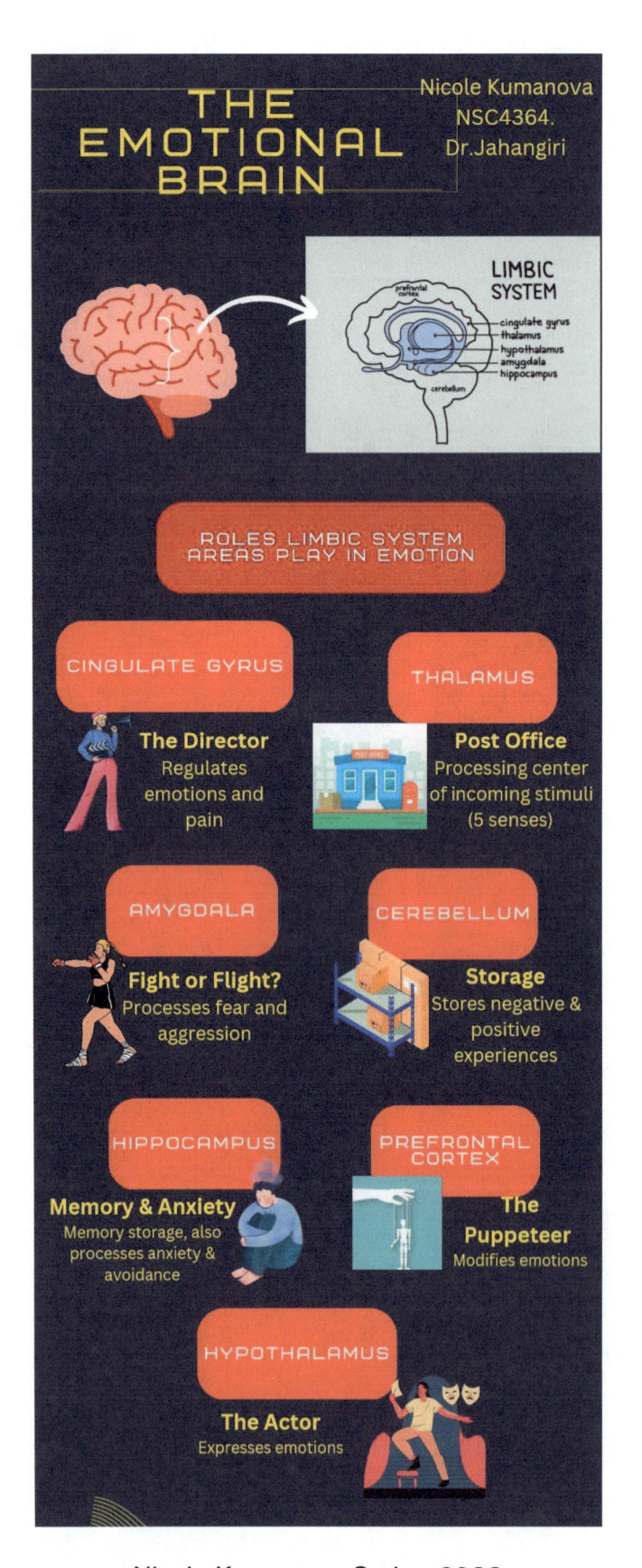

Nicole Kumanova, Spring 2023

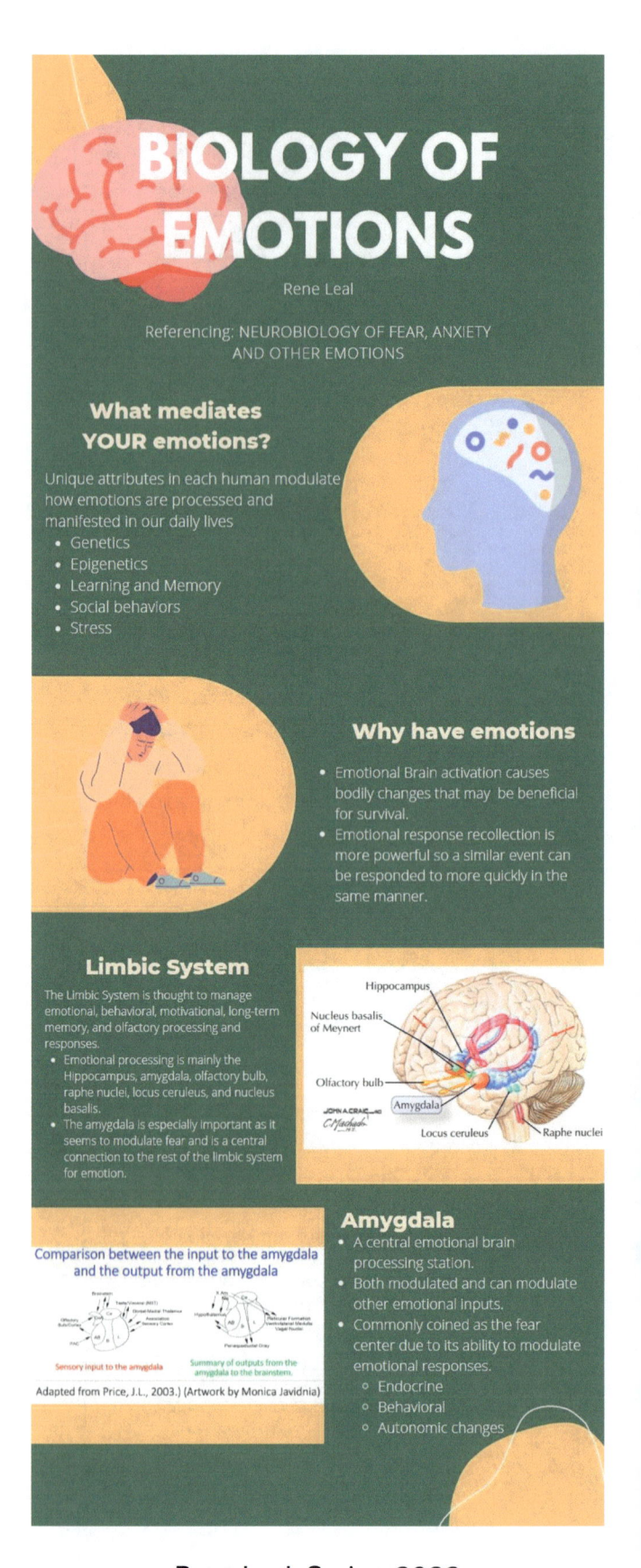

Rene Leal, Spring 2023

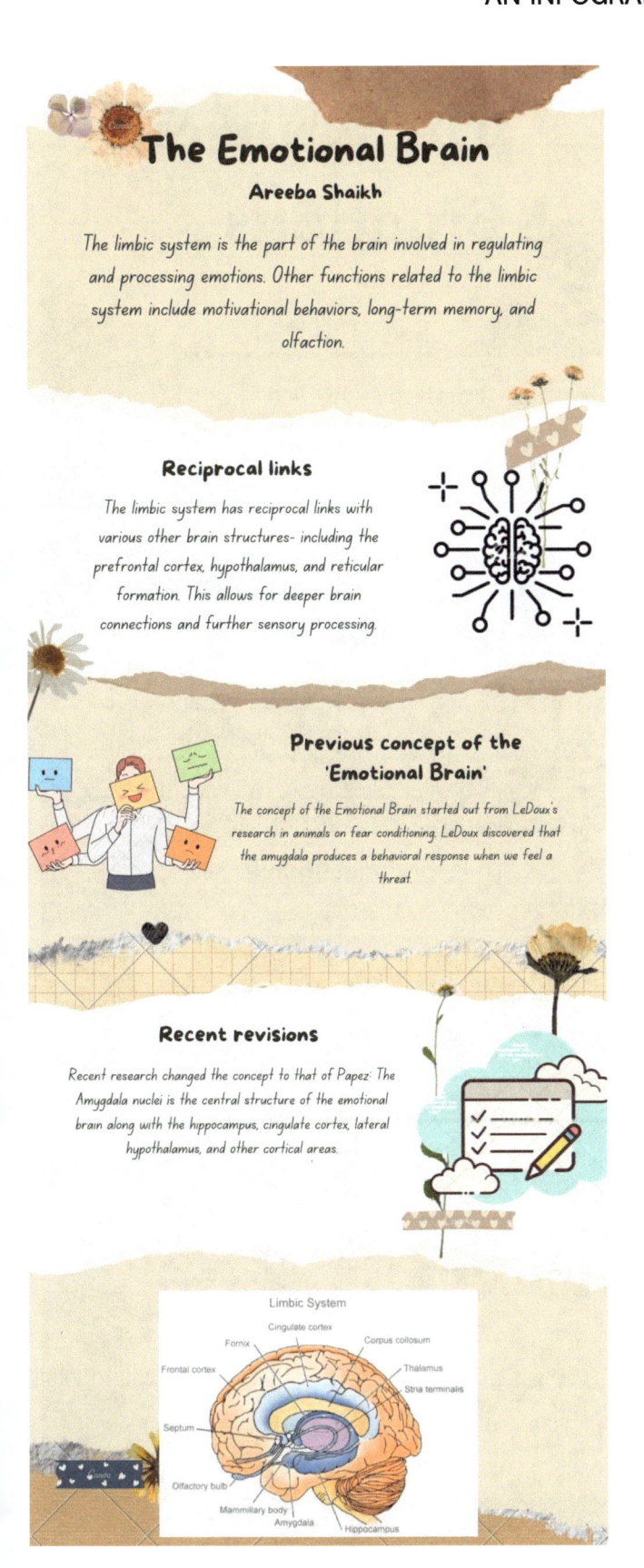

AN INFOGRAPHIC JOURNEY

The Emotional Brain
Areeba Shaikh

The limbic system is the part of the brain involved in regulating and processing emotions. Other functions related to the limbic system include motivational behaviors, long-term memory, and olfaction.

Reciprocal links
The limbic system has reciprocal links with various other brain structures- including the prefrontal cortex, hypothalamus, and reticular formation. This allows for deeper brain connections and further sensory processing.

Previous concept of the 'Emotional Brain'
The concept of the Emotional Brain started out from LeDoux's research in animals on fear conditioning. LeDoux discovered that the amygdala produces a behavioral response when we feel a threat.

Recent revisions
Recent research changed the concept to that of Papez: The Amygdala nuclei is the central structure of the emotional brain along with the hippocampus, cingulate cortex, lateral hypothalamus, and other cortical areas.

Areeba Shaikh, Spring 2023

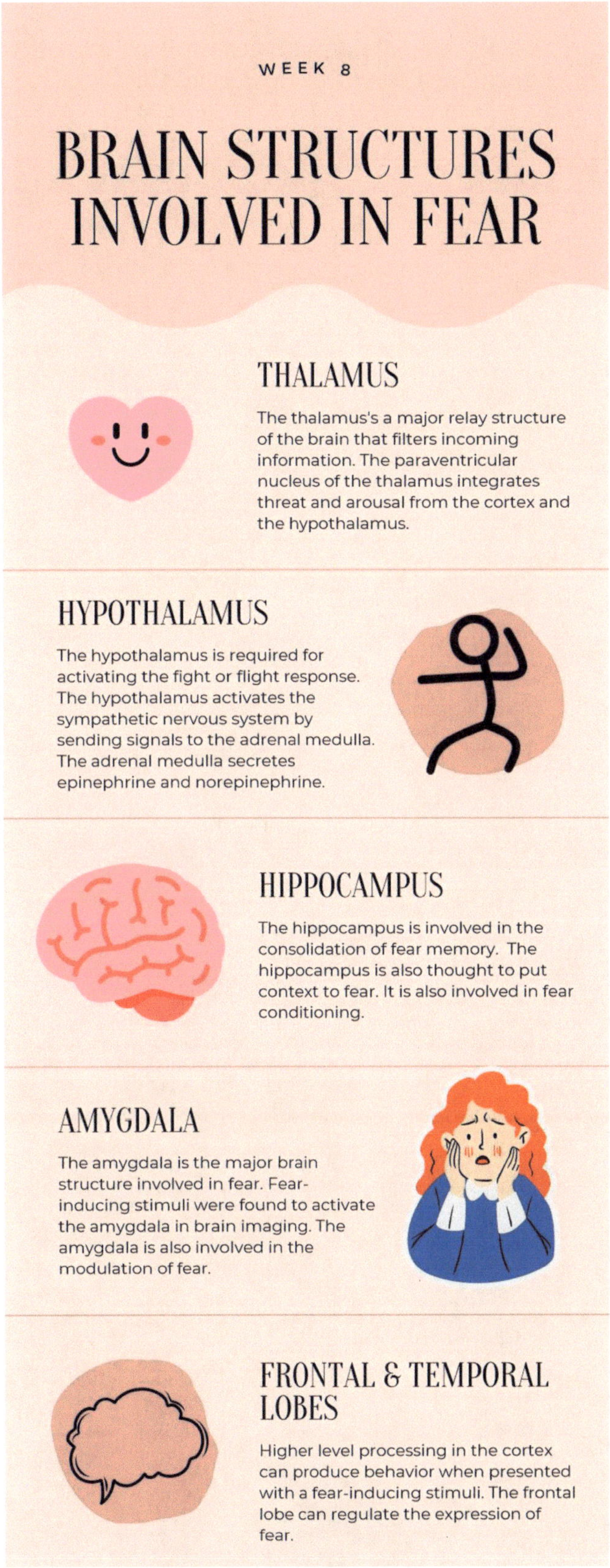

WEEK 8

BRAIN STRUCTURES INVOLVED IN FEAR

THALAMUS
The thalamus's a major relay structure of the brain that filters incoming information. The paraventricular nucleus of the thalamus integrates threat and arousal from the cortex and the hypothalamus.

HYPOTHALAMUS
The hypothalamus is required for activating the fight or flight response. The hypothalamus activates the sympathetic nervous system by sending signals to the adrenal medulla. The adrenal medulla secretes epinephrine and norepinephrine.

HIPPOCAMPUS
The hippocampus is involved in the consolidation of fear memory. The hippocampus is also thought to put context to fear. It is also involved in fear conditioning.

AMYGDALA
The amygdala is the major brain structure involved in fear. Fear-inducing stimuli were found to activate the amygdala in brain imaging. The amygdala is also involved in the modulation of fear.

FRONTAL & TEMPORAL LOBES
Higher level processing in the cortex can produce behavior when presented with a fear-inducing stimuli. The frontal lobe can regulate the expression of fear.

Hanah Kim, Spring 2023

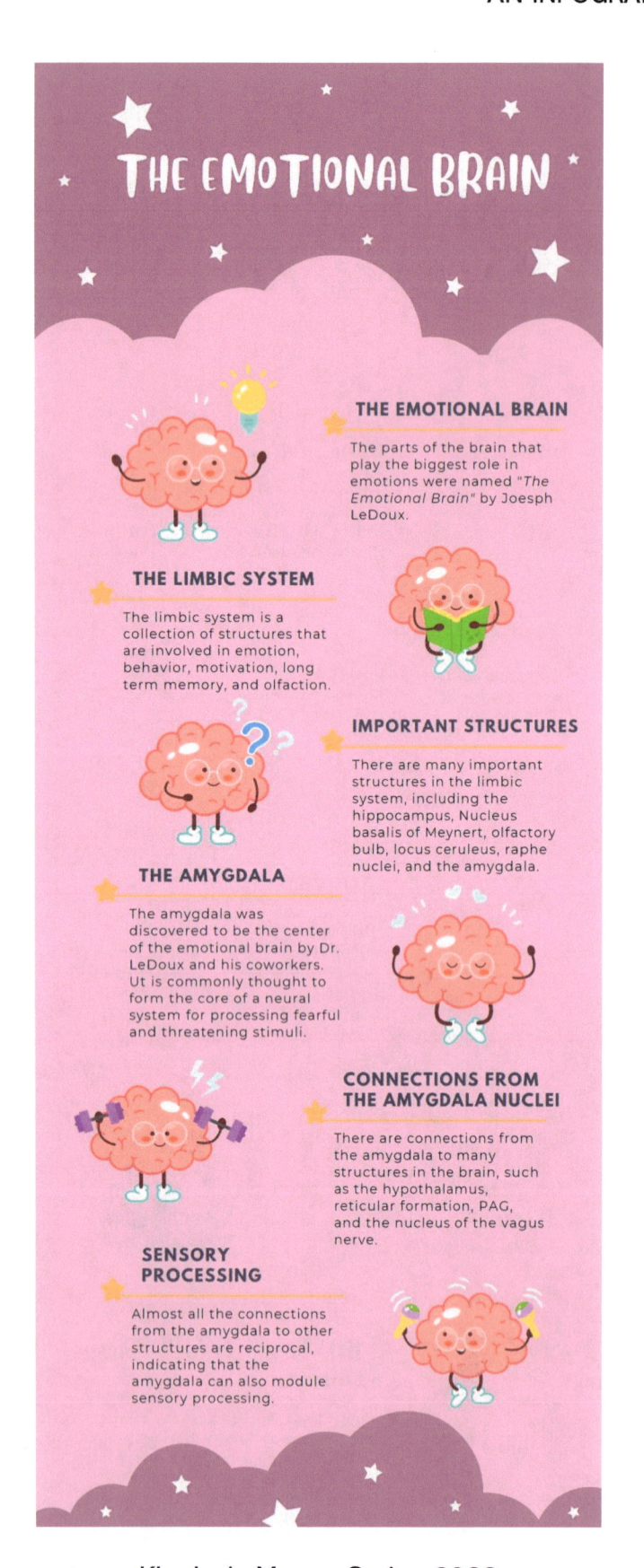

AN INFOGRAPHIC JOURNEY

THE EMOTIONAL BRAIN

THE EMOTIONAL BRAIN
The parts of the brain that play the biggest role in emotions were named *"The Emotional Brain"* by Joesph LeDoux.

THE LIMBIC SYSTEM
The limbic system is a collection of structures that are involved in emotion, behavior, motivation, long term memory, and olfaction.

IMPORTANT STRUCTURES
There are many important structures in the limbic system, including the hippocampus, Nucleus basalis of Meynert, olfactory bulb, locus ceruleus, raphe nuclei, and the amygdala.

THE AMYGDALA
The amygdala was discovered to be the center of the emotional brain by Dr. LeDoux and his coworkers. Ut is commonly thought to form the core of a neural system for processing fearful and threatening stimuli.

CONNECTIONS FROM THE AMYGDALA NUCLEI
There are connections from the amygdala to many structures in the brain, such as the hypothalamus, reticular formation, PAG, and the nucleus of the vagus nerve.

SENSORY PROCESSING
Almost all the connections from the amygdala to other structures are reciprocal, indicating that the amygdala can also module sensory processing.

Khadeeja Moosa, Spring 2023

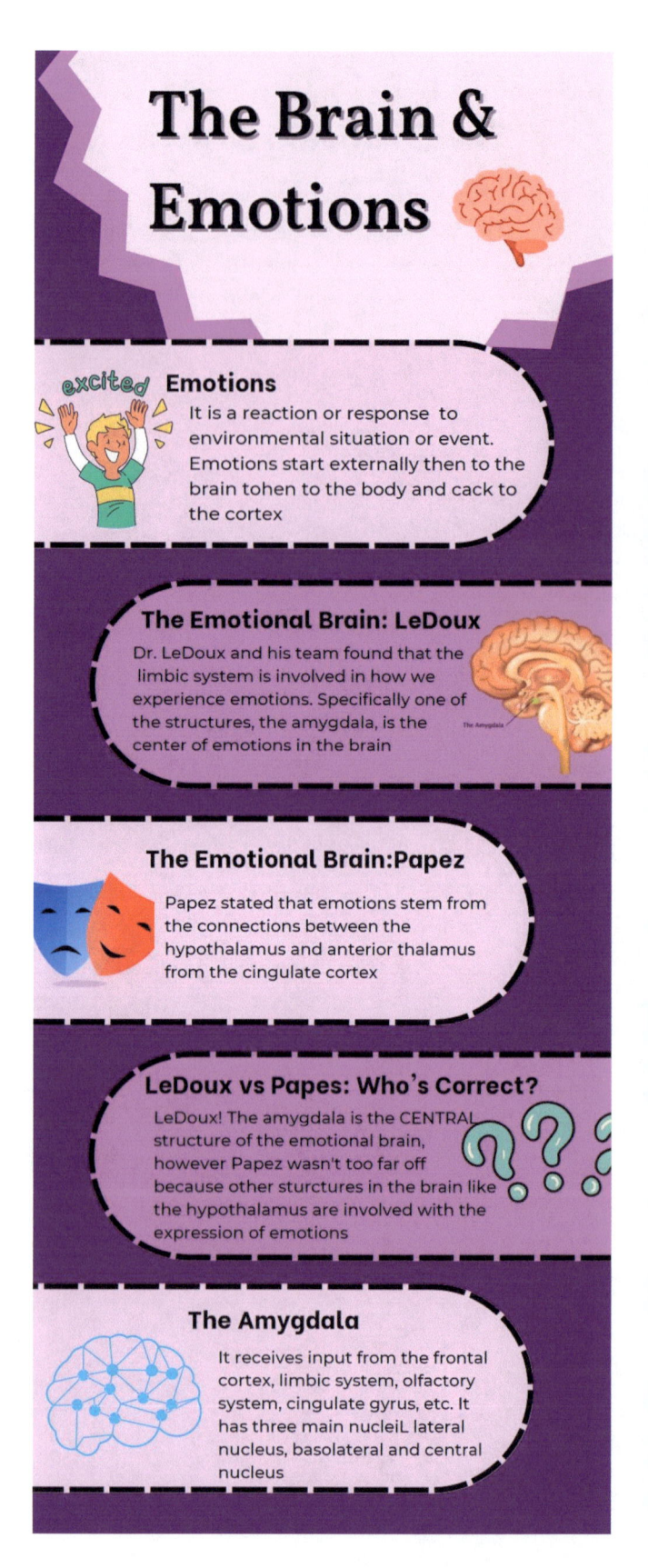

The Brain & Emotions

Emotions
It is a reaction or response to environmental situation or event. Emotions start externally then to the brain tohen to the body and cack to the cortex

The Emotional Brain: LeDoux
Dr. LeDoux and his team found that the limbic system is involved in how we experience emotions. Specifically one of the structures, the amygdala, is the center of emotions in the brain

The Emotional Brain: Papez
Papez stated that emotions stem from the connections between the hypothalamus and anterior thalamus from the cingulate cortex

LeDoux vs Papes: Who's Correct?
LeDoux! The amygdala is the CENTRAL structure of the emotional brain, however Papez wasn't too far off because other sturctures in the brain like the hypothalamus are involved with the expression of emotions

The Amygdala
It receives input from the frontal cortex, limbic system, olfactory system, cingulate gyrus, etc. It has three main nucleiL lateral nucleus, basolateral and central nucleus

Lilly Neguse, Spring 2023

AN INFOGRAPHIC JOURNEY

THE FUNCTIONAL ASPECTS OF EMOTION

1. CRUCIAL STRUCTURES
The thalamus, hypothalamus, hippocampus, frontal and temporal lobes, and the amygdala are crucial structures involved in creating the reactions to fear

2. FUNCTIONAL ASPECTS OF THE AMYGDALA
The amygdala plays an important role in evaluating emotional stimuli. It also works together with the orbitofrontal cortex to organize emotional responses and translate them into actions.

3. THE AMYGDALA'S INPUTS
The amygdala receives 2 main sensory system inputs: rapid and crudely processed information from the dorsomedial thalamus, and slower and more processed information from the ventral thalamus.

4. EVALUATION OF STIMULI
Stimuli goes through the sensory thalamus where information is processed and then relayed to the amygdala. The amygdala then creates connections with the conscious mind in order to create an appropriate response.

5. DIFFERENT EMOTIONAL RESPONSES
The central nucleus of the amygdala has outputs to different regions of the brain resulting in different responses. For example, the output to the lateral thalamus results in sympathetic activation.

6. THE AMYGDALA NUCLEI
The activity in amygdala nuclei can be modulated by signals from other structures. Activity in threat-related neural networks is increased in people with anxiety disorders, as well as in persons exhibiting high levels of trait anxiety.

7. THE AMYGDALA & MEMORY
The amygdala attaches emotional significance to memories, which results in greater permanence. The amygdala also plays a key role in forming new memories specifically related to fear. Fearful memories are able to be formed after only a few repetitions (Queensland Brain Institute).

8. CITATIONS
Queensland Brain Institute. "Where Are Memories Stored in the Brain?" Uq.edu.au, The University of Queensland, 23 July 2018, qbi.uq.edu.au/brain-basics/memory/where-are-memories-stored.

Jeffy Jackson, Fall 2023

FUNCTIONAL ASPECTS OF EMOTION

SEQUENCE OF EVENTS THAT CAUSE "RAGE IN THE BRAIN"

1. Amygdala alerted by external stimuli
2. Signal bypasses logic center and directly transmits to primitive brain
3. Brain triggers testosterone and adrenaline hormones "under attack"
4. Blood pumps faster
5. More hormones produced due to blood pumping faster creating more anger/rage
6. Takes approximately 20 minutes to transition from emotional to thinking brain again

THE AMYGDALA AS A CENTER FOR EMOTIONAL EVALUATION

The amygdala receives:
- Rapid and crudely processed information from the dorso-medial thalamus and the nucleus (Non-Classical Sensory Pathways) of the solitary tract
- Slower and more processed information from the ventral thalamus and successive stages of cortical processing (Classical Sensory Pathways)

EXPRESSION OF DIFFERENT EMOTIONAL RESPONSES BY AMYGDALA

- Emotional Stimulus > Thalamus > Cortical Structures > Lateral Nucleus of Amygdala
- Main Nuclei of Amygdala > Other Brain Structures
- "the amygdala is a critical substrate in the neural system necessary for triggering somatic states from primary inducers" (Bechara et al. 2006).

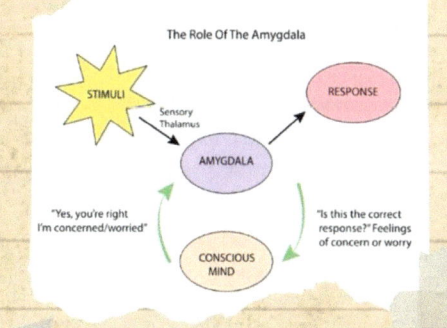

The Role Of The Amygdala

STIMULI → Sensory Thalamus → AMYGDALA → RESPONSE
AMYGDALA ↔ CONSCIOUS MIND
"Yes, you're right I'm concerned/worried"
"Is this the correct response?" Feelings of concern or worry

MODULATION OF ACTIVITY IN AMYGDALA NUCLEI

- People with anxiety disorders display increased activity in threat-related neural networks
- Tendency to report and experience negative emotions such as fear, anxiety, and worry across many situations.

Armaan Sood, Fall 2023

AN INFOGRAPHIC JOURNEY

CHAPTER 12

Detection of Threats

Stress, Anxiety, HPA Axis

By Erica Nah & Praniya Syona Jakkamsetti, Spring 2024

In today's fast-paced and constantly evolving world, stress has become increasingly prevalent, significantly impacting individuals' daily lives and overall well-being. The constant exposure to societal pressures and the demands of modern life have contributed to the rise of these conditions, affecting people of all ages and backgrounds. Highlighting the urgency of this issue, the World Health Organization reported that the global prevalence of anxiety disorders increased by 25% in the first year of the COVID-19 pandemic alone (World Health Organization, 2022). These statistics highlight the need to address stress and anxiety, as their effects can influence individuals' quality of life.

To better understand this widespread phenomenon, exploring the concept of stress and its various manifestations is essential. Stress is a physiological and psychological response to perceived threats or challenges, manifesting in various forms, such as anxiety, fear, and worry. According to the World Health Organization, stress is "the state of worry or mental tension caused by a difficult situation... A natural human response that prompts us to address challenges and threats in our lives" (World Health Organization, 2023). While stress is a natural response, research has identified several factors that can exacerbate its impact on mental well-being, including academic pressure, family obligations, financial concerns, and societal expectations (Slimmen et al., 2022).

At the core of the body's stress response lies the hypothalamic pituitary adrenal (HPA) axis, a complex neuroendocrine system responsible for regulating the secretion of stress hormones, particularly cortisol. A cascade of hormonal signals is initiated when a perceived threat or stressor is noted. The hypothalamus releases corticotropin-releasing hormone (CRH), which stimulates the anterior pituitary gland to release adrenocorticotropic hormone (ACTH). ACTH, in turn, triggers the adrenal glands to produce cortisol, the primary stress hormone. The HPA axis is regulated through a feedback mechanism to prevent prolonged stress responses, with cortisol acting on the hypothalamus and pituitary gland to suppress further release of CRH and ACTH, respectively (Tsigos & Chrousos, 2002). This system highlights the body's ability to maintain homeostasis during stress.

While the HPA axis plays a significant role, the physiological mechanisms underlying stress and anxiety involve various neurotransmitters and hormones. For example, adrenaline or epinephrine, released primarily by the adrenal medulla, is important in triggering the "fight or flight" response, preparing the body to cope with stressful situations. The regulation of the HPA axis involves a balance of neuronal and endocrine factors, with the hippocampus, amygdala, and prefrontal cortex modulating the stress response through their connections with the hypothalamus and other brain regions (Herman et al., 2016). Moreover, feedback mechanisms involving glucocorticoid receptors in the brain and pituitary gland help regulate the activity of the HPA axis, preventing prolonged stress responses (Tsigos & Chrousos, 2002).

While the body's stress response is a natural mechanism, chronic stress and dysregulation in the HPA axis can affect physical and mental well-being. Numerous studies have linked chronic stress and elevated cortisol levels to an increased risk of mood disorders, metabolic diseases, cardiovascular disease, and cognitive impairments (Chrousos, 2009; Juruena et al., 2020). Furthermore, environmental stressors, such as maternal stress during pregnancy, can influence the development of the fetal HPA axis, potentially increasing the risk of adult disease (Juruena et al., 2020). These findings underscore the importance of addressing stress and anxiety, as their impact can extend far beyond the immediate experience.

The prevalence of anxiety disorders, closely linked to stress and HPA axis dysregulation, is a growing public health concern. According to the National Institute of Mental Health (NIMH), anxiety disorders affect approximately 19.1% of adults in the United States each year (NIMH, 2022). However, the burden of these conditions is not evenly distributed. Higher rates of anxiety disorders are observed among females, younger adults, and individuals with lower socioeconomic status (Bandelow & Michaelis, 2015). Additionally, cultural and societal factors, as well as exposure to traumatic events, can contribute to the development of anxiety disorders (Hofmann & Hinton, 2014). This variability in prevalence highlights the need for targeted interventions and a deeper understanding of the underlying risk factors.

Given the significant impact of stress, anxiety, and HPA axis dysregulation, various treatment modalities have been developed to address these conditions. Pharmacological interventions, such as selective serotonin reuptake inhibitors (SSRIs) and serotonin-norepinephrine reuptake inhibitors (SNRIs), target neurotransmitter systems involved in anxiety regulation (Baldwin et al., 2014). Complementing these approaches, psychotherapeutic techniques like cognitive-behavioral therapy (CBT) and mindfulness-based interventions have demonstrated efficacy in reducing anxiety symptoms and improving coping strategies (Hofmann & Smits, 2008; Khoury et al., 2013).

However, the quest for more effective treatments continues. Emerging therapeutic approaches, including brain stimulation techniques and novel pharmacological agents targeting the HPA axis or specific neurotransmitter systems, are currently being investigated as potential solutions for anxiety disorders (Juruena et al., 2020). To measure the influence of HPA axis functioning on cortisol levels, various tests, such as the dexamethasone suppression test and CRH stimulation test, have been employed (Carvalho & Pariante, 2008). These assessments can help identify dysregulation associated with stress-related disorders and inform treatment strategies.

As research in this field progresses, ongoing efforts aim to elucidate further the complex interplay between the HPA axis, neurotransmitter systems, and anxiety disorders. Advances in neuroimaging techniques and molecular biology may provide valuable insights into the neurobiological mechanisms underlying these conditions (Juruena et al., 2020). Additionally, the development of personalized treatment approaches based on individual differences in HPA axis functioning and genetic factors could lead to more targeted and effective interventions for anxiety disorders (Ising & Holsboer, 2006). These advancements hold promise for improving the lives of those affected by stress and anxiety disorders.

In modern society, stress and anxiety have emerged as significant public health concerns, with far-reaching impacts on individuals' mental and physical well-being. Understanding the neurobiological mechanisms underlying these conditions, particularly the role of the HPA axis and stress hormones, is crucial for developing effective prevention and treatment strategies. While significant progress has been made, addressing stress and anxiety requires a multifaceted approach that combines pharmacological interventions, psychotherapeutic techniques, and lifestyle modifications. By prioritizing mental health research and implementing evidence-based interventions, we can work towards reducing the burden of anxiety disorders and promoting a more resilient and mentally healthy society. Ultimately, this endeavor not only benefits individuals but also contributes to the overall well-being of communities and societies as a whole.

References

1. World Health Organization. (n.d.). *Covid-19 pandemic triggers 25% increase in prevalence of anxiety and depression worldwide*. World Health Organization. https://www.who.int/news/item/02-03-2022-covid-19-pandemic-triggers-25-increase-in-prevalence-of-anxiety-and-depression-worldwide

2. World Health Organization. (n.d.-b). *Stress*. World Health Organization. https://www.who.int/news-room/questions-and-answers/item/stress
3. Slimmen, S., Timmermans, O., Mikolajczak-Degrauwe, K., & Oenema, A. (2022, November 7). *How stress-related factors affect mental wellbeing of university students a cross-sectional study to explore the associations between stressors, perceived stress, and mental wellbeing.* PloS one. https://www.ncbi.nlm.nih.gov/pmc/articles/PMC9639818/
4. GP;, T. C. (n.d.). *Hypothalamic-pituitary-adrenal axis, neuroendocrine factors and stress*. Journal of psychosomatic research. https://pubmed.ncbi.nlm.nih.gov/12377295/
5. Herman, J. P., McKlveen, J. M., Ghosal, S., Kopp, B., Wulsin, A., Makinson, R., Scheimann, J., & Myers, B. (2016, March 15). *Regulation of the hypothalamic-pituitary-adrenocortical stress response.* Comprehensive Physiology. https://www.ncbi.nlm.nih.gov/pmc/articles/PMC4867107/
6. GP;, C. (n.d.). *Stress and disorders of the stress system*. Nature reviews. Endocrinology. https://pubmed.ncbi.nlm.nih.gov/19488073/
7. AH;, J. M. F. A. (n.d.). *The role of early life stress in Hpa Axis and anxiety*. Advances in experimental medicine and biology. https://pubmed.ncbi.nlm.nih.gov/32002927/
8. U.S. Department of Health and Human Services. (n.d.). *Any anxiety disorder*. National Institute of Mental Health. https://www.nimh.nih.gov/health/statistics/any-anxiety-disorder
9. S;, B. B. (n.d.). *Epidemiology of Anxiety Disorders in the 21st Century*. Dialogues in clinical neuroscience. https://pubmed.ncbi.nlm.nih.gov/26487813/
10. Hofmann, S. G., & Hinton, D. E. (2014, June). *Cross-cultural aspects of anxiety disorders*. Current psychiatry reports. https://www.ncbi.nlm.nih.gov/pmc/articles/PMC4037698/
11. Baldwin DS;Anderson IM;Nutt DJ;Allgulander C;Bandelow B;den Boer JA;Christmas DM;Davies S;Fineberg N;Lidbetter N;Malizia A;McCrone P;Nabarro D;O'Neill C;Scott J;van der Wee N;Wittchen HU; (n.d.-b). *Evidence-based pharmacological treatment of anxiety disorders,*
12. *post-traumatic stress disorder and obsessive-compulsive disorder: A revision of the 2005 guidelines from the British Association for Psychopharmacology.* Journal of psychopharmacology (Oxford, England). https://pubmed.ncbi.nlm.nih.gov/24713617.
13. JA;, H. S. (n.d.). *Cognitive-behavioral therapy for adult anxiety disorders: A meta-analysis of randomized placebo-controlled trials.* The Journal of clinical psychiatry. https://pubmed.ncbi.nlm.nih.gov/18363421/
14. Khoury B;Lecomte T;Fortin G;Masse M;Therien P;Bouchard V;Chapleau MA;Paquin K;Hofmann SG; (n.d.). *Mindfulness-based therapy: A comprehensive meta-analysis*. Clinical psychology review. https://pubmed.ncbi.nlm.nih.gov/23796855/
15. CM;, C. L. (n.d.). *In vitro modulation of the glucocorticoid receptor by antidepressants*. Stress (Amsterdam, Netherlands). https://pubmed.ncbi.nlm.nih.gov/19065455/
16. F;, I. M. (n.d.). *Genetics of stress response and stress-related disorders*. Dialogues in clinical neuroscience. https://pubmed.ncbi.nlm.nih.gov/17290801/

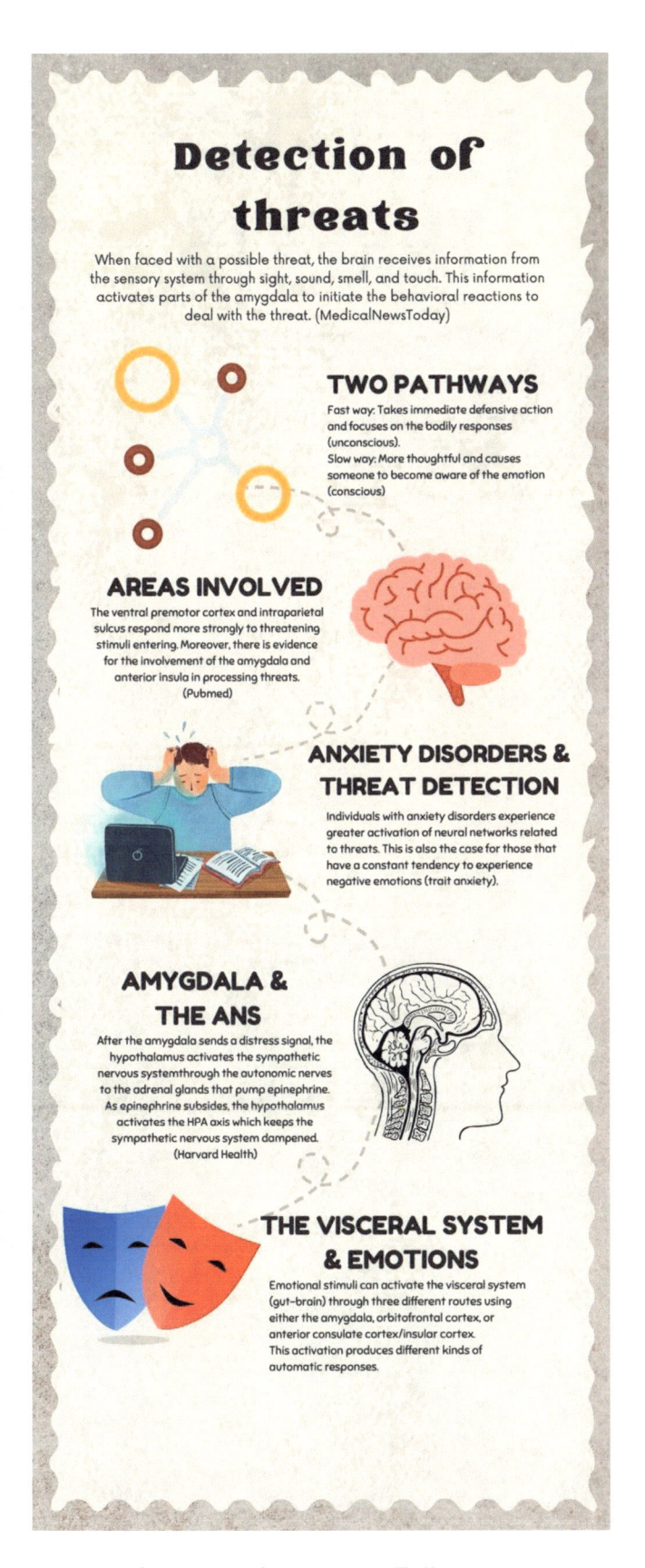

Detection of threats

When faced with a possible threat, the brain receives information from the sensory system through sight, sound, smell, and touch. This information activates parts of the amygdala to initiate the behavioral reactions to deal with the threat. (MedicalNewsToday)

TWO PATHWAYS
Fast way: Takes immediate defensive action and focuses on the bodily responses (unconscious).
Slow way: More thoughtful and causes someone to become aware of the emotion (conscious)

AREAS INVOLVED
The ventral premotor cortex and intraparietal sulcus respond more strongly to threatening stimuli entering. Moreover, there is evidence for the involvement of the amygdala and anterior insula in processing threats.
(Pubmed)

ANXIETY DISORDERS & THREAT DETECTION
Individuals with anxiety disorders experience greater activation of neural networks related to threats. This is also the case for those that have a constant tendency to experience negative emotions (trait anxiety).

AMYGDALA & THE ANS
After the amygdala sends a distress signal, the hypothalamus activates the sympathetic nervous system through the autonomic nerves to the adrenal glands that pump epinephrine. As epinephrine subsides, the hypothalamus activates the HPA axis which keeps the sympathetic nervous system dampened.
(Harvard Health)

THE VISCERAL SYSTEM & EMOTIONS
Emotional stimuli can activate the visceral system (gut-brain) through three different routes using either the amygdala, orbitofrontal cortex, or anterior consulate cortex/insular cortex. This activation produces different kinds of automatic responses.

Samiksha Sivakumar, Fall 2023

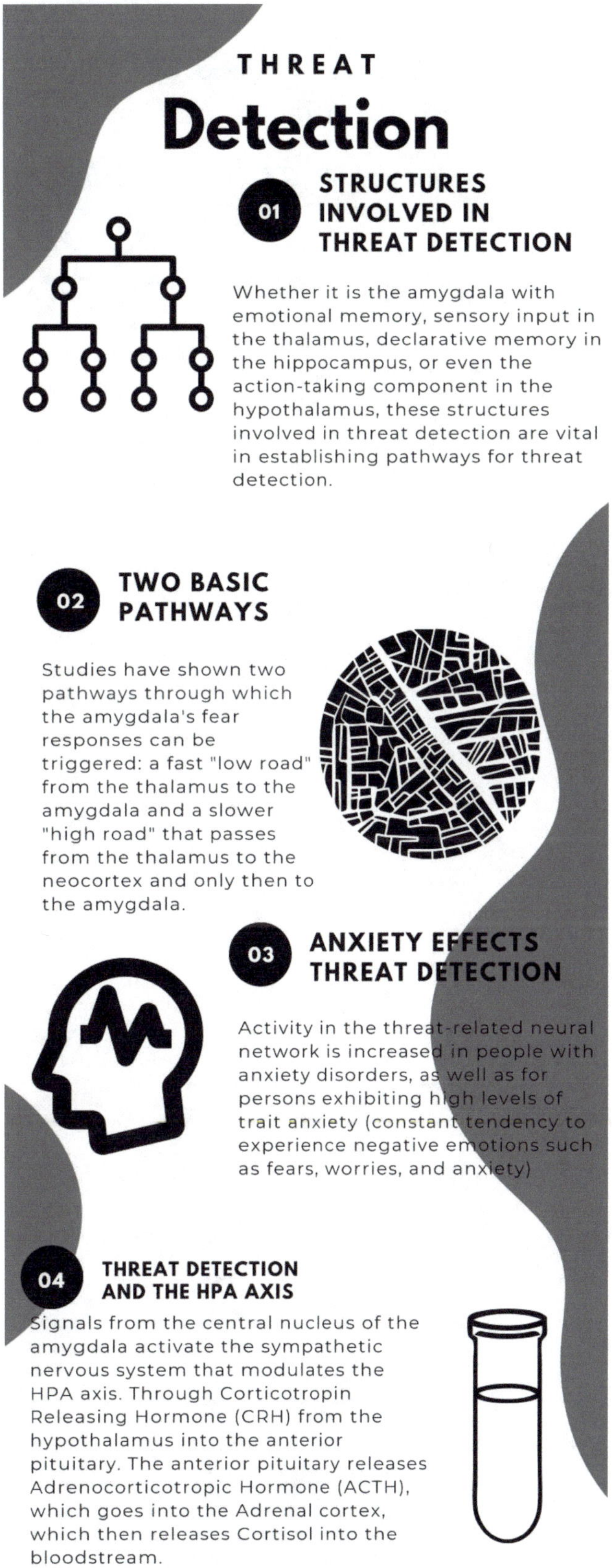

THREAT Detection

01 STRUCTURES INVOLVED IN THREAT DETECTION
Whether it is the amygdala with emotional memory, sensory input in the thalamus, declarative memory in the hippocampus, or even the action-taking component in the hypothalamus, these structures involved in threat detection are vital in establishing pathways for threat detection.

02 TWO BASIC PATHWAYS
Studies have shown two pathways through which the amygdala's fear responses can be triggered: a fast "low road" from the thalamus to the amygdala and a slower "high road" that passes from the thalamus to the neocortex and only then to the amygdala.

03 ANXIETY EFFECTS THREAT DETECTION
Activity in the threat-related neural network is increased in people with anxiety disorders, as well as for persons exhibiting high levels of trait anxiety (constant tendency to experience negative emotions such as fears, worries, and anxiety)

04 THREAT DETECTION AND THE HPA AXIS
Signals from the central nucleus of the amygdala activate the sympathetic nervous system that modulates the HPA axis. Through Corticotropin Releasing Hormone (CRH) from the hypothalamus into the anterior pituitary. The anterior pituitary releases Adrenocorticotropic Hormone (ACTH), which goes into the Adrenal cortex, which then releases Cortisol into the bloodstream.

Nicolas Gambardella, Spring 2023

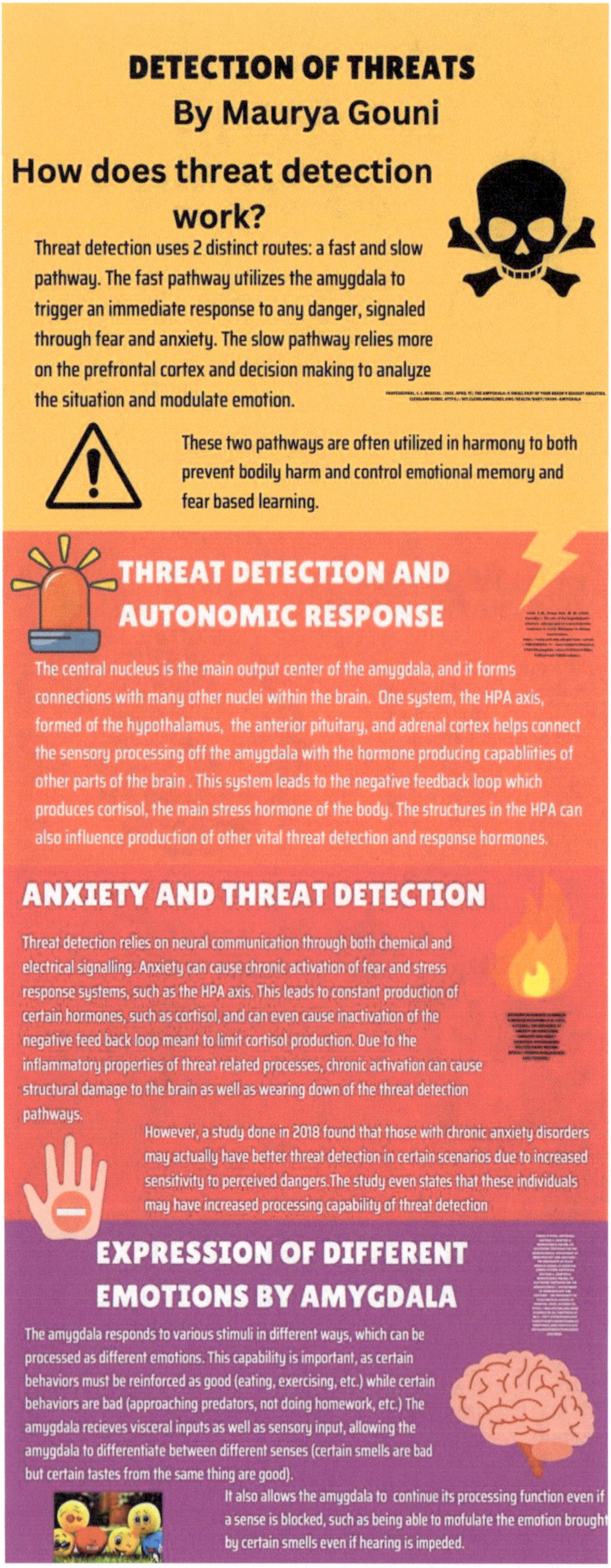

AN INFOGRAPHIC JOURNEY

DETECTION OF THREATS
By Maurya Gouni

How does threat detection work?

Threat detection uses 2 distinct routes: a fast and slow pathway. The fast pathway utilizes the amygdala to trigger an immediate response to any danger, signaled through fear and anxiety. The slow pathway relies more on the prefrontal cortex and decision making to analyze the situation and modulate emotion.

These two pathways are often utilized in harmony to both prevent bodily harm and control emotional memory and fear based learning.

THREAT DETECTION AND AUTONOMIC RESPONSE

The central nucleus is the main output center of the amygdala, and it forms connections with many other nuclei within the brain. One system, the HPA axis, formed of the hypothalamus, the anterior pituitary, and adrenal cortex helps connect the sensory processing off the amygdala with the hormone producing capabilities of other parts of the brain. This system leads to the negative feedback loop which produces cortisol, the main stress hormone of the body. The structures in the HPA can also influence production of other vital threat detection and response hormones.

ANXIETY AND THREAT DETECTION

Threat detection relies on neural communication through both chemical and electrical signalling. Anxiety can cause chronic activation of fear and stress response systems, such as the HPA axis. This leads to constant production of certain hormones, such as cortisol, and can even cause inactivation of the negative feed back loop meant to limit cortisol production. Due to the inflammatory properties of threat related processes, chronic activation can cause structural damage to the brain as well as wearing down of the threat detection pathways.

However, a study done in 2018 found that those with chronic anxiety disorders may actually have better threat detection in certain scenarios due to increased sensitivity to perceived dangers. The study even states that these individuals may have increased processing capability of threat detection.

EXPRESSION OF DIFFERENT EMOTIONS BY AMYGDALA

The amygdala responds to various stimuli in different ways, which can be processed as different emotions. This capability is important, as certain behaviors must be reinforced as good (eating, exercising, etc.) while certain behaviors are bad (approaching predators, not doing homework, etc.) The amygdala recieves visceral inputs as well as sensory input, allowing the amygdala to differentiate between different senses (certain smells are bad but certain tastes from the same thing are good).

It also allows the amygdala to continue its processing function even if a sense is blocked, such as being able to mofulate the emotion brought by certain smells even if hearing is impeded.

Maurya Gouni, Fall 2023

FEAR FROM THREATS

A threat is an external stimulus that triggers fear and anxiety responses in the brain.

1. Neural Pathways of Threat Responses
- The amygdala, thalamus, and sensory cortices are neural pathways that activate fear responses in reaction to threats.

2. Threat Awareness
- The amygdala, particularly the lateral nucleus, plays a crucial role in recognizing threats and initiating fear responses.

3. Phasic vs. Sustained Fear
- Limited research on specific phobias indicates unique neural networks and heightened neural activity for phasic and sustained fear.

4. History of Amygdala Research
- Early research, such as Klüver and Bucy's 1939 monkey study, linked amygdala damage to fearlessness, enhanced resilience, and altered limbic pathways.

References
Møller, A. R. (2019). *Neurobiology of Fear, Anxiety and other Emotions.*

Natalie Laguer Torres, Fall 2023

AN INFOGRAPHIC JOURNEY

Distinguishing between Threats *vs* Non-Threats

Pathways for Reaction to Stimulus
Our unconscious mechanism to deal with threats involved 2 pathways: defensive response (fast) & consciousness response (slow)

Important Brain Regions
Our brain separates stimulus into threat & safety. A threatful stimulus evokes a response in our amygdala causing inflammation. Safety responses evoke our autonomic nervous system.

HPA Axis System
The central nucleus of the amygdala stimulates the sympathetic nervous system in part of the HPA Axis. The output stimulates fear and reward circuitries.

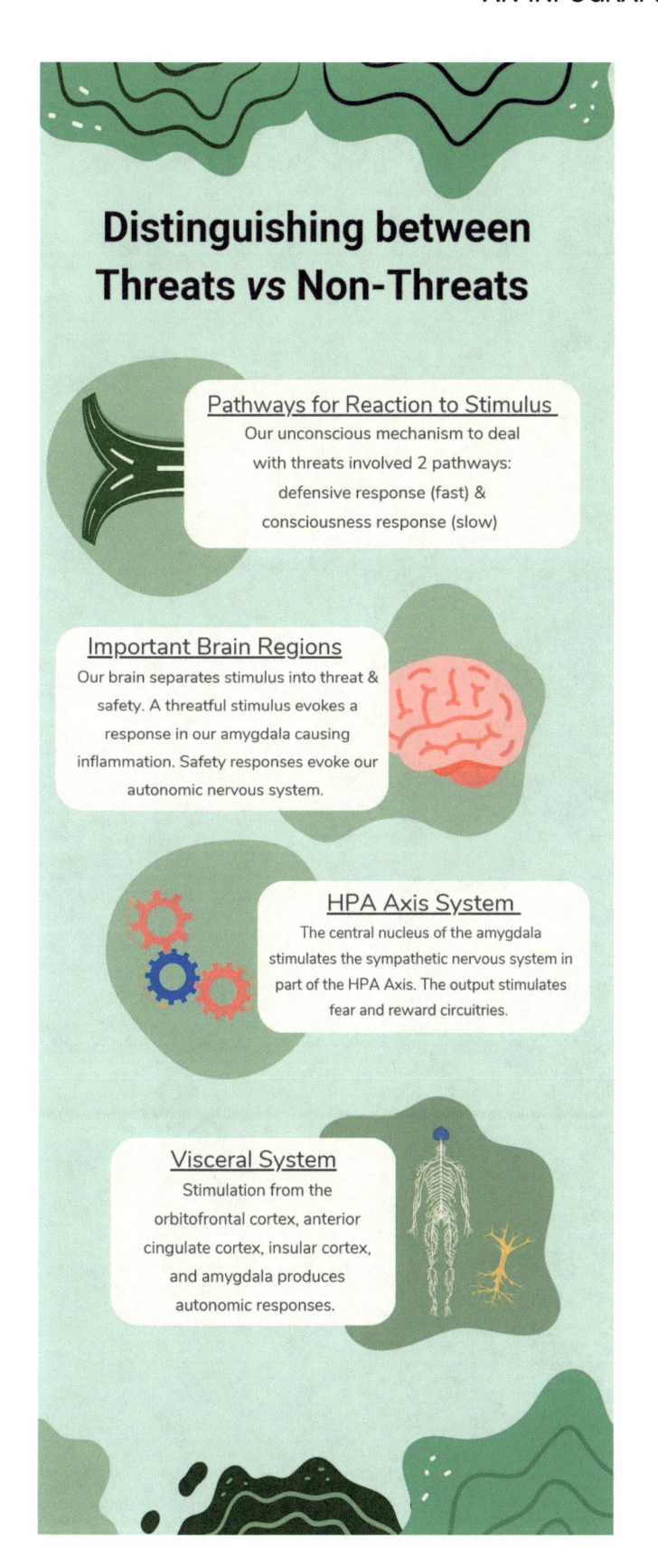

Visceral System
Stimulation from the orbitofrontal cortex, anterior cingulate cortex, insular cortex, and amygdala produces autonomic responses.

Dhruv Patel, Spring 2023

THREAT DETECTION AND ANXIETY

GAD AND THREAT SENSITIVITY
Anxiety disorders often mean an enhancement of threat-related information processing in the brain. This may lead to exaggerated threat sensitivity in the long run.

THREAT PROCESSING IN ANXIOUS VS NON-ANXIOUS INDIVIDUALS

1 Anxious individuals detect threatening stimuli more quickly than non-anxious individuals

2 Anxious individuals are more likely to regard both ambiguous and threatening stimuli as more threatening than they actually are

3 Anxious individuals engage in avoidance behaviors in response to perceived threats.

CORRELATION BETWEEN SEVERITY OF ANXIETY DIOSRDER AND THREAT REACTIVITY

STUDY DETAILS
A study by Armony et al measured threat reactivity by presenting normal and PTSD diagnosed individuals with masked fearful and happy faces and measuring amygdala activation

RESULTS
The difference in responses to masked fearful and happy faces was significantly correlated with the severity of PTSD

MAIN TAKEAWAY
Threat detection and reactivity is positively correlated with the severity of anxiety symptoms

10.1016/j.neubiorev.2012.10.013
By: Neha Bhupathiraju

Neha Bhupathiraju, Spring 2023

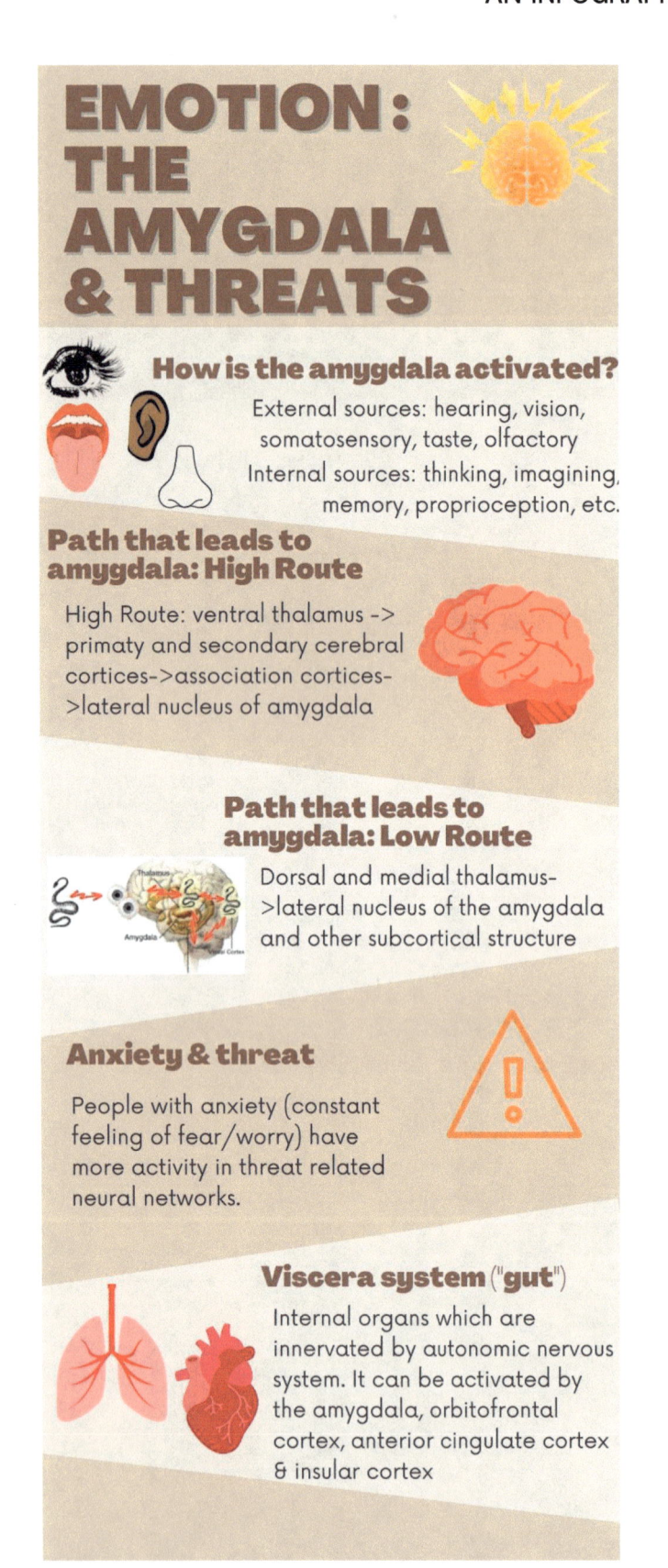

EMOTION: THE AMYGDALA & THREATS

How is the amygdala activated?
External sources: hearing, vision, somatosensory, taste, olfactory
Internal sources: thinking, imagining, memory, proprioception, etc.

Path that leads to amygdala: High Route
High Route: ventral thalamus -> primaty and secondary cerebral cortices -> association cortices -> lateral nucleus of amygdala

Path that leads to amygdala: Low Route
Dorsal and medial thalamus -> lateral nucleus of the amygdala and other subcortical structure

Anxiety & threat
People with anxiety (constant feeling of fear/worry) have more activity in threat related neural networks.

Viscera system ("gut")
Internal organs which are innervated by autonomic nervous system. It can be activated by the amygdala, orbitofrontal cortex, anterior cingulate cortex & insular cortex

Lilly Neguse, Spring 2023

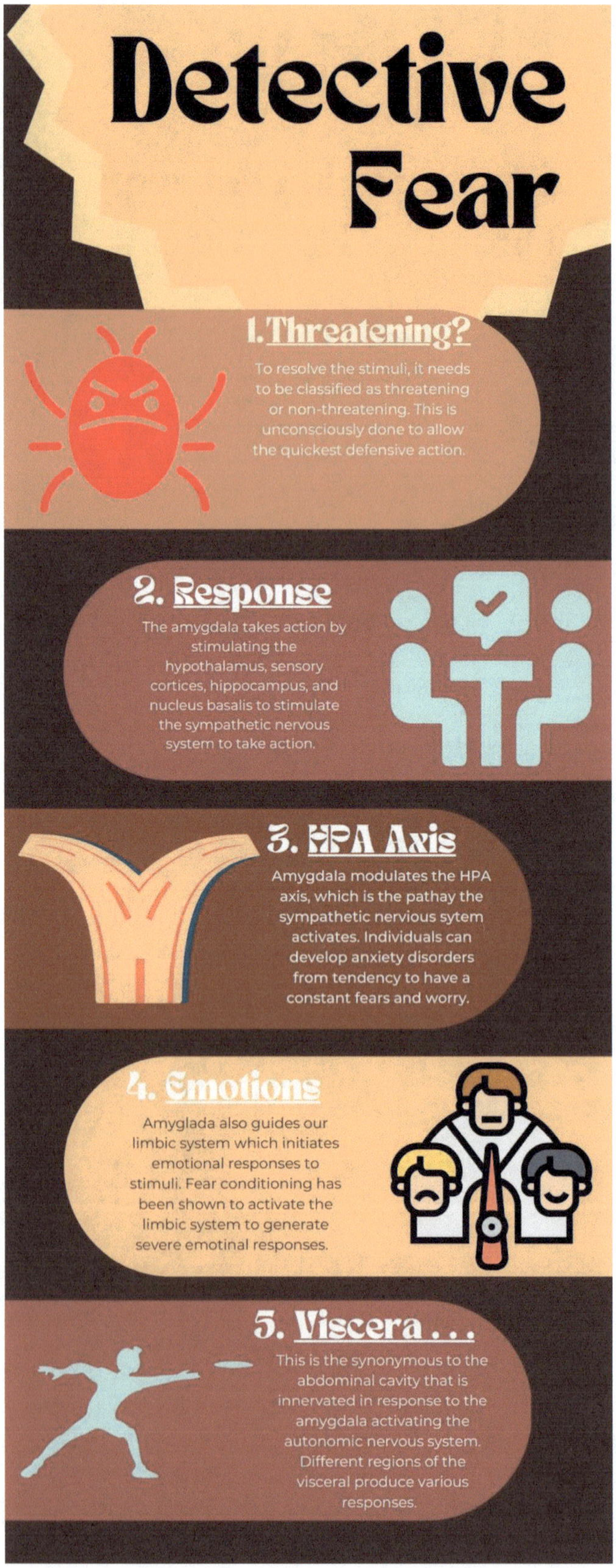

Detective Fear

1. Threatening?
To resolve the stimuli, it needs to be classified as threatening or non-threatening. This is unconsciously done to allow the quickest defensive action.

2. Response
The amygdala takes action by stimulating the hypothalamus, sensory cortices, hippocampus, and nucleus basalis to stimulate the sympathetic nervous system to take action.

3. HPA Axis
Amygdala modulates the HPA axis, which is the pathay the sympathetic nervous sytem activates. Individuals can develop anxiety disorders from tendency to have a constant fears and worry.

4. Emotions
Amyglada also guides our limbic system which initiates emotional responses to stimuli. Fear conditioning has been shown to activate the limbic system to generate severe emotinal responses.

5. Viscera...
This is the synonymous to the abdominal cavity that is innervated in response to the amygdala activating the autonomic nervous system. Different regions of the visceral produce various responses.

Dhruv Patel, Spring 2023

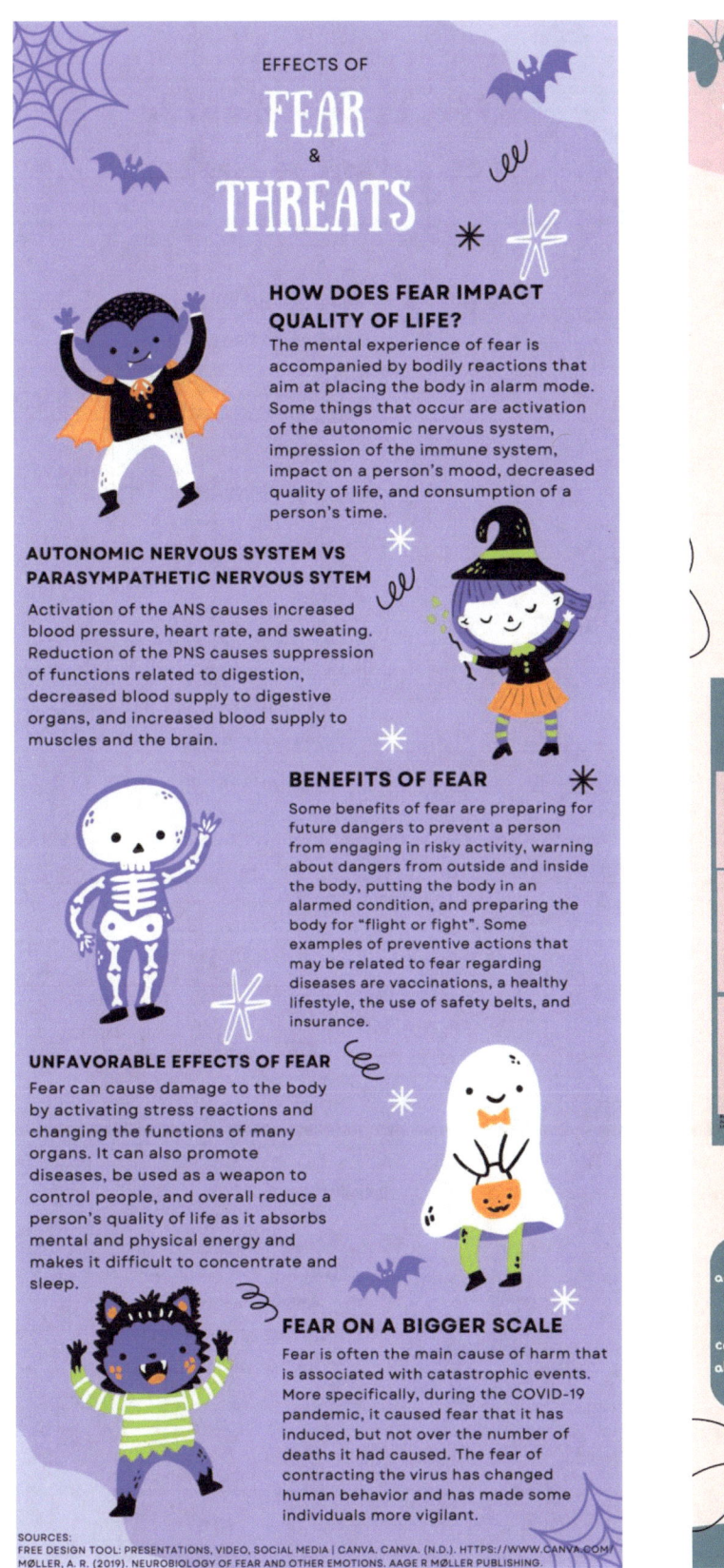

AN INFOGRAPHIC JOURNEY

EFFECTS OF FEAR & THREATS

HOW DOES FEAR IMPACT QUALITY OF LIFE?
The mental experience of fear is accompanied by bodily reactions that aim at placing the body in alarm mode. Some things that occur are activation of the autonomic nervous system, impression of the immune system, impact on a person's mood, decreased quality of life, and consumption of a person's time.

AUTONOMIC NERVOUS SYSTEM VS PARASYMPATHETIC NERVOUS SYTEM
Activation of the ANS causes increased blood pressure, heart rate, and sweating. Reduction of the PNS causes suppression of functions related to digestion, decreased blood supply to digestive organs, and increased blood supply to muscles and the brain.

BENEFITS OF FEAR
Some benefits of fear are preparing for future dangers to prevent a person from engaging in risky activity, warning about dangers from outside and inside the body, putting the body in an alarmed condition, and preparing the body for "flight or fight". Some examples of preventive actions that may be related to fear regarding diseases are vaccinations, a healthy lifestyle, the use of safety belts, and insurance.

UNFAVORABLE EFFECTS OF FEAR
Fear can cause damage to the body by activating stress reactions and changing the functions of many organs. It can also promote diseases, be used as a weapon to control people, and overall reduce a person's quality of life as it absorbs mental and physical energy and makes it difficult to concentrate and sleep.

FEAR ON A BIGGER SCALE
Fear is often the main cause of harm that is associated with catastrophic events. More specifically, during the COVID-19 pandemic, it caused fear that it has induced, but not over the number of deaths it had caused. The fear of contracting the virus has changed human behavior and has made some individuals more vigilant.

SOURCES:
FREE DESIGN TOOL: PRESENTATIONS, VIDEO, SOCIAL MEDIA | CANVA. CANVA. (N.D.). HTTPS://WWW.CANVA.COM/
MØLLER, A. R. (2019). NEUROBIOLOGY OF FEAR AND OTHER EMOTIONS. AAGE R MØLLER PUBLISHING.

Tiffany Nouanesengsy, Fall 2023

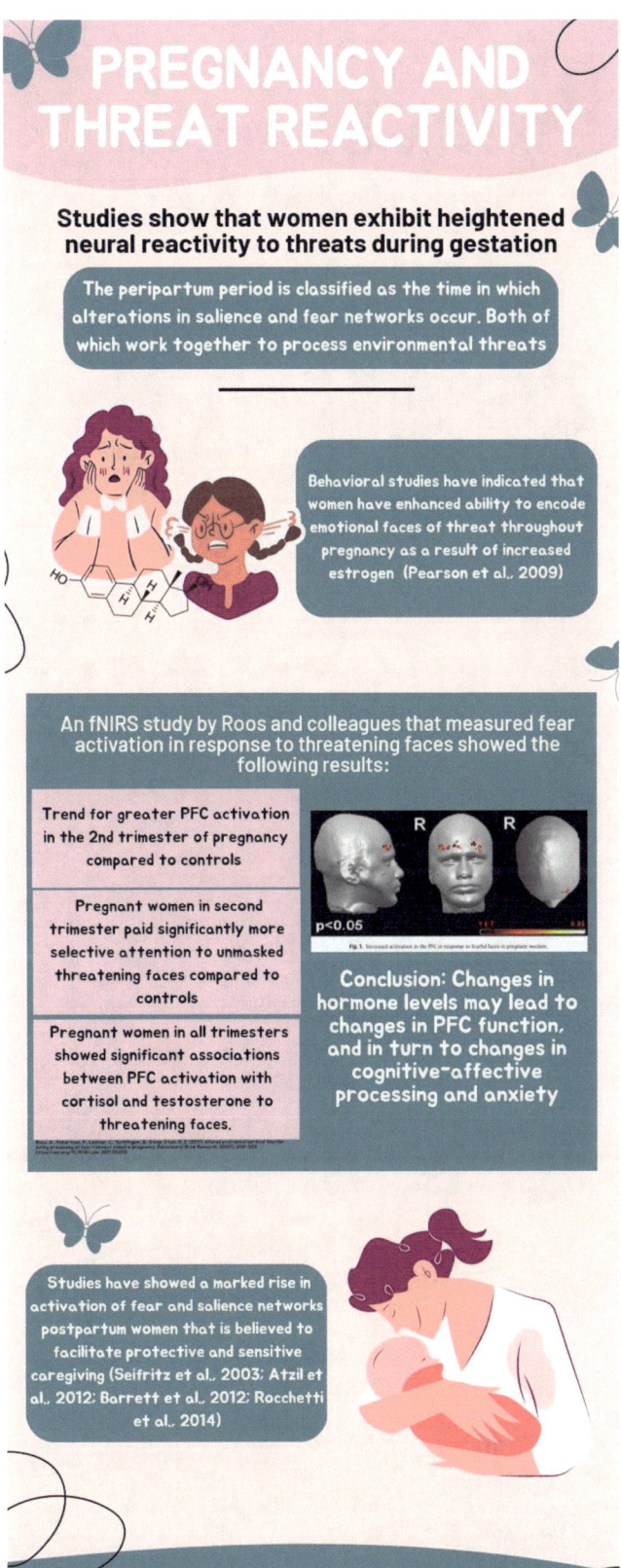

PREGNANCY AND THREAT REACTIVITY

Studies show that women exhibit heightened neural reactivity to threats during gestation

The peripartum period is classified as the time in which alterations in salience and fear networks occur. Both of which work together to process environmental threats

Behavioral studies have indicated that women have enhanced ability to encode emotional faces of threat throughout pregnancy as a result of increased estrogen (Pearson et al., 2009)

An fNIRS study by Roos and colleagues that measured fear activation in response to threatening faces showed the following results:

- Trend for greater PFC activation in the 2nd trimester of pregnancy compared to controls
- Pregnant women in second trimester paid significantly more selective attention to unmasked threatening faces compared to controls
- Pregnant women in all trimesters showed significant associations between PFC activation with cortisol and testosterone to threatening faces.

$p < 0.05$

Conclusion: Changes in hormone levels may lead to changes in PFC function, and in turn to changes in cognitive-affective processing and anxiety

Studies have showed a marked rise in activation of fear and salience networks postpartum women that is believed to facilitate protective and sensitive caregiving (Seifritz et al., 2003; Atzil et al., 2012; Barrett et al., 2012; Rocchetti et al., 2014)

By: Neha Bhupathiraju

Neha Bhupathiraju, Spring 2023

AN INFOGRAPHIC JOURNEY

The Effects of Repeated Activation of Stress

Three Effects in Sequence:
1. Alarm
2. Resistance
3. Exhaustion

Alarm!
The body will release stress hormones. However, if the source of the stressor is removed, there is no long-term damage.

Resistance
The body will attempt to return to its normal state. The immune system will be affected as an effect.

Exhaustion
Our ability to resist stress will be gone. Memory, emotional states, and our organs will become fatigued.

Machenzie Park, Fall 2022

Effects of Repeated Activation of Stress

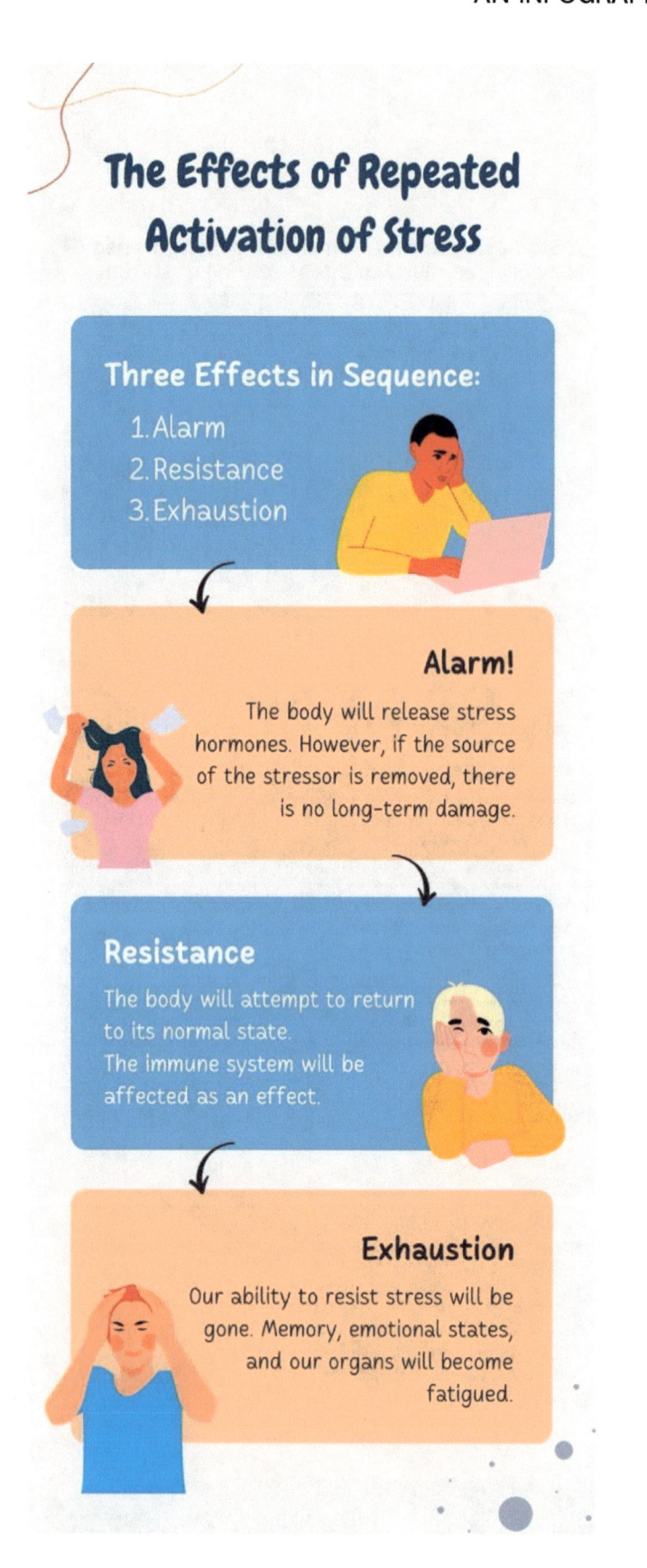

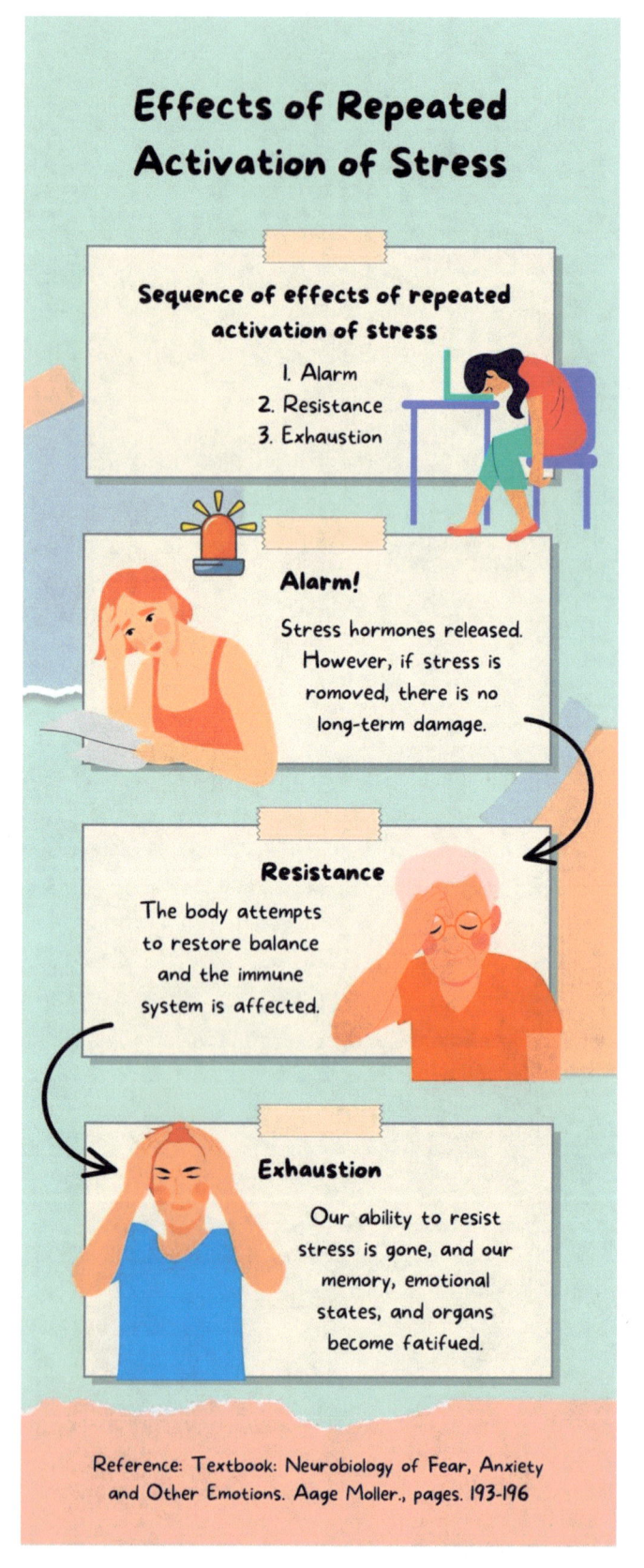

Sequence of effects of repeated activation of stress
1. Alarm
2. Resistance
3. Exhaustion

Alarm!
Stress hormones released. However, if stress is romoved, there is no long-term damage.

Resistance
The body attempts to restore balance and the immune system is affected.

Exhaustion
Our ability to resist stress is gone, and our memory, emotional states, and organs become fatifued.

Reference: Textbook: Neurobiology of Fear, Anxiety and Other Emotions. Aage Moller., pages. 193-196

Hyeonji Lee, Fall 2023

AN INFOGRAPHIC JOURNEY

STRESS AND DISEASES

1. Fear and anxiety are common causes of stress. Activation of stress is one of the risk factors for many diseases including the metabolic syndrome caused by insulin resistance.

2. Chronic stress can lead to the development of the metabolic syndrome and many other diseases. Activating the stress system affects the function of several organs including the immune system.

3. Acute stress may trigger neuropsychiatric manifestations such as anxiety, depression, executive and cognitive dysfunction, cognitive dysfunctions, panic attacks, psychotic episodes, and various body signs such as allergic reactions.

4. The sequence of effects of repeated activation of stress goes from Alarm, Stress hormones released to resistance, the body attempts to restore balance, to finally exhaustion, the ability to resist stress is gone.

5. Lasting effects of trauma on the brain, showing long-term dysregulation of norepinephrine and cortisol systems and vulnerable areas of the hippocampus, amygdala, and medial prefrontal cortex affect many organ systems of the body.

tabatha V. Nieves

Stress and Diseases

STRESS ARISES FROM FEAR

Activation of the stress response can be a risk factor for numerous illnesses, including diabetes related to obesity. Stress can also lead to low physical exercise and overeating which can also serve as a risk factor for cardiovascular diseases and ischemic strokes, etc.

Stress Triggers Neuropsychiatric Symptoms

Anxiety and depression can lead to cognitive dysfunction which can show many different bodily signs: migraines, pain, and GI syndromes

Seek Help Immidiately

It is always recommended to seek help if someone is going through fear and anxiety as it is very dangerous to our health and wellbeing

Tabatha Nieves, Spring 2023   Tamjeed Islam, Spring 2023

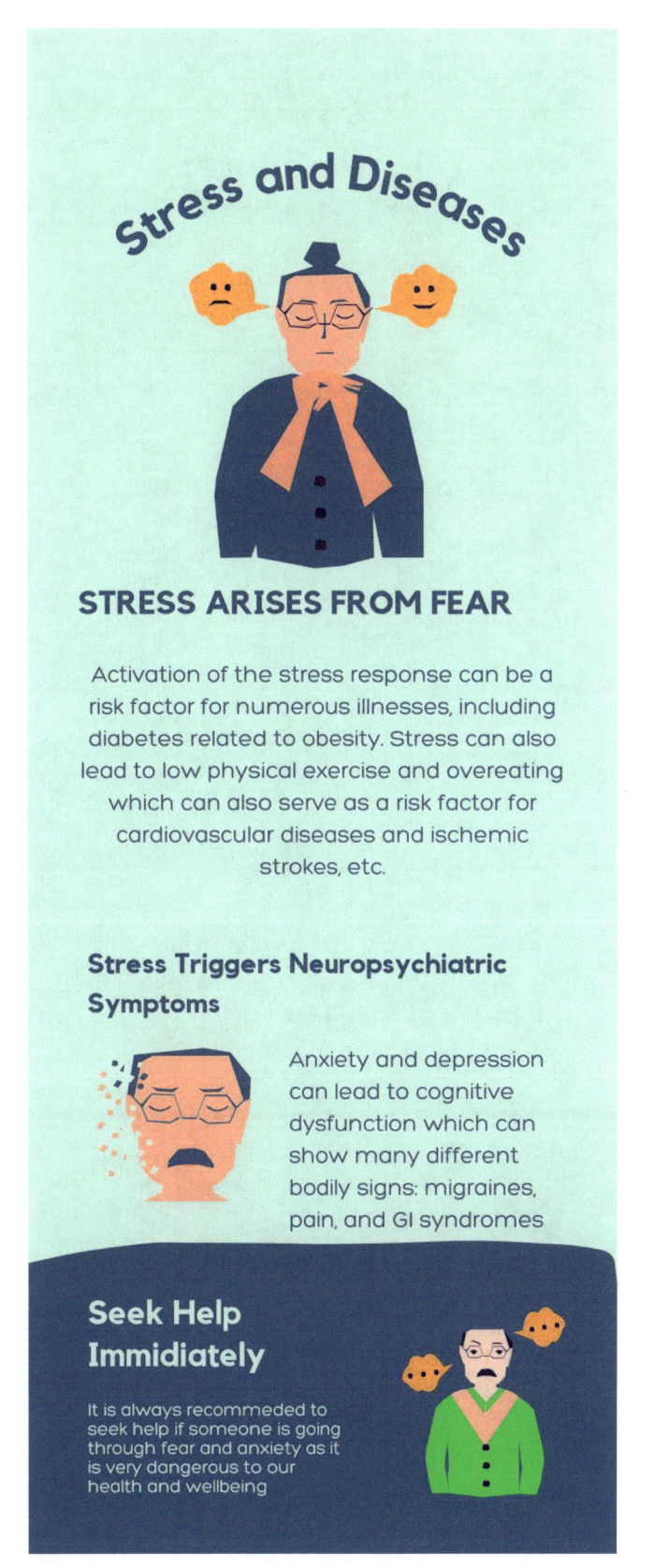

AN INFOGRAPHIC JOURNEY

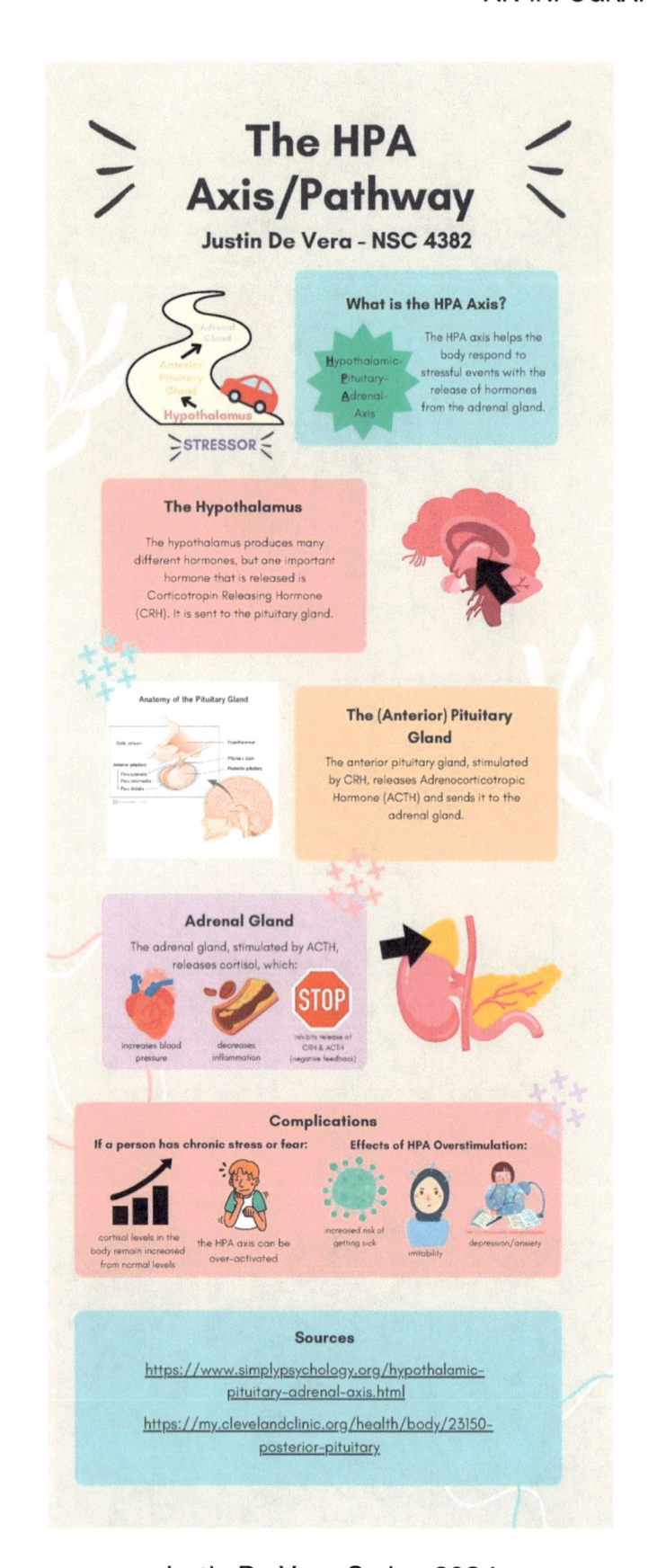

Justin De Vera, Spring 2024

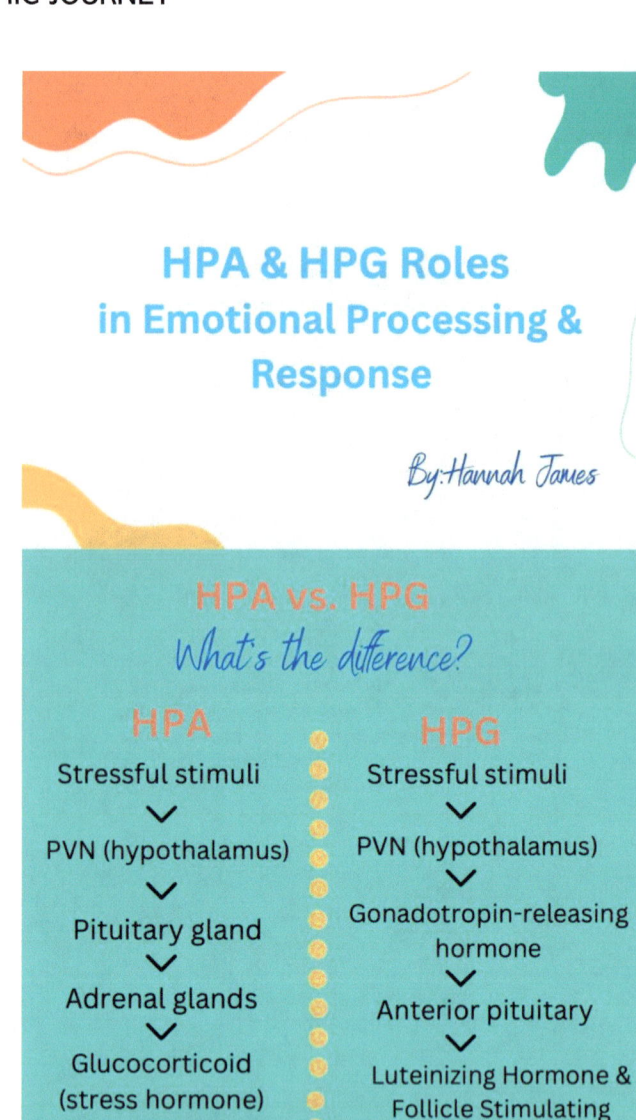

Hannah James, Fall 2023

HPA Axis

The Hpothalamic-pituitary-adrenal (HPA) axis is one of various systems involved in producing the stress response

The HPA axis is activated whenever we perceive a threat

Chronic activation of the HPA axis will increase inflammation

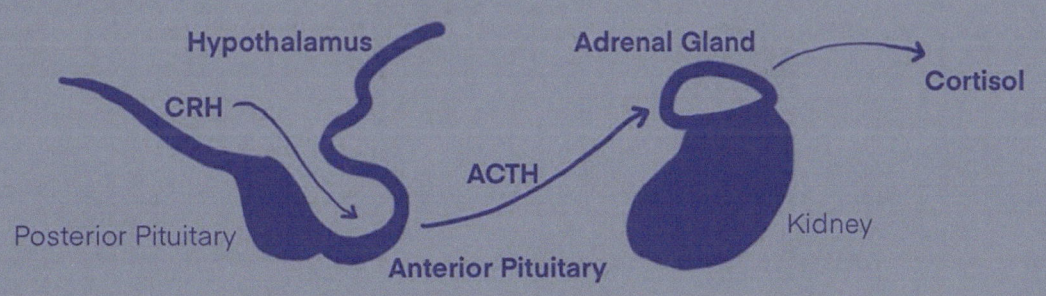

Hypothalamus — CRH — Posterior Pituitary — Anterior Pituitary — ACTH — Adrenal Gland — Cortisol — Kidney

The Hypothalamus releases Coticotropin-releasing hormone (CRH) which stimulates the posterior pituitary to produce and secrete Adrenocorticotropic hormone (ACTH) into the blood stream. ACTH will then act on the adrenal glands above the kidneys to release stress hormones.

Citation:
https://www.ncbi.nlm.nih.gov/pmc/articles/PMC3181830/

Kaden Kobernat, Fall 2023

AN INFOGRAPHIC JOURNEY

CHAPTER 13

Oxytocin and Other Molecules

Hormones Affecting Emotions

By Justin De Vera

Understanding the role of hormones in regulating our emotions is crucial, especially for women and menstruating women who undergo numerous challenges and changes to their bodies and their emotions. Whether these effects are positive or negative, this understanding can explain our behaviors and empower us to seek the proper tools or guidance to help us cope with the changes we are experiencing. It's not just about knowing what's happening in our bodies, but also about feeling in control of our emotional well-being.

Oxytocin is one hormone that has been cited to play an important role in the reproductive system and a role in affecting the body in many different emotional aspects. According to *Oxytocin: The love hormone* by Harvard Health Publishing (2023), it is one of the many hormones made in the hypothalamus, transferred to the posterior pituitary gland, and sent to appropriate parts of the body (para. 1). The hypothalamus is the origin of a wide variety of endocrine hormones controlling functions such as water retention, heart rate, and metabolism. Harvard Health Publishing (2023) also states that oxytocin is commonly known as the "love hormone" or the "cuddle hormone" (para. 3). Its production helps create and promote positive sexual behaviors between two partners. A process called social buffering is closely related to the production of oxytocin. According to a study called *Social Buffering: Relief from Stress and Anxiety* by Takefumi Kikisui, James Winslow, and Yuji Mori (2006), socially interacting with a partner can help reduce the impact of stress and the release of cortisol, a crucial stress hormone part of the hypothalamic-pituitary-adrenal (HPA) axis (Clinical Aspects para. 1). Even though some of the research in the study is focused on animals, these behaviors are also tested and applied with humans. Bodily responses to stress noticeably decrease due to the inhibition of the effects of cortisol. While it is common knowledge that social or romantic relationships can benefit us, many interesting hormonal effects can help us become healthier. According to *Neurobiology of Fear and Other Emotions* by Aage Møller (2019), oxytocin can help a person relax but make the amygdala less reactive to stressful social stimuli. This further highlights the effects of decreased cortisol, as shown through this anxiolytic effect (Chapter 3). In addition, the hormone can help pair bonding between a mother and baby. Pair bonding can be achieved through actions like breastfeeding, where milk from the mother is released from the nipple for the baby to drink.

Estradiol is a primary form of the hormone estrogen, which plays a crucial role as a female sex hormone. Like oxytocin, it is involved in the female reproductive system and the regulation of emotional states. According to the article "Estradiol" by Lana Hariri and Anis Rehman (2023), estradiol is essential for managing the menstrual cycle, maintaining the skeletal system, and regulating the vascular system (Indications para. 1). A deficiency of estrogen/estradiol in the body can lead to emotional discomfort and affect the systems mentioned above. Recent research studies suggest that estradiol is also implicated in the process of fear extinction. Specifically, the study "Estrogen and Extinction of Fear Memories: Implications for Posttraumatic Stress Disorder Treatment" by Ebony Glover, Tanja Jovanovic, and Seth Davin Norrholm (2015) cites other research indicating links between low levels of estradiol and impaired fear extinction (Role of sex hormones in conditioned fear extinction para. 3). This suggests that individuals with low levels of estradiol or estrogen might find it more challenging to eliminate fearful behaviors or to prevent their recurrence. These findings have contributed to the development of treatments for conditions such as anxiety disorders or post-traumatic stress disorder (PTSD). Managing fear extinction can be beneficial in reducing the strain on brain structures, particularly the amygdala, associated with fear and anxiety.

Vasopressin, also known as antidiuretic hormone, is another commonly known hormone that helps play a role in emotions. According to the *National Cancer Institute's* definition of the hormone, vasopressin/antidiuretic hormone is responsible for balancing the salt and water content of the body, which in turn affects urine content and blood pressure (p. 1). Since vasopressin influences blood pressure, one might assume that vasopressin is involved in fear circuits and the function of the amygdala. The study *Balance of Brain Oxytocin and vasopressin: Implications for anxiety, depression, and Social Behaviors* by Inga Neumann and Rainer Landgraf (2012) shows that vasopressin was associated with creating an anxiogenic or anxiety-inducing effect in the body, and overexposure to it early in life could create hyper anxiety (OXT and AVP: anxiety and social phobia para. 3). This is opposite to the effects of oxytocin, which creates a relaxing effect. According to *Aage Møller* (2019), vasopressin's functions are very similar to oxytocin, as they are both connected to brain regions that control social behaviors such as bonding and social buffering. They are also associated with the milk letdown reflex and vasoconstriction (Chapter 3). There could be many reasons as to how or why they have very similar functions. One could theorize that since they are both released by the posterior pituitary gland, they develop similar functions. In any case, understanding the complexities of these hormones and their overlaps can further elucidate emotional states.

The average person may not always consider the impact of hormones on their behavior, but hormones play a significant role in our daily lives. The amygdala, a key part of the brain responsible for emotions, is influenced by various body circuits and pathways, shaping our responses to both positive and stressful situations. Understanding the influence of hormones on human behavior could pave the way for innovative treatments for emotional disorders. For instance, further exploration of how hormones interact with the amygdala could reveal new approaches to treating conditions such as depression and anxiety.

References

1. Glover, E. M., Jovanovic, T., & Norrholm, S. D. (2015). Estrogen and Extinction of Fear Memories: Implications for Posttraumatic Stress Disorder Treatment. *Biological Psychiatry (1969), 78*(3), 178–185. https://doi.org/10.1016/j.biopsych.2015.02.007

2. Hariri, L., & Rehman, A. (2023, June 28). Estradiol. StatPearls [Internet]. https://www.ncbi.nlm.nih.gov/books/NBK549797/#:~:text=Estradiol%20is%20a%20med ication%20used,%2C%20dysuria%2C%20and%20many%20more.

3. Kikusui, T., Winslow, J. T., & Mori, Y. (2006). Social buffering: relief from stress and anxiety. *Philosophical Transactions of the Royal Society of London. Series B. Biological Sciences, 361*(1476), 2215–2228. https://doi.org/10.1098/rstb.2006.1941

4. Møller, A. (2019). *Neurobiology of Fear, Anxiety and Other Emotions*. Aage R Møller Publishing.

5. *NCI Dictionary of Cancer terms- Antidiuretic hormone.* Comprehensive Cancer Information - NCI. https://www.cancer.gov/publications/dictionaries/cancer-terms/def/antidiuretic-hormone

6. Neumann, I. D., & Landgraf, R. (2012). Balance of brain oxytocin and vasopressin: implications for anxiety, depression, and social behaviors. *Trends in Neurosciences (Regular Ed.), 35*(11), 649–659. https://doi.org/10.1016/j.tins.2012.08.004

7. *Oxytocin: The love hormone.* Harvard Health. (2023, June 13). https://www.health.harvard.edu/mind-and-mood/oxytocin-the-love-hormone

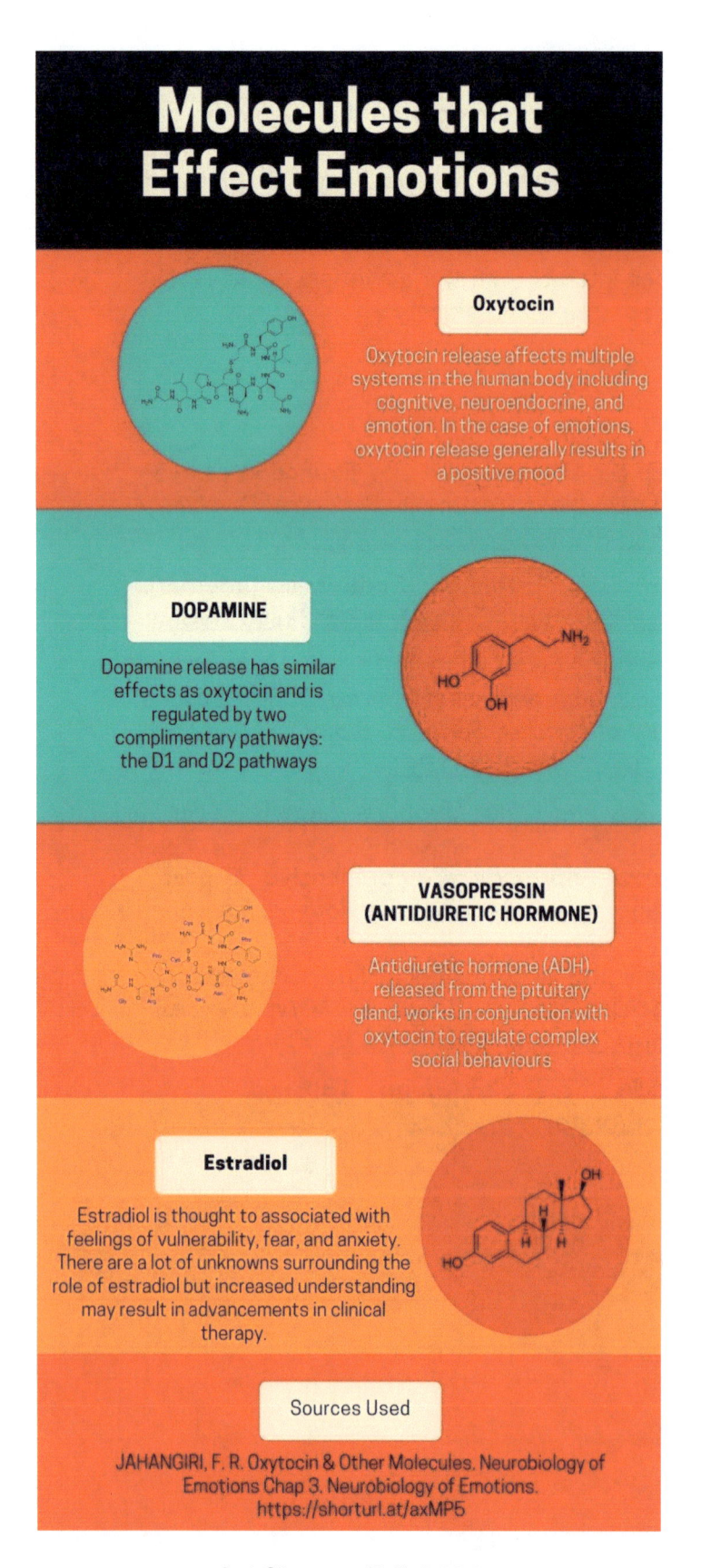

AN INFOGRAPHIC JOURNEY

Molecules that Effect Emotions

Oxytocin
Oxytocin release affects multiple systems in the human body including cognitive, neuroendocrine, and emotion. In the case of emotions, oxytocin release generally results in a positive mood

DOPAMINE
Dopamine release has similar effects as oxytocin and is regulated by two complimentary pathways: the D1 and D2 pathways

VASOPRESSIN (ANTIDIURETIC HORMONE)
Antidiuretic hormone (ADH), released from the pituitary gland, works in conjunction with oxytocin to regulate complex social behaviours

Estradiol
Estradiol is thought to associated with feelings of vulnerability, fear, and anxiety. There are a lot of unknowns surrounding the role of estradiol but increased understanding may result in advancements in clinical therapy.

Sources Used
JAHANGIRI, F. R. Oxytocin & Other Molecules. Neurobiology of Emotions Chap 3. Neurobiology of Emotions. https://shorturl.at/axMP5

Ani Sharma, Fall 2023

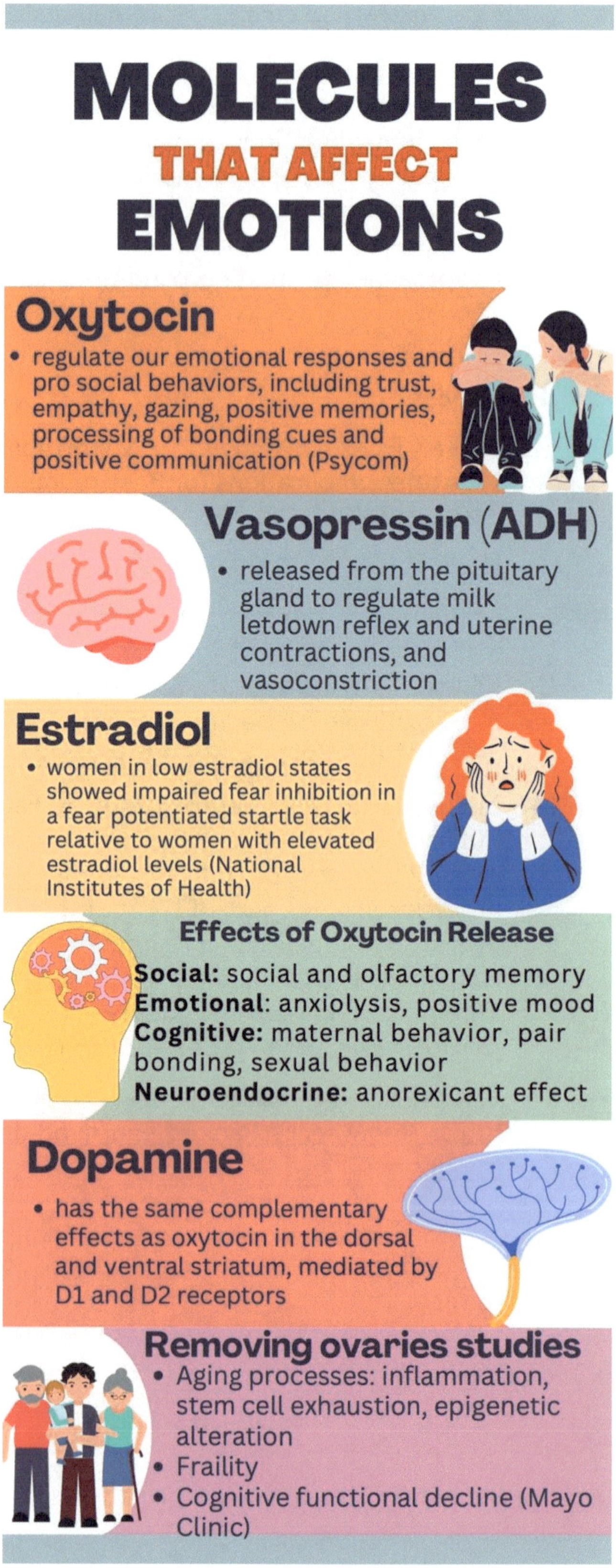

MOLECULES THAT AFFECT EMOTIONS

Oxytocin
- regulate our emotional responses and pro social behaviors, including trust, empathy, gazing, positive memories, processing of bonding cues and positive communication (Psycom)

Vasopressin (ADH)
- released from the pituitary gland to regulate milk letdown reflex and uterine contractions, and vasoconstriction

Estradiol
- women in low estradiol states showed impaired fear inhibition in a fear potentiated startle task relative to women with elevated estradiol levels (National Institutes of Health)

Effects of Oxytocin Release
Social: social and olfactory memory
Emotional: anxiolysis, positive mood
Cognitive: maternal behavior, pair bonding, sexual behavior
Neuroendocrine: anorexicant effect

Dopamine
- has the same complementary effects as oxytocin in the dorsal and ventral striatum, mediated by D1 and D2 receptors

Removing ovaries studies
- Aging processes: inflammation, stem cell exhaustion, epigenetic alteration
- Fraility
- Cognitive functional decline (Mayo Clinic)

Samiksha Sivakumar, Fall 2023

AN INFOGRAPHIC JOURNEY

MOLECULES that Affect Emotion

OXYTOCIN (OT)
Oxytocin reduces amygdala and HPA axis reactivity to social stressors. It is known as the "love hormone," since it is induced during social interaction to mediate anxiolytic and stress-protective effects.

OXYTOCIN STRUCTURE

DOPAMINE (DA)
Just as how OT may increase gain in the amygdala and decrease sensory precision in the hypothalamus, DA has complementary effects mediated by the D1 (go pathway) and D2 (no-go pathway) receptors.

DOPAMINE STRUCTURE

DEFICITS TO OT AND DA
According to Quattrocki (2014), deficits of oxytocin leads to a failure of interoceptive processing, while dopamine deficits hinder proprioceptive processing and the initiation of action (Parkinson's).

VASOPRESSIN (ADH)
OT and ADH are involved in the milk letdown reflex and uterine contractions in females, as well as vasoconstriction and water retention in males. It regulates complex social behaviors such as mating, bonding, and parenting.

VASOPRESSIN STRUCTURE

ESTRADIOL
There is a correlation between estradiol levels and vulnerability for fear and anxiety disorders. Since it is known to modulate fear extinction, further studies will investigate what pathways this modulation innervates.

ESTRADIOL STRUCTURE

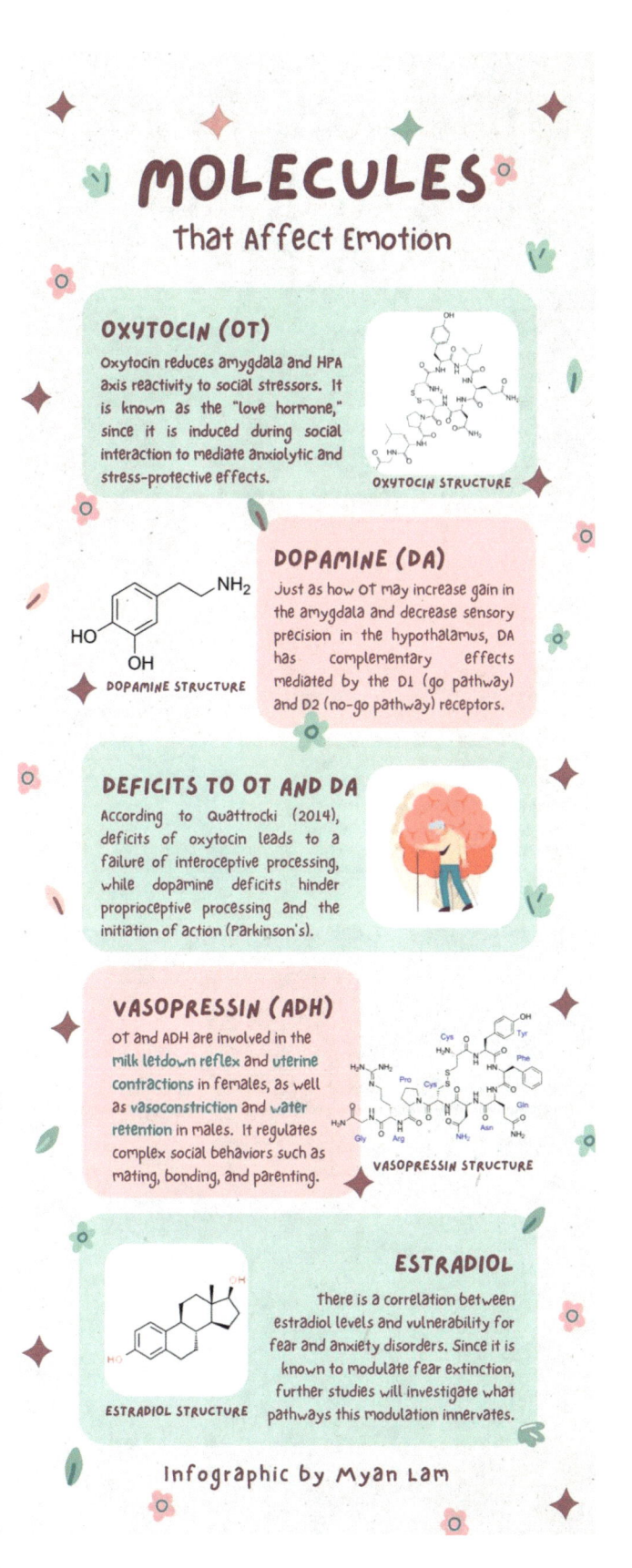

Infographic by Myan Lam

Myan Lam, Spring 2023

MODULATION OF EMOTIONS

THERE ARE MANY FACTORS THAT CAN MODULATE THE NEURAL RESPONSES TO EMOTIONS

EMOTIONS & THE IMMUNE SYSTEM
One's emotions have a direct impact on one's health. For example, stress can affect inflammatory processes and cancer. The list of diseases where the immune system plays an important, role continues to increase.

ROLE OF THE IMMUNE SYSTEM
The immune system impacts functions in the spinal cord, and the brain and the CNS affect the immune system. In terms of maladaptive neuroplasticity, it plays a role in severe tinnitus, spasticity, and chronic neuropathic pain.

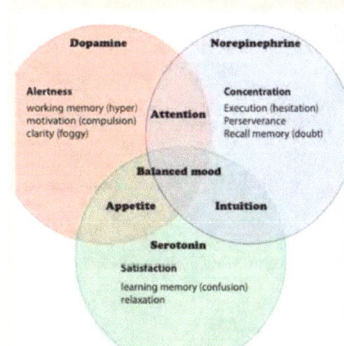

NEUROTRANSMITTERS INVOLVED IN EMOTIONS AND MOOD DISEASES
Many functions of dopamine, norepinephrine, and serotonin are directly and indirectly related to emotions and the diseases of mood.

PAIN CAN MODULATE EMOTIONS
Pain and emotion/cognition both influence one another as they can both be facilitating or suppressing. If one has a negative emotional state, it may lead to increased pain. and if one has a positive emotional state, it may decrease the pain. Cognitive states such as attention and memory also have a direct impact on pain.

SOURCES:
FREE DESIGN TOOL: PRESENTATIONS, VIDEO, SOCIAL MEDIA | CANVA. CANVA. (N.D.). HTTPS://WWW.CANVA.COM/ MØLLER, A. R. (2019). NEUROBIOLOGY OF FEAR AND OTHER EMOTIONS. AAGE R MØLLER PUBLISHING.

Tiffany Nouanesengsy, Fall 2023

AN INFOGRAPHIC JOURNEY

MOLECULES OF EMOTION
By Syed Naqvi

01 Oxytocin
Used in emotional, social, autoregulation, cognitive, and neuroendocrine regulation. important for feed forward interactions

02 Vasopressin
Also known as antidiuretic hormone. Used for vasoconstriction and controls many social behaviors.

03 Estradiol
Studies show that estradiol might be responsible for fear and anxiety disorders. possible future target for therapies

04 Epinephrine
Most know for the fight or flight response. Involved in many feed forward loops. Main goal to keep prevent harm and self preservation

05 Dopamine
Used in complex neuromodulatory signaling, has effects mediated by D1 and D2 receptors. Issues with dopamine may cause Parkinson's

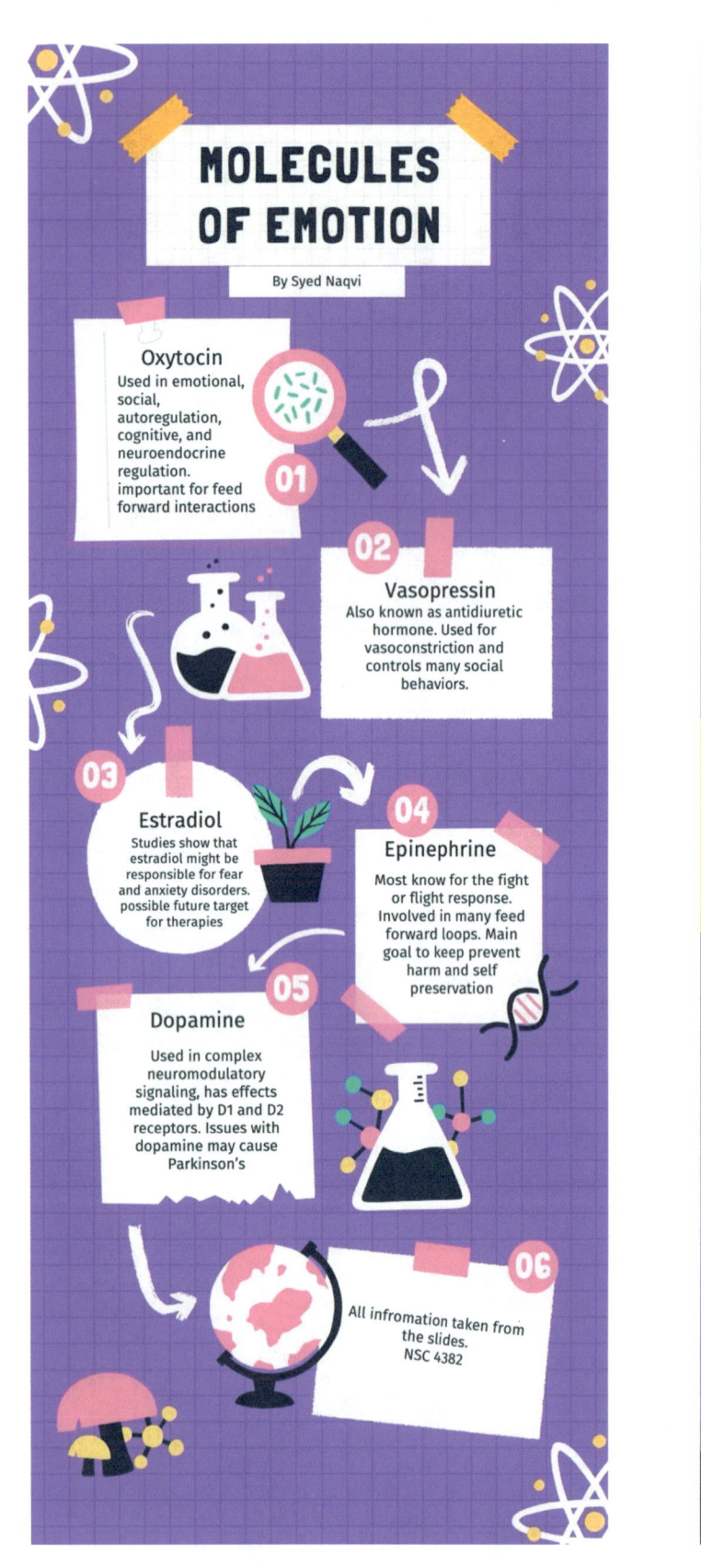

06
All infromation taken from the slides.
NSC 4382

Syed Naqvi, Fall 2023

HORMONAL IMPACT ON FEAR AND ANXIETY

Understanding how oxytocin reduces amygdala reactivity, influences social interactions, and shapes socio-sexual behavior is essential for managing fear and anxiety. Oxytocin and vasopressin impact fear regulation.

1 Oxytocin in Anxiety Reduction
- Oxytocin is an anxiolytic agent that reduces amygdala reactivity
- Positive social interactions trigger oxytocin release, offering stress protection through "social buffering," thereby reducing fear and anxiety

2 Oxytocin in Fear Reduction
- Oxytocin's anxiolytic effects extend to fear reduction, impacting the amygdala and hypothalamic regions
- Early postnatal experiences can influence oxytocin's effects on reducing anxiety and fear-related behaviors, contributing to emotional well-being

3 Oxytocin and Learning for Fear Management
- Oxytocin's influence on sensory attenuation and emotional awareness contributes to effective fear management
- Oxytocin also mediates successful reproduction and affects various brain regions, which can play a role in mitigating fear and anxiety

4 Oxytocin vs. Vasopressin in Fear Regulation
- Oxytocin and vasopressin share functions in peripheral regulation and complex social behaviors, including fear responses
- They differ in their specific roles related to fear and anxiety, contributing to a nuanced understanding of hormonal influence

Reference
Møller, A. R. (2019). *Neurobiology of Fear, Anxiety and other Emotions.*

Natalie Laguer Torres, Fall 2023

THE ROLE OF OXYTOCIN

OXYTOCIN AND DOPAMINE:
- Oxytocin can cause augmentation in the gain of the amygdala and decrease sensory precision
- Dopamine has the same complementary effects mediated by the **D1 (go pathway)** and **D2 (no-go pathway)** receptors
  - in both, context sensitive neuromodulatory signaling is sent by **descending projections** from cortical regions in emotion regulation (**oxytocin**) or action selection (**dopamine**)

DEFICITS OF OXYTOCIN:
- Deficient OXT: failure of **interoceptive processing**
- Deficient DA: compromise **proprioceptive processing** and **initiation of action**

OXYTOCIN AND ADH
- Vasopressin (ADH) and oxytocin are released from **pituitary gland** into circulation for regulation of peripheral functions
  - ex. milk let down reflex, uterine contractions, **vasoconstriction** and **water retention**
- OXT and ADH released throughout brain to regulate **important social behaviors**
  - social recognition, mating, bonding, parenting, etc.

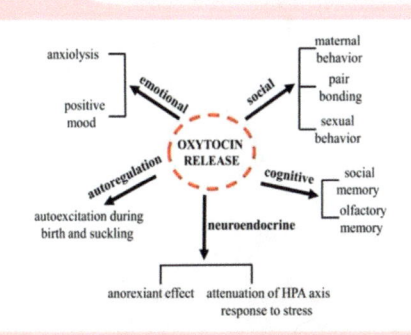

SOME EFFECTS OF OXYTOCIN RELEASE

Alyssa Tran, Fall 2023

AN INFOGRAPHIC JOURNEY

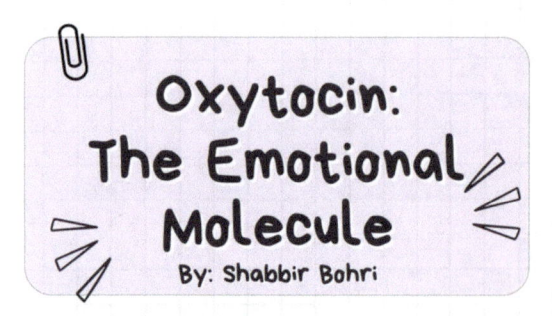

Oxytocin: The Emotional Molecule
By: Shabbir Bohri

Oxytocin v.s. Dopamine
These both have the same effects, as oxytocin on the amygdala while dopamine in the ventral and dorsal striatum both cause neuromodulatory signaling with descending projections that helps with emotional regulation.

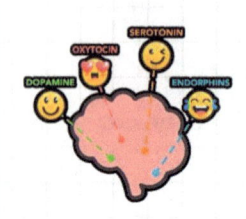

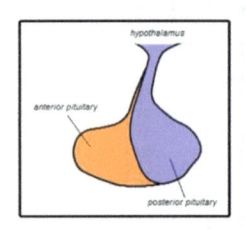

Oxytocin and ADH
Both are hormones released from the pituitary gland, and help in regulating the peripheral functions. For example, oxytocin is released during childbirth in women to help with contractions, while ADH assists in water retention during dehydration.

Effects of Oxytocin
Oxytocin has many effects. Cognitively, it can affect sexual behavior and maternal bonding. Emotionally, it can stimulate the feeling of a good mood. Socially, it helps in social and olfactory memory. Oxytocin as a hormone has target receptors everywhere in the body due to this.

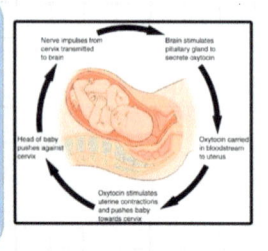

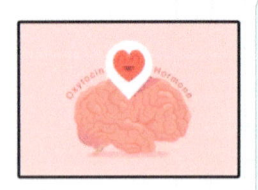

Lack of Oxytocin
A lack of oxytocin will lead to the decrease of good mood, assistance in contractions and milk ejection from breasts, and the other social and cognitive benefits it offers. It can also lead to a failure in interaoperative processing.

All info from Dr. Jahangiri's lecture slides. All photos from Google Images.

Shabbir Bohri, Fall 2023

OXYTOCIN: THE LOVE HORMONE
BY: ALIFIYA SHAIKH

WHAT IS OXYTOCIN?
Oxytocin is a hormone made in the brain and released by the pituitary gland. Some of its functions include increasing ocntractions during labor, and enhancing positive emotions and relationship attachments.

HOW IT FUNCTIONS IN THE BODY
Oxytocin plays a big role in recognition, building trust and interpersonal relationships, increasing parental-infant bonding, and sexual arousal. In reproduction, it increases flow of glandular breast milk and increases uterine contractions in labor

LACK OF OXYTOCIN?
Low oxytocin can result in irritability and lack of affection, high levels of anxiety, sleep problems, and low sexual drive as well.

NATURAL WAYS TO INCREASE OXYTOCIN
Some activities to increase this hormone include exercise, listening to positive/upbeat music, playing with animals, being in nature, and physical touch with a loved one.

Source:
Healthdirect Australia. (n.d.). Oxytocin. healthdirect.
https://www.healthdirect.gov.au/oxytocin

Alifiya Shaikh, Fall 2023

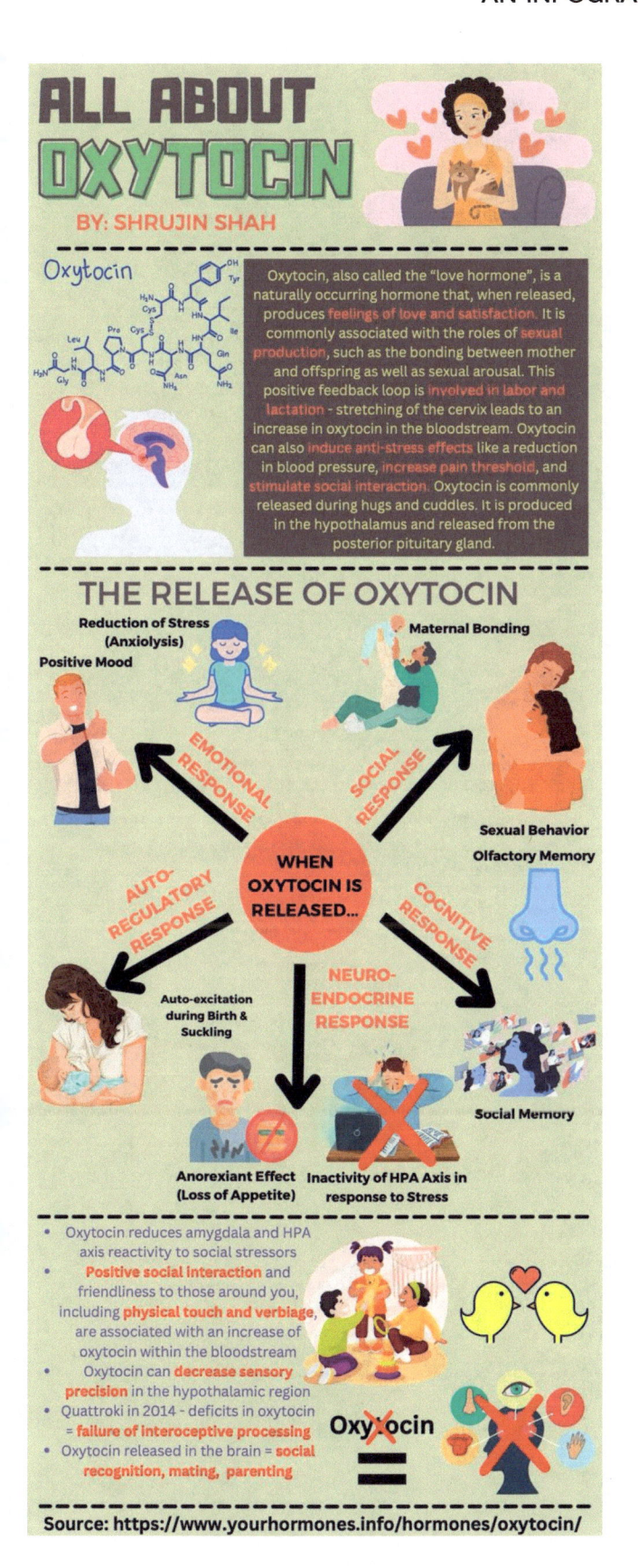

Shrujin Shah, Fall 2023

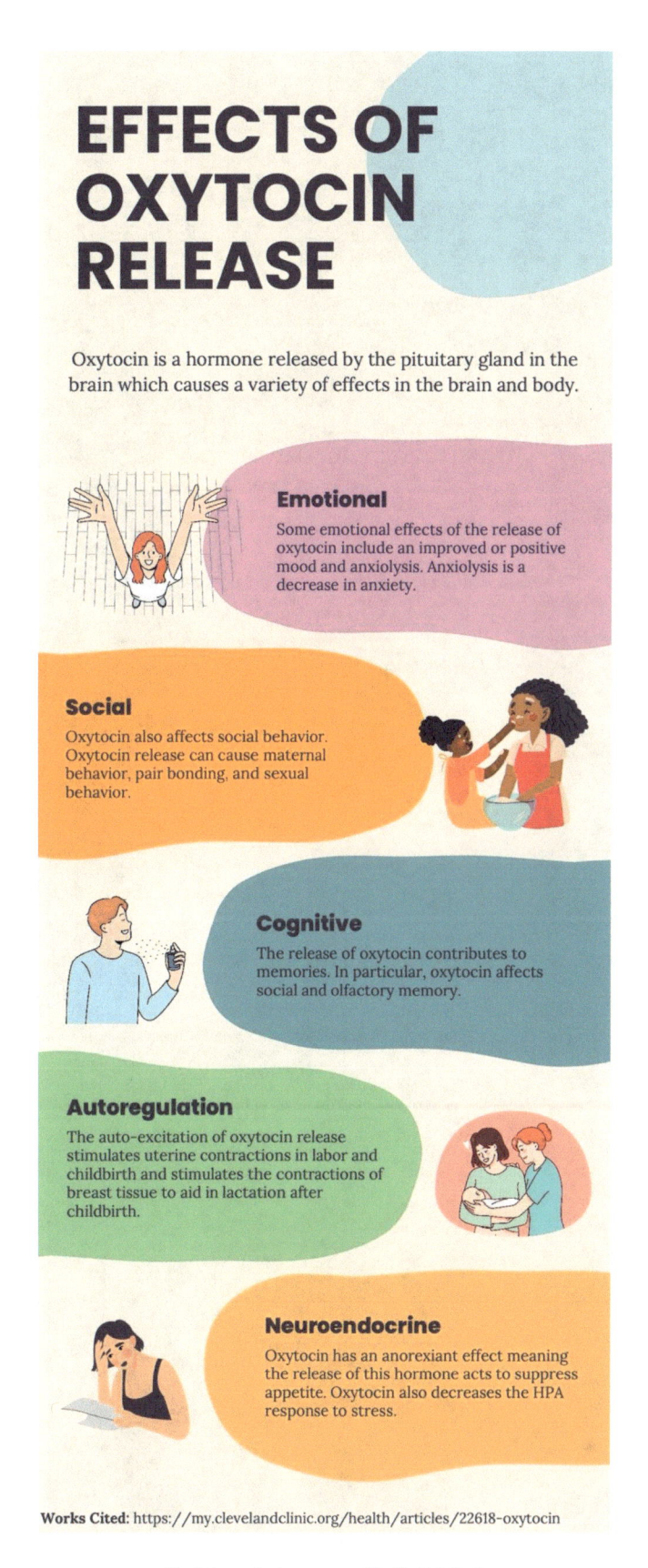

Rohita Arjarapu, Fall 2023

239

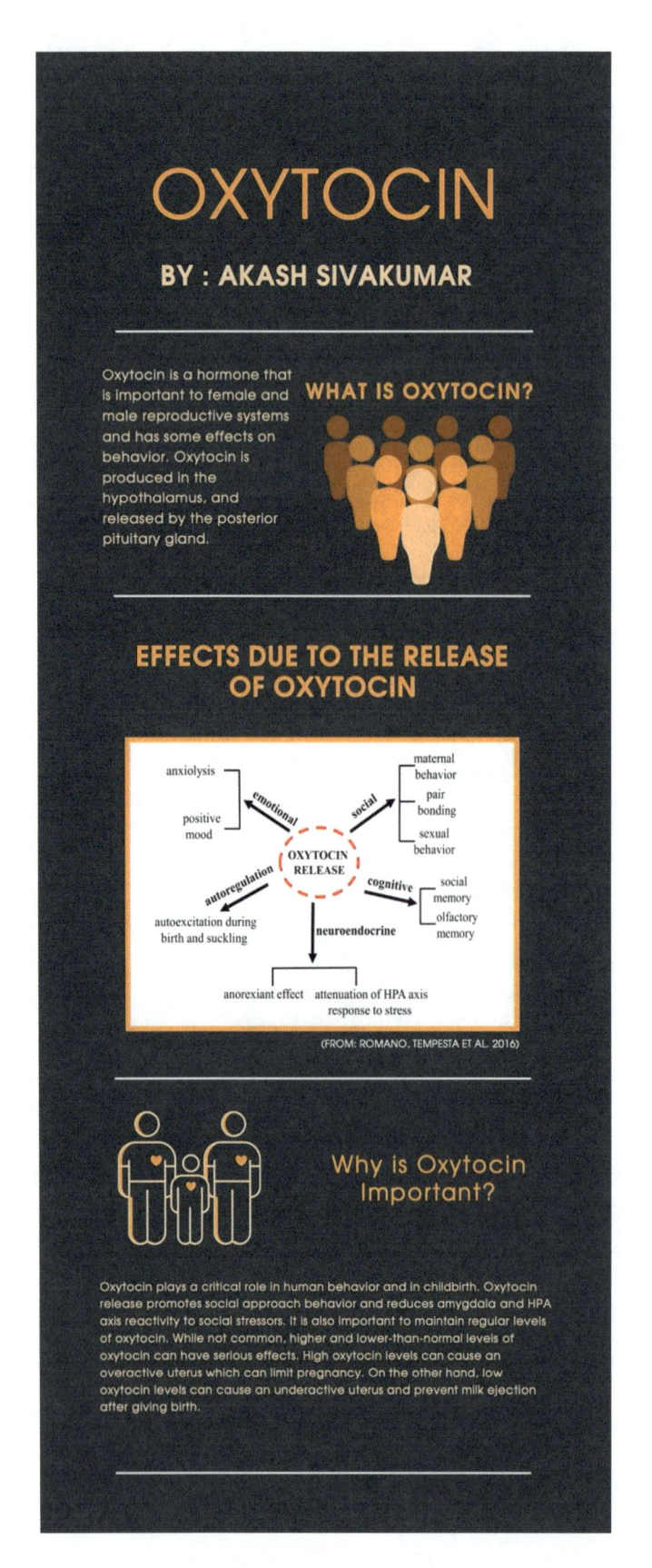

AN INFOGRAPHIC JOURNEY

OXYTOCIN
BY : AKASH SIVAKUMAR

WHAT IS OXYTOCIN?

Oxytocin is a hormone that is important to female and male reproductive systems and has some effects on behavior. Oxytocin is produced in the hypothalamus, and released by the posterior pituitary gland.

EFFECTS DUE TO THE RELEASE OF OXYTOCIN

Oxytocin release effects:
- emotional: anxiolysis, positive mood
- social: maternal behavior, pair bonding, sexual behavior
- cognitive: social memory, olfactory memory
- neuroendocrine: anorexiant effect, attenuation of HPA axis response to stress
- autoregulation: autoexcitation during birth and suckling

(FROM: ROMANO, TEMPESTA ET AL. 2016)

Why is Oxytocin Important?

Oxytocin plays a critical role in human behavior and in childbirth. Oxytocin release promotes social approach behavior and reduces amygdala and HPA axis reactivity to social stressors. It is also important to maintain regular levels of oxytocin. While not common, higher and lower-than-normal levels of oxytocin can have serious effects. High oxytocin levels can cause an overactive uterus which can limit pregnancy. On the other hand, low oxytocin levels can cause an underactive uterus and prevent milk ejection after giving birth.

Akash Sivakumar, Fall 2023

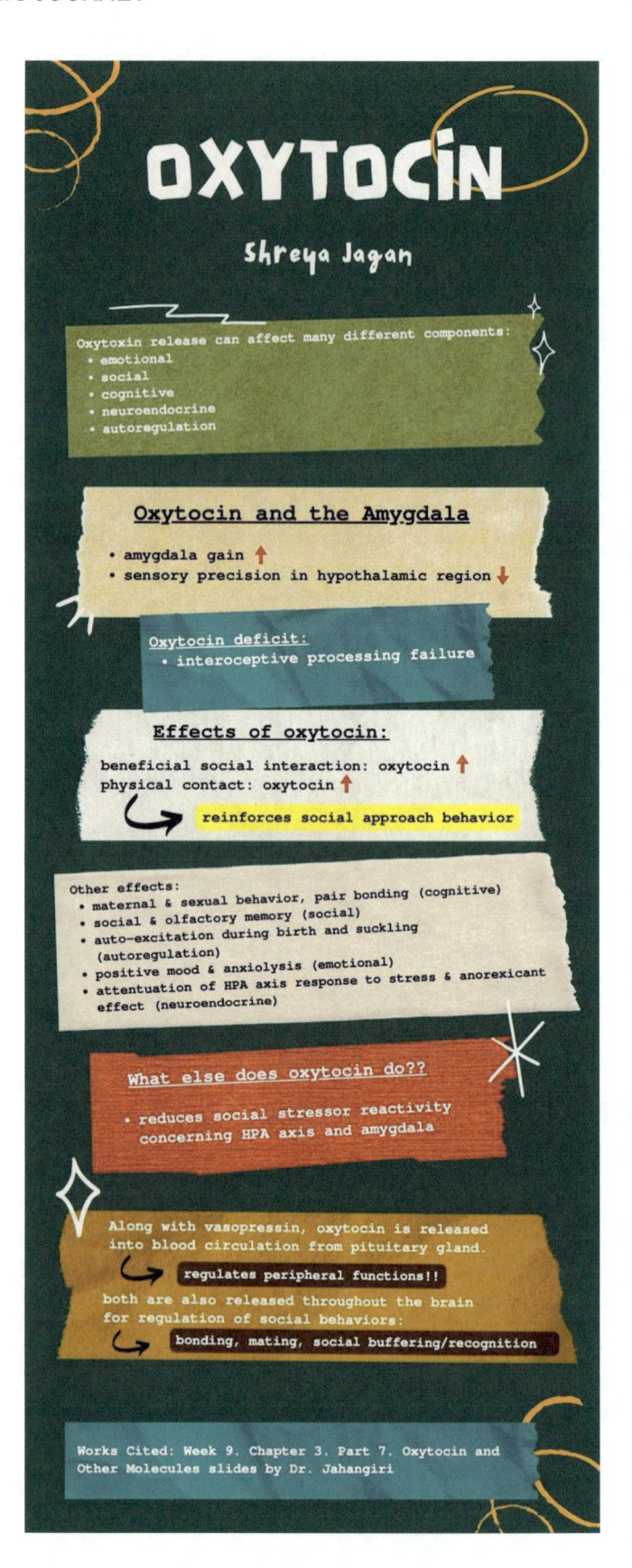

OXYTOCIN
Shreya Jagan

Oxytoxin release can affect many different components:
- emotional
- social
- cognitive
- neuroendocrine
- autoregulation

Oxytocin and the Amygdala
- amygdala gain ↑
- sensory precision in hypothalamic region ↓

Oxytocin deficit:
- interoceptive processing failure

Effects of oxytocin:
beneficial social interaction: oxytocin ↑
physical contact: oxytocin ↑
→ reinforces social approach behavior

Other effects:
- maternal & sexual behavior, pair bonding (cognitive)
- social & olfactory memory (social)
- auto-excitation during birth and suckling (autoregulation)
- positive mood & anxiolysis (emotional)
- attenuation of HPA axis response to stress & anorexicant effect (neuroendocrine)

What else does oxytocin do??
- reduces social stressor reactivity concerning HPA axis and amygdala

Along with vasopressin, oxytocin is released into blood circulation from pituitary gland.
→ regulates peripheral functions!!
both are also released throughout the brain for regulation of social behaviors:
→ bonding, mating, social buffering/recognition

Works Cited: Week 9, Chapter 3, Part 7, Oxytocin and Other Molecules slides by Dr. Jahangiri

Shreya Jagan, Fall 2023

AN INFOGRAPHIC JOURNEY

The Role of Oxytocin

What is Oxytocin?

Oxytocin is a hormone that effects **mood** and has many functions related to **reproduction**. Oxytocin is released from the pituitary gland into the blood stream.

Some Effects of Oxytocin Release:

- Oxytocin **reduces** amygdala and HPA axis reactivity, promoting social bonding.
- **Cognitive** effects: maternal behavior, pair bonding, and sexual behavior
- **Emotional** effects: anxiolysis and positive mood

A **deficiency** in oxytocin may impact interoceptive processing, potentially affecting emotional regulation.

Oxytocin and Dopamine in the Amygdala

Oxytocin and dopamine play **complementary** roles in the amygdala. Oxytocin augments the gain in the amygdala, enhancing emotional responses, while dopamine has similar effects in the dorsal and ventral striatum through D1 and D2 receptors.

In both cases, signals that adjust to the specific situation come from the brain's **emotional control areas** for oxytocin and **action choices** for dopamine. These signals help fine-tune our responses to fit the circumstances.

Oxytocin and Vasopressin (ADH):

Oxytocin and vasopressin, also known as antidiuretic hormone (ADH), play a vital role in social behaviors.
- Regulate **peripheral functions** such as the milk letdown reflex and uterine contractions in females.
- Leads to **vasoconstriction** and **water retention** in both males and females.
- They affect the brain, influencing social recognition, mating, bonding, parenting, and social buffering.

Resource: All information is from Week 9 Lecture by Dr. Jahangiri & TA as well as Chapter 3 from **Neurobiology of Fear and other Emotions** by Dr. Moller

Haniya Qavi, Fall 2023

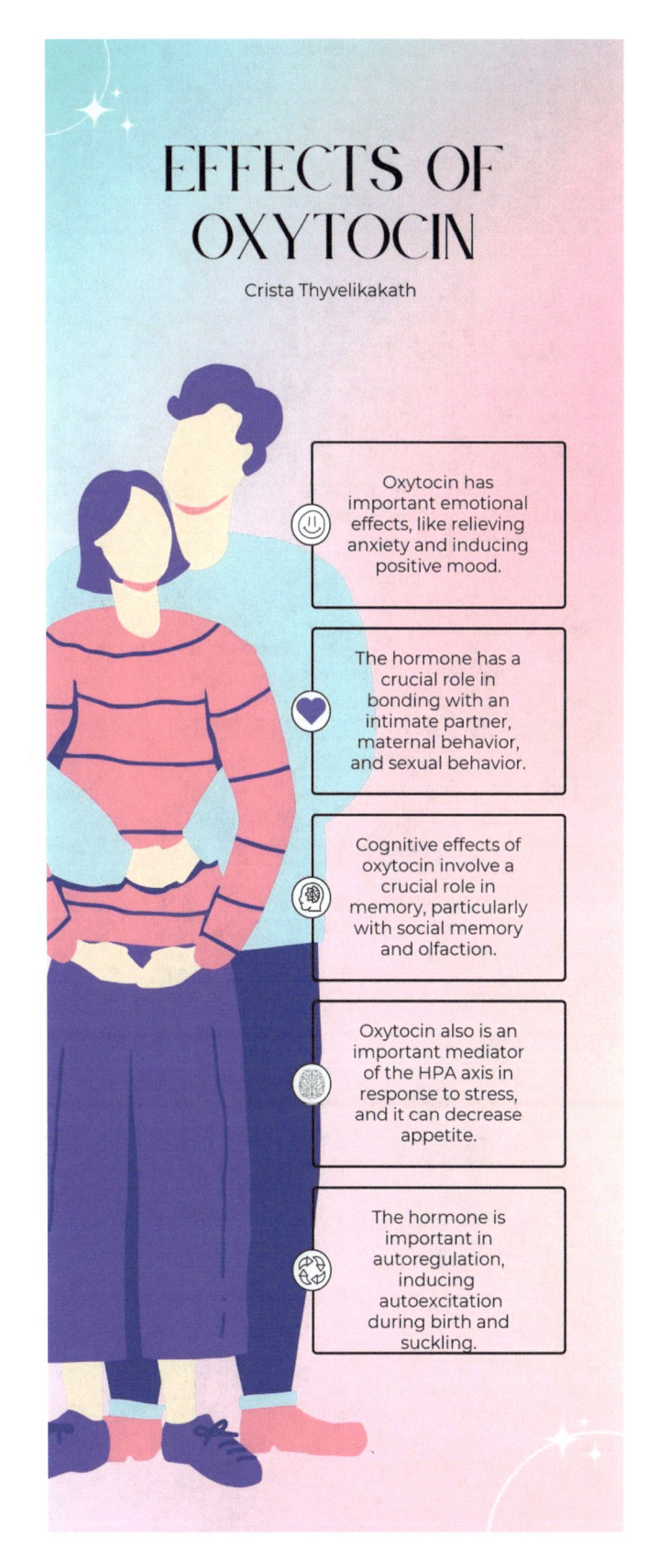

EFFECTS OF OXYTOCIN

Crista Thyvelikakath

- Oxytocin has important emotional effects, like relieving anxiety and inducing positive mood.
- The hormone has a crucial role in bonding with an intimate partner, maternal behavior, and sexual behavior.
- Cognitive effects of oxytocin involve a crucial role in memory, particularly with social memory and olfaction.
- Oxytocin also is an important mediator of the HPA axis in response to stress, and it can decrease appetite.
- The hormone is important in autoregulation, inducing autoexcitation during birth and suckling.

Crista Thyvelikakath, Spring 2023

AN INFOGRAPHIC JOURNEY

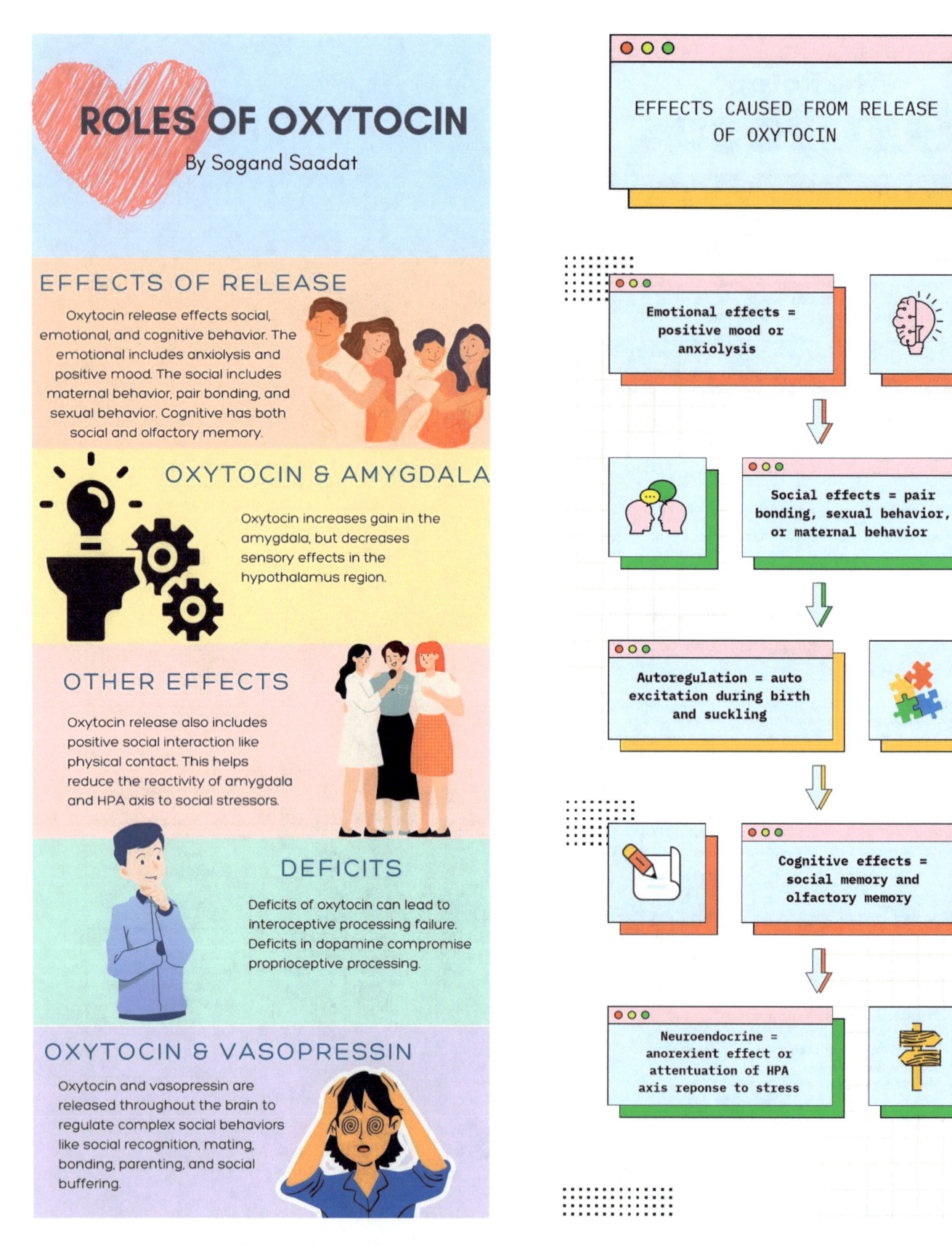

ROLES OF OXYTOCIN
By Sogand Saadat

EFFECTS OF RELEASE
Oxytocin release effects social, emotional, and cognitive behavior. The emotional includes anxiolysis and positive mood. The social includes maternal behavior, pair bonding, and sexual behavior. Cognitive has both social and olfactory memory.

OXYTOCIN & AMYGDALA
Oxytocin increases gain in the amygdala, but decreases sensory effects in the hypothalamus region.

OTHER EFFECTS
Oxytocin release also includes positive social interaction like physical contact. This helps reduce the reactivity of amygdala and HPA axis to social stressors.

DEFICITS
Deficits of oxytocin can lead to interoceptive processing failure. Deficits in dopamine compromise proprioceptive processing.

OXYTOCIN & VASOPRESSIN
Oxytocin and vasopressin are released throughout the brain to regulate complex social behaviors like social recognition, mating, bonding, parenting, and social buffering.

Sogand Saadat, Spring 2023

EFFECTS CAUSED FROM RELEASE OF OXYTOCIN

- Emotional effects = positive mood or anxiolysis
- Social effects = pair bonding, sexual behavior, or maternal behavior
- Autoregulation = auto excitation during birth and suckling
- Cognitive effects = social memory and olfactory memory
- Neuroendocrine = anorexient effect or attentuation of HPA axis reponse to stress

Kayla Pham, Spring 2023

AN INFOGRAPHIC JOURNEY

Oxytocin's Function

By: Ayaan Ahmed

Oxytocin as a Social Enabler

- Serves as a anxiolysis (stress remover) and contributes to a positive mood.
- Known as the bonding hormone and promotes sexual behavior.
- Promotes social recognition, mating, and parenting.
- Autoexcitation by suckling contributes to mother-baby bonding.

Dopamine Connection

- Deficits of Oxytocin lead to failure of feeling what goes on inside your body whereas failure of dopamine processing can compromise movement and lead to Parkinson's.
- Both are involved in context-sensitive neuromodulatory signaling.

Vasopressin Connection

- Regulate milk let down reflex and uterine contractions.
- Help in vasoconstriction and water retention in both genders.

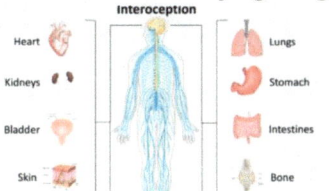

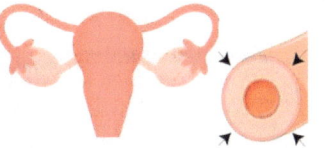

References

Ayaan Ahmed, Spring 2023

Role of Oxytocin

Oxytocin is colloquially known as the "love hormone," however there are many other social and emotion roles it plays beyond sexual and romantic attraction!

Maternal Behaviour

When oxytocin and vasopressin are released from the pituitary gland into the bloodstream, they regulate peripheral functions including the milk letdown relfex in mothers.

Positive Mood

Oxytocin reinforce positive mood, as it's releases is promoted by positive social interactions. However, current research supports oxytocin releases with strengthening bad memories.

Social Buffering

Oxytocin mediatess social buffering, the phenomenon in which the presence of a familiar individual reduces (maybe even eliminates) stress

Deficits

Deficits in oxytocin are associated with interoception. In other words, internal body modulators such as hunger, body-temperature control, urinary tract may be inaccurately sensed.

Kathy Nguyen, Spring 2023

AN INFOGRAPHIC JOURNEY

OXYTOCIN, THE BRAIN, AND EMOTIONS

OXYTOCIN
When oxytocin is released there is a rise in positive mood, maternal behavior, social memory, and an increase in the gain in the amygdala

OXYTOCIN AND VASOPRESSIN
They are peptide molecules that are released from the pituitary gland and into the blood circulation to regulate peripheral functions and also have a role in social processes and behavior

MELATONIN
Melatonin is a hormone and antioxidant that is secreted by the pineal gland (mainly) and helps with our circadian rhythm. It does not initiate sleep but it signals when it is time to sleep

AUTONOMIC NERVOUS SYSTEM
The autonomic nervous system is a part of the peripheral nervous system. The autonomic nervous system plays a role in regulating blood pressure, breathing and heart rate, respiration, etc.

HYPOTHALAMUS PITUITARY ADRENAL AXIS (HPA)
The hypothalamus pituitary adrenal axis plays a role in regulating stress responses. Metabolism, immune responses and physiological process are just some things that are regulated by the HPA when the body is in stress

Lilly Neguse, Spring 2023

AMBERLYN HAQUE
OXYTOCIN RELEASE

emotional
Emotional effects of this release are anxiolysis, which is anxiety relief, and a positive mood.

social
Emotional effects of this release are olfactory memory, such as scents, and social memory.

cognitive
Emotional effects of this release are pair bonding, which is the selection between two individuals in the same species, sexual behavior, and maternal, or motherly, behavior.

neuroendocrine
Emotional effects of this release are effects that are anorexicant and an attenuation of HPA, also known as hypothalamic-pituitary-adrenal, axis response to stress

autoregulation
Emotional effects of this release are autoexcitatory effects during situations like suckling and birth.

REFERENCES
Neurobiology of Fear and other Emotions by Aage R. Møller, PhD
"Anxiolytics." Cleveland Clinic, my.clevelandclinic.org/health/treatments/24776-anxiolytics.
Blumenthal, Sarah A, and Larry J Young. "The Neurobiology of Love and Pair Bonding from Human and Animal Perspectives." Biology, U.S. National Library of Medicine, 12 June 2023, www.ncbi.nlm.nih.gov/pmc/articles/PMC10295201/#:~:text=Pair%20bonds%20refer%20to%20selective,sexually%20involved%20or%20sexually%20exclusive.

Amberlyn Haque, Fall 2023

AN INFOGRAPHIC JOURNEY

THE EFFECTS OF OXYTOCIN

NEUROENDOCRINE EFFECTS
Oxytocin causes an augmentation of the gain in the amygdala and attenuates HPA axis reactivity to stress. Oxytocin also has an anorexiant effect as it suppresses appetite.

EMOTIONAL EFFECTS
Oxytocin affects emotions such as fear and anxiety. Oxytocin enables the neural plasticity required to establish the perception of the emotional and social "self".

SOCIAL EFFECTS
Oxytocin mediates social buffering. Positive social interaction, such as physical touch, is associated with oxytocin release. This further promotes social approach behavior.

COGNITIVE EFFECTS
Oxytocin is involved in maternal behavior, pair bonding, and sexual behavior. Oxytocin is also crucial to establishing a normal socio-sexual behavior by affecting parts of the brain.

DEFICITS OF OXYTOCIN
Dopamine has complementary effects to oxytocin, and is mediated by the D1 (go pathway) and D2 (no-go pathway) receptors. Deficits of oxytocin may lead to a failure of interoceptive processing, while dopamine deficits compromise proprioceptive processing and the initiation of action.

Moller, Aage R. Neurobiology of Fear, Anxiety and Other Emotions. 31 July 2019

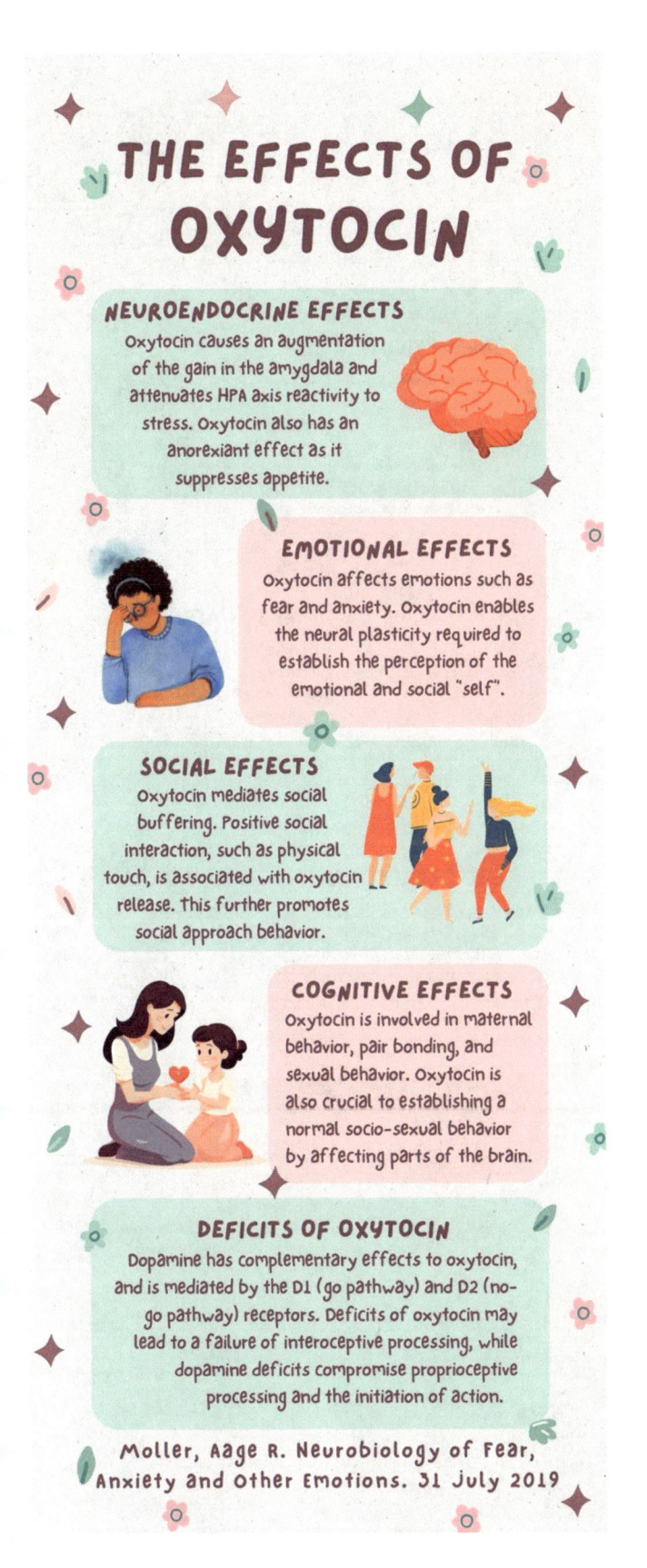

Megha Akkineni, Fall 2023

About Oxytocin
NSC 4382. Lucie Nguyen.

EFFECTS OF RELEASE
- Regulates milk letdown reflex and uterine contractions in females
- Reduces amygdala and HPA axis with stress and anxiety
- Affects emotions + mood
- Social and olfactory memory
- Maternal behavior, pair bonding, sexual behavior

OXYTOCIN

OXYTOCIN + AMYGDALA
- Augment the function of the amygdala
- Plays a role in emotion
- inhibitory roles with the HPA axis, suppress fear response
- Decrease anxiety

DEFICIENCIES
- Failure of interoceptive processing
- Can stop uterine contractions during birthing
- Low levels have been linked to both depressive and autism spectrum disorder but further research is needed

OXYTOCIN + VASOPRESSIN
- Role in social behavior such as mating, offspring bonds, etc.
- Both from pituitary gland and involved in uterine contractions and milk let down reflex in females
- Role in water retention

COOL FACTS
- Dogs produce lots of oxytocin when making eye contact with humans
- Oxytocin in meerkats make them more altruistic
- Oxytocin has been found to lower blood pressure

Moller, R. (2019). Neurobiology of Fear, Anxiety and Other Emotions.
Cleveland Clinic Medical. (n.d.). Retrieved from https://my.clevelandclinic.org/health/articles/22618-oxytocin
Riley, J. (n.d.) 6 fascinating facts about the "Love hormone": BBC Earth. https://www.bbcearth.com/news/six-fascinating-facts-about-the-love-hormone

Lucie Nguyen, Fall 2023

Effects of Taking Acetaminophen

Liver Failure
In the US, studies have shown that injesting acetaminophen regularly can lead to the severe side effect of liver failure.

Brain development
Studies have reported that acetaminophen is a common pain reliever for children. The use of it by children may lead to impairments of brain developement.

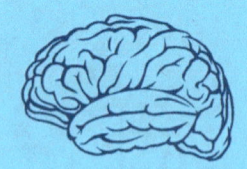

Asthma
Another side effect that has been investigated is asthma. It has been shown that acetaminophen can increase the risk of developing asthma by up to 40% in children.

Behavioral issues
The results of studies have concluded that ADHD could be associated with acetaminohen. Even at low amounts of intake, it can cause side effects up to seven years later.

Response impairment
Acetaminophen can also affect the adult brain in ways such as stunting their responses to positive and negative stimuli. This effect can lead to risky situations as they will not notice harmful stimuli they may be experiencing.

Emily Lopez, Spring 2024

ACETAMINOPHEN

DEFINITION & USE
Acetaminophen, also known by its brand name Tylenol, is commonly used as an over the counter pain reliever due to the medication being advertised as having less side effects than other medicines.

RISKS IN ADULTS
Despite its common usage, acetaminophen has severe side effects, including liver toxicity. The medication causes oxidative stress response at high dosages (4.000 mg).

RISKS IN CHILDREN
A study has shown acetaminophen may affect early brain development in children. In addition, acetaminophen may increase the risk of developing asthma or ADHD.

WHAT SHOULD YOU DO?

RECOMMENDATIONS
- Always read the side effects of a medication.
- Never take high or prolonged dosages of acetaminophen.
- Increase preventative care practices, such as getting vaccinated or wearing a mask.

Reference:
"Neurobiology of Fear, Anxiety, and Other Emotions" Møller, A.R.

Maryam Imam, Fall 2023

AN INFOGRAPHIC JOURNEY

EVERYTHING ABOUT ACETAMINOPHEN
By Saad Tanwir

WHAT IS ACETAMINOPHEN?

It is one of the active ingredients found in the medication Tylenol which mostly used for headaches and pain such as toothache.

WHAT DOES IT DONE?

It is known to be the most common type of pain and fever reliever. It does that by elevating the body's overall pain threshold which makes you feel less pain and lowers the fever by eliminating the excess heat.

WHAT DOES IT TREAT?

it mostly treats headache, back pain, pain of arthritis, muscular aches, premenstrual, and menstrual cramps.

WHO SHOULD TAKE THIS?

Patients who suffer with a kidney disease, stomach problems, and on heart therapy should consider taking it.

SIDE EFFECTS?

This medication can cause really bad liver damage if a patient takes more than 4,000 mg within 24 hours especially with alcohol consumption.

MORE SIDE SEVERE SIDE EFFECTS?

It can also cause skin reactions which can be like reddening of the skin, blisters, and rash. It can cause problems in urine, diarrhea, sweating, nausea, and stomach cramps.

Saad Tanwir, Spring 2024

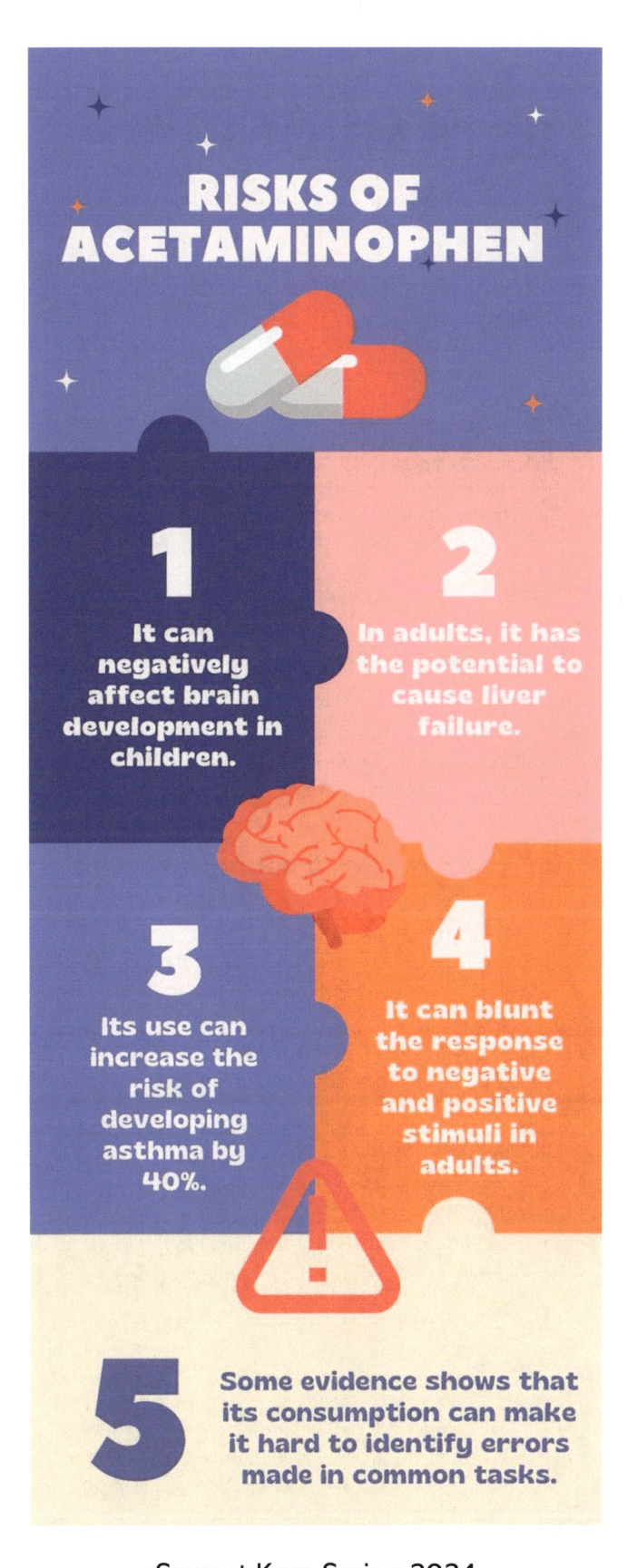

RISKS OF ACETAMINOPHEN

1 It can negatively affect brain development in children.

2 In adults, it has the potential to cause liver failure.

3 Its use can increase the risk of developing asthma by 40%.

4 It can blunt the response to negative and positive stimuli in adults.

5 Some evidence shows that its consumption can make it hard to identify errors made in common tasks.

Supreet Kaur, Spring 2024

AN INFOGRAPHIC JOURNEY

ESTRADIOL

for fear and anxiety

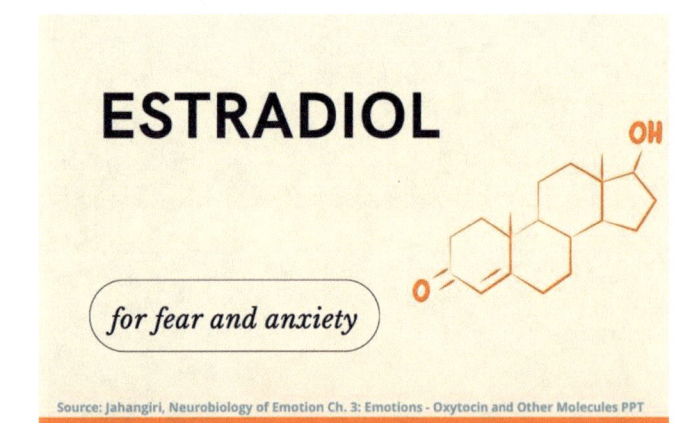

Source: Jahangiri, Neurobiology of Emotion Ch. 3: Emotions - Oxytocin and Other Molecules PPT

01. ESTRADIOL IN FEAR

There is a correlation between estradiol concentration and fear and anxiety disorders. Understanding this relationship could aid in developing more targeted and effective treatments for fear and anxiety.

02. OOPHORECTOMY

Bilateral removal of ovaries, oophorectomy, led to an increase in mental health, cardiovascular, and/or metabolic conditions such as, coronary artery disease, congestive heart failure, COPD, and PKD.

03. ACCELERATED AGING

Women who had a bilateral oophorectomy experienced accelerated aging leading to multi morbidity and mortality.

04. IMPACT OF OOPHORECTOMY

Bilateral removal of the ovaries causes the premature loss of estrogen and other ovarian hormones. Behavioral and environmental factors can also have an impact of the estrogen concentration. A decrease in ovarian hormones can cause stem cell exhaustion among other dysfunctions leading to frailty and multi morbidities in mental health, cardiovascular, and somatic conditions.

05. FUTURE DIRECTION

Asking how estradiol is affecting fear extinction induced cellular and molecular mechanisms, where is estradiol changing the neural function, and when will treatment be more effective will help develop decode the effect of estradiol and how treatmetns would take advantage of this system.

Sarah Padani, Fall 2023

Pranavi Maddipatla

FUNCTIONS OF ESTRADIOL

1. Estrogen
Estrogen is one of the main reproductive hormones and plays a key role is sexuality and fertility.

2. Estradiol
Estradiol is one of the 3 forms of estrogen, along with estrone and estriol.

3. When is it used?
Estradiol is the most potent form of estrogen and is present in the body during child-bearing years.

4. What does it control?
Estradiol controls sexual desire, lipid metabolism, brain function, and bone and skin health.

5. Role in fear
Estradiol plays a role in fear extinction, and some studies have shown that low levels are associated with impaired fear extinction.

References
- Cover, K. K., Maeng, L. Y., Lebron-Milad, K. & Milad, M. R. (2014). Mechanisms of estradiol in fear circuitry: implications for sex differences in psychopathology. Translational Psychiatry, 4(8), e422. https://doi.org/10.1038/tp.2014.67
- Society, E. (2022). Reproductive hormones. Endocrine Society. https://www.endocrine.org/patient-engagement/endocrine-library/hormones-and-endocrine-function/reproductive-hormones#:~:text=Estradiol%20has%20several%20functions%20in,a%20fertilized%20egg%20to%20implant.

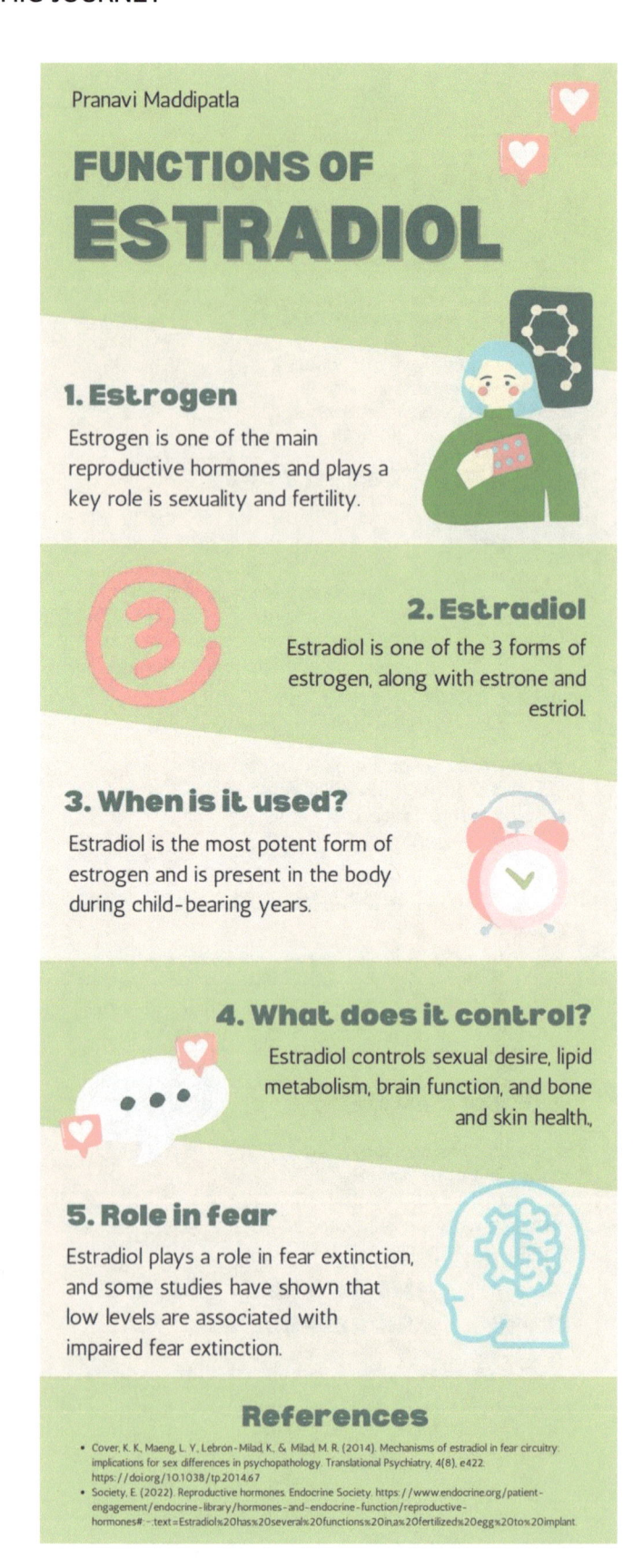

Pranavi Maddipatla, Fall 2023

AN INFOGRAPHIC JOURNEY

COMPLEMENTARY EFFECTS OF DOPAMINE PATHWAYS

By Sahiti Pydimarri

D1 PATHWAY (GO)
- Activation of D1 receptors leads to **increase of intracellular cAMP** levels
- Associated with **Direct Pathway** of basal ganglia
- Facilitates movement
- Generally **excitatory** and promotes motor function, cognition, and motivation
- Dysfunction can lead to **Parkinson's disease**

D2 PATHWAY (NO GO)
- Activation of D2 receptors leads to decrease of intracellular cAMP levels
- Associated with Indirect Pathway of basal ganglia
- Generally inhibitory and contols excessive unwanted movements and regulates motor functioning
- Dysfunction can lead to schizophrenia and other movement disorders

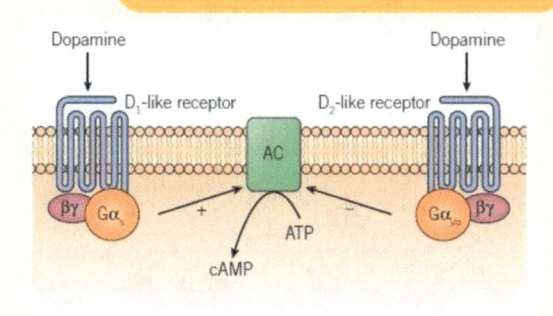

Sources: https://www.ncbi.nlm.nih.gov/pmc/articles/PMC5509068/

Sahiti Pydimarri, Fall 2023

METHAMPHETAMINE
ITS USES AND RISK OF HARM

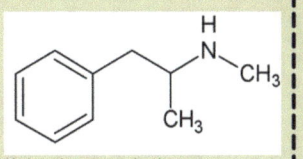

ABOUT
- Class: Stimulants
- Schedule II Controlled Substance
- Indirect agonist of dopamine, norepinephrine, and serotonin

Methamphetamine molecular structure

MEDICINAL USES
- Treatment for ADHD & Obesity
- Treatment for narcolepsy and idiopathic hypersomnia
- Elevate mood
- Increase alertness, concentration and energy in fatigued individuals

RISK OF HARM
Low Doses
- Rapid unexplained weight loss
- Increased BP

High doses
- Psychosis
- Skeletal muscle breakdown
- Seizures
- Brain Bleed

Chronic high-doses
- Increased Risk of Parkinson's Disease
- Reduced Gray Matter
- Increased risk of contracting infectious diseases
- Hallucinations/Delirium
- Violent behavior

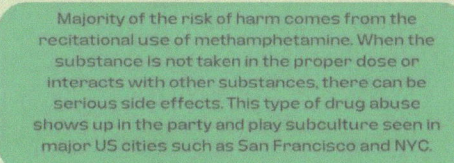

Majority of the risk of harm comes from the recitational use of methamphetamine. When the substance is not taken in the proper dose or interacts with other substances, there can be serious side effects. This type of drug abuse shows up in the party and play subculture seen in major US cities such as San Francisco and NYC.

BY: NEHA BHUPATHIRAJU

Neha Bhupathiraju, Spring 2023

AN INFOGRAPHIC JOURNEY

RISKS OF MEDICATIONS
By: Masa Jallad

Risk of Common Medications

Despite strong evidence of numerous serious side effects, especially adult liver failure, acetaminophen is nevertheless promoted as having fewer side effects than other nonsteroidal anti-inflammatory pain medications. A study found that the liver toxicity of acetaminophen in the US much outweighs that of other causes of acute liver failure.

Acetaminophen

Research has indicated that acetaminophen, the most commonly prescribed drug for children, may have an impact on early brain development. This is the case even though the drug is easily accessible for infants in an over-the-counter form that is labeled as "safe, gentle, and effective," with no warnings about possible negative effects other than allergic reactions.

Acetaminophen Risks

- Acetaminophen has a profound effect on adult brain function.
- Acetaminophen may blunt the response to both negative and positive stimuli.
- Blunted response to threatening stimuli and a reduction in behavioral responses to social rejection
- May impair the ability of most adults to identify errors made during the performance of simple or common tasks.

Statistics of Effects of Acetaminophen

40%

- According to the findings of a global study including over 200,000 children, acetaminophen use may up the risk of asthma development and maintenance by 40%.
- Acetaminophen began to replace aspirin in the early 1980s, which coincided with a notable rise in autism, asthma, and ADHD.
- Acetaminophen consumption may be linked to ADHD. Seven years later, acetaminophen, even in small dosages, can have an impact on behavior.

References
Week 12 Lecture by Dr. Jahangiri

Masa Jallad, Spring 2024

Overlooked Risks: Medication & Fear

Commonly Used Medications Have Risks

- Acetaminophen: Despite being advertised as safer than other pain relievers, it can lead to severe side effects including liver failure and increased risk of asthma and ADHD.
- Brain Function: Acetaminophen may also affect brain function in adults, blunting responses to stimuli and impairing error identification during tasks.

Deaths from Preventable Diseases

- Influenza: Preventable deaths vary widely annually, reaching up to 80,000 in some seasons.
- Healthcare: Estimates suggest preventable deaths range from 98,000 to 200,000 annually in the US.

Fear as a Manipulator

- Inducing Fear: Fear can be used to manipulate and control people, influencing behaviors and decisions.
- Fearmongering: Deliberately arousing public fear or alarm can be used to enforce laws or spread misinformation.

Examples of Fear's Power

- Paralyzing Nations: Fear can paralyze entire nations, affecting decision-making and behavior.
- Fearmongering Impact: Once fear is induced, it's difficult to reverse its effects.

Effect on Perception and Behavior

- Threat Perception: Prolonged threat perception leads to activation of threat-related neural circuitry and elevated inflammation.
- Cognitive State Anxiety: Exaggerated sensitivity to threats can result in sustained threat perception and cognitive-behavioral responses.

Emma Siddiqui, Spring 2024

CHAPTER 14

Neuroplasticity

Neuroplasticity

Sneha Sharma & Saad Tanwir, Spring 2024

A newborn baby eagerly gazes at his mother taking in his new environment. The ecstatic family surrounds the infant, calling his name, which sounds like mere whispers and a jumbled mess. However, with each passing day, the intricate web of neurons activates, reorganizes, and forms strengthened connections allowing the infant to adapt to the highly stimulating environment. As a toddler, he can now process and understand the sounds making up his name as well as other words spoken by his family.

Language acquisition exemplifies the innate, crucial, and transformative power of neuroplasticity, or the brain's ability to adapt throughout one's lifetime by the formation of neural connections. The first few years of human life are where the most rapid neuronal growth is seen, starting from around 2,500 synapses and jumping to 15,000 by three years old (Cherry). This critical period of development requires exposure to certain stimuli and inputs to properly develop, however, this process slows down in adolescence and adults. It is not completely stopped since it is needed for future adaptation needs and instead manifests as synaptic pruning: the strengthening of frequently used connection pathways and elimination of rarely used ones.

So, why is neuroplasticity such an integral part of development? Since the brain can reorganize itself, we can learn new things and recover from traumatic brain injuries or strokes. Furthermore, our existing capabilities can be enhanced in response to the loss of other cognitive functions. Many stroke rehabilitation programs help patients regain functioning by tapping into this instinctive process and encouraging physical activity that activates the damaged regions of the brain. They also couple it with mental stimulation, exhibiting that neuroplasticity is an all-encompassing and multifaceted system within us (Awasthi).

Neuroplasticity is an innate ability humans have, but there are a variety of external factors that can influence it. According to Dr. Kolb and Dr. Gibb at the University of Lethbridge, they identified the eight principles that impact neuroplastic processes: sensory stimuli, psychoactive drugs, gonadal hormones, parental-child relationships, peer relationships, early stress, intestinal flora, and diet. These factors demonstrate not all neuroplasticity is good and, as the name "plastic" suggests, is an ever-changing process. For example, puppies raised alone in a cage showed abnormal behaviors compared to those raised in an environment with positive stimuli/ experiences, (Kolb and Gibb). Drugs can have adverse effects both pre- and postnatally with specific classes targeting different regions of the brain. Overall, the connections made tend to be weaker with reduced spine density and dendritic length.

There are countless measures one can take to enrich one's environment and promote healthy brain stimulation, such as taking part in creative pursuits, reading, traveling, or actively learning new hobbies, to name a few. Learning and repeated activation of specific neural circuits leads to a process called long-term potentiation (LTP). It is responsible for increasing the efficiency of synaptic transmission and some suggest it has a hand in memory encoding and retention.

There are two types of neuroplasticity, the first being functional neuroplasticity which plays a role in moving the brain function from an area in the brain that is damaged to an area that is not damaged. Functional neuroplasticity has four different forms such as cross-modal reassignment, homologous area adaptation, map expansion, and compensatory masquerade. Cross-modal reassignment helps the region of a brain that lacks important input and provides new inputs. Such as the study was done, "the images such as positron emission tomography of tactile discrimination showed that people who had a vision loss in early childhood but did their testing as adults, the new somatosensory inputs were directed in occipital cortex" (Grafman).

Homologous area adaptation is a form of an area that suggests that the area of the brain that has gone under some sort of damage and lacks functional and cognitive operations, can be overcome by shifting all these operations to another part of the brain. The map expression, on the other hand, suggests that the brain has some flexible regions for any kind of skill, knowledge, skill, and cognitive operation. The brain regions that have these operations can be enlarged with repeated exposure to that stimulus and practice of any skill. Compensatory masquerade is related to our daily tasks in life, which we repeat every day, such as driving to work, which trains our cognitive process to perform that task.

The second type of neuroplasticity is structural plasticity, which allows the human brain to adapt to any new kind of disease they develop, the new skill they learn, and the new environment, and helps repair any sought-after lesions. Most of its functions lie within the hippocampus such as memory, learning, anxiety, and stress regulation. Such as when a person is trying to learn a new skill like playing the piano, which helps a person learn and remember the new chords with repeated practice.

There were unique early theories regarding neuroplasticity that any changes the brain goes through are limited to only occurring in early childhood and infancy. And once the brain has fully developed its structure, it doesn't go through any changes in adulthood. "The psychiatrist Norman Doidge explained to us the reasons behind these theories that people believed that the brain is like a working machine that can never develop or grow. Also, the reason that some people experienced brain injuries never end up recovering from them" (Cherry). By the time of 1960, the modern theories set to arise when the researchers started doing studies on people with strokes and found that patients who experienced stroke were able to regain their brain functioning which suggested that the brain is more than capable of growing in adulthood as well.

In conclusion, neuroplasticity does play many critical roles in our lives from being able to adapt to a new environment, learn new things, enhance our existing cognitive capabilities, and help patients recover from traumatic brain injuries and strokes. With so many benefits we can utilize it even more by enhancing it by rewiring our cognitive pathways by exercising, sleeping well, doing challenging tasks such as learning to juggle, and expanding our vocabulary. Mainly, neuroplasticity has such great ability, and enhancing it through physical activity has such benefits that it can help patients suffering from traumatic brain injuries gain function.

References

1. Author links open overlay panel Jordan Grafman, et al. "Conceptualizing Functional Neuroplasticity." Journal of Communication Disorders, Elsevier, 14 Sept. 2000, www.sciencedirect.com/science/article/abs/pii/S0021992400000307.

2. Kendra Cherry, MSEd. "How Brain Neurons Change over Time from Life Experience." Verywell Mind, www.verywellmind.com/what-is-brain-plasticity-2794886. Accessed 28 Apr. 2024.

3. Kolb, Bryan, and Robbin Gibb. "Brain Plasticity and Behaviour in the Developing Brain." Journal of the Canadian Academy of Child and Adolescent Psychiatry = Journal de l'Academie Canadienne de Psychiatrie de l'enfant et de l'adolescent, U.S. National Library of Medicine, Nov. 2011, www.ncbi.nlm.nih.gov/pmc/articles/PMC3222570/#:~:text=Eight%20basic%20principles%20of%20brain,%2C%20intestinal%20flora%2C%20and%20diet.

4. L;, La Rosa C;Parolisi R;Bonfanti. "Brain Structural Plasticity: From Adult Neurogenesis to Immature Neurons." Frontiers in Neuroscience, U.S. National Library of Medicine, pubmed.ncbi.nlm.nih.gov/32116519/#:~:text=Brain%20structural%20plasticity%20is%2 0an,disease%2C%20and%20to%20slow%20aging. Accessed 28 Apr. 2024.

5. Leuner, Benedetta, and Elizabeth Gould. "Structural Plasticity and Hippocampal Function." Annual Review of Psychology, U.S. National Library of Medicine, 2010, www.ncbi.nlm.nih.gov/pmc/articles/PMC3012424/.

6. "Neuroplasticity." Encyclopædia Britannica, Encyclopædia Britannica, inc., 24 Apr. 2024, www.britannica.com/science/neuroplasticity.

7. SITNFlash. "Neuroplasticity: How Lost Skills Can Be Regained after Injury or Illness." Science in the News, 3 Apr. 2023, sitn.hms.harvard.edu/flash/2023/neuroplasticity-how-lost- skills-can-be-regained-after-injury-or-illness/.

8. Thompson, Jonathan. "9 Neuroplasticity Exercises to Boost Productivity." Work Life by Atlassian, 17 Mar. 2022, www.atlassian.com/blog/productivity/neuroplasticity-train- your-brain.

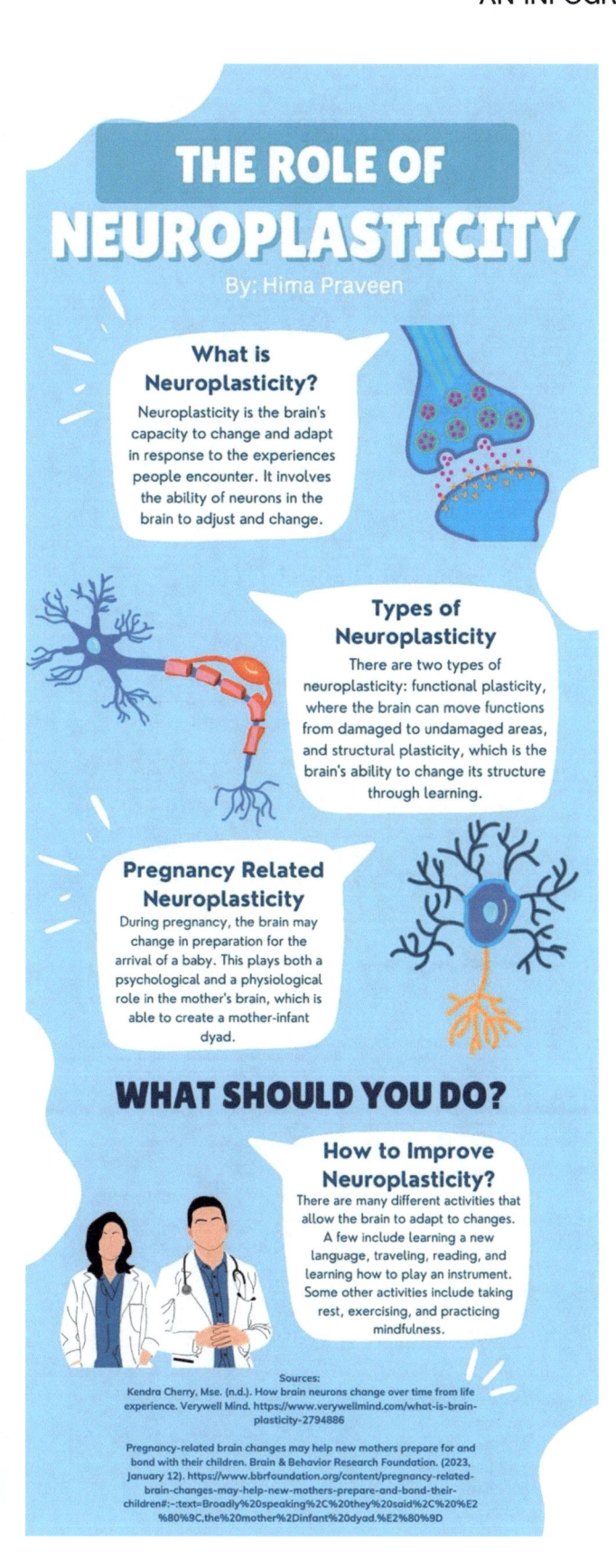

AN INFOGRAPHIC JOURNEY

THE ROLE OF NEUROPLASTICITY
By: Hima Praveen

What is Neuroplasticity?
Neuroplasticity is the brain's capacity to change and adapt in response to the experiences people encounter. It involves the ability of neurons in the brain to adjust and change.

Types of Neuroplasticity
There are two types of neuroplasticity: functional plasticity, where the brain can move functions from damaged to undamaged areas, and structural plasticity, which is the brain's ability to change its structure through learning.

Pregnancy Related Neuroplasticity
During pregnancy, the brain may change in preparation for the arrival of a baby. This plays both a psychological and a physiological role in the mother's brain, which is able to create a mother-infant dyad.

WHAT SHOULD YOU DO?

How to Improve Neuroplasticity?
There are many different activities that allow the brain to adapt to changes. A few include learning a new language, traveling, reading, and learning how to play an instrument. Some other activities include taking rest, exercising, and practicing mindfulness.

Sources:
Kendra Cherry, Mse. (n.d.). How brain neurons change over time from life experience. Verywell Mind. https://www.verywellmind.com/what-is-brain-plasticity-2794886

Pregnancy-related brain changes may help new mothers prepare for and bond with their children. Brain & Behavior Research Foundation. (2023, January 12). https://www.bbrfoundation.org/content/pregnancy-related-brain-changes-may-help-new-mothers-prepare-and-bond-their-children#:~:text=Broadly%20speaking%2C%20they%20said%2C%20%E2%80%9C,the%20mother%2Dinfant%20dyad.%E2%80%9D

Hima Praveen, Fall 2023

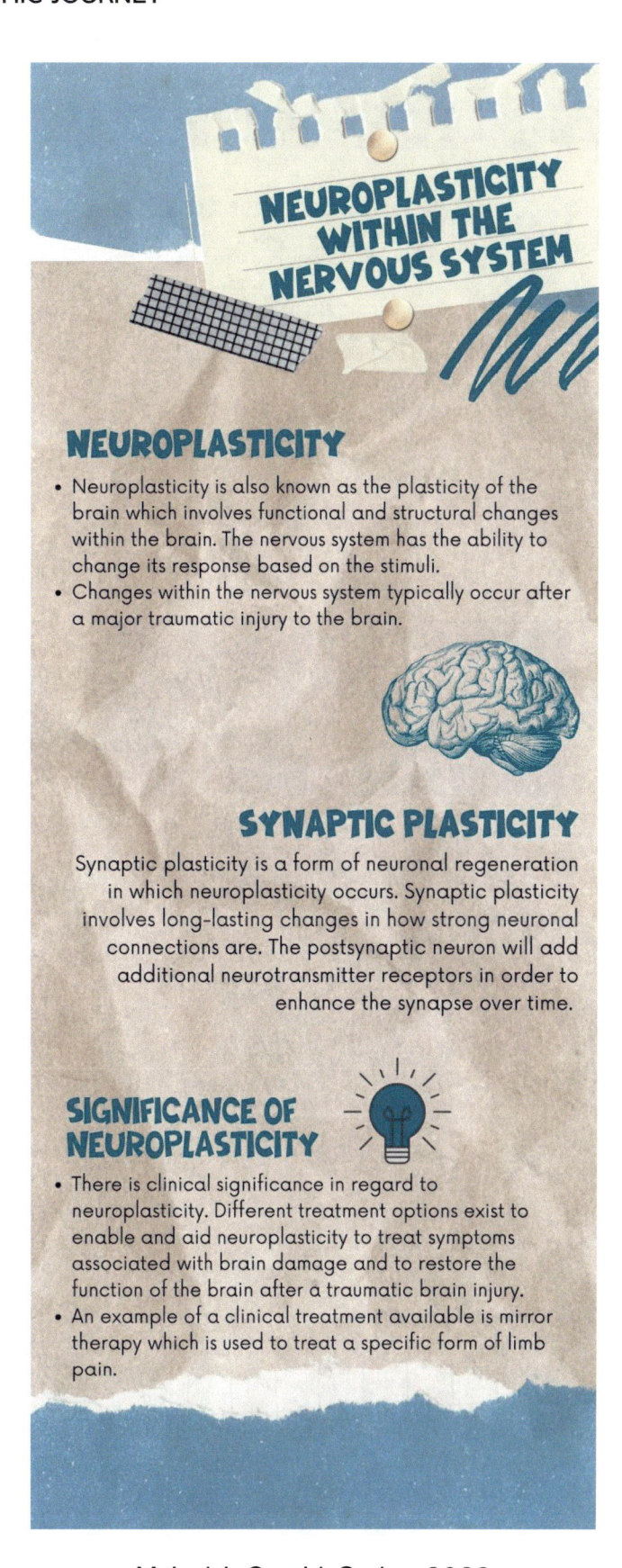

NEUROPLASTICITY WITHIN THE NERVOUS SYSTEM

NEUROPLASTICITY
- Neuroplasticity is also known as the plasticity of the brain which involves functional and structural changes within the brain. The nervous system has the ability to change its response based on the stimuli.
- Changes within the nervous system typically occur after a major traumatic injury to the brain.

SYNAPTIC PLASTICITY
Synaptic plasticity is a form of neuronal regeneration in which neuroplasticity occurs. Synaptic plasticity involves long-lasting changes in how strong neuronal connections are. The postsynaptic neuron will add additional neurotransmitter receptors in order to enhance the synapse over time.

SIGNIFICANCE OF NEUROPLASTICITY
- There is clinical significance in regard to neuroplasticity. Different treatment options exist to enable and aid neuroplasticity to treat symptoms associated with brain damage and to restore the function of the brain after a traumatic brain injury.
- An example of a clinical treatment available is mirror therapy which is used to treat a specific form of limb pain.

Mahwish Quadri, Spring 2023

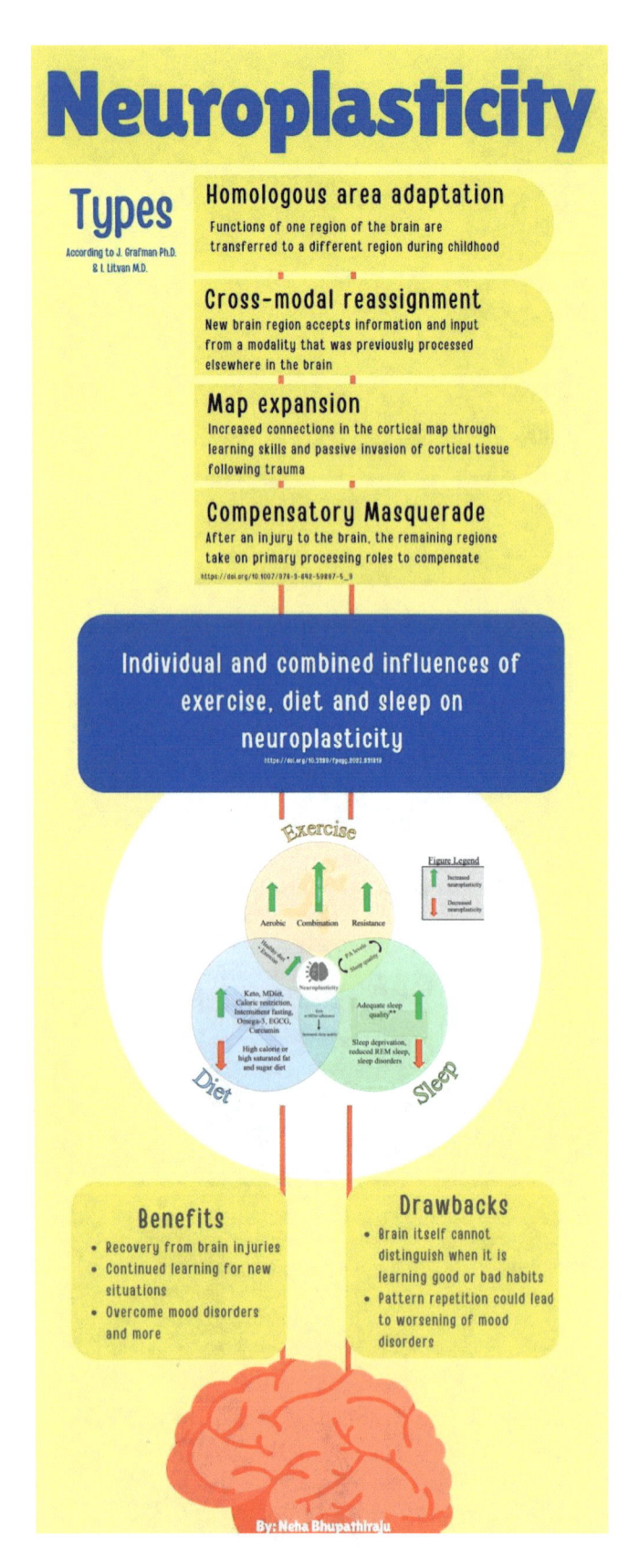

Neha Bhupathiraju, Spring 2023

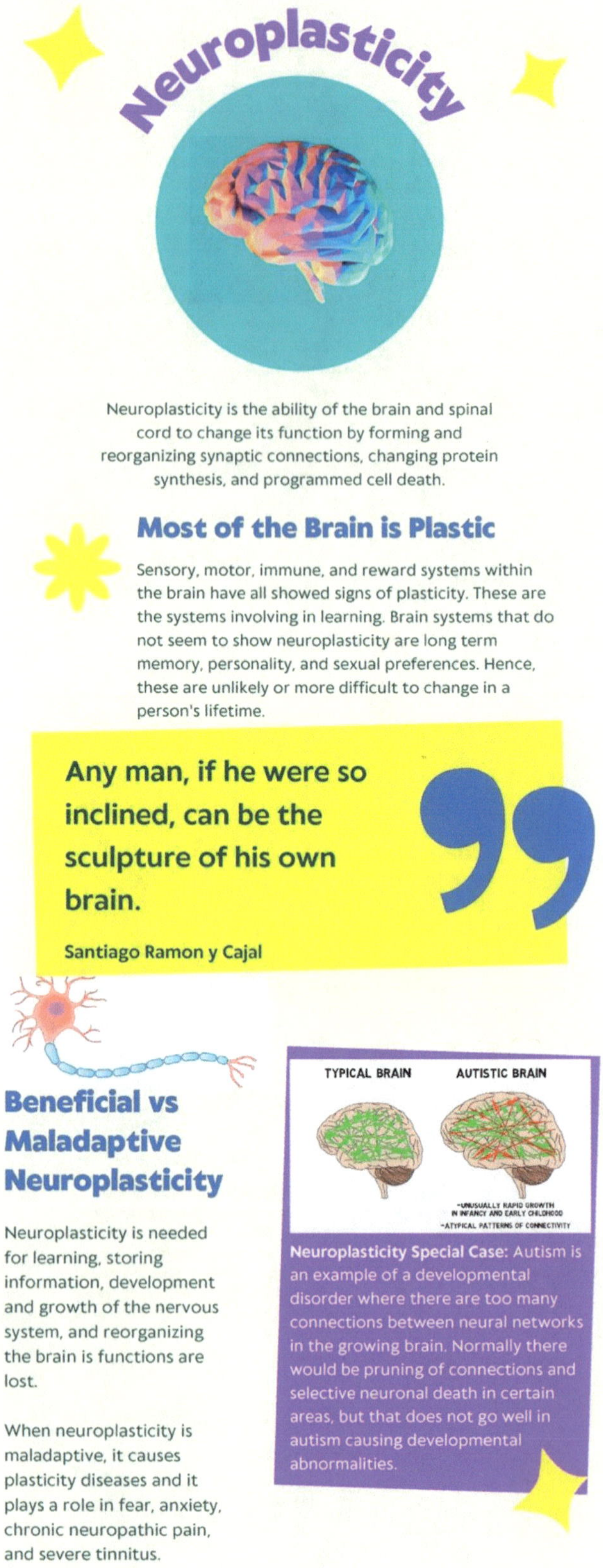

Sara Saravanan, Fall 2022

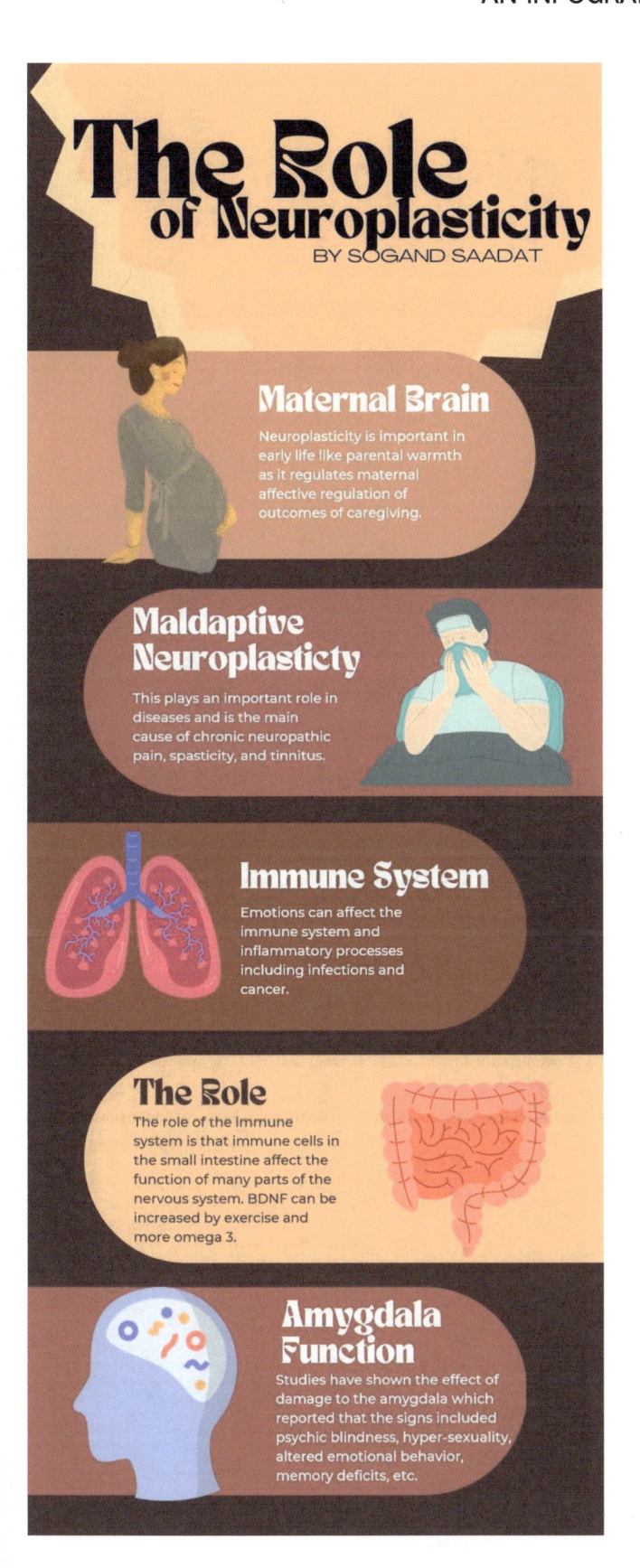

AN INFOGRAPHIC JOURNEY

The Role of Neuroplasticity
BY SOGAND SAADAT

Maternal Brain
Neuroplasticity is important in early life like parental warmth as it regulates maternal affective regulation of outcomes of caregiving.

Maldaptive Neuroplasticty
This plays an important role in diseases and is the main cause of chronic neuropathic pain, spasticity, and tinnitus.

Immune System
Emotions can affect the immune system and inflammatory processes including infections and cancer.

The Role
The role of the immune system is that immune cells in the small intestine affect the function of many parts of the nervous system. BDNF can be increased by exercise and more omega 3.

Amygdala Function
Studies have shown the effect of damage to the amygdala which reported that the signs included psychic blindness, hyper-sexuality, altered emotional behavior, memory deficits, etc.

Sogand Saadat, Spring 2023

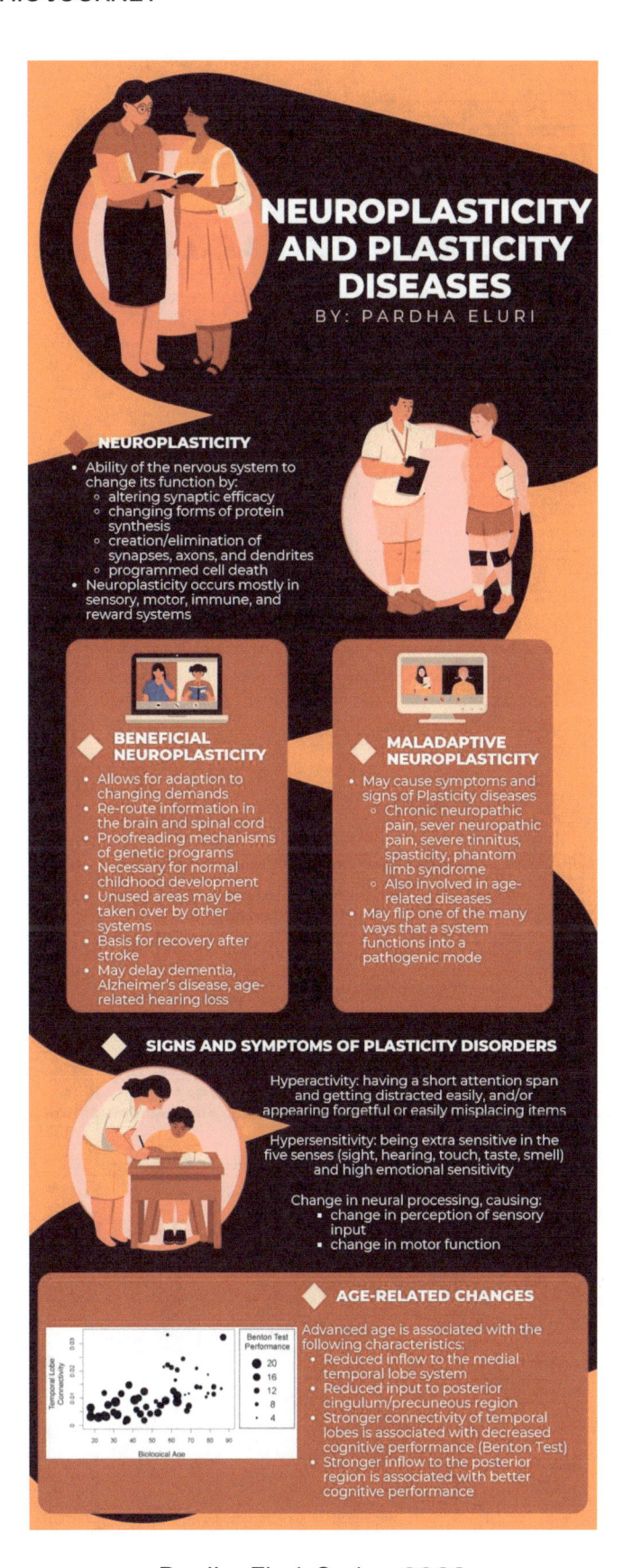

NEUROPLASTICITY AND PLASTICITY DISEASES
BY: PARDHA ELURI

NEUROPLASTICITY
- Ability of the nervous system to change its function by:
  - altering synaptic efficacy
  - changing forms of protein synthesis
  - creation/elimination of synapses, axons, and dendrites
  - programmed cell death
- Neuroplasticity occurs mostly in sensory, motor, immune, and reward systems

BENEFICIAL NEUROPLASTICITY
- Allows for adaption to changing demands
- Re-route information in the brain and spinal cord
- Proofreading mechanisms of genetic programs
- Necessary for normal childhood development
- Unused areas may be taken over by other systems
- Basis for recovery after stroke
- May delay dementia, Alzheimer's disease, age-related hearing loss

MALADAPTIVE NEUROPLASTICITY
- May cause symptoms and signs of Plasticity diseases
  - Chronic neuropathic pain, sever neuropathic pain, severe tinnitus, spasticity, phantom limb syndrome
  - Also involved in age-related diseases
- May flip one of the many ways that a system functions into a pathogenic mode

SIGNS AND SYMPTOMS OF PLASTICITY DISORDERS

Hyperactivity: having a short attention span and getting distracted easily, and/or appearing forgetful or easily misplacing items

Hypersensitivity: being extra sensitive in the five senses (sight, hearing, touch, taste, smell) and high emotional sensitivity

Change in neural processing, causing:
- change in perception of sensory input
- change in motor function

AGE-RELATED CHANGES
Advanced age is associated with the following characteristics:
- Reduced inflow to the medial temporal lobe system
- Reduced input to posterior cingulum/precuneous region
- Stronger connectivity of temporal lobes is associated with decreased cognitive performance (Benton Test)
- Stronger inflow to the posterior region is associated with better cognitive performance

Pardha Eluri, Spring 2023

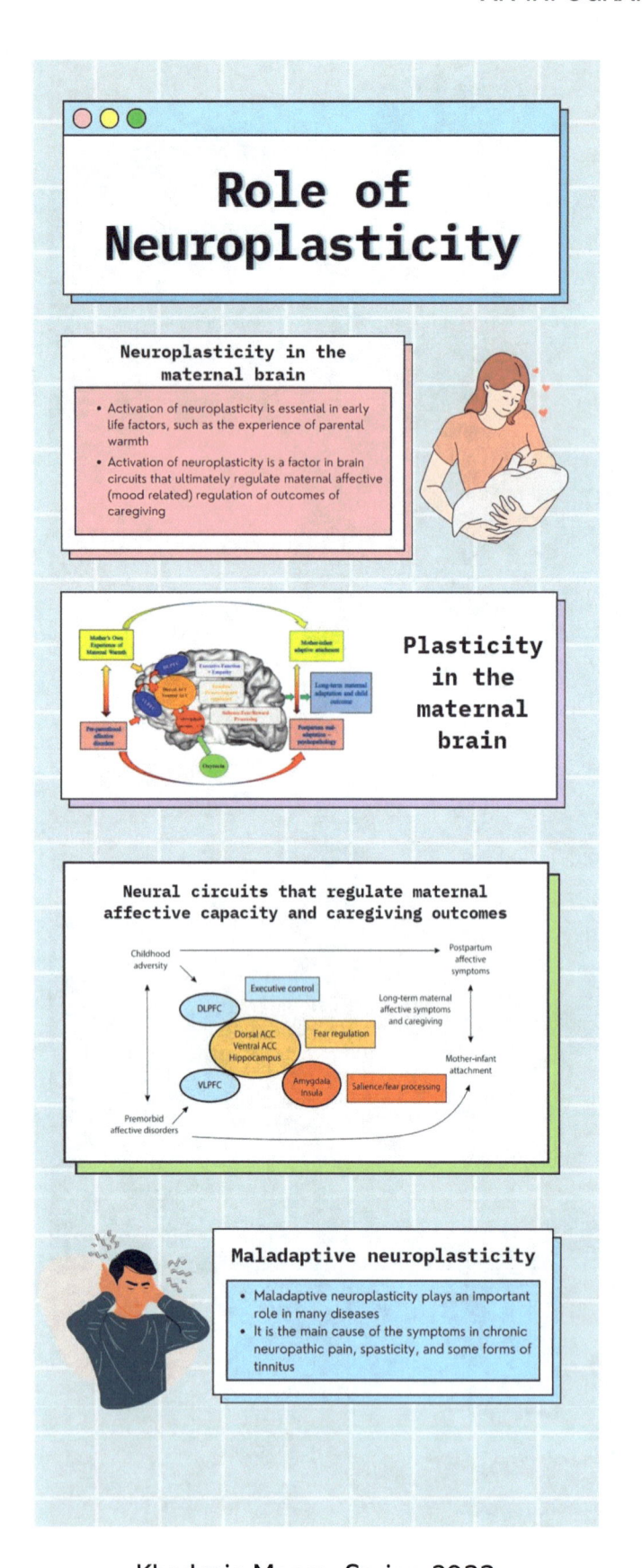

AN INFOGRAPHIC JOURNEY

Khadeeja Moosa, Spring 2023

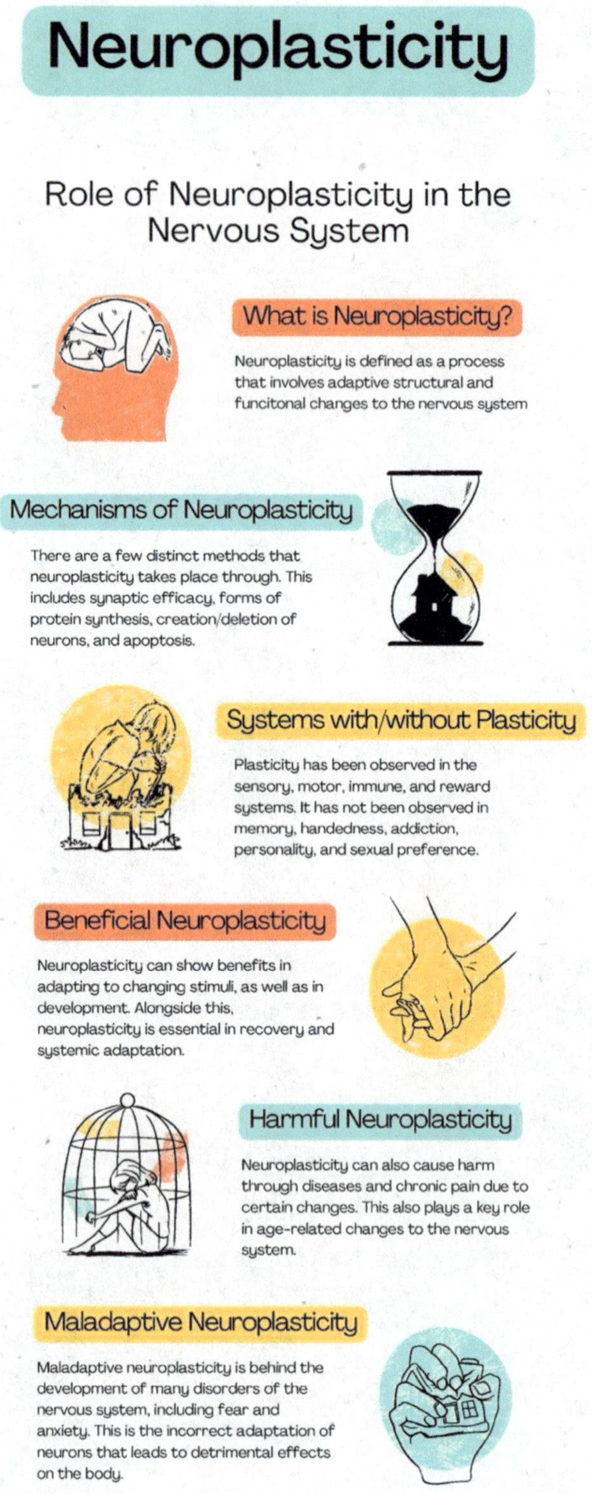

Edwin Phillip, Spring 2024

AN INFOGRAPHIC JOURNEY

ALL ABOUT Neuroplasticity

Neuroplasticity refers to the brain's ability to adapt to stimuli by reorganizing synaptic connections, programmed cell death, modifying protein synthesis pathways, etc.

NOT ALL OF THE BRAIN IS PLASTIC.

The sensory, motor, immune, and reward (addiction-related) systems have all shown plasticity. The following functions are not shown to be plastic: long-term memory, handedness, sexual preferences, personality, etc.

THE NECESSITY OF PLASTICITY

Neuroplasticity is necessary to learn new skills, store information, normal development of the nervous system, and reorganize the nervous system to compensate for or replace loss of function.

Beneficial forms of neuroplasticity
- adaptation to changing directions or demands
- changes part of normal childhood development
- unused areas may be taken over by other systems
- basis of recovery after stroke and other neurological conditions
- can delay onset of neurodegenerative diseases

Harmful forms of neuroplasticity
Has been found to be the main cause of:
- neuropathic pain
- severe tinnitus
- spasticity
- phantom limb syndromes
- negative physiological changes due to aging
- fibromyalgia
- chronic fatigue syndrome

Did you know?
Phantom sensations are caused by maladaptive neuroplasticity through increased activation of the primary somatosensory cortices.

ENVIRONMENTAL FACTORS

In addition to genetic factors, the environment can influence plasticity through the modulation of gene expression, or epigenetics.

Neuroplasticity is an umbrella term.
It refers to several different types of morphological changes in the brain involving various structures on the synaptic and molecular level, including microglia, neurons, and vascular cells.

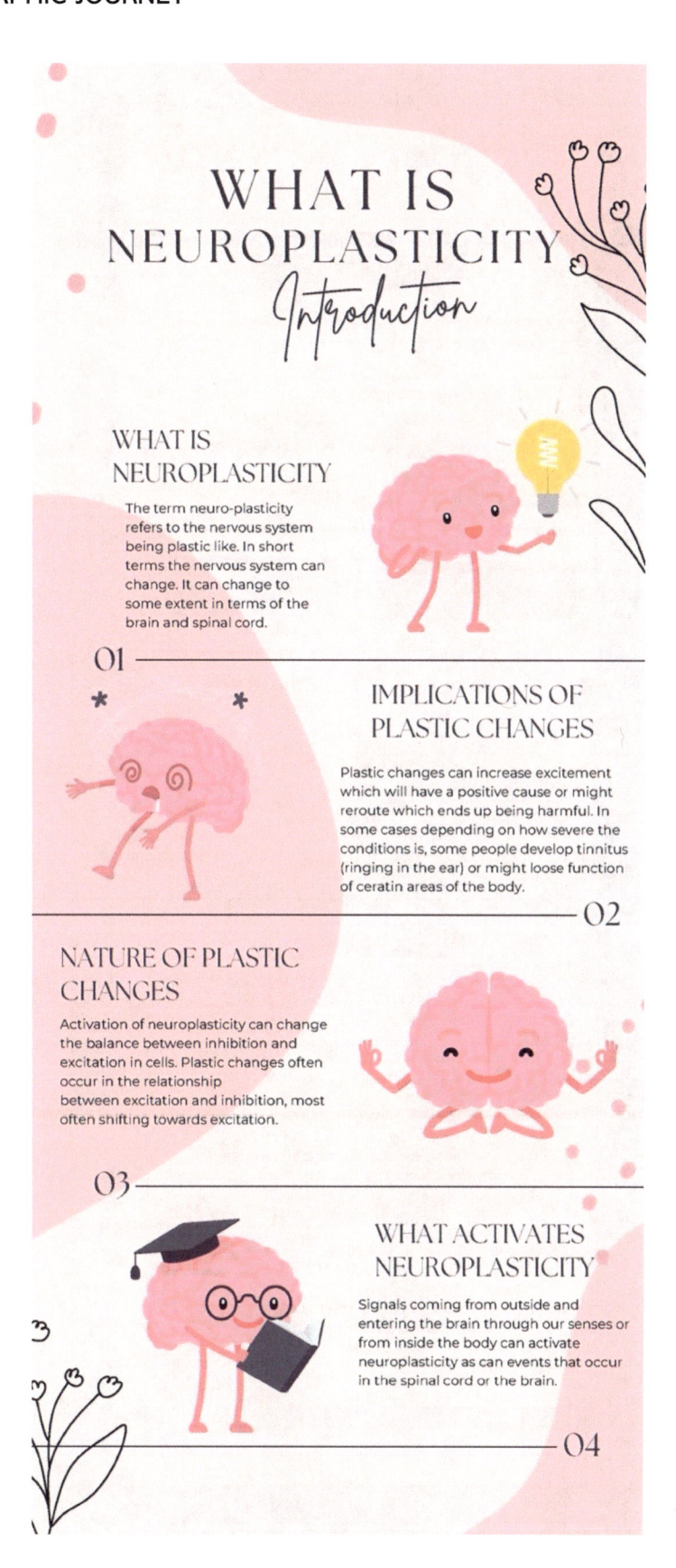

NSC 4382

Shreya Jupelly, Spring 2024

WHAT IS NEUROPLASTICITY
Introduction

WHAT IS NEUROPLASTICITY

The term neuro-plasticity refers to the nervous system being plastic like. In short terms the nervous system can change. It can change to some extent in terms of the brain and spinal cord.

01

IMPLICATIONS OF PLASTIC CHANGES

Plastic changes can increase excitement which will have a positive cause or might reroute which ends up being harmful. In some cases depending on how severe the conditions is, some people develop tinnitus (ringing in the ear) or might loose function of ceratin areas of the body.

02

NATURE OF PLASTIC CHANGES

Activation of neuroplasticity can change the balance between inhibition and excitation in cells. Plastic changes often occur in the relationship between excitation and inhibition, most often shifting towards excitation.

03

WHAT ACTIVATES NEUROPLASTICITY

Signals coming from outside and entering the brain through our senses or from inside the body can activate neuroplasticity as can events that occur in the spinal cord or the brain.

04

Inioluwa Adenekan, Spring 2024

AN INFOGRAPHIC JOURNEY

NEUROPLASTICITY

What is Neuroplasticity?

Neuroplasticity is the ability of the nervous system to change its function by:

- Changing synaptic efficacy
- Changing forms of protein synthesis
- Creation and elimination of synapses, axons, and dendrites
- Programmed cell death (apoptosis)

Systems that show plasticity:

- Sensory Systems
- Motor Systems
- Immune System
- Reward System (addictions)

Functions that do not seem to be plastic:

- Long Term Memory
- Handedness
- Sexual Preferences
- Some Forms of Addictions
- Personality

Good Plasticity

- Activation of good plasticity makes it possible to adapt to changing demands
- Necessary for learning new skills and storing information
- Necessary for normal childhood development
- Unused areas may be taken over by other systems
- Basis for recovery after stroke
- May delay dementia and Alzheimer's disease, and perhaps age-related hearing loss

Bad Plasticity

- Activation of bad (maladaptive) plasticity may cause symptoms and signs of diseases
- Main cause of diseases such as chronic neuropathic pain, severe tinnitus, spasticity, and phantom limb symptoms

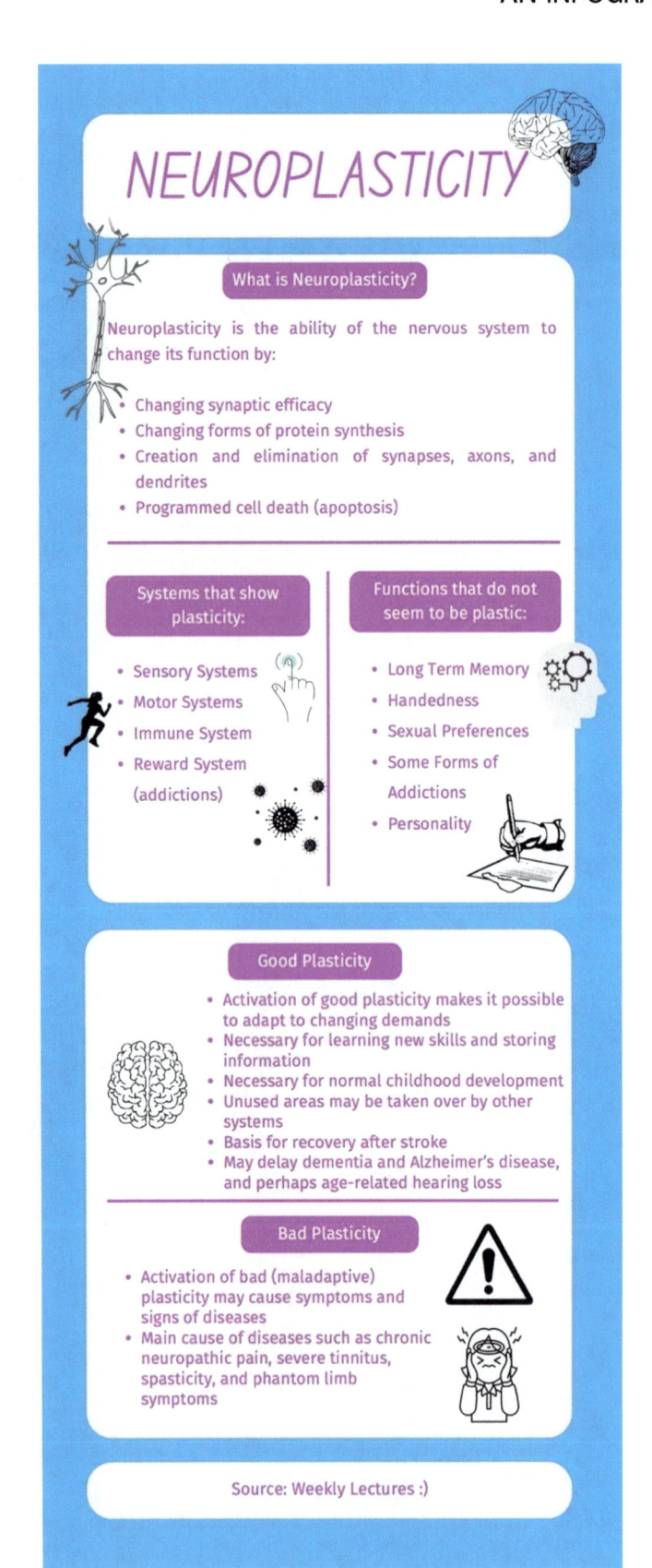

Source: Weekly Lectures :)

Audrey Villanueva, Fall 2023

NEUROPLASTICITY
HELEN NGUYEN

NEUROPLASTICITY IN THE MATERNAL BRAIN

- Activation of neuroplasticity is essential in early life factors, such as the experience of parental warmth
- Activation of neuroplasticity is a factor in brain circuits that ultimately regulate maternal affective (mood related) regulation of outcomes of caregiving

MALADAPTIVE NEUROPLASTICITY

- Maladaptive neuroplasticity plays an important role in many diseases
- It is the main cause of the symptoms in chronic neuropathic pain, spasticity, and some forms of tinnitus
- It is a contributing factor in many other diseases

THE ROLE OF THE IMMUNE SYSTEM

- Emotions can affect inflammatory processes and perhaps infections and cancer
- Factors implicating in the causes of the symptoms of these diseases have also grown and now include BDNF in addition to maladaptive plasticity
- This is a favorable development in that these factors can be affected by relatively simple means

INFLAMMATORY REFLEX

- Neuronal interconnections between the NTS, A P, DMN, NA, and higher forebrain regions integrate afferent signaling and efferent vagus nerve-mediated immunoregulatory output.
- Microglia are the primary recipients of peripheral inflammatory signals as they reach the brain
- Stress, pain, and depression lead to excessive and untimely release of corticotropin-releasing hormone (CRH), adrenocorticotropic hormone (ACTH) and glucocorticoids

EFFECT OF DAMAGE TO THE AMYGDALA

- human amygdala is indispensable to:
  - recognize fear in facial expressions
  - recognize multiple emotions in a single facial expression
  - it is NOT required for recognizing personal identity from faces.
- These results suggest that damage restricted to the amygdala causes particular recognition impairments, and thus forces the notion that the amygdala is involved in emotion" (Adolphs, 1994).

SOURCES:
BLACKBOARD. (2020). WEEK 8, CHAPTER 3, PART 6 NEUROPLASTICITY - NSC _ RETRIEVED OCTOBER 14, 2023, FROM UTDALLAS.EDU WEBSITE: HTTPS://ELEARNING.UTDALLAS.EDU/WEBAPPS/BLACKBOARD/EXECUTE/CONTENT/FILE?CMD=VIEW&CONTENT_ID=_7107583_1&COURSE_ID=_335276_1

Helen Nguyen, Fall 2023

AN INFOGRAPHIC JOURNEY

CLOSER LOOK AT NEUROPLASTICITY

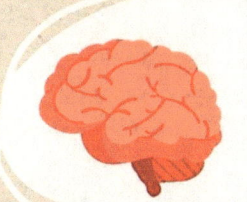

WHAT IS NEUROPLASTICITY?
The ability of the nervous system to change its function by changing synaptic efficacy, changing forms of protein synthesis, creation and elimination of synapses, axons, & dendrites, and programmed cell death.

PLASTIC AND NOT PLASTIC
Sensory systems, motor systems, immune systems, and reward systems have shown plasticity. Long term memory, handedness, sexual preferences, some forms of addiction, and personality do not seem to be plastic.

GOOD NEUROPLASTICITY
It makes it possible to adapt to changing demands, re-routes information in the brain and spinal cord, and provides "mid-course corrections" of genetic programs.

MALADAPTIVE NEUROPLASTICITY
May cause diseases such as chronic neuropathic pain, phantom limb symptoms, or disorders associated with fear and anxiety.

AGING
Studied have found that some age-related changes in resting state connectivity is related to cognitive changes, such as reduced inflow to the medial temporal lobe or stronger inflow to posterior region.

Sources: Møller, A.R. Sensory Systems: Anatomy and Physiology, Aage R. Møller Publishing, 2014

Sarvani Ganapavarapu, Fall 2023

Neuroplasticity

JUSTIN DE VERA- NSC 4382

WHAT IS NEUROPLASTICITY?
Neuroplasticity explains the process in which the functions of the nervous system are altered through changes in synapses, protein sythesis, and cell death.

SYSTEMS THAT SHOW PLASTICITY
- Sensory systems
- Motor systems
- Immune system

BENEFICIAL NEUROPLASTICITY
- Allows for normal nervous system development/repair
- Chance to delay conditions such as dementia
- Useful in stroke recovery

MALADAPTIVE NEUROPLASTICITY
can create certain disorders such as:
- Severe tinnitus
- Phantom limb syndrome
- Chronic neuropathic pain

SOURCES
Møller, A.R. "Neurobiology of Fear, Anxiety and other Emotions" Chapter 6

Justin De Vera, Spring 2024

AN INFOGRAPHIC JOURNEY

Neurobiology of Emotion
Neuroplasticity

1. Overview
Neuroplasticity is the ability of the cells of the nervous system to change their function through different ways (lecture). It is key for learning, memory, and key in restoring body functions at the neuronal level (PubMed)

2. Mechanisms
Neurons can change their function by adjusting synaptic connections (synaptogenesis, strengthening, or pruning), or by destroying cells internally (via apoptosis) (lecture).

3. Plastic Tissue
Almost all neurons in the nervous system can exhibit neuroplasticity. Cells in the primary motor and somatosensory cortex have been shown to experience neuroplasticity to account for motor and sensory deficits.

4. Good Plasticity
Positive neuroplasticity allows the brain to adapt to changing demands. In tissue death due to stroke, the surrounding tissue can take over functions of the dead tissue. This allows some degree of recovery (lecture)

5. Bad Plasticity
Neuroplasticity can act in harmful ways in chronic neuropathic pain, tinnitus, and muscle spasm. Some signs of maladaptive neuroplasticity are hyperactivity/hypersensitivity, and changes in sensation (lecture)

Hussam Asim, Fall 2023

WHAT IS NEUROPLASTICITY

Neuroplasticity is defined to be the ability of the nervous system to change its function by: changing synaptic efficacy; changing forms of protein synthesis; creation and elimination of synapses, axons, and dendrites; and programmed cell death (termed apoptosis).

Type 1: Structural Plasticity
Structural plasticity allows the brain to change its physical structure as a result of experiences and memories. This facilitates learning and development, especially throughout child development.

Type 2: Functional Plasticity
Functional plasticity allows the brain to maintain its functional capacity by moving brain functions from a damaged area to an undamaged area.

Systems That Show Plasticity
- Sensory Systems
- Motor Systems
- Immune System
- Reward Systems (addictions)

Systems That Do Not Show Plasticity
- Long-term Memory
- Handedness
- Sexual Preferences
- Some Forms of Addictions
- Personality

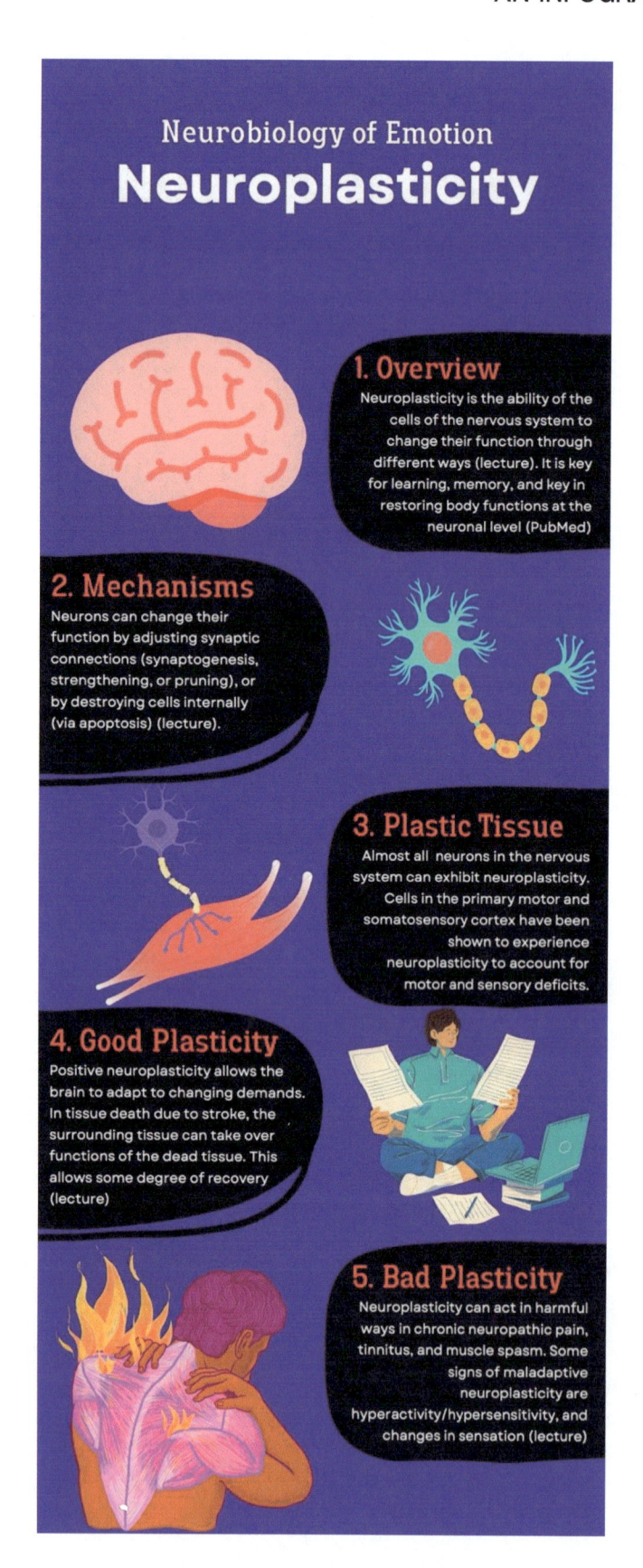

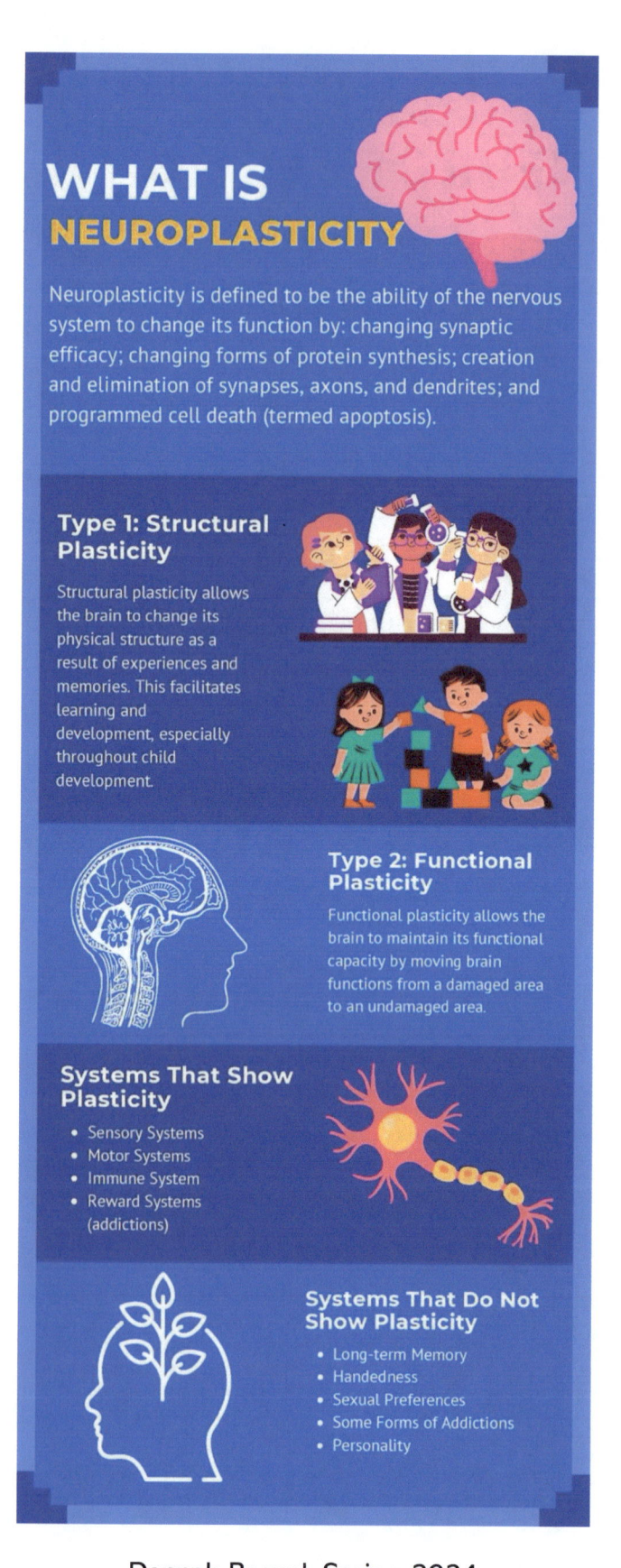

Dannah Bagcal, Spring 2024

AN INFOGRAPHIC JOURNEY

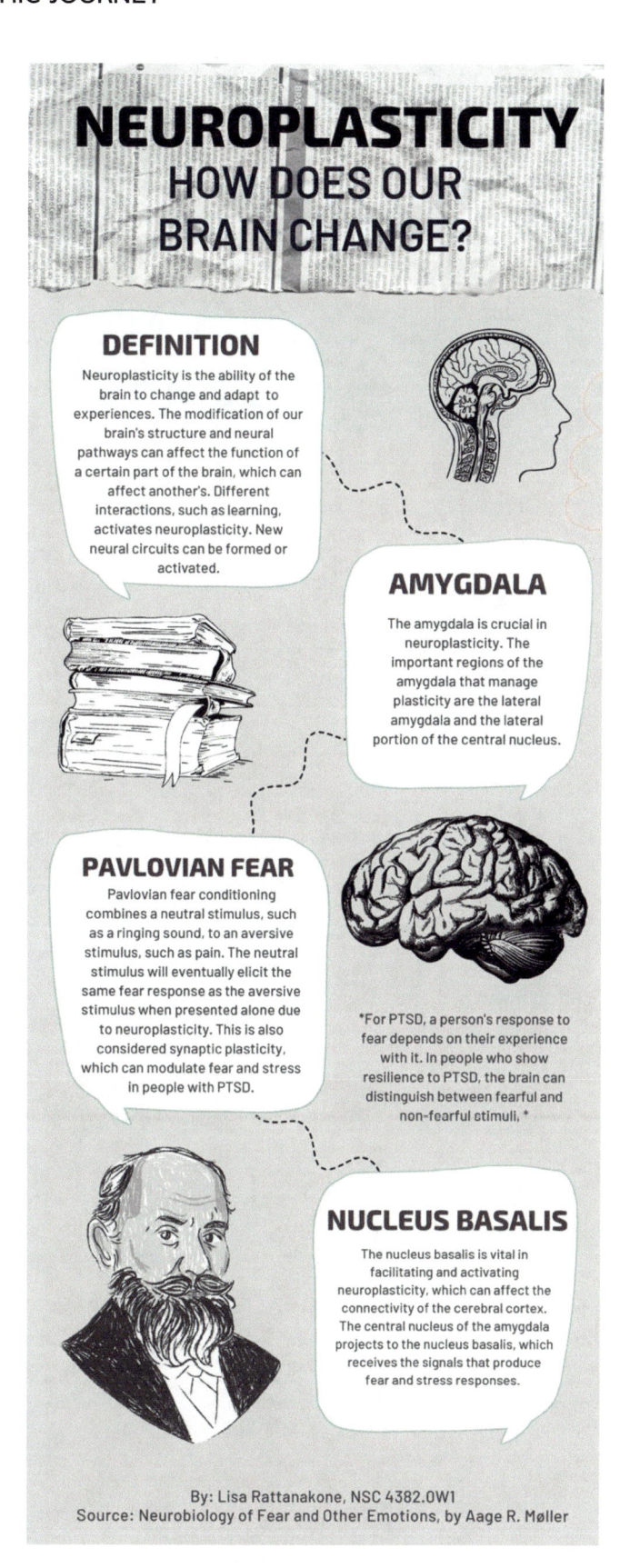

Rohita Arjarapu, Fall 2023

Lisa Rattankone, Fall 2022

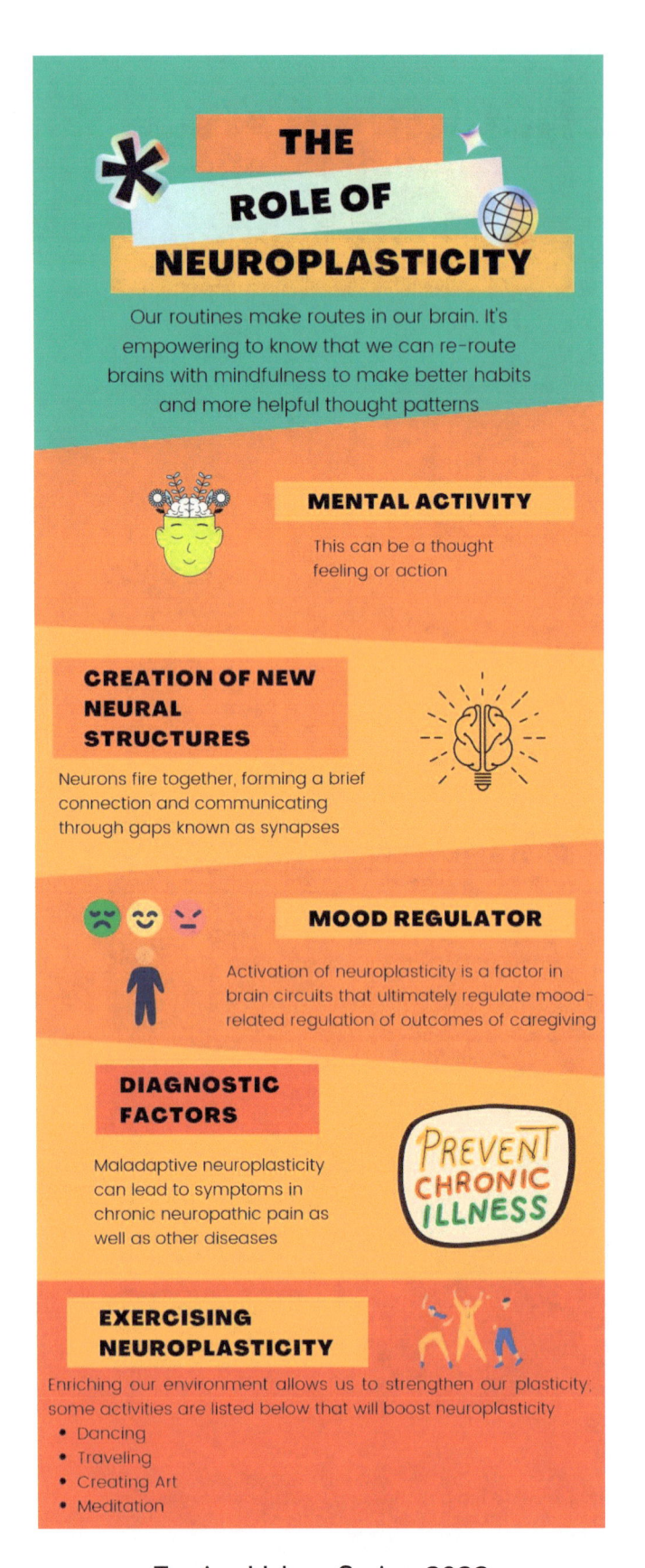

AN INFOGRAPHIC JOURNEY

THE ROLE OF NEUROPLASTICITY

Our routines make routes in our brain. It's empowering to know that we can re-route brains with mindfulness to make better habits and more helpful thought patterns

MENTAL ACTIVITY
This can be a thought feeling or action

CREATION OF NEW NEURAL STRUCTURES
Neurons fire together, forming a brief connection and communicating through gaps known as synapses

MOOD REGULATOR
Activation of neuroplasticity is a factor in brain circuits that ultimately regulate mood-related regulation of outcomes of caregiving

DIAGNOSTIC FACTORS
Maladaptive neuroplasticity can lead to symptoms in chronic neuropathic pain as well as other diseases

PREVENT CHRONIC ILLNESS

EXERCISING NEUROPLASTICITY
Enriching our environment allows us to strengthen our plasticity; some activities are listed below that will boost neuroplasticity
- Dancing
- Traveling
- Creating Art
- Meditation

Tamjeed Islam, Spring 2023

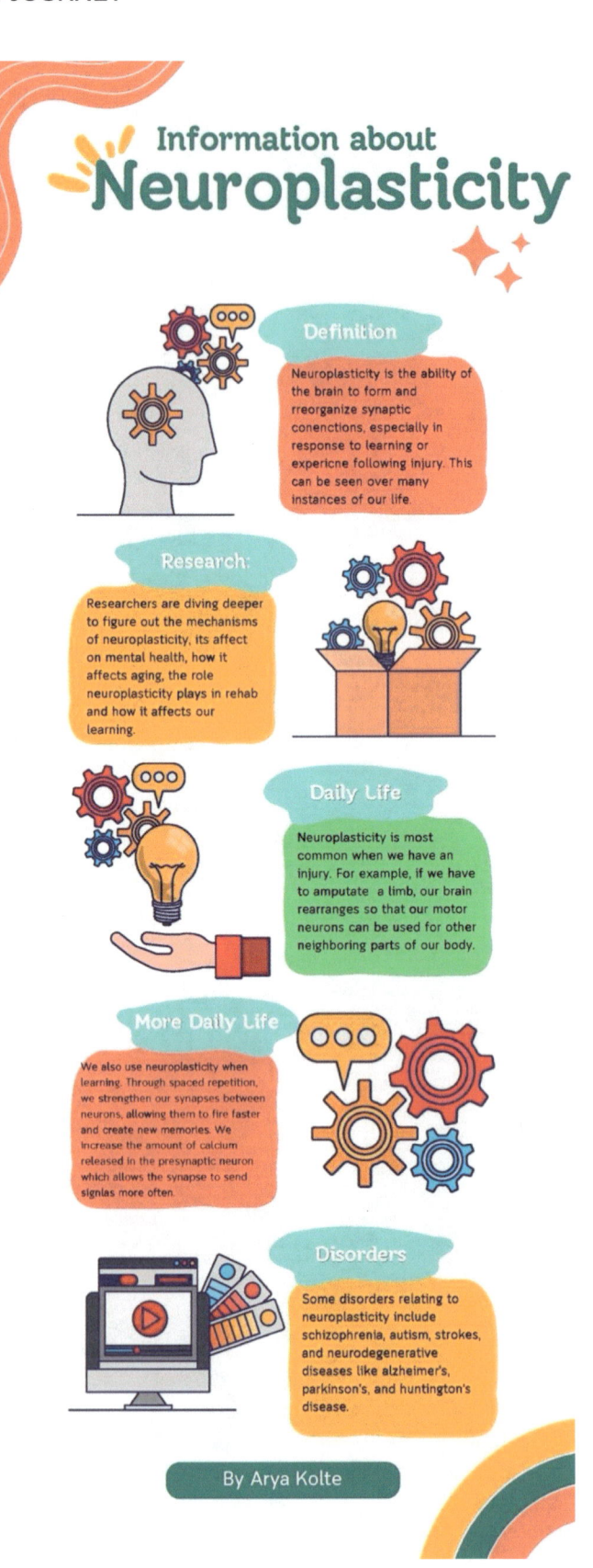

Information about Neuroplasticity

Definition
Neuroplasticity is the ability of the brain to form and reorganize synaptic conenctions, especially in response to learning or expericne following injury. This can be seen over many instances of our life.

Research:
Researchers are diving deeper to figure out the mechanisms of neuroplasticity, its affect on mental health, how it affects aging, the role neuroplasticity plays in rehab and how it affects our learning.

Daily Life
Neuroplasticity is most common when we have an injury. For example, if we have to amputate a limb, our brain rearranges so that our motor neurons can be used for other neighboring parts of our body.

More Daily Life
We also use neuroplasticity when learning. Through spaced repetition, we strengthen our synapses between neurons, allowing them to fire faster and create new memories. We increase the amount of calcium released in the presynaptic neuron which allows the synapse to send signlas more often.

Disorders
Some disorders relating to neuroplasticity include schizophrenia, autism, strokes, and neurodegenerative diseases like alzheimer's, parkinson's, and huntington's disease.

By Arya Kolte

Arya Kolte, Spring 2024

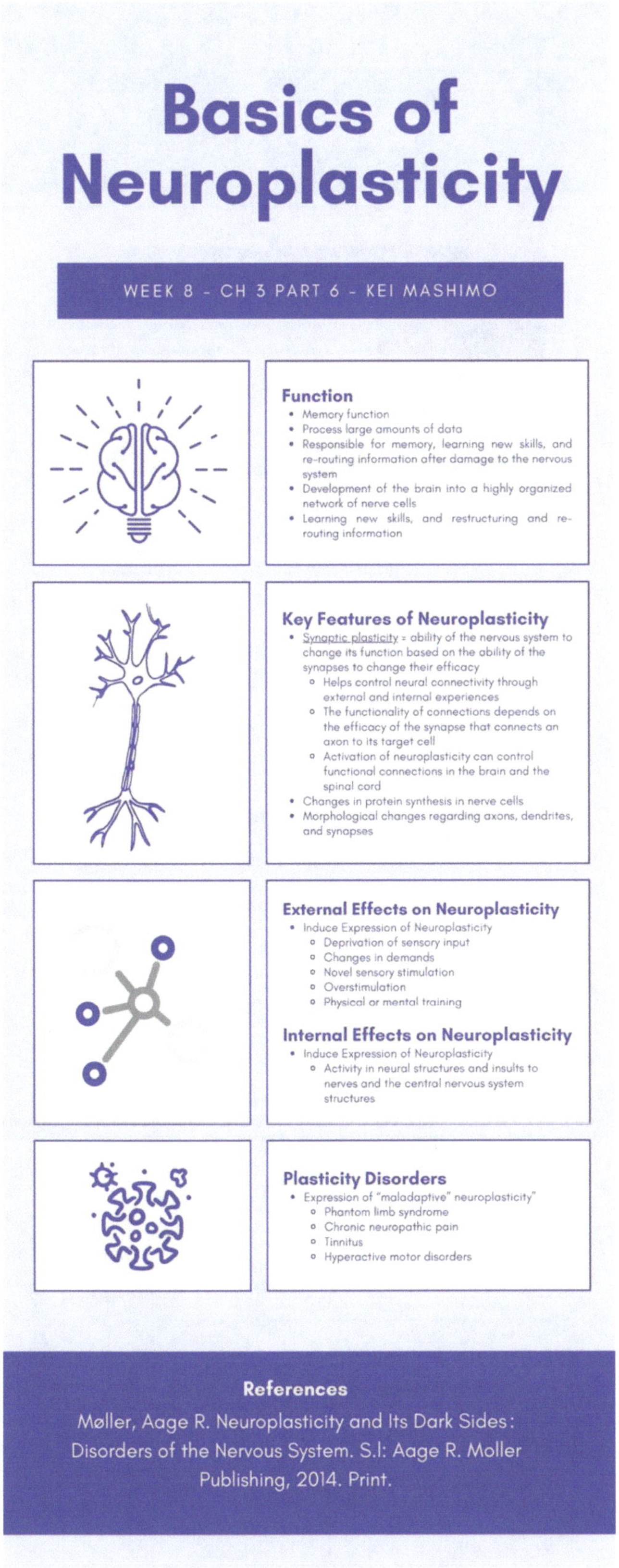

AN INFOGRAPHIC JOURNEY

Basics of Neuroplasticity

WEEK 8 – CH 3 PART 6 – KEI MASHIMO

Function
- Memory function
- Process large amounts of data
- Responsible for memory, learning new skills, and re-routing information after damage to the nervous system
- Development of the brain into a highly organized network of nerve cells
- Learning new skills, and restructuring and re-routing information

Key Features of Neuroplasticity
- Synaptic plasticity = ability of the nervous system to change its function based on the ability of the synapses to change their efficacy
  - Helps control neural connectivity through external and internal experiences
  - The functionality of connections depends on the efficacy of the synapse that connects an axon to its target cell
  - Activation of neuroplasticity can control functional connections in the brain and the spinal cord
- Changes in protein synthesis in nerve cells
- Morphological changes regarding axons, dendrites, and synapses

External Effects on Neuroplasticity
- Induce Expression of Neuroplasticity
  - Deprivation of sensory input
  - Changes in demands
  - Novel sensory stimulation
  - Overstimulation
  - Physical or mental training

Internal Effects on Neuroplasticity
- Induce Expression of Neuroplasticity
  - Activity in neural structures and insults to nerves and the central nervous system structures

Plasticity Disorders
- Expression of "maladaptive" neuroplasticity
  - Phantom limb syndrome
  - Chronic neuropathic pain
  - Tinnitus
  - Hyperactive motor disorders

References
Møller, Aage R. Neuroplasticity and Its Dark Sides: Disorders of the Nervous System. S.l: Aage R. Moller Publishing, 2014. Print.

Kei Mashimo, Fall 2022

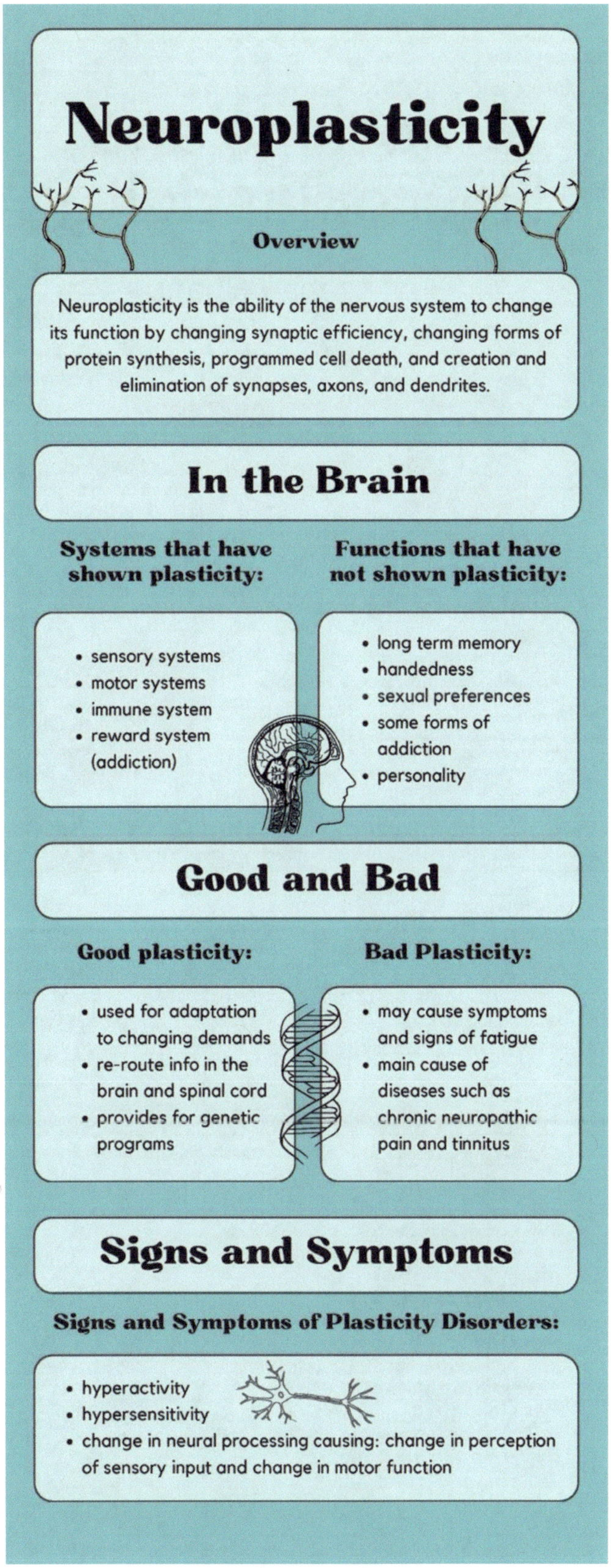

Neuroplasticity

Overview
Neuroplasticity is the ability of the nervous system to change its function by changing synaptic efficiency, changing forms of protein synthesis, programmed cell death, and creation and elimination of synapses, axons, and dendrites.

In the Brain

Systems that have shown plasticity:
- sensory systems
- motor systems
- immune system
- reward system (addiction)

Functions that have not shown plasticity:
- long term memory
- handedness
- sexual preferences
- some forms of addiction
- personality

Good and Bad

Good plasticity:
- used for adaptation to changing demands
- re-route info in the brain and spinal cord
- provides for genetic programs

Bad Plasticity:
- may cause symptoms and signs of fatigue
- main cause of diseases such as chronic neuropathic pain and tinnitus

Signs and Symptoms

Signs and Symptoms of Plasticity Disorders:
- hyperactivity
- hypersensitivity
- change in neural processing causing: change in perception of sensory input and change in motor function

Aisha Ali, Spring 2024

AN INFOGRAPHIC JOURNEY

Emotions and Neuroplasticity

By: Madhav Bhatt

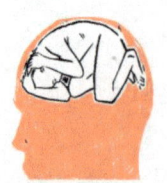

Neuroplasticity

Neuroplasticity is the brain's remarkable ability to form new connections and pathways throughout life. It enables learning, memory, and recovery from brain injuries.

Anatomy of Our Emotional Brain

- Amygdala: Central to processing emotions like fear and pleasure.
- Prefrontal Cortex: Involved in decision-making, personality expression, and moderating social behavior.
- Anterior Cingulate Cortex: Plays a role in empathy, impulse control, and emotion.

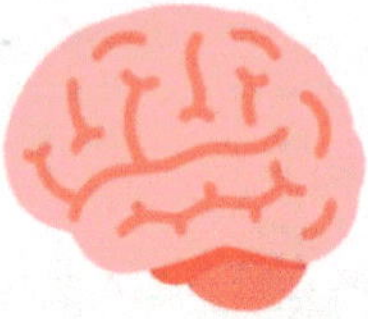

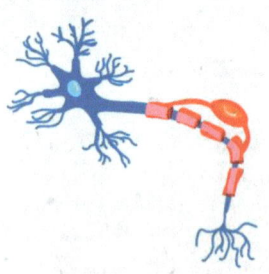

Emotional Expressions and the Amygdala

- Sensory Processing: The amygdala evaluates sensory information through both fast, direct pathways (for immediate reactions) and slower, more analytical pathways (for complex evaluations).
- Behavioral Responses: It helps mediate various emotional responses, from instinctual fear to complex social interactions, showcasing the amygdala's pivotal role in our emotional lives.

The Dark Side of Neuroplasticity

- Maladaptive Changes: Sometimes, neuroplasticity can lead to negative outcomes, such as chronic pain or tinnitus, when the brain 'mislearns' or reinforces harmful pathways.
- Mental Health: Understanding maladaptive neuroplasticity is crucial for developing treatments for various mental health conditions, showing that the brain's adaptability can have both positive and negative effects.

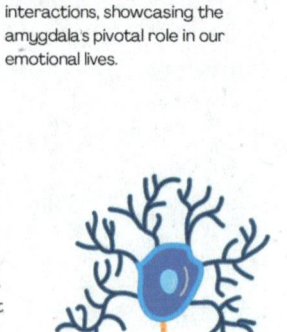

Madhav Bhatt, Spring 2024

NEUROPLASTICITY AND EMOTIONS
RIDA HAMID

WHAT IS NEUROPLASTICITY?
This is the brain's ability to rebuild and reform its synaptic connections in order to adapt to new situations, learn from them, and grow.

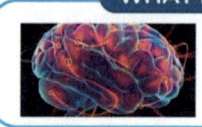

PURPOSE OF NEUROPLASTICITY
Neuroplasticity is activated with mood-related situations, especially caregiving. This can stem from maternal relations, especially at birth and the first few months of life.

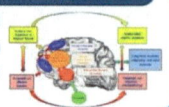

MALADAPTIVE NEUROPLASTICITY
This is a process where although neural connections are created and do change, they are not helpful, and are in fact detrimental. It can lead to other diseases, and is the number one cause of chronic neuropathic pain.

THE IMMUNE SYSTEM
The immune system plays a role in all parts of the body, and it includes cells from the small intestine that have a connection to the nervous system.

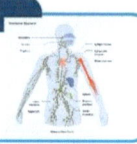

EXAMPLES
The inflammatory reflex is where areas of the forebrain create connections in order to reduce inflammation and control the immune system. The vagus nerve plays a big role in this as well.

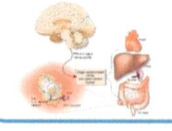

AMYGDALA DAMAGE
Amygdala damage can lead to various syndromes and disorders. For example, the Klüver-Bucy syndrome is where the cortical connections in the amygdala is damaged, leading to various memory and behavioral changes, often disruptive.

BI- VS. UNILATERAL
Bilateral damage is often more severe than unilateral, since bilateral is where both are damaged. Bilateral damage leads to judgement differences for fear expression, as well as processing some emotions (but not all).

Rida Hamid, Fall 2023

An Infographic Journey

Neuroplasticity: The Good and Bad

What Is Neuroplasticity?
- The ability of the nervous system to change structurally or functionally in response to experience
- Mechanisms of neuroplasticity:
  - Changes in synaptic strengths
  - Changes in numbers of synapses and which cells are connected by synapses
  - Changes in protein synthesis
  - Elimination of unused neurons

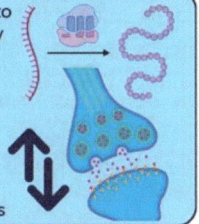

When Is Neuroplasticity Adaptive?

ADAPTIVE
- Allows people of all ages to learn and adapt to new situations
- During development, neuroplasticity helps children to quickly learn helpful skills
- After injuries, like stroke or traumatic brain injury, neuroplasticity helps rewire functions to areas that were not damaged, allowing some cognitive functions to recover

MALADAPTIVE
- Unwanted and unhelpful changes to the nervous system often arise after injury or trauma, producing pain and other disruptive effects
- After amputation, nerve cells responsible for the sensation of the amputated limb may adapt in a way that causes pain, seemingly in the severed limb (phantom limb pain)
- After hearing loss, neuroplasticity in auditory processing regions can cause severe tinnitus

What Systems and Functions Are Most Susceptible To Plastic Changes?

Not all brain functions are equally adaptable. While many systems of the brain are able to adapt to new circumstances and restore their functions after injury through neuroplasticity, others are relatively fixed once you reach adulthood.

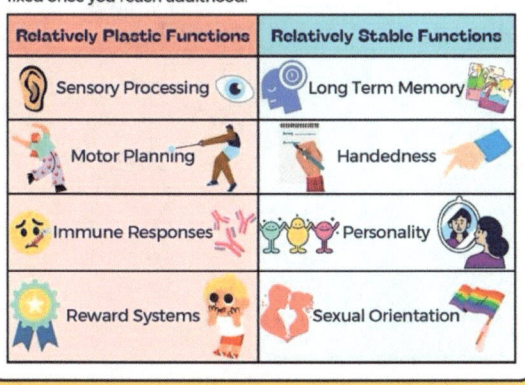

Relatively Plastic Functions	Relatively Stable Functions
Sensory Processing	Long Term Memory
Motor Planning	Handedness
Immune Responses	Personality
Reward Systems	Sexual Orientation

Allyson Macfee, Spring 2024

Adaptive vs Maladaptive Neuroplasticity

Pranavi Maddipatla

ADAPTIVE	MALADAPTIVE
General definition — Adaptation refers to a positive change that occurs in response to event that is helpful to an individual.	**General definition** — Maladaptation occurs when an adaptation or a responsive change to an even becomes harmful rather than helpful.
In neuroplasticity — The brain adapts in beneficial ways to changing needs and requirements	**In neuroplasticity** — The brain adapts in harmful ways to changing requirements
Example - stroke — This includes changes that allow patients to better recover limb function	**Example - stroke** — This includes changes that cause the development of an undesirable symptom that prevents limb function recovery
Example - maternal brain — Experience of maternal warmth prior to motherhood can lead to adaptive strong infant-mother attachments	**Example - maternal brain** — Pre-parental affective disorders can result in post-partum maladaptive psychopathology

References
- Kim, P., Strathearn, L., & Swain, J. E. (2016). The maternal brain and its plasticity in humans. Hormones and behavior, 77, 113–123. https://doi.org/10.1016/j.yhbeh.2015.08.001
- Nava, E., & Röder, B. (2011). Adaptation and maladaptation insights from brain plasticity. Progress in brain research, 191, 177–194. https://doi.org/10.1016/B978-0-444-53752-2.00005-9

Pranavi Maddipatla, Fall 2023

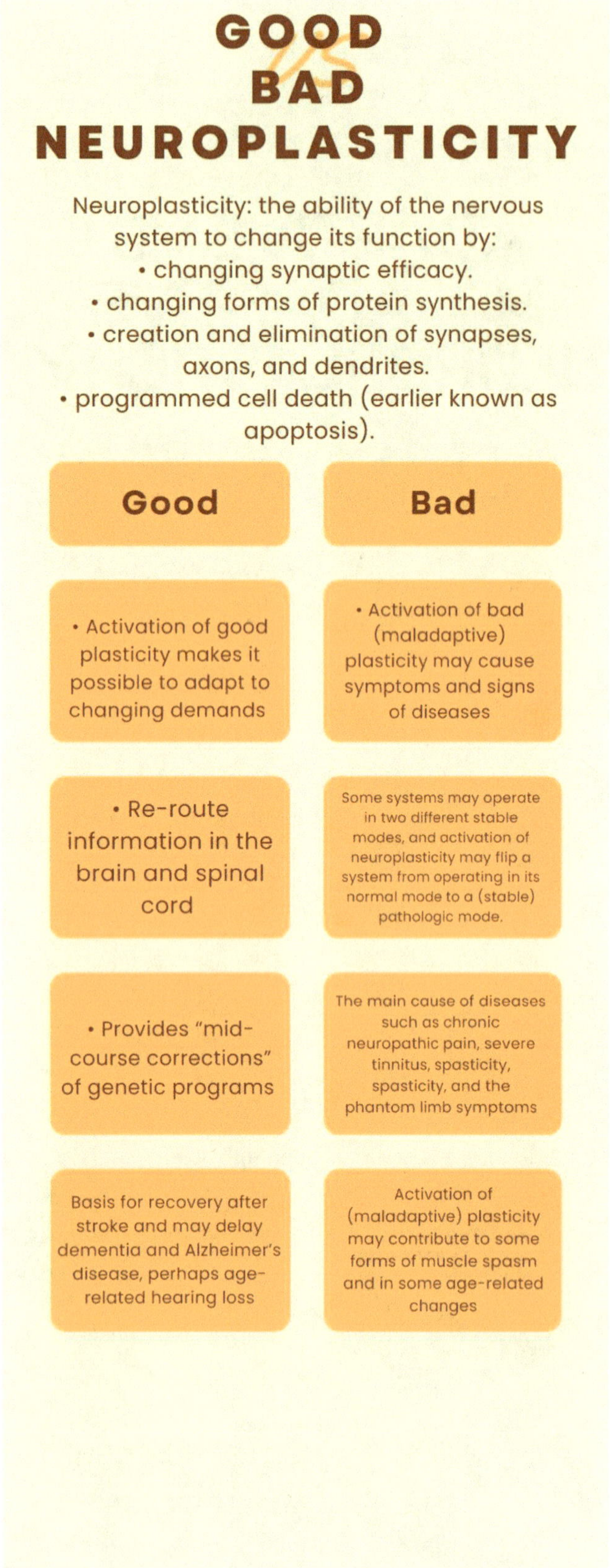

AN INFOGRAPHIC JOURNEY

GOOD vs BAD NEUROPLASTICITY

Neuroplasticity: the ability of the nervous system to change its function by:
- changing synaptic efficacy.
- changing forms of protein synthesis.
- creation and elimination of synapses, axons, and dendrites.
- programmed cell death (earlier known as apoptosis).

Good	Bad
• Activation of good plasticity makes it possible to adapt to changing demands	• Activation of bad (maladaptive) plasticity may cause symptoms and signs of diseases
• Re-route information in the brain and spinal cord	Some systems may operate in two different stable modes, and activation of neuroplasticity may flip a system from operating in its normal mode to a (stable) pathologic mode.
• Provides "mid-course corrections" of genetic programs	The main cause of diseases such as chronic neuropathic pain, severe tinnitus, spasticity, spasticity, and the phantom limb symptoms
Basis for recovery after stroke and may delay dementia and Alzheimer's disease, perhaps age-related hearing loss	Activation of (maladaptive) plasticity may contribute to some forms of muscle spasm and in some age-related changes

Priya Upadhyaya, Spring 2023

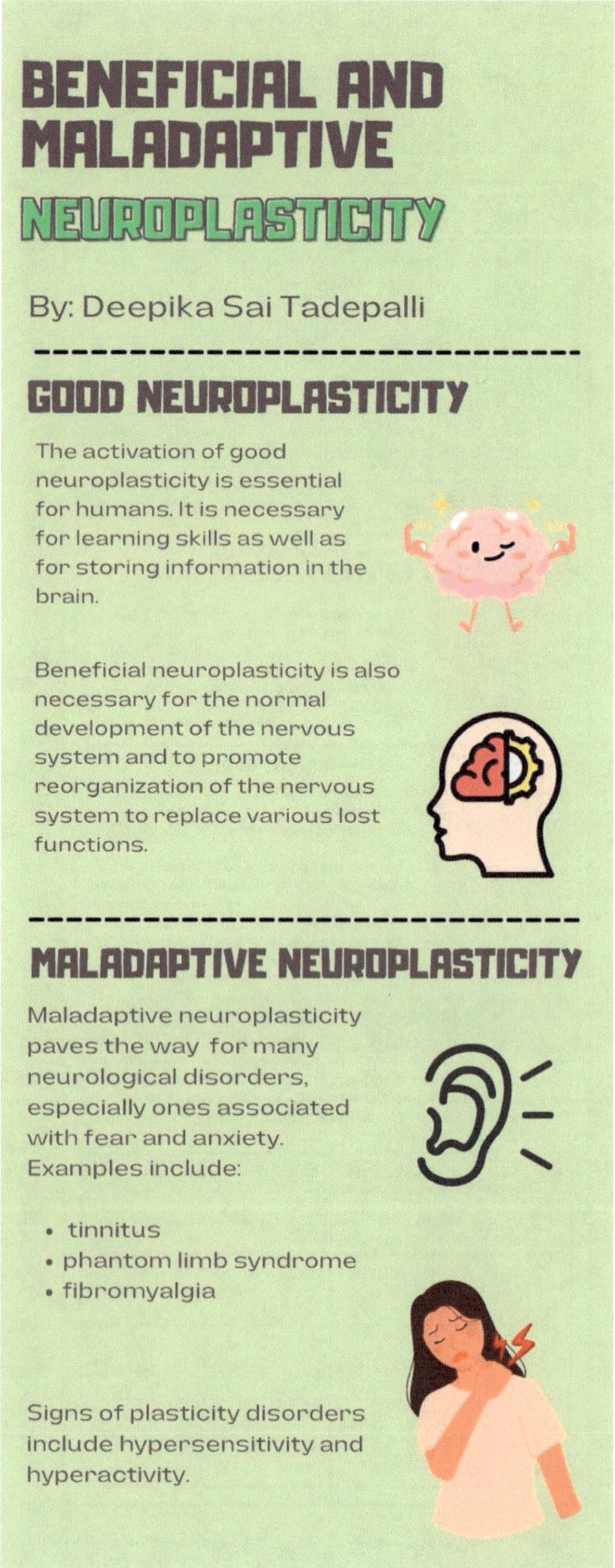

BENEFICIAL AND MALADAPTIVE NEUROPLASTICITY

By: Deepika Sai Tadepalli

GOOD NEUROPLASTICITY

The activation of good neuroplasticity is essential for humans. It is necessary for learning skills as well as for storing information in the brain.

Beneficial neuroplasticity is also necessary for the normal development of the nervous system and to promote reorganization of the nervous system to replace various lost functions.

MALADAPTIVE NEUROPLASTICITY

Maladaptive neuroplasticity paves the way for many neurological disorders, especially ones associated with fear and anxiety. Examples include:

- tinnitus
- phantom limb syndrome
- fibromyalgia

Signs of plasticity disorders include hypersensitivity and hyperactivity.

Deepika Sai Tadepalli, Spring 2024

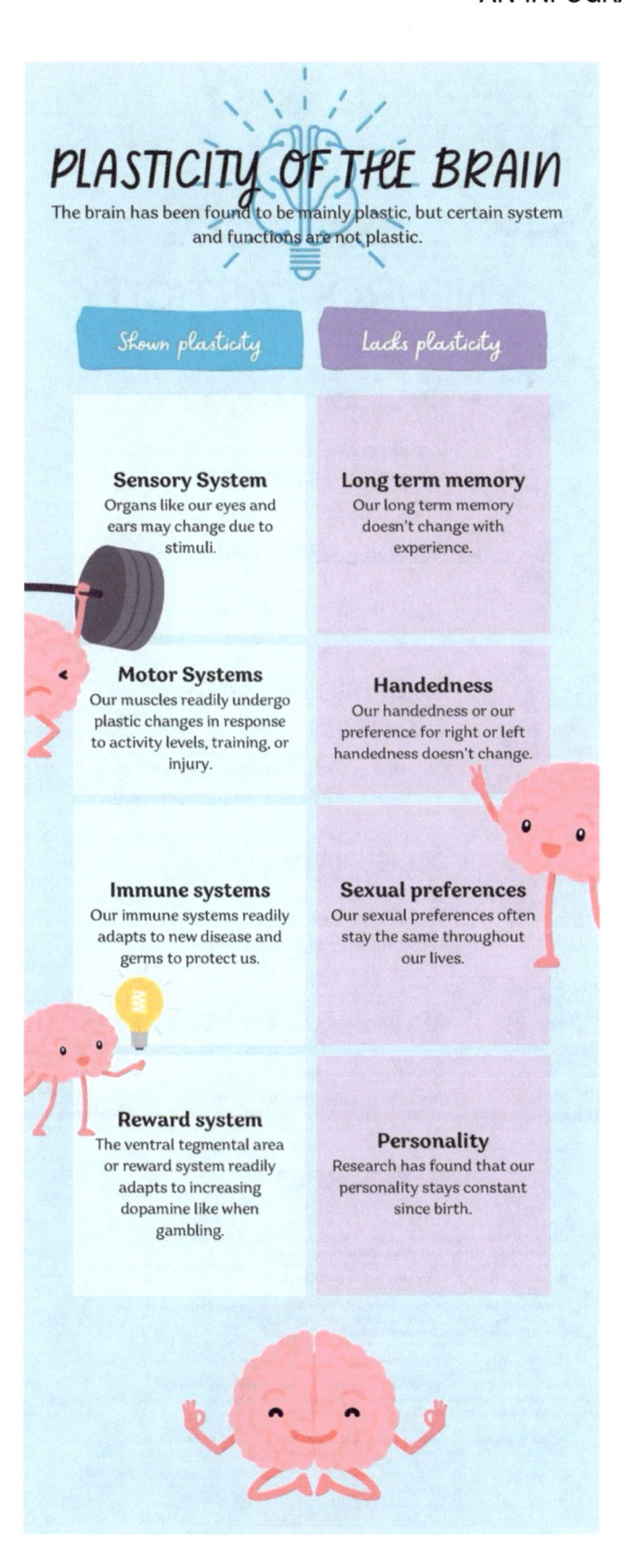

PLASTICITY OF THE BRAIN

The brain has been found to be mainly plastic, but certain system and functions are not plastic.

Shown plasticity

Sensory System
Organs like our eyes and ears may change due to stimuli.

Motor Systems
Our muscles readily undergo plastic changes in response to activity levels, training, or injury.

Immune systems
Our immune systems readily adapts to new disease and germs to protect us.

Reward system
The ventral tegmental area or reward system readily adapts to increasing dopamine like when gambling.

Lacks plasticity

Long term memory
Our long term memory doesn't change with experience.

Handedness
Our handedness or our preference for right or left handedness doesn't change.

Sexual preferences
Our sexual preferences often stay the same throughout our lives.

Personality
Research has found that our personality stays constant since birth.

Bowen Liu, Spring 2024

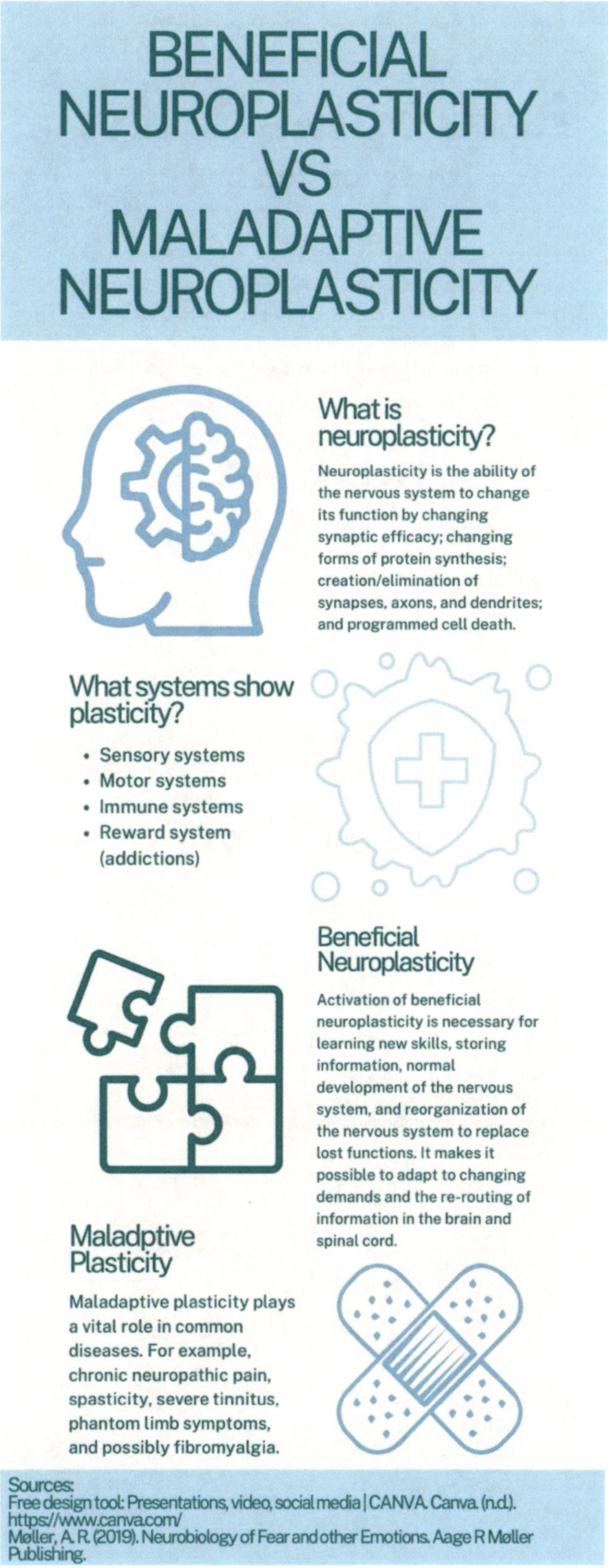

BENEFICIAL NEUROPLASTICITY VS MALADAPTIVE NEUROPLASTICITY

What is neuroplasticity?
Neuroplasticity is the ability of the nervous system to change its function by changing synaptic efficacy; changing forms of protein synthesis; creation/elimination of synapses, axons, and dendrites; and programmed cell death.

What systems show plasticity?
- Sensory systems
- Motor systems
- Immune systems
- Reward system (addictions)

Beneficial Neuroplasticity
Activation of beneficial neuroplasticity is necessary for learning new skills, storing information, normal development of the nervous system, and reorganization of the nervous system to replace lost functions. It makes it possible to adapt to changing demands and the re-routing of information in the brain and spinal cord.

Maladptive Plasticity
Maladaptive plasticity plays a vital role in common diseases. For example, chronic neuropathic pain, spasticity, severe tinnitus, phantom limb symptoms, and possibly fibromyalgia.

Sources:
Free design tool: Presentations, video, social media | CANVA. Canva. (n.d.). https://www.canva.com/
Møller, A. R. (2019). Neurobiology of Fear and other Emotions. Aage R Møller Publishing.

Tiffany Nouanesengsy, Fall 2023

AN INFOGRAPHIC JOURNEY

neuroplasticity: the good and bad

Neuroplasticity refers to the ability of the nervous system to change its function by: changing synaptic efficacy, changing forms of protein synthesis, creation and elimination of synapses, axons, and dendrites, and programmed cell death.

two types

Adaptive

the ability of the brain to reorganize neural connectivity in response to experience and develop new information and skills. adaptive changes compensate or improve the function

Maldaptive

when the brain's reorganization leads to a loss of function or to other negative consequences. It plays an important role in many neurologic disorders, including disorders associated with fear and anxiety.

plasticity

good vs bad

activation of good neuroplasticity:
- Necessary for learning new skills
- Necessary for storing information
- Necessary for normal development of the nervous system
- necessary for adaptation to changing demands
- Reorganize the nervous system to replace lost functions

activation of bad neuroplasticity:
- the main cause of diseases such as chronic neuropathic pain, severe tinnitus, spasticity, spasticity, and the phantom limb symptoms
- leads to individuals showing signs and symptoms of hyperactivity, hypersensitivity, and change in neural processing

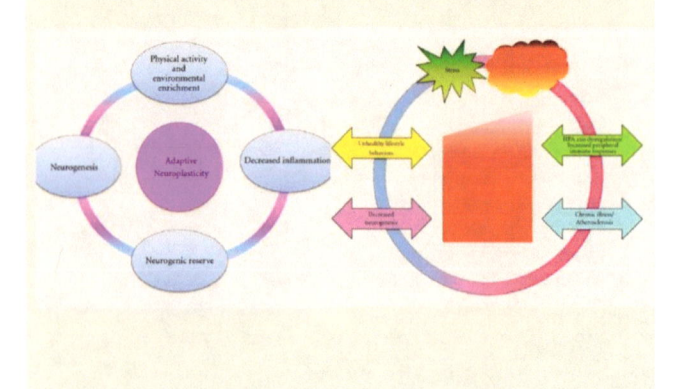

Zainab Ali, Spring 2024

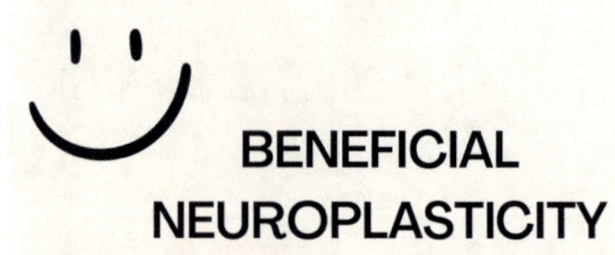

BENEFICIAL NEUROPLASTICITY

CHILDHOOD BLINDNESS
Blindness during a sensitive period may modify the neural basis for language in visual cortices

STROKE RECOVERY
Synaptic plasticity and axon growth Lost function recovery after injury

PARKINSON'S DISEASE TREATMENT
Cognitively demanding exercise and deep brain stimulation may increase plasticity

DEMENTIA DELAY
Aerobic exercise and cognitive stimulating activities may slow dementia's effects

APHASIA RECOVERY
Homologous adaptation and recruitment of other brain regions for language functions

SOURCES

Dorszewska, Jolanta, et al. "Neuroplasticity in the Pathology of Neurodegenerative Diseases." Neural Plasticity, U.S. National Library of Medicine, 27 May 2020, www.ncbi.nlm.nih.gov/pmc/articles/PMC7273406/#:~:text=Neuroplasticity%20in%20pathological%20conditions%20include,Parkinson's%20disease%2C%20and%20Huntington's%20disease.

Fandakova, Yana, and Catherine A. Hartley. "Mechanisms of Learning and Plasticity in Childhood and Adolescence." NIH, U.S. National Library of Medicine, Apr. 2020, www.ncbi.nlm.nih.gov/pmc/articles/PMC7013153/.

Hill, Nikki L, et al. "Plasticity in Early Alzheimer's Disease: An Opportunity for Intervention." NIH, U.S. National Library of Medicine, Oct. 2011, www.ncbi.nlm.nih.gov/pmc/articles/PMC3419487/#:~:text=Plasticity%20processes%20are%20believed%20to,of%20cognitive%20abilities%20during%20aging.&text=Recently%2C%20there%20has%20been%20interest,delay%20the%20progression%20of%20dementia.

Thompson, Cynthia K. "Neuroplasticity: Evidence from Aphasia." NIH, U.S. National Library of Medicine, 2000, www.ncbi.nlm.nih.gov/pmc/articles/PMC3086401/.

Devaditya Ray, Fall 2023

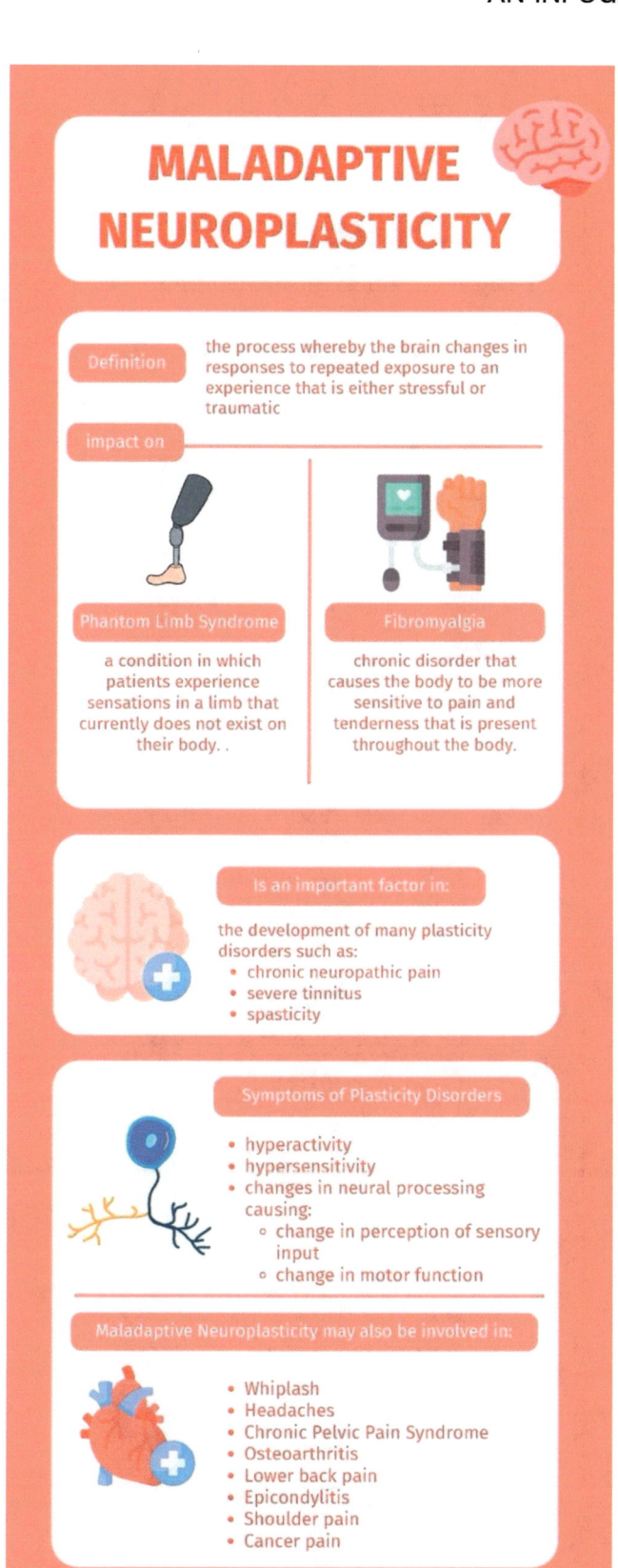

AN INFOGRAPHIC JOURNEY

MALADAPTIVE NEUROPLASTICITY

Definition: the process whereby the brain changes in responses to repeated exposure to an experience that is either stressful or traumatic

Impact on:

Phantom Limb Syndrome — a condition in which patients experience sensations in a limb that currently does not exist on their body.

Fibromyalgia — chronic disorder that causes the body to be more sensitive to pain and tenderness that is present throughout the body.

Is an important factor in:
the development of many plasticity disorders such as:
- chronic neuropathic pain
- severe tinnitus
- spasticity

Symptoms of Plasticity Disorders
- hyperactivity
- hypersensitivity
- changes in neural processing causing:
  - change in perception of sensory input
  - change in motor function

Maladaptive Neuroplasticity may also be involved in:
- Whiplash
- Headaches
- Chronic Pelvic Pain Syndrome
- Osteoarthritis
- Lower back pain
- Epicondylitis
- Shoulder pain
- Cancer pain

Zaara Siddiki, Spring 2024

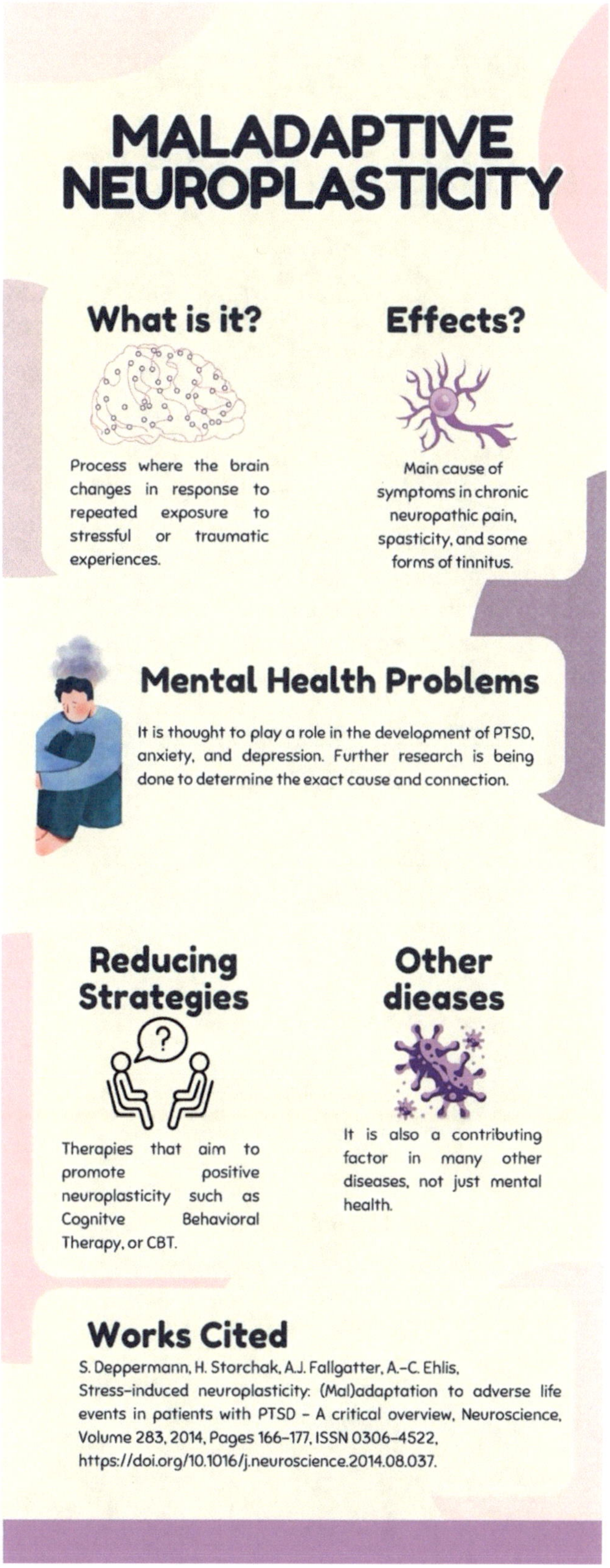

MALADAPTIVE NEUROPLASTICITY

What is it?
Process where the brain changes in response to repeated exposure to stressful or traumatic experiences.

Effects?
Main cause of symptoms in chronic neuropathic pain, spasticity, and some forms of tinnitus.

Mental Health Problems
It is thought to play a role in the development of PTSD, anxiety, and depression. Further research is being done to determine the exact cause and connection.

Reducing Strategies
Therapies that aim to promote positive neuroplasticity such as Cognitve Behavioral Therapy, or CBT.

Other dieases
It is also a contributing factor in many other diseases, not just mental health.

Works Cited
S. Deppermann, H. Storchak, A.J. Fallgatter, A.-C. Ehlis, Stress-induced neuroplasticity: (Mal)adaptation to adverse life events in patients with PTSD – A critical overview, Neuroscience, Volume 283, 2014, Pages 166–177, ISSN 0306-4522, https://doi.org/10.1016/j.neuroscience.2014.08.037.

Zaara Siddiki, Spring 2024

AN INFOGRAPHIC JOURNEY

MALADAPTIVE NEUROPLASTICITY

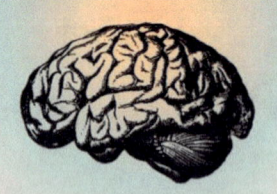

WHAT IS MALADAPTIVE NEUROPLASTICITY?

Maladaptive neuroplasticity refers to changes in the structure and function of the brain that contribute to dysfunctional or maladaptive behaviors, thoughts, or cognitive processes.

ROLE IN DEVELOPMENT OF DISEASES

This phenomena can lead to maladaptive outcomes such as diseases. Some research suggests that maladaptive neuroplasticity may also contribute to anxiety & depression

CHRONIC PAIN

Maladaptive neuroplastic can change where pain signals become amplified or prolonged. This can cause chronic pain.

THERAPIES

Therapies such as cognitive-behavioral therapy & mindfulness-based interventions, target cognitive & emotional patterns associated with various conditions. These approaches promote adaptive changes in brain function & improve symptom management for individuals affected by disorders like depression, anxiety, and PTSD.

BY: JAZA MALIK

Jaza Malik, Spring 2024

MALADAPTIVE NEURAL PLASTICITY

Neuralplasticity is a property of the central nervous system to adapt and change.

HOW IT HAPPENS?

Plastic changes occur through:
- changes in synaptic efficacy
- changes in forms of protein synthesis
- Creation/elimination of axons/dendrites and synapses
- programmed cell death

WHERE?

Plasticity has been observed in the motor, sensory, immune and reward systems.

WHEN IT GOES RIGHT...

Activation of good plasticity is crucial for learning new skills, storing information, normal development of the nervous system and, in the case of disease or injury, reorganization of the nervous system to replace lost functions.

WHEN IT GOES WRONG...

Activation of maladaptive plasticity can trigger a switch to a stable but pathologic condition causing signs and symptoms of a group of diseases known as plasticity diseases.

SOME MALADAPTIVE DISEASES

- chronic neuropathic pain
- severe tinnitus
- spasticity
- phantom limb symptoms

BUT WAIT, THERE'S MORE!!!

Maladaptive neuralplasticity is also a suspected culprit in ...
- Fibromyalgia
- Whiplash
- Chronic Fatigue Syndrome
- Epicondylitis
- Cancer Pain

Iris Downing, Spring 2023

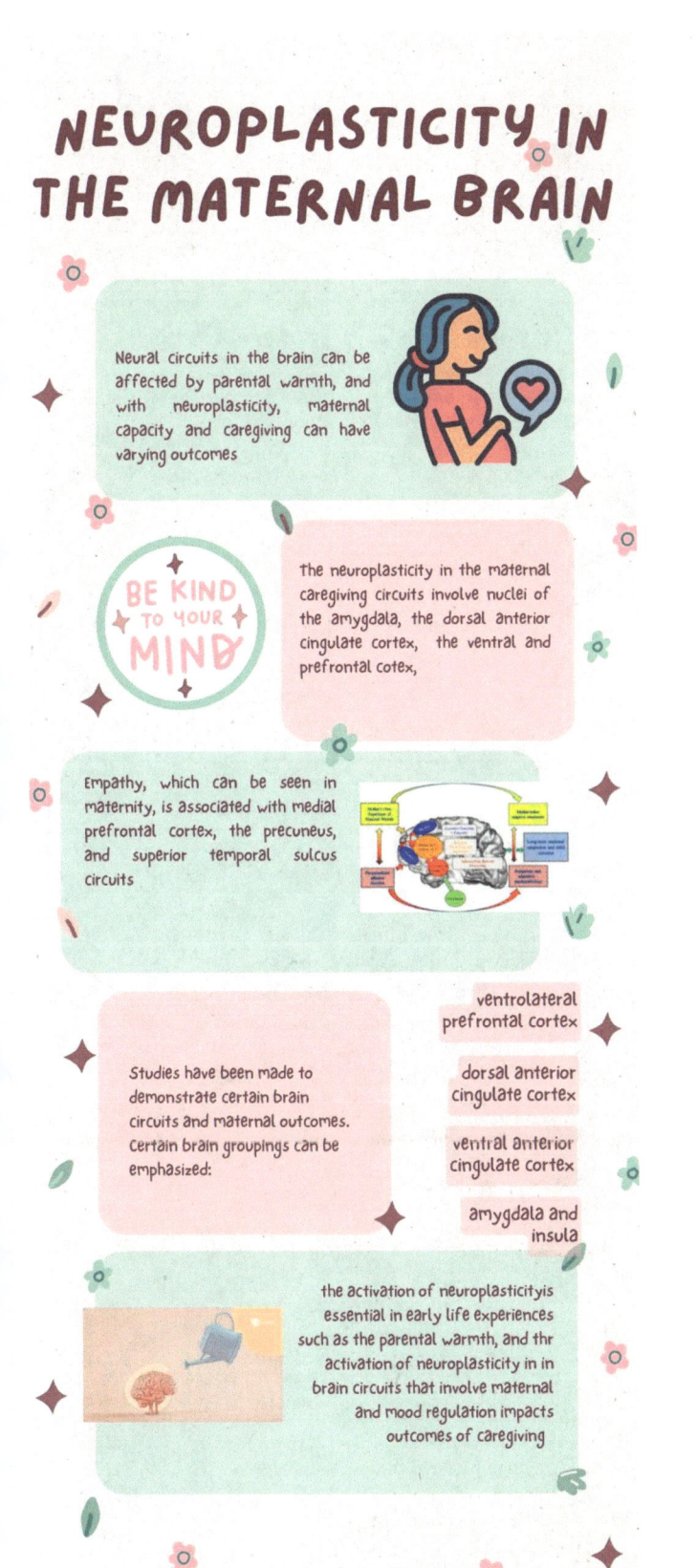

AN INFOGRAPHIC JOURNEY

NEUROPLASTICITY IN THE MATERNAL BRAIN

Neural circuits in the brain can be affected by parental warmth, and with neuroplasticity, maternal capacity and caregiving can have varying outcomes

BE KIND TO YOUR MIND

the neuroplasticity in the maternal caregiving circuits involve nuclei of the amygdala, the dorsal anterior cingulate cortex, the ventral and prefrontal cotex,

Empathy, which can be seen in maternity, is associated with medial prefrontal cortex, the precuneus, and superior temporal sulcus circuits

Studies have been made to demonstrate certain brain circuits and maternal outcomes. Certain brain groupings can be emphasized:
- ventrolateral prefrontal cortex
- dorsal anterior cingulate cortex
- ventral anterior cingulate cortex
- amygdala and insula

the activation of neuroplasticity is essential in early life experiences such as the parental warmth, and thr activation of neuroplasticity in in brain circuits that involve maternal and mood regulation impacts outcomes of caregiving

Natalia Brzezinski, Spring 2023

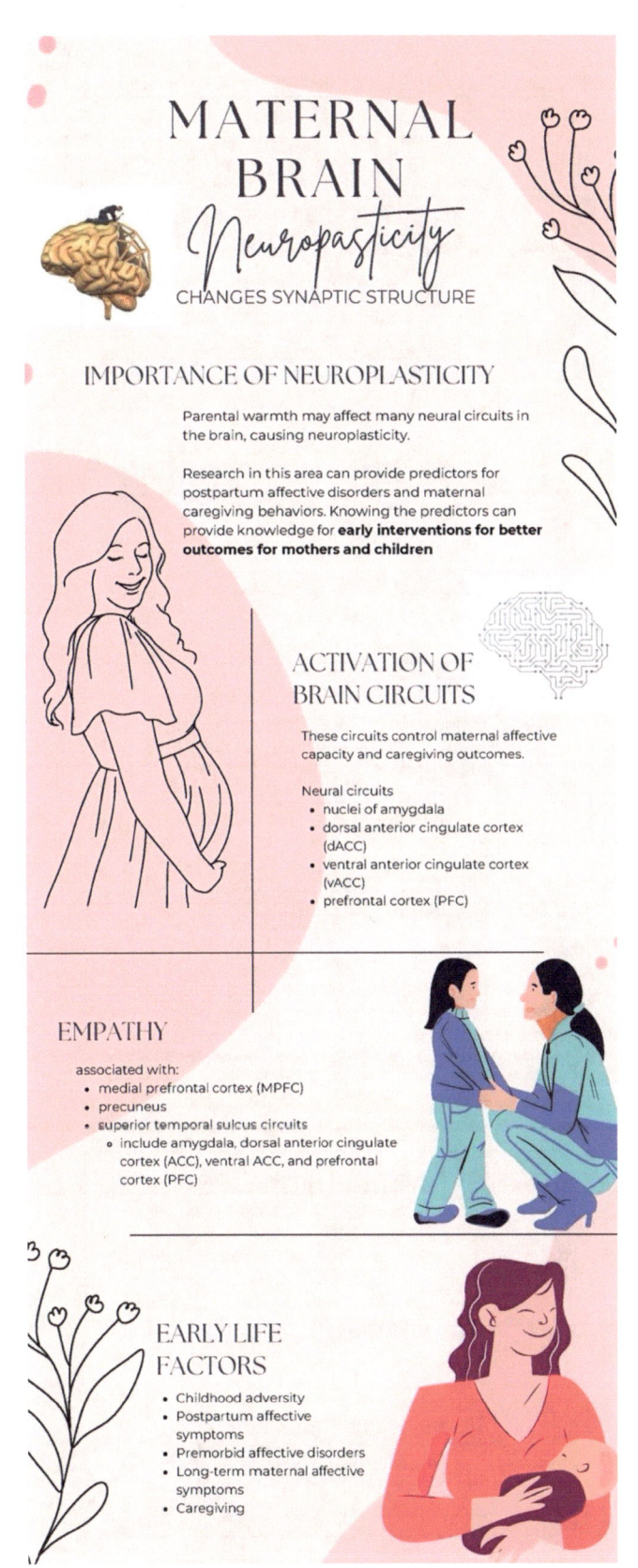

MATERNAL BRAIN Neuroplasticity
CHANGES SYNAPTIC STRUCTURE

IMPORTANCE OF NEUROPLASTICITY

Parental warmth may affect many neural circuits in the brain, causing neuroplasticity.

Research in this area can provide predictors for postpartum affective disorders and maternal caregiving behaviors. Knowing the predictors can provide knowledge for **early interventions for better outcomes for mothers and children**

ACTIVATION OF BRAIN CIRCUITS

These circuits control maternal affective capacity and caregiving outcomes.

Neural circuits
- nuclei of amygdala
- dorsal anterior cingulate cortex (dACC)
- ventral anterior cingulate cortex (vACC)
- prefrontal cortex (PFC)

EMPATHY

associated with:
- medial prefrontal cortex (MPFC)
- precuneus
- superior temporal sulcus circuits
  - include amygdala, dorsal anterior cingulate cortex (ACC), ventral ACC, and prefrontal cortex (PFC)

EARLY LIFE FACTORS

- Childhood adversity
- Postpartum affective symptoms
- Premorbid affective disorders
- Long-term maternal affective symptoms
- Caregiving

Jasha Dela Cruz, Spring 2024

AN INFOGRAPHIC JOURNEY

THE ROLE OF NEUROPLASTICITY IN MOTHERS

MATERNAL BRAIN
Activation of neuroplasticity is important in motherhood. This creates a warmth experience and it regulates maternal moods

NEURAL CIRCUITS INVOLVED
The medial prefrontal cortex (MPFC), which is associated with empathy as well as precunexus, and superior temporal sulcus circuits

NEURAL CIRCUITS AND CAREGIVING OUTCOMES
Child adversity affects the dorsolateral prefrontal cortex (DLPFC), Hippocampus, ad Amygdala Insula which can cause postpartum affective symptoms.

ABNORMALITIES IN NEURAL SYSTEM
The left-sided ventromedial prefrontal cortical (VMPFC) regions have beven associated with abnormalities in the regulation of emotions. Examples of some emotion instability is bipolar disorders.

EMOTIONAL EVALUATION
The amygdala can receive rapid and processed information from the dorso-medial thalamus from a stimuli from a child which in exchange can cause a response such as fear.

Andrea Pinto, Spring 2023

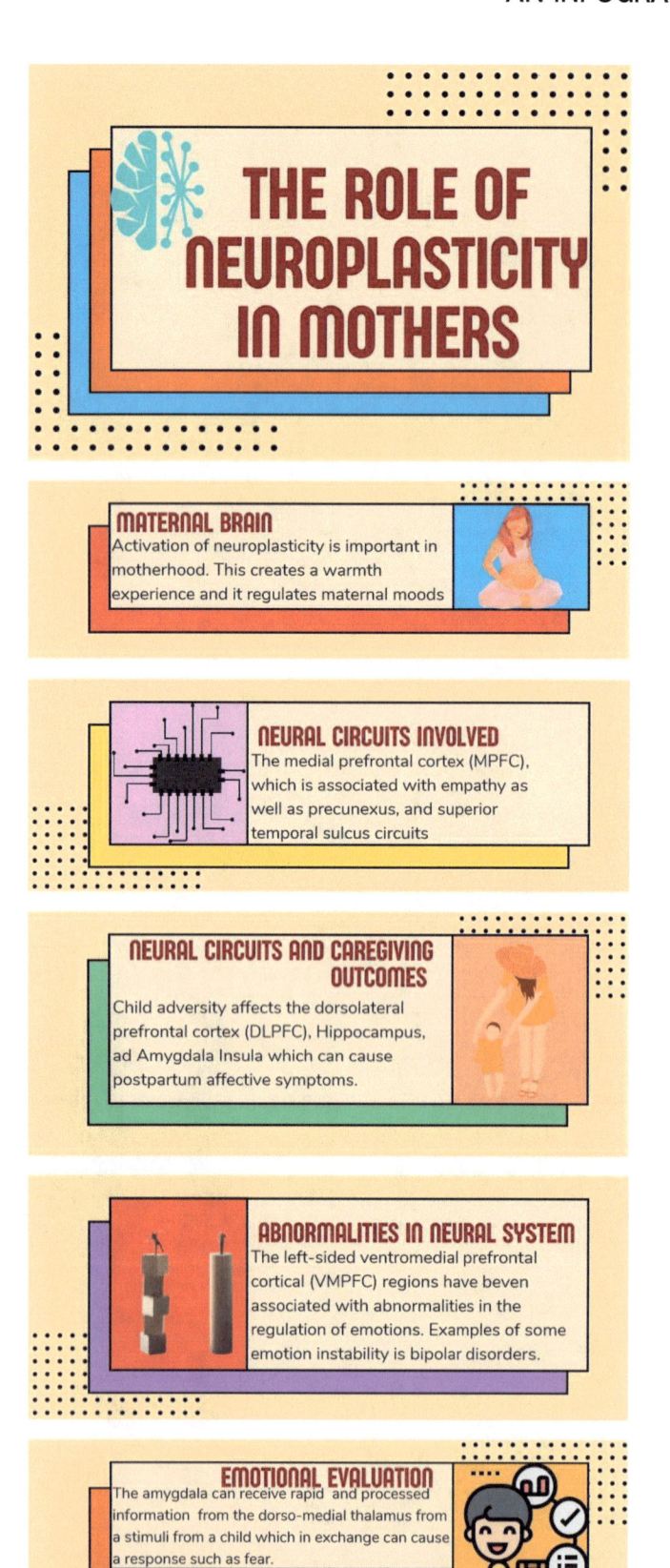

MATERNAL BRAIN NEUROPLASTICITY

Neuroplasticity
Neuroplasticity is essential in early life factors, like the experience of parental warmth.

Maternal Brain
Neuroplasticity in the maternal brain plays a role in regulating affect during caregiving.

Brain Adaptation During Pregnancy
- Increased caution to threats --> Enhanced ability to protect the infant.
- Increased sensitivity to infant cues.
- Increased feelings of fetal emotional attachment.

Brain Adaptation During Postpartum
- Heightened behavioral sensitivity toward infant cues (i.e. cries, smells, & smiles)
- Increased levels of parental preoccupation (i.e, frequently checking on the infant)

Outcome
Neuroplasticity in the maternal brain promotes more connection between the mother and her baby. It leads to more attentiveness and drive to protect her child. Ultimately, this helps with strengthening the communication between mother and infant.

Dannah Bagcal, Spring 2024

CHAPTER 15

Diseases of the Nervous System

Maladaptive Neuroplasticity and Plasticity Disorders

By Khyra White, Spring 2024

Typically, when the topic of neuroplasticity is brought up, it is used with a positive connotation. Oftentimes, only the benefits of neuroplasticity are discussed; however, this aspect of our nervous system can harm our brain and body just as much as it can help. Now what exactly is neuroplasticity? It is the ability of your nervous system to adapt to your experiences by changing the efficacy of neuron synapses, changing the forms in which proteins are made, and creating or destroying connections of neurons throughout the nervous system. The reason this ability is highly valued is the fact that not every system in our brain has it. The systems that are lucky enough to have plasticity are the sensory system, motor system, immune system, and reward systems. Functions that do not have this ability to adapt and change include an individual's long-term memory, handedness, sexual preferences, and personality.

Now that we've established how important neuroplasticity is, let's delve into why it's so important and necessary. For starters, being able to create and change connections between neurons and synapses allows us to learn new skills and store more information by essentially clearing out what we no longer need. Both functions are vital for normal development of the nervous system. Another benefit of this ability to reorganize the nervous system is to replace any lost function caused by a stroke or other injury. An interesting example of this is in patients who receive a hemispherectomy when one hemisphere of the brain is removed. As explained in a study conducted in 2020 by Höller et. al., this replacement of lost function is so effective to the point that "the interhemispheric connectivity in brains with only one hemisphere is strikingly similar to the functional network organization in brains with two hemispheres." Although there are obviously many upsides to neuroplasticity, this ability of our nervous system to adapt and change can also become maladaptive.

One of the major effects of maladaptive neuroplasticity is the role it plays in different disorders and diseases, also known as plasticity disorders. These types of disorders and diseases differ from others because they are caused by functional changes as opposed to morphological or biochemical changes. One example of a plasticity disorder is phantom limb syndrome, which occurs post-amputation of a limb. Essentially, once an individual's limb is removed, the nerves at the site of amputation continue to fire signals through the nervous system. This firing makes the individual feel as if the limb is still attached to their body and can sometimes cause pain in the "phantom" limb. Although these plasticity disorders can greatly hinder an individual's quality of life, there is a possibility of their signs and symptoms being relieved. This is because plasticity disorders are caused by functional changes within the nervous system. Functional changes have a higher chance of being reversible, hence the possibility of alleviating symptoms without surgery or prescriptions.

A second example of plasticity disorders and their effect is chronic neuropathic pain. To start off, there are three types of pain. First, there is physiological pain which is caused by the stimulation of pain receptors. Next is pathological pain which is when receptors in pathological tissue are stimulated. Oftentimes, pathological pain is caused by any functional changes in the nervous system. Finally, there is inflammatory pain. This type of pain is a sort of combination of pathological and physiological pain and can be caused by things like inflammation, stimulation of pain receptors, and different kinds of chemicals. Now that you know all of the main ways in which your body can hurt, let's delve into what exactly chronic neuropathic pain is. It's essentially a combination of all types of pain being experienced throughout the nervous system; from the nerves in your limbs to your central nervous system (brain and spine). This typically occurs when there are changes in function of the central nervous system caused by neuroplasticity, which is typically caused by acute pain. Unfortunately, chronic neuropathic pain is difficult to treat and doesn't really respond to pain relievers. The level of pain that is experienced with this plasticity disorder severely hinders a person's quality of life to the point that there is a heightened risk of depression.

A more commonly known example of a different plasticity disorder is tinnitus; however, it is a bit more severe than the tinnitus you may have experienced. Tinnitus can be described as hearing different random noises that are not coming from your outside environment, such as your ear ringing; however, tinnitus comes in a variety of forms and varies from person to person. The two symptoms or effects of tinnitus are your brain perceiving a sound that is not there as well as a decrease in the individual's quality of life due to the sounds being a nuisance or, in worse cases, extremely painful. Similarly to chronic neuropathic pain, severe tinnitus is often caused by the activation of neuroplasticity and does not show any visible, physical signs of a disease. To emphasize the severity of this level of tinnitus, we will go through the 3 different grades: mild, moderate, and severe. The mildest level of tinnitus does not have any major hindrance on the individual's daily life and doesn't occur very often, to the point where it's nearly unnoticeable. Moderate tinnitus may happen more often and interfere enough to be displeasing and annoying, yet still not enough to cause any major life effects. Finally, severe tinnitus greatly hinders a person's life with how often and severely it occurs. In the most extreme cases, the pain is so severe that the individual develops phonophobia, the fear of sound.

Neuroplasticity is very beneficial to our quality of life and allows us to experience the world by giving us the ability to learn new skills and retain more information. Not only is it valuable for experiencing our environment, it's also necessary for our development in learning how to walk and talk as we grow up on top of the development of our nervous system overall. Although neuroplasticity has all of these uses and is essential for our development, as you have learned, it can also harm us by being almost too efficient. The overactivation of this neuroplasticity is the main cause in all of these debilitating plasticity disorders that affect so many people, diminishing their quality of life.

References

1. Höller, Y., Versace, V., Trinka, E., & Nardone, R. (2020). Functional connectivity after hemispherectomy. Quantitative imaging in medicine and surgery, 10(5), 1174–1178. https://doi.org/10.21037/qims.2020.03.17.
2. Moller, A. R. (2019). *Neurobiology of Fear, Anxiety and other Emotions*. Aage R Moller Publishing.

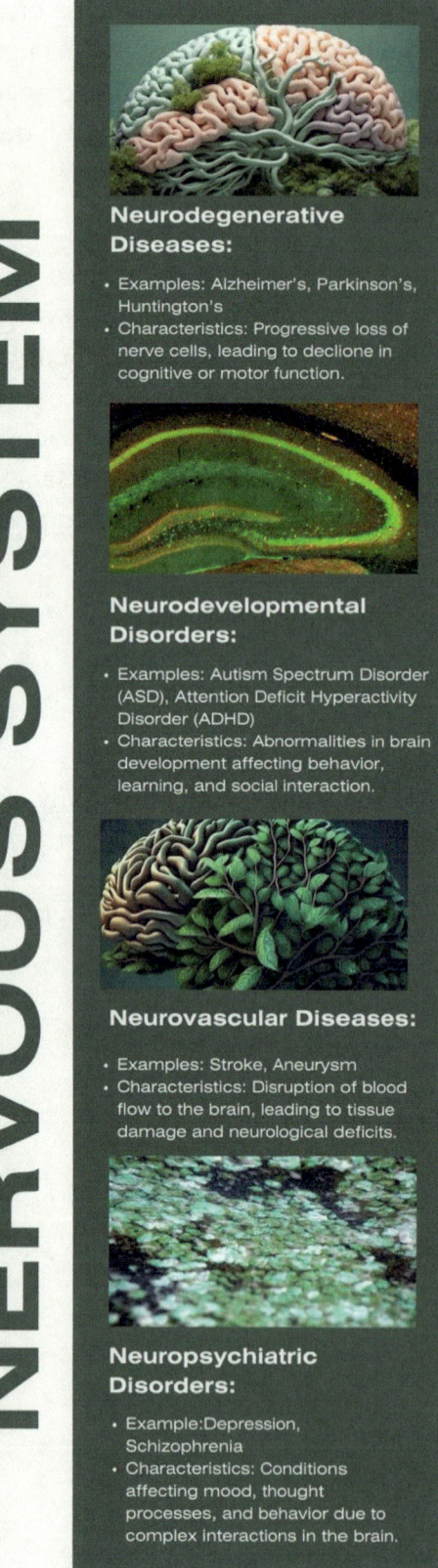

AN INFOGRAPHIC JOURNEY

DISEASES OF THE NERVOUS SYSTEM

Neurodegenerative Diseases:
- Examples: Alzheimer's, Parkinson's, Huntington's
- Characteristics: Progressive loss of nerve cells, leading to declione in cognitive or motor function.

Neurodevelopmental Disorders:
- Examples: Autism Spectrum Disorder (ASD), Attention Deficit Hyperactivity Disorder (ADHD)
- Characteristics: Abnormalities in brain development affecting behavior, learning, and social interaction.

Neurovascular Diseases:
- Examples: Stroke, Aneurysm
- Characteristics: Disruption of blood flow to the brain, leading to tissue damage and neurological deficits.

Neuropsychiatric Disorders:
- Example: Depression, Schizophrenia
- Characteristics: Conditions affecting mood, thought processes, and behavior due to complex interactions in the brain.

Sandra Cuenca

Diseases of The NERVOUS SYSTEM
By Krish Patel

Neuroplasticity is the ability of the nervous system to modify its function through mechanisms such as changing synaptic efficiency, changing forms of protein synthesis, or the creation of synapses/axons/dendrites

Good Plasticity

Activation of good plasticity allows for the nervous system to adapt to changing demands and it is crucial for normal childhood development and recovery after stroke. It can delay dementia and Alzheimer

Maladaptive Plasticity

This is often the main cause of symptoms and diseases such as chronic neuropathic pain, tinnitus, spasticity, and phantom limb. It is also involved in age related changes and fibromyalgia

Symptoms of Plasticity Disorder:
- hyperactivity
- hypersensitivity
- change in perception of sensory input
- change in motor function

Cognitive change and age
- reduced inflow to medial temporal lobe
- reduced input to posterior cingulum/precuneous region
- stronger connectivity of temporal lobe
- stronger inflow to posterior regions

Source: Dr. Jahangiri Lecture

Sandra Cuenca, Spring 2024 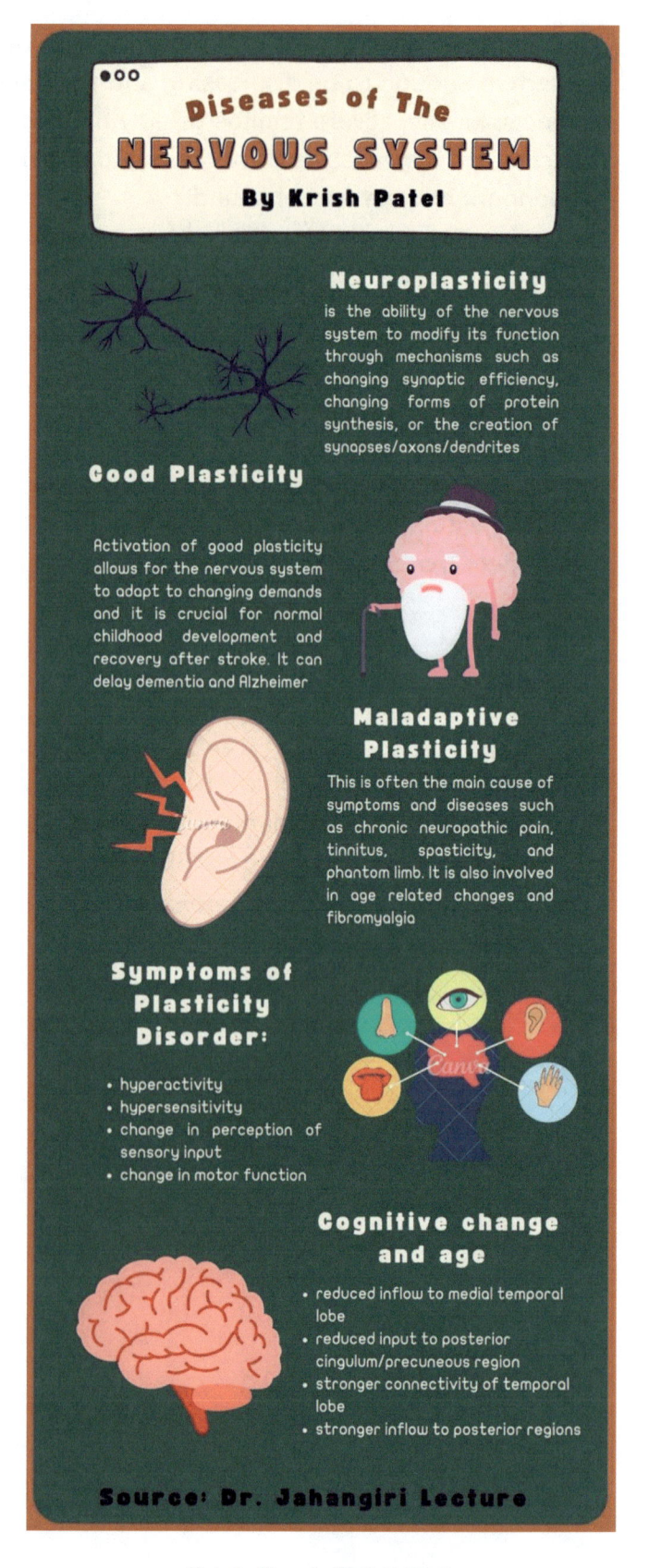   Krish Patel, Fall 2023

AN INFOGRAPHIC JOURNEY

DISEASES OF THE NERVOUS SYSTEM
BY: MANA ZANDI

OLD VS NEW CONCEPT
In the old viewpoint, it was seen that symptoms were caused by a specific part of the nervous system, but the new viewpoint states that symptoms are caused by a network of dysfunction, and the immune system plays a huge part in neurological diseases.

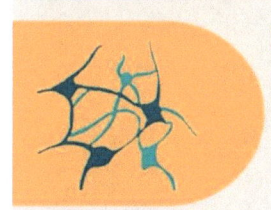

NEUROPLASTICITY
This is the ability of the nervous system to change its function by cell death, efficacy, and synthesis. It is involved in the sensory, motor, immune, and reward systems. It is not involved in personality or long-term memory.

GOOD VS BAD
Neuroplasticity can be good in adapting to changes, re-routing the information in the brain and spinal cord and recovery after a stroke, dealing with age-related diseases. it can be also bad like maladaptive plasticity and changing operations from normal to pathologic.

MALADAPTIVE PLASTICITY
This is the main cause of chronic neuropathic pain or tinnitus. It is also seen in the phantom limb syndrome and can be a cause that leads to Fibromyalgia or Alzheimer's disease. Some of its symptoms may include hyperactivity, hypersensitivity, and change in perception of sensory input and motor function.

AGE
Changes in resting-state connectivity can be related to reduced inflow to the medial temporal lobe and input to the posterior cingulum. It can be related to stronger connectivity of the temporal lobe, Benton test, and stronger input to the posterior leading to decreased and better cognitive performance.

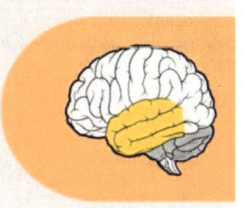

PHANTOMS
They are caused by maladaptive neuroplasticity activation. The over-activation of the sensory cortexes by the destruction of the sensory afferent neurons.

Reference: NSC 4382, Week 11, Diseases of the Nervous System

Mana Zandi, Fall 2023

DISEASES RELATED TO THE EMOTIONAL BRAIN

There are a couple of different diseases that can affect the emotional brain. The following points will cover some examples and their characteristics.

Plasticity Disorders
Plastic disorders are characterized by their main cause being the activation of neuroplasticity. Some common examples of this are:
- Chronic neuropathic pain
- Tinnitus
- Spasticity

Chronic Neuropathic Pain
There are 3 main types of pain:
- Physiological pain
  - Pain receptors in tissues are activated
- Pathological pain
  - Stimulation of pain receptors in pathological tissue
- Inflammatory pain

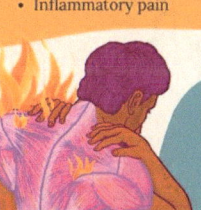

Physiological Pain
Under the umbrella of physiological pain there are more definitions of pain:
- Somatic pain
  - Pain from tissues of the body and/or head
- Visceral pain
  - Pain from the internal organs
- Inflammatory pain
  - Pain from inflamed tissue

Neuropathic Pain
- This type of pain does not come from the activation of pain receptors
- Originates from changes in function of the spinal cord and brain
- Belongs to a group of disorders where maladaptive neuroplasticity plays an important role

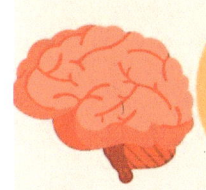

Structures that may be Involved
- Somatosensory cortex
- Anterior cingulate cortex
- Amygdala
- Insular cortex
- Pre-frontal cortex

https://www.webmd.com/pain-management/pain-management-psychogenic-pain

Ajay Tunikipati, Fall 2023

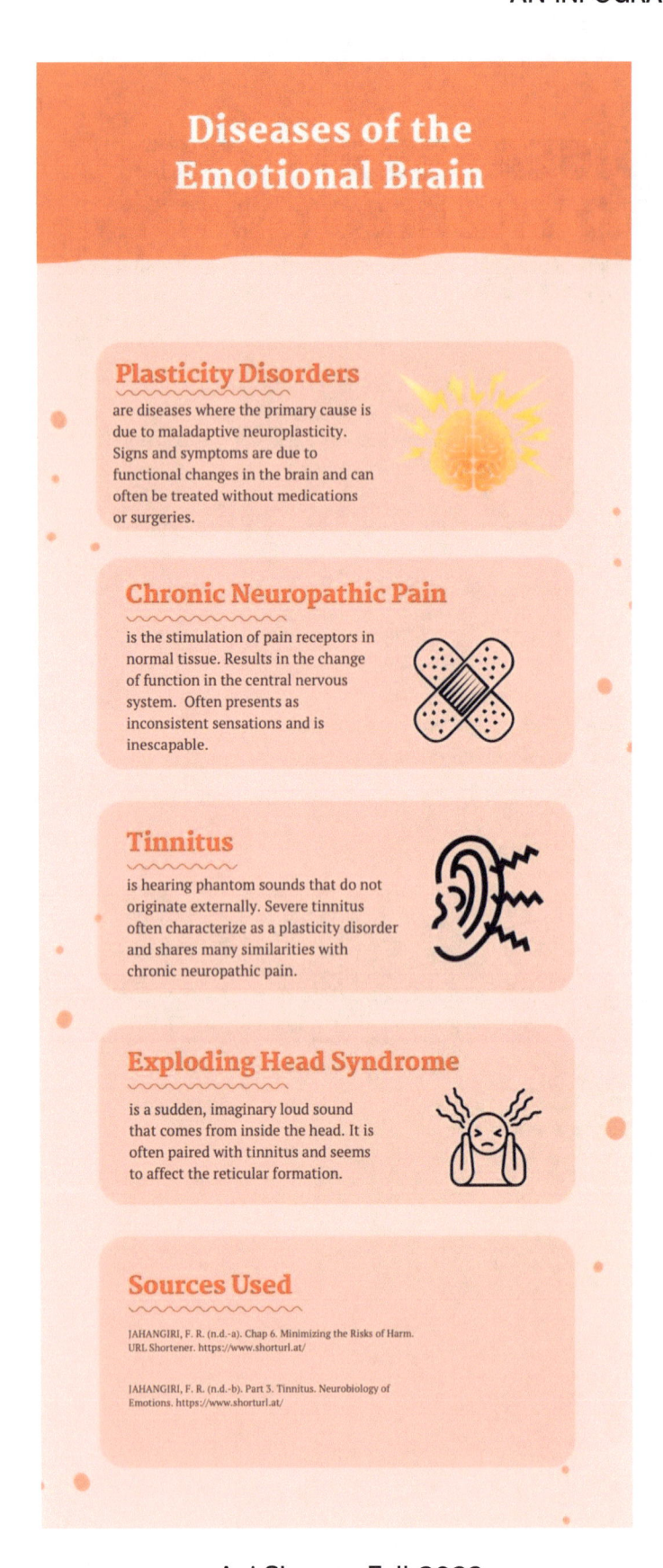

AN INFOGRAPHIC JOURNEY

Diseases of the Emotional Brain

Plasticity Disorders are diseases where the primary cause is due to maladaptive neuroplasticity. Signs and symptoms are due to functional changes in the brain and can often be treated without medications or surgeries.

Chronic Neuropathic Pain is the stimulation of pain receptors in normal tissue. Results in the change of function in the central nervous system. Often presents as inconsistent sensations and is inescapable.

Tinnitus is hearing phantom sounds that do not originate externally. Severe tinnitus often characterize as a plasticity disorder and shares many similarities with chronic neuropathic pain.

Exploding Head Syndrome is a sudden, imaginary loud sound that comes from inside the head. It is often paired with tinnitus and seems to affect the reticular formation.

Sources Used

JAHANGIRI, F. R. (n.d.-a). Chap 6. Minimizing the Risks of Harm. URL Shortener. https://www.shorturl.at/

JAHANGIRI, F. R. (n.d.-b). Part 3. Tinnitus. Neurobiology of Emotions. https://www.shorturl.at/

Ani Sharma, Fall 2023

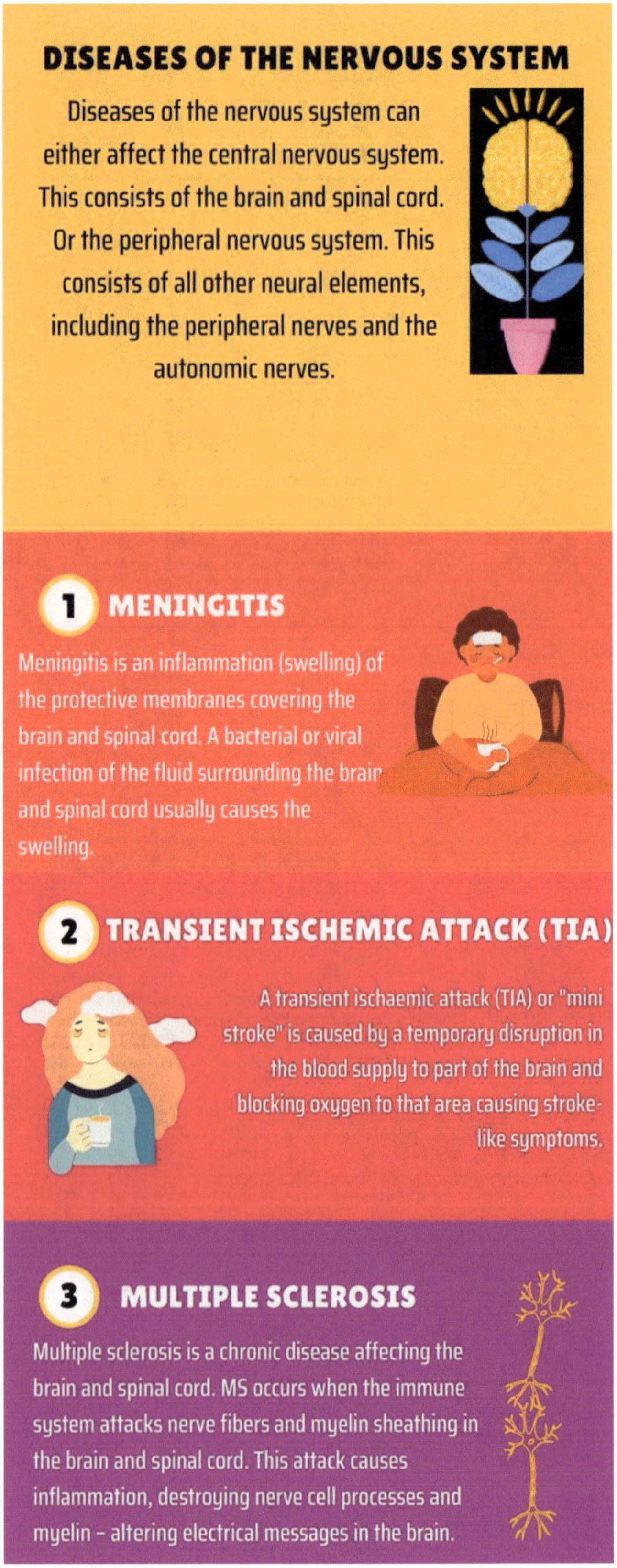

DISEASES OF THE NERVOUS SYSTEM

Diseases of the nervous system can either affect the central nervous system. This consists of the brain and spinal cord. Or the peripheral nervous system. This consists of all other neural elements, including the peripheral nerves and the autonomic nerves.

1 MENINGITIS
Meningitis is an inflammation (swelling) of the protective membranes covering the brain and spinal cord. A bacterial or viral infection of the fluid surrounding the brain and spinal cord usually causes the swelling.

2 TRANSIENT ISCHEMIC ATTACK (TIA)
A transient ischaemic attack (TIA) or "mini stroke" is caused by a temporary disruption in the blood supply to part of the brain and blocking oxygen to that area causing stroke-like symptoms.

3 MULTIPLE SCLEROSIS
Multiple sclerosis is a chronic disease affecting the brain and spinal cord. MS occurs when the immune system attacks nerve fibers and myelin sheathing in the brain and spinal cord. This attack causes inflammation, destroying nerve cell processes and myelin – altering electrical messages in the brain.

Suhina Khalid, Fall 2022

AN INFOGRAPHIC JOURNEY

NERVOUS SYSTEM DISORDERS

1. FOUNDATION FOR DISORDERS

Disorders are specific to their pathways. The symptoms are used to determine which pathway, which regions of the brain/spinal cord, or other segments of the nervous system are affected. The changes to the composition of the Nervous system are related to the symptoms.

2. FEAR/ANXIETY DISEASES

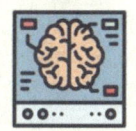

The base for these diseases is a dysfunction in the functional networks of the nervous system. Neuroimaging is not heavily used for the diagnosis of fear or anxiety disorders as these rely more on psychological impacts. The limbic system is investigated for these specific diseases.

3. NEUROPLASTICITY

The brain is able to change its connections, which is referred to as neuroplasticity. Changes can be positive and negative consequences like learning or severe tinnitus. Diseases are called plasticity diseases which can be age-related or due to trauma.

3. MALADAPTIVE NEUROPLASITICTY

There is abundant evidence that maladaptive plasticity (bad neuroplasticity) is the major contributor to disorders. Pain disorders like phantom limb syndrome are due to neuroplasticity changes. This disorder causes hyperactivity and hypersensitivity from changes in motor function/preception of input resulting form an amputated limb.

Dhruv Patel, Spring 2023

Diseases of the Nervous System

By: Hima Praveen

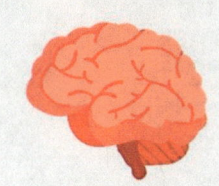

Vascular disorders

The nervous system can be damaged by various factors, including vascular disorders such as strokes, hemorrhages, transient ischemic attacks (TIAs), and hematomas.

Infections

Infections, such as meningitis (an infection of the meninges that cover the brain and spinal cord), polio (a viral infection), and an epidural abscess, can cause damage to the nervous system.

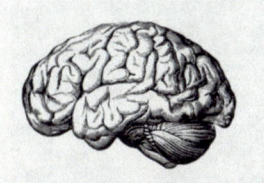

Structural disorders

Some structural disorders include brain/spinal cord injury, Bell's palsy (which causes spontaneous paralysis in the facial muscles), brain or spinal cord tumors, and peripheral neuropathy.

Functional disorders

Functional disorders of the nervous system include headaches, epilepsy, dizziness, and neuralgia. It is important to look for signs that indicate a change in headaches.

Degeneration

Many nervous system disorders cause degeneration. These disorders include Parkinson's disease, multiple sclerosis, Huntington's disease, and Alzheimer's disease. It is important to look for signs of memory loss or impaired mental ability.

Sources:
"Overview of Nervous System Disorders." Johns Hopkins Medicine, 28 July 2021, www.hopkinsmedicine.org/health/conditions-and-diseases/overview-of-nervous-system-disorders#:~:text=Disorders%20of%20the%20nervous%20system,-Disorders%20of%20the&text=Infections%2C%20such%20as%20meningitis%2C%20encephalitis,neuropathy%2C%20and%20Guillain%2DBarr%C3%A9%20syndrome.

Hima Praveen, Fall 2023

AN INFOGRAPHIC JOURNEY

DISEASES RELATED TO THE EMOTIONAL BRAIN

FORMS OF PAIN

There are three types of pain: physiological, pathological, and inflammatory. Physiological pain is stimulation of pain receptors in normal tissue, it can be from the body/head, internal organs, or inflamed tissue. Pathological pain is stimulation of receptors inpathological tissue, includes changes in nervous system function. Inflammatory pain is caused by stimulation of pain receptors, inflammation, and chemicals

CHRONIC NEUROPATHIC PAIN

Chronic neuropathic pain is a plasticity disorder. it is not caused by the stimulation of pain receptors instead it is caused by changes in the function of the spinal cord and the brain.

AFFECTS OF PAIN

Some ways that severe pain can affect someones life is that it can prevent or disturb sleep, it can interfere or prevent intellectual work, it can cause suicide, and it can cause abnormal sensations from touch. Pain may also be beneficial because it can be protective

TINNITUS

It is a plasticity disease causes sounds that dont come from the outside and can effect the quality of life depeding on what grade it is.

TREATMENT OF AFFECTIVE DISORDERS

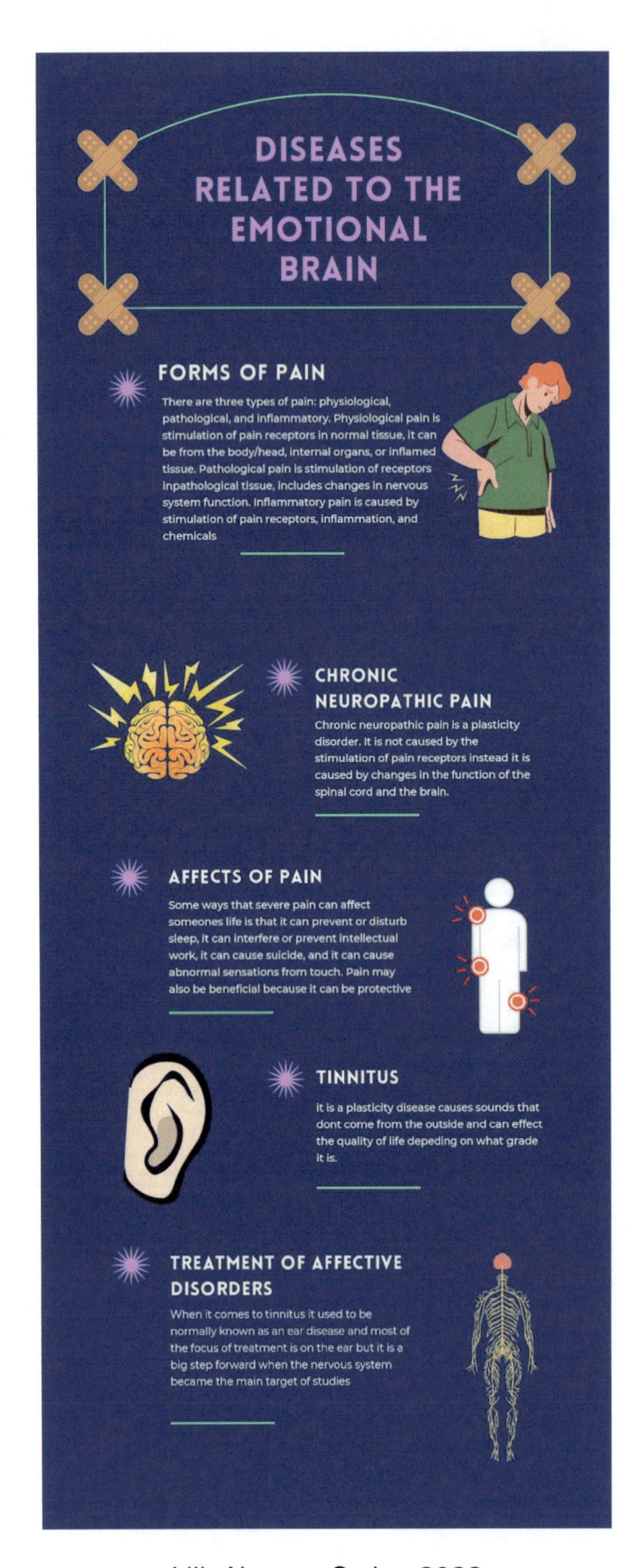

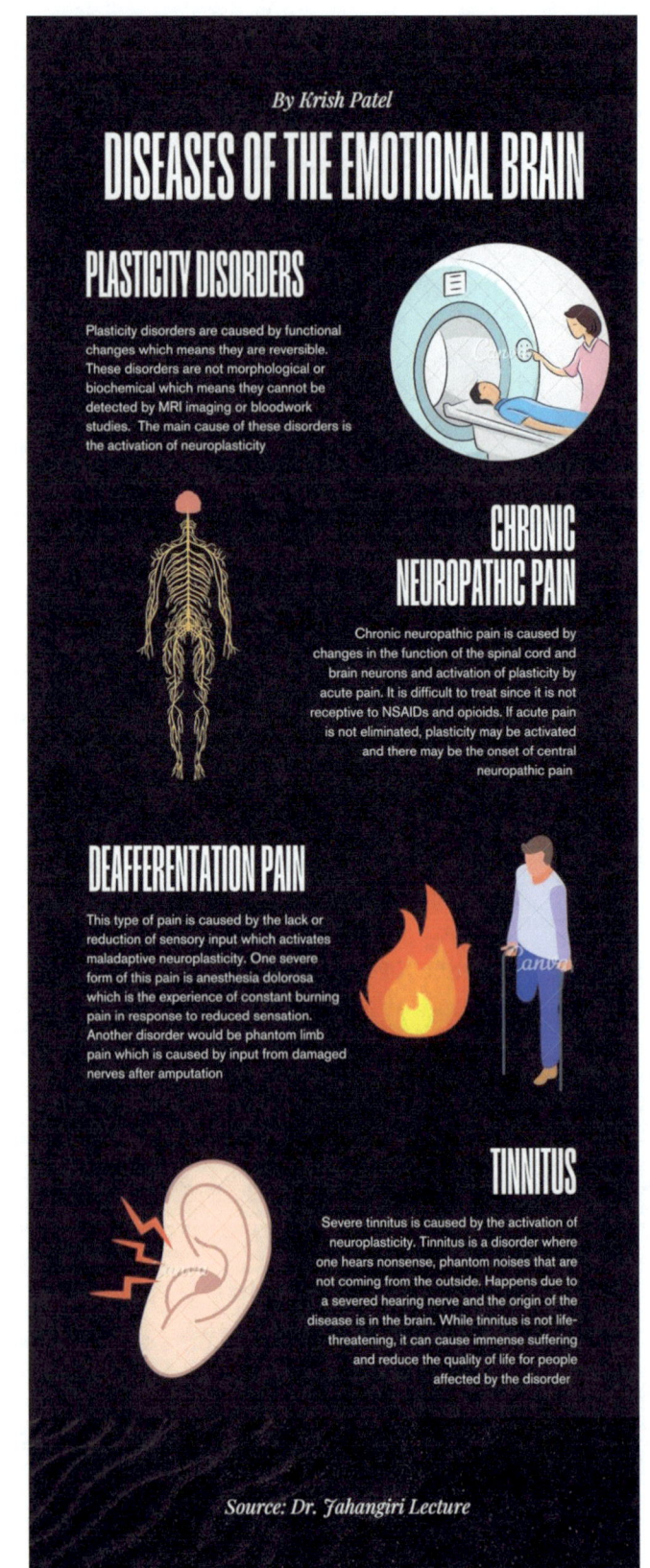

When it comes to tinnitus it used to be normally known as an ear disease and most of the focus of treatment is on the ear but it is a big step forward when the nervous system became the main target of studies

Lilly Nguyen, Spring 2023

By Krish Patel

DISEASES OF THE EMOTIONAL BRAIN

PLASTICITY DISORDERS

Plasticity disorders are caused by functional changes which means they are reversible. These disorders are not morphological or biochemical which means they cannot be detected by MRI imaging or bloodwork studies. The main cause of these disorders is the activation of neuroplasticity

CHRONIC NEUROPATHIC PAIN

Chronic neuropathic pain is caused by changes in the function of the spinal cord and brain neurons and activation of plasticity by acute pain. It is difficult to treat since it is not receptive to NSAIDs and opioids. If acute pain is not eliminated, plasticity may be activated and there may be the onset of central neuropathic pain

DEAFFERENTATION PAIN

This type of pain is caused by the lack or reduction of sensory input which activates maladaptive neuroplasticity. One severe form of this pain is anesthesia dolorosa which is the experience of constant burning pain in response to reduced sensation. Another disorder would be phantom limb pain which is caused by input from damaged nerves after amputation

TINNITUS

Severe tinnitus is caused by the activation of neuroplasticity. Tinnitus is a disorder where one hears nonsense, phantom noises that are not coming from the outside. Happens due to a severed hearing nerve and the origin of the disease is in the brain. While tinnitus is not life-threatening, it can cause immense suffering and reduce the quality of life for people affected by the disorder

Source: Dr. Jahangiri Lecture

Krish Patel, Fall 2023

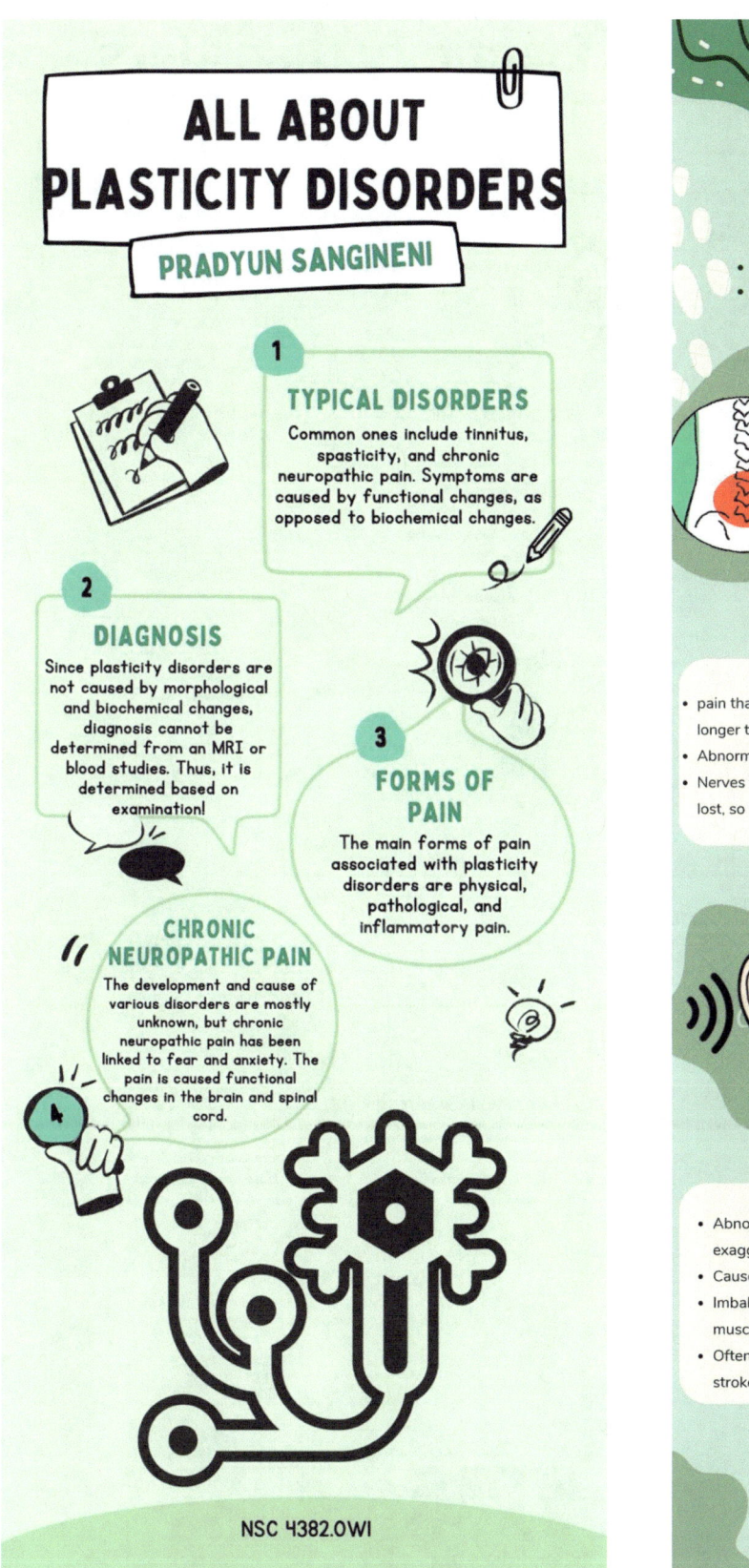

AN INFOGRAPHIC JOURNEY

ALL ABOUT PLASTICITY DISORDERS
PRADYUN SANGINENI

1. TYPICAL DISORDERS
Common ones include tinnitus, spasticity, and chronic neuropathic pain. Symptoms are caused by functional changes, as opposed to biochemical changes.

2. DIAGNOSIS
Since plasticity disorders are not caused by morphological and biochemical changes, diagnosis cannot be determined from an MRI or blood studies. Thus, it is determined based on examination!

3. FORMS OF PAIN
The main forms of pain associated with plasticity disorders are physical, pathological, and inflammatory pain.

4. CHRONIC NEUROPATHIC PAIN
The development and cause of various disorders are mostly unknown, but chronic neuropathic pain has been linked to fear and anxiety. The pain is caused functional changes in the brain and spinal cord.

NSC 4382.0WI

Pradyun Sangineni, Fall 2023

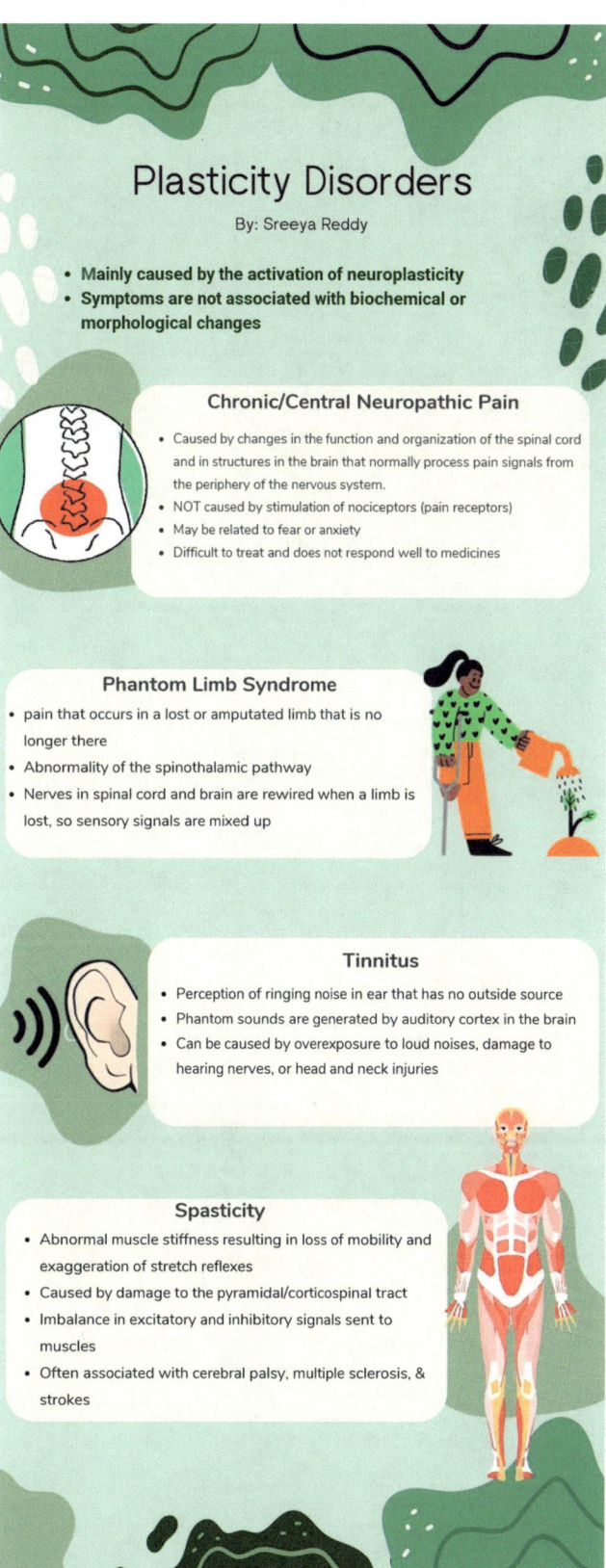

Plasticity Disorders
By: Sreeya Reddy

- Mainly caused by the activation of neuroplasticity
- Symptoms are not associated with biochemical or morphological changes

Chronic/Central Neuropathic Pain
- Caused by changes in the function and organization of the spinal cord and in structures in the brain that normally process pain signals from the periphery of the nervous system.
- NOT caused by stimulation of nociceptors (pain receptors)
- May be related to fear or anxiety
- Difficult to treat and does not respond well to medicines

Phantom Limb Syndrome
- pain that occurs in a lost or amputated limb that is no longer there
- Abnormality of the spinothalamic pathway
- Nerves in spinal cord and brain are rewired when a limb is lost, so sensory signals are mixed up

Tinnitus
- Perception of ringing noise in ear that has no outside source
- Phantom sounds are generated by auditory cortex in the brain
- Can be caused by overexposure to loud noises, damage to hearing nerves, or head and neck injuries

Spasticity
- Abnormal muscle stiffness resulting in loss of mobility and exaggeration of stretch reflexes
- Caused by damage to the pyramidal/corticospinal tract
- Imbalance in excitatory and inhibitory signals sent to muscles
- Often associated with cerebral palsy, multiple sclerosis, & strokes

Sreeya Reddy, Spring 2023

AN INFOGRAPHIC JOURNEY

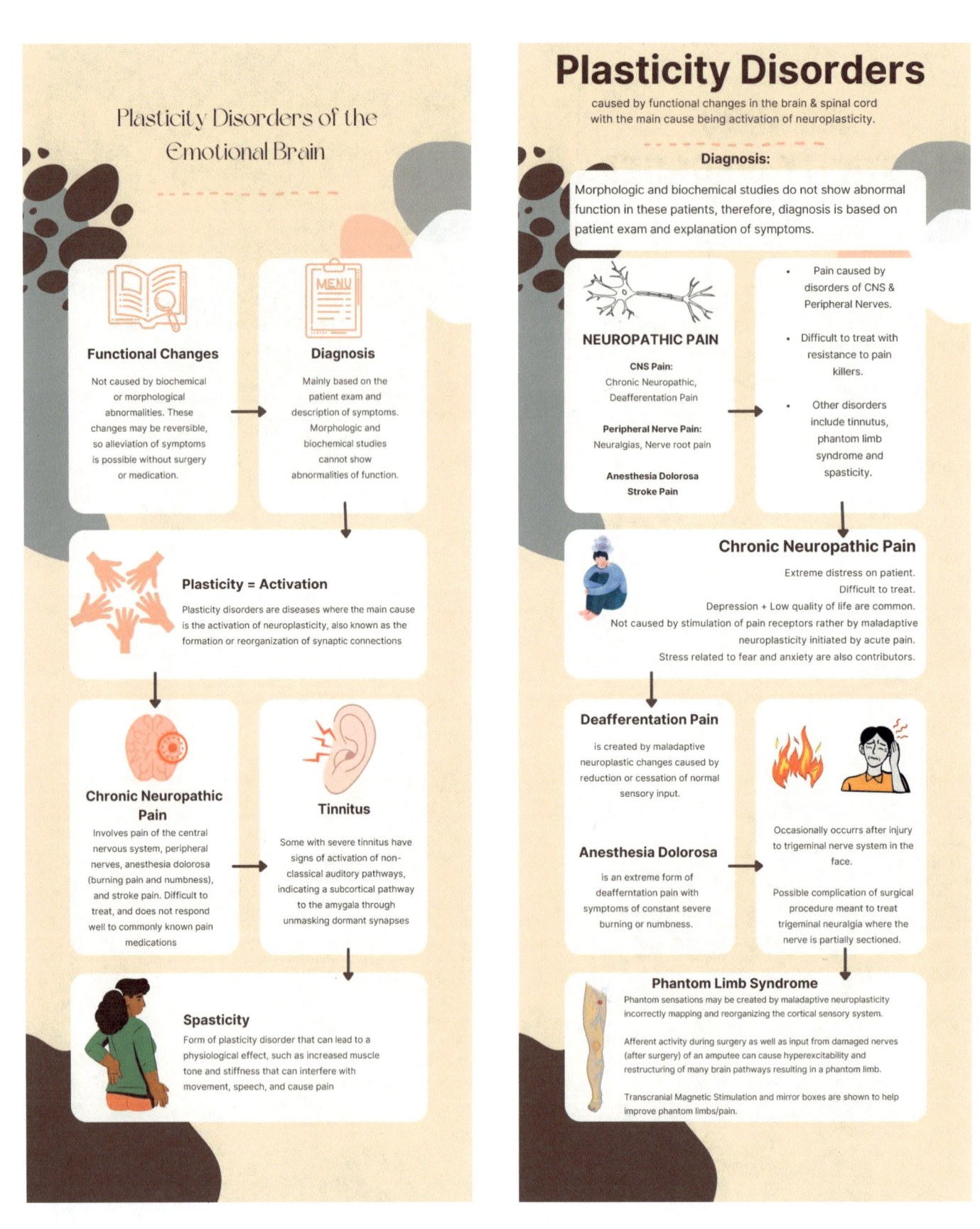

Plasticity Disorders of the Emotional Brain

Functional Changes
Not caused by biochemical or morphological abnormalities. These changes may be reversible, so alleviation of symptoms is possible without surgery or medication.

Diagnosis
Mainly based on the patient exam and description of symptoms. Morphologic and biochemical studies cannot show abnormalities of function.

Plasticity = Activation
Plasticity disorders are diseases where the main cause is the activation of neuroplasticity, also known as the formation or reorganization of synaptic connections

Chronic Neuropathic Pain
Involves pain of the central nervous system, peripheral nerves, anesthesia dolorosa (burning pain and numbness), and stroke pain. Difficult to treat, and does not respond well to commonly known pain medications

Tinnitus
Some with severe tinnitus have signs of activation of non-classical auditory pathways, indicating a subcortical pathway to the amygala through unmasking dormant synapses

Spasticity
Form of plasticity disorder that can lead to a physiological effect, such as increased muscle tone and stiffness that can interfere with movement, speech, and cause pain

Crystal Peraza, Spring 2023

Plasticity Disorders
caused by functional changes in the brain & spinal cord with the main cause being activation of neuroplasticity.

Diagnosis:
Morphologic and biochemical studies do not show abnormal function in these patients, therefore, diagnosis is based on patient exam and explanation of symptoms.

NEUROPATHIC PAIN

CNS Pain:
Chronic Neuropathic, Deafferentation Pain

Peripheral Nerve Pain:
Neuralgias, Nerve root pain

Anesthesia Dolorosa
Stroke Pain

- Pain caused by disorders of CNS & Peripheral Nerves.
- Difficult to treat with resistance to pain killers.
- Other disorders include tinnutus, phantom limb syndrome and spasticity.

Chronic Neuropathic Pain
Extreme distress on patient.
Difficult to treat.
Depression + Low quality of life are common.
Not caused by stimulation of pain receptors rather by maladaptive neuroplasticity initiated by acute pain.
Stress related to fear and anxiety are also contributors.

Deafferentation Pain
is created by maladaptive neuroplastic changes caused by reduction or cessation of normal sensory input.

Anesthesia Dolorosa
is an extreme form of deafferntation pain with symptoms of constant severe burning or numbness.

Occasionally occurs after injury to trigeminal nerve system in the face.

Possible complication of surgical procedure meant to treat trigeminal neuralgia where the nerve is partially sectioned.

Phantom Limb Syndrome
Phantom sensations may be created by maladaptive neuroplasticity incorrectly mapping and reorganizing the cortical sensory system.

Afferent activity during surgery as well as input from damaged nerves (after surgery) of an amputee can cause hyperexcitability and restructuring of many brain pathways resulting in a phantom limb.

Transcranial Magnetic Stimulation and mirror boxes are shown to help improve phantom limbs/pain.

Cambree Yedica, Spring 2023

AN INFOGRAPHIC JOURNEY

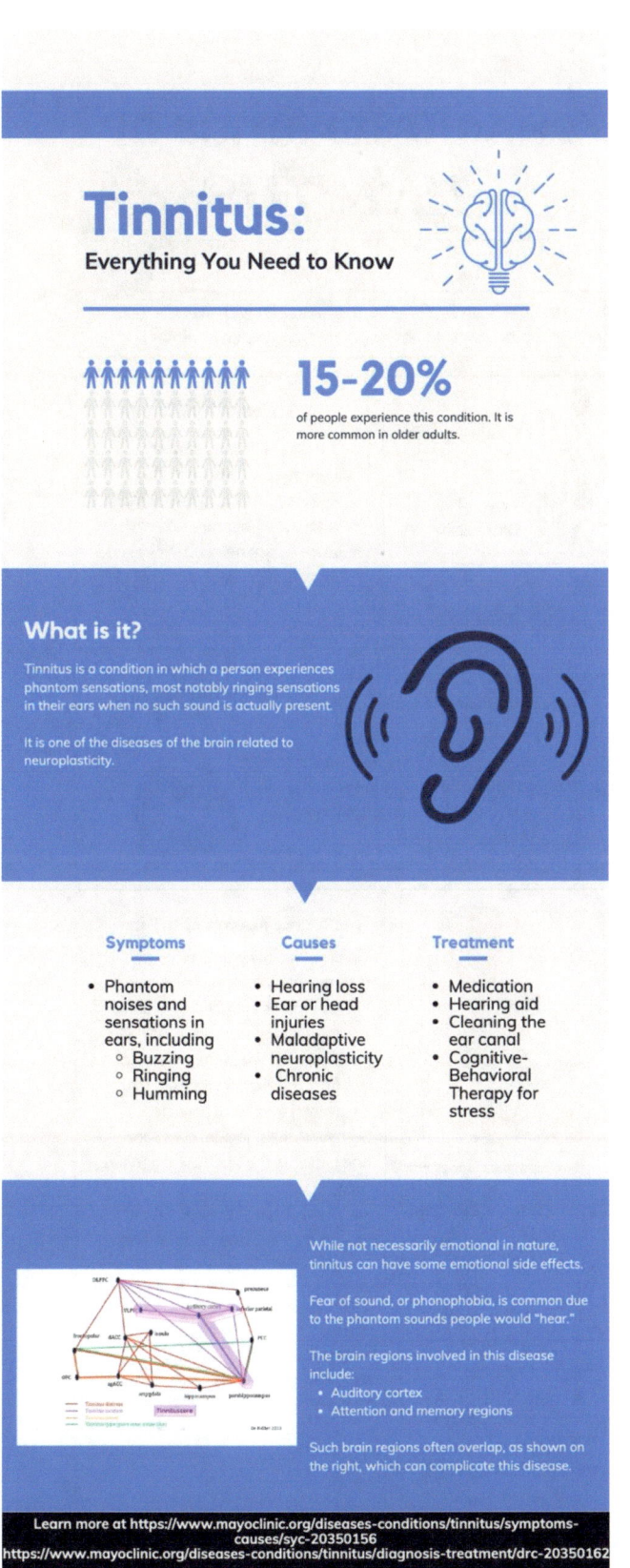

Hana Ahmad, Fall 2023

Gauri Surendran, Fall 2023

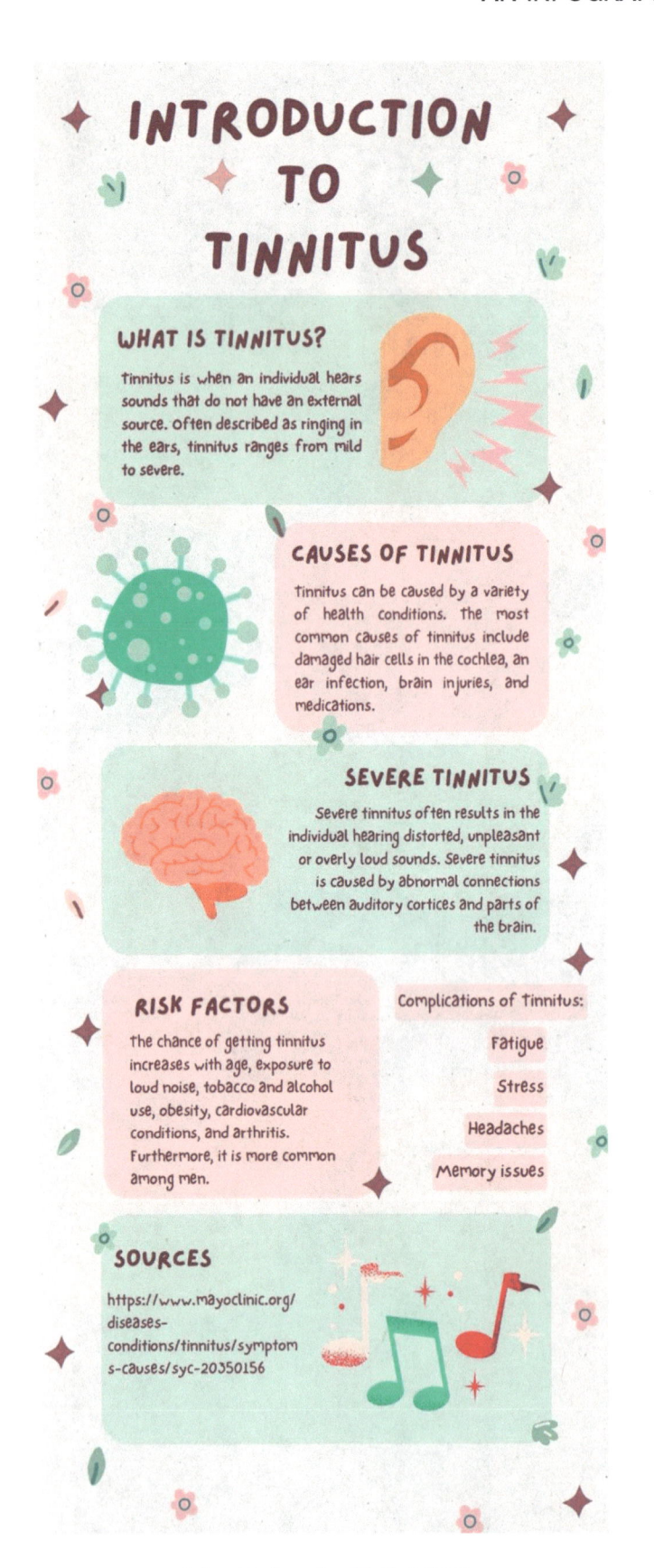

AN INFOGRAPHIC JOURNEY

INTRODUCTION TO TINNITUS

WHAT IS TINNITUS?
Tinnitus is when an individual hears sounds that do not have an external source. Often described as ringing in the ears, tinnitus ranges from mild to severe.

CAUSES OF TINNITUS
Tinnitus can be caused by a variety of health conditions. The most common causes of tinnitus include damaged hair cells in the cochlea, an ear infection, brain injuries, and medications.

SEVERE TINNITUS
Severe tinnitus often results in the individual hearing distorted, unpleasant or overly loud sounds. Severe tinnitus is caused by abnormal connections between auditory cortices and parts of the brain.

RISK FACTORS
The chance of getting tinnitus increases with age, exposure to loud noise, tobacco and alcohol use, obesity, cardiovascular conditions, and arthritis. Furthermore, it is more common among men.

Complications of Tinnitus:
- Fatigue
- Stress
- Headaches
- Memory issues

SOURCES
https://www.mayoclinic.org/diseases-conditions/tinnitus/symptoms-causes/syc-20350156

Isha Rojanala, Fall 2023

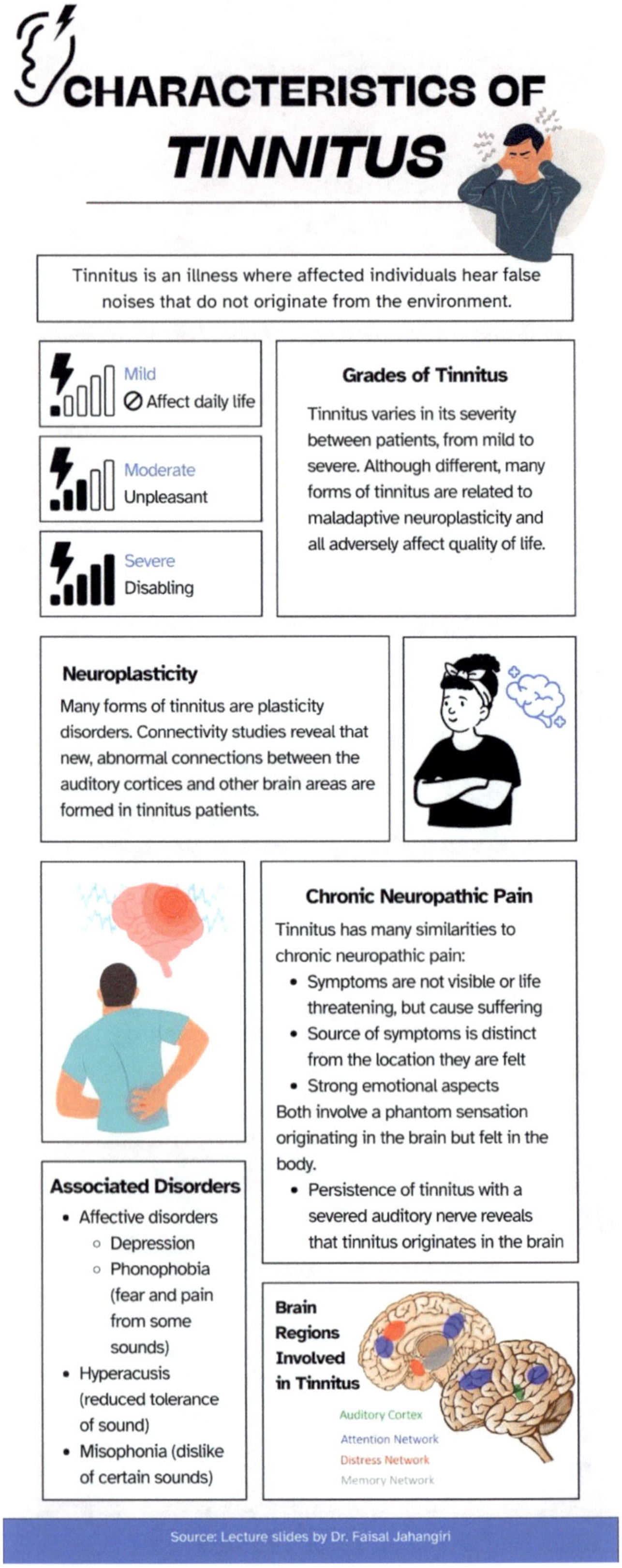

CHARACTERISTICS OF TINNITUS

Tinnitus is an illness where affected individuals hear false noises that do not originate from the environment.

- Mild — Affect daily life
- Moderate — Unpleasant
- Severe — Disabling

Grades of Tinnitus
Tinnitus varies in its severity between patients, from mild to severe. Although different, many forms of tinnitus are related to maladaptive neuroplasticity and all adversely affect quality of life.

Neuroplasticity
Many forms of tinnitus are plasticity disorders. Connectivity studies reveal that new, abnormal connections between the auditory cortices and other brain areas are formed in tinnitus patients.

Chronic Neuropathic Pain
Tinnitus has many similarities to chronic neuropathic pain:
- Symptoms are not visible or life threatening, but cause suffering
- Source of symptoms is distinct from the location they are felt
- Strong emotional aspects

Both involve a phantom sensation originating in the brain but felt in the body.
- Persistence of tinnitus with a severed auditory nerve reveals that tinnitus originates in the brain

Associated Disorders
- Affective disorders
  - Depression
  - Phonophobia (fear and pain from some sounds)
- Hyperacusis (reduced tolerance of sound)
- Misophonia (dislike of certain sounds)

Brain Regions Involved in Tinnitus
- Auditory Cortex
- Attention Network
- Distress Network
- Memory Network

Source: Lecture slides by Dr. Faisal Jahangiri

Vijaya Dutt, Fall 2023

AN INFOGRAPHIC JOURNEY

TINNITUS

What is Tinnitus
Tinnitus is when an individual hears phantom sounds that are not coming from the environment which leads to suffering and a decreased quality of life

Causes of Tinnitus
Tinnitus is caused by activation of neuroplasticity in the brain and abnormal connections between brain structures. For example, the auditory cortex of people with tinnitus has additional connections.

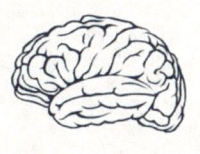

Types of Tinnitus
- Mild Tinnitus: does not interfere with day to day life
- Moderate Tinnitus: may cause some unpleasant feelings
- Severe Tinnitus: interferes with life and can be disabling

Symptoms associated with Tinnitus
- Hyperacusis: reduced tolerance of sounds
- Phonophobia: A fear of certain sounds
- Misophonia: A dislike of specific sounds

Effects on a person
Severe Tinnitus can impact a person's life in major ways. It can lead to sleep disturbances, difficulty focusing and working, a fear of sounds, and even depression.

Reference: "Neurobiology of Fear, Anxiety, and Other Emotions" Møller, A.R.

Maryam Imam, Fall 2023

Tinnitus: 4 different types

BY: JANA ELKHODARI

Subjective Tinnitus
This is the most common type. It is characterized by earing noises that are not caused by external sources. It can be caused by exposure to very loud noises.

Neurological Tinnitus
This type of tinnitus is associated with underlying conditions of the brain. Due to this, it becomes more difficult to hear clearly, and may cause dizziness and nausea.

Somatic Tinnitus
In this type of tinnitus, it is linked to the sensory system and is often associated with movement and touch. It typically triggered by muscle spasms, or other mechanical issues.

Objective Tinnitus
This is the rarest type of tinnitus. It can be heard by other people, including audiologists and external observers. Most cases are caused by involuntary muscle contraction.

References
https://siouxlandhearing.com/the-4-different-types-of-tinnitus/#:~:text=There%20are%20four%20types%20of%20tinnitus%2C%20including%20subjective%2C%20neurological%2C,seek%20advice%20from%20your%20audiologist.

Jana Elkhodari, Fall 2023

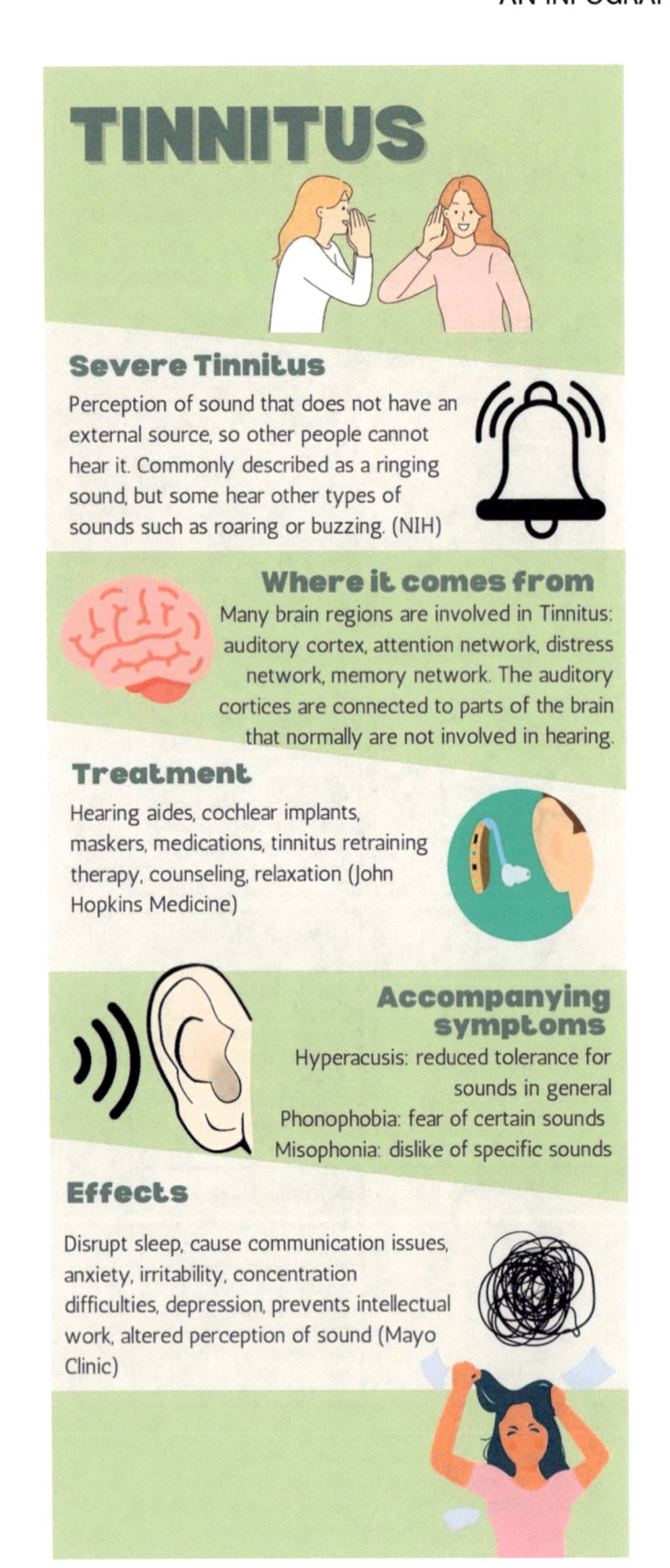

TINNITUS

Severe Tinnitus
Perception of sound that does not have an external source, so other people cannot hear it. Commonly described as a ringing sound, but some hear other types of sounds such as roaring or buzzing. (NIH)

Where it comes from
Many brain regions are involved in Tinnitus: auditory cortex, attention network, distress network, memory network. The auditory cortices are connected to parts of the brain that normally are not involved in hearing.

Treatment
Hearing aides, cochlear implants, maskers, medications, tinnitus retraining therapy, counseling, relaxation (John Hopkins Medicine)

Accompanying symptoms
Hyperacusis: reduced tolerance for sounds in general
Phonophobia: fear of certain sounds
Misophonia: dislike of specific sounds

Effects
Disrupt sleep, cause communication issues, anxiety, irritability, concentration difficulties, depression, prevents intellectual work, altered perception of sound (Mayo Clinic)

Samiksha Sivakumar, Fall 2023

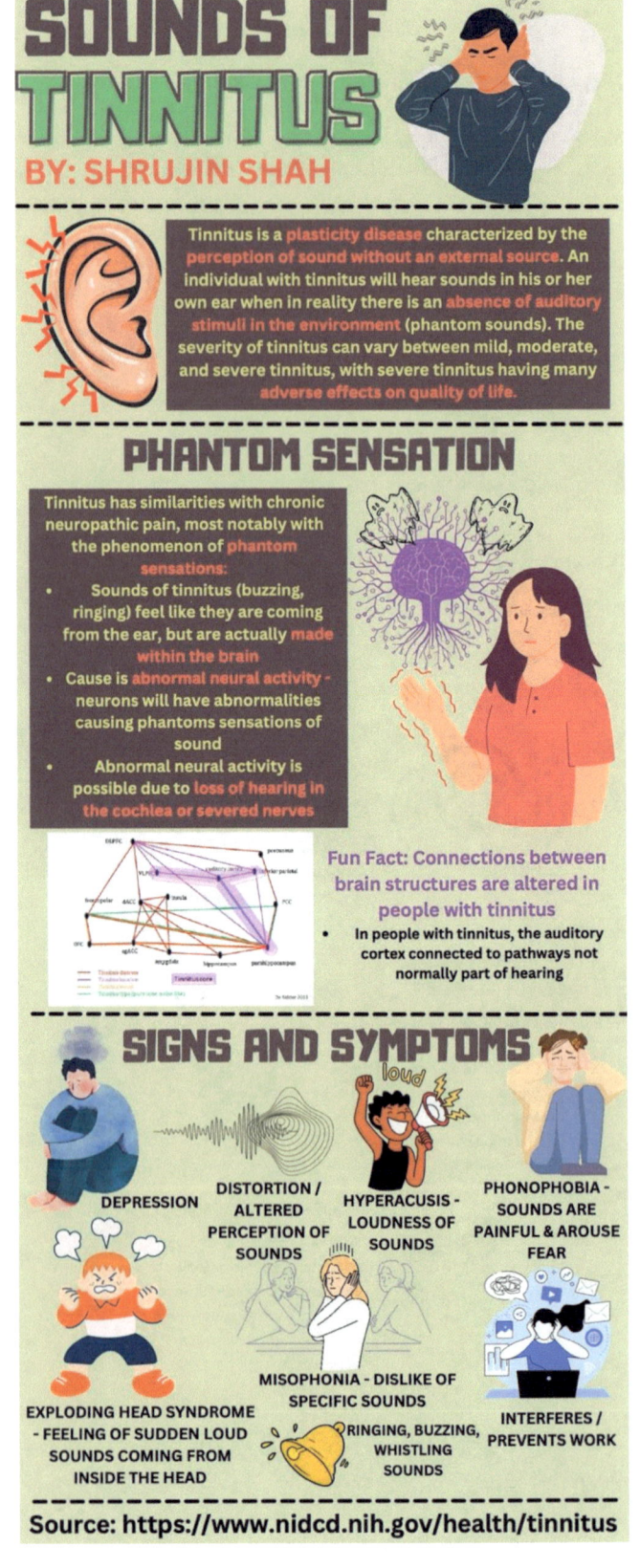

SOUNDS OF TINNITUS
BY: SHRUJIN SHAH

Tinnitus is a **plasticity disease** characterized by the perception of sound without an external source. An individual with tinnitus will hear sounds in his or her own ear when in reality there is an **absence of auditory stimuli in the environment** (phantom sounds). The severity of tinnitus can vary between mild, moderate, and severe tinnitus, with severe tinnitus having many adverse effects on quality of life.

PHANTOM SENSATION

Tinnitus has similarities with chronic neuropathic pain, most notably with the phenomenon of **phantom sensations**:
- Sounds of tinnitus (buzzing, ringing) feel like they are coming from the ear, but are actually **made within the brain**
- Cause is **abnormal neural activity** - neurons will have abnormalities causing phantoms sensations of sound
- Abnormal neural activity is possible due to **loss of hearing in the cochlea or severed nerves**

Fun Fact: Connections between brain structures are altered in people with tinnitus
- In people with tinnitus, the auditory cortex connected to pathways not normally part of hearing

SIGNS AND SYMPTOMS

- **DEPRESSION**
- **DISTORTION / ALTERED PERCEPTION OF SOUNDS**
- **HYPERACUSIS - LOUDNESS OF SOUNDS**
- **PHONOPHOBIA - SOUNDS ARE PAINFUL & AROUSE FEAR**
- **EXPLODING HEAD SYNDROME - FEELING OF SUDDEN LOUD SOUNDS COMING FROM INSIDE THE HEAD**
- **MISOPHONIA - DISLIKE OF SPECIFIC SOUNDS**
- **RINGING, BUZZING, WHISTLING SOUNDS**
- **INTERFERES / PREVENTS WORK**

Source: https://www.nidcd.nih.gov/health/tinnitus

Shrujin Shah, Fall 2023

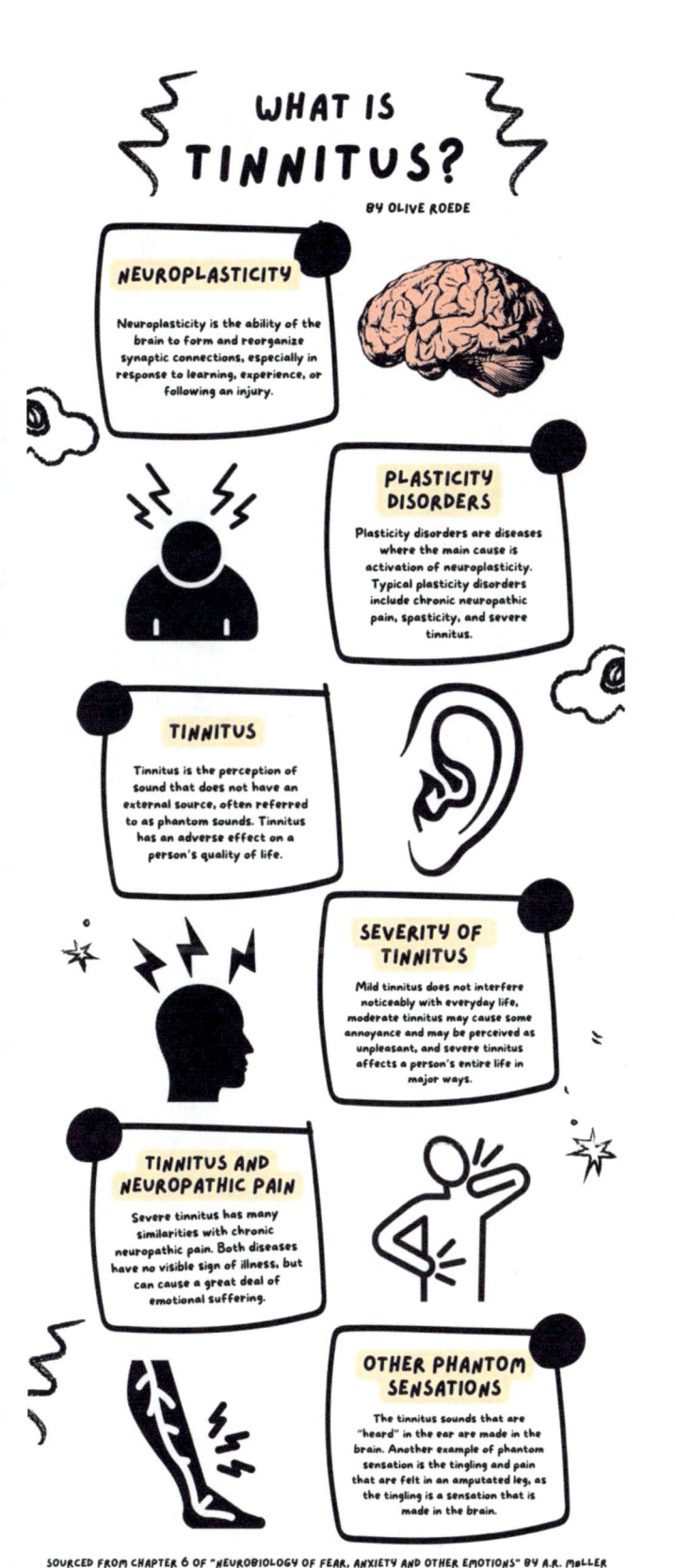

AN INFOGRAPHIC JOURNEY

WHAT IS TINNITUS?
BY OLIVE ROEDE

NEUROPLASTICITY
Neuroplasticity is the ability of the brain to form and reorganize synaptic connections, especially in response to learning, experience, or following an injury.

PLASTICITY DISORDERS
Plasticity disorders are diseases where the main cause is activation of neuroplasticity. Typical plasticity disorders include chronic neuropathic pain, spasticity, and severe tinnitus.

TINNITUS
Tinnitus is the perception of sound that does not have an external source, often referred to as phantom sounds. Tinnitus has an adverse effect on a person's quality of life.

SEVERITY OF TINNITUS
Mild tinnitus does not interfere noticeably with everyday life, moderate tinnitus may cause some annoyance and may be perceived as unpleasant, and severe tinnitus affects a person's entire life in major ways.

TINNITUS AND NEUROPATHIC PAIN
Severe tinnitus has many similarities with chronic neuropathic pain. Both diseases have no visible sign of illness, but can cause a great deal of emotional suffering.

OTHER PHANTOM SENSATIONS
The tinnitus sounds that are "heard" in the ear are made in the brain. Another example of phantom sensation is the tingling and pain that are felt in an amputated leg, as the tingling is a sensation that is made in the brain.

SOURCED FROM CHAPTER 6 OF "NEUROBIOLOGY OF FEAR, ANXIETY AND OTHER EMOTIONS" BY A.R. MØLLER

Olive Roede, Fall 2023

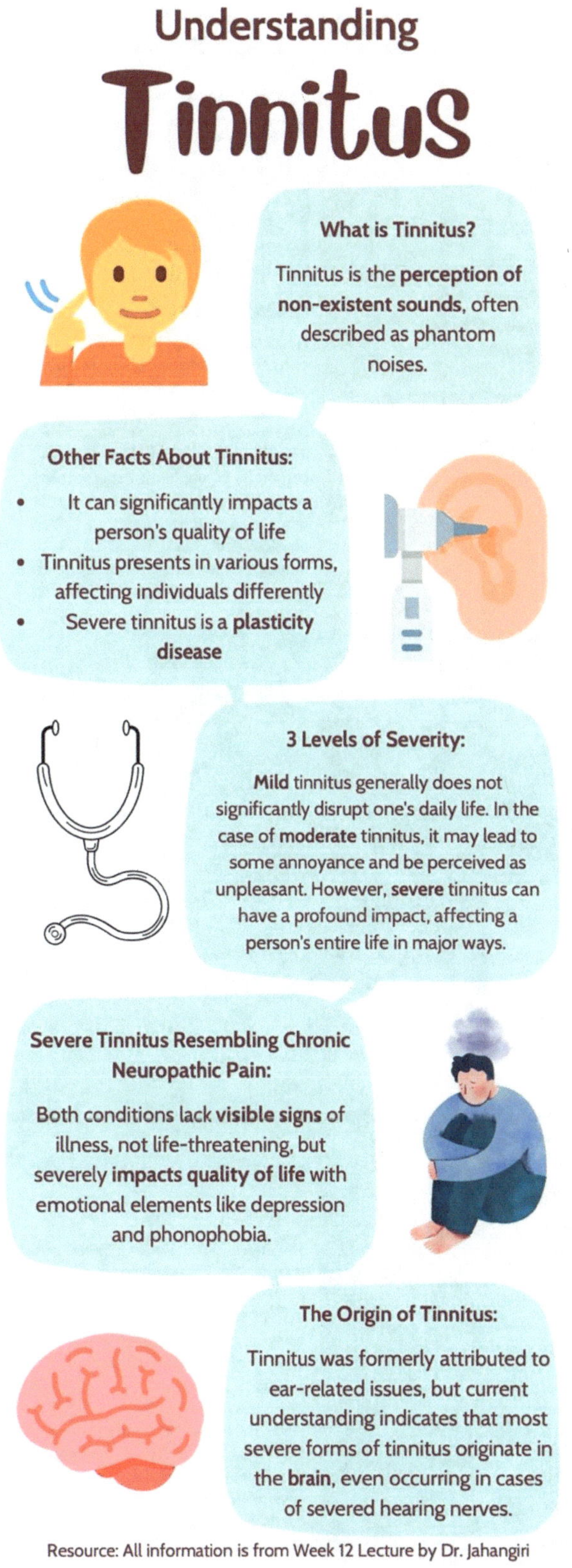

Understanding Tinnitus

What is Tinnitus?
Tinnitus is the **perception of non-existent sounds**, often described as phantom noises.

Other Facts About Tinnitus:
- It can significantly impacts a person's quality of life
- Tinnitus presents in various forms, affecting individuals differently
- Severe tinnitus is a **plasticity disease**

3 Levels of Severity:
Mild tinnitus generally does not significantly disrupt one's daily life. In the case of **moderate** tinnitus, it may lead to some annoyance and be perceived as unpleasant. However, **severe** tinnitus can have a profound impact, affecting a person's entire life in major ways.

Severe Tinnitus Resembling Chronic Neuropathic Pain:
Both conditions lack **visible signs** of illness, not life-threatening, but severely **impacts quality of life** with emotional elements like depression and phonophobia.

The Origin of Tinnitus:
Tinnitus was formerly attributed to ear-related issues, but current understanding indicates that most severe forms of tinnitus originate in the **brain**, even occurring in cases of severed hearing nerves.

Resource: All information is from Week 12 Lecture by Dr. Jahangiri

Haniya Qavi, Fall 2023

AN INFOGRAPHIC JOURNEY

TINNITUS

1. What is Tinnitus?

Tinnitus is a condition characterized by the perception of noise or ringing in the ears, even when there is no real noise present. Patients often describe this "phantom noise" as ringing, buzzing, or whistling.

Causes for tinnitus may vary, from high exposure to loud noises, age-related hearing loss, certain medications, sinus infections, jaw joint disorders, and more. However, many forms of severe tinnitus have similarities with central neuropathic pain.

Severe tinnitus is characterized by no visible signs of illness, not life-threatening BUT affects the quality of life, the cause is not where the symptoms are felt, and has a strong emotional component

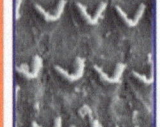

Healthy Hair Cells / Damaged Hair Cells

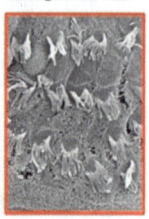

Figure 1. The image on the left shows microscopic imaging of healthy hair cells. The image on the right shows microscopic imaging of damaged hair cells found in tinnitus patients. This image shows an example of tinnitus caused by a peripheral issue. Milder versions of tinnitus are commonly associated with peripheral physiological changes, such as damaged hair cells, which may have been caused by constant exposure to loud noises

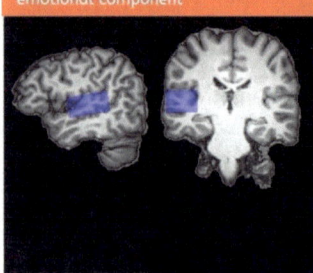

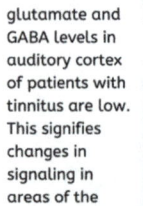

Figure 1: Studies show that glutamate and GABA levels in auditory cortex of patients with tinnitus are low. This signifies changes in signaling in areas of the brain.

2. Tinnitus and the Brain

Tinnitus often originates in the auditory system, which includes the ears and the auditory nerve. Furthermore, neural changes in the circuits of the brain associated with hearing and sound processing may be a factor in chronic tinnitus. For example, studies have shown that the auditory cortices of people with tinnitus are connected to parts of the brain that are not normally involved in hearing. Furthermore, neuroplastic changes may occur as the brain tries to adjust to the altered auditory input. This can lead to the persistence of tinnitus even after the initial trigger has been addressed. Finally, tinnitus can also trigger brain regions associated with emotions, attention and stress

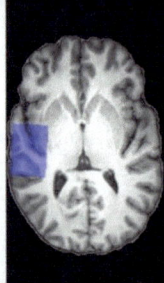

5. Reaction to Tinnitus

Severe tinnitus is commonly involved in affective mood disorders, such as depression and phonophobia. Most people either catastrophize or confront the tinnitus and its effects. With a catastrophizing mindset, the patient will believe that there is nothing that can be done to cure it. On the other hand, non-catastrophizing patients will seek treatment and will learn to cope with it.

Citations

The Physiological Society. "How Loud Is Loud: The Physiology of Ear Ringing." The Physiological Society, 13 Mar. 2019, www.physoc.org/blog/how-loud-is-loud-the-physiology-of-ear-ringing/.

Tinnitus." Mayo Clinic, Mayo Foundation for Medical Education and Research, 30 Nov. 2022, www.mayoclinic.org/diseases-conditions/tinnitus/symptoms-causes/syc-20350156.

Vyshnavi Poruri, Fall 2023

TINNITUS
By: Neha Kazani

01 WHAT IS TINNITUS
- Hearing nonsesnse sounds that do not come from the outside, aka phantom sounds
- A plasticity disease

02 FORMS OF TINNITUS
- Mild tinnitus: does not noticeably interfere with everyday life
- Moderate tinnitus: may be annoying/unpleasant
- Severe tinnitus: may be severely disabling

03 SIMILARITIES TO CHRONIC NEUROPATHIC PAIN
- No visible signs of illness
- Not life-threatening
- Affects quality of life
- Strong emotional components including depression and phonophobia (fear of sound)

04 LOCATION OF ILLNESS
- Severe chronic tinnitus: phantom sensation that is made in the brain
- The tinnitus sound that is felt coming from the ear is made in the nervous system

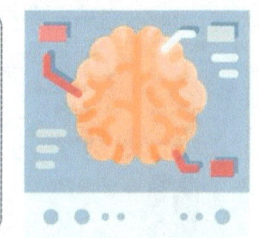

Works Cited: Jahangiri, Faisal, November, 2023, Neurobiology of Emotions Chapter 6 Pt. 3: Minimizing the Risks of Harm, Tinnitus, School of Brain and Behavioral Sciences, University of Texas at Dallas

Neha Kazani, Fall 2023

AN INFOGRAPHIC JOURNEY

TINNITUS

- Severe tinnitus is often caused by the activation of neuroplasticity
- Many forms of severe tinnitus have similarities with central neuropathic pain
- Tinnitus has many different forms. Large individual variations in severity

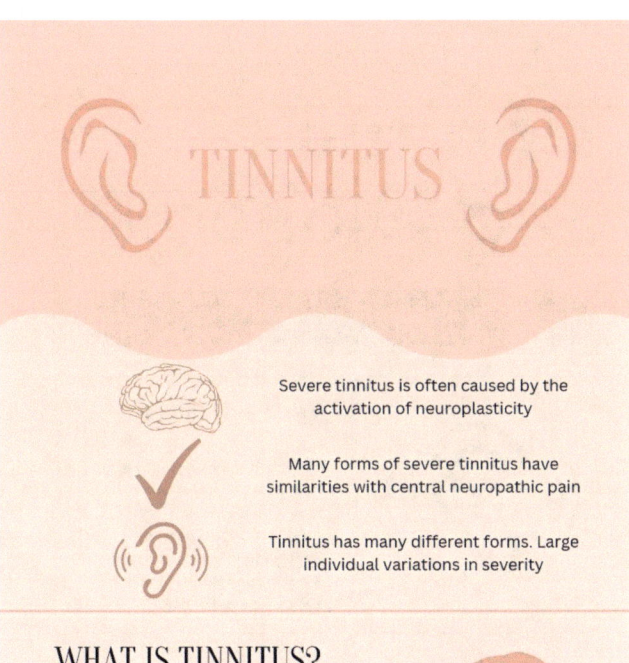

WHAT IS TINNITUS?

- Hearing (nonsense) sounds that do not come from the outside (phantom sounds)
- An adverse effect on a person QUALITY OF LIFE

Tinnitus has many forms.

THERE ARE MANY GRADES OF TINNITUS

- <u>Mild tinnitus</u>: Does not interfere noticeably with everyday life
- <u>Moderate tinnitus</u>: May cause some annoyance and may be perceived as unpleasant
- <u>Severe tinnitus</u>: Affects a person's entire life in major ways

WHERE DOES TINNITUS COME FROM?

- Earlier it was believed that tinnitus came from the ear, and it was concluded that the cause of tinnitus was something wrong with the ear
- Now we know that most forms of severe tinnitus come from the brain.
- Tinnitus can occur with a severed hearing nerve

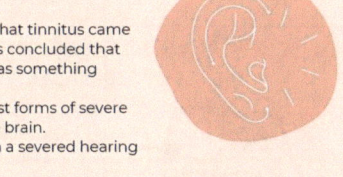

ACCOMPANYING SYMPTOMS TO TINNITUS

- Hyperacusis
  - Reduced tolerance for sounds in general
  - Involvement of non-classical pathways?
  - Cause and pathophysiology unknown
- Phonophobia
  - Fear of certain sounds
  - Cause and pathophysiology unknown
- Misophonia
  - Misophonia is "dislike of specific sounds"
  - Object ("what") stream problem?
  - Together with tinnitus or a separate disease?
  - Cause and pathophysiology unknown

Shreena Desai, Spring 2023

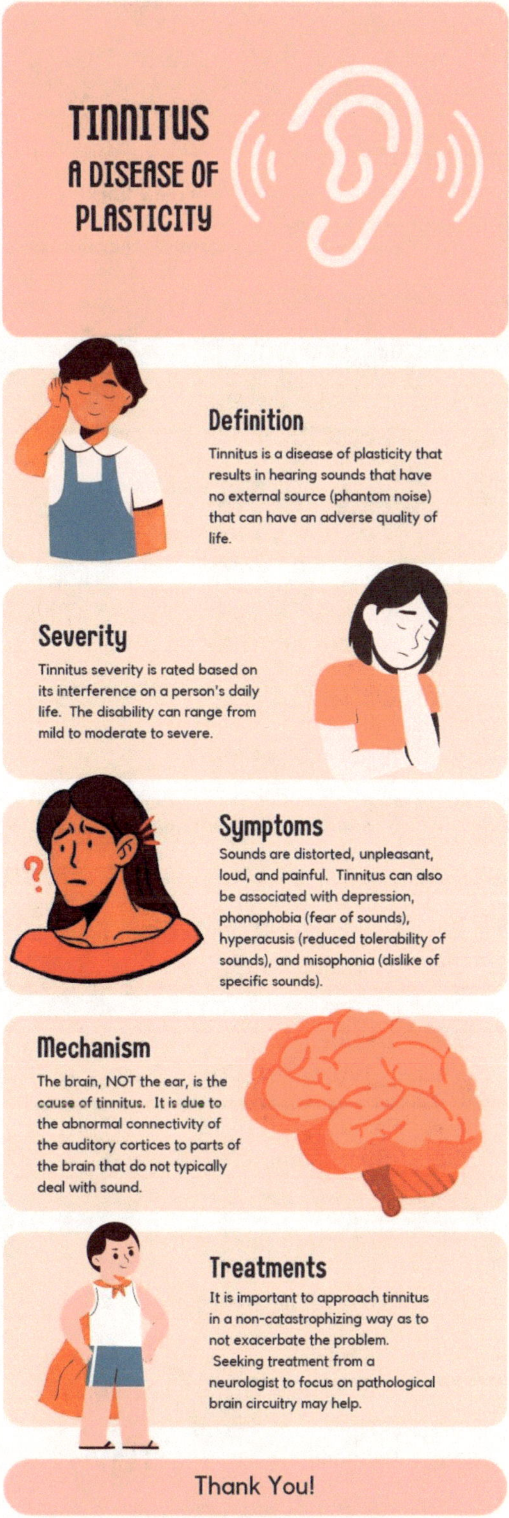

TINNITUS
A DISEASE OF PLASTICITY

Definition
Tinnitus is a disease of plasticity that results in hearing sounds that have no external source (phantom noise) that can have an adverse quality of life.

Severity
Tinnitus severity is rated based on its interference on a person's daily life. The disability can range from mild to moderate to severe.

Symptoms
Sounds are distorted, unpleasant, loud, and painful. Tinnitus can also be associated with depression, phonophobia (fear of sounds), hyperacusis (reduced tolerability of sounds), and misophonia (dislike of specific sounds).

Mechanism
The brain, NOT the ear, is the cause of tinnitus. It is due to the abnormal connectivity of the auditory cortices to parts of the brain that do not typically deal with sound.

Treatments
It is important to approach tinnitus in a non-catastrophizing way as to not exacerbate the problem. Seeking treatment from a neurologist to focus on pathological brain circuitry may help.

Thank You!

Katelyn Bonvillain, Spring 2023

AN INFOGRAPHIC JOURNEY

TINNITUS SUMMARY

What is Tinnitus?
- Hearing nonsensical sounds that do not come from the outside (also known as phantom sounds)
- Tinnitus has many forms and has a adverse effect on quality of life
- Many forms of tinnitus are plasticity disorders

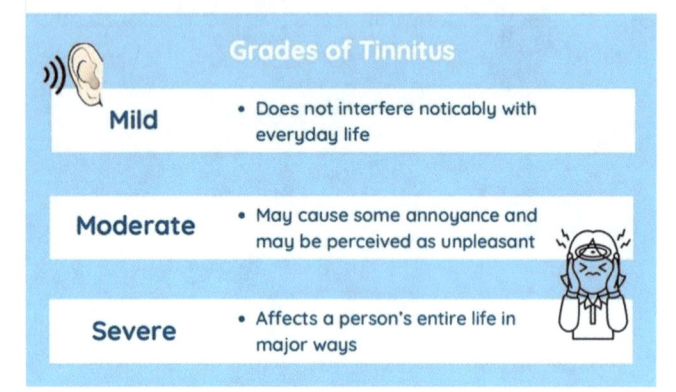

Grades of Tinnitus

Mild	Does not interfere noticably with everyday life
Moderate	May cause some annoyance and may be perceived as unpleasant
Severe	Affects a person's entire life in major ways

Where does tinnitus come from?
- Earlier it was believed that tinnitus came from the ear, and it was concluded that the cause of tinnitus was something wrong with the ear
- Now we know that most forms of severe tinnitus comes from the brain.
- Tinnitus can occur with a severed hearing nerve

Accompanying Symptoms

Hyperacusis
- Reduced tolerance for sounds in general

Phonophobia
- Fear of certain sounds

Misophonia
- "dislike of specific sounds"

Cause and pathophysiology unknown

Negative Affects on Life
- Prevents or disturbs sleep
- Interferes with or prevents Intellectual work
- Often accompanied by an altered perception of sound

Source: Weekly Lectures :)

Audrey Villanueva, Fall 2023

Tinnitus at a Glance

BY: HIMA PRAVEEN

What Is Tinnitus?

Tinnitus is the experience of hearing a ringing or some type of noise in one's ear. It affects 15-20% of people mainly found in older adults. Keep in mind this ringing is not an external sound.

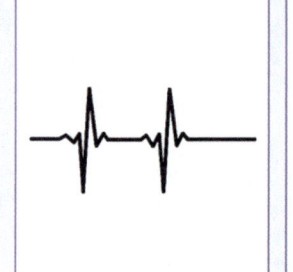

Symptoms

Most of the time tinnitus is categorized as ringing in the ears, but other sounds such as buzzing, roaring, clicking, hissing, or humming can be a symptom as well. Rarely, it can be heard in the form of rhythmically pulsing and whooshing.

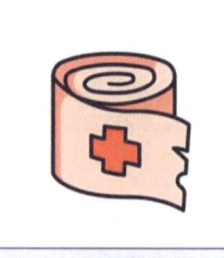

Causes

In many people, some causes of tinnitus Include hearing loss, ear Infection/ear canal blockage, head/neck Injuries, muscle spasms in the inner ear, ear bone changes and/or medications.

Complications

Some complications that arise In people who have tinnitus are fatigue, stress, sleep problems, trouble concentrating, memory problems, depression, anxiety and irritability, headaches, and problems with work and family life.

References
"Tinnitus." Mayo Clinic, Mayo Foundation for Medical Education and Research, 30 Nov. 2022, www.mayoclinic.org/diseases-conditions/tinnitus/symptoms-causes/syc-20350156.

Hima Praveen, Fall 2023

AN INFOGRAPHIC JOURNEY

CHAPTER 16

Pain

Understanding Phantom Pain

By Emma Siddiqui, Spring 2024

Introduction:
Phantom pain, a phenomenon where individuals feel sensations such as pain in limbs that are no longer there, is a fascinating and intriguing human experience. Phantom pain affects a significant number of people who have gone through limb amputations, impacting their daily lives and functions in several ways. Despite the condition's prevalence, phantom pain often remains misunderstood by the public and others who do not face the condition. Here, we will delve deeper into the complexities of phantom pain, understanding where it begins, emotional impacts, management strategies, and current research.

What is Phantom Pain?
Phantom pain is a sensory phenomenon experienced by individuals who have undergone limb amputations. The brain continues to receive signals that create sensations of pain or discomfort originating from the missing body part despite the absence of the amputated limb. The sensations under phantom limb pain can vary, ranging from tingling, throbbing, and itching to sharp stabbing pains in the limb that is no longer present. In the United States, around 79.9% of amputees reported phantom pains (Hanyu-Deutmeyer et al.). Phantom pains are more common in the upper and lower extremities (Hanyu-Deutmeyer et al.). Additionally, some individuals might experience sensations where the missing limb feels like it is still there, and they can feel the limb and move it, making the condition even more complicated. In the United States, around 79.9% of amputees reported phantom pains (Hanyu-Deutmeyer et.al).

Understanding How Phantom Pain Begins:
To understand the phenomenon of phantom pain, it is vital to explore the changes that happen in the nervous system after a limb is lost. The brain's changes following limb loss,

which are frequently connected to phantom limb pain, have been investigated by scientists in recent years. In this process, the portions of the brain that formerly represented the missing limb are taken up by nearby regions. Neuroplasticity, the brain's ability to reorganize networks, is caused when the normal flow of sensory information to the brain is disrupted by amputations (Erlenwein J et al.). The brain reorganizes and compensates for the loss of sensory information from the amputated limb to create adaptive changes in the brain. Sometimes, these adaptive changes in the brain can result in maladaptive rewiring, which creates the perception of phantom sensations such as pain. The peripheral nervous system (PNS) and central nervous system (CNS) have also changed, which causes the phantom pains to continue. This brain alteration explains why stimulation of nerves in the remaining portion of the missing leg might cause sensations and discomfort. Individuals may experience more discomfort as their brain rearranges (Hanyu-Deutmeyer et al.).

Different Ways Phantom Pain Presents Itself:
Phantom pain symptoms can vary for each area of the limb, making it a very complex condition. Symptoms may range from mild discomfort or tingling sensations to severe debilitating pain that significantly impacts one's daily life consisting of simple tasks. Their types of pain and strength can change over time, and people may experience other things, such as phantom limb sensations. Phantom limb sensations occur when it feels like the missing limb is present, and the limb appears to change in size and shape. People must understand the unique differences in pain and how it can change over time to treat these pains effectively.

Emotional Impacts of Phantom Pains:
Phantom pains not only impact an individual physically but also impact a person emotionally. The chronic pains caused by phantom pain can lead to feelings of anxiety, depression, frustration, and decreased quality of life (Hanyu-Deutmeyer et al.). Since phantom pains are unpredictable and change over time, the uncertainty of the condition can create more significant challenges than just adapting to life without a limb. Individuals coping with phantom pain do not only need physical support but also need mental health care to cope with their condition better.

Managing and Caring for Phantom Pains:
Managing phantom pain needs a holistic approach that can address all the aspects of the condition, such as physical and emotional pains. Pain relievers, antidepressants, and anticonvulsants are some medications that may be prescribed to lessen the pain and adjust signals in the brain. Additionally, physical, mirror and virtual reality therapy can help teach the brain's perception of the missing limb and reduce phantom sensations (Hanyu-Deutmeyer et al.). Interventions such as cognitive-behavioral therapy and mindfulness approaches are some psychological ways to assist individuals in coping with emotional challenges. These interventions and changes can help improve an individual's quality of life

and decrease the burden of the impacts of phantom pains. However, it is essential to create treatment plans that fit each individual's needs while considering their symptoms, goals, and preferences.

Current Research:

Researchers are actively seeking new information on understanding and managing phantom pains, but there is still much more to learn. Current researchers' goals are to understand the mechanisms of phantom pain further and develop new treatment approaches.

Advances in neuroimaging, such as functional magnetic resonance imaging and positron emission tomography, provide researchers with more bottomless pictures of neural correlations with phantom pain (Erlenwein J). Furthermore, innovations such as brain-computer interfaces and neuromodulation devices have been shown to modulate pain signals and store sensory functions in individuals with the condition. With the help of new research studies and findings we can understand phantom pain better and improve the outcomes of the people affected by the condition.

Conclusion:

Phantom pain remains a complex and compelling aspect of the human body, impacting individuals who have undergone amputations in several ways. While it may seem confusing, understanding its origins, presentation, emotional impact, and management strategies is essential for supporting and caring for those who experience the condition. By creating awareness, compassion, and collaboration, we can create a more inclusive and supportive environment for those navigating the challenges of phantom pain after those of a limb. Continued research, education and advocacy can further our understanding of phantom pain and develop more effective interventions to improve the daily lives of those affected by the condition.

References

1. Hanyu-Deutmeyer AA, Cascella M, Varacallo M. Phantom Limb Pain. [Updated 2023 Aug 4]. In: StatPearls [Internet]. Treasure Island (FL): StatPearls Publishing; 2024 Jan-. Available from: https://www.ncbi.nlm.nih.gov/books/NBK448188/
2. Erlenwein J, Diers M, Ernst J, Schulz F, Petzke F. Clinical updates on phantom limb pain. Pain Rep. 2021 Jan 15;6(1):e888. doi: 10.1097/PR9.0000000000000888. PMID: 33490849; PMCID:
3. PMC7813551. https://www.ncbi.nlm.nih.gov/pmc/articles/PMC7813551/

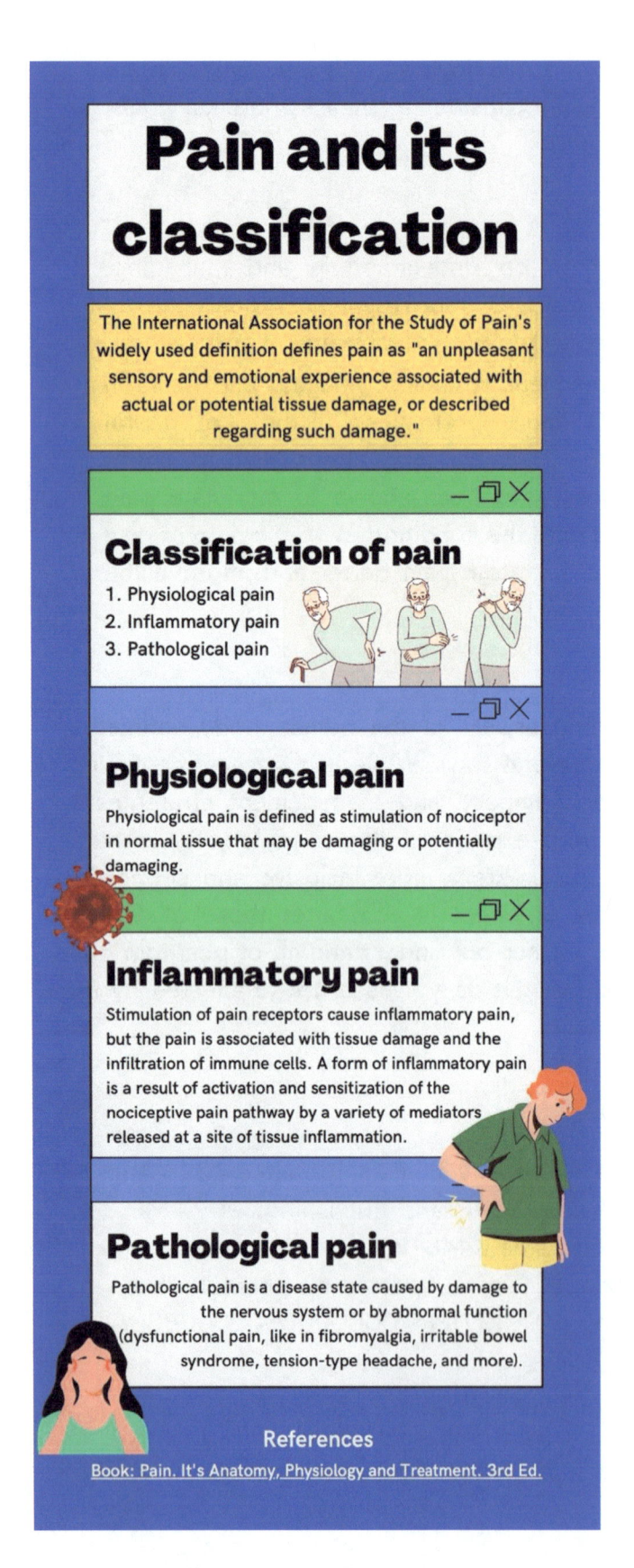

Hyeonji Lee, Fall 2023

Sharanya Swaminathan, Fall 2022

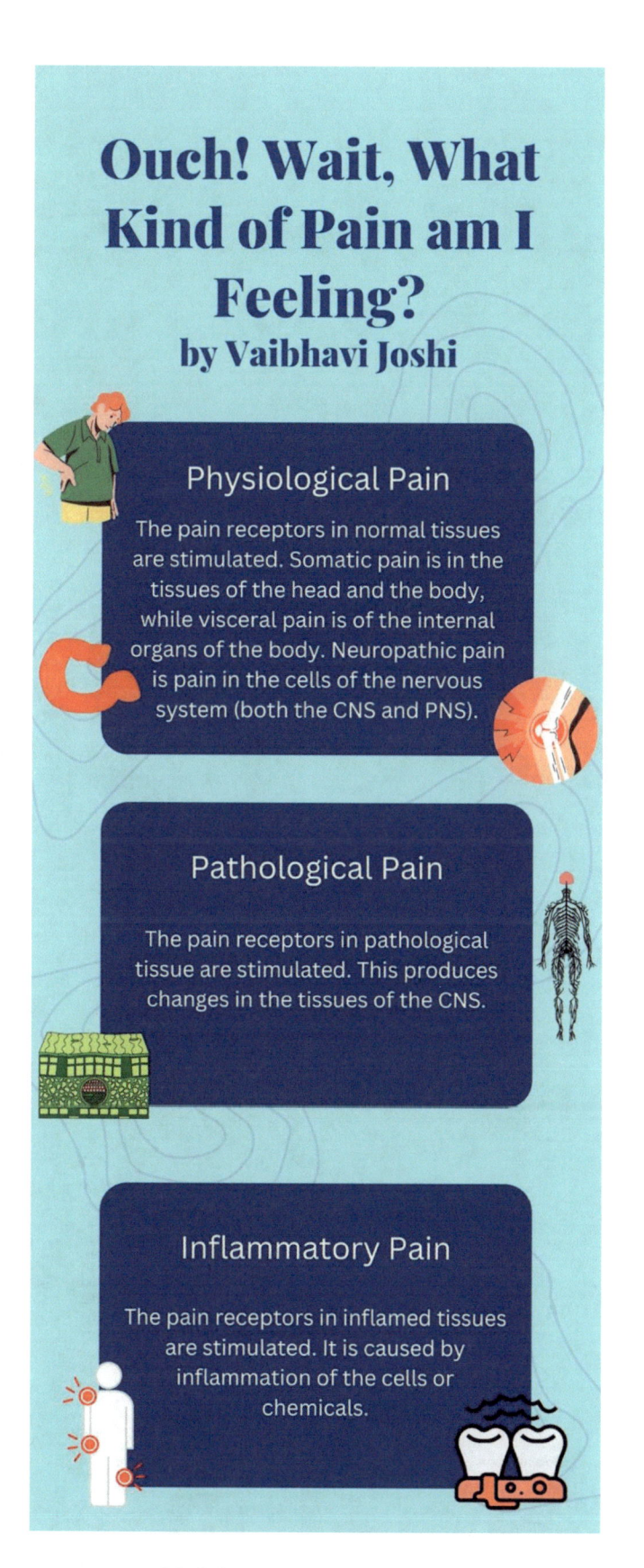

AN INFOGRAPHIC JOURNEY

Ouch! Wait, What Kind of Pain am I Feeling?
by Vaibhavi Joshi

Physiological Pain
The pain receptors in normal tissues are stimulated. Somatic pain is in the tissues of the head and the body, while visceral pain is of the internal organs of the body. Neuropathic pain is pain in the cells of the nervous system (both the CNS and PNS).

Pathological Pain
The pain receptors in pathological tissue are stimulated. This produces changes in the tissues of the CNS.

Inflammatory Pain
The pain receptors in inflamed tissues are stimulated. It is caused by inflammation of the cells or chemicals.

Vaibhavi Joshi, Fall 2022

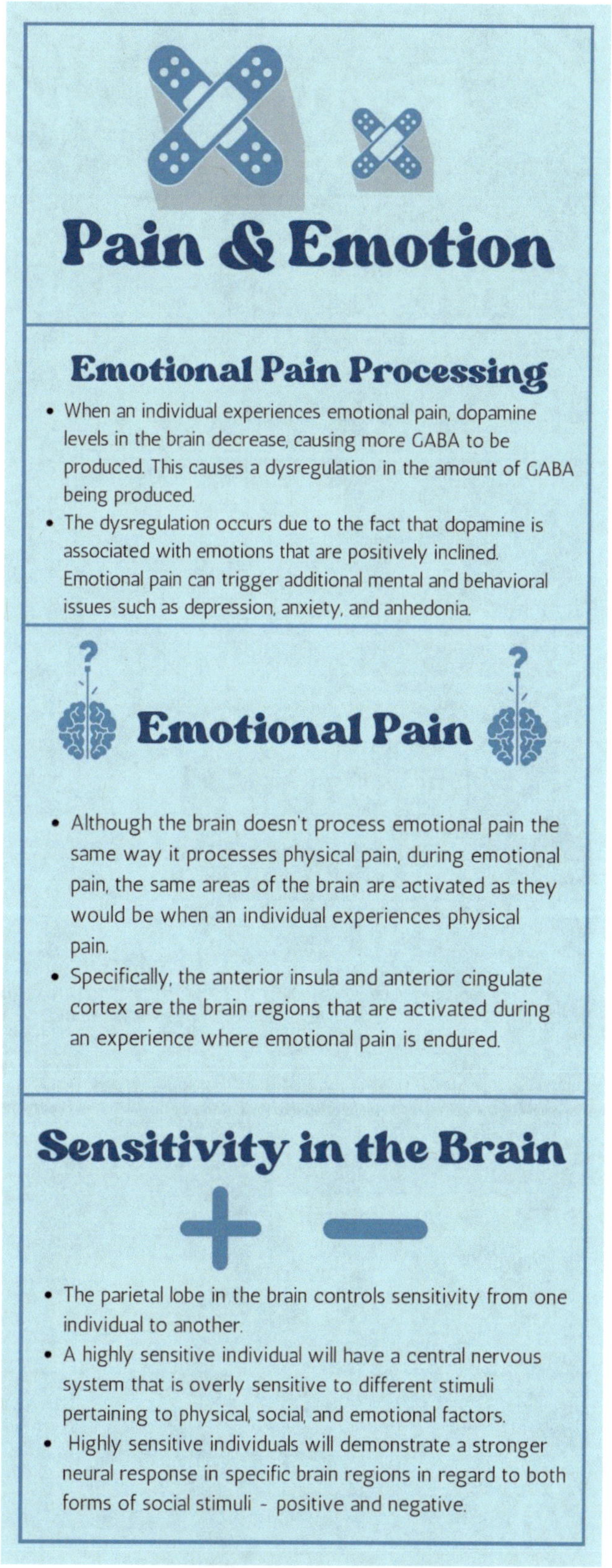

Pain & Emotion

Emotional Pain Processing
- When an individual experiences emotional pain, dopamine levels in the brain decrease, causing more GABA to be produced. This causes a dysregulation in the amount of GABA being produced.
- The dysregulation occurs due to the fact that dopamine is associated with emotions that are positively inclined. Emotional pain can trigger additional mental and behavioral issues such as depression, anxiety, and anhedonia.

Emotional Pain
- Although the brain doesn't process emotional pain the same way it processes physical pain, during emotional pain, the same areas of the brain are activated as they would be when an individual experiences physical pain.
- Specifically, the anterior insula and anterior cingulate cortex are the brain regions that are activated during an experience where emotional pain is endured.

Sensitivity in the Brain
- The parietal lobe in the brain controls sensitivity from one individual to another.
- A highly sensitive individual will have a central nervous system that is overly sensitive to different stimuli pertaining to physical, social, and emotional factors.
- Highly sensitive individuals will demonstrate a stronger neural response in specific brain regions in regard to both forms of social stimuli - positive and negative.

Mahwish Quadri, Spring 2023

Forms of Pain

01. Somatic

Somatic pain is pain from nociceptors of intact tissue of the body and the head. Afferent nociceptive information enters the brain from pain receptors.

02. Visceral

Visceral pain is pain from internal organs characterized by inconsistent sensations. There's sometimes referred pain to the body's surface. This pain often feels inescapable to those experiencing it.

03. Inflammatory

Inflammatory pain is caused by the stimulation of pain receptors and inflammation of various kinds. Inflammatory pain can be caused by various chemicals.

04. Neuropathic

Neuropathic pain can be caused by pain in the central nervous system, peripheral nervous system, anesthesia dolorosa (burning pain and numbness) and stoke pain.

05. Pathological

This type of pain is caused by the stimulation of pain receptors in pathological tissue. Changes in the function of the nervous system (spinal cord and the brain).

Works Cited: https://www.beaumont.org/services/pain-management-services/types-of-pain; Dr. Jahangiri's Slides

Rohita Arjarapu, Fall 2023

Types of pain

01 PHYSIOLOGICAL PAIN

Afferent nociceptive information enters the brain from pain receptors in the body and the head (somatic pain) and internal organs (visceral pain). Afferent pathways carry signals to the thalamus and then go to primary somatosensory cortex (S1), and secondary somatosensory cortex (S2), the insula, anterior cingulate cortex (ACC), the lateral nucleus of the amygdala (AMY).

02 INFLAMMATORY PAIN

inflammatory pain is caused by stimulation of pain receptors, inflammation in various tissue, and chemicals. It is in between physiological and pathological pain.

03 PATHOLOGICAL PAIN

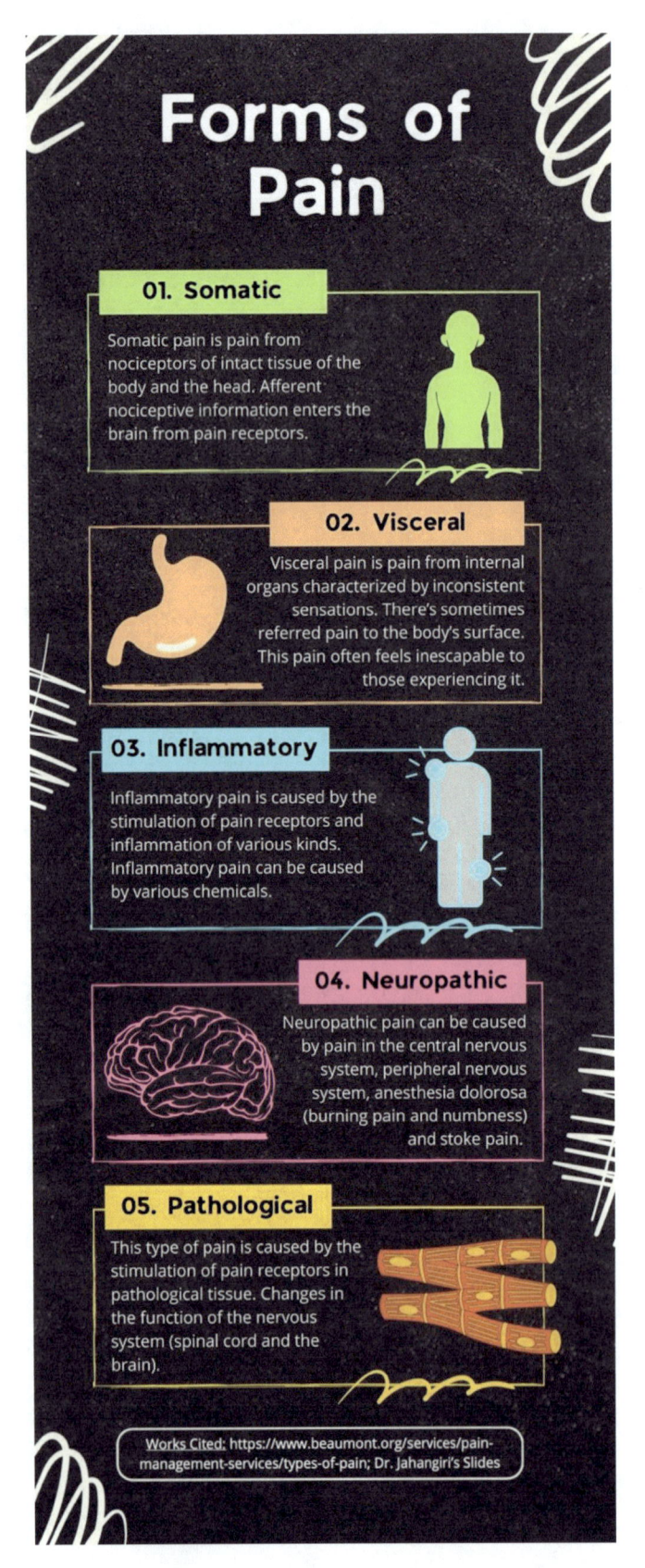

Neuropathological pain results from maladaptive neuroplasticity, which makes it difficult to treat with common pain medications. examples of maladaptive neuroplasticity disorders include tinnitus and phantom limb syndrome. Chronic neuropathological pain is caused by changes in the function of the spinal cord and the brain, not pain receptors.

04 DID YOU KNOW?

Although capsaicin is associated with burning and irritation from chili peppers, it is also used as a topical treatment to reduce neuropathic pain. Capsaicin selectively activates TRPV1, a Ca^{2+}-permeable cationic ion channel that is enriched in the terminals of certain nociceptors. Activation is followed by a prolonged decreased response to noxious stimuli (Chung and Campbell).

citation:
Chung, Man-Kyo, and James N Campbell. "Use of Capsaicin to Treat Pain: Mechanistic and Therapeutic Considerations." Pharmaceuticals (Basel, Switzerland) vol. 9,4 66. 1 Nov. 2016, doi:10.3390/ph9040066

Jeffy Jackson, Fall 2023

AN INFOGRAPHIC JOURNEY

PAIN
NSC 4382. LUCIE NGUYEN.

What is Pain?
- Unpleasant, noxious signal
- Can activate many different circuits
- Severe pain can activate emotional brain
- Can cause stress that decreases effect of immune system
- Pain perception can be influenced by expectations and evaluations

Classifications
Pain can be classified:
- By anatomical structure that creates the symptoms (peripheral and cranial nerves)
- Different body systems affected
- Anatomical location
- Inflammatory, nociceptive
- Length of Time

Physiological Pain
Stems from stimulation of stimuli that may be damaging or potentially damaging. Pain from nociceptors located in the body and head. Information for this pain is routed through the thalamus and is projected to somatosensory cortex and emotional brain.

Inflammatory Pain
Stimulation of these receptors is triggered by tissue damage or activation of immune cells. This pain lies between physiological and pathological pain. Other causes can be various chemicals like interleukins, tumor necrosis factors, chemokines, reactive oxygen species and more!

Pathological Pain
Pathological pain is also known as neuropathic pain. This pain stems from all pains of the peripheral and central nervous system.
- Causes include disease, lesion, or sensory abnormalities
- Neuroplasticity plays a role
- Chronic neuropathic pain is NOT caused by stimulation of pain receptors thus harder to treat

Effects of Pain
- Sleep disruptions
- Suicide
- Interfere with work
- Diminish quality of life
- Can lead to stress which decreases immune system function

References
Møller, A.R. (2014) Pain: Its anatomy, physiology and treatment. Richardson, TX: Aage R. Møller Publishing.

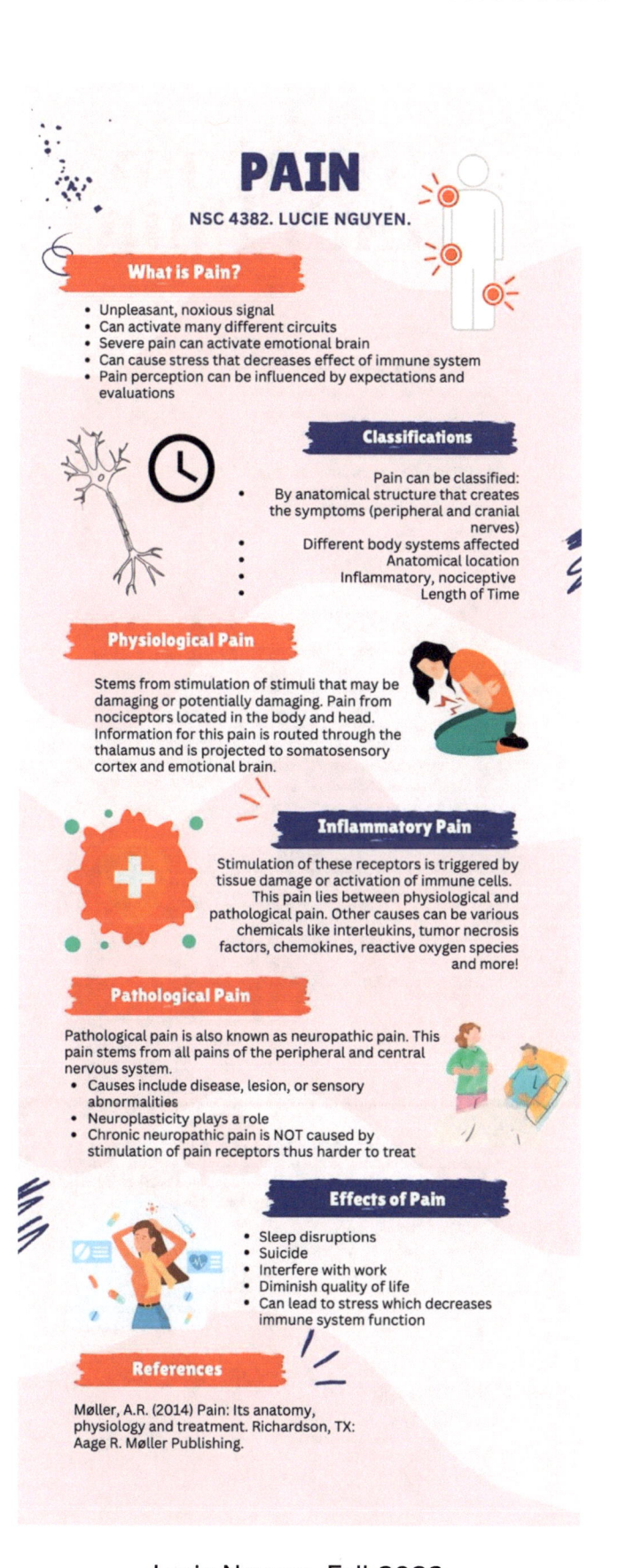

Lucie Nguyen, Fall 2023

The Body's Protective Mechanisms

The "Freezing" Mechanism
Sometimes, dangerous situations can trigger a "freezing" response in people. Though freezing has the disadvantage of leaving a person in a state where they cannot run away, it can sometimes be advantageous to not move because it can ward off an attack. The alternative to this is the "fight" aspect of the fight or flight response, in which the sympathetic nervous system is activated, causing blood pressure and heart rate to go up in anticipation of fighting off a threat.

Neuroplasticity
Neuroplasticity plays an important role in allowing people to learn from past experiences and adapt their behavior accordingly. Neuroplasticity confers a survival advantage to people since they can improve their survival mechanisms based on what they have encountered before. For instance, after surviving a certain life or death situation, your brain may be more attuned to picking up on certain cues of danger in future situations.

Pain
The ability to feel pain is also a major protective mechanism of the body. Pain alerts us to threats and helps us respond appropriately to avoid injury. For instance, feeling pain when putting your hand on a hot stove alerts you to withdraw your hand from the stove in order to prevent a major burn. This is where neuroplasticity also plays a role because that experience teaches you that touching the stove is not advisable. People born with a congenital insensitivity to pain often suffer many injuries because their body does not have an alarm system to alert them to threats.

Laiba Ali, Fall 2022

5 PHANTOM RISKS

1. Airport Security Scanners
People tend to be worried about radiation exposure even though it is considered to be minimal and safe.

2. Vaccination Risks
People fear vaccines because of the link between them and diseases, even though many are considered safe.

3. Electric Vehicles
There are concerns about battery safety but the risk of battery-related accidents is relatively low.

4. Cell Phone radiation
There are fears about the radiation emitted from cell phones causing ill health, even though no direct link has been proven.

5. Genetically Modified Organisms
People are worried about the consumption of GMO's even though there is extensive research proving otherwise.

Neha Gannapaneni, Spring 2024

Phantom Limb Pain

1. Overview
Amputees may develop a condition called phantom limb pain (PLP), where pain is felt in a missing limb. The pain ranges from mild to severe and can last anywhere from seconds to days. Approximately 8 out of 10 people who lose a limb experience PLP to some degree.

2. Causes
The pathophysiology of PLP remains poorly understood, though the general idea is that pain results from a mix-up and misinterpretation of nervous signals. The predominant theory entails the irritation of the severed nerve endings, but modern research progress shows evidence of central nervous system involvement as well.

Proposed Mechanisms
- Neuromas causing hyperexcitability of neurons
- Central sensitization of the spinal cord
- Cortical reorganization
- Psychogenic factors

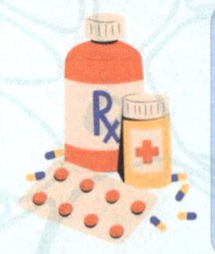

3. Management
PLP treatment focuses on easing symptoms. These include...
- Nonsteroidal anti-inflammatory drugs
- Pain Relievers
- Muscle Relaxers
- Antiseizure medications
- Beta Blockers
- Neurostimulation

4. Diagnosis
Because the diagnosis of PLP is primarily one of exclusion and dependent on a patient's history, physicians may order blood tests or imaging scans in order to rule out residual limb pain

Phantom Sensations
- Missing limb feels like it's still part of the body
- Classified as neuropathic pain

Residual Limb Pain
- Pain in remaining part of limb where amputation occurred
- Often has a medical reason
- Classified as nociceptive pain

References
Hanyu-Deutmeyer AA, Cascella M, Varacallo M. Phantom Limb Pain. [Updated 2023 Aug 4]. In: StatPearls [Internet]. Treasure Island (FL): StatPearls Publishing; 2023 Jan-. Available from: https://www.ncbi.nlm.nih.gov/books/NBK448188/

Ashley Tran, Fall 2023

AN INFOGRAPHIC JOURNEY

TYPES OF phantom sensations

Pranavi Maddipatla

Kinetic
Kinetic phantom sensations are related to, perceived movements. One example of this could be an individual feeling their toes flexing while nothing has actually changed.

Kinesthetic
Kinesthetic phantom sensations are related to size, shape, or positioning of body parts. One example of could be mistakenly feeling one's fingers are crossed.

Exteroceptive
Exteroceptive phantom sensations are related to sensory information such as touch, pressure, temperature, itch, and vibration that could be felt by a previously amputated body part.

References
Cohut, M., PhD. (2019, June 18). Phantom sensations: The mystery of how brains process touch. *Medical News Today*. https://www.medicalnewstoday.com/articles/325496#3-factors-contribute-to-phantom-sensations

Pranavi Maddipatla, Fall 2023

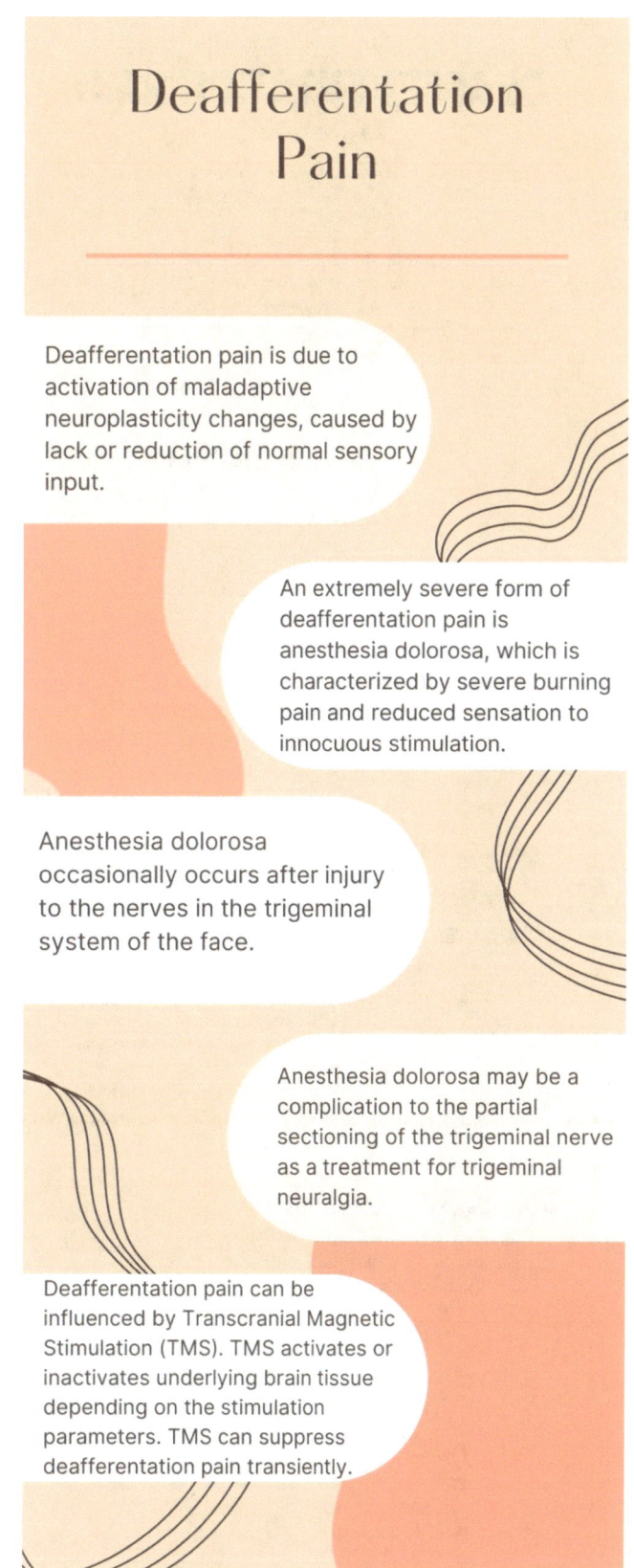

Deafferentation Pain

Deafferentation pain is due to activation of maladaptive neuroplasticity changes, caused by lack or reduction of normal sensory input.

An extremely severe form of deafferentation pain is anesthesia dolorosa, which is characterized by severe burning pain and reduced sensation to innocuous stimulation.

Anesthesia dolorosa occasionally occurs after injury to the nerves in the trigeminal system of the face.

Anesthesia dolorosa may be a complication to the partial sectioning of the trigeminal nerve as a treatment for trigeminal neuralgia.

Deafferentation pain can be influenced by Transcranial Magnetic Stimulation (TMS). TMS activates or inactivates underlying brain tissue depending on the stimulation parameters. TMS can suppress deafferentation pain transiently.

Allison Scott, Spring 2023

AN INFOGRAPHIC JOURNEY

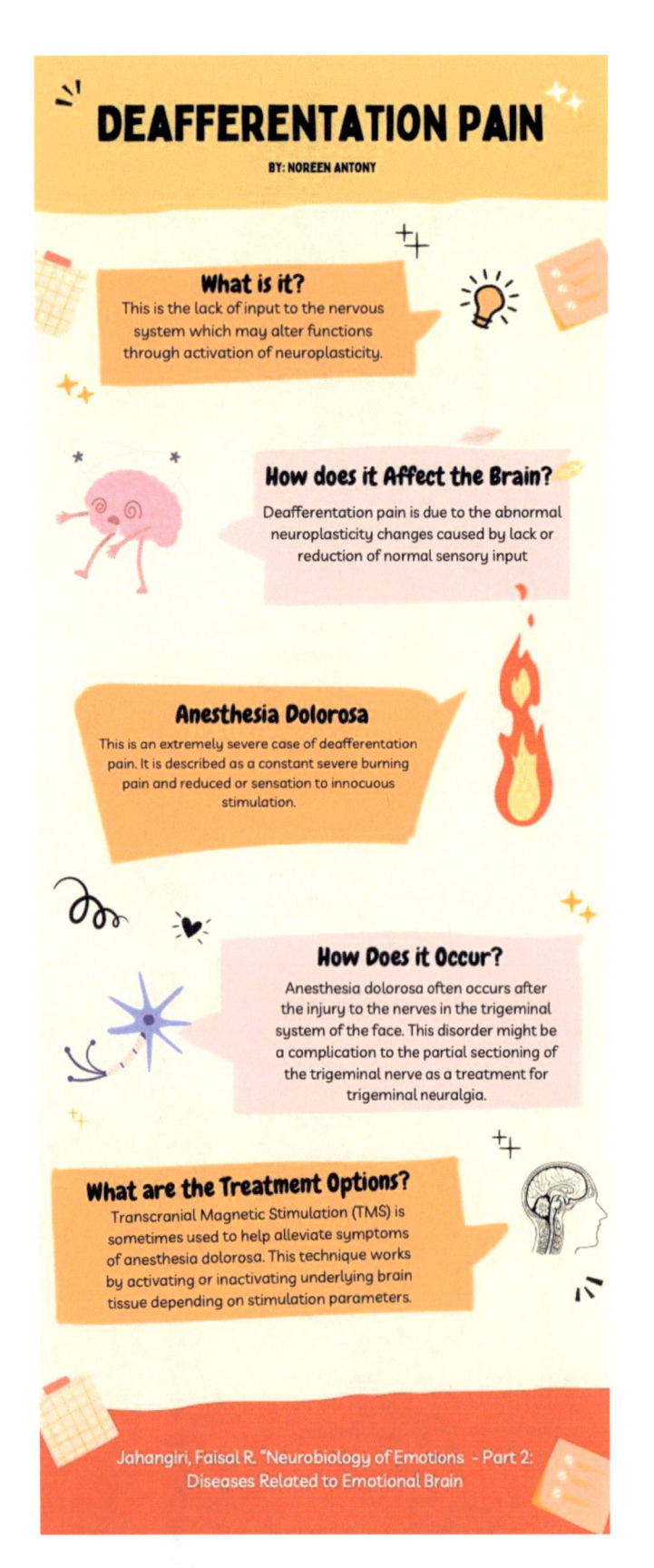

DEAFFERENTATION PAIN
BY: NOREEN ANTONY

What is it?
This is the lack of input to the nervous system which may alter functions through activation of neuroplasticity.

How does it Affect the Brain?
Deafferentation pain is due to the abnormal neuroplasticity changes caused by lack or reduction of normal sensory input

Anesthesia Dolorosa
This is an extremely severe case of deafferentation pain. It is described as a constant severe burning pain and reduced or sensation to innocuous stimulation.

How Does it Occur?
Anesthesia dolorosa often occurs after the injury to the nerves in the trigeminal system of the face. This disorder might be a complication to the partial sectioning of the trigeminal nerve as a treatment for trigeminal neuralgia.

What are the Treatment Options?
Transcranial Magnetic Stimulation (TMS) is sometimes used to help alleviate symptoms of anesthesia dolorosa. This technique works by activating or inactivating underlying brain tissue depending on stimulation parameters.

Jahangiri, Faisal R. "Neurobiology of Emotions - Part 2: Diseases Related to Emotional Brain

Noreen Antony, Fall 2023

Deafferentation Pain
By: Elisa Kapunan

Lack of input to the nervous system may alter functions through activation of neuroplasticity

Deafferentation pain is due to activation of maladaptive neuroplasticity changes caused by lack or reduction of normal sensory input

An extremely severe form of deafferentation pain is **anesthesia dolorosa**, which is characterized by constant severe burning pain and/or reduced sensation to innocuous stimulation

Anesthesia dolorosa occasionally occurs after injury to the nerves in the trigeminal system of the face

Anesthesia dolorosa may be a complication to the partial sectioning of the trigeminal nerve as a treatment for trigeminal neuralgia

Elisa Kapunan, Spring 2023

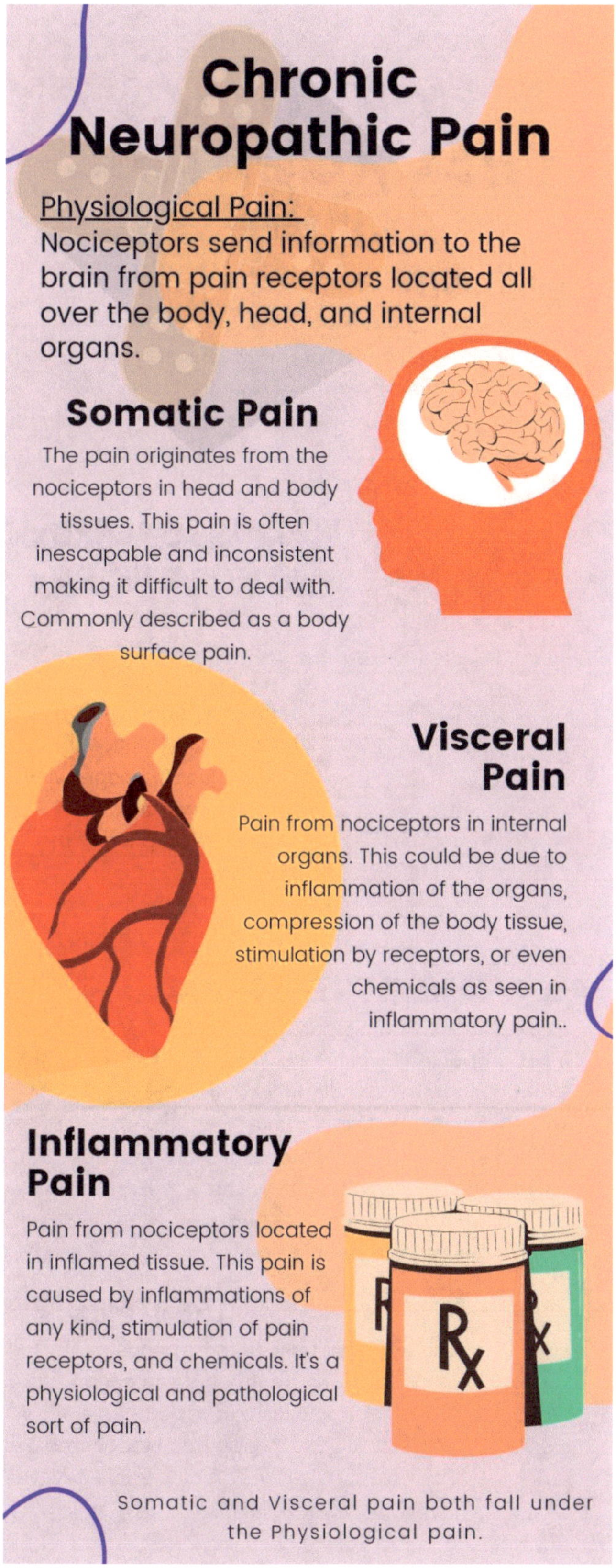

Chronic Neuropathic Pain

Physiological Pain: Nociceptors send information to the brain from pain receptors located all over the body, head, and internal organs.

Somatic Pain

The pain originates from the nociceptors in head and body tissues. This pain is often inescapable and inconsistent making it difficult to deal with. Commonly described as a body surface pain.

Visceral Pain

Pain from nociceptors in internal organs. This could be due to inflammation of the organs, compression of the body tissue, stimulation by receptors, or even chemicals as seen in inflammatory pain..

Inflammatory Pain

Pain from nociceptors located in inflamed tissue. This pain is caused by inflammations of any kind, stimulation of pain receptors, and chemicals. It's a physiological and pathological sort of pain.

Somatic and Visceral pain both fall under the Physiological pain.

Alicia Gonzalez, Spring 2023

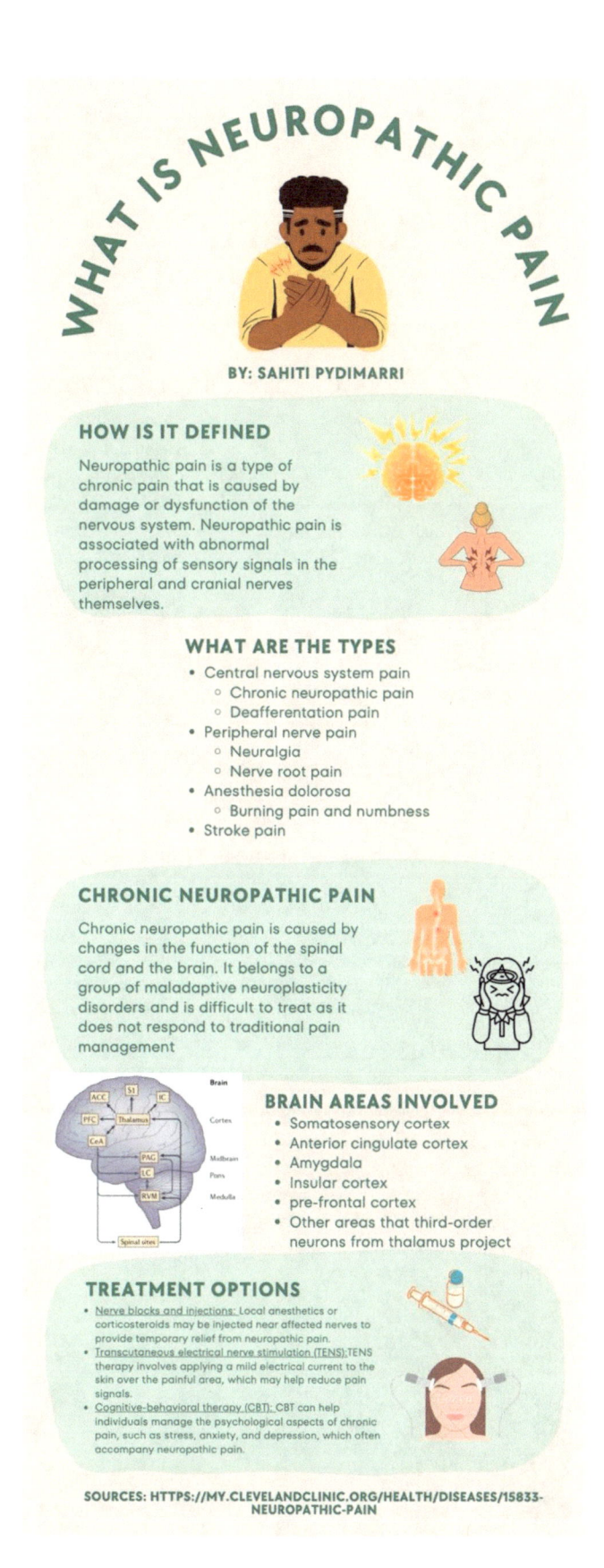

WHAT IS NEUROPATHIC PAIN

BY: SAHITI PYDIMARRI

HOW IS IT DEFINED

Neuropathic pain is a type of chronic pain that is caused by damage or dysfunction of the nervous system. Neuropathic pain is associated with abnormal processing of sensory signals in the peripheral and cranial nerves themselves.

WHAT ARE THE TYPES

- Central nervous system pain
  - Chronic neuropathic pain
  - Deafferentation pain
- Peripheral nerve pain
  - Neuralgia
  - Nerve root pain
- Anesthesia dolorosa
  - Burning pain and numbness
- Stroke pain

CHRONIC NEUROPATHIC PAIN

Chronic neuropathic pain is caused by changes in the function of the spinal cord and the brain. It belongs to a group of maladaptive neuroplasticity disorders and is difficult to treat as it does not respond to traditional pain management

BRAIN AREAS INVOLVED

- Somatosensory cortex
- Anterior cingulate cortex
- Amygdala
- Insular cortex
- pre-frontal cortex
- Other areas that third-order neurons from thalamus project

TREATMENT OPTIONS

- **Nerve blocks and injections:** Local anesthetics or corticosteroids may be injected near affected nerves to provide temporary relief from neuropathic pain.
- **Transcutaneous electrical nerve stimulation (TENS):** TENS therapy involves applying a mild electrical current to the skin over the painful area, which may help reduce pain signals.
- **Cognitive-behavioral therapy (CBT):** CBT can help individuals manage the psychological aspects of chronic pain, such as stress, anxiety, and depression, which often accompany neuropathic pain.

SOURCES: HTTPS://MY.CLEVELANDCLINIC.ORG/HEALTH/DISEASES/15833-NEUROPATHIC-PAIN

Sahiti Pydimarri, Fall 2023

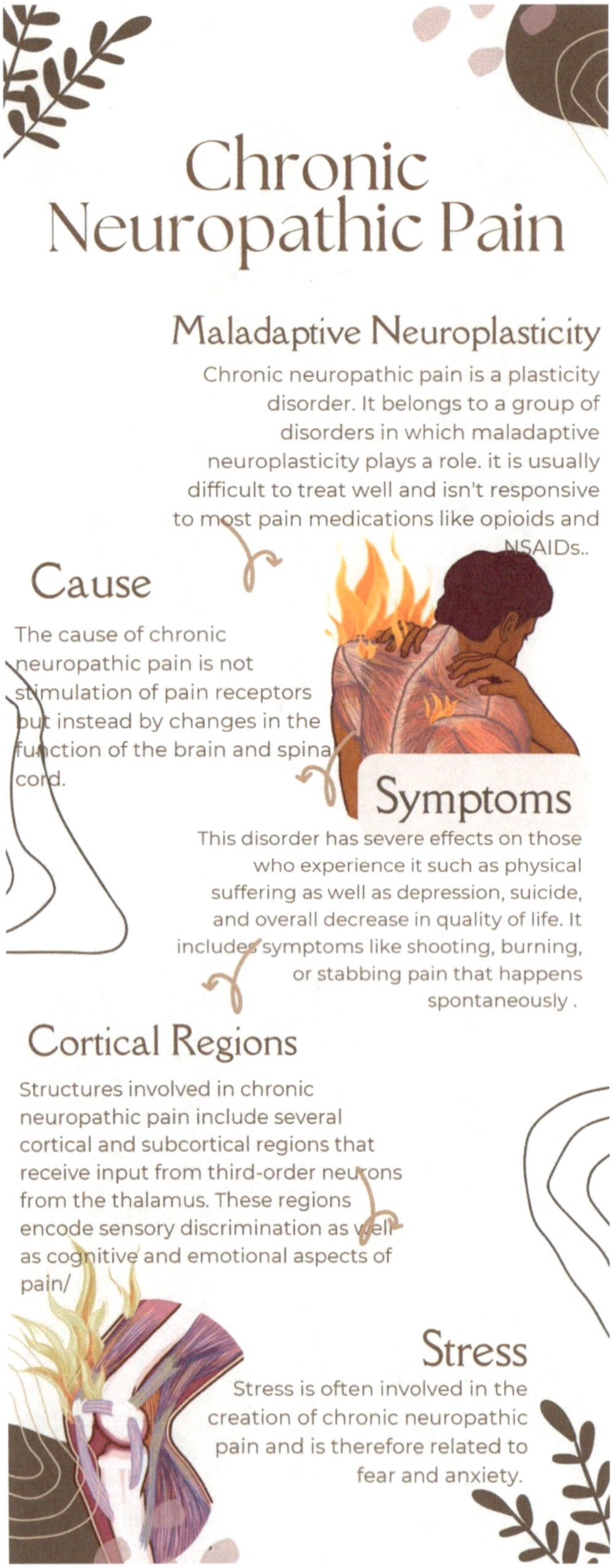

AN INFOGRAPHIC JOURNEY

Chronic Neuropathic Pain

Maladaptive Neuroplasticity
Chronic neuropathic pain is a plasticity disorder. It belongs to a group of disorders in which maladaptive neuroplasticity plays a role. it is usually difficult to treat well and isn't responsive to most pain medications like opioids and NSAIDs..

Cause
The cause of chronic neuropathic pain is not stimulation of pain receptors but instead by changes in the function of the brain and spinal cord.

Symptoms
This disorder has severe effects on those who experience it such as physical suffering as well as depression, suicide, and overall decrease in quality of life. It includes symptoms like shooting, burning, or stabbing pain that happens spontaneously.

Cortical Regions
Structures involved in chronic neuropathic pain include several cortical and subcortical regions that receive input from third-order neurons from the thalamus. These regions encode sensory discrimination as well as cognitive and emotional aspects of pain/

Stress
Stress is often involved in the creation of chronic neuropathic pain and is therefore related to fear and anxiety.

Jayda Simon, Spring 2023

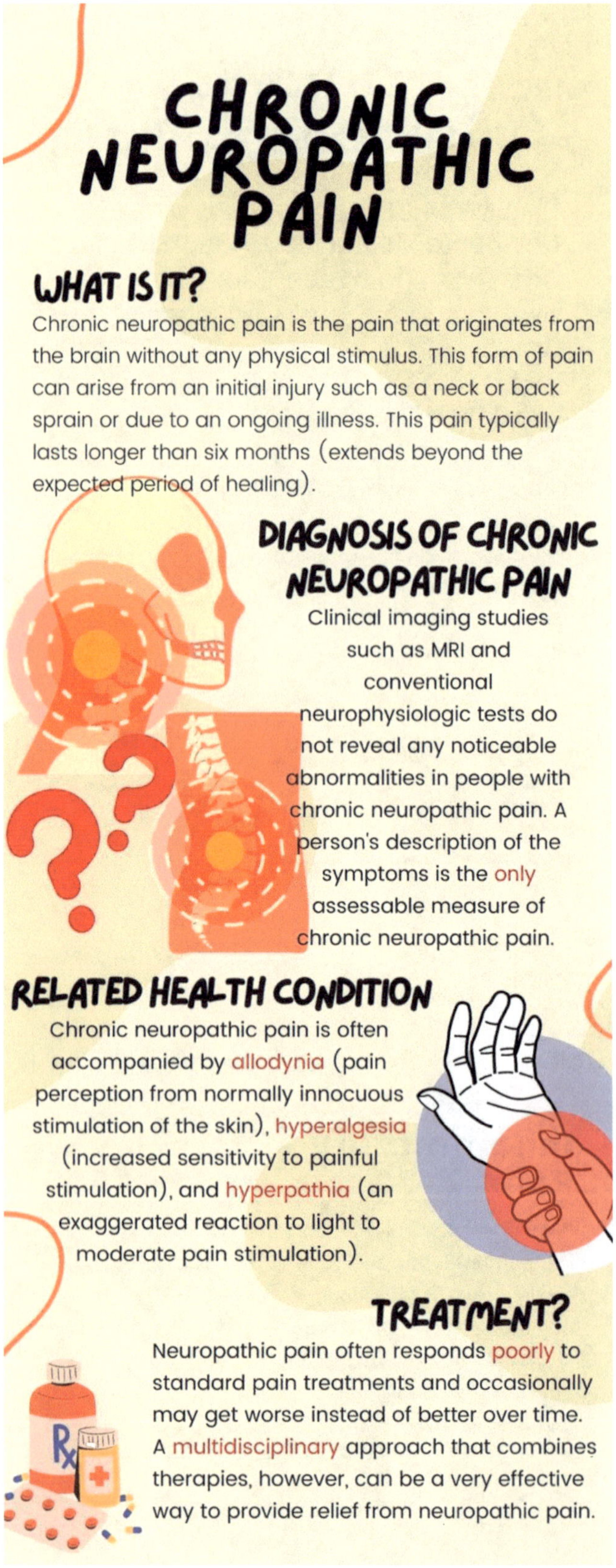

CHRONIC NEUROPATHIC PAIN

WHAT IS IT?
Chronic neuropathic pain is the pain that originates from the brain without any physical stimulus. This form of pain can arise from an initial injury such as a neck or back sprain or due to an ongoing illness. This pain typically lasts longer than six months (extends beyond the expected period of healing).

DIAGNOSIS OF CHRONIC NEUROPATHIC PAIN
Clinical imaging studies such as MRI and conventional neurophysiologic tests do not reveal any noticeable abnormalities in people with chronic neuropathic pain. A person's description of the symptoms is the only assessable measure of chronic neuropathic pain.

RELATED HEALTH CONDITION
Chronic neuropathic pain is often accompanied by allodynia (pain perception from normally innocuous stimulation of the skin), hyperalgesia (increased sensitivity to painful stimulation), and hyperpathia (an exaggerated reaction to light to moderate pain stimulation).

TREATMENT?
Neuropathic pain often responds poorly to standard pain treatments and occasionally may get worse instead of better over time. A multidisciplinary approach that combines therapies, however, can be a very effective way to provide relief from neuropathic pain.

Huong Nguyen, Fall 2022

AN INFOGRAPHIC JOURNEY

CHRONIC NEUROPATHIC PAIN
By: Dhara Sheth

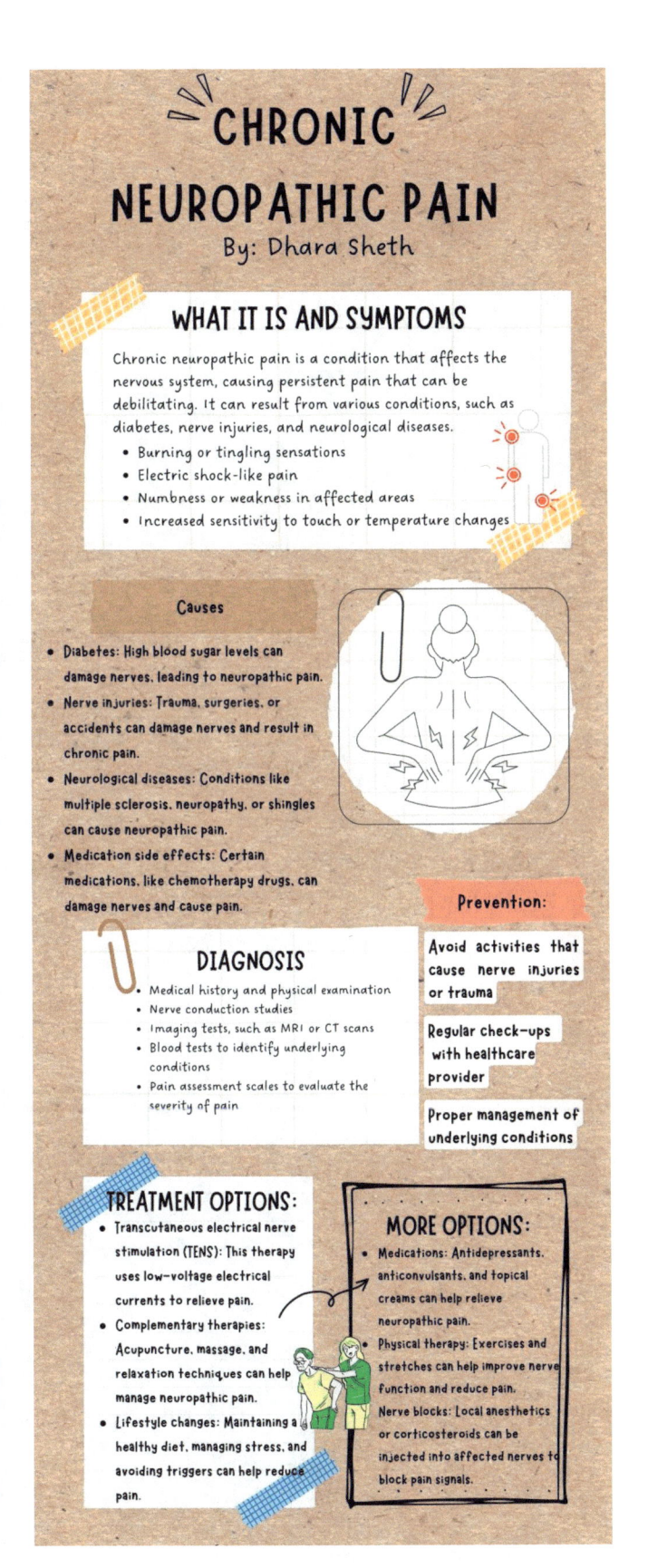

WHAT IT IS AND SYMPTOMS

Chronic neuropathic pain is a condition that affects the nervous system, causing persistent pain that can be debilitating. It can result from various conditions, such as diabetes, nerve injuries, and neurological diseases.
- Burning or tingling sensations
- Electric shock-like pain
- Numbness or weakness in affected areas
- Increased sensitivity to touch or temperature changes

Causes
- **Diabetes:** High blood sugar levels can damage nerves, leading to neuropathic pain.
- **Nerve injuries:** Trauma, surgeries, or accidents can damage nerves and result in chronic pain.
- **Neurological diseases:** Conditions like multiple sclerosis, neuropathy, or shingles can cause neuropathic pain.
- **Medication side effects:** Certain medications, like chemotherapy drugs, can damage nerves and cause pain.

DIAGNOSIS
- Medical history and physical examination
- Nerve conduction studies
- Imaging tests, such as MRI or CT scans
- Blood tests to identify underlying conditions
- Pain assessment scales to evaluate the severity of pain

Prevention:
- Avoid activities that cause nerve injuries or trauma
- Regular check-ups with healthcare provider
- Proper management of underlying conditions

TREATMENT OPTIONS:
- **Transcutaneous electrical nerve stimulation (TENS):** This therapy uses low-voltage electrical currents to relieve pain.
- **Complementary therapies:** Acupuncture, massage, and relaxation techniques can help manage neuropathic pain.
- **Lifestyle changes:** Maintaining a healthy diet, managing stress, and avoiding triggers can help reduce pain.

MORE OPTIONS:
- **Medications:** Antidepressants, anticonvulsants, and topical creams can help relieve neuropathic pain.
- **Physical therapy:** Exercises and stretches can help improve nerve function and reduce pain.
- **Nerve blocks:** Local anesthetics or corticosteroids can be injected into affected nerves to block pain signals.

Dhara Sheth, Spring 2023

NEUROPATHIC PAIN

WHAT IS NEUROPATHIC PAIN?
Neuropathic pain can be described as a chronic shooting or burning pain.

WHAT CAUSES IT?
Neuropathic pain is typically associated with maladaptive neuroplasticity. Neuropathic pain can appear due to nerve misfires because of improper connections following nerve damage.

Specific causes can include amputation, chemotherapy, HIV, Multiple Sclerosis, diabetes, alchoholism, etc.

SYMPTOMS
- Shooting and burning pain
- Tingling and numbness
- Gradual onset that spreads
- Extreme touch sensitivity
- Muscle weakness
- Lack of coordination
- Heat intolerance
- Drops in blood pressure
- Excessive sweating or not being able to sweat

DIAGNOSIS
A diagnosis can be done by conducting a neurologic exam and an interview. Questions would be asked about the description of pain, occurrence of pain, and triggers of pain. History would also be taken to see risk factors.

TREATMENT
- Physical therapy
- Working with a counselor
- Relaxation therapy
- Massage therapy
- Acupuncture

The first line of treatment for neuropathic pain is typically anticonvulsants and antidepressants. Pain medication along with electrical stimulation may also be used to mediate specific pain symptoms.

PHANTOM LIMB SYNDROME
One example of neuropathic pain is phantom limb pain which is a condition that arises after amputation. The brain continues to send pain signals even after removal of an arm or a leg. The nerves misfire and cause pain as if the limb was still there.

Zaynah Bawa, Spring 2023

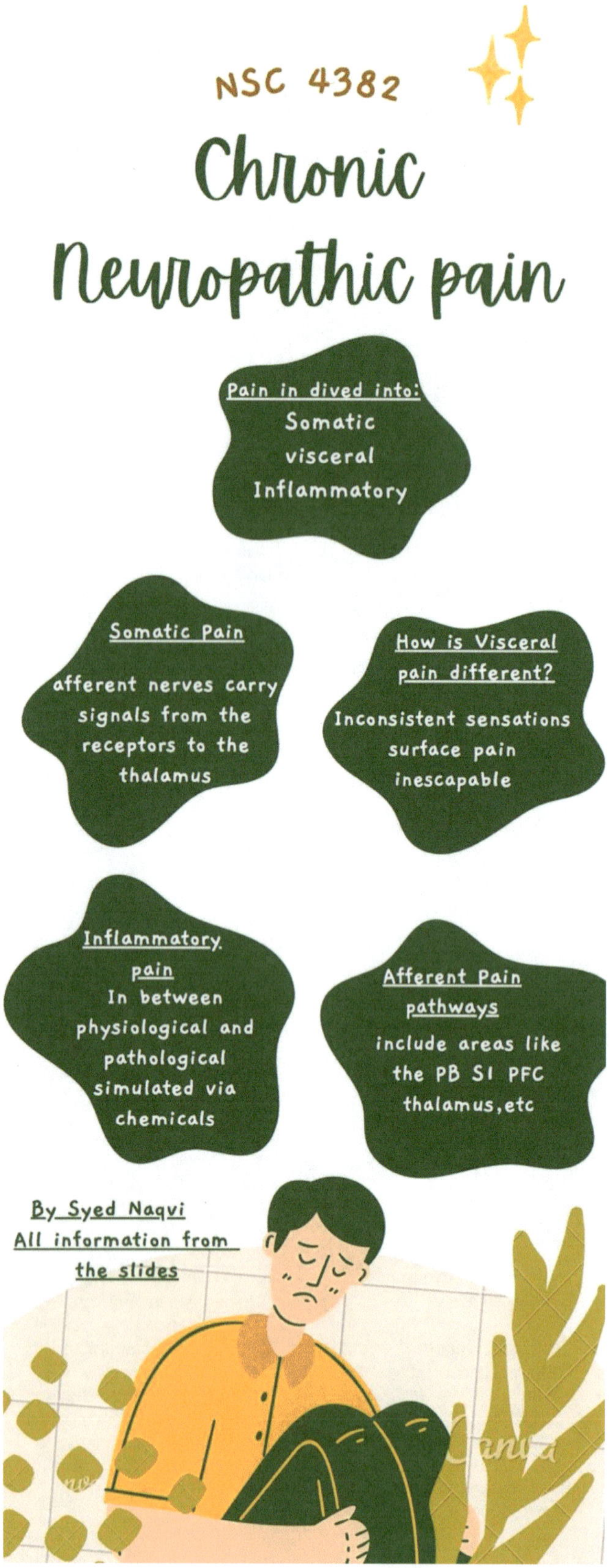

AN INFOGRAPHIC JOURNEY

Chronic Neuropathic pain

NSC 4382

Pain is dived into:
Somatic
visceral
Inflammatory

Somatic Pain
afferent nerves carry signals from the receptors to the thalamus

How is Visceral pain different?
Inconsistent sensations
surface pain
inescapable

Inflammatory pain
In between physiological and pathological simulated via chemicals

Afferent Pain pathways
include areas like the PB SI PFC thalamus, etc

By Syed Naqvi
All information from the slides

Syed Naqvi, Fall 2023

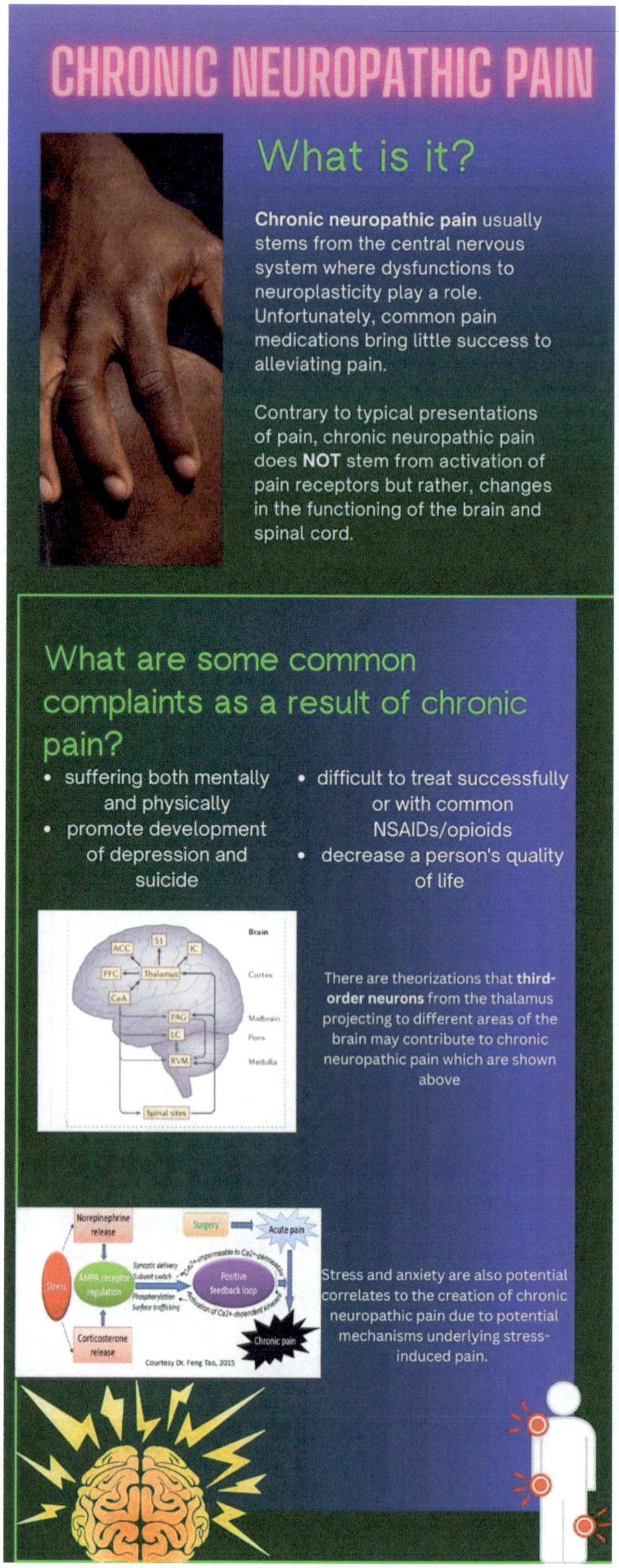

CHRONIC NEUROPATHIC PAIN

What is it?

Chronic neuropathic pain usually stems from the central nervous system where dysfunctions to neuroplasticity play a role. Unfortunately, common pain medications bring little success to alleviating pain.

Contrary to typical presentations of pain, chronic neuropathic pain does **NOT** stem from activation of pain receptors but rather, changes in the functioning of the brain and spinal cord.

What are some common complaints as a result of chronic pain?

- suffering both mentally and physically
- promote development of depression and suicide
- difficult to treat successfully or with common NSAIDs/opioids
- decrease a person's quality of life

There are theorizations that **third-order neurons** from the thalamus projecting to different areas of the brain may contribute to chronic neuropathic pain which are shown above

Stress and anxiety are also potential correlates to the creation of chronic neuropathic pain due to potential mechanisms underlying stress-induced pain.

Lydia Ta, Fall 2022

AN INFOGRAPHIC JOURNEY

Chronic Neuropathic Pain
Deepti Nandakumar

DEAFFERENTIATION PAIN
Definition: Lack of input to the sensory system causes maladaptive neuroplasticity, resulting in altered functions

NEUROPATHIC PAIN *01*

Chronic Neuropathic Pain is a plasticity disorder of the peripheral and cranial nerves that causes pain in the body. Deafferentiation pain is a specific type of chronic neuropathic pain.

02 **ANESTHESIA DOLOROSA**

One disorder caused by lack of input to the sensory system is anesthesia dolorosa which is characterized by constant severe burning pain and reduced sensation to innocuous stimulation.

PHANTOM LIMB PAIN *03*

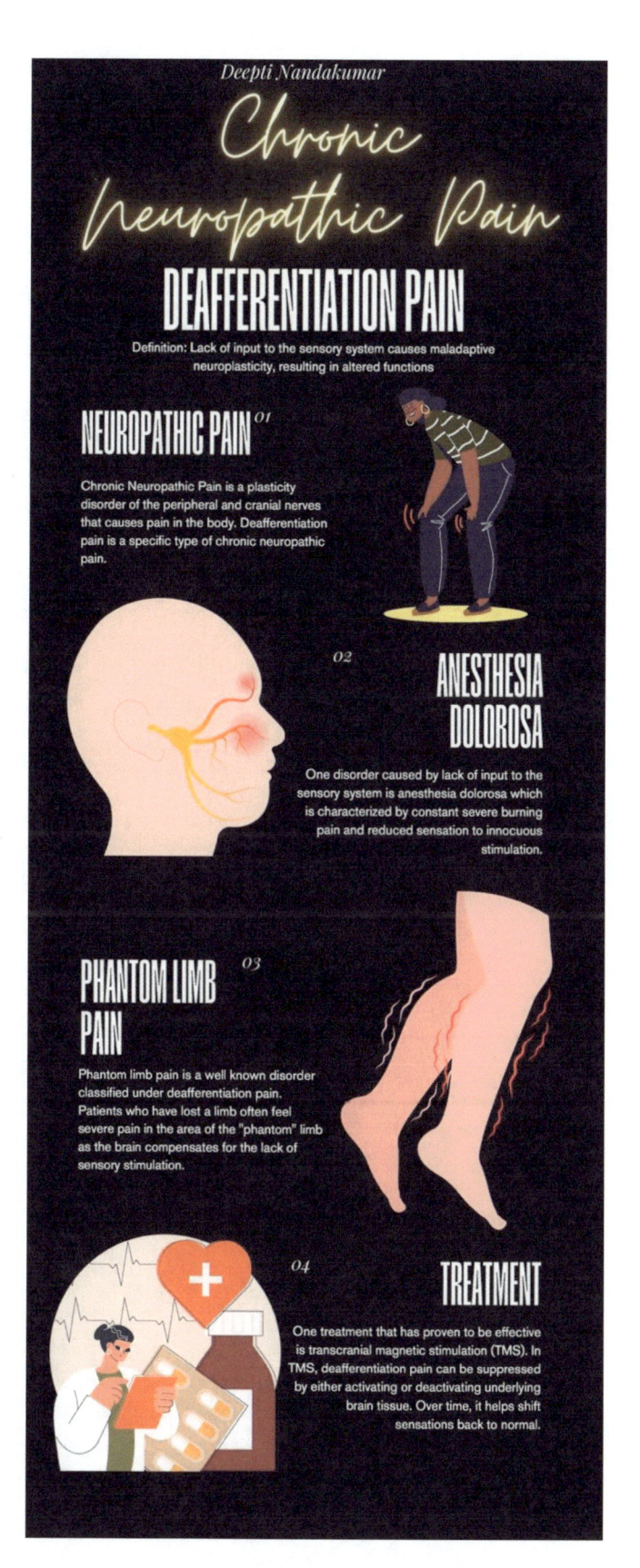

Phantom limb pain is a well known disorder classified under deafferentiation pain. Patients who have lost a limb often feel severe pain in the area of the "phantom" limb as the brain compensates for the lack of sensory stimulation.

04 **TREATMENT**

One treatment that has proven to be effective is transcranial magnetic stimulation (TMS). In TMS, deafferentiation pain can be suppressed by either activating or deactivating underlying brain tissue. Over time, it helps shift sensations back to normal.

Deepti Nandakumar, Spring 2024

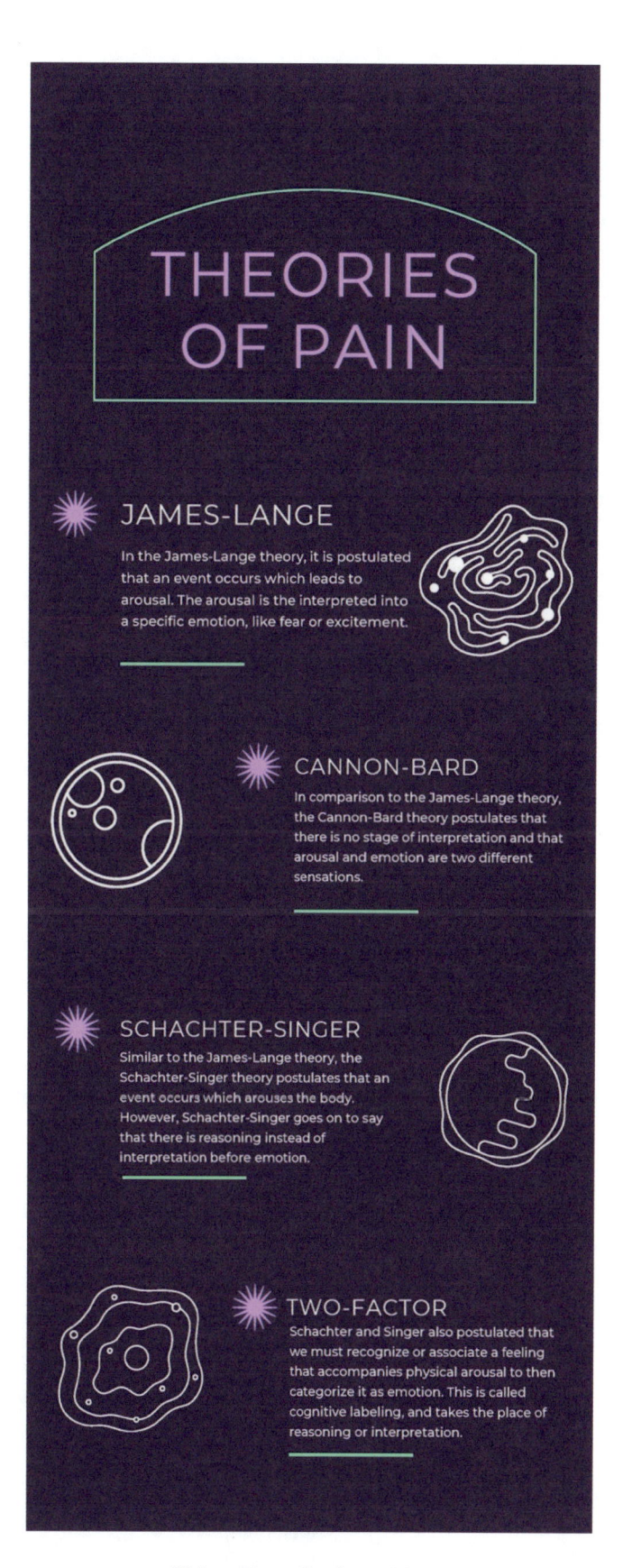

THEORIES OF PAIN

JAMES-LANGE
In the James-Lange theory, it is postulated that an event occurs which leads to arousal. The arousal is the interpreted into a specific emotion, like fear or excitement.

CANNON-BARD
In comparison to the James-Lange theory, the Cannon-Bard theory postulates that there is no stage of interpretation and that arousal and emotion are two different sensations.

SCHACHTER-SINGER
Similar to the James-Lange theory, the Schachter-Singer theory postulates that an event occurs which arouses the body. However, Schachter-Singer goes on to say that there is reasoning instead of interpretation before emotion.

TWO-FACTOR
Schachter and Singer also postulated that we must recognize or associate a feeling that accompanies physical arousal to then categorize it as emotion. This is called cognitive labeling, and takes the place of reasoning or interpretation.

Chloe Tee, Spring 2024

AN INFOGRAPHIC JOURNEY

CHAPTER 17

Treatment and Technology

Enhancing Fear Memory Extinction Through Vagus Nerve Stimulation

By Anonymous, Spring 2024

In the online lectures, Dr. Faisal Jahangiri delved into the role of the amygdala, a pivotal limbic system component, in recognizing and responding to fear. This brain region processes emotions by responding to diverse stimuli, including sensory inputs from our environment and internal cues related to memories and the autonomic functions coordinated by the Vagus nerve. This relationship between the amygdala and our recollections enables it to elicit responses based on our past—effectively bridging our memories with our emotions. These interactions underscore the amygdala's important role in fear memory management. Upon encountering a fear-associated stimulus, the amygdala is instrumental in encoding and recalling the memory of fear, reinforcing emotional responses from these past experiences. This functionality is essential for immediate threat responses and shaping long-term behavioral adaptations in reaction to fear-inducing situations. Additionally, the Vagus nerve, a key player in the parasympathetic nervous system, modulates emotional and fear responses by interacting with the amygdala. This neurological interplay is particularly relevant in conditions like PTSD or post-traumatic stress disorder, which is deeply rooted in the mechanisms of fear memory.

PTSD, or post-traumatic stress disorder, has a profound connection to fear memory, arising often after an individual encounters or witnesses a traumatic event, leading to intense and persistent fear responses. These fear memories, if not processed correctly, can give rise to prolonged emotional and physiological reactions, which manifest as the symptoms commonly associated with PTSD, such as flashbacks and severe anxiety. A prevalent form of treatment is exposure therapy, which, through gradual and repeated exposure to traumatic memory, aims to reduce the fear response. However, this approach has high dropout rates and can be less effective for some individuals. Vagus Nerve Stimulation (VNS)—an established treatment for epilepsy—is being explored as a therapeutic avenue for a variety of neurological conditions, including depression, mood disorders, and migraines. This paper aims to examine the potential of VNS in bolstering memory enhancement, specifically in the extinguishing of fear memories.

Research, such as the 2017 study by Christa McIntyre and colleagues, has investigated augmenting exposure therapy with Vagus Nerve Stimulation (VNS) to improve PTSD treatment outcomes potentially. In their study, PTSD-like symptoms in rats were diminished/impaired when VNS was integrated into fear extinction protocols, suggesting significant therapeutic potential. The study utilized a model known as Single Prolonged Stress (SPS) to induce PTSD- like symptoms in rats, which involved a sequence of stressors and a period of isolation.

Following this, the rats underwent auditory fear conditioning, linking a neutral auditory cue (tone) with an aversive experience (shock), establishing a conditioned fear response. Typically, fear responses decrease over time with extinction training—repeated exposure to the cue without the aversive experience. However, rats with SPS maintained their fear responses, echoing challenges faced by PTSD patients in overcoming fear memories.

Introducing VNS during extinction training markedly improved the reduction of fear responses in these rats. The treatment involved pairing VNS with exposure to the conditioned cue, likely aiding the formation of extinction memories. After the treatment, rats exhibited reduced fear responses during training (freezing less—which is an indication of fear in rats), and they also displayed fewer PTSD-like behaviors in subsequent assessments. These findings suggest that VNS could influence the brain's neural pathways associated with fear memory, perhaps affecting the amygdala and its connections to brain areas like the prefrontal cortex, which are responsible for emotional regulation. VNS seems to enhance neural plasticity, which can improve the efficacy of psychological treatments, such as exposure therapy.

A 2016 paper released by Christa McIntyre wanted to explore the possible mechanisms behind VNS-enhanced extinction. They found that VNS-enhanced extinction is linked to changes in how brain cells connect and communicate along a specific neural pathway between the infralimbic cortex (IL) and the basolateral amygdala (BLA). Specifically, high-frequency stimulation of the IL during this therapy leads to more robust and more lasting connections (known as long-term potentiation, or LTP) in the BLA, which is a crucial area for processing fear. The study also found that VNS enhances extinction by increasing proteins that strengthen synaptic connections, thereby enhancing extinction learning. It also reduces the protein (Arc) levels linked to weakening these connections. Additionally, an increase in a specific receptor (GluN2B) in the brain region involved in fear (BLA) is crucial for this process. Activation of another protein (p-CaMKII) in this context further boosts synaptic strength, enhancing the overall efficacy of VNS in reducing learned fear responses.

The implications of this study reach beyond PTSD. The assistance VNS provides in fear memory extinction could apply to various anxiety-related disorders. This highlights the potential of neuromodulation techniques, used alongside psychological therapies, to treat disorders that are marked by dysfunctional fear memories effectively. Such disorders include generalized anxiety disorder, social anxiety disorder, and specific phobias, where intrusive fear memories often lead to significant distress and impairment. Moving forward, research must continue to evaluate the use of VNS as an adjunctive therapy in exposure treatments for PTSD and other anxiety disorders. Future studies should mainly focus on optimizing the timing and intensity of VNS to maximize therapeutic benefits while minimizing potential treatment dropout rates. Understanding the ideal parameters for VNS application can enhance its efficacy and increase patient adherence to treatment protocols. Incorporating VNS into therapeutic protocols may represent a significant leap forward in treating disorders characterized by maladaptive fear memories. Additionally, exploring the mechanistic pathways through which VNS affects the nervous system could further refine its application, making it a more precise tool in neuropsychiatric treatment. By potentially resetting the neurological patterns associated with fear, VNS promises to facilitate more enduring therapeutic outcomes, reduce long-term reliance on pharmacological solutions, and improve the overall quality of life for patients suffering from these complex disorders. This innovative approach heralds a new era in the integration of technology and psychological treatment, offering hope for more effective management of anxiety disorders.

References

1. Dr. Faisal Jahangiri, NSC 4382, Neurobiology of emotions: Week 5, chapter 3 "Connections from the amygdala

2. Alvarez-Dieppa AC, Griffin K, Cavalier S, McIntyre CK. Vagus Nerve Stimulation Enhances Extinction of Conditioned Fear in Rats and Modulates Arc Protein, CaMKII, and GluN2B-Containing NMDA Receptors in the Basolateral Amygdala. Neural Plast. 2016;2016:4273280. doi: 10.1155/2016/4273280. Epub 2016 Nov 9. PMID: 27957346; PMCID: PMC5120198.

3. https://www.ncbi.nlm.nih.gov/pmc/articles/pmid/27957346/

4. Noble LJ, Gonzalez IJ, Meruva VB, Callahan KA, Belfort BD, Ramanathan KR, Meyers E, Kilgard MP, Rennaker RL, McIntyre CK. Effects of vagus nerve stimulation on extinction of conditioned fear and post-traumatic stress disorder symptoms in rats. Transl Psychiatry. 2017 Aug 22;7(8):e1217. doi: 10.1038/tp.2017.191. PMID: 28892066; PMCID: PMC5611754.

5. https://pubmed.ncbi.nlm.nih.gov/28892066/

AN INFOGRAPHIC JOURNEY

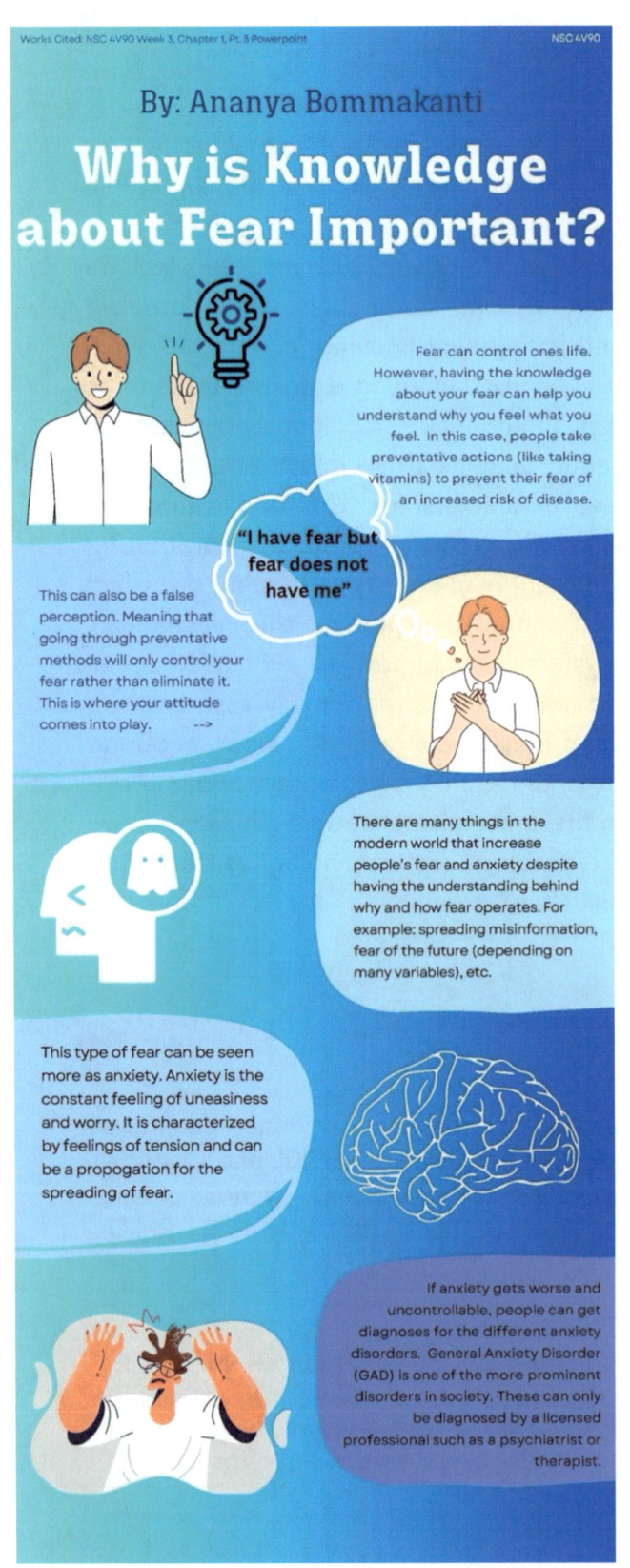

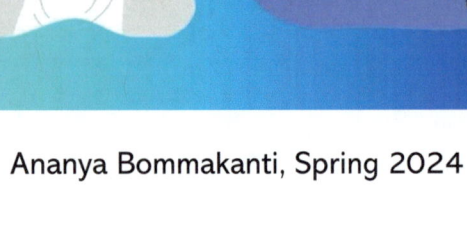

Ananya Bommakanti, Spring 2024

Ranime Goual, Spring 2024

AN INFOGRAPHIC JOURNEY

Masa Jallad, Spring 2024

Lilly Neguse, Spring 2023

AN INFOGRAPHIC JOURNEY

THE IMPORTANCE OF KNOWLEDGE TO UNDERSTAND FEAR & ANIETY

1. KEEP AN OPEN MIND
Learning more about something can actually reduce some forms of fear in people. For example, as people learned to treat and prevent diseases, the fear of illness has been reduced

2. MINDFULNESS OF HEALTH
When someone takes necessary precautions against what they fear, then there is a reduced chance that it can become reality. This can be evident in mothers who take folic acid during pregnancy since the risk of deficits in a child is lowered with the intake of folic acid.

3. MEDICATION & PREVENTION
Medications to treat disease with little to no side effects are a high priority. However, there are prevention methods anyone can take to reduce fear and anxiety about their health like exercising and taking vitamins.

4. FEAR HAS INCREASED
Despite the vast access to information and knowledge we currently have, fear and anxiety has increased. Misinformation, high costs of living, low access to health care, and increased crime and loss have resulted in the rise of anxiety and fear of what life has in store.

5. UNDERSTAND YOURSELF
Understanding why we feel a certain way can make it easier to manage things when we become afraid (NHS). Slowly being exposed to what makes one anxious and afraid can garner more knowledge on how to reduce fear (NHS).

CITATIONS
NHS. "Facing Your Fears - Self-Help CBT Techniques - Every Mind Matters." Nhs.uk, 26 Sept. 2022, www.nhs.uk/every-mind-matters/mental-wellbeing-tips/self-help-cbt-techniques/facing-your-fears/.

Jeffy Jackson, Fall 2023

THE IMPORTANCE OF KNOWLEDGE

Knowledge can help us plan for the future
Cancer risk could be reduced by as much as 50% if people take 4,000 IU of vitamin D3 daily. Keeping a person's blood pressure under control would reduce the risk of cerebral strokes and heart problems.

Knowledge can reduce fear
This includes knowledge about how to live a healthy life, vaccinations, and the risk of giving birth to a child with severe deficits such as autism, spina bifida, or cleft palate can be lowered by the mother taking folic acid before and during pregnancy.

Knowledge can cause fear
The knowledge that a person has a disease can cause fear. Waiting for a test result about a particular condition may cause fear and anxiety. Incorrect information can be spread widely, causing fear of matters that do not pose any risk

Knowledge can make life better
Knowledge can allow for a better and more rewarding occupation. Knowledge makes it possible to reduce the risk of bodily injuries and diseases. Knowledge can increase the quality of life in general.

Knowledge has compound interest
Knowledge allows us to "know" how to learn, how best to retain information, and most importantly, how to frame our perspective e to continue learning and growing in life.

Nicolas Gambardella, Spring 2023

AN INFOGRAPHIC JOURNEY

Knowledge's Impact on Fear

1. Reduced Fear
In some cases have more knowledge about a topic can reduce fear. Some examples are knowledge about vaccines, healthy lifestyle, and how to prevent birth defects.

2. Perceived Reduced Fear
Having more knowledge does not always equate to reduced fear. Sometimes more knowledge makes people feel a false sense of security. For example, routine check-ups as well as annual check-ups.

3. Increased Fear
Often times obtaining more knowledge can cause an increase in fear mostly pertaining to negative topics. For example, getting diagnosed with a deadly disease or even being informed that you are failing a class

4. Factors contributing to fear
Additional factors that contribute to fear such as misinformation, anxiety of the future, and increased cost of living.

5. Anxiety
Anxiety is characterized by a feeling of nervousness and inability to concentrate. Often times the more people know the more anxious thoughts they tend to have leading to more fear of the unknown or the future.

HTTPS://WWW.MAYOCLINIC.ORG/DISEASES-CONDITIONS/ANXIETY/SYMPTOMS-CAUSES/SYC-20350961

Ajay Tunikipati, Fall 2023

Benefits of Knowledge of your Emotions

Knowing what you are feeling can give great insight to yourself.

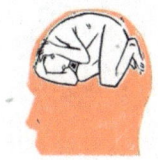

What is emotional intelligence?
Having emotional intelligence allows you to manage your emotions and understand the emotions of people that you surround yourself with.

First Benefits
Knowledge of emotions can allow you to sympathize and create more meaningful relationships. Empathy is also created when you understand how other people feel which builds a sense of care.

Characteristics
The 5 characteristics of emotional intelligence are self awareness, self regulation, motivation, empathy, and social skills. These are present in individuals who know how to manage their emotions.

How to Achieve it
To be in touch with your feelings, you should think about your feelings, forgive, control your thoughts, and apologize. You must recognize where you are lacking emotionally and work towards shifting your mindset to create one that is aware of your feelings.

More Benefits
Having knowledge of your emotions can relieve stress, communicate effectively, and overcome challenges. This helps you in all aspects of life. Professionally, if you communicate better, you can from more connections.

Relating to Emotions
Most people shut down their emotions after going through a traumatic event. This leads to a lot of mental health problems, but it can be fixed by trying to understand your emotions. If you know what makes you feel a certain way, you can deal with a situation in a better way.

Arya Kolte, Spring 2024

AN INFOGRAPHIC JOURNEY

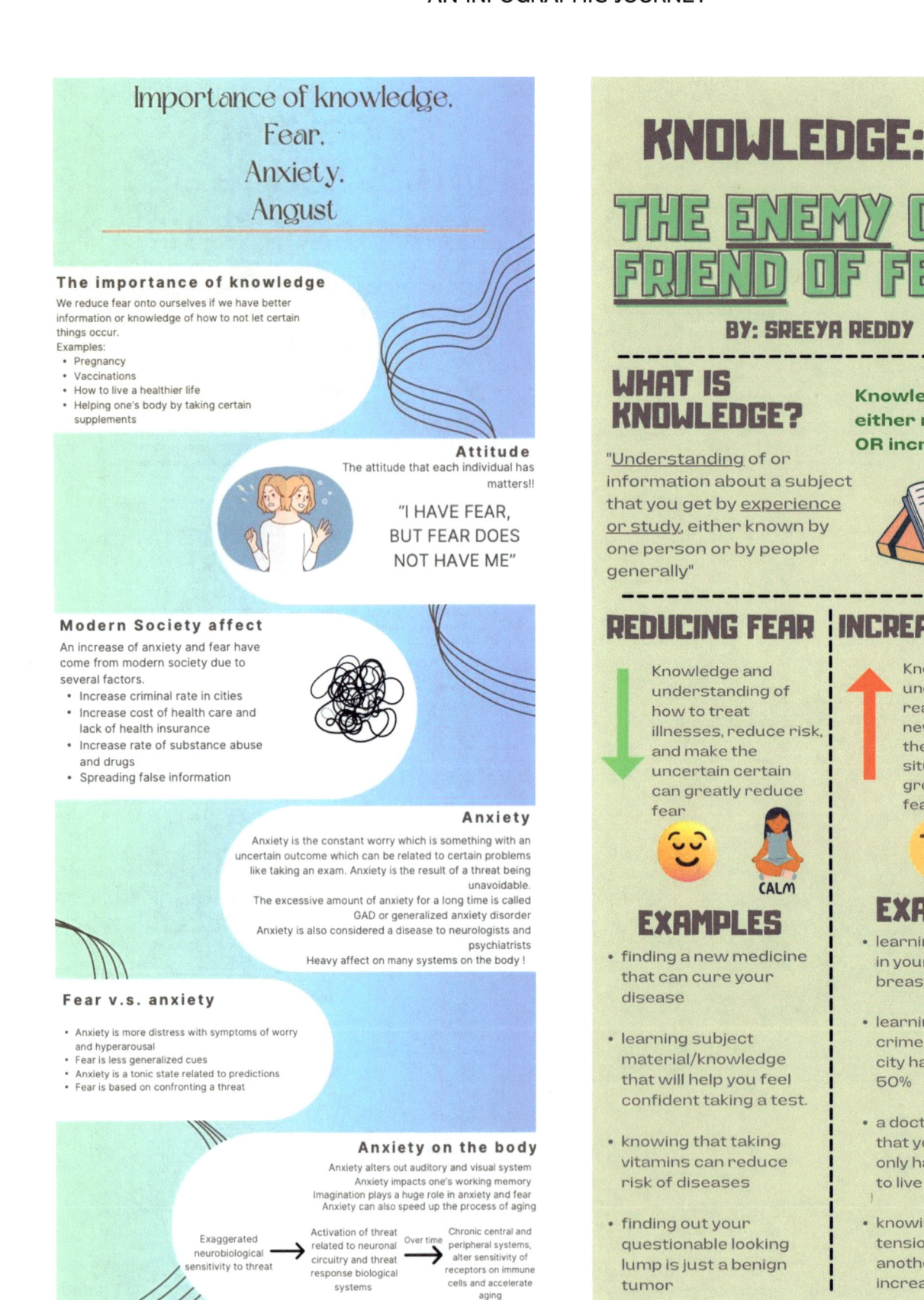

Importance of knowledge. Fear. Anxiety. Angust

The importance of knowledge
We reduce fear onto ourselves if we have better information or knowledge of how to not let certain things occur.
Examples:
- Pregnancy
- Vaccinations
- How to live a healthier life
- Helping one's body by taking certain supplements

Attitude
The attitude that each individual has matters!!

"I HAVE FEAR, BUT FEAR DOES NOT HAVE ME"

Modern Society affect
An increase of anxiety and fear have come from modern society due to several factors.
- Increase criminal rate in cities
- Increase cost of health care and lack of health insurance
- Increase rate of substance abuse and drugs
- Spreading false information

Anxiety
Anxiety is the constant worry which is something with an uncertain outcome which can be related to certain problems like taking an exam. Anxiety is the result of a threat being unavoidable.
The excessive amount of anxiety for a long time is called GAD or generalized anxiety disorder
Anxiety is also considered a disease to neurologists and psychiatrists
Heavy affect on many systems on the body !

Fear v.s. anxiety
- Anxiety is more distress with symptoms of worry and hyperarousal
- Fear is less generalized cues
- Anxiety is a tonic state related to predictions
- Fear is based on confronting a threat

Anxiety on the body
Anxiety alters out auditory and visual system
Anxiety impacts one's working memory
Imagination plays a huge role in anxiety and fear
Anxiety can also speed up the process of aging

Exaggerated neurobiological sensitivity to threat → Activation of threat related to neuronal circuitry and threat response biological systems → Over time → Chronic central and peripheral systems, alter sensitivity of receptors on immune cells and accelerate aging

Emily Gutierrez, Fall 2023

KNOWLEDGE: THE ENEMY OR FRIEND OF FEAR?

BY: SREEYA REDDY

WHAT IS KNOWLEDGE?
"Understanding of or information about a subject that you get by experience or study, either known by one person or by people generally"

Knowledge can either reduce fear OR increase fear.

REDUCING FEAR
Knowledge and understanding of how to treat illnesses, reduce risk, and make the uncertain certain can greatly reduce fear

INCREASING FEAR
Knowing and understanding a reality, diagnosis, new information, or the uncertainty of a situation can greatly increase fear.

EXAMPLES
- finding a new medicine that can cure your disease
- learning subject material/knowledge that will help you feel confident taking a test.
- knowing that taking vitamins can reduce risk of diseases
- finding out your questionable looking lump is just a benign tumor

EXAMPLES
- learning that a lump in your armpit is breast cancer
- learning that the crime rate in your city has increased by 50%
- a doctor explaining that your loved one only has months left to live
- knowing that political tensions with another country are increasing

Sreeya Reddy, Spring 2023

AN INFOGRAPHIC JOURNEY

The benefits of therapy in response to fear

1. Have more mental clarity

Talking to someone can have even the most ordinary of benefits, getting rid of a burden and providing a safe space to work through fear

2. Saying fears out loud makes them less scary

Some fears once said aloud, are already less scary and thus discussing them with a therapist will help improve the coping strategies to deal with fear

3. Therapy is safe

Therapy is a place to feel safe and protected because it can turn any maladaptive behaviors into positive thoughts and actions

4. Dig Deeper with the emotions

The path in therapy is not linear but it allows one to know themself more deeply, having more awareness of themself and their emotions.

Tamjeed Islam, Spring 2023

AN INFOGRAPHIC JOURNEY

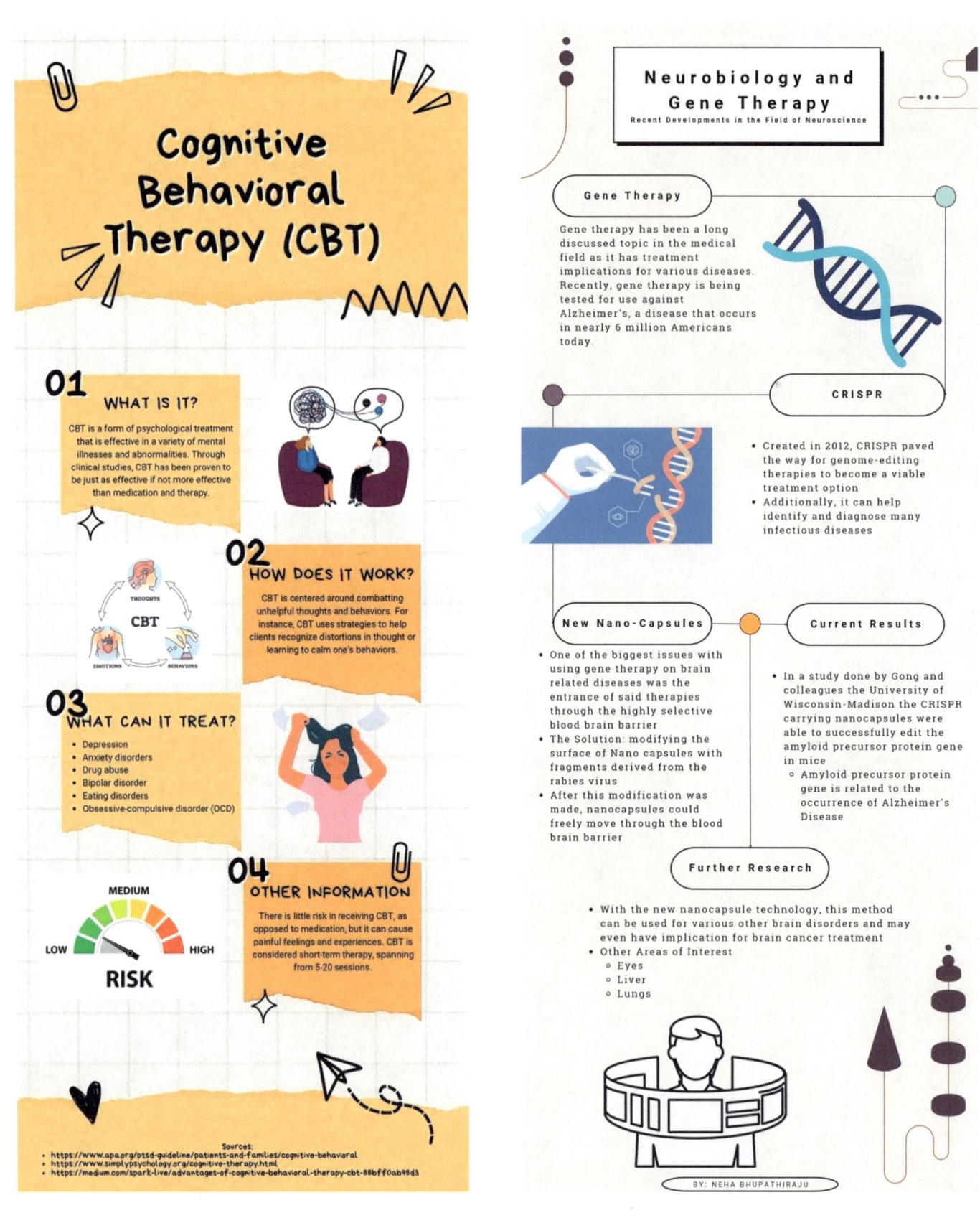

Allen Liang, Spring 2024

Neha Bhupathiraju, Spring 2023

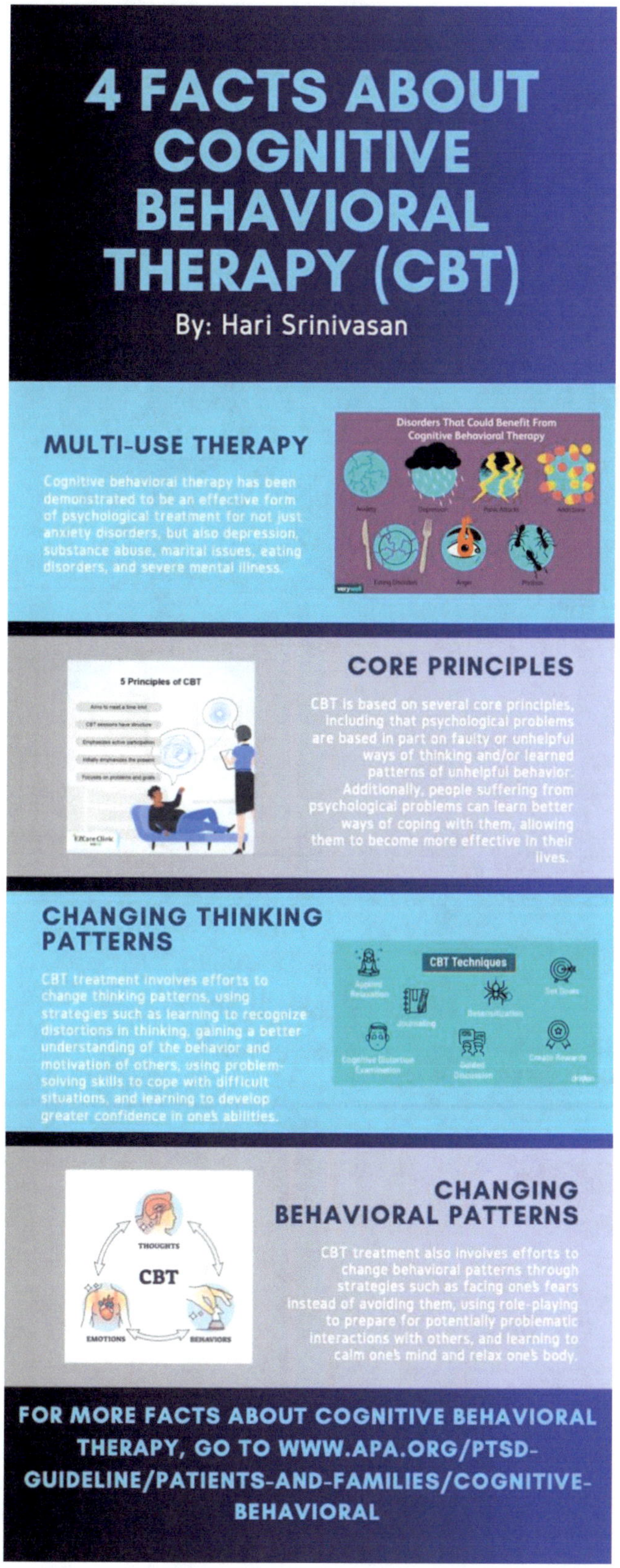

AN INFOGRAPHIC JOURNEY

4 FACTS ABOUT COGNITIVE BEHAVIORAL THERAPY (CBT)

By: Hari Srinivasan

MULTI-USE THERAPY

Cognitive behavioral therapy has been demonstrated to be an effective form of psychological treatment for not just anxiety disorders, but also depression, substance abuse, marital issues, eating disorders, and severe mental illness.

CORE PRINCIPLES

CBT is based on several core principles, including that psychological problems are based in part on faulty or unhelpful ways of thinking and/or learned patterns of unhelpful behavior. Additionally, people suffering from psychological problems can learn better ways of coping with them, allowing them to become more effective in their lives.

CHANGING THINKING PATTERNS

CBT treatment involves efforts to change thinking patterns, using strategies such as learning to recognize distortions in thinking, gaining a better understanding of the behavior and motivation of others, using problem-solving skills to cope with difficult situations, and learning to develop greater confidence in one's abilities.

CHANGING BEHAVIORAL PATTERNS

CBT treatment also involves efforts to change behavioral patterns through strategies such as facing one's fears instead of avoiding them, using role-playing to prepare for potentially problematic interactions with others, and learning to calm one's mind and relax one's body.

FOR MORE FACTS ABOUT COGNITIVE BEHAVIORAL THERAPY, GO TO WWW.APA.ORG/PTSD-GUIDELINE/PATIENTS-AND-FAMILIES/COGNITIVE-BEHAVIORAL

Hari Srinivasan, Fall 2023

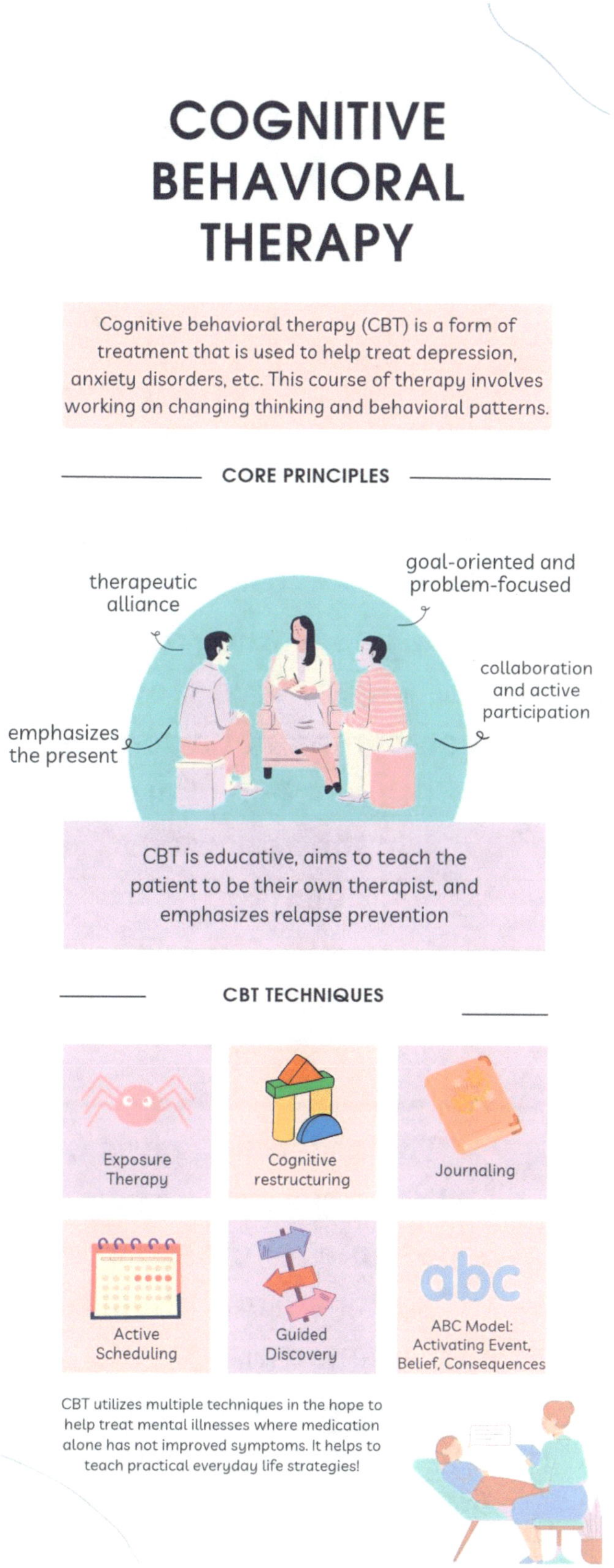

COGNITIVE BEHAVIORAL THERAPY

Cognitive behavioral therapy (CBT) is a form of treatment that is used to help treat depression, anxiety disorders, etc. This course of therapy involves working on changing thinking and behavioral patterns.

CORE PRINCIPLES

- therapeutic alliance
- goal-oriented and problem-focused
- emphasizes the present
- collaboration and active participation

CBT is educative, aims to teach the patient to be their own therapist, and emphasizes relapse prevention

CBT TECHNIQUES

- Exposure Therapy
- Cognitive restructuring
- Journaling
- Active Scheduling
- Guided Discovery
- ABC Model: Activating Event, Belief, Consequences

CBT utilizes multiple techniques in the hope to help treat mental illnesses where medication alone has not improved symptoms. It helps to teach practical everyday life strategies!

Zaynah Bawa, Spring 2023

AN INFOGRAPHIC JOURNEY

THE VAGUS NERVE

The vagus nerve provides two-way connections between the brain and many organs in the body, including the heart

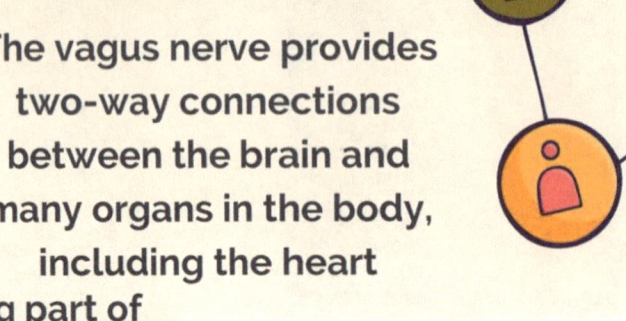

The descending part of the vagus nerve provides parasympathetic control of the function of organs in the abdomen, including the heart

The ascending parts of the vagus nerve make it possible for organs in the abdomen and chest to influence many parts of the brain, including the emotional brain.

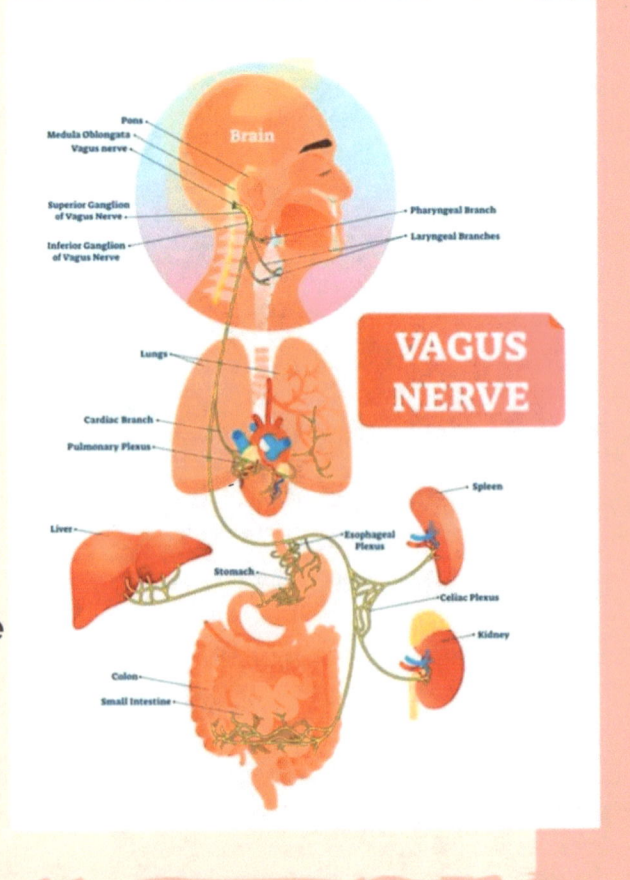

Samrah Akhter, Fall 2022

AN INFOGRAPHIC JOURNEY

Vagus Nerve

By Gloria Geevarghese

The vagus nerve provides two-way connections between the brain and many organs in the body

ascending

The ascending parts of the vagus nerve allow for abdominal organs and the chest to influence parts of the brain, including the emotional brain

descending

The descending part of the vagus nerve provides parasympathetic control for abdominal organs, including the heart

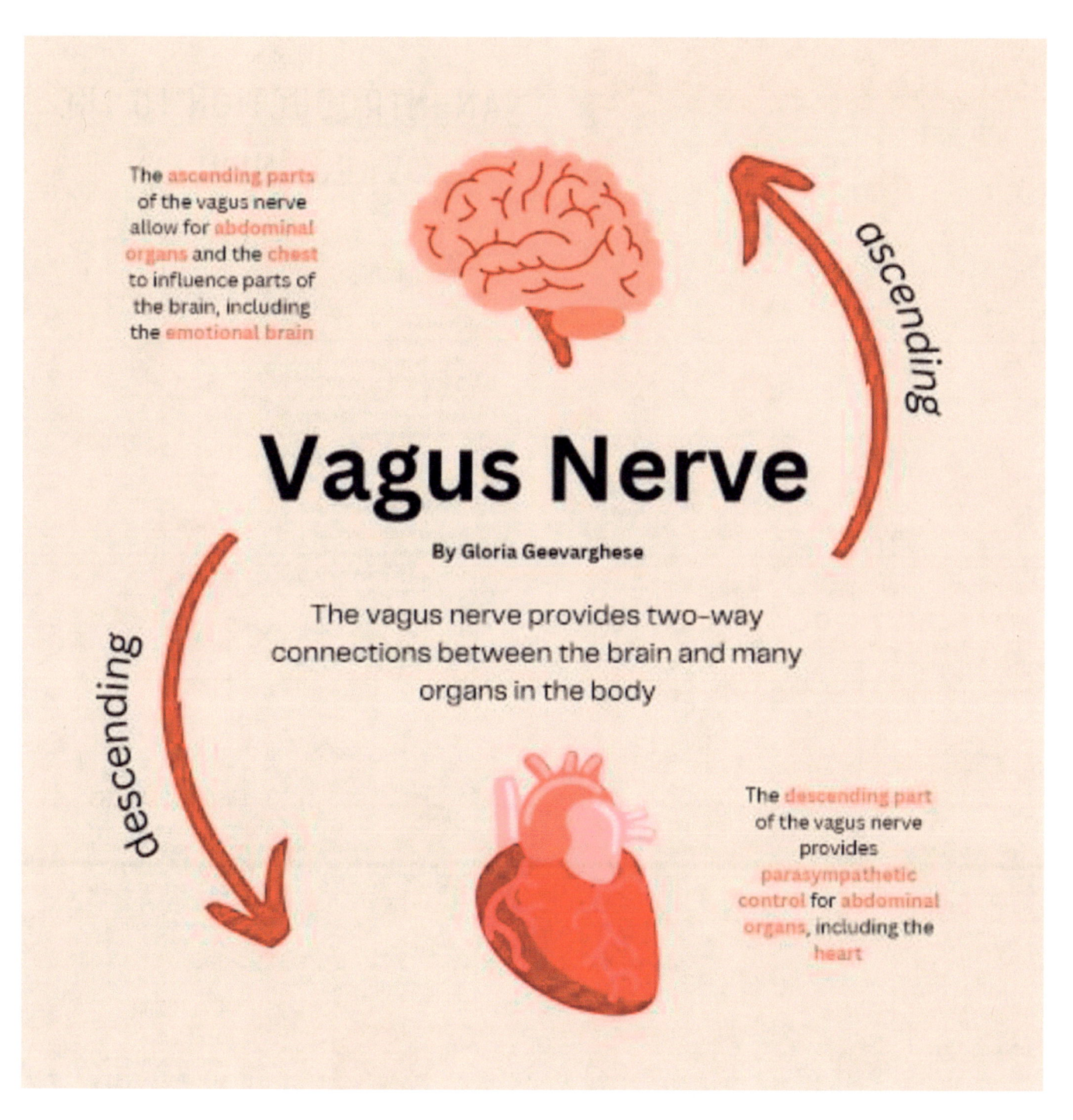

Gloria Geevarghese, Spring 2023

AN INFOGRAPHIC JOURNEY

The Vagus Nerve and the Human Body

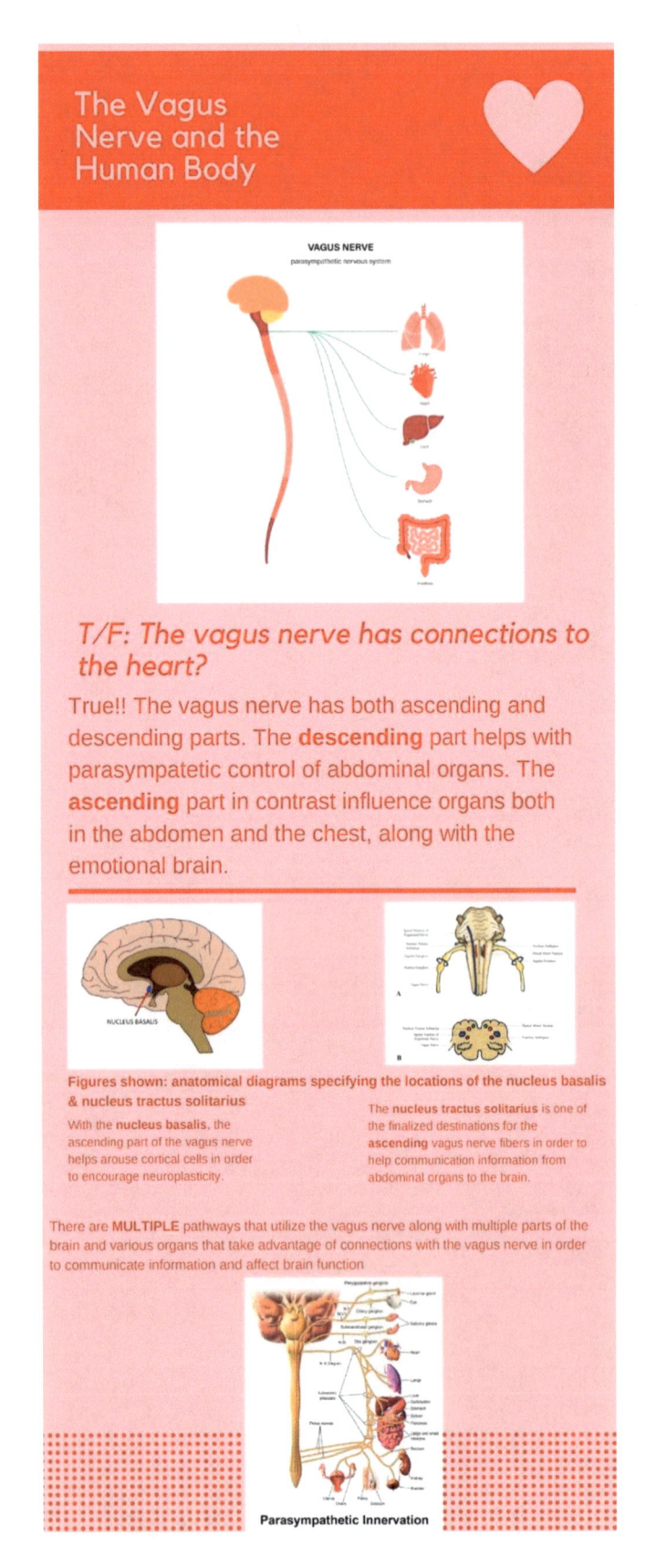

T/F: The vagus nerve has connections to the heart?

True!! The vagus nerve has both ascending and descending parts. The **descending** part helps with parasympatetic control of abdominal organs. The **ascending** part in contrast influence organs both in the abdomen and the chest, along with the emotional brain.

Figures shown: anatomical diagrams specifying the locations of the nucleus basalis & nucleus tractus solitarius

With the **nucleus basalis**, the ascending part of the vagus nerve helps arouse cortical cells in order to encourage neuroplasticity.

The **nucleus tractus solitarius** is one of the finalized destinations for the **ascending** vagus nerve fibers in order to help communication information from abdominal organs to the brain.

There are MULTIPLE pathways that utilize the vagus nerve along with multiple parts of the brain and various organs that take advantage of connections with the vagus nerve in order to communicate information and affect brain function

Parasympathetic Innervation

Lydia Ta, Fall 2022

Week 10

AN INTRODUCTION TO THE VAGUS NERVE
Hanah Kim

1. INTRODUCTION
The vagus nerve is cranial nerve X, It is a mixed nerve that carries both sensory and motor functions of the body. This nerve also carries preganglionic parasympathetic fibers to important visceral organs. the vagus enrve exist the skull through thejugular foramen.

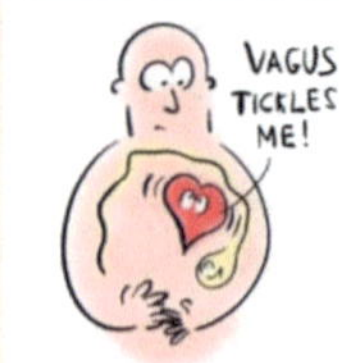

VAGUS TICKLES ME!

2. MOTOR FUNCTIONS
The vagus nerve controls muscles of the soft palate, pharynx, and larynx. A lesion to the vagus nerve can cause the ipsilateral side of the soft palate to lose muscle tone and droop down.

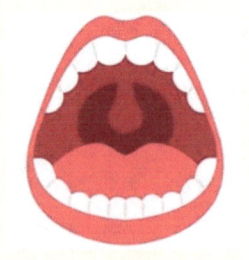

3. SENSORY FUNCTIONS
The vagus nerve carries general sensation from the larynx, pharynx, and middle ear. It also carries taste sensation from the epiglottis and base of the tongue. Additionally, it carries visceral sensation from the heart, lungs, and abdominal organs

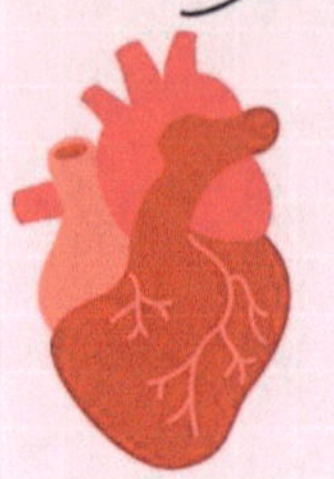

4. AUTONOMIC
CN X carries parasympathetic fibers to cardiac muscles of the heart and smooth muscle of the respiratory and digestive systems.

Hanah Kim, Spring 2023

DEEP BRAIN STIMULATION
TECH ORIGINS, USES, AND CURRENT RESEARCH

What is Deep Brain Stimulation?
This technology uses a pacemaker-like device to send electrical stimulation to areas within the brain

Components

- **Lead (electrode)** – wire inserted through a small opening in the skull and implanted in the brain. Tip of the electrode targets a specific brain area, depending on the disorder
- **Extension** – wire passed under skin of head, neck and shoulder that connects the lead to the pulse generator
- **Implantable Pulse Generator** – implanted under the skin near collarbone, in chest, or under skin in abdomen

Origins and Timeline

- **1947** Spiegel & Wycis introduce stereotactic technology for ablative procedures
- **1953** Cooper notes ligation of anterior choroidal artery reduced tremor
- **1987** Benabid, Pollak and team performed first DBS in thalamus
- **1994** First case series of pallidal DBS published by Siegfried and Lippitz for PD
- **2002** FDA approved DBS for PD

- **1939** Meyers performs partial caudate resection to control unilateral tremor
- **1953** Pallidotomies performed by Narabayashi & Okuma and Guiot & Brion – Hiatus in surgery
- **1968** Cotzias introduces levodopa
- **1993** First case of STN DBS for PD published by Benabid and Pollak
- **1997** FDA approved DBS for ET

Current Uses
- Parkinson's
- Essential Tremor
- Dystonia
- Epilepsy

BY: NEHA BHUPATHIRAJU

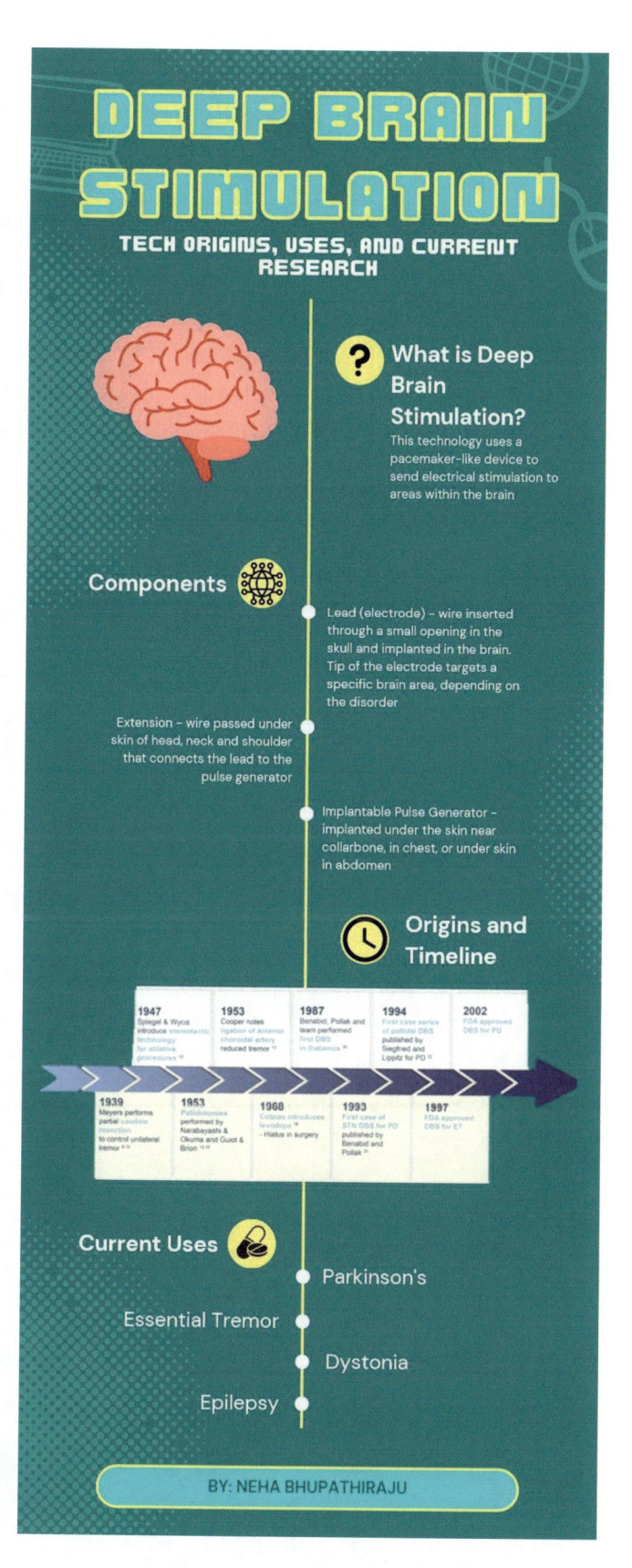

Neha Bhupathiraju, Spring 2023

AN INFOGRAPHIC JOURNEY

AN INFOGRAPHIC JOURNEY

Contributors

Name	Page
Abhi Patel	112
Aditi Manjrekar	154
Afrosa Islam	127, 158
Aisha Ali	66, 264
Ajay Tunikipati	6, 278, 315
Akash Sivakumar	15, 53, 239
Akshara Rao	138, 188
Alaina Chenault	44, 164
Alana Simpson	89
Alicia Gonzalez	33, 139, 150, 303
Alifiya Shaikh	89, 151, 237
Allen Liang	45, 95, 163, 166, 318
Allison Scott	301
Allyson Judge	86, 134
Arshad Manzar	109, 114, 138, 161, 172
Arya Kolte	58, 263, 315
Ashley Brizuela	83, 160
Ashley Kiser	100, 150, 163, 164
Ashley Tran	115, 135, 162, 171, 300
Asif Lakhani	55, 133, 202
Audrey Villanueva	49, 91, 137, 157, 259, 291
Austin Sprouse	54, 113, 146
Avalon De Curtis	111, 174
Ayaan Ahmed	84, 242
Bernice David	68
Bowen Liu	268
Bridget Manu	192
Cambree Yedica	283
Cheng Hao	178
Chenghao Liu	70
Emily Leung	149, 204
Emily Lopez	56, 245
Emma Siddiqui	30, 249, 292
Erica Nah	206, 215
Esha Kanna	153
Falisha Leava	49
Gauri Surendran	42, 284
Gloria Geevarghese	190, 321
Haley Reynolds	101
Hana Ahmad	118, 284
Hanah Kim	65, 212, 322
Haniya Qavi	129, 155, 240, 288
Hannah James	186, 227
Hannah Nguyen	182
Hari Srinivasan	25, 319
Helen Nguyen	38, 80, 129, 259
Judith James	48
Jumeynah Firdaus	191

Name	Page
Allyson Macfee	29, 86, 110, 136, 145, 266
Alyssa Tran	39, 77, 180, 236
Aman Mohammad	25, 181
Aman Baig	118
Amberlyn Haque	160, 183, 243
Amitha Prattipati	64
Ananya Bommakanti	47, 312
Andrea Pinto	210, 273
Ani Sharma	125, 233, 279
Anisah Bakshi	9, 200
Anisha Reddy	78, 112
Anna Awa	12
Areeba Shaikh	212
Armaan Sood	46, 181, 201, 214
Chloe Tee	44, 85, 307
Crista Thyvelikakath	14, 240
Crystal Peraza	283
Dannah Bagcal	7, 27, 47, 261, 273
Deepika Sai Tadepalli	267
Deepti Nandakumar	307
Devaditya Ray	29, 187, 269
Devapriya Baiju	33, 51, 70, 76
Dhara Sheth	81, 185, 305
Dhruv Patel	75, 222, 223, 280
Diya Thapa	79, 158
Dominique Ortiz	148
Edwin Phillip	257
Elisa Kapunan	149, 302
Elsa Chittet	31, 126, 175
Emily Gutierrez	87, 174, 316
Hima Praveen	9, 151, 254, 280, 291
Huong Nguyen	304
Hussam Asim	65, 261
Hyeonji Lee	102, 183, 225, 296
Ibrahim Khalilullah	52, 83
Inioluwa Adenekan	258
Iris Downing	271
Isha Rojanala	137, 177, 285
Jagannath Ravindran	50
Jana Elkhodari	286
Jasha Dela Cruz	56, 57, 76, 140, 272
Javeria Ahmed	79, 92
Jayda Simon	101, 304
Jaza Malik	104, 116, 124, 271
Jeffy Jackson	214, 298, 314
Jesse Idemudia	104, 106, 166
Khadeeja Moosa	92, 124, 176, 213, 257
Khyra White	209, 274

325

AN INFOGRAPHIC JOURNEY

Name	Page	Name	Page
Justin De Vera	108, 117, 171, 191, 227, 229, 260	Krish Patel	277, 281
Juveria Ali	24	Laiba Ali	299
Kaden Kobernat	228	Lilly Neguse	213, 223, 243, 313
Kaeli Nguyen	57, 94	Lisa Rattankone	262
Kailyn Endres	127	Lucie Nguyen	90, 131, 156, 244, 299
Kajal Patel	105, 132, 147, 180, 193	Lydia Ta	306, 322
Kani Mirza	64	Machenzie Park	225
Karina Slobodkin	109, 176, 208	Madhav Bhatt	119, 265
Katelin Tran	91	Mahwish Quadri	66, 200, 254, 297
Katelyn Bonvillain	80, 110, 290	Mana Zandi	165, 173, 198, 278
Kathy Nguyen	209, 242	Manha Chaudhry	184, 198, 206
Kayla Pham	16, 31, 241	Manuel Jagan	204
Kei Mashimo	264	Mark Nguyen	34, 46
Maryam Imam	75, 156, 245, 286	Nehal Dave	13
Masa Jallad	71, 77, 249, 313	Nhi Nguyen	159, 167
Maurya Gouni	221	Nicolas Gambardella	113, 220, 314
Megan Russell	69, 131	Nicole Kumanova	54, 211
Megha Akkineni	8, 130, 244	Noreen Antony	302
Melanie Cruz	38	Nupoor Shah	69, 100, 165
Minaal Atif	18, 114, 145	Olive Roede	50, 179, 288
Mohammad Ali	182	Pardha Eluri	82, 136, 256
Myan Lam	122, 189, 234	Pradyun Sangineni	7, 282
Namitha Mariam Jaimson	188	Pranavi Maddipatla	15, 41, 116, 146, 247, 266, 301
Naomi Kurian	27, 119	Preena Desai	135, 179
Natalia Brzezinski	272	Priya Upadhyaya	132, 267
Natalie Laguer Torres	10, 134, 184, 205, 221, 235	Rahil Howlader	82
Neha Bhupathiraju	19, 222, 224, 248, 255, 318, 323	Rakshak Ravichandran	55, 185
Neha Gannapaneni	102, 300	Ranime Goual	199, 312
Neha Kazani	289	Rashed Daka	94
Rene Leal	211	Sarah Padani	88, 247
Rida Hamid	173, 265	Sarvani Ganapavarapu	42, 123, 175, 203, 260
Rohita Arjarapu	51, 67, 238, 262, 298	Seema Arjuna	88, 106
Rola Mukhtar	153	Seth Abraham	123
Saad Tanwir	90, 130, 246, 250	Shabbir Bohri	237
Saara Ahmad	205	Shani Hibbert	154
Sahana Dhananjayan	40	Sharanya Swaminathan	296
Sahiti Pydimarri	68, 115 248, 303	Shohini Ghosh	32
Saloni Nehra	10	Shreena Desai	290
Samiksha Sivajumar	78	Shreya Jagan	239
Samrah Akhter	320	Shreya Jupelly	147, 207, 258
Sandra Cuenca	277	Shreya Saride	26
Sanya Bhatt	190	Shrujin Shah	18, 28, 107, 238, 287
Sara Hasan	43	Skyla Lopez	26, 178
Sara Saravanan	255	Sneha Sharma	28, 67, 84, 108, 161, 250
		Sogand Saadat	241, 256
Sreeya Reddy	282, 316	Vaibhavi Joshi	297
Stefanie Favaro	87, 202	Valentina Grijalba	117
Suhina Khalid	279	Valeria Viveros	80, 208

AN INFOGRAPHIC JOURNEY

Name	Page	Name	Page
Supreet Kaur	246	Varun Thavanampalli	157
Susana Kudsi	139	Victor Onuorak Jr	103
Syed Naqvi	43, 186, 235, 306	Vijaya Dutt	6, 53, 285
Syeda Alvi	110	Vivian Wang	125
Tabatha Nieves	226	Vyshnavi Poruri	5, 8, 208, 289
Tabatha Vaca Nieves	30, 199	Zaara Siddiki	102, 271
Taha Ahmed	5, 48, 133, 201	Zahra Khan	93, 167
Talha Maqsood	11	Zahra Zafar	17
Tamjeed Islam	14, 103, 226, 263, 317	Zainab Ali	270
Tarik Ehsan	128	Zaki Khan	17
Tejas Devata	45, 95	Zaynah Bawa	163, 305, 319
Tiffany Nouanesengsy	32, 41, 122, 172, 225, 235, 269		
Tommu Vu	40		

AN INFOGRAPHIC JOURNEY

About the Authors

Dr. Faisal R. Jahangiri is a distinguished neurophysiologist based in Dallas, Texas, internationally renowned for his Intraoperative Neurophysiological Monitoring (IONM) expertise. As the President and CEO of Global Innervation LLC, Dr. Jahangiri has made substantial contributions to the field, particularly in enhancing the safety and efficacy of neurosurgical procedures.

Dr. Jahangiri's academic journey began at Khyber Medical College in Peshawar, Pakistan, where he earned his medical degree in 1991. He furthered his education in the United States, undertaking postgraduate studies in Biomedical Engineering at Case Western Reserve University in Cleveland, Ohio. His early research focused on Functional Electrical Stimulation (FES), EEG, and 3-D imaging for reconstructive plastic surgery, laying a robust foundation for his future work in neurophysiology.

With over three decades of clinical experience, Dr. Jahangiri has monitored and supervised more than 17,000 surgical procedures across over 300 hospitals in the United States, the Middle East, and Pakistan. His expertise includes neurosurgical, orthopedic, otolaryngology (ENT), vascular, and general surgeries. He is also skilled in interventional procedures, intensive care units (ICU), and epilepsy monitoring units (EMU).

Dr. Jahangiri's commitment to education is evident in his role as an Assistant Professor of Instruction at the Department of Neuroscience, School of Behavioral and Brain Sciences, The University of Texas at Dallas, Texas, and Adjunct Professor at Labouré College of Healthcare in Massachusetts, where he teaches neurophysiology and neuroscience courses. He has also developed and led online diploma and postdoctoral fellowship programs in Surgical Neurophysiology. These programs are designed to train the next generation of neurophysiologists, emphasizing theoretical knowledge and practical skills.

His contributions to the field have been recognized with numerous awards. These include the Outstanding Publication in a Peer-Reviewed Journal Award from the American Society of Neurophysiological Monitoring (ASNM) and the Excellence in Education Award from the Association of Physicians of Pakistani Descent of North America (APPNA). He is also a fellow of the ASNM and the Neurodiagnostic Society (ASET).

Dr. Jahangiri has a prolific academic output, with over 60 research publications and over 200 invited speeches/research presentations. He has authored several books, including the well-regarded "Surgical Neurophysiology," "Mapping of the Brain," and "Introduction to Neurophysiology." His work is frequently featured at national and international conferences, where he is a sought-after speaker and course director.

In addition to his clinical and academic roles, Dr. Jahangiri is actively involved in professional organizations. He chaired the membership committee of the ASNM from 2014-2024 and is a member of the North American Spine Society's (NASS) section on IONM. His involvement in these organizations underscores his dedication to advancing high-quality, evidence-based neuromonitoring practices.

Dr. Faisal Jahangiri's extensive experience, dedication to education, and commitment to advancing the field of neurophysiology make him a pivotal figure in the medical community. Dr. Jahangiri's work continues to set high neurophysiology standards to enhance surgical procedures' safety and outcomes, benefiting countless patients and inspiring future generations of neurophysiologists.

Haniya Qavi is completing her Bachelor of Science in Biology and a Master of Science in Healthcare Leadership and Management at the University of Texas at Dallas. She conducts research in the Habit Learning Lab to better understand the mechanisms of Vagus nerve stimulation for enhanced motor learning and its connection to the gut.

Haniya has also gained valuable experience volunteering in the Emergency Department and Operating Room and shadowing physicians from various specialties. These experiences have deepened her passion for medicine and patient care, inspiring her to pursue a medical career. Through her work, she aims to bridge the gap between research and clinical practice through patient education to improve patient outcomes.

Khadeeja Moosa recently graduated from the University of Texas at Dallas, where she double majored and earned her Bachelor of Science in Psychology and Child Learning & Development. While at the university, Khadeeja was a research intern at the Psychoneuroendocrine Research Program and worked as a volunteer emergency medical technician for the University Emergency Medical Response (UEMR).

In addition to her academic work, Khadeeja is actively involved in professional organizations such as the American Muslim Women Physician Association, in which she served as the founder and vice president of the UT Dallas chapter. She enjoys volunteering at community health fairs and actively raising awareness about the critical role of preventive medicine in maintaining public health. Khadeeja is currently interested in exploring the effects of eating disorders and plans to apply for medical school. Throughout her career, she aims to remain actively involved in her community, continuing her dedication to service and volunteerism.

About the Illustrator

Zainab Qavi is currently completing her Bachelor of Science in Biology at the University of Texas at Dallas. She is involved in research at the Center of Advanced Pain Studies (CAPS) at UTD, where she, under the mentorship of Dr. Joesph Lesnak, is studying the role of cytokines in the generation of chronic pain states, such as diabetic peripheral neuropathy.

In her free time, Zainab enjoys painting, photography, design, and more. She is the founder of Qavi Creations, a small business that sells Arabic Calligraphy art and donates a part of the proceeds to charity. She also enjoys creating art pieces for on-campus charity auctions and connecting with people through creative hobbies.

Zainab also has a deep passion for volunteering at community medical clinics for uninsured individuals. She strives to serve those in need, offering her time and expertise to connect with people worldwide and provide essential support. She hopes to apply for medical school and dedicate her career to leading through service, advocating for patient's needs, and traveling the world to provide medical care to patients in underserved localities. She hopes to make the world a better place using her art and heart.

Made in the USA
Columbia, SC
21 July 2024